BEOWULF

HWÆT WE GARD
na in gear dagum. þeod cyninga
þrym ge frunon hu ða æþelingas elle
fre medon. Oft scyld scefing sceaþe
þreatum monegū mægþum meodo setla
of teah egsode eorl syððan ærest wear
fea sceaft funden he þæs frofre geba
weox under wolcnum weorð myndum þah
oð þ him æghwylc þara ymb sittendra
ofer hron rade hyran scolde gomban
gyldan þ wæs god cyning. ðæm eafera wæs
æfter cenned geong in geardum þone god
sende folce to frofre fyren ðearfe on
geat þ hie ær drugon aldor[illegible]se. lange
hwile him þæs lif frea wuldres wealde[illegible]
worold are for geaf. beowulf wæs bre[illegible]
blæd wide sprang scyldes eafera sce[illegible]
landum in. Swa sceal [illegible] gode
ge wyrcean fromum feoh [illegible]

MS. Cott. Vit. A. xv. (reduced) fol. 129a (132a)

HWÆT WE GARDE

na inȝear daȝum. þeod cyninȝa

þrym ȝe frunon huða æþelinȝas elle[n]

fre medon. Oft scyld scefinȝ sceaþe[na]

5 þreatum moneȝu*m* mæȝþum meodo setla

of teah eȝsode eorl syððan ærest wear[ð]

fea sceaft funden he þæs frofre ȝeba[d]

weox under wolcnum weorð myndum þah.

oð *þæt* him æȝhwylc þara ymb sittendra

10 ofer hron rade hyran scolde ȝomban

ȝyldan *þæt* wæs ȝod cyninȝ. ðæm eafera wæs

æfter cenned ȝeonȝ in ȝeardum þone ȝod

sende folce tofrofre fyren ðearfe on

ȝeat *þæt* hie ær druȝon aldor [le]ase. lanȝe

15 hwile him þæs lif frea wuldres wealdend

worold are for ȝeaf. beowulf wæs breme

blæd wide spranȝ scyldes eafera scede

landum in. Swa sceal [ȝeonȝ ȝ]uma ȝode

ȝe wyrcean fromum feoh ȝiftum. on fæder

BEOWULF

with

THE FINNSBURG FRAGMENT

Edited by

A. J. WYATT

NEW EDITION REVISED
WITH INTRODUCTION AND NOTES
by

R. W. CHAMBERS

Cambridge:
at the University Press
1968

Published by the Syndics of the Cambridge University Press
Bentley House, 200 Euston Road, London N.W.1
American Branch: 32 East 57th Street, New York, N.Y. 10022

Standard Book Number: 521 06882 7

First Edition **1914**
Reprinted **1920**
1925
1933
1943
1948
1952
1968

First printed in Great Britain at The University Press, Cambridge
Reprinted in Great Britain by Lowe & Brydone (Printers) Ltd., London

CONTENTS

ON THE TEXT OF *BEOWULF*

THE editors of *Beowulf* have, with rare exceptions, concentrated their attention upon the problem of fixing and interpreting the text, and have avoided discussing the literary history of the poem. Theories as to the origin and structure of *Beowulf* have been developed, not in editions, but in monographs such as those of ten Brink, Müllenhoff, and Boer.

This practice is probably sound: and in accordance with it I have made no pretence here to deal with questions of the "higher criticism." I hope to attempt this in an *Introduction to the Study of Beowulf*, which is to be issued separately. But an editor ought to give an account of the principles upon which he has worked, and the relation of his text to the MS. This duty is particularly incumbent upon him, when he is revising a standard text.

THE MANUSCRIPT

The *Beowulf* has been preserved in one manuscript only written about the year 1000: a feature which it shares with most extant Old English poetry. As to the history of this manuscript we have no information, till we find it in the collection formed by Sir Robert Cotton, which is now in the British Museum. From its position in the book-cases of this collection the MS. containing *Beowulf* received the name and number (*Cotton Vitellius A.* 15) by which it is still known. Our first record of it dates from 1705, when Wanley in his Catalogue of Anglo-Saxon Manuscripts described our poem as telling of the wars which a Dane, Beowulf, waged against the Kings of Sweden.

Twenty-six years later occurred the disastrous fire in which so many of the Cottonian MSS. were either destroyed or, like the *Beowulf* MS., damaged.

It was not till the eighteenth century was drawing to a close that any serious attempt was made to master the poem. Thorkelin, an Icelander by birth, inspired by that revival of historical studies which marked the close of the eighteenth century in Denmark, and doubtless led by Wanley's misdescription of the MS., came to England, made a transcript of the MS., and caused a second transcript to be made. After twenty years of labour his edition was nearing completion, when in 1807 "the Englishman came, the damnèd thief[1]," bombarded Copenhagen, and incidentally destroyed Thorkelin's translation and notes. The much more valuable transcripts of the MS. fortunately escaped. But the work had all to be done again, and it was not till 1815 that the first edition of the *Beowulf* appeared, under the title of *De Danorum rebus gestis...poema Danicum, dialecto Anglo-saxonica.*

Thorkelin's ignorance has been harshly censured by later students, who have often forgotten that, by his two transcripts, made more than forty years before any Englishman cared to study the poem, the Scandinavian scholar had done a service, the value of which cannot be exaggerated. For after Thorkelin's time the MS. continued to deteriorate steadily, by the dropping away of its charred edges[2]. Thorkelin's mistranslations simply do not matter to us. What does matter is that he recorded what was to be read in the MS. at the time he saw it. He, and, to a greater extent, the transcriber whom he employed, made many mistakes: but the two transcripts correct each other: and the mistakes are of a type easily detected and explained. Indeed Thorkelin's ignorance of Anglo-Saxon, and the ignorance of his scribe, add immensely to the value of their transcripts. Had they

[1] *Aa det var Aaret atten hundrede aa syv*
Da Engelsmanden kom, den forbandede Tyv—

[2] More than thirty years ago, further destruction was prevented by the MS. being rebound, and the parchment inset: but the paper which now surrounds each parchment leaf necessarily covers letters or portions of letters, especially on the back.

known more, they would have been tempted to fill in from conjecture such gaps as they did find, and this would have deprived their testimony of its value.

Thorkelin's transcripts are generally referred to as A (the copy made by Thorkelin's order) and B (the copy which he made personally). Both belong to the year 1787: they are preserved in the Royal Library at Copenhagen.

In 1830 the MS. was again copied by Thorpe, who however did not publish till a quarter of a century later. In 1833 (and more correctly in a second edition, in 1835) Kemble published the results of his inspection. In 1861 N. F. S. Grundtvig published a text based upon an examination both of the MS. and of Thorkelin's transcripts. In 1876 Kölbing published collations in *Herrigs Archiv* (LVI.), and both Wülker (1881) and Holder (1881: from his notes made in 1876) prefixed to their texts a transcription of the MS., letter by letter.

Finally, in 1882, a facsimile of the MS. was published by the Early English Text Society, with a transcription by Prof. Zupitza (quoted in the notes below as "Zupitza"). This transcription embodies more than Zupitza's personal reading of the MS.; for he endeavoured "to give the text as far as possible in that condition in which it stood in the MS. a century ago." He weighed the evidence of all the scholars, enumerated above, who had examined the MS. before him, and he had the advantage of comparing the MS. itself with Thorkelin's two transcripts, which were sent to the British Museum for the purpose.

The MS. having thus been collated and recollated by eight scholars, each in his day peculiarly competent, it might well seem that nothing further remained to be done. And in fact most recent students have been content to take the facsimile, and Zupitza's transliteration, as final. But in the study of a MS. which has suffered as the *Beowulf* MS. has, finality is indeed hardly to be reached; and Dr Sedgefield has shown in his recent edition what good results may yet be produced by an editor who will look at the MS. for himself. *Cotton Vitellius A.* 15 is still a field in which a student, particularly if armed with much patience and a strong lens, may have, "on the whole, not a bad day's sport."

The facsimile is indeed an excellent one: but when it is remembered that the MS. has often to be turned many ways, and examined under many lights, before the stroke of a letter can be distinguished from some accidental crease, it is clear that no facsimile can be an adequate substitute for examination of the MS. itself. One example of this will suffice. An American scholar observed from the facsimile that the word *heaðo* in an admittedly defective passage (ll. 62–3) was apparently written over an erasure. Since the necessity for an erasure pointed to some kind of confusion in the mind of the scribe, he concluded that consequently it was here, and not, as generally supposed, at an earlier point, that the corruption had crept into the text, and that therefore the generally accepted emendations must be given up, and an attempt made to solve the crux by starting from the point where the "erasure" occurs.

Having made up his mind from the autotype that there *was* an erasure, he subsequently examined the MS. at the British Museum, and whilst thinking that the erasure was not as manifest in the MS. as in some copies of the autotype, he adhered to his position. The appearance of an erasure is indeed so strong in the *facsimile* that no one has disputed it: and I was therefore greatly surprised, when consulting the MS. itself, to find that it showed no trace of that roughening of the surface which was to be expected. On the parchment being held up to the light, all the dim marks, which in the facsimile (and at first sight in the MS. also) look like fragments of an erased word, turned out to be nothing more than strokes of the word on the other side of the leaf, which (as so often in the *Beowulf* MS.) shine through the parchment. Yet over the reading of these "erased letters" there has been considerable, and heated, controversy: and the discussion of the "erased word" and of the theories built upon it has been the subject of seven contributions to a philological periodical[1], consisting

[1] See *M.L.N.* xix. 121, 122: xx. 9: xxi. 143, 255: xxii. 96, 160.

altogether of about ten thousand printed words. It is painful to think that the time of skilled compositors should have been thus wasted.

A facsimile is given of two pages of the MS., and of the pages in Thorkelin's transcripts A and B corresponding to the second of these.

The facsimiles of the MS. should be compared with the corresponding passage in the text. Such a comparison will show the student what are the main difficulties which beset the editor, and how he is helped by Thorkelin's transcripts. Several things will at once be obvious:

(1) The lines of the MS. do not correspond to the verse lines of the poem. This does not, however, cause any serious trouble, for so uniform is Old English metre that cases where there can be any real doubt as to the division of the lines very seldom occur. Holthausen would put *geaf* at the end of l. 2430: Schücking at the beginning of l. 2431.

(2) The punctuation of the MS. is meagre and unreliable. The full stop is, indeed, sometimes used as we should use it: *e.g.* after the word *cyning* in l. 11 of p. 1; but it is often placed in the middle of a sentence, as after *aldorlēase,* three lines below.

(3) Though the first word after a full stop is not infrequently written with a capital, proper names are not written with capital letters. Hence, for instance, the dispute whether *hondsciō* (l. 2076) is, or is not, a personal name.

(4) Vowel length is only rarely marked. Hence difficulties like that of determining whether *gæst* stands for *găst* 'stranger' or *gǣst,* 'spirit[1].'

(5) One word is sometimes written as two or even three words, and two words are often written as one. Hyphens are unknown to the scribes. Hence *eofor lic scionon* (l. 303) has been read both as *eofor-līc scionon* and *eofor līc-scionon.* And in addition to the difficulty of interpreting such gaps as the scribe did undoubtedly leave, we have the further

[1] A list is given below of the vowels marked long in the MS.

difficulty of deciding when he did, and when he did not, intend the vague and indeterminate space which he left between letters to be regarded as a gap separating two words.

(6) Though there are no glaring examples on the pages reproduced, it appears that the scribes worked mechanically, sometimes altering the entire meaning of a sentence by omitting little words, like *ne*, 'not.' The painfully slow care with which the Old English letters were traced would tend to make the scribe lose the general drift of what he was writing.

(7) The spelling is inconsistent: *moncynn* appears as *mancynne* (dat.) in l. 110, as *moncynnes* (gen.) in l. 196, and as *mon cynnes* (gen.) in l. 1955. Yet, compared with that of many a Middle English MS. or Tudor printed book, the spelling might almost be called uniform.

(8) It will be seen that both pages of the MS., but more particularly the second, are badly damaged at the edges and corners. With the facsimile of the second page should be compared the facsimile of the corresponding passage from Thorkelin's transcripts. When these transcripts were made the damage cannot have extended beyond the margins, and the written page must have been, like the transcript, complete[1]. At the present day, out of 108 words, 26 are either quite gone or damaged. This will give some measure of the value of Thorkelin's transcripts. Of course even without them we should still be able to get much information from the texts of Kemble and Thorpe as to what the MS. was like in its less damaged state: but, as it is, we depend mainly upon Thorkelin. As explained above, the mechanical nature of these transcripts is their greatest merit. It is quite clear that the transcriber of A had no knowledge whatsoever of Old English. This is proved by spellings like *relite* for *rehte*, *riga* for *wiga*, *criðan* for *cwiðan*. How slight Thorkelin's own knowledge must have been at the time he made his transcript is shown by similar misspellings, e.g. *gloguðe* for *geoguðe*.

The handwriting of the second page reproduced from the *Beowulf* MS. differs from that of the first. The second hand

[1] Thorkelin could not read the first word of l. 8, but the transcriber got it right.

Scilding fela fricgende feorran rehte
hwilum hilde deor hearpan wynne go
mel wudu grette hwilum gyd awræc soð
and sarlic hwilum syllic spell. rehte æfter
rihte rum heort cyning. hwilum eft
ongan eldo gebunden gomel guðwiga
glogude cwidan hilde strengo hreðer
.. me weoll. þonne he wintrum frod worn ge
munde swa we þær inne and langne
dæg mode naman oððæt niht becwom
oðer to yldum þa wæs eft hraðe gearo
sorh full sunu dead fornam wig hete
wedra wif unhyre hyre bearn gewræc
beorn acwealde ellenlice þær wæs æsc
here frodan fyrn witan feorh uð
genge. noðær hy hine nemoston syððan
mergen cwom dead werigne denia
leode. (erasum..). bronde for barnan
ne on bel hladan leofne mannan
gyrn wræce grendeles modor sidode ——

Beowulf: Thorkelin's Transcript B. (reduced), ll. 2105—2127.

[illegible]
[illegible]lde deor hearpan wynne go
[illegible]udu grette hwilum gyd awræc. soð
[illegible]lic hwilum syllic spell. rehte æfter
[illegible]e rum heort cyning. hwilum eft
[illegible]n eldo gebunden gomel guð wiga
[illegible]de cwiðan hilde strengo hreðer
[illegible]e weoll. þon he wintrum frod worn
[illegible]nde. swa we þær inne andlangne
[illegible]ode naman oððæt niht becwom.
[illegible]to yldum þa wæs eft hraðe gearo
[illegible]wræce grendeles modor. siðode
[illegible]h full sunu deað fornam wig hete
[illegible]a wif unhyre hyre bearn gewræc
[illegible]n acwealde ellenlice þær wæs æsc
[illegible]frodan fyrn witan feorh uð
[illegible]ge. noðer hy hine nemoston syððan
[illegible]gen cwom deað werigne dena
[illegible]de. [illegible] bronde forbærnan
[illegible]n bel hladan. leofne mannan

MS. Cott. Vit. A. xv. (reduced) fol. 176[b] (179[b]) (= ll. 2105—2127)

Transliteration, ll. 2105—2127.

[scildinȝ f]ela fricȝ[ende feorran] r[ehte] **Fol. 176v.**

[hwilu*m* h]ilde deor hearpan wynne ȝo

[mel]wudu ȝrette hwilu*m* ȝyd awræc. soð

[*ond* sar]líc hwilu*m* syllic spell. rehte æfter

[ri]hte rum heort cyninȝ. hwilu*m* eft

[onȝa]n eldo ȝebunden ȝomel ȝuð wiȝa

[ȝioȝ]uðe cwiðan hilde strenȝo hreðer

[inn]e weoll þon*ne* he wintru*m* frod worn

[ȝem]unde swa we þær inne *and*lanȝne

[dæȝ] niode naman oððæt niht becwom.

[oðer] to yldum þa wæs eft hraðe ȝearo

[ȝyrn] wræce. ȝrendeles modor. Siðode

[sor]h full sunu deað fornam wiȝ hete

[wed]ra wif unhyre hyre bearn ȝewræc

[beo]rn acwealde ellenlice þær wæs æsc

[her]e frodan fyrn-witan feorh uð

[ȝen]ȝe. noðer hy hine nemoston syððan

[m]erȝen cwom deað weriȝ ne denia

[leo]de. bronde for bærnan

[n]e on bęl hladan. leofne mannan

Letters now entirely lost, or so far lost as to be very difficult to read, are placed within square brackets.

ƿear. dade. hand on hiorte ⁊ he hean ðonan modes geomor mere grund —

gefeoll meþone ƿæl ƿæs ƿine scildunga. fættan golde fela leano de...

manegū maðmū syððan mergen cōm. ⁊ ƿe to symble geseten hæfdon.

þær ƿæs gidd ⁊ gleo gomela scilding fela fricgende feorran relire.....

hƿilū hilde deor hearpan ƿynne go mel ƿudu grette hƿilū gyd arræc. soð

⁊ sarlīc hƿilū syllic spell. rehte æfter rihte rum heort cyning. hƿilū ..

eft ongan eldo gebunden gomel guð ƿiga giogude cƿiðan hilde ...

strengo hreðer inne ƿeoll. þon he ƿintrū frod ƿorn gemunde spaþeþær

inne ⁊ langne dæg. niode naman oððæt niht bæƿoin. oðer to yldum

þa ƿæs eft hraðe gearo gyrn ƿræce. grendeles modor. Sidode...

sorh full sunu deað fornam ƿighete ƿedra ƿif unhyre hyre bearn ..

geƿræc beorn acƿealde ellenlice þær ƿæs æsc here frodan fyrn ƿitan

feorh uð genge. noðer hy hine nemoston syððan mergen cƿom deað....

ƿerigne dena leode bronde for bærnan neon bel hladan. leofne ....

mannan hio þlic æt bær feondes fæð

der firgen stream. þ ƿæs hroð hreopa tornost þara

þe leod fru man lange begeate. þa se ðeoden mic ðine life healsode

hreoh mod þ ic on holma gering eorl scipe efnde ealdre genedde.

mærdo fremede heme mede geher ic ðaðær ƿælmes þe is ƿide cuð

62 grimme

Beowulf: Thorkelin's Transcript A. (reduced), ll. 2098—2136.

begins with *mōste* in l. 1939. *Judith,* which follows *Beowulf* in the composite MS. *Cotton Vitellius A.* 15, is asserted on good authority to be also in this second hand. This is important, for with the second hand many variations in spelling are introduced into *Beowulf.* Our first instinct would be to attribute these altered spellings to the new copyist: but since they do not occur in the *Judith,* this can hardly be the correct explanation, *if* he also transcribed that poem. In that case it would seem rather that the second scribe copied his original more exactly, and therefore retained features which the first scribe was prone to obliterate. The peculiarities of spelling which meet us in the later portion of *Beowulf* seem, then, to be derived from the MS. from which our existing copy was transcribed[1].

The abbreviations used by the scribes are neither numerous nor difficult. Instead of *ond,* which occurs only three times (ll. 600, 1148, 2040), the symbol 7 is almost invariably used. For *þæt,* ꝥ is similarly found. It has been disputed whether ꝥ can also stand for *þā* (see note to l. 15): if it cannot there are certainly instances in *Beowulf* where ꝥ and *þā* have been confused by a natural scribal blunder. Sense is much improved by reading ꝥ as *þā* in ll. 15, 1833, 3134 (cf. 2701) and *þā* as ꝥ in l. 2629.

To signify *m,* especially final *m,* the scribe drew a heavy hooked line over the preceding vowel.

From the times of the earliest O.E. glosses this symbol is also used occasionally to signify *n.* The *Beowulf* scribe, like the scribe of the almost contemporary *Exeter Book,* does not normally use the mark for *n*[2]. But the older MS. which he was copying perhaps did so, and this would account for such a blunder as *hrūsam* for *hrūsan* (2279) and for the frequent omission of an *n* in our manuscript[3].

[1] See Davidson, and MacClumpha, *Differences between the scribes of Beowulf,* in *M.L.N.*, v. 87—89, 245, 378.

[2] In ll. 2645, 2741, read *forðam* rather than *forðan.* In *þon̄* (=*þonne*) the mark is used for *ne,* and for *en* on the abnormally contracted last page of the MS.

[3] Ll. 60, 70, 255, 418, 591, 673, 1176, 1510, 1697, 1883, 2259, 2307, 2545, 2996, 3121, 3155. When final, this may be due to the original having been in a Northern dialect [Sievers$_3$, § 188. 2].

Textual Emendation

It is most important that the student should study the two facsimile pages of the *Beowulf* MS. sufficiently to familiarize himself with the forms of the Anglo-Saxon script, for it is only by this means that he will be able to weigh the value of the different conjectural emendations. A conjecture which seems a very violent one when expressed in modern type may yet appear very reasonable when we picture the form of the Old English letters. From this point of view it is a pity that we have abandoned the custom, so generally followed at the beginning of Old English studies, of printing Old English texts in type which was a conventionalized facsimile of the Old English hand. The letters are picturesque, and can be learnt in five minutes.

Much work was done in the emendation and elucidation of the text by Grundtvig, Kemble, Thorpe and Ettmüller. The constant occurrence of the name of Grundtvig in the textual notes bears witness to the frequency with which he cleared up some desperate place in the MS. But these emendations only represent a portion of Grundtvig's achievement. Working from Thorkelin's inaccurate text, he made many conjectures which, on a more careful examination, were found to be actually the readings of the MS. Such success naturally aroused confidence in his conjectural restorations.

The great bulk of Grundtvig's emendations were appended to the *translation* which he published in 1820. Other emendations were made in his *edition*, published in 1861. These two books have not been sufficiently distinguished by editors of *Beowulf*. Yet in discussing the priority of an emendation it is obviously important to know in which of two books, separated by more than forty years, a scholar may have made his conjectures. In this edition, therefore, the word 'Grundtvig,' followed by the number of a page, refers invariably to the translation of 1820; references to the edition of 1861 are specified as such.

Grundtvig had contributed a large number of these

emendations to a Copenhagen paper during the year 1815[1]. The perfect editor would no doubt go through these articles, and note exactly where each emendation first appeared. But life is short and there is much to do: I have therefore only referred to these periodical articles of Grundtvig where it appeared that there was some useful purpose to be gained by so doing. Generally speaking I have taken Grundtvig's publication of 1820 as summing up the results of his early work, and have not striven to go behind it.

The student must not be surprised if he finds the same emendation attributed by different scholars sometimes to Kemble and sometimes to Thorpe, since frequently Kemble's emendations were only suggested in the notes of his second volume, but were first given *in the text* by Thorpe; and there was so much intercommunication between the two scholars that it is not easy to say to whom belongs the credit of some particular emendations.

Much confusion has also resulted from the differences between the first edition of Kemble's *Beowulf* (1833: limited to 100 copies) and the second revised edition of 1835. For instance, Zupitza—than whom no one knew more of the history of *Beowulf* criticism, and whose premature death was a loss to *Beowulf* scholarship from which we are still suffering—charged other editors with inaccuracy in their quotations of Kemble[2]: the explanation is that they were using the one edition, and he was using the other, and that the two editions differ very widely. I have therefore thought it better to differentiate. 'Kemble $_{(1)}$' refers to the edition of 1833; 'Kemble $_{(2)}$' to that of 1835; 'Kemble $_{(3)}$' to the list of emendations which Kemble appended to his translation in 1837. 'Thorpe' refers, of course, to Thorpe's edition of 1855.

The labours of Ettmüller covered a period little shorter than those of Grundtvig. In my notes, 'Ettmüller $_{(1)}$' refers to the translation of 1840: 'Ettmüller $_{(2)}$' to the abbreviated *Beowulf* which appeared in the book of extracts entitled

[1] Some eight articles in the *Nyeste Skilderie af Kjöbenhavn.*

[2] *Archiv*, xciv. 328.

Engla and Seaxna Scopas and Bôceras, 1850: 'Ettmüller$_{(3)}$' to the edition (still abbreviated) of 1875.

A new era begins with the publication of Grein's complete corpus of Anglo-Saxon poetry, between 1857 and 1864 (4 vols.). Grein's actual text of *Beowulf,* both in the first volume of this *Bibliothek,* and in his subsequent separate edition, is not without its faults: but the great lexicon given in the last two volumes of the *Bibliothek* brought to bear upon the interpretation of *Beowulf* the whole store of knowledge of Old English poetic speech. The student who has made some progress, and hopes to make more, will still find his best course to be the looking up in Grein's *Sprachschatz* of parallels for the usage of any words puzzling him. In quoting I differentiate 'Grein$_{(1)}$' (1857); 'Grein$_{(2)}$' (1867); 'Grein$_{(3)}$' (Grein's hand-copy, corrected, as used by Wülker).

Since Grein's day the edition of Heyne (1863, etc.), constantly revised, has continued to hold its own (English translation, Harrison and Sharp, 1882, etc.), rivalled for two decades by that of Holder (1881, etc.: last edit., 1899). Kluge added valuable conjectures to Holder's edition: to these 'Kluge' if quoted in my notes, without details, refers[1]. Wülker's revision of Grein's *Bibliothek* (1883, etc.) by giving scrupulously accurate texts, with full collations, remedied the one fault of Grein's great work. In recent years four editions have been published: (1) Trautmann's (1904), distinguished by bold alterations of the text; (2) Holthausen's (third edit. 1912–13), invaluable for its closely packed references and bibliographies: Holthausen's treatment of the text represents a middle course between the violent alterations of Trautmann and the conservative text of (3) Schücking, whose revision of Heyne (nominally the eighth edit., 1908: tenth, 1913: but amounting in fact almost to a new work) has restored its place of honour to that classic text; whilst (4) Dr Sedgefield's text (second edit., 1913) has gone far to remove from English scholarship the reproach of neglect of the earliest monuments of our literature.

[1] But 'Kluge' followed by a figure refers to *P.B.B.* IX. See p. xxxii.

Aim of the Present Edition

Text. In revising the text I have made it my aim to retain that conservatism which characterised Mr Wyatt's edition. In fifty places I have, however, felt compelled, mainly on metrical grounds, to desert the MS., where Mr Wyatt adhered to it. But this is balanced by the fact that in fifty-one places I undertake the defence of the MS., even where Mr Wyatt had abandoned it.

When Mr Wyatt's edition was first issued in 1894 it was necessary for him to protest against wanton alterations of the MS. such as *fāmigheals* for *fāmiheals*. Such alterations are now no longer tolerated: and even to argue against them would be an anachronism: Mr Wyatt has the greatest reward that can befall a controversialist, that of finding his protest so generally accepted as to be out of date.

But with the increased knowledge of Old English metre which we owe to the genius of Sievers, a new reason for deserting the MS. has been approved, to some extent at least, by most recent editors. In places where the metre shows that the original poet must have used a form different from that in our extant MS., it is now usual to put that form back: to write e.g. *frēga* for *frēa*, *gāan* for *gān*, *dōið* for *dōð*.

To the present editor there seems to be no middle course between, on the one hand, leaving the language of the poem in the form given to it by its last transcribers, and, on the other hand, attempting to rewrite the whole poem in the language of the eighth century. The rule "to emend the text where the metre shows the form given in the MS. to be wrong" sounds simple, but is, in practice, not possible. For the suspected form may occur in a line which is absolutely unmetrical, in one which is merely hard to parallel, or in one which is of a type usually avoided, but undoubtedly to be found. Are we to alter in all three cases, or only in the first? And having altered a form in a place where it is unmetrical, what are we to do when we meet the identical form in a place where it is possible?

Unless we make changes right through, we merely produce a text which is an inconsistent mixture of eighth and tenth century forms.

But, it may be said, the MS. itself is not consistent, for the last transcribers here and there retained earlier forms. They did, and these forms may be of the greatest value in enabling us to trace the history of the poem. For that very reason the issues should not be confused by inserting into the text a number of ancient forms which are *not* in the MS. If we scatter these over the page, the student is led to believe that he has come across forms like *frēga, gāan, dōið* in his reading of *Beowulf*. All the typographical devices of italics and brackets cannot prevent this: in a poem of over three thousand lines no student can be expected to remember for very long exactly what letters are printed in italic, and exactly what in roman type.

Besides, though we may be certain, on metrical grounds, that the word *gān* in *hāt in gān* (l. 386) represents an earlier word of two syllables, we cannot be certain whether that word was *gāan* or *gangan*.

The difficulty that monosyllables in the text have to do duty as disyllables can be met quite simply. Where the metre shows that a long vowel or diphthong, such as *gān, frēa* was originally disyllabic, I write it with the circumflex: *gân, frêa*; in other cases the makron is used: *hū, ðā*. This method suffices to draw the student's attention to the metrical fact: at the same time he is not misled by seeing in the text a form for which there is no MS. authority, and which the original author may, after all, not have used.

To attempt to reinsert these earlier forms is indeed to carry into text editing the mistake of the architects of half a century ago, who, finding a fourteenth century church which showed traces of having been remodelled out of a twelfth century one, proceeded to knock out the Decorated tracery in order to insert their conjectural restoration of the original Norman lights. By so doing they merely falsified the history of the building, and left us with windows which are neither 'Decorated' nor 'Norman' but architectural lies.

Experience has now taught our church restorers that, however much we may regret the work of the fourteenth century remodeller, we cannot escape from it. And the same is true of the text-restoration of *Beowulf*. To put back into the text a few sporadic ancient forms is merely to increase confusion. To put back the whole poem into the language of about the year 700 is impossible[1]. How impossible can best be shown by means of a comparison. In the case of *Piers Plowman* (A text) we have fifteen MSS., some belonging to a period but little later than the author's lifetime. Most of these MSS. are excellent ones, and by a comparison of them it is possible to reconstruct a text immensely better than even the best of these MSS. Yet, whilst the *wording* of this text can be fixed with considerable certainty, it is impossible to reconstruct *the exact dialectical colouring* in a form which would command any measure of general consent. How can we hope to do so, then, in the case of a text extant in one MS., transcribed nearly three centuries after the poem was first composed?

It does not follow that we need print the text exactly as it stands, relegating all attempts at emendation to the notes. It seems possible to distinguish between those changes in spelling and grammatical form which the scribes deliberately made with fair consistency, and those rarer cases where they have, generally owing to carelessness or misunderstanding, altered the *wording* of a passage. If the critic thinks he can emend such passages, he has every right to do so. To correct blunders which the scribes made inadvertently, and which they themselves corrected when they noticed them, is quite a different thing from putting back the language which the scribes deliberately adopted into that which they deliberately rejected.

The degree of faithfulness at which the scribe aimed of course varied greatly with individual cases. It may be admitted that some ancient scribes had almost as little respect for the MS. before them as some modern editors. But an

[1] Holthausen's specimen of a restored text should be compared by all students. In 25 lines over 100 alterations are needed.

accurate scribe did not as a rule depart from the *wording* of his original except as a result of oversight. On the other hand, even an accurate scribe did not hesitate to alter the spelling and form of words.

Accordingly, whilst it is often possible from MS. evidence to aim at reconstructing the exact *words* of a text, it is an immeasurably more difficult task, unless we have some external help, to aim at reconstructing the original *dialect.*

The rule which I have followed is therefore this. Where there is reason to think that the spelling or the dialectal form has been tampered with, I do not try to restore the original, such a task being at once too uncertain and too far-reaching. But where there is reason to think that the scribe has departed from the wording and grammatical construction of his original, and that this can be restored with tolerable certainty, I do so.

And here again the study of metre is of the greatest help. There can be no possible doubt that a half-line like *secg betsta* (l. 947) is unmetrical: that the half-line originally ran *secga betsta.* No device of circumflex accents can help us here, and it appears to me that the editor has no choice but to write the words as they originally stood. Yet caution is advisable: where there is even a sporting chance of the MS. reading being correct I retain it: in some instances I retain the MS. reading, though firmly believing that it is wrong; because none of the emendations suggested is satisfactory.

"I have indulged but sparingly," Mr Wyatt wrote, "in the luxury of personal emendations, because they are obviously the greatest disqualification for discharging duly the functions of an editor." This view was strongly disputed at the time, notably by Zupitza, who urged, quite truly, that it is the duty of an editor to bring all his powers to bear upon the construction of a correct text; that, for instance, one of the greatest merits of Lachmann as an editor lay precisely in his personal emendations. Yet here discrimination is desirable. We do not all possess the genius of Lachmann, and if we did, we have not the advantage he had in being early in the field. On the contrary, we find the study of *Beowulf* littered with hundreds of conjectural emendations. All these the unfortunate editor must judge, admitting some few to a place in his text, according more a cursory reference in his notes, but of necessity dismissing the majority without mention. It will be easier for the magistrate, if he has to sit in judgment upon none of his own offspring. True, there are editors, inflexible as Lucius Junius Brutus, who have filled many pages of periodicals with conjectural emendations, but who yet, when they accept the responsibility of editorship, admit that few or none of their own conjectures are worthy of serious consideration. But such integrity is rare; and where an editor has to judge between the emendations of so many capable scholars, he may do well for his own part to adopt a self-denying ordinance. Especially is this desirable when he is editing a text on strictly conservative lines: it would be impertinent for me, whilst excluding from the text a number of the really brilliant conjectures of recent students, to allow a place to my own very inferior efforts. I have therefore followed, and indeed bettered, Mr Wyatt's example: he made few personal emendations: I have made none.

For, indeed, conjectural emendation has been allowed to run riot. Advocates of a conservative text are often taunted with credulous belief in the letter of the manuscript—"Buchstaben-glauben." But, in fact, the charge of superstitious credulity might more justly be brought against those who believe that, with the miserably inadequate means at our disposal, we *can* exactly restore the original text. Prof. Trautmann assures us that the extant manuscript is grossly faulty, and on the strength of this belief puts forth an edition full of the most drastic and daring alterations. But, if we grant (for the sake of argument) that the manuscript is as grossly erroneous as Prof. Trautmann's emendations postulate, then it follows that it is too bad to afford a sound basis for conjectural emendation at all. If Prof. Trautmann's premises were correct, the only course open to the editor would be to remove merely those obvious and surface blemishes of the manuscript as to which there can be little or no doubt, and then to say: "This is the best that can be done with a text so peculiarly corrupt. I therefore leave it at that, and if I must work at text-criticism, I will choose some other text, where there is better material at my disposal, and where I can consequently proceed by critical methods rather than by guess-work."

And, without going as far as this, we may reasonably regret that much of the scholarship and acumen squandered on the conjectural emendation of *Beowulf* has not been devoted to certain Middle English texts. There the evidence is often abundant, and of a kind which, if properly investigated and utilized, would enable us to make indisputable corrections of important texts in hundreds of places.

Type. The chief innovation, and one which will, I expect, be generally disapproved, is the introduction into the text of the Old Eng. symbol ʒ. Against this ʒ most teachers seem to cherish an unreasoning antipathy. Now, in itself, it surely matters little whether we reproduce an Old Eng. consonant by the Mod. Eng. form, or by a facsimile of the Old Eng. form. By general consent *þ* and ð are used: yet it would not matter if we were to write *th* instead. But it does matter if the symbol misleads the student. Now, whilst most consonants have much the same value in Old as in Mod. Eng., Mod. Eng. *g* fulfils one only of the three functions of Old Eng. ʒ. To the elementary student it is really helpful to have a constant reminder of this fact. He should not be misled by the spellings *hiʒ* or *wiʒʒe*, as he is only too likely to be by the spellings *hig* or *wigge*.

Besides, as has been pointed out by Sievers, with the end of the Anglo-Saxon period both ʒ and *g* came into use: ʒ to signify the spirant, *g* the stop. To write *g* in Anglo-Saxon texts conveys the idea that the symbol ʒ was added in Middle English to signify the spirant; when in reality it was the ʒ which was used all along and the *g* which was added later to denote the stopped sound.

In the text I have therefore followed the Old English usage, and have written the ʒ wherever it occurs in the MS.

But where the scribe actually used *G*, as a capital, I have retained it. In the *Introduction, Notes* and *Glossary* I write *g*, as a matter of convenience.

Hyphens and Punctuation. As to the use of hyphens and the general principles of punctuation there is no change from the practice advocated by Mr Wyatt in the first edition:

It will have been seen that the MS. gives no help in one of the most difficult problems that beset the editor of O. E. poems, the question of the use of hyphens. Grein and Sweet discard them altogether. I cannot but question whether this is not to shirk one's duty. At least it is a method that I have not been able at present to bring myself to adopt, tempting as it is. The difficulty of course is as to "where to draw the line"—where to use a hyphen or to write as one word, where to use a hyphen or write as two words. The former is the chief difficulty, and here as elsewhere I have endeavoured to find the path "of least resistance." Prepositional prefixes in my text are not marked off by a hyphen from the following word; on the other hand, adverbial prefixes, such as *ūp* in *ūp-lang*, *ūt* in *ūt-weard*, are so marked off. This then is where I have, not without misgivings, "drawn the line." Where the two parts of a compound seem to preserve their full notional force I have used a hyphen; where the force of one part seems to be quite subordinate to that of the other, I have written them as one word. It is the familiar distinction of compounds and derivatives over again, but at a stage of the language when some compounds were in course of becoming derivatives. Doubtless there are mistakes and inconsistencies. I need hardly say I shall be glad to have them pointed out.

The punctuation of *Beowulf* has hitherto been largely traditional, as it were, and largely German, and German punctuation of course differs in some respects from English. Some editors have shown daring originality in the substitution of colons for the semi-colons, and marks of exclamation for the full-stops, of previous editors. Periods have usually been held too sacred to question. I may say at once that, although I have been extremely conservative in my handling of the text, I have felt and have shown scant courtesy for much of the traditional punctuation. Let me state here the principles, right or wrong, upon which I have acted. First, I have made the punctuation as *simple* as possible. I have therefore done away with the somewhat fine distinction between the colon and the semicolon, and have restricted the use of the former to marking the opening of an *oratio recta*, and to a very few similar *loci*, such as ll. 801, 1392, 1476. In the same way, I have, wherever possible, done away with parentheses, and with our modern meretricious marks of exclamation. If the reader's sense or emotions do not tell him where he ought to feel exclamatory, he must suffer the consequences. Secondly, I have attempted to make the punctuation *logical*, especially by the use of *pairs of commas* wherever the sequence of a sentence is interrupted by parallelisms. This may be made clearer by a reference to ll. 1235–7, 1283–4, 3051–2. But, on the other hand, I have as far as possible avoided breaking up the metrical unit of the half line with a comma.

Notes. The chief difference between this edition and its predecessor will be found in the greater diffuseness of the notes, which have been almost entirely rewritten. "The infelicity of our times" has compelled me, as revising editor, to depart from Mr Wyatt's practice of quoting but sparsely the emendations which he did not accept. In the last eighteen years the number of emendations and interpretations has multiplied enormously, and many of these it is impossible to neglect.

To discuss at length the pros and cons of these disputed points is impossible in a text-book: such task must be left to the lecturer: but if no information on the subject is given in the text-book, the task both of lecturer and student is made unnecessarily heavy. Authorities are therefore quoted rather freely: and in the manner of quoting them a difficulty arose. To quote arguments at any length would have been to swell this book unduly; but to quote the name of the scholar who has originated any conjecture without further particulars, is to encourage the student in the pestilent superstition that he is expected to know which scholar holds which particular view: whereas in reality all that concerns him is the *ground* upon which a particular view is held.

The student who reads the seventeen pages in which Sievers defends the reading *egsode eorlas* (l. 6) will have had a lesson which should be of permanent value to him: a lesson in Old English metre, in Old English syntax, in critical methods, and above all in the truth that a man should do with his might that which his hand findeth to do, even though it be nothing better than the emending of a doubtful line. The student who understands, if only in broadest outline, the grounds upon which Kock defends the MS. reading *eorl*, and Sievers declares *eorl* impossible, has acquired a piece of grammatical and metrical knowledge which should be of constant use to him, as he works through his *Beowulf.* The student who, hoping to get marks in an examination, commits to memory the fact that Kock supports *eorl,* Sievers *eorlas,* has done nothing save degrade his intelligence to the level of that of a dog, learning tricks for a lump of sugar.

For this reason, in quoting the names of the proposers or defenders of emendations or interpretations, I have indicated (as briefly as possible) the place where further particulars can be found. Not that I wish to add to the already heavy yoke of the student by expecting him to look up all, or indeed any great proportion, of such references. Even if he looks up none, a constant reminder that these *are* references, not formulae to be learnt by heart, is worth giving. For even the most exacting teacher will hardly demand that the student should commit to memory the year, periodical and page in which each emendation appeared. All such references are placed between square brackets, and elementary students should skip these portions of the notes.

To the advanced student it is hoped that the references may be useful: and in small classes where the lecturer uses the "Seminar" method, and expects each member of the class in turn to study specially some section or aspect of the poem, they may be worked profitably. If a student is led by these references to turn only to Klaeber's articles in *Modern Philology,* or Sievers' monographs in the *Beiträge,* they will not have been given in vain.

In references to editions and translations, where the comment will be found under the appropriate line, no further details are given. The modern editions quoted in the notes are

Grein-Wülker = Bibliothek der angelsächsischen Poesie, begründet von C. W. M. Grein, neu bearbeitet von R. P. Wülker. Bd. I. Beowulf, etc., 1883 (1 Hälfte, 1881).

Holthausen = Beowulf, herausgegeben von F. Holthausen. Dritte Auflage, 1912–13.

Trautmann = Das Beowulflied. Bearbeiteter Text u. deutsche Uebersetzung von M. Trautmann. Bonn, 1904.

Heyne-Schücking = Bēowulf, herausgegeben von M. Heyne. Zehnte Auflage bearbeitet von L. L. Schücking, 1913.

Sedgefield = Beowulf, edited by W. J. Sedgefield. Second edit., 1913.

The following translations into English, with commentaries, need special mention:

Earle = The Deeds of Beowulf...done into modern prose...by John Earle, 1892.

Morris and Wyatt = The tale of Beowulf translated by William Morris and A. J. Wyatt, 1895.

Gummere = The Oldest English Epic. Beowulf, etc., translated in the original metres...by Francis B. Gummere, 1909.

Clark Hall = Beowulf...a translation into Modern English prose by J. R. Clark Hall. New edition, 1911.

But the most important contributions to the study of the text of *Beowulf* have appeared of recent years not so much in editions, as in monographs, and chiefly in periodicals.

Eleven of these, which have to be referred to with special frequency, are quoted by the author's name and the page alone. Such abbreviations are to be interpreted thus[1]:

Bugge[1], etc. = Studien über das Beowulfepos, in *P.B.B.* xii. 1—112, 360—375.

Cosijn[1], etc. = Aanteekeningen op den Beowulf, 1892.

Holthausen[113], etc. = Beiträge zur Erklärung des alteng. Epos, in *Z.f.d.Ph.*, xxxvii. 113—125[2].

Klaeber[235], etc. = Studies in the Textual Interpretation of *Beowulf*, in *Mod. Phil.*, iii. 235—265, 445—465.

Kluge[187], etc. = Zum Beowulf, in *P.B.B.*, ix. 187—192.

Möller, *VE.*[1], etc. = Das altenglische Volksepos. 1883.

Müllenhoff[1], etc. = Beovulf. Untersuchungen. 1889.

Rieger[381], etc. = Zum Beowulf, in *Z.f.d.Ph.*, iii. 381—416.

Sedgefield[286], etc. = Notes on Beowulf, in *M.L.R.*, v. 286—288.

ten Brink[1], etc. = Beowulf. Untersuchungen. 1888. (*Q.F.* 62.)

Trautmann[121], etc. = Berichtigungen, Vermutungen und Erklärungen zum Beowulf, in the *Bonner Beiträge*, II. 121—192.

'Sievers,' when quoted without further details than the section, refers to the *Grammatik* (third edition, German, 1898;

[1] No attempt is made here to give a bibliography of *Beowulf* criticism, which I hope to essay in the separately published *Introduction to Beowulf*.

[2] Note that 'Holthausen' without fuller particulars refers to the edition: 'Holthausen[113]' to the article in the *Z.f.d.Ph.*

English, 1903): 'Bülbring' to Bülbring's *Elementarbuch*, 1902: 'Brandl' to the monograph on *Englische Literatur* in the second edition of Paul's *Grundriss* (1908).

Any further articles are quoted according to the periodical in which they are to be found. The title of the periodical or series is, however, given in an abbreviated form.

A.f.d.A. = Anzeiger für deutsches Altertum, 1876, etc.
Anglia = Anglia, Zeitschrift für Englische Philologie, 1878, etc.
Archiv = (Herrigs) Archiv für das Studium der neueren Sprachen und Litteraturen, 1846, etc.
Engl. Stud. = Englische Studien, 1877, etc.
Germania = Germania, Vierteljahrsschrift für deutsche Altertumskunde, 1856-92.
I.F. = Indogermanische Forschungen, 1891, etc.
{*J.G.Ph.* = Journal of Germanic Philology, 1897-1902: subsequently,
{*J.E.G.Ph.* = Journal of English and Germanic Philology, 1903, etc.
M.L.N. = Modern Language Notes, 1886, etc.
M.L.R. = The Modern Language Review, 1906, etc.
Mod. Phil. = Modern Philology, 1903, etc.
P.B.B. = Beiträge zur Geschichte der deutschen Sprache und Litteratur herausgeg. v. H. Paul u. W. Braune, 1874, etc.
Pub. Mod. Lang. Assoc. Amer. = Publications of the Modern Language Association of America, 1889, etc.
Q.F. = Quellen und Forschungen...1874, etc.
Tidsskr. = Tidsskrift for Philologi og Pædagogik, 1860, etc.
Z.f.d.A. = Zeitschrift für deutsches Altertum, 1841, etc.
Z.f.d.Ph. = (Zachers) Zeitschrift für deutsche Philologie, 1869, etc.
Z.f.ö.G. = Zeitschrift für die österreichischen Gymnasien, 1850, etc.
Z.f.v.S. = Zeitschrift für vergleichende Sprachforschung, 1852, etc.

Glossary. Here I have tried to depart as little as possible from the plan laid down by Mr Wyatt. The glossary makes no attempt at being a complete verbal and grammatical index to the poem. It is desirable that such an index should exist: that there should be a place where a scholar who wishes to know exactly in what places even the commonest word is used in *Beowulf*, should be able to find the information he seeks. Such an index is supplied in Holder's edition, where all the instances in which even *ond* occurs will be found recorded: it is also supplied, on a slightly different plan, in the editions of Holthausen,

Heyne-Schücking, and Sedgefield. Finally Mr A. S. Cook has produced a *Concordance to Beowulf* (Halle, 1911). The work having been done so often and so well, it would have been useless to attempt to convert the glossary to this edition into yet another complete index to the poem; and the space saved can be utilized in explaining matters more necessary perhaps to the elementary student. Indeed, as Mr Wyatt remarked, a too elaborate glossary may "rob the work of much of its educative value": it is better to "furnish the requisite amount of help and no more."

One of the chief difficulties which beset English students of Anglo-Saxon is that of preventing their knowledge of modern English from leading them astray. When we meet with the word *æfter*, we must remember that 'after' only gives one specialized meaning of the O.E. word: *fǣr* would seldom be correctly translated by 'fear.' Another difficulty is the wide range of meanings possessed by the O.E. poetic vocabulary, and the ease with which a highly abstract passes into a very concrete idea. Thus *duguþ* signifies doughtiness, excellence: again, it signifies that body of tried veterans from whom the quality of *duguþ* is particularly to be expected. But we can hardly translate *duguþ* simply as 'warriors': for the abstract meaning reacts upon the concrete: they must be *doughty* warriors. A very close parallel is supplied by the English word 'chivalry,' though here the original sense is concrete. Starting with the signification of a body of horsemen, the word comes to signify the quality which should distinguish a knight. Then the abstract meaning reflects upon the concrete. When Milton speaks of 'paynim chivalry,' or Byron of the 'chivalry' gathered in Brussels before the field of Waterloo, the word means more than merely 'warriors.' So with *duguþ*. I have elsewhere suggested translating it by 'chivalry,' to which, in both its meanings, it closely approximates: *cūþe hē duguðe þēaw* "he knew the rule of chivalry[1]."

[1] I cannot agree with M. Huchon (on *Widsith*, l. 98) "rendre *duguþe* par '*chivalry*' au lieu de '*grown up men*' ou de '*warriors*' parait peu exact." *Duguþ* is much more than 'grown up men.' Thralls and churls half trained

To avoid dogmatism, and steadily to compare one passage with another, is the only way of safety. It is by the comparative method that Klaeber has been able to throw so much light upon many dark places in the text. Many alterations have been made in the glossary in view of the arguments produced by Klaeber: but in the main the glossary remains Mr Wyatt's work, though of course I take full responsibility for it in its present form.

The MS. has been carefully examined for the purposes of this edition. Whenever Zupitza's opinion as to the reading of the MS. is quoted, it may be taken, unless the contrary is indicated, that I read the MS. in the same way, though Zupitza is quoted for authority. With regard to Thorkelin's transcripts, however, although I have examined these at Copenhagen, I have trusted mainly to Zupitza, since they are too clear to leave much room for dispute.

I have to thank many scholars for their generous cooperation.

The proofs of the Introduction, Text and Notes have been read by my former teacher Prof. W. P. Ker, and by my colleague, Mr J. H. G. Grattan. To both of them, for performing this friendly office amid great pressure of work, my most grateful thanks are due. I am indebted to them for a large number of corrections and suggestions.

Mr Wyatt most kindly placed in my hands all the material he had collected for a new edition, including a copy of Heyne's edition of 1879, with copious MS. notes by Dr T. Miller, the editor of the O.E. *Bede*. These MS. notes would well repay a careful investigation, and to publish gleanings from them would be an act of piety to the memory of a good scholar. I regret that through lack of time I have not been able to make as much use of them for this edition as I had hoped. Mr Wyatt has further read the proofs throughout, with scrupulous care, and I am deeply indebted to him in many ways.

in war may be grown up, and may on occasion even be warriors, but they are not *duguþ*.

If the text should be found to be typographically accurate, thanks are largely due to two old pupils of mine, Miss E. V. Hitchcock and Mr E. Emson, and also to the Cambridge Press reader. Prof. Sedgefield kindly placed at my disposal a set of the proofs of his second edition, which has enabled me to bring up to date my references to his most valuable work.

Like every student of *Beowulf*, I have been particularly indebted to the bibliographical notes of Holthausen, the Heyne-Schücking glossary, the metrical researches of Sievers, and the syntactical studies of Klaeber. The footnotes give the names of the originators of emendations adopted in the text: and I have tried to give fairly exhaustive information of all readings adopted in any recent standard edition: for a student ought so to study *Beowulf* as to be able to translate not one particular text, but any.

Lastly, I regret that I have not been in a position to take the excellent advice recently given by one editor of *Beowulf* to another: that he should let his edition mature for the nine years recommended by Horace. Had I been permitted to spend so long in revising my proofs, the result would, I hope, have been a better edition: the printer's bill for corrections would certainly have been enormous. But it is well to stop weighing pros and cons, as Mosca de' Lamberti said, since "a thing done hath an end."

For giving which evil counsel, Dante saw the mutilated form of Mosca in the ninth pit of the eighth circle of Hell. If I have closured any discussion by a too hasty application of the principle 'cosa fatta capo ha' I hope my punishment may be more lenient. And so, in the pious words of an editor of four centuries ago, "If any faute be, I remyt the correctyon thereof to them that discretly shall fynde any reasonable defaute; and in their so doynge I shall pray god to sende them the blysse of heven."

R. W. CHAMBERS.

UNIVERSITY COLLEGE, LONDON,
Aug. 8, 1914.

NOTE

The following vowels are the only ones *certainly* marked long in the MS.:

út-, 33; án, 100; -wát, 123; wóp, 128; -wát, 210; bát, 211; bád, 264; hál, 300; bád, 301; ár, 336; -hár, 357; hát, gán, 386; mót, 442; án-, 449; sǽ, 507; gár-, 537; sǽ(-), 544, 564, 579; mót, 603; gád, 660; nát, 681; sǽ-, 690; -stód, 759; ábeag, 775; bán-, 780; wíc, 821; sǽ-, 895; -fón, 911; sár, 975; fáh, 1038; dón, 1116; sǽ-, 1149; mód, 1167; brúc, 1177; ǽr, 1187; rǽd, 1201; sǽ, 1223; wín, 1233; -wát, 1274; -wíc, 1275; hád, 1297; hár, 1307; bád, 1313; rún-, 1325; wát, 1331; ǽr, 1371, 1388; áris, 1390; gá, 1394; hám, 1407; bán-, 1445; dóm, 1491, 1528; brún-, 1546; gód, 1562; ǽr, 1587; -bád, 1720; lác, 1863; gód, 1870; sǽ-, 1882; rád, 1883; scír-, 1895; sǽ-, 1896, 1924; gár-, 1962; scán, 1965; fús, 1966; -hwíl, 2002; líc, 2080; róf, 2084; síd, 2086; -dón, 2090; cóm, 2103; sarlíc, 2109; dóm, 2147; Hroðgár, 2155; -stól, 2196; án, 2210 (see note); fǽr, 2230 (see note); -pád, -bád, 2258; án, 2280; -wóc, 2287; -bád, 2302; fór, 2308; -gód, 2342; wíd-, 2346; -dóm, 2376; sár, 2468; mán-, 2514; hárne stán, 2553; -swát, 2558; -swáf, 2559; bád, 2568; -wác, 2577; -swác, 2584; -gód, 2586; wíc-, 2607; Wigláf, 2631; gár-, 2641; fáne, 2655; -réc, 2661; stód, 2679; fýr-, 2689, 2701; wís-, 2716; bád, 2736; líf, 2743, 2751; stód, 2769; dóm, 2820, 2858; -rád, 2898; (-)cóm, 2944, 2992; ád-, 3010; fús, 3025; -róf, 3063; Wigláf, 3076; -bád, 3116; fús, 3119; ád, 3138; -réc, 3144; bán-, 3147.

The following are *probably* to be included, but there is some doubt:

bát, 742; bán-, 1116; blód, 1121; gán, 1163; ár-, 1168; sǽ-, 1652; sǽ-, 1850 (now either gone or covered by the paper); wát, 1863; gár-, 2043; hrán, 2270; gár-, 2674; -swác, 2681; -hróf, 3123; -hús, 3147.

On the other hand, the supposed mark over the following is *possibly* quite accidental: the scribes scattered little dots of ink not infrequently over the page:

brim-, 222; fus-, 232; me, 472; win, 1162; woc, 1960; dom, 2666, 2964.

With even more certainty the following supposed cases of marking may be dismissed:

we, 270; ancre, 303; hat, 897; al-walda, 955; ænig, 1099; þa, 1151; feonda, 1152 (the supposed mark is that of *ár*-, 1168, shining through the page); ac, 2477; he, 2704.

Schücking adds to the list of vowels marked long *till*, 2721 and *un*(*riht*), 2739. But the mark over these vowels is quite unlike the mark of length: it occurs again over *up*, 2893.

The latest and most careful scrutiny of the MS. is that of Dr Sedgefield, and I have collated my results with his.

Of the vowels which I have classed as *undoubtedly* marked long, Sedgefield regards many as doubtful, and others as too uncertain to be mentioned at all.

(*a*) *Marked doubtful by Sedgefield*: fáh, 1038; dón, 1116; hár, 1307; ǽr, 1371; án, 2280; -bád, 2302; dóm, 2376; wís-, 2716.

(*b*) *Entirely omitted by Sedgefield*: án, 100; mót, 442; sǽ-, 544; -fón, 911; dóm, 1528; gár-, 1962; síd, 2086; dóm, 2147; -stól, 2196; -pád, 2258; -wóc, 2287; -réc, 2661.

After careful and repeated scrutiny under a strong lens, I have no doubt as to the vowels in both these classes (*a*) and (*b*) being in every case marked long. Many of them appear to me even more clearly so marked than do some of those which Sedgefield agrees to be certainly marked long, such as sár, 975; stód, 2679; bán, 3147.

Of the vowels which I have classed as *probable*, bát, 742; bán-, 1116; blód, 1121; ár-, 1168; -swác, 2681 are classed as doubtful by Sedgefield: but gán, 1163; sǽ-, 1652, 1850; wát, 1863; gár-, 2043; hrán, 2270; gár-, 2674; -hróf, 3123; -hús, 3147, are regarded by him as too doubtful to be recorded at all.

The mark of length consists of a heavy dot, with a stroke sloping from it over the vowel. This stroke is very faint, and has often faded: in which case the mark of length can only be distinguished from an accidental blot by noting the position and shape of the dot, or by a microscopic search for traces of the stroke.

Complete certainty cannot be arrived at, since a stroke is sometimes perceptible only in certain lights. For example, after repeated scrutiny I had classed *gár*- (l. 2674) as one of the supposed cases of marking which might be dismissed. On a final examination I had to alter this, as I could make out the stroke fairly clearly.

BEOWULF

HWÆT, WĒ GĀR-DEna in ȝēar-daȝum Fol. 129ᵃ.
þēod-cyninȝa þrym ȝefrunon,
hū ðā æþelinȝas ellen fremedon.
Oft Scyld Scēfinȝ sceaþena þrēatum,
5 moneȝum mǣȝþum meodo-setla oftēah,
eȝsode eorl[*as*], syððan ǣrest wearð

Letters supplied in the text, but found neither in the MS. nor in Thorkelin's transcripts, are printed within square brackets. When it is clear that the absence of these letters from the manuscript is *not* due to the damage which the MS. has sustained, and that the letters can never have stood there, both square brackets and italics are used. Other deviations from the MS. are indicated in the text by italics alone, and the reading of the MS. is given in a footnote. The term 'MS. reading' must not however be taken to imply that the letters can all be read in the MS. in its present condition; but only that there is satisfactory evidence that they once stood there.

Certain letters and words which, though found in the MS., were presumably not in the original, but were added by the scribes, have been placed between brackets thus: ⟨þāra⟩.

Long syllables which can be proved on metrical grounds to represent an earlier disyllable are marked by the circumflex: *gân* representing an older *gāan* or perhaps having been substituted for the cognate *gangan*.

2. The original text presumably had *gefrugnon*, the combination of consonants making the syllable long, as, in conformity with metrical law, it should be.

5. Two distinct verbs seem to be confused in *oftēon*: (1) **oftīhan*, 'to deny' (cf. Goth. *teihan*) construed with gen. of thing and dat. of person, as here; (2) **oftēohan*, 'to tug, draw away' (cf. Goth. *tiuhan*) taking an acc. of the thing, as in l. 2489. [Cf. Sievers in *P.B.B.* xxix. 306.]

Whether *oftēah* mean 'denied' or 'drew away' the mead-benches, it equally indicates a reduction to servitude. Cf. l. 11 below, and the statement of Saxo Grammaticus concerning Scioldus that 'he subdued the whole race of the Allemanni and compelled them to pay tribute.' [Ed. Holder, p. 12.]

6. *eorl*[*as*], Kemble$_1$: MS. *eorl*. This correction seems desirable (1) metrically, because the type ⏊⏑̀ × ⏊, though found in the second half-line (cf. ll. 463, 623, *etc.*), is not elsewhere found in the first; and (2) syntactically, because *egsian* is elsewhere transitive, and to take *eorl* here as = 'many an earl' seems rather forced: l. 795 is not quite parallel [cf. Sievers in *P.B.B.* xxix. 560–576]. Yet *eorl* may be defensible [cf. Kock in *Anglia* xxvii. 219, *etc.*; xxviii. 140, *etc.*; Klaeber[249]].

fēa-sceaft funden; hē þæs frōfre ʒebād,
wēox under wolcnum, weorð-myndum þāh,
oð þæt him ǣʒhwylc ⟨þāra⟩ ymb-sittendra
10 ofer hron-rāde hȳran scolde,
ʒomban ʒyldan; þæt wæs ʒōd cyninʒ.
Đǣm eafera wæs æfter cenned
ʒeonʒ in ʒeardum, þone ʒod sende
folce tō frōfre; fyren-ðearfe onʒeat,
15 þæt hīe ǣr druʒon aldor-[lē]ase
lanʒe hwīle. Him þæs Līf-frêa,
wuldres Wealdend, worold-āre forʒeaf;
Bēowulf wæs brēme —blǣd wīde spranʒ—
Scyldes eafera Scede-landum in.
20 Swā sceal [ʒeonʒ ʒ]uma ʒōde ʒewyrcean,
fromum feoh-ʒiftum, on fæder |[bea]rme, Fol. 129b.

7. *fēa-sceaft*, 'as a helpless child.' See *Index of Persons*: Scyld; and cf. *umbor-wesende* below.

þæs frōfre, 'consolation for that,' i.e. for his helplessness.

9. *þāra* is presumably the addition of a scribe, being opposed to the usage of *Beowulf* both (1), metrically, since *ymbsittendra* makes a complete half-line, and the preceding *þāra* is not only otiose, but irregular [see Sievers in *P.B.B.* x. 256]; and (2), syntactically, since *sē*, *sēo*, *þæt* is in *Beowulf* a demonstrative, and is very seldom used as a mere article. [See *Introduction to Beowulf.*]

15. *þæt*: MS. ꝥ, which is normally used as an abbreviation for *þæt*. Since the antecedent *fyren-ðearf* is fem., some would take ꝥ here as an abbreviation for *þā*: 'the dire need which they had suffered.' Zupitza supports this interpretation of ꝥ, although dubiously.

aldor-[lē]ase. MS. defective; but there is no reason to doubt that the missing letters were *le*. Holthausen, to avoid the syntactical difficulty of *þæt* (see above), reads *aldor-[lē]as[t]e*, and takes *þæt* as a conjunction: 'He [God] knew their cruel need: how that, before, they long had suffered want of a lord.' But we can take *þæt* as a conj. without this change: 'that, being without a lord, they had before experienced a long time of sorrow': for *drugon lange hwīle* cf. l. 87, *þrāge geþolode*.

For the explanation of *aldor-lēase* see *Index of Persons*: Heremod.

16. *Him*, pl.; *þæs*, 'in compensation for that,' i.e. the evil days.

frēa. The metre demands a disyllabic form, such as *frēga* [Sievers]; and most recent editors insert this form in the text.

18. *Bēowulf*. Not the hero of the poem.

18, 19. *eafera* is in apposition with *Bēowulf*. Trautmann, Heyne-Schücking and Holthausen follow the emendation of Kemble$_1$

Bēowulf wæs brēme, blǣd wide sprang
Scyldes eafera[n] Scede-landum in.

='the glory of the son of Scyld spread far and wide.' The alteration is not necessary [cf. Klaeber in *Engl. Stud.* xxxix. 428].

20. MS. defective. Grein's reading adopted in text.

21. MS. defective at corner. The respective merits of the restorations attempted by the earlier editors have been zealously canvassed ever since. These restorations are:

feorme, 'while yet in his father's support' [Kemble$_1$];

þæt hine on ylde eft ȝewuniȝen
wil-ȝesīþas, þonne wīȝ cume,
lēode ȝelǣsten; lof-dǣdum sceal
25 in mǣȝþa ȝehwǣre man ȝeþēon.
Him ðā Scyld ȝewāt tō ȝescæp-hwīle
fela-hrōr fēran on Frēan wǣre;
hī hyne þā ætbǣron tō brimes faroðe,
swǣse ȝesīþas, swā hē selfa bæd,
30 þenden wordum wēold wine Scyldinȝa;
lēof land-fruma lanȝe āhte.

bearme, 'bosom' [Bouterwek, Thorpe: so Holthausen$_{2,3}$];
wine, 'to his father's friends' [Grundtvig, 1861, p. 1];
ærne, 'in his father's house' [Grein$_1$: so Sedgefield, Schücking];
leofne, 'sustenance' [Trautmann].

We are dealing here, not with conjectural emendation, but with attempts to decipher a MS. reading which has been partially lost. The data which can still be ascertained are:

First a space ($\frac{5}{16}$ in.) for two or three letters;

Then a fragment of a letter involving a long down stroke (i.e. either *f*, *r*, *s*, *þ*, or *w*; this letter was seen fully only by the five earliest transcribers or collators, who unanimously describe it as *r*; the fact that Thorkelin in his edition chose to read *þina*, and altered the *r* of his transcript to *þ* in conformity with his theory, in no way invalidates this evidence);

Then something which can now be read either as *m*, *in*, or blank space followed by *n* (the earliest transcribers support only the readings *m* or *in*);

Then *e*.

Wine and *ærne* are, then, opposed to the evidence of the earliest transcribers, and cannot be read into the MS. even in its present condition, for they fail to make the line come up to the margin, which the scribe (with only the rarest exceptions, e.g. l. 1753) keeps precisely.

leofne fills the space, but is syntactically faulty [cf. Sievers in *P.B.B.* xxix. 306] and the *f* is inconsistent with the early transcriptions.

feorme gives unsatisfactory sense and is metrically impossible as involving double alliteration in the second half-line;

bearme fits exactly (the *bea*, for instance, of l. 40 just fills the necessary $\frac{5}{16}$ in.), and gives satisfactory sense, especially if, with Klaeber [*J.E.G.Ph.* vi. 190], we render 'in his father's possession': the young prince gives treasures from his father's store—which, as Klaeber (following Sievers) remarks, would agree excellently with Saxo's description of Scioldus: '*proceres*...domesticis *stipendiis colebat*....'

25. Here and elsewhere, as Sievers points out [*P.B.B.* x. 485], metre demands, instead of the fem. *gehwǣre*, the form *gehwām*, which in the older language is used with feminines as well as with masculines and neuters. Cf. Sievers$_3$ § 341, N. 4.

31. *āhte* needs an object, expressed or understood. We may either supply mentally *swǣse gesīþas* or *hī* [Klaeber[446]] or we may insert *hī* in the text: *lange hī āhte*, 'long he ruled them' [Holthausen]. Many emendations have been suggested in order to supply an object to *āhte*: *līf* in place of *lēof*, 'the chief long possessed his life' [Rieger[382]]; *lǣndagas āhte*, 'possessed these transitory days' [Kluge[188]]; *lān* [or *lǣn*] *geāhte* 'possessed the grant, the land lent by God' [Kock in *Anglia*, xxvii. 223. For many other emendations and interpretations see Cosijn[1]; Bright in *M.L.N.* x. 43 (*geweald* for *weold*); Child in *M.L.N.* xxi. 175; Sievers in *P.B.B.* xxix. 308].

þǣr æt hȳðe stōd hrinȝed stefna
īsiȝ ond ūt-fūs, æþelinȝes fær;
ālēdon þā lēofne þēoden,
35 bēaȝa bryttan on bearm scipes,
mǣrne be mæste. Þǣr wæs mādma fela
of feor-weȝum frætwa ȝelǣded.
Ne hȳrde ic cȳmlīcor cēol ȝeȝyrwan
hilde-wǣpnum ond heaðo-wǣdum,
40 billum ond byrnum; him on bearme læȝ
mādma mæniȝo, þā him mid scoldon
on flōdes ǣht feor ȝewītan.
Nalæs hī hine lǣssan lācum tēodan,
þēod-ȝestrēonum, þon[*ne*] þā dydon,
45 þe hine æt frum-sceafte forð onsendon
ǣnne ofer ȳðe umbor-we|sende. Fol. 130ª.
Þā ȝȳt hīe him āsetton seȝen ȝ[yl]denne
hēah ofer hēafod, lēton holm beran,
ȝēafon on ȝār-secȝ; him wæs ȝeōmor sefa,
50 murnende mōd. Men ne cunnon
secȝan tō sōðe, sele-rǣden*de*,
hæleð under heofenum, hwā þǣm hlæste onfēnȝ.

I ÐĀ wæs on burȝum Bēowulf Scyldinȝa,
lēof lēod-cyninȝ lonȝe þrāȝe
55 folcum ȝefrǣȝe —fæder ellor hwearf,

33. *isig*, 'covered with ice' [cf. Sievers in *P.B.B.* xxxvi. 422].
38. *gegyrwan*. In modern English the passive inf. would be used.
44. *þon*[*ne*]. Thorkelin's emendation: MS. *þon*.
46. *umbor-wesende*. Uninflected. Cf. Sievers$_3$ § 305, N. 1. Cf. l. 372.
47. MS. defective at corner; missing letters supplied by Kemble$_1$.
48–9. Cf. Sievers in *P.B.B.* xxviii. 271.
51. *sele-rǣdende*, Kemble$_3$ following l. 1346: MS. *sele rædenne*.
52. The nearest parallel to the burial of Scyld is that of Baldr in the *Prose Edda* (chap. 48): 'But the gods took the body of Baldr, and carried it to the seashore. Baldr's ship was named Hringhorni: it was the greatest of all ships, and the gods sought to launch it, and to build the pyre of Baldr on it...Then was the body of Baldr borne out onto the ship...Odin laid on the pyre the gold ring named Draupnir...and Baldr's horse with all his trappings was placed on the pyre.'
In historic times the chiefs were still burnt or buried in ships.
For the voyage of the dead, cf. the stories of Sinfjǫtli (O.E. Fitela), whose body is wafted away by a mysterious ferryman (see *Index of Persons*); of Elaine (the lady of Shalott); and of Arthur himself, who, like Scyld, goes "from the great deep to the great deep."
53. *Bēowulf*. Still the prince of l. 18: to be distinguished from the hero of the poem.

aldor of earde— oþ þæt him eft onwōc
hēah Healfdene; hēold þenden lifde,
ʒamol ond ʒūð-rēouw, ʒlæde Scyldinʒas.
Ðǣm fēower bearn forð ʒerīmed
60 in worold wōcun, weoroda rǣswa[*n*],
Heoroʒār ond Hrōðʒār ond Hālʒa til;
hȳrde ic, þæt [........ *wæs On*]elan cwēn
Heaðo-Scilfinʒas heals-ʒebedda.
Þā wæs Hrōðʒāre here-spēd ʒyfen,
65 wīʒes weorð-mynd, þæt him his wine-māʒas
ʒeorne hȳrdon, oðð þæt sēo ʒeoʒoð ʒewēox,
maʒo-driht micel. Him on mōd be-arn,

57–8. *hēah* and *gamol* are both conventional epithets for Healfdene, found also in O.N. (*Halfdan gamle—Skáldskaparmál*, 73: *Halfdan hǽstr Skjolldunga—Hyndluljóð*, 14).

gūð-rēouw shows the *w* on the way to becoming a vowel and causing the triphthong *ēou* [cf. Zupitza in *Z.f.d.A.* xxi. 10].

glæde may be an adverb 'gladly,' but is more probably an adjective agreeing with *Scyldingas*, 'the gracious, lordly Scyldings' [cf. Klaeþer in *Anglia*, xxix. 378–9].

60. *rǣswa*[*n*], Kemble$_2$: MS. *rǣswa*. Kemble's emendation has been widely accepted. The change is exceedingly slight, cf. note to l. 1176. Indeed in the Anglian original of *Beowulf* the final *n* of the oblique cases of weak nouns may already have been lost, and the scribe who put the poem into W.S. would not in that case recognize the form as a plural [Cosijn^{25}]. Cf. note to l. 1543.

62. ...[*On*]*elan*, Grundtvig [*Brage*, IV. 500]; Bugge [*Tidsskr.* viii. 43] supported this and supplied *wæs*: the name of the lady and part of that of her consort were omitted by the scribe, who wrote *hyrde ic ꝥ elan cwen*, without anything to indicate at what point in the sentence the omission may have occurred.

As the husband is a Swede (*Heaðoscilfing*, cf. l. 2205) the coincidence between *elan* and the name of the Swedish king *Onela* is too remarkable to be overlooked, especially as it relieves us from having to postulate a Germanic princess with the extraordinary name of *Elan*. The reading of the text, which leaves the lady's name unknown, is therefore preferable to the theory [of Grein$_2$, Ettmüller$_3$, Sedgefield$_1$, *etc.*] which makes Elan the name of the queen, and supplies Ongentheow, father of Onela, as the husband:

hȳrde ic þæt Elan cwēn [*Ongenþēowes wæs*]
Heaðo-Scilfingas heals-gebedda.

There is no external evidence for either alliance: chronologically either is possible.

Kluge [*Engl. Stud.* xxii. 144], following the *Saga of Rolf Kraki*, where Halfdan has a daughter Signy, who weds earl Saevil, suggested:

hȳrde ic þæt [*Sigenēow wæs Sǣw*]*elan cwēn*.

So Sedgefield$_2$ and Schücking. But Saevil was not a king of Sweden. [For a full discussion of the passage see Trautmann in *Anglia, Beiblatt*, x. 259.]

63. For gen. sg. in *as*, cf. ll. 2453, 2921; Sievers$_3$ § 237, N. 1. For *gebedda*, masc. in form, but here fem. in meaning (as *foregenga*, applied to Judith's female attendant, *Judith*, 127), cf. Sievers$_3$ § 278, N. 4.

67. *be-arn* from *be-iernan*, *q.v.*

þæt heal-reced hātan wolde,
|medo-ærn micel, men ʒewyrcean, **Fol. 130b.**
70 þon[*n*]e yldo bearn ǣfre ʒefrunon,
ond þǣr on innan eall ʒedǣlan
ʒeonʒum ond ealdum, swylc him ʒod sealde,
būton folc-scare ond feorum ʒumena.
Đā ic wīde ʒefræʒn weorc ʒebannan
75 maniʒre mǣʒþe ʒeond þisne middan-ʒeard,
folc-stede frætwan. Him on fyrste ʒelomp
ǣdre mid yldum, þæt hit wearð eal ʒearo,
heal-ærna mǣst; scōp him Heort naman,
sē þe his wordes ʒeweald wīde hæfde.
80 Hē bēot ne āleh, bēaʒas dǣlde,
sinc æt symle. Sele hlīfade
hēah ond horn-ʒēap; heaðo-wylma bād
lāðan līʒes. Ne wæs hit lenʒe þā ʒēn,

68. Rask [*Angelsaksisk Sproglære*, 1817] and Kemble$_1$, followed by most of the older editors, read *þæt* [*hē*] *heal-reced*. But *hē* need not be expressed: it is understood from *him* in the preceding line.

70. *þon*[*n*]*e* is an emendation of Grein$_1$ and Grundtvig (1861, p. 3). If in other respects we retain the MS. reading, 'greater' must be understood from *micel* in the preceding line. Parallels have often been adduced for this usage of the positive where we should expect the comparative. But Bright has shown [*M.L.N.* xxvii. 181–3] that the clearest of these parallels [*Psalms*, 117, 8–9: *Ps.* 118 in our reckoning] is due simply to a literal translation of a biblical idiom, and that in other cases [e.g. *Elene*, 647] the text is very probably corrupt. Bright would alter the text here to *medo-ærn micle māre gewyrcean þonne*... 'a hall much greater than'.... See also Cosijn[1].

yldo bearn, 'the children of men.' Such gen. pls. in *o* are rare, but undoubted. See Sievers$_3$ § 237, N. 4. [For a collection of instances, cf. Klaeber in *M.L.N.* xvi. 17–18.]

73. Cf. Tacitus [*Germ.* VII.]: 'The kings have not despotic or unlimited power.'

77. *ǣdre mid yldum*, 'presently amid men.' Earle's rendering 'with a quickness surprising to men' is forced.

78. Heorot is probably so named from the horns on the gable, cf. *horn-gēap*, l. 82. But possibly *horn* simply means 'corner,' 'gable,' and *horn-gēap* 'wide-gabled' [cf. Miller in *Anglia*, xii. 396].

83. Two interpretations of *lenge* are offered:

(1) 'the time was not yet at hand that...,' *lenge* being an adj. meaning 'pertaining to'; *gelenge* in this sense is not uncommon, but there is no certain instance of *lenge*, and to take 'pertaining to' in the sense of 'at hand' is forced. However this interpretation [Rieger[382]] has been followed widely, and recently by Schücking, Sedgefield and Holthausen$_3$.

Or (2) *lenge* may be another form of the comparative adv. *leng* (Grein). The comparative here (where Mod. Eng. would use a positive) would be paralleled by ll. 134, 2555. The meaning would then be 'the time was not very distant.' [So Klaeber[246].]

Holthausen$_2$ reads *longe*.

þæt se *ecᵹ*-hete āþum-swerian
85 æfter wæl-nīðe wæcnan scolde.
Ðā se ellen-ᵹǣst earfoðlīce
þrāᵹe ᵹeþolode, sē þe in þȳstrum bād,
þæt hē dōᵹora ᵹehwām drēam ᵹehȳrde
hlūdne in healle; þǣr wæs hearpan swēᵹ,
90 swutol sanᵹ scopes. Sæᵹde sē þe cūþe
frumsceaft fīra feorran reccan,
|cwæð þæt se Ælmihtiᵹa eorðan worh[te], Fol. 132a.
wlite-beorhtne wanᵹ, swā wæter bebūᵹeð;
ᵹesette siᵹe-hrēþiᵹ sunnan ond mōnan
95 lēoman tō lēohte land-būendum,
ond ᵹefrætwade foldan scēatas
leomum ond lēafum; līf ēac ᵹesceōp
cynna ᵹehwylcum, þāra ðe cwice hwyrfaþ.
Swā ðā driht-ᵹuman drēamum lifdon
100 ēadiᵹlīce, oð ðæt ān onᵹan
fyrene fre[m]man, fēond on helle;

84. *ecg-hete*, $Grein_1$: MS. *secghete*. Cf. l. 1738, and *Seafarer*, 70.
āþum-swerian: *āþum*='son-in-law,' *swēor*='father-in-law.' It is clear that we have to do with a compound, meaning 'son- and father-in-law,' comparable to *suhtergefæderan* (l. 1164), *suhtorfædran* (*Widsith*, 46), 'nephew and uncle.' All recent editors follow Trautmann in altering *āþum-swerian* to *ābum-swēorum*; and it may well be that this was the original reading, and that the scribe misunderstood *āþum* as 'oaths' and so came to miswrite *swēorum* as *swerian* 'to swear.' Yet *swerian* may perhaps be defended as =*swerigum* from **sweriga* 'father-in-law,' a form not elsewhere recorded, but standing to *swēor* much as *suhtriga* to *suhtor*, both meaning 'nephew' (cf. *Genesis*, 1775, *his suhtrian wif*). [Bugge, *Tidsskr*. viii. 45–6 defended *swerian*, comparing Goth. *brōþrahans* and Icel. *feðgar*.]
The reference is to the contest between Hrothgar and his son-in-law Ingeld (cf. ll. 2020–69). Possibly the hall was burnt in this contest, which took place, as we know from *Widsith*, '*æt Heorote*.' But more probably l. 82 refers to the later struggle among the kin of Hrothgar, when the hall was burnt over Hrothulf's head. See *Index of Persons*: Hrothulf.
86. *ellen-gǣst*. $Grein_1$ and Rieger[383] emend to the more usual *ellor-gǣst*, which is also adopted by Earle and Sedgefield; cf. ll. 807, 1617, *etc*. See note to l. 102.
87. *þrāge*, 'a hard time' (Klaeber[254], comparing *Juliana*, 464, *is þēos þrāg ful strong*). See also *Beowulf*, l. 2883 [cf. Cosijn[6]].
92. *worh*[*te*], $Kemble_1$: MS. defective at corner.
93. *swā*, relative: see *Glossary*.
101. *frem*[*m*]*an*, $Kemble_1$: MS. defective at edge.
Earle adopts the emendation [of Bugge[80]], *healle* for *helle*, because it is 'so simple, and gives so much relief.' On the other hand, in l. 142 he adopts *hel-ðegnes* for *heal-ðegnes* [as suggested tentatively by $Ettmüller_1$ but not adopted by him]. Both changes are needless.
fēond on helle is simply 'hell-fiend' [Cosijn[3]]. Cf. *helle hæfton*, l. 788.

wæs se ʒrimma ʒǣst ʒrendel hāten,
mǣre mearc-stapa, sē þe mōras hēold,
fen ond fæsten; fīfel-cynnes eard
105 won-sǣlī wer weardode hwīle,
siþðan him Scyppend forscrifen hæfde.
In Cāines cynne þone cwealm ʒewræc
ēce Drihten, þæs þe hē Ābel slōʒ.
Ne ʒefeah hē þǣre fǣhðe, ac hē hine feor forwræc,
110 Metod for þȳ māne, man-cynne fram.
Þanon untȳdras ealle onwōcon,
eotenas ond ylfe ond orcnêas,
swylce ʒī|ʒantas, þā wið ʒode wunnon Fol. 132b.

102. *gæst.* This ambiguous word may stand for *gāst* 'spirit,' or *giest*, *gist*, *gyst*, 'stranger'; *giest* is, of course, akin to the Latin *hostis*, and sometimes acquires the sense of 'hostile stranger,' 'foe' (e.g. ll. 1441, 1522, 1545 *sele-gyst*, 2560 *gryre-giest*).

In ll. 1800, 1893 there can be no doubt that *gæst* stands for *giest*, 'stranger.' In l. 2073 and in *inwit-gæst* (2670) the word is connected with *nēos[i]an* 'to visit,' which makes it highly probable that it means *giest* and is used with grim irony. In the last instance we have confirmation from the fact that *gryre-giest* is applied to the dragon in l. 2560; and I should be inclined also to take *gæst* (2312), *nīð-gæst* (2699) as = *giest*, *nīð-giest*. The dragon is not regarded as a spirit of hell, but as a strange phenomenon. Grendel and his mother, on the contrary, *are* regarded as diabolic spirits (cf. 1266); and when applied to them I take *gæst* = *gāst* 'spirit' (102: *wæl-gǣst*, 1331, 1995: *ellor-gǣst*, 1349, 1617). This is confirmed by the fact that ll. 807, 1621 give (*ellor*)-*gāst*, which can only mean 'spirit.'

In l. 1123 *gæsta* = *gāsta*.

104. Moor and fen were the appropriate dwelling-places of misbegotten beings. Jordanes, recording Gothic traditions, mentions the offspring of witches and evil spirits: a race 'which was of old amid the fens.' Cf. note to l. 426.

106–8. Sievers [*P.B.B.* ix. 137]:

...*forscrifen hæfde*
in Caines cynne (*þone cwealm gewræc*
ēce Drihten)...

'Had proscribed him amid the race of Cain (the eternal Lord avenged that death) for that he slew Abel.'

109. *hē*...*hē hine* = Cain...God, Cain.

112. *orcnēas.* The meaning 'sea-monster' is often attributed to this word (e.g. by Heyne and Schücking), on the theory that it is a compound, the first element connected with Icel. *ørkn* 'a kind of seal' [cf. Lat. *orca* 'a kind of whale'], and the second with O.E. *eoh*, 'horse.' [Kluge in *P.B.B.* ix. 188, in part following Heyne.]

But the context seems to demand 'evil spirit,' rather than 'sea-horse.' From the Lat. *Orcus* 'Hell, Death' was derived the O.E. *orc* 'giant' or 'devil,' as is proved by the gloss '*orcus*: *orc*, *þyrs oððe hel-deofol*.' *Orc-nēas* may be a compound of *orc* with *nē* 'corpse' (cf. *nē-fugol*, 'carrion-bird,' *Gen.* 2158; *dryht-nēum*, 'host of corpses,' *Exod.* 163; and Goth. *náus*, 'a corpse'). [See Bugge[80–82] and in *Z.f.d.Ph.*, iv. 193; and cf. ten Brink[10]; Sievers in *P.B.B.* xxxvi. 428.]

lange þrāȝe; hē him ðæs lēan forȝeald.
II 115 Gewāt ðā nēosian, syþðan niht becōm,
hêan hūses, hū hit Hrinȝ-Dene
æfter bēor-þeȝe ȝebūn hæfdon.
Fand þā ðǣr inne æþelinȝa ȝedriht
swefan æfter symble; sorȝe ne cūðon,
120 wonsceaft wera. Wiht unhǣlo,
ȝrim ond ȝrǣdiȝ, ȝearo sōna wæs,
rēoc ond rēþe, ond on ræste ȝenam
þrītig þeȝna; þanon eft ȝewāt
hūðe hrēmiȝ tō hām faran,
125 mid þǣre wæl-fylle wīca nēosan.
Ðā wæs on ūhtan mid ǣr-dæȝe
Ȝrendles ȝūð-cræft ȝumum undyrne;
þā wæs æfter wiste wōp ūp āhafen,
micel morȝen-swēȝ. Mǣre þēoden,
130 æþeling ǣr-ȝōd, unblīðe sæt,
þolode ðrȳð-swȳð, þeȝn-sorȝe drēah,
syðþan hīe þæs lāðan lāst scēawedon,

115. *nēosian.* Sievers reads *nēosan*, for metrical reasons. Cf. l. 125. See *Introduction to Beowulf*.

116. *hēan.* The weak adj. without definite art. is a feature of early O.E. poetry. See *Introduction to Beowulf*.

120. Sievers [*P.B.B.* ix. 137] reads *wera*[*s*], 'the men knew not sorrow.' Some edd. put the stop after *unhǣlo*, 'they knew not sorrow, aught of evil.' But with this punctuation *Grim ond grǣdig* makes a very abrupt beginning of the next sentence; and I see no reason to doubt that *wiht unhǣlo* can mean 'the creature of evil, Grendel'; cf. *hǣlo-bearn*, 'Saviour-child' in *Crist*, 586, 754. [See also Klaeber, *Christ. Elementen*, in *Anglia*, xxxv. 252.]

128. *æfter wiste*, 'after their weal,' or 'after their feasting,' followed lamentation. This seems a more likely interpretation than that there was lamentation concerning Grendel's feasting upon the thirty thanes. [Cf. Kock in *Anglia*, xxvii. 223.]

131. *ðrȳð-swȳð*. Earle takes this as a noun, 'mighty pain,' 'majestic rage,' comparing Icel. *sviði*, 'a smart from burning.' Surely this is seeking trouble, for there is no evidence for any O.E. noun *swȳð*, 'pain, smart,' whilst the adj. *swȳð*, 'strong,' is common. It seems, then, natural to take *ðrȳð-swȳð* as an adj., 'strong in might,' parallel to *earm-swīð*, *mōd-swīð*, which are indisputably adjs., meaning 'strong in arm,' 'strong in mind,' not nouns meaning 'arm-pain,' 'mind-pain.' Context too supports the adjectival rendering 'strong in might'; for it is at least as satisfactory here as 'mighty pain,' and more so in l. 736, the only other passage where *þrȳð-swȳð* occurs. If we thus make *þrȳð-swȳð* an adj., we have to take *þolian* as intransitive. But there is no difficulty about this: cf. l. 2499, and *Maldon*, 307. [Earle quotes Grein in support of his interpretation: yet Grein$_2$ renders 'stark an Kraft.']

werȝan ȝāstes; wæs þæt ȝewin tō stranȝ,
lāð ond lonȝsum. Næs hit lenȝra |fyrst, Fol. 133ª.
135 ac ymb āne niht eft ȝefremede
morð-beala māre ond nō mearn fore,
fæhðe ond fyrene; wæs tō fæst on þām.
Þā wæs ēað-fynde, þe him elles hwǣr
ȝerūmlīcor ræste [*sōhte*],
140 bed æfter būrum, ðā him ȝebēacnod wæs,
ȝesæȝd sōðlīce, sweotolan tācne
heal-ðeȝnes hete; hēold hyne syðþan
fyr ond fæstor, sē þǣm fēonde ætwand.
Swā rīxode ond wið rihte wan
145 āna wið eallum, oð þæt īdel stōd
hūsa sēlest. Wæs sēo hwīl micel;
twelf wintra tīd torn ȝeþolode
wine Scyld*inȝ*a, wēana ȝehwelcne,
sīdra sorȝa; forðam [*syðþan*] wearð
150 ylda bearnum undyrne cūð,
ȝyddum ȝeōmore, þætte Ȝrendel wan
hwīle wið Hrōþȝār, hete-nīðas wæȝ,
fyrene ond fæhðe fela missēra,

133. It is not easy to be certain whether *wergan*, here and in l. 1747, is the weak form of *wērig*, 'weary,' or is to be read short, *werga*, 'accursed.' The latter seems to be the more probable. Cf. *wergan*, *wyrgan*, 'to curse' [and see Hart in *M.L.N.* xxii. 220, *etc.*; and Earle, 168].

136. *māre* 'further,' 'additional' murder—does not of course imply that the second attack was more murderous than the first. [Cf. Klaeber[449].]

morð-beala for *morð-bealu*. Some edd. alter, but see note to l. 1914. [Cf. Bugge in *Z.f.d.Ph.* IV. 194 and Sievers in *P.B.B.* xxix. 312.]

138. The typical understatement of O.E. verse: 'It was easy to find one who sought rest outside the hall,' amounts to saying that all deserted it.

139. [*sōhte*] Grein$_1$; no gap in MS.

140. *æfter būrum*. The bowers lie *outside* the hall, as in the 'Cynewulf and Cyneheard' episode in the *Anglo-Saxon Chronicle*. The retainers, who would normally sleep in the hall, prefer a bed by the bowers, which are free from Grendel's attack.

142–3. The survivors held themselves 'the safer the further away.'

146–7. Sievers [*P.B.B.* ix. 137]:
hūsa sēlest (*wæs sēo hwīl micel*)
twelf wintra tīd...

147. *twelf*: MS. .XII.

148. *Scyldinga*, Grundtvig[269], Kemble$_2$: MS. *scyldenda*.

149. No gap in MS.: [*syðþan*] supplied by Kemble$_2$, following private communication from Thorpe. Cf. ll. 1453, 2175. Some stop-gap is required for the alliteration. Klaeber [*J.E.G.Ph.* vi. 191] supplies *secgum*, so too Schücking; Holthausen$_{2,3}$ *sōna*; Bugge[367], *sārcwidum*; Sievers [*P.B.B.*

sinȝāle sæce; sibbe ne wolde
155 wið manna hwone mæȝenes Deniȝa,
feorh-bealo feorran, fēa þingian;
nē þǣr nǣniȝ witena wēnan þorfte
beorhtre bōte tō ban*an* folmum.
|[Atol] ǣȝlǣca ēhtende wæs, **Fol. 133b.**
160 deorc dēaþ-scūa, duȝuþe ond ȝeoȝoþe,
seomade ond syrede, sin-nihte hēold
mīstiȝe mōras; men ne cunnon,
hwyder hel-rūnan hwyrftum scrīþað.
Swā fela fyrena fēond man-cynnes,
165 atol ān-ȝenȝea, oft ȝefremede,
heardra hȳnða; Heorot eardode,
sinc-fāȝe sel sweartum nihtum;
nō hē þone ȝif-stōl ȝrētan mōste,
māþðum for Metode, ne his myne wisse.

xxix. 313], *for þām sōcnum*: cf. l. 1777. Klaeber, following Sievers' suggestion, substitutes *forðan*, the form usual in *Beowulf*.

154–5. *sibbe* and *feorh-bealo feorran* are possibly parallel, 'he wished not for peace, or to remove the life-bale,' the verbal phrase explaining the noun more fully, as in ll. 185–6, *frōfre...wihte gewendan* [cf. Bugge[82]; Klaeber[238]]. We can, however, construe *sibbe* as an instrumental, in which case there should be no comma after *Deniga*: 'he would not out of compassion to any man remove the life-bale.' [Cf. Grein; Sievers, *P.B.B.* xxix. 317.]

156. *fēa*. Kemble$_2$ normalized to *fēo*, and has been followed by all the editors. Yet *ēa* for *ēo* is a common Anglian (especially Northumbrian) peculiarity. See Sievers$_3$ § 150. 3.

157–8. *wēnan tō*, 'to expect from.' See *Glossary*: *wēnan*, and cf. l. 1396.

158. *beorhtre* is, of course, not comparative, as taken by many editors and translators, but gen. fem., agreeing with *bōte*, after *wēnan*.

banan, Kemble$_2$: miswritten in MS. *banū*. The error possibly arose through the influence of *folmū* (cf. l. 2961); or possibly *banā* (=*banan*) in an older MS. was written with an open *a* and this, as so often, was wrongly transcribed as *u* (cf. ll. 581, 2821, 2961).

159. MS. defective. [*Atol*] Thorpe; [*ac sē*], without a period, Rieger[384].

163. *hel-rūnan*. The fem. *hel-rūne*, 'witch,' occurs in several glosses: the Gothic equivalent is recorded by Jordanes: Filimer, King of the Goths, found among his people certain witches, '*quas patrio sermone Haliurunnas is ipse cognominat*' [*Getica*, cap. xxiv.]. It is not clear whether in this passage in *Beowulf* we have the fem., or a corresponding masc., *hel-rūna*, not elsewhere recorded.

167–9. *for Metode* is generally taken 'on account of the Lord': cf. l. 706, *þā Metod nolde*. Holtzmann [*Germania*, viii. 489] makes *hē* refer to Hrothgar: 'he could not touch his throne, his treasure, by reason of God's prohibition, nor have joy in it.' But this seems very difficult, since Grendel has been the subject for the last fifteen lines. Most probably, then, *hē* refers to Grendel, who 'was not suffered to outrage Hrothgar's throne by reason of God's prohibition: he knew not His mind' (i.e. the fate in store for him).

But the phrase may mean simply that Grendel is a fiend rejected by God,

170 þæt wæs wrǣc micel wine Scyldinȝa,
mōdes brecða. Moniȝ oft ȝesæt
rīce tō rūne, rǣd eahtedon,
hwæt swīð-ferhðum sēlest wǣre
wið fǣr-ȝryrum tō ȝefremmanne.
175 Hwīlum hīe ȝehēton æt *hærȝ*-trafum
wīg-weorþunȝa, wordum bǣdon,
þæt him ȝāst-bona ȝēoce ȝefremede
wið þēod-þrēaum. Swylc wæs þēaw hyra,
hǣþenra hyht; helle ȝemundon
180 in mōd-sefan, Metod hīe ne cūþon,
dǣda Dēmend, ne wiston hīe Drihten ȝod,
|ne hīe hūru heofena Helm herian ne cūþon, Fol. 134ᵃ.
wuldres Waldend. Wā bið þǣm ðe sceal
þurh slīðne nīð sāwle bescūfan
185 in fȳres fæþm, frōfre ne wēnan,
wihte ȝewendan; wel bið þǣm þe mōt
æfter dēað-dæȝe Drihten sēcean,
ond tō Fæder fæþmum freoðo wilnian.
III Swā ðā mǣl-ceare maȝa Healfdenes

and hence cannot approach *God's* throne or receive a gift in the presence of his Creator. In this case, it is suggested by Klaeber [*J.E.G.Ph.* viii. 254] that *ne his myne wisse* means 'nor did He (God) take thought of him (Grendel).' [Parallels for this are given by Klaeber, *Christ. Elementen*, in *Anglia*, xxxv. 254, e.g. *Exeter Gnomic Verses*, 162, *wǣrlēas mon ond wonhȳdig þæs ne gȳmeð God.*] Anyway the contrast is between the loyal thane who approaches the throne to do homage and receive gifts, and such a 'hall-thane' (cf. l. 142) as Grendel.

[Cf. also Cosijn[5]; Kock in *Anglia*, xxvii. 225; Pogatscher in *P.B.B.* xix. 544, who suggests *formetode* as a verb from **formetian*: 'he despised the giving of treasure'; Sievers in *P.B.B.* xxix. 319. Kölbing in *Engl. Stud.* iii. 92.]

175. *hærg*: MS. *hrærg*: Kemble$_2$ corrected to *hearg*: Grundtvig (1861, p. 6) kept nearer to the MS. by retaining the spelling *hærg*. This heathen term had perhaps become less intelligible when our MS. was transcribed, whence the scribe's error.

It has often been objected that these lines are not consistent with the Christian sentiments uttered by leading characters elsewhere in the poem: that Hrothgar, for instance, does not talk like a pagan (cf. e.g. ll. 1724, *seq.*). Attempts have been made to harmonize the discrepancy by supposing that the Danes are regarded as Christians, but as having in time of stress relapsed, like the East Angles in the seventh century. [Klaeber, *Christ. Elementen*, in *Anglia*, xxxv. 134: Bright in Routh's *Ballad Theory*, 1905, 54, *footnote*.] But this supposition is unnecessary, for such Christian sentiments as Hrothgar or Beowulf do utter are vague and undogmatic, not unlike the godly expressions that Chaucer puts into the mouth of his pious heathen. [See *Introduction to Beowulf*.]

189. *mǣl-ceare*, 'the sorrow of this time' (i.e. the time spoken of above):

190 singāla sēað; ne mihte snotor hæleð
wēan onwendan; wæs þæt gewin tō swȳð,
lāþ ond longsum, þe on ðā lēode becōm,
nȳd-wracu nīþ-grim, niht-bealwa mǣst.

Þæt fram hām gefrægn Higelāces þegn,
195 gōd mid Gēatum, Grendles dǣda;
sē wæs mon-cynnes mægenes strengest
on þǣm dæge þysses līfes,
æþele ond ēacen. Hēt him ȳð-lidan
gōdne gegyrwan; cwæð, hē gūð-cyning
200 ofer swan-rāde sēcean wolde,
mǣrne þēoden, þā him wæs manna þearf.
Ðone sīð-fæt him snotere ceorlas
lȳt-hwōn lōgon, |þēah hē him lēof wǣre; Fol. 134b.
hwetton hige-[r]ōfne, hǣl scēawedon.
205 Hæfde se gōda Gēata lēoda
cempan gecorone, þāra þe hē cēnoste
findan mihte; fīftēna sum
sund-wudu sōhte; secg wīsade,
lagu-cræftig mon, land-gemyrcu.

mōd-ceare, the emendation of Trautmann[137], is unnecessary [cf. Sievers in *P.B.B.* xxix. 321]: *mǣl-ceare* is probably acc. after *sēað*, 'brooded over the care'; but might be instrumental, 'seethed with care' [Earle].

194. *fram hām*: 'from' indicates that Beowulf's home is different from the scene of Grendel's deeds: Earle rightly renders 'in his distant home.' Cf. l. 410.

197. *þǣm* can bear the alliteration because emphatic.

203. This, by the customary understatement (cf. ll. 2738, 3029), means that they heartily approved of his enterprise, as is shown by l. 415. [Cf. Klaeber in *M.L.N.* xvii. 323, and Cosijn[5].]

204. *[r]ōfne* is the conjecture of Rask [Grundtvig[270]] and is certain. The MS. is defective: only the lower part of the first letter is left, and this may have been *r*, *þ*, *f*, *s*, or *w*. The letter must have been only half legible even in Thorkelin's time; transcript A has *þofne*, B *forne*.

hǣl scēawedon, 'watched the omens.' Tacitus notes the attention paid to auspices and the methods of divination by the ancient Germans. [*Germ.* x.: *Auspicia sortesque, ut qui maxime, observant.*]

The conjecture of Sedgefield[286] *hǣl geēawedon*, 'gave him a farewell greeting,' seems unnecessary. [Cf. Klaeber, *Engl. Stud.* xliv. 123.]

207. *fīftēna*: MS. *xv^na*. 'With fourteen companions.' Cf. l. 3123.

209. *lagu-cræftig mon.* This is often taken to refer to a pilot, but more probably it relates to Beowulf himself. Seamanship is a characteristic of the perfect hero, as of Sîfrît in the *Nibelungen Lied.*

wīsade...land-gemyrcu has been rendered 'pointed out the land-marks' [Earle, Clark-Hall]; but the travellers do not appear to be as yet afloat.

210 Fyrst forð ʒewāt; flota wæs on ȳðum,
bāt under beorʒe. Beornas ʒearwe
on stefn stiʒon; strēamas wundon,
sund wið sande; secʒas bǣron
on bearm nacan beorhte frætwe,
215 ʒūð-searo ʒeatolīc; ʒuman ūt scufon,
weras on wil-sīð, wudu bundenne.
ʒewāt þā ofer wǣʒ-holm winde ʒefȳsed
flota fāmī-heals fuʒle ʒelīcost,
oð þæt ymb an-tīd ōþres dōʒores
220 wunden-stefna ʒewaden hæfde,
þæt ðā līðende land ʒesāwon,
brim-clifu blīcan, beorʒas stēape,
sīde sǣ-næssas; þā wæs sund liden
eoletes æt ende. Þanon ūp hraðe
225 Wedera lēode on wanʒ stiʒon,
sǣ-wudu sǣldon; syrcan hrysedon,
ʒūð-ʒewǣdo; ʒode þancedon,

(*Sund-wudu sōhte*, l. 208, means 'he proceeded to the ship,' not necessarily 'went on board.') We must therefore either translate 'led them to the land-boundary' (the shore) [cf. Sievers in *P.B.B.* xxix. 322; Klaeber[451]], or we must [as has been suggested to me by Mr Grattan] take the phrase *wisade land-gemyrcu* quite generally: Beowulf 'was their pilot on this expedition.'

Cf. l. 2409.

210. *Fyrst forð gewāt*, 'the time' between the arrival at the shore, and the embarkation 'had passed': or, quite generally, 'time passed on.'

216. *bundenne*, 'well-braced.'

218. *fāmi-heals*. See Sievers$_3$ § 214, 5.

219. *an-tid*: MS. *an tid*. Grein, *ān-tīd* f. = *hora prima*, 'erste Stunde,' comparing 'nōn-tīd' *hora nona*. Cosijn [*P.B.B.* viii. 568, following Ettmüller] contends for *an-tīd* = *and-tīd* or *ond-tīd*, 'corresponding time,' 'the same time,' so that the phrase would mean 'about the same hour of the second day.'

Sievers [*P.B.B.* xxix. 322, *etc.*] regards *āntīd* as 'due time,' comparing O.N. *eindagi*, 'agreed time, term,' and points out that *ymb*, when used to mark time, means rather 'after' than 'about'; hence: 'after the lapse of due time, on the next day.' Earle arrives at the same rendering, though on different grounds, which to me are not clear.

224. *eoletes*. The word occurs here only. The sense seems to demand 'sea'; 'then was the sound traversed at the far side of the sea.' Yet this passive use of *liden* is difficult—a difficulty which Thorpe sought to avoid by reading *sund-lida ēa-lāde æt ende*, 'the sea-sailer (i.e. boat) at the end of its watery way.' Bugge [*Tidsskr.* viii. 47] interpreted 'stormy sea' (O.N. *él*, 'storm'). But the first element, *eo*, in *eolet* may, by the Anglian confusion of *ĕo* and *ĕa*, be the same as *ēa*, 'river' (Lat. *aqua*, Goth. *aƕwa*). Others suppose the word to mean 'labour' (cognate with Greek ἐλαύνω), or else to be a mere 'ghost-word,' the result of a scribe's blunder. [Sedgefield[286].]

þæs þe him ȳþ-lāde ēaðe wurdon.
|Þā of wealle ȝeseah weard Scildinȝa, **Fol. 135a.**
230 sē þe holm-clifu healdan scolde,
beran ofer bolcan beorhte randas,
fyrd-searu fūslicu; hine fyrwyt bræc
mōd-ȝehyȝdum, hwæt þā men wǣron.
Ȝewāt him þā tō waroðe wicȝe rīdan
235 þeȝn Hrōðȝāres, þrymmum cwehte
mæȝen-wudu mundum, meþel-wordum fræȝn:
"Hwæt syndon ȝē searo-hæbbendra
byrnum werede, þe þus brontne cēol
ofer laȝu-strǣte lǣdan cwōmon,
240 hider ofer holmas? [*Hwæt, ic hwī*]le wæs
ende-sǣta, ǣȝ-wearde hēold,
þē on land Dena lāðra nǣniȝ
mid scip-herȝe sceðþan ne meahte.
Nō hēr cūðlīcor cuman onȝunnon
245 lind-hæbbende; ne ȝē lēafnes-word
ȝūð-fremmendra ȝearwe ne wisson,
māȝa ȝemēdu. Nǣfre ic māran ȝeseah
eorla ofer eorþan, ðonne is ēower sum,
secȝ on searwum; nis þæt seld-ȝuma
250 wǣpnum ȝeweorðad, næf*n*e him his wlite lēoȝe,

230. *scolde*, 'whose office it was'; cf. l. 251.
232. See note to l. 1426.
240. [*Hwæt, ic hwī*]*le wæs*, the reading of Sievers [*Anglia*, xiv. 146], following in part that of Bugge[83]:

hider ofer holmas? [*Hwīle ic on weal*]*le*
wæs ende-sǣta.

MS. *hider ofer holmas le wæs, etc.*, without any gap. Thorkelin read the *le* as *Ic*, Kemble as *Ie*, but there can be no doubt that it is *le*, and this makes Wülker's conjecture unlikely:

hider ofer holmas [*hringed-stefnan*]*?*
Ic wæs ende-sǣta....

The same applies to that of Ettmüller$_2$:

hider ofer holmas [*helmas bǣron*]*?*

hwīle, 'a long time.'
244. *cuman* is possibly a noun (cf. l. 1806). 'Never have strangers, warriors, made themselves more at home.' [Bugge in *Tidsskr.* viii. 290.] For this use of *onginnan*, = 'behave,' Klaeber [*Anglia*, xxviii. 439] compares *ēaðmōdlīce onginnað*, *Cura Pastoralis*, 421, 26; and advocates the old reading *gelēafnes-word* for *gē lēafnes-word*, taking *wisson* (l. 246) as 3rd pers.
245–6. *ne...ne.* Note that in O.E. syntax two negatives do *not* make an affirmative.
249–50. 'Yon weapon-decked man is no mere retainer.' *Seld-guma*, 'hall-man,' i.e. house-carl, retainer. Other suggestions are that it means

ǣnlīc an-sȳn. Nū ic ēower sceal
frum-cyn witan, ǣr ȝē fyr |heonan, Fol. 135b.
lēas-scēaweras, on land Dena
furþur fēran. Nū ȝē feor-būend,
255 mere-līðende, mīn[*n*]e ȝehȳrað
ān-fealdne ȝeþōht; ofost is sēlest
tō ȝecȳðanne, hwanan ēowre cyme syndon."
IV Him se yldesta ondswarode,
werodes wīsa, word-hord onlēac:
260 "Wē synt ȝum-cynnes Ȝēata lēode
ond Hiȝelāces heorð-ȝenēatas.
Wæs mīn fæder folcum ȝecȳþed,
æþele ord-fruma Ecȝþēow hāten;
ȝebād wintra worn, ǣr hē on weȝ hwurfe
265 ȝamol of ȝeardum; hine ȝearwe ȝeman
witena wel-hwylc wīde ȝeond eorþan.
Wē þurh holdne hiȝe hlāford þīnne,
sunu Healfdenes, sēcean cwōmon,
lēod-ȝebyrȝean; wes þū ūs lārena ȝōd.
270 Habbað wē tō þǣm mǣran micel ǣrende
Deniȝa frêan; ne sceal þǣr dyrne sum
wesan, þæs ic wēne. ū wāst ȝif hit is,

'one who remains within the *seld*,' 'stay-at-home,' 'carpet-knight,' or that it indicates a peasant, one who possesses only a *seld*. But the *seld* was a hall or palace, occupied by warriors and owned by kings, so that these explanations are less satisfactory. [Cf. Bugge in *Tidsskr.* viii. 290–1.]

250. *næfne*, Kemble$_2$: MS. *næfre.*

253. *lēas-scēaweras*, the MS. reading, meaning 'evil spies,' has been emended to *lēase scēaweras* [Ettmüller$_2$, Thorpe, followed by all the older editors]. But this gives a type of line (Expanded D*) which, unless with double alliteration, is unparalleled. It seems therefore better to keep the MS. reading.

So abusive a word is surprising in the middle of an otherwise courteous conversation. But, perhaps, the drift is, as Sievers suggests: 'It is my duty to (*ic sceal*) enquire: tell me, rather than (*ǣr*), by going further, bring yourselves under suspicion of being false spies.' [*P.B.B.* xxix. 329: cf. also Klaeber in *Anglia*, xxix. 379–80.]

255. *mīn[n]e*, Kemble$_2$: MS. *mine.*

258. *yldesta*, 'chief'; cf. l. 363.

262. Holthausen$_2$ reads *Wæs mīn [frōd] fæder*: Holthausen$_3$, *Wæs mīn fæder folcum [feor] gecȳþed.* This improves the alliteration. From the point of view of scansion alteration is not essential, since a personal pronoun can take the stress: cf. ll. 345, 346, 353, 1934, 1984, 2160. This is not a mere licence, but usually corresponds to a fine shade of meaning.

269. *lārena gōd*, 'good to us in guidance.'

swā wē sōþlīce |secʒan hȳrdon, Fol. 136ᵃ
þæt mid Scyldinʒum sceaðona ic nāt hwylc,
275 dēoʒol dǣd-hata, deorcum nihtum
ēaweð þurh eʒsan uncūðne nīð,
hȳnðu ond hrā-fyl. Ic þæs Hrōðʒār mæʒ
þurh rūmne sefan rǣd ʒelǣran,
hū hē frōd ond ʒōd fēond oferswȳðeþ,
280 ʒyf him ed-wendan ǣfre scolde
bealuwa bisiʒu, bōt eft cuman,
ond þā cear-wylmas cōlran wurðaþ;
oððe ā syþðan earfoð-þrāʒe,
þrēa-nȳd þolað, þenden þǣr wunað
285 on hēah-stede hūsa sēlest."
Weard maþelode, ðǣr on wicʒe sæt,
ombeht unforht: "Ǣʒhwæþres sceal
scearp scyld-wiʒa ʒescād witan,
worda ond worca, sē þe wel þenceð.
290 Ic þæt ʒehȳre, þæt þis is hold weorod
frēan Scyldinʒa. ʒewītaþ forð beran
wǣpen ond ʒewǣdu, ic ēow wīsiʒe;
swylce ic maʒu-þeʒnas mīne hāte
wið fēonda ʒehwone flotan ēowerne,

274. *sceaðona*, in Thorkelin's transcript A only: now only *scea* left.

275. *dǣd-hata.* Grein hesitated whether to regard this word as *dǣd-hǣta*, 'one who hates or persecutes by deeds' [so Grein$_2$] or *dǣd-hāta*, 'one who promises deeds.' Earle adopts the latter reading, and translates 'author of deeds.' The former is, however, the more probable: *hatian* means not merely 'to hate' but 'to pursue with hatred, persecute'; cf. l. 2466 [see Klaeber[260]].

276. *þurh egsan*, 'in dread wise': for *þurh* marking attendant circumstances, cf. l. 1335, and perhaps l. 184. [Cf. Klaeber[451] and in *Archiv*, cxv. 178.] Above, l. 267, and below, l. 278, *þurh* retains more clearly its meaning of cause or instrument. And *þurh egsan* may mean 'by reason of the awe he inspires.' Cf. *Seafarer*, 103 [and see Cosijn[6]].

280. *edwendan* MS. Bugge [*Tidsskr.* viii. 291] suggested the noun *edwenden*, in which case we must take *bisigu* as gen. dependent upon it: 'a change of his trouble.' [So Holthausen and Sedgefield: already in 1861 Grundtvig (p. 117) took the passage in this way, though retaining the spelling *edwendan*, which he interpreted as a noun = *edwenden.*] The emendation *edwenden* is exceedingly probable, since the verb *edwendan* occurs nowhere else: for in l. 1774, where the MS. gives *edwendan*, it is necessary to read this as *edwenden*; *him edwenden...bealuwa bisigum* has been suggested: cf. l. 318, *sīða gesunde*, and l. 2170, *nīða heardum.*

286. Sievers [*P.B.B.* ix. 137], followed by Holthausen and Sedgefield, would supply [*hē*] after *þǣr*. But this seems unnecessary: cf. l. 1923. [See Pogatscher, in *Anglia*, xxiii. 265.]

295 nīw-tyrwydne nacan on sande,
ārum healdan, oþ þæt eft byreð
ofer laȝu-strēa|mas lēofne mannan **Fol. 136b.**
wudu wunden-hals tō Weder-mearce,
ȝōd-fremmendra swylcum ȝifeþe bið
300 þæt þone hilde-rǣs hāl ȝedīȝeð."
Ȝewiton him þā fēran; flota stille bād,
seomode on sāle sīd-fæþmed scip,
on ancre fæst. Eofor-līc scionon
ofer hlēor-ber[ȝ]an, ȝehroden ȝolde;
305 fāh ond fȳr-heard ferh-wearde hēold
ȝūþmōdȝ*um* m*en*. Ȝuman ōnetton,

297-9. *lēofne mannan* and *swylcum* may refer to the whole band, 'to whomsoever it shall be granted' [Kemble, Thorpe]. For a full defence of this rendering see Klaeber[250]: *lēofne mannan* would be a singular used collectively: cf. *eorl* (l. 795), *æþelinge* (l. 1244). Most recent translators make of ll. 299, 300, an assertion relating to Beowulf: 'to such a valiant man it will be granted....' It has been objected that this is to attribute to the coast-guard a statement which is absurd—a view refuted 'by all the brave men who have ever fallen in battle' [Rieger[385]]. Yet he may reasonably say 'Valiant men like your captain are destined to win.'

299. *gōd-fremmendra.* Grundtvig's emendation *gūð-fremmendra* [1861, p. 10] is needless.

300. Here, too, Sievers, followed by Sedgefield, would supply [*hē*] after *þæt.*

302. *sāle*, Ettmüller$_2$; cf. ll. 226, 1906, and 1917, and modern 'riding *on* a hawser.' It has been suggested that the MS. reading *sole* is not impossible, and that it might be interpreted as from *sol*, mod. Kent. *sole*, 'a muddy pool.' But surely this is a libel upon the Cattegat.

303, *etc. scionon=scinon*, 'they shone,' by u-umlaut, just as *riodan* (l. 3169)=*ridon*, 'they rode' (Sievers$_3$ § 376): there seems no sufficient reason to reject this explanation, and, with Grein, to invent a verb *scānan*, *scēon*, or with Sedgefield to take *scīonon* as an adj. (=*scīenan*, 'bright'), agreeing with *eofor-līc.*

hlēor-ber[*g*]*an*, 'cheek-guards,' Ettmüller$_3$, Gering [*Z.f.d.Ph.* xii. 123: he compares *cinberg*, *Exod.* 175]: MS. *hleor beran.* If we retain the MS. reading we must either take *beran*=*bǣron*, 'they bore over their faces,' or else, with Grein, assume a noun *hlēor-bera*, 'visor'; Sedgefield$_2$ reads *ofer hleoþu bēran*, 'they bore, over the hill-sides....'

The latter part of l. 305 has been widely read *ferh wearde hēold*, 'the pig' (*ferh* for *fearh*, parallel to *eofor-līc*) 'held guard': but the expression *ferh*, 'pig' for *eofor*, 'boar' is strange [Cosijn[7]]. The reading of the text *ferhwearde hēold* (*ferh* for *feorh*) involves a rapid change from pl. to sg.: but in O.E. poetry this is no insuperable difficulty. Translate 'the gleaming and tempered [helm] held guard of life over the valiant man (*gūþmōdgum men*).'

The MS. reading, *gūþmōd grummon*, hardly admits of interpretation. If a verb, *grummon* must be from *grimman*, 'to rage, roar,' which gives no satisfactory sense; the meaning 'hasten' is generally applied to it here, but this is forced; why should 'to roar' mean 'to hasten'? And *gūþmōd* as subject (=*gūþmōd*(*i*)*ge* 'the valiant ones') is almost equally unsatisfactory, even if we follow Kemble$_2$ and alter to *gūþ-mōd*[*e*].

Sedgefield suggests *grimmon* (Dat. pl.), 'over the fierce ones': Bright

sizon ætsomne, oþ þæt hȳ [*s*]æl timbred,
zeatolīc ond zold-fāh, onzyton mihton;
þæt wæs fore-mǣrost fold-būendum
310 receda under roderum, on þǣm se rīca bād;
līxte se lēoma ofer landa fela.
Him þā hilde-dēor [*h*]of mōdizra
torht zetǣhte, þæt hīe him tō mihton
zeznum zanzan; zūð-beorna sum
315 wicz zewende, word æfter cwæð:
"Mǣl is mē tō fēran; Fæder al-walda
mid ār-stafum ēowic zehealde
sīða zesunde! Ic tō sǣ wille
wið |wrāð werod wearde healdan." Fol. 137a.
V 320 Strǣt wæs stān-fāh, stīz wīsode
zumum ætzædere. zūð-byrne scān
heard hond-locen, hrinz-īren scīr
sonz in searwum, þā hīe tō sele furðum
in hyra zryre-zeatwum zanzan cwōmon.
325 Setton sǣ-mēþe sīde scyldas,
rondas rezn-hearde, wið þæs recedes weal,
buzon þā tō bence; byrnan hrinzdon,

[*M.L.N.* x. 43] had made the same emendation, but with adverbial meaning, 'grimly.'

Tacitus notes these boar-helmets: but as a characteristic, not of the Germans proper, but of the Æstii [*Germ.* XLV.: *Insigne superstitionis formas aprorum gestant*].

The straightening out of this passage, so far as it admits of explanation, is mainly due to Bugge[83] [and in *Z.f.d.Ph.* iv. 195, *etc.*], who proposed:

eofor līc-scionon
ofer hlēorberan gehroden golde
fāh ond fȳrheard ferh-wearde hēold
gūþ-mōdgum men.

'The boar, over the visor, adorned with gold, gleaming and tempered, held guard of life over the valiant man, fair of body (*līc-scīonon*).' Bugge's interpretation, at least of ll. 305, 306, seems likely, and has been adopted by Schücking and Holthausen$_2$; cf. Klaeber[451].

307. [*s*]*æl timbred*, Kemble$_2$: MS. *æltimbred.*

308. For infinitives in *on* cf. ll. 2167, 2842, and Sievers$_3$ § 363, N. 1.

312. [*h*]*of*, Kemble$_2$: MS. *of.* Both sense and alliteration demand the change.

315. *æfter*, 'thereupon.'

326. *regn-hearde. Regn* (Goth. *ragin*, 'counsel,' *raginōn*, 'to rule') comes in *O.N.* (*regin*) to be a synonym for the gods. Here it is used simply to intensify. Cf. the proper name Reginhart (Reynard), appropriately applied to that 'thoroughly hardened sinner,' the fox.

ʒūð-searo ʒumena; ʒāras stōdon,
sǣ-manna searo, samod ætʒædere,
330 æsc-holt ufan ʒrǣʒ; wæs se īren-þrēat
wǣpnum ʒewurþad. Þā ðǣr wlonc hæleð
ōret-mecʒas æfter *æþelum* fræʒn:
"Hwanon feriʒeað ʒē fǣtte scyldas,
ʒrǣʒe syrcan ond ʒrīm-helmas,
335 here-sceafta hēap? Ic eom Hrōðʒāres
ār ond ombiht. Ne seah ic el-þēodiʒe
þus maniʒe men mōdiʒlīcran.
Wēn ic þæt ʒē for wlenco, nalles for wrǣc-sīðum
ac for hiʒe-|þrymmum, Hrōðʒār sōhton." Fol. 137[b].
340 Him þā ellen-rōf andswarode,
wlanc Wedera lēod word æfter spræc,
heard under helme: "Wē synt Hiʒelāces
bēod-ʒenēatas; Bēowulf is mīn nama.
Wille ic āsecʒan sunu Healfdenes,
345 mǣrum þēodne, mīn ǣrende,
aldre þīnum, ʒif hē ūs ʒeunnan wile,
þæt wē hine swā ʒōdne ʒrētan mōton."
Wulfʒār maþelode —þæt wæs Wendla lēod,
wæs his mōd-sefa maneʒum ʒecȳðed,
350 wīʒ ond wīs-dōm— "Ic þæs wine Deniʒa,
frēan Scildinʒa, frīnan wille,
bēaʒa bryttan, swā þū bēna eart,
þēoden mǣrne, ymb þīnne sīð,
ond þē þā ondsware ǣdre ʒecȳðan,
355 ðe mē se ʒōda āʒifan þenceð."
Hwearf þā hrædlīce, þǣr Hrōðʒār sæt
eald ond *a*nhār mid his eorla ʒedriht;

332. *æþelum*, $Grein_1$ (cf. l. 392, and for the sense ll. 251–2): MS. *hæle[h]um*—evidently a scribal blunder due to the *hæleð* of the previous line. For *ōret-*, see $Sievers_3$ § 43, N. 4.

338. *Wēn.* Some editors write this *wēn'* (=*wēne*). Cf. ll. 442 and 525.

344. *sunu.* The editors from $Kemble_2$ downwards have adopted the more usual form of the dat., *suna*; but see $Sievers_3$ §§ 270 and 271, N. 2.

357. *anhār*: MS. *unhar.* Bugge [*Z.f.d.Ph.* iv. 197] suggests that the *un* intensifies: 'very hoary'; so Cosijn[18] and Schücking: but the parallels quoted in support are not satisfactory. $Sedgefield_1$ retains *unhār*, but translates 'with hair not yet white.' But the emendation *anhār* [Bugge in *Tidsskr.*

ēode ellen-rōf, þæt hē for eaxlum ȝestōd
Deniȝa frêan; cūþe hē duȝuðe þēaw.
360 Wulfȝār maðelode |tō his wine-drihtne: Fol. 138[a].
"Hēr syndon ȝeferede, feorran cumene
ofer ȝeofenes beȝanȝ, Ȝēata lēode;
þone yldestan ōret-mecȝas
Bēowulf nemnað. Hȳ bēnan synt,
365 þæt hīe, þēoden mīn, wið þē mōton
wordum wrixlan; nō ðū him wearne ȝetēoh
ðīnra ȝeȝn-cwida, ȝlædman Hrōðȝār.
Hȳ on wīȝ-ȝetāwum wyrðe þinceað
eorla ȝeæhtlan; hūru se aldor dēah,
370 sē þǣm heaðo-rincum hider wīsade."
VI Hrōðȝār maþelode, helm Scyldinȝa:
"Ic hine cūðe cniht-wesende;
wæs his eald fæder Ecȝþēo hāten,
ðǣm tō hām forȝeaf Hrēþel Ȝēata
375 ānȝan dohtor; is his eafor*a* nū

viii. 71; Trautmann: adopted by Holthausen] is simple and final. A similar bad spelling occurs in the *Dream of the Rood*, 117: the MS. has *unforht*, which is nonsense, and has been emended to *anforht* 'timid.' Such scribal mistakes were easily made at a period when, the top of the *a* being left open, it was hardly distinguishable from *u*: another example is *wudu* for *wadu*, below (l. 581). For *anhar*, cf. *ansund* (l. 1000).

367. *glædman*, indisputably the MS. reading: Thorkelin's transcript B reads *glædnian* [cf. Rieger[386]].

Bugge[84] defends *glædman*, quoting the gloss '*Hilaris*: *glædman*.' The best interpretation of the word seems, then, to be 'cheerful.' Other suggestions have been that it is the oblique case of a noun *glædma*, 'gladness,' or that it should be read as two words, *glæd man*. *Glæd*, 'gracious,' is a stock epithet of princes. Grundtvig's emendation [1861, p. 13] *glæd-mōd* is followed by $\text{Holthausen}_{1,2}$ and Sedgefield.

368. *wig-getāwum*. Note the spelling here, and in ll. 395, 2636: the editors generally alter into the more usual form *wig-geatwum*, *etc.*, and this emendation is supported here by metrical considerations. *Geatwe* is generally supposed to be a corruption (Sievers_3 § 43, N. 4) of *getāwe*. It would seem, then, that the more primitive form, *getāwum*, has been, by a scribal error, inserted here, although the metre shows that the form actually used was the corrupt *geatwe*. Yet it has been maintained that the two words, *geatwe* and *getāwe*, are from distinct roots (*geatwe* cognate with *frætwe*; *getāwe* with *tāwian*, 'to prepare'). If so, they were certainly confused and interchanged by the scribes. [Cf. von Grienberger in *Z.f.ö.G.* 1905, 753.]

372. *cniht-wesende*, uninflected; see note to l. 46, above.

373. *eald fæder*: MS. *ealdfæder*. This compound, meaning 'grandfather, ancestor,' occurs in the forms *ealdfæder*, *ealdefæder*; but its use here is a strain to the meaning of the passage, and we may safely assume that the scribe has run two words into one, as in numerous other instances. *Eald fæder* makes excellent sense.

375. *eafora*, Grundtvig[272], Kemble_1: MS. *eaforan*.

heard hēr cumen, sōhte holdne wine.
Ðonne sæʒdon þæt sǣ-līþende,
þā ðe ʒif-sceattas ʒēata fyredon
þyder tō þance, þæt hē þrī|tiʒes Fol. 138b.
380 manna mæʒen-cræft on his mund-ʒripe
heaþo-rōf hæbbe. Hine hāliʒ ʒod
for ār-stafum ūs onsende,
tō West-Denum, þæs ic wēn hæbbe,
wið ʒrendles ʒryre; ic þǣm ʒōdan sceal
385 for his mōd-þræce mādmas bēodan.
Bēo ðū on ofeste, hāt in ʒân
sēon sibbe-ʒedriht samod ætʒædere;
ʒesaʒa him ēac wordum, þæt hīe sint wil-cuman
Deniʒa lēodum." [*þā wið duru healle*
390 *Wulfʒār ēode,*] word inne ābēad;
"Ēow hēt secʒan siʒe-drihten mīn,
aldor East-Dena, þæt hē ēower æþelu can,
ond ʒē him syndon ofer sǣ-wylmas,
heard-hicʒende, hider wil-cuman.
395 Nū ʒē mōton ʒanʒan in ēowrum ʒūð-ʒeatawum,

378–9. Thorpe, *Gēatum*, adopted by Bugge[86] and Earle. The change is not necessary, because the genitive can be objective: 'presents for the Geatas.' [So Klaeber[452].]

þyder. Cosijn[7] would alter to *hyder*, and make the Danes the recipients of the treasure: but this weakens the alliteration. We need not assume that either nation was tributary to the other. Tacitus records similar interchange of gifts between neighbouring tribes: *Gaudent praecipue finitimarum gentium donis, quae non modo a singulis sed publice mittuntur, electi equi, magna arma, phalerae torquesque.* [*Germ.* xv.] Cf. too l. 472, below.

379. *þrītiges*: MS. ·xxx· *tiges*.

386–7. The demands of the metre show that *gān* stands for some disyllabic form, *gāan* or *gangan*.

sibbe-gedriht may refer to Beowulf's men, 'bid this company come into my presence' (cf. l. 729), but this compels us to give a forced rendering to *sēon*: more probably therefore *sibbe-gedriht* refers to the Danes, and is the object of *sēon*, 'bid them come in and see our company.' We must supply *hi* mentally after *in gān*.

Bright [*M.L.N.* x. 44] suggests *hāt* [*þæt*] *in gā sēo sibbegedriht* 'bid that company (Beowulf's) to go in.' This emendation is supported by *Exodus*, 214, but is not necessary.

389–90. [*þā...ēode*], Grein_1: no gap in MS., though the lack of alliteration seems conclusive as to a defect in the text.

inne, 'speaking from inside.'

395. *gūð-geatawum*. See note to l. 368 and Sievers_3 § 260, Notes 1, 2. The emendation of Ettmüller_2 *gūð-getawum* has the advantage of avoiding the abnormal double alliteration in the second half line: for *ge-* of course does not alliterate.

under here-ʒrīman, Hrōðʒār ʒesēon;
lǣtað hilde-bord hēr onbīdan,
wudu, wæl-sceaftas, worda ʒeþinʒes."
Ārās þā se rīca, ymb hine rinc maniʒ,
400 þrȳðlīc þeʒna hēap; sume þǣr bidon,
heaðo-rēaf hēoldon, swā him se |hearda bebēad. Fol.
Snyredon ætsomne, þā secʒ wīsode, 139^a.
under Heorotes hrōf; [*hyʒe-rōf ēode,*]
heard under helme, þæt hē on hēoðe ʒestōd.
405 Bēowulf maðelode —on him byrne scān,
searo-net seowed smiþes or-þancum—
"Wæs þū, Hrōðgār, hāl! Ic eom Hiʒelāces
mǣʒ ond maʒo-ðeʒn; hæbbe ic mǣrða fela
onʒunnen on ʒeoʒoþe. Mē wearð ʒrendles þinʒ
410 on mīnre ēþel-tyrf undyrne cūð;
secʒað sǣ-līðend, þæt þæs sele stande,
reced sēlesta, rinca ʒehwylcum
īdel ond unnyt, siððan ǣfen-lēoht
under heofenes hador beholen weorþeð.

397. *onbīdan.* The scribe seems to have written *onbidman*, and to have erased the *m* very carelessly, so that one stroke, resembling an *i*, remains. Some editors read *onbidian.*

402. *þā* is metrically excessive [Sievers in *P.B.B.* x. 256], the only parallel being ⟨*þāra*⟩*ymbsittendra*, where we can be certain that *þāra* was not original (see note to l. 9). Holthausen omits *þā* here also.

403. [*hyge-rōf ēode*], Grein$_1$: no gap in MS.

404. *hēoðe.* The emendation *heo*[*r*]*ðe* [Kemble$_2$, suggested by Thorpe] is adopted by Holthausen and Sedgefield$_2$. Holtzmann [*Germ.* viii. 490] showed, by a parallel passage from the *Egils saga*, how the hearth was in front of the high seat in a Germanic hall. Beowulf, before the throne of Hrothgar, would then be on or near the hearth.

On hēoðe has been taken to mean 'in the interior' (cf. *hel-hēoðo*), or 'on the dais' (from *hēah*). This last interpretation is difficult to demonstrate.

407. *Wæs*; *æ* for *e*: cf. *spræc* (l. 1171). See Sievers$_3$ § 427, N. 10; Bülbring § 92. 1.

411. Most editors have followed Thorkelin and Kemble$_1$ in normalizing to *þes*. But *þæs* is a possible Northern form of the nom. masc. [Sievers$_3$ § 338, N. 4].

As in the *Hildebrand Lay*, news is brought by seafaring folk (*sēolīdante*).

414. *hador.* If we retain the MS. reading we must take *hador* as either (1) 'brightness,' which is unprecedented (*hādor* being elsewhere an adj.) and does not give good sense, or (2) 'vault of heaven,' connecting with a word twice recorded in the *Riddles*, which seems to mean 'receptacle' or 'confinement' (lxv. [lxvi.] 3, *on headre*; xx. [xxi.] 13, *on heaþore*; cf. Goth. *hēþjō*, 'chamber': some editors emend to *haðor* here in *Beowulf*). Cf. ll. 860, 1773, *under swegles begong*.

Sedgefield$_1$ transposes the words and reads *hādor under heofene*, trans-

415 þā mē þæt ȝelǣrdon lēode mīne,
þā sēlestan, snotere ceorlas,
þēoden Hrōðȝār, þæt ic þē sōhte,
forþan hīe mæȝenes cræft mīn[*n*]e cūþon;
selfe ofersāwon, ðā ic of searwum cwōm,
420 fāh from fēondum, þǣr ic fīfe ȝeband,
ȳðde eotena cyn, ond on ȳðum slōȝ
niceras nihtes, nearo-þearfe drēah,
wræc |Wedera nīð —wēan āhsodon— Fol. 139b.
forȝrand ȝramum; ond nū wið Grendel sceal,
425 wið þām āȝlǣcan, āna ȝehēȝan
ðinȝ wið þyrse. Ic þē nū ðā,
breȝo Beorht-Dena, biddan wille,
eodor Scyldinȝa, ānre bēne,
þæt ðū mē ne forwyrne, wīȝendra hlēo,
430 frēo-wine folca, nū ic þus feorran cōm,
þæt ic mōte āna [*ond*] mīnra eorla ȝedryht,
þes hearda hēap, Heorot fǣlsian.
Hæbbe ic ēac ȝeāhsod, þæt se ǣȝlǣca
for his won-hȳdum wǣpna ne recceð;
435 ic þæt þonne forhicȝe, swā mē Hiȝelāc sīe,

lating 'after the bright evening light is hidden under the sky.' [But cf. Klaeber in *Engl. Stud.* xliv. 124.] Sedgefield[2] *under heofene hādor.*

418. *mīn*[*n*]*e*, Grein[1]: MS. *mine*. Cf. l. 255.

420. *þǣr ic fīfe geband.* The emendation *þǣra* for *þǣr* [Rieger[399]] is unnecessary: *þǣr* can mean 'when'; Klaeber[452] compares ll. 513, 550.

Unless 'eotens' and 'nicers' are different beasts, there is a discrepancy, since later Beowulf claims to have *slain nine* nickers (l. 575). It seems possible that *fīfe* is either a form (as Grein thought), or, more probably, a corruption, of *fīfel*, 'sea-monster.' There are several conjectures based upon this, the oldest of which is Bugge's *þǣr ic on fīfel-geban.* Bugge[367] supposes this to have been the reading of a very early MS., which was later misunderstood and corrupted: *geban* would be the older form of *geofon*, and the phrase would be parallel to *ofer fīfel-wǣg* (*Elene*, 237), *etc.*

422. *niceras.* The word seems to have been used by the different Germanic peoples for any strange water-being they might meet, from a mermaid to a hippopotamus.

423. Cf. note to l. 1206.

426. *þyrse.* Cf. the *Cottonian Gnomic Verses*, l. 42:
"*þyrs sceal on fenne gewunian*
āna innan lande."

431–2. *āna* [*ond*]...*þes*: MS. *ana minra eorla gedryht* 7 *þes, etc.* Kemble[2] transposed the 7 (=*ond*).

434. Cf. ll. 681, *etc.*, 801, *etc.*

435. *sīe.* In O.E. poetry the metre sometimes demands that *sīe*, *sȳ*

mīn mon-drihten, mōdes blīðe,
þæt ic sweord bere oþðe sīdne scyld,
ȝeolo-rand tō ȝūþe; ac ic mid ȝrāpe sceal
fōn wið fēonde, ond ymb feorh sacan
440 lāð wið lāþum; ðǣr ȝelȳfan sceal
Dryhtnes dōme sē þe hine dēað nimeð.
Wēn ic þæt hē wille, ȝif hē wealdan mōt,
in þǣm ȝūð-sele ȝēotena lēode
etan unforhte, swā hē |oft dyde Fol. 140a.
445 mæȝen Hrēð-manna. Nā þū mīnne þearft
hafalan hȳdan, ac hē mē habban wile
d[*r*]ēore fāhne, ȝif mec dēað nimeð;
byreð blōdiȝ wæl, byrȝean þenceð,
eteð ān-ȝenȝa unmurnlīce,
450 mearcað mōr-hopu; nō ðū ymb mīnes ne þearft
līces feorme lenȝ sorȝian.

should be monosyllabic, sometimes disyllabic: the spelling is no guide. Here it is monosyllabic; the verse is of the B type, with resolution of first accented syllable (× × ⏑́ × | × ⏑́). For cases where *sie* is disyllabic, see ll. 1831, 2649 [cf. Sievers in *P.B.B.* x. 477].

Hygelac is brought in because, as Beowulf's chief, he shares the credit of his achievements. [Cf. Tacitus, *Germ.* xv., and note to l. 1968, below.]

440–1. *gelȳfan...Dryhtnes dōme.* Earle renders 'resign himself to': for similar sentiment, cf. ll. 685, *etc.*

þe hine, 'whom.'

443. *Gēotena.* Many editors alter to the normal form *Gēata.* But (1) the dialectal confusion of *ēo* and *ēa* [Sievers₃ § 150. 3] is peculiarly apt to survive in proper names, and (2) weak and strong forms of proper names alternate; *Bēaw* compared with *Bēowa* exemplifies both changes. *Gēotena* is, then, a conceivable form, and the MS. reading should be retained.

Those who hold that the Geatas are Jutes have seen in this form a confirmation of their theory; and (though I do not share that view) this is an additional reason for not tampering with the MS. reading.

445. To avoid the difficulty of the alliteration falling on the second element in the compound, Schücking reads *mægen-hrēð manna*, 'the pride of men.' *Hrǣdas* is an ancient epic title of the Goths: it became *Hrēðas* by false analogy with *hrēð*, 'glory'; but the term *Hrēð-menn* here cannot signify 'Goths.' It may possibly refer to the Geatas, whose king is *Hrēðel*, in which case a comma must be inserted after *dyde.* But I rather take it to mean the Danes, part of whose kingdom is in Icelandic called *Reið-Gotaland*; this gives a more satisfactory sense: 'he thinks to treat the Geatas as he did the Danes.' Cf. l. 601.

446. *hafalan hȳdan*, referring to the rites of burial. It does not necessarily follow, as has been argued, that there is any reference to the custom, once prevalent, at any rate in Scandinavian countries, of covering with a cloth the face of the dead [Konrath in *Archiv*, xcix. 417].

That Beowulf is declining a guard of honour (*hēafod-weard*), as Schücking supposes, seems very improbable.

447. *d*[*r*]*ēore*, Grundtvig[273]: MS. *deore.*

450–1. 'Thou needst care no more about my body's sustenance.'

Onsend Hiȝelāce, ȝif mec hild nime,
beadu-scrūda betst, þæt mīne brēost wereð,
hræȝla sēlest; þæt is Hrǣdlan lāf,
455 Wēlandes ȝeweorc. Ȝǣð ā wyrd swā hīo scel."
VII Hrōðȝār maþelode, helm Scyldinȝa:
F*or* [*ȝ*]*ew*y[*r*]htum þū, wine mīn Bēowulf,
ond for ār-stafum ūsic sōhtest.
Ȝeslōh þīn fæder fǣhðe mǣste,
460 wearþ hē Heaþolāfe tō hand-bonan
mid Wilfinȝum; ðā hine *Wede*ra cyn
for here-brōȝan habban ne mihte.
Þanon hē ȝesōhte Sūð-Dena folc
ofer ȳða ȝewealc, Ār-|Scyldinȝa; **Fol. 140b.**
465 ðā ic furþum wēold folce Deni*ȝa*,
ond on ȝeoȝoðe hēold ȝimme-rīce
hord-burh hæleþa. Đā wæs Hereȝār dēad,

454. *Hrǣdlan.* There is no need to alter *Hrǣdlan* into *Hrēðles.* For *ǣd* alternating with *ēð*, cf. note to l. 445 above. The alternation of weak and strong forms (*Hors* and *Horsa*) is common, especially in the names of ancestral heroes. See note to l. 443 above.

457. *F*[*or gewyr*]*htum*: MS. *fere fyhtum.* Grundtvig (1861) suggested *F*[*or w*]*ere-fyhtum*, 'for defensive fighting.' More than a dozen emendations have been proposed: that in the text is by Trautmann [in his edition: otherwise Trautmann[152]], and we must render, with Klaeber [*J.E.G.Ph.* vi. 191], 'because of deeds done,' i.e. owing to the ancestral ties mentioned below. [Cf. also Sievers in *P.B.B.* xxxvi. 401; Klaeber[453]]. Thorpe, followed by Schücking, reads *fore fyhtum*, and emended *wine* to *frēond*, so as to alliterate. But the error obviously lies in *fere fyhtum*, which should be, and is not, parallel to *ond for ār-stafum* [Sievers, *P.B.B.* ix. 138].

459. Holthausen, followed by recent editors, reads for metrical reasons, *þīn fæder geslōh.*

Klaeber[262] translates 'thy father brought about by fight the greatest of feuds.' Schücking, following Klaeber, similarly renders *geslēan*, 'durch Schlagen verursachen.' But (1) *geslēan* conveys an idea of finality, and means 'to achieve' rather than 'to cause' by blows; and (2) since Ecgtheow escapes safely, and the Wylfingas have to be content with a money payment from a third party, such ineffective vengeance could not be described as 'the greatest of feuds'; for the honours go to the side which last slays its man. I take the *fǣhð* to be a blood-feud *preceding* and culminating in the slaying of Heatholaf, by which slaying Ecgtheow 'achieves' the feud: cf. *Widsith*, 38, *Offa geslōg cynerica mǣst*, 'won, achieved by blows, the greatest of kingdoms.' [For *geslēan* cf. Kock in *Anglia*, xxvii. 226–7.]

461. *Wedera*, Grundtvig (1861, p. 16): MS. *gara*: see ll. 225, 423, *etc.*

462. *for here-brōgan*, 'because of the terror of war.'

465. *Deniga*, Kemble$_2$: MS. *deninga*: see ll. 155, 271, *etc.*

466. *ginne rice*, 'my ample kingdom,' and *gumena rice* have been proposed.

467. *Heregār.* *Heorogār* is of course meant. Many editors alter the name accordingly. When names are confused, it is frequently found, as

mīn yldra mǣᵹ   unlifiᵹende,
bearn Healfdenes;   sē wæs betera ðonne ic.
470 Siððan þā fǣhðe   fēo þinᵹode;
sende ic Wylfinᵹum   ofer wæteres hrycᵹ
ealde mādmas;   hē mē āþas swōr.
Sorh is mē tō secᵹanne   on sefan mīnum
ᵹumena ǣnᵹum,   hwæt mē ᵹrendel hafað
475 hȳnðo on Heorote   mid his hete-þancum,
fǣr-nīþa ᵹefremed;   is mīn flet-werod,
wīᵹ-hēap, ᵹewanod;   hīe wyrd forswēop
on ᵹrendles ᵹryre.   ᵹod ēaþe mæᵹ
þone dol-sceaðan   dǣda ᵹetwǣfan.
480 Ful oft ᵹebēotedon   bēore druncne
ofer ealo-wǣᵹe   ōret-mecᵹas,
þæt hīe in bēor-sele   bīdan woldon
ᵹrendles ᵹūþe   mid ᵹryrum ecᵹa.
Đonne wæs þēos medo-heal   on morᵹen-tīd,
485 driht-sele drēor-fāh,   þonne dæᵹ līxte,
eal |benc-þelu   blōde bestȳmed,   Fol. 141a.
heall heoru-drēore;   āhte ic holdra þȳ lǣs,
dēorre duᵹuðe,   þē þā dēað fornam.
Site nū tō symle   ond onsǣl meoto,
490 siᵹe-hrēð secᵹum,   swā þīn sefa hwette."

here, that the first (alliterating) letter, and the second element, are kept intact. Cf. *Sigeferð* and *Sǣferð*, *Ordlāf* and *Ōslāf, etc.*

470. *fēo* instrumental. The *ic* of l. 471 is to be understood also with *þingode* [cf. Kock in *Anglia*, xxvii. 227].

473. The metre demands *tō secgan* [so Holthausen, Schücking, and Sedgefield]: similarly in ll. 1724, 1941, 2093, 2562. The uninflected form is preserved in ll. 316, 2556.

479. *-sceaðan*: MS. *sc^e^aðan*, the *e* in a different hand.

488. *þē...fornam*, 'since death had taken them away.' [Klaeber[453], comparing *Riddles*, ix. [x.] 11.]

489–90. *onsǣl...secgum*: MS. *on sæl meoto sige hreð secgū.* The MS. reading has in the past been very generally defended [e.g. by Leo, Heyne, Bugge in *Tidsskr.* viii. 292, Grein$_2$, Dietrich, Wülker, Kluge[188]], and is retained by Trautmann[154]: *onsǣl* has been taken as the imperative of the verb, and *meoto* as fem. sg. (Grein, *Sprachschatz*) or neut. pl. (Grein$_2$, Bugge) of some word not elsewhere recorded, meaning either 'measure,' 'thought,' or 'speech': so *onsǣl meoto*='relax the ties of etiquette' or 'unknit thy thoughts.' The difficulty is that a verb, unless emphatic, should not take the alliteration. Those who retain the MS. reading generally take *sigehrēð* as an adj.=*sige-hrēðig*, 'victory famed' (so Heyne, Trautmann: but it is surely a noun), or make *sigehrēðsecgum* one word.

Holthausen suggested [*Z.f.d.Ph.* xxxvii. 114] *on sǣlum weota sigehrēðgum*

þā wæs ȝēat-mæcȝum ȝeador ætsomne
on bēor-sele benc ȝerȳmed;
þǣr swīð-ferhþe sittan ēodon,
þrȳðum dealle. þeȝn nytte behēold,
495 sē þe on handa bær hroden ealo-wǣȝe,
scencte scīr wered. Scop hwīlum sanȝ
hādor on Heorote; þǣr wæs hæleða drēam,
duȝuð unlȳtel Dena ond Wedera.

VIII ⟨H⟩VNferð maþelode, Ecȝlāfes bearn,
500 þe æt fōtum sæt frēan Scyldinȝa,
onband beadu-rūne —wæs him Bēowulfes sīð,
mōdȝes mere-faran, micel æf-þunca,
forþon þe hē ne ūþe, þæt ǣniȝ ōðer man
ǣfre |mǣrða þon mā middan-ȝeardes Fol. 141b.
505 ȝehēdde under heofenum þonne hē sylfa—
"Eart þū se Bēowulf, sē þe wið Brecan wunne,
on sīdne sǣ ymb sund flite,
ðǣr ȝit for wlence wada cunnedon,
ond for dol-ȝilpe on dēop wæter
510 aldrum nēþdon? Nē inc ǣniȝ mon,
ne lēof ne lāð, belēan mihte
sorh-fullne sīð, þā ȝit on sund rêon;

secgum..., *weota* being from *witian*: 'in happiness ordain to these victorious men as thy soul bids thee.'

The reading *on sǣl meota sige-hrēð secga* [Klaeber in *J.E.G.Ph.* vi. 192] is an improvement upon Holthausen's, being much nearer to the MS., and giving better sense: 'in joyful time think upon victory of men.' This has since been adopted by Holthausen$_2$. The verb **metian* is not elsewhere recorded, but may be inferred from the Goth. *mitōn*, 'consider.'

Sedgefield$_1$ suggests *on sǣl mota sigehrēð[ig] secgum*: 'when time suits speak, victorious one, to the men': Sedgefield$_2$ *on sǣlum tēo* (award) *sigehrēð secgum*.

Cosijn[10] would read *Sigehrēðsecgum*=*Hrēðmonnum*='unto the Danes.'

499. *Unferð*: always written with an *h* in the MS., although alliterating with vowels.

505. *gehēdde*. This is usually interpreted 'obtain' or 'achieve,' and is explained either as a compound of *hȳdan*, 'to hide' (Bosworth-Toller; cf. ll. 2235, 3059), or of *hēdan*, 'to heed' (so Sedgefield). But it may be, as Holthausen (who reads *gehēgde*) and Schücking suppose [cf. Sievers, *P.B.B.* ix. 293], from *gehēgan* (l. 425), 'to carry out,' in which case *mǣrða*='deeds of glory.' Grein adopted all three interpretations in turn.

507. *sund flite*. The older editors took this as one word, 'swimming contest.' It is better, however, to render 'didst strive in swimming.' [Cf. Bugge in *Tidsskr.* viii. 48.]

512. *rēon*. The metre demands a disyllable, here and in l. 539.

þǣr ȝit ēaȝor-strēam earmum þehton,
mǣton mere-strǣta, mundum bruȝdon,
515 ȝlidon ofer ȝār-secȝ; ȝeofon ȳþum wēol,
wintrys wylm[*e*]. Ȝit on wæteres ǣht
seofon niht swuncon; hē þē æt sunde oferflāt,
hæfde māre mæȝen. Þā hine on morȝen-tīd
on Heaþo-Rǣm*as* holm ūp ætbær;
520 ðonon hē ȝesōhte swǣsne ēðel,
lēof his lēodum lond Brondinȝa,
freoðo-burh fǣȝere, þǣr hē folc āhte,
burh ond bēaȝas. |Bēot eal wið þē — Fol. 142a.
sunu Bēanstānes sōðe ȝelǣste.
525 Ðonne wēne ic tō þē wyrsan ȝeþinȝea,
ðēah þū heaðo-rǣsa ȝehwǣr dohte,
ȝrimre ȝūðe, ȝif þū Ȝrendles dearst
niht-lonȝne fyrst nêan bīdan."
Bēowulf maþelode, bearn Ecȝþēowes:
530 "Hwæt! þū worn fela, wine mīn ⟨H⟩unferð,
bēore druncen ymb Brecan sprǣce,
sæȝdest from his sīðe. Sōð ic taliȝe,
þæt ic mere-strenȝo māran āhte,
earfeþo on ȳþum, ðonne ǣniȝ ōþer man.

516. *wylm*[*e*], Thorpe: MS. *wylm*. The alteration is demanded by the metre, and betters the sense; *wylm*[*um*] or [*þurh*] *wintrys wylm* have also been suggested.

For the gen. sg. *wintrys* see Sievers$_3$ § 44, N. 2: *winter* properly belongs to the *u*-declension, Sievers$_3$ § 273.

517. Tacitus [*Germ.* XI.] notes this reckoning by nights instead of days: *Nec dierum numerum, ut nos, sed noctium computant.* Cf. 'a sennight, fortnight.'

519. *Heaþo-Rǣmas*, Grein$_1$: MS. *heaþoræmes*. The most correct form of the name, *Heaþo-Rēamas*, occurs in *Widsith* (l. 63) and some editors would substitute it here.

520. *ēðel*: MS. ᛟ. The O.E. name of this runic character ᛟ was *ēðel*; hence the character is used here and in l. 913 for the word *ēðel*.

525. Either we must take *wyrsan* as gen. pl. for *wyrsena*, a form which would be extraordinary, but not quite unprecedented (cf. *flotan and sceotta*, *Brunanburh*, 32), or we must alter *geþingea* into *geþinges* [Rieger[389]].

The meaning is 'I expect from thee a worse issue.' Cf. l. 1396 [and see Kock in *Anglia*, xxvii. 224].

528. *nēan*: a disyllable. Note the characteristic syntax, 'to await from near at hand.' So Beowulf hears of Grendel's deeds, not *æt hām*, but *from hām*; see l. 194.

530. *Unferð*: see note to l. 499.

534. *earfeþo*, 'stress,' is not a good parallel to *mere-strengo*, so that many editors have altered to *eafeþo*, 'strength.'

535 Wit þæt ȝecwǣdon cniht-wesende
ond ȝebēotedon —wǣron bēȝen þā ȝīt
on ȝeoȝoð-fēore— þæt wit on ȝār-secȝ ūt
aldrum nēðdon; ond þæt ȝeæfndon swā.
Hæfdon swurd nacod, þā wit on sund rêon,
540 heard on handa; wit unc wið hron-fixas
werian þōhton. Nō hē wiht fram mē
flōd-ȳþum feor flēotan meahte,
hraþor on holme; nō ic fram him wolde.
Ðā wit æt|somne on sǣ wǣron Fol. 142b.
545 fīf nihta fyrst, oþ þæt unc flōd tōdrāf,
wado weallende; wedera cealdost,
nīpende niht ond norþan wind,
heaðo-ȝrim ondhwearf; hrēo wǣron ȳþa.
Wæs mere-fixa mōd onhrēred;
550 þǣr mē wið lāðum līc-syrce mīn,
heard hond-locen, helpe ȝefremede;
beado-hræȝl brōden on brēostum læȝ,
ȝolde ȝeȝyrwed. Mē tō ȝrunde tēah
fāh fēond-scaða, fæste hæfde
555 ȝrim on ȝrāpe; hwæþre mē ȝyfeþe wearð,
þæt ic āȝlǣcan orde ȝerǣhte,
hilde-bille; heaþo-rǣs fornam
mihtiȝ mere-dēor þurh mīne hand.
VIIII Swā mec ȝelōme lāð-ȝetēonan
560 þrēatedon þearle. Ic him þēnode
dēoran sweorde, swā hit ȝedēfe wæs;
næs hīe ðǣre fylle ȝefēan hæfdon,
mān-fordǣdlan, þæt hīe mē þēȝon,
symbel ymb-sǣton sǣ-ȝrunde nēah;
565 ac on merȝenne mēcum |wunde Fol. 143a.

543. *him* can take the alliteration because emphatic. Cf. l. 197.

548. *ondhwearf*: MS. ⁊*hwearf*; for the use of this symbol with compound verbs, cf. ⁊*swarode*, l. 258. Grein takes *hwearf* to be an adj., which he glosses '*versatilis, volubilis*,' and compares Icel. *hverfr*, 'shifty.'

565. Some grammarians have seen in *mēcum* (l. 565), *sweordum* (l. 567), *mǣgum* (l. 2353), perhaps *māgum* (l. 2614), *hēafdum* (Rood, 63), *etc.*, a survival of an old instrumental *singular*. This, however, is exceedingly doubtful [cf. Osthoff, *I.F.* xx. 163–218].

The use of pl. for sg. is to be found in Latin, Greek and O.E.: cf.

be ȳð-lāfe uppe lǣᵹon,
sweo[*r*]dum āswefede, þæt syðþan nā
ymb brontne ford brim-līðende
lāde ne letton. Lēoht ēastan cōm,
570 beorht bēacen ᵹodes; brimu swaþredon,
þæt ic sǣ-næssas ᵹesēon mihte,
windiᵹe weallas. Wyrd oft nereð
unfǣᵹne eorl, þonne his ellen dēah.
Hwæþere mē ᵹesǣlde, þæt ic mid sweorde ofslōh
575 niceras niᵹene. Nō ic on niht ᵹefræᵹn
under heofones hwealf heardran feohtan,
ne on ēᵹ-strēamum earmran mannon;
hw*æ*þere ic fāra fenᵹ fēore ᵹedīᵹde,
sīþes wēriᵹ. Ðā mec sǣ oþbær,
580 flōd æfter faroðe, on Finna land,
w*a*du weallendu. Nō ic wiht fram þē
swylcra searo-nīða secᵹan hȳrde,
billa brōᵹan; Breca nǣfre ᵹīt
æt heaðo-lāce, ne ᵹehwæþer incer,

l. 1074, *bearnum ond brōðrum.* Similarly here the plural has become almost an epic formula, which is used, although logically inaccurate, since Breca's sword had no share in this slaughter. [Cf. Cosijn[11]. This seems better than to suppose with Heinzel that Breca and Beowulf *together* slaughter the monsters, and that the apparent inconsistency with the preceding lines, 544, *etc.*, where the separation of Beowulf and Breca is told, is due to that O.E. 'harking back,' which he justly emphasizes. See *A.f.d.A.* x. 220.]

567. *sweo*[*r*]*dum*, Kemble$_1$: MS. defective at corner, having only *swe* and part of *o*. Thorkelin's transcript A has *sweodum.*

568. *brontne.* Similarly Icel. *brattr* is used of 'lofty' waves. No alteration of the text is necessary.

572–3. 'Fate often saves a man if he is not doomed, *and* if his courage holds.' The paradox is a favourite one in Germanic literature. Cf. ll. 670, 1056, 1552, where Beowulf is saved by God *and* his mail; *Laxdæla saga*, xv., where two fugitives, crossing a swollen river in winter, are saved 'because they were brave *and because* longer life was granted to them.' [Cf. Klaeber in *Archiv*, cxv. 179.] Cook [*M.L.N.* viii. 118] quotes many parallels for the dogma that 'hap helpeth hardy man,' including *Andreas*, 459, *etc.* (which may be imitated from this passage).

574. *Hwæþere.* Some critics [e.g. Bugge in *Tidsskr.* viii. 48] have objected that there is no need for any contrast here. Sievers [*P.B.B.* ix. 138] justifies the text, comparing the Mod. Eng. use of 'however,' resuming after a digression, without, necessarily, any idea of contrast.

577. *mannon* for *mannan*, cf. ll. 788, 849.

578. *hwæþere*, Thorpe; MS. *hwaþere.*

580. *Finna land* may be Lapland; but at this date there were still '*Finns*' in the South, and localities in Southern Sweden have been suggested which harmonize better with *Heaþo-Rǣmas* than Lapland does.

581. *wadu*, Grundtvig[275] and Kemble$_2$: MS. *wudu.* See l. 546.

585 swā dēorlīce dǣd ʒefremede
fāʒum sweordum —nō ic þæs [*ʒeflites*] ʒylpe—
þēah ðū þīnum brōðrum tō banan wurde,
hēafod-mǣʒum; þæs þū in |helle scealt **Fol. 143[b].**
werhðo drēoʒan, þēah þīn wit duʒe.
590 Secʒe ic þē tō sōðe, sunu Ecʒlāfes,
þæt nǣfre Ʒre[*n*]del swā fela ʒryra ʒefremede,
atol ǣʒlǣca, ealdre þīnum,
hȳnðo on Heorote, ʒif þīn hiʒe wǣre,
sefa swā searo-ʒrim, swā þū self talast;
595 ac hē hafað onfunden, þæt hē þā fǣhðe ne þearf,
atole ecʒ-þræce, ēower lēode
swīðe onsittan, Sige-Scyldinʒa;
nymeð nȳd-bāde, nǣneʒum ārað
lēode Deniʒa, ac hē lust wiʒeð,
600 swefeð ond sendeþ, secce ne wēneþ
tō Ʒār-Denum. Ac ic him Ʒēata sceal

586. [*geflites*] Kluge: Grein$_1$ suggested [*fela*]. Heyne assumed the loss of two half lines after *sweordum*, with the unpleasant consequence that the numbers of his lines were one too many throughout the rest of the poem. This has been corrected in the latest revision of Heyne: but students must be prepared to find most references to *Beowulf* in monographs following Heyne's old numbering.

587. The same taunt is hurled by Gothmund against Sinfjǫtli (Fitela): *Helga kviþa Hundingsbana*, i. 38. *There* it is an instance of "flyting," mere irresponsible abuse. That it is not to be so taken here appears from ll. 1167, *etc.* It is quoted by Beowulf with serious and bitter irony as Unferth's greatest achievement. [Cf. Cosijn[12].]

591. *Gre*[*n*]*del*, Thorkelin's emendation: MS. *gre del.*

596. If we retain *ēower*, we must take it as gen. of *gē* 'ye' dependent upon *lēode*. Trautmann, Holthausen$_{1,2}$ and Sedgefield alter to *ēowre*.

599. Kemble$_3$ suggested *hē* [*on*] *lust wigeð*, 'he warreth as it pleaseth him,' which is supported by l. 618, *hē on lust geþeah.* Bugge [*Tidsskr.* VIII. 49] would read *þigeð* here likewise, 'he helps himself at will.'

But the MS. can be defended: 'Grendel feels pleasure': *wigeð* is then from *wegan*, 'to bear'; cf. ll. 1777, 1931, 2464.

600. *sendeþ* is the MS. reading, but the meaning is not clear. Leo translated 'feasteth': but though *sand* often means 'a course,' 'mess,' or 'dish,' there is no authority for *sendan*='to feast.' Schücking [in his edition: also in *Engl. Stud.* XXXIX. 103: so Holthausen$_3$] renders *sendeþ* 'sends to destruction'=*forsendeþ* (cf. l. 904), but this is not satisfactory.

Yet the emendations proposed are equally inconclusive: Bosworth-Toller, *scendeþ*, 'puts to shame,' which fails to alliterate; Trautmann[158], *swelgeþ*, 'swallows'; Holthausen$_{1,2}$, *swenceþ*, 'torments'; Sedgefield, *serweþ*, 'lies in wait' (*sierwan*), cf. l. 161.

secce, a dialectal form; see Sievers$_3$ § 151: Thorkelin and Thorpe normalized to *sæcce*, followed by older editors.

601. Thorpe and Heyne$_2$ *etc.* suppress *ic*. Thorpe (followed by Earle) then makes *Gēata* (weak form) the subject, and *eafoð ond ellen* the object. Heyne

eafoð ond ellen unȝēara nū
ȝūþe ȝebēodan. Ȝǣþ eft sē þe mōt
tō medo mōdiȝ, siþþan morȝen-lēoht
605 ofer ylda bearn ōþres dōȝores,
sunne sweȝl-wered, sūþan scīneð."
Þā wæs on sālum sinces brytta,
ȝamol-feax ond ȝūð-rōf; ȝēoce ȝelȳfde
|breȝo Beorht-Dena; ȝehȳrde on Bēowulfe Fol. 144a.
610 folces hyrde fæst-rǣdne ȝeþōht.
Ðǣr wæs hæleþa hleahtor, hlyn swynsode,
word wǣron wynsume. Ēode Wealhþēow forð,
cwēn Hrōðȝāres, cynna ȝemyndiȝ,
ȝrētte ȝold-hroden ȝuman on healle;
615 ond þā frēolīc wīf ful ȝesealde
ǣrest Ēast-Dena ēþel-wearde,
bæd hine blīðne æt þǣre bēor-þeȝe,
lēodum lēofne; hē on lust ȝeþeah
symbel ond sele-ful, siȝe-rōf kyninȝ.
620 Ymb-ēode þā ides Helminȝa
duȝuþe ond ȝeoȝoþe dǣl ǣȝhwylcne,
sinc-fato sealde, oþ þæt sǣl ālamp,
þæt hīo Bēowulfe, bēaȝ-hroden cwēn,
mōde ȝeþunȝen, medo-ful ætbær;
625 ȝrētte Ȝēata lēod, Ȝode þancode
wīs-fæst wordum, þæs ðe hire se willa ȝelamp,
þæt hēo on ǣniȝne eorl ȝelȳfde
fyrena frōfre. Hē þæt ful ȝeþeah,
wæl-rēow wiȝa, |æt Wealhþēon, Fol. 144b.
630 ond þā ȝyddode ȝūþe ȝefȳsed;
Bēowulf maþelode, bearn Ecȝþēowes:

takes *eafoð ond ellen Gēata* as subject, *gūðe* as object, and gives as his reason for suppressing *ic*, that we can hardly construe *ic Gēata* as 'I of the Geatas,' or 'I among the Geatas.' This is true, but, as a previous editor has remarked, it 'is what Coleridge calls the "wilful ingenuity of blundering." What is to prevent *ic* being taken as the subject, and *eafoð ond ellen Gēata* as the object?'

603. *gūþe* may be parallel to *eafoð ond ellen*, or may mean 'in battle.'
605. *ōþres dōgores*, adverbial, 'on the next day,' as in l. 219.
612. Compare the picture of the gracious lady in the *Exeter Book Gnomic Verses*, 85, *etc.*
617. The verb 'to be' is understood after *blīðne*, as frequently.
629. The metre demands the uncontracted *Wealhþēowan*.

"Ic þæt hoᵹode, þā ic on holm ᵹestāh,
sǣ-bāt ᵹesæt mid mīnra secᵹa ᵹedriht,
þæt ic ānunᵹa ēowra lēoda
635 willan ᵹeworhte, oþðe on wæl crunᵹe
fēond-ᵹrāpum fæst. Ic ᵹefremman sceal
eorlīc ellen, oþðe ende-dæᵹ
on þisse meodu-healle mīnne ᵹebīdan."
Ðām wīfe þā word wel līcodon,
640 ᵹilp-cwide Ᵹēates; ēode ᵹold-hroden
frēolicu folc-cwēn tō hire frēan sittan.
Þā wæs eft swā ǣr inne on healle
þrȳð-word sprecen, ðēod on sǣlum,
siᵹe-folca swēᵹ, oþ þæt semninᵹa
645 sunu Healfdenes sēcean wolde
ǣfen-ræste; wiste þǣm āhlǣcan
tō þǣm hēah-sele hilde ᵹeþinᵹed,
siððan hīe sunnan lēoht ᵹesēon [*ne*] meahton,
oþðe nīpende niht ofer ealle,
650 scadu-helma ᵹesceapu scrīðan cwōman,
wan under wolcnum. Werod eall ārās;
[*ᵹe*]ᵹrētte þā ᵹuma ōþerne,
Hrōðᵹār Bēowulf, ond him hǣl ābēad
wīn-ærnes |ᵹeweald, ond þæt word ācwæð: Fol. 145ᵃ.
655 "Nǣfre ic ǣneᵹum men ǣr ālȳfde,

644. *Semninga* must not be taken, as it is by several translators, to imply a hurried retreat. Precisely as in Mod. Eng. 'presently' (which indeed well renders *semninga*), the strict force of 'immediately' must not be pressed, either here or in ll. 1640 and 1767.

648. [*ne*], Thorpe's simple emendation, now generally adopted. Bugge [*Tidsskr.* viii. 57] proposed, in addition, to regard *oþðe* (l. 649) as equivalent to *ond*, as in l. 2475, and the suggestion was adopted by Heyne: 'and the darkness of night [''was'' understood, Bugge[89]] over all.' This is more satisfactory than Earle's defence of the usual meaning 'or': 'There is something of alternative between twilight and the dead of night.' Trautmann[160] and Holthausen regard *gesēon* [*ne*] *meahton* as metrically incorrect. It is unusual, but not quite without precedent. [Cf. Sievers, *P.B.B.* x. 234, and l. 1504.] Holthausen$_2$ emends *sēon* [*ne*] *meahton*; Holthausen$_3$ *gesēon* [*ne*] *magon*.

651. *wan* has changed its meaning from 'dark' to 'pale.' The modern meaning is inappropriate here. In other phrases, such as 'waters wan,' the appropriateness of the adjective has been rather increased by the change in meaning.

652. [*ge*]*grētte*. The half line is metrically defective, and the addition of *ge* [Grundtvig[276]] is the simplest and now the generally accepted remedy (cf. l. 2516). Grein$_2$ supplied [*glædmōd*], Heyne$_2$, *etc.* [*giddum*].

655, *etc.* The alleged inconsistency between these lines and ll. 480–8 was

siþðan ic hond ond rond hebban mihte,
ðrȳþ-ærn Dena būton þē nū ðā.
Hafa nū ond ʒeheald hūsa sēlest,
ʒemyne mǣrþo, mæʒen-ellen cȳð,
660 waca wið wrāþum. Ne bið þē wilna ʒād,
ʒif þū þæt ellen-weorc aldre ʒedīʒest."
x ÐĀ him Hrōþʒār ʒewāt mid his hæleþa ʒedryht,
eodur Scyldinʒa, ūt of healle;
wolde wīʒ-fruma Wealhþēo sēcan,
665 cwēn tō ʒebeddan. Hæfde Kyninʒ-wuldor
ʒrendle tō-ʒēanes, swā ʒuman ʒefrunʒon,
sele-weard āseted; sundor-nytte behēold
ymb aldor Dena, eoton-weard ābēad.
Hūru ʒēata lēod ʒeorne trūwode
670 mōdʒan mæʒnes, Metodes hyldo.
Ðā hē him of dyde īsern-byrnan,
helm of hafelan, sealde his hyrsted sweord,
īrena cyst, ombiht-þeʒne,
ond ʒehealdan hēt hilde-ʒeatwe.
675 ʒespræc þā se ʒōda ʒylp-worda sum,
Bēowulf |ʒēata, ǣr hē on bed stiʒe: Fol. 145b.
"Nō ic mē an here-wǣsmun hnāʒran taliʒe

one of the arguments of Müllenhoff[116] against unity of authorship. The discrepancy is only apparent. The Danish hall had never before been entrusted by its king to a *stranger*. [For the explanation of this, and similar 'inconsistencies,' cf. Jellinek and Kraus in *Z.f.d.A.* xlv. 265, *etc.*]

665. MS. *kyning*, at end of line: there is room for an *a*, but no trace of one. Most editors, however, follow Kemble$_3$ and read *kyning*[*a*] *wuldor*. Bugge[368], Klaeber[454], and Schücking argue for the MS. reading. In any case we must follow Müllenhoff[117] in interpreting *Kyning-wuldor*, *etc.*, as 'God': see *Elene*, 5; *Judith*, 155. [Cf. Holthausen, *Anglia*, *Beiblatt*, xiii. 204.]

668. Thorpe *eoton* (acc.) *weard* (nom.) *ābēad*; Heyne *eoton* (dat.) *weard* (acc.) *ābēad*. The difficulty of the uninflected acc., *eoton-weard*, seems less than the difficulties presented by these readings. The *e* of *weard*[*e*] is elided before the vowel: cf. l. 1932. [See Klaeber[454].]

Beowulf is the subject of *behēold*, *ābēad*.

Sedgefield reads *ābād* and takes *eoton-weard* as referring to Beowulf: 'the watcher against the monster stayed behind.'

669. *trūwode*. The metre demands *trēowde* instead of the Southern form *trūwode*, here and in ll. 1533, 1993, 2322, 2370, 2540, 2953. In l. 1166 *trēowde* has been retained by the scribe. [Cf. Sievers in *P.B.B.* x. 233.]

670. *mōdgan* may refer to God, or to Beowulf, or may agree with *mægnes*.

673. *īrena*. Metre demands that the second syllable should be long [cf. note to l. 6]; hence here and in l. 1697 Sievers corrects to *īrenna* (cf. ll. 802, 2259) [*P.B.B.* x. 308; xxix. 568].

677. *wǣsmun*; Grundtvig[277], Kemble$_2$, *etc.* normalize to *wǣstmum*.

ʒūþ-ʒeweorca þonne ʒrendel hine;
forþan ic hine sweorde swebban nelle,
680 aldre benēotan, þēah ic eal mæʒe.
Nāt hē þāra ʒōda, þæt hē mē onʒēan slêa,
rand ʒehēawe, þēah ðe hē rōf sîe
nīþ-ʒeweorca; ac wit on niht sculon
secʒe ofersittan, ʒif hē ʒesēcean dear
685 wīʒ ofer wǣpen, ond siþðan wītiʒ ʒod
on swā hwæþere hond, hāliʒ Dryhten,
mǣrðo dēme, swā him ʒemet þince."
Hylde hine þā heaþo-dēor, hlēor-bolster onfēnʒ
eorles andwlitan, ond hine ymb moniʒ
690 snellīc sǣ-rinc sele-reste ʒebēah.
Nǣniʒ heora þōhte, þæt hē þanon scolde
eft eard-lufan ǣfre ʒesēcean,
folc oþðe frēo-burh, þǣr hē āfēded wæs:
ac hīe hæfdon ʒefrunen, þæt hīe ǣr tō fela micles
695 in þǣm wīn-sele wæl-dēað fornam,
Deniʒea lēode. Ac him Dryhten forʒeaf
wīʒ-spēda ʒewiofu, |Wedera lēodum Fol. 146ᵃ.
frōfor ond fultum, þæt hīe fēond heora
ðurh ānes cræft ealle ofercōmon,
700 selfes mihtum; sōð is ʒecȳþed,
þæt mihtiʒ ʒod manna cynnes
wēold *w*īde-ferhð. Cōm on wanre niht
scrīðan sceadu-ʒenʒa. Scēotend swǣfon,
þā þæt horn-reced healdan scoldon,
705 ealle būton ānum. Þæt wæs yldum cūþ,

Grein to *wǣsmum*. But the spelling, though unusual, is not unprecedented. For *un* in place of *um* cf. *wīcun*, l. 1304.

681. *þāra gōda*, 'of those gentle practices,' i.e. 'swordmanship,' Earle.

þæt, 'to enable him to.'

The text has been doubted, but its syntax is confirmed by a parallel quoted by Klaeber[455] from Ælfric, who, after referring to the Redemption, continues '*þæt folc ne cūþe þǣra gōda, þæt hī cwǣdon þæt hē God wǣre.*'

slēa. Subjunctive. The metre demands a disyllable, *slāe*, which many editors [Holthausen, Schücking, following Kaluza] substitute in the text.

684. *secge*, from *secg*, 'sword.'

hē, Kemble$_2$: MS. *het.*

694. *hīe ǣr.* Thorpe, *hyra ǣr*: Kluge[189], followed by Sedgefield, reads *hiera*: an unnecessary change; since *hīe* and *fela* are coordinate. [Cf. Klaeber[455].]

702. *wīde*, Grundtvig[277]. Thorkelin's transcripts, *ride*: now nothing left but part of the perpendicular stroke of the first letter.

þæt hīe ne mōste, þā Metod nolde,
se s[c]yn-scaþa under sceadu breʒdan;
ac hē wæccende wrāþum on andan
bād bolʒen-mōd beadwa ʒeþinʒes.
XI 710 Ðā cōm of mōre under mīst-hleoþum
Ʒrendel ʒonʒan, ʒodes yrre bær;
mynte se mān-scaða manna cynnes
sumne besyrwan in sele þām hēan.
Wōd under wolcnum, tō þæs þe hē wīn-reced,
715 ʒold-sele ʒumena, ʒearwost wisse,
fǣttum fāhne; ne wæs þæt forma sīð,
þæt hē Hrōþʒāres hām ʒesōhte.
Nǣfre hē on aldor-daʒum ǣr |ne siþðan **Fol. 146b.**
heardran hǣle heal-ðeʒnas fand.
720 Cōm þā tō recede rinc sīðian
drēamum bedǣled; duru sōna onarn,
fȳr-bendum fæst, syþðan hē hire folmum [æthr]ān;
onbrǣd þā bealo-hȳdiʒ, ðā [hē ʒe]bolʒen wæs,

707. *s[c]yn-scaþa*, Grein: MS. *synscaþa*. If we keep the MS. reading, the parallel of *mān-scaða* (l. 712) favours the derivation of the first element from *synn*, 'crime,' rather than (as in *sin-here*, *syn-snǣd*) from *sin-*, 'incessant.' But the alliteration is incorrect [cf. Schröder in *Z.f.d.A.* xliii. 365–6]. The second element in a compound noun is the less important, and therefore should not take the alliteration when the first does not, and accordingly Grein, followed by Holthausen, Trautmann[164], Schücking, emended to *scinscaþa*, or *scyn-sceaþa*, 'spectral foe.'

708. *hē*, Beowulf.

719. *heardran hǣle* we may render 'with worse omen' [Holthausen in *Anglia*, xxiv. 267], or 'with sterner greeting.' If we read *heardran hæle*, 'braver men,' we have an exceptional type of line [cf. Sievers in *P.B.B.* x. 275]. Holthausen$_2$, after numerous earlier attempts, finally (ii. 170) reads *heardran hæle[scipes]*, 'more doughty valour,' Schücking *heardran hæle[þas]*, 'more doughty champions.' [For other conjectures cf. Bugge[368], Trautmann[165].]

722. MS. defective at edge. Zupitza's transliteration of the MS. has [*gehr*]*an*; *hr* can be made out, though with much difficulty and some uncertainty. The preceding letters have been lost, but as there *must* have been two preceding letters we can hardly, with Schücking and Sedgefield, read *hrān*.

The contention that the simple form is preferable, because whilst *hrīnan* usually governs the dat., *gehrīnan* more commonly takes the acc., can be met by reading [*æthr*]*ān* (*æthrīnan* takes the gen. and would therefore suit the context). This excellent suggestion was made by Grundtvig[277] in 1820, but has been generally overlooked.

723. MS. faded. *ðā hē gebolgen wæs* was conjectured by Grundtvig[277] in 1820 and is adopted by recent edd. Kemble and the older edd. read *ðā hē ābolgen wæs*. Zupitza says: 'Now *bolgen* is still distinct, and before it I think I see traces of two letters of which the first seems to have been *g*' [I can see nothing of this]: 'but what preceded this is entirely faded.

recedes mūþan. Raþe æfter þon
725 on fāȝne flōr fēond treddode,
ēode yrre-mōd; him of ēaȝum stōd
liȝȝe ȝelīcost lēoht unfǣȝer.
ȝeseah hē in recede rinca maniȝe,
swefan sibbe-ȝedriht samod ætȝædere,
730 maȝo-rinca hēap. Þā his mōd āhlōȝ;
mynte þæt hē ȝedǣlde, ǣr þon dæȝ cwōme,
atol āȝlǣca, ānra ȝehwylces
līf wið līce, þā him ālumpen wæs
wist-fylle wēn. Ne wæs þæt wyrd þā ȝēn,
735 þæt hē mā mōste manna cynnes
ðicȝean ofer þā niht. Þrȳð-swȳð behēold
mǣȝ Hiȝelāces, hū se mān-scaða
under fǣr-ȝripum ȝefaran wolde.
Nē þæt se āȝlǣca yldan þōhte,
740 ac hē ȝe|fēnȝ hraðe forman sīðe — Fol. 131a.
slǣpendne rinc, slāt unwearnum,
bāt bān-locan, blōd ēdrum dranc,
syn-snǣdum swealh; sōna hæfde
unlyfiȝendes eal ȝefeormod,
745 fēt ond folma. Forð nēar ætstōp,
nam þā mid handa hiȝe-þihtiȝne
rinc on ræste, rǣhte *tōȝēan[es]*
fēond mid folme; hē onfēnȝ hraþe
inwit-þancum ond wið earm ȝesæt.

726. Note the rhyme.
727. *ligge* = *lige*. Cf. note to l. 1085.
736. *þrȳð-swȳð*. See note to l. 131.
738. *under fǣr-gripum*, 'during' or 'in his attack.' Compare the use of *under þǣm*, 'during that,' in the Orosius. [See Cosijn, *P.B.B.* xix. 455.]
739. *Nē*. Grundtvig (1861) altered *Nē þæt* to *Nō þǣr*, and Holthausen$_{1,2}$ adopts *nō*, on the ground that *ne* should immediately precede its verb. But, as Klaeber [*Engl. Stud.* xxxix. 430] points out, we have here the emphatic *nē*, 'nor,' which, in Old as in Mod. Eng., is not necessarily preceded by a negative sentence. Cf. ll. 510, 1071.
741. *slǣpendne rinc* = Hondscioh: see ll. 2076, *etc.*
742. 'feet, hands, and all.' Cf. l. 2080. [See Cosijn[14].]
747. *tōgēanes*, Sievers: MS. *ongean*. The change is metrically essential, and has been adopted by all recent editors.
748. *fēond* is nom. and refers to Grendel, Beowulf is never so called: *hē* must then refer to Beowulf, not to Grendel, since the situation of ll. 750–754 would be impossible if Beowulf up to that had remained passive.
748–9. *onfēng...inwit-þancum*. Klaeber[253] would understand 'him': 'He

750 Sōna þæt onfunde fyrena hyrde,
þæt hē ne mētte middan-ȝeardes,
eorþan scēatta, on elran men
mund-ȝripe māran; hē on mōde wearð
forht on ferhðe; nō þȳ ǣr fram meahte.
755 Hyȝe wæs him hin-fūs, wolde on heolster flēon,
sēcan dēofla ȝedræȝ; ne wæs his drohtoð þǣr,
swylce hē on ealder-daȝum ǣr ȝemētte.
Ȝemunde þā se *m*ōd[*ȝ*]a mǣȝ Hiȝelāces
ǣfen-sprǣce, ūp-lanȝ āstōd
760 ond him fæste wiðfēnȝ; finȝras burston;
eoten wæs ūt-weard; eorl furþur stōp.
Mynte se mǣra, |[þ]ǣr hē meahte swā, Fol. 131b.
wīdre ȝewindan ond on weȝ þanon
flēon on fen-hopu; wiste his finȝra ȝeweald

(Beowulf) received him (Grendel) with hostile intent,' *i.e.* he did not flinch or try to avoid the attack but came to grips with Grendel whilst still lying down. This is the best rendering of *onfēng*, and is the situation implied in ll. 750 ff. Against this it is objected (Schücking) that *inwit* has a signification of malice and treachery which makes it unsuitable to Beowulf, and that we should render: 'Beowulf took, perceived, his (Grendel's) treacherous hostility.' Cosijn[14] conjectures *inwit-þanculum* (dat. of adj. *inwit-þancol*, 'hostile in intent,' referring to Grendel). Grein took *inwit-þanc* as an adj. agreeing with 'Grendel' understood: but in the five other passages where the word occurs in O.E. poetry it is a substantive.

749. *wið earm gesæt* has been taken to mean (1) that Beowulf settled upon Grendel's arm [so, *e.g.*, Clark-Hall]; (2) that he propped himself on his own arm [so, *e.g.*, Grein, Gummere]. The second meaning is supported by *The Harrowing of Hell*, 67 (*Christ and Satan*, 432). Mr Grattan writes to me: 'Have you never tried to throw off a bigger man than yourself who has got you down? Beowulf is at a disadvantage, having been attacked while supine. He, *with great difficulty*, of course, gets one shoulder up, supported on one arm; and later, when his grip has alarmed the aggressor and caused him to pull away, he succeeds in getting on to his legs (l. 759). When once he has done this, Grendel's chance is up. Beowulf gets a clean grip on him (l. 760). All this is the language of wrestling, which is employed again later in the struggle with Grendel's mother.'

752. *scēatta.* Many editors normalise to *scēata.* But see Sievers$_3$ § 230.

756. *gedræg*, 'tumult': the word can be used both in an abstract and in a concrete sense, 'noisy bearing' or 'a noisy assembly.'

758. *mōd[g]a*, Rieger: MS. *goda.* The emendation is necessary for the sake of the alliteration, and is followed by recent editors: Holthausen, Schücking, Sedgefield.

762. *mǣra*, 'notorious': cf. l. 103. For other instances see Bosworth-Toller.

þǣr. MS. defective at corner: only the lower part of the *r* is now left: but Thorkelin's transcripts agree upon the last two letters, *ær.* As to the preceding letters, A has a blank, B records *hw*, but with another ink, and crossed out in pencil. With evidence so confused, the parallel of l. 797 tells in favour of *þær*, which is read by most editors.

765 on ȝrames ȝrāpum; þæt wæs ȝēocor sīð,
þæt se hearm-scaþa tō Heorute ātēah.
Dryht-sele dynede; Denum eallum wearð,
ceaster-būendum, cēnra ȝehwylcum,
eorlum ealu-scerwen. Yrre wǣron bēȝen
770 rēþe ren-weardas. Reced hlynsode;
þā wæs wundor micel, þæt se wīn-sele
wiðhæfde heaþo-dēorum, þæt hē on hrūsan ne fēol,
fǣȝer fold-bold; ac hē þæs fæste wæs
innan ond ūtan īren-bendum
775 searo-þoncum besmiþod. Þǣr fram sylle ābēaȝ
medu-benc moniȝ, mīne ȝefrǣȝe,
ȝolde ȝereȝnad, þǣr þā ȝraman wunnon;
þæs ne wēndon ǣr witan Scyldinȝa,
þæt hit ā mid ȝemete manna ǣniȝ,
780 *b*etlīc ond bān-fāȝ, tōbrecan meahte,
listum tōlūcan, nymþe līȝes fæþm

765. *þæt wæs*, Grein$_1$: MS. *þæt he wæs*. The emendation is generally accepted.

765–6. Since *sīð* is masc., *ātēah* is probably intransitive, and the second *þæt* a conj., not a pronoun, as in l. 717, *etc*. Translate 'that was a hard journey, when the ravager betook himself to Heorot.'

769. *ealu-scerwen*. A similar word, *meodu-scerwen*, occurs in the *Andreas* (1526). The meaning apparently is 'terror as at the loss of ale,' 'mortal panic.' Confusion has ensued because (through an early and remarkably long-lived error) the word in the *Andreas* has been read *meodu-scerpen*. On the theory that this was the right spelling, a derivation from *scearp*, with the meaning of 'sharpening, ferment, bitterness,' has been advocated [by Sedgefield; von Grienberger in *P.B.B.* xxxvi. 84; and Baskervill in his *Andreas*]. Wülker's facsimile of the *Vercelli Book* shows clearly that the right reading in the *Andreas* (as in *Beowulf*) is *scerwen* [cf. Sievers in *P.B.B.* xxxvi. 410; Klaeber in *Engl. Stud.* xliv. 125].

Apparently we must connect the word with *bescerwan*=*bescerian*, 'to deprive,' a 'deprivation of mead' being synonymous with the greatest distress. Bugge [*Tidsskr.* viii. 294–5] connects with *scirian*, 'to dispense' (taken ironically, 'they were given to drink of a deadly wine').

770. *ren-weardas*. This has usually been read *rēn* (=*regn*) *weardas*, 'mighty guardians': cf. *regn-heard* in l. 326. Holthausen and Klaeber [*J.E.G.Ph.* vi. 193] have independently suggested that *ren*=*ern*=*ærn*, 'house,' by the common metathesis of *r* (Sievers$_3$ § 179, 1); *rendegn* [*ren-þegn*]=*aedis minister* occurs in the *Erfurt Glossary*. 'The guardians of the house' gives the more satisfactory sense.

779. *mid gemete*. Klaeber[455] argues for the meaning 'in any wise,' rather than 'with strength,' comparing Bede, 86. 8, *ealle gemete*=*omnimodo*, *etc*.

780. *betlīc*, Grundtvig[278]: MS. *hetlic*. Cf. l. 1925.

781. Cf. ll. 82–5, and the note there.

swulȝe on swaþule. Swēȝ |ūp āstāȝ   Fol. 147ᵃ.
nīwe ȝeneahhe; Norð-Denum stōd
atelic eȝesa, ānra ȝehwylcum,
785 þāra þe of wealle wōp ȝehȳrdon,
ȝryre-lēoð ȝalan ȝodes ondsacan,
siȝe-lēasne sanȝ, sār wāniȝean
helle hæfton. Hēold hine fæste,
sē þe manna wæs mæȝene strenȝest
790 on þǣm dæȝe þysses līfes.
XII Nolde eorla hlēo ǣniȝe þinȝa
þone cwealm-cuman cwicne forlǣtan,
ne his līf-daȝas lēoda ǣniȝum
nytte tealde. Þǣr ȝenehost bræȝd
795 eorl Bēowulfes ealde lāfe,
wolde frēa-drihtnes feorh ealȝian,
mǣres þēodnes, ðǣr hīe meahton swā.
Hīe þæt ne wiston, þā hīe ȝewin druȝon,
heard-hicȝende hilde-mecȝas,
800 ond on healfa ȝehwone hēawan þōhton,
sāwle sēcan: þone syn-scaðan
ǣniȝ ofer eorþan īrenna cyst,
ȝūð-billa nān, ȝrētan nolde;

782. *swaþule.* Form and meaning seem alike to connect this word with *sweoloðe* (l. 1115) and *swioðole* (MS. *swicðole*, l. 3145). Context demands the meaning 'flame' and this is supported by the forms *swoloð* [see Bosworth-Toller] and *swoþel* [*Anglia*, viii. 452], both of which are given in glosses as equivalent to *cauma* ['burning'] *vel aestus.* The meaning 'smoke' often attributed to these words [Dietrich *Z.f.d.A.* v. 216] is possibly due to an attempt to connect the word with *sweoþol*, 'band, swaddling cloth,' through the meaning of 'enveloping smoke.' But context and the evidence of the glosses seems conclusive in favour of 'flame': cf. O.E. *swelan*, *swǣlan* 'burn'; O.H.G. *suilizo*, '*ardor, cauma.*'

788. Zupitza and others *helle-hæfton*; but nothing is gained by making the words a compound. For *-an* of the weak declension *-on* is not uncommon (cf. l. 849). Holthausen, following a parallel passage in the *Andreas* (1342), reads *helle hæftling.*

Almost all editors insert [*tō*] before *fæste*; and indeed the word may once have stood at the end of the line in the MS., though there is now no trace of it, and neither of Thorkelin's transcripts records it.

801. *sāwle sēcan.* Gering and Klaeber [*Christ. Elementen*, in *Anglia*, xxxv. 465] point out that this looks like a learned phrase: a translation of the biblical *animam quaerere*; yet it may have been a native idiom also (cf. l. 2422).

þæt understood before *þone*; cf. l. 199.

syn-scaðan. See note to l. 707.

ac hē siᵹe-wǣpnum |forsworen hæfde, Fol. 147b.
805 ecᵹa ᵹehwylcre. Scolde his aldor-ᵹedāl
on ðǣm dæᵹe þysses līfes
earmlīc wurðan, ond se ellor-ᵹāst
on fēonda ᵹeweald feor sīðian.
Ðā þæt onfunde, sē þe fela ǣror
810 mōdes myrðe manna cynne
fyrene ᵹefremede, hē fāᵹ wið Ᵹod,
þæt him se līc-homa lǣstan nolde,
ac hine se mōdeᵹa mǣᵹ Hyᵹelāces
hæfde be honda; wæs ᵹehwæþer ōðrum
815 lifiᵹende lāð. Līc-sār ᵹebād
atol ǣᵹlǣca; him on eaxle wearð
syn-dolh sweotol; seonowe onsprunᵹon,
burston bān-locan. Bēowulfe wearð
ᵹūð-hrēð ᵹyfeþe; scolde Ᵹrendel þonan
820 feorh-sēoc flêon under fen-hleoðu,
sēcean wyn-lēas wīc; wiste þē ᵹeornor,
þæt his aldres wæs ende ᵹeᵹonᵹen,
dōᵹera dæᵹ-rīm. Denum eallum wearð
æfter þām wæl-rǣse willa ᵹelumpen.
825 Hæfde þā ᵹefǣlsod, sē þe ǣr feorran cōm,
snotor ond swȳð-ferhð sele Hrōðᵹāres,
ᵹenered wið |nīðe; niht-weorce ᵹefeh, Fol. 148a.
ellen-mǣrþum. Hæfde Ēast-Denum
Ᵹēat-mecᵹa lēod ᵹilp ᵹelǣsted,
830 swylce oncȳþðe ealle ᵹebētte,

804. *forsworen*, not that Grendel had 'forsworn,' 'renounced' the use of swords, but that he had 'laid a spell' on the swords of his foes. If we translate *forsworen* as 'forsworn' then *hē* must be Beowulf: others tried to slay Grendel with the sword, but he, knowing better, had forsworn weapons [and trusted to his grip]. This is quite a possible rendering, for although below (l. 805) *his* must again refer to Grendel, such rapid transitions can easily be paralleled in O.E. syntax.

For the blunting of swords by the glance, see Saxo, Bk. VI. (ed. Holder, p. 187).

810. Holthausen would connect *myrðe* with *mierran* (Goth. *marzjan*), and interpret 'destructiveness,' but it is unnecessary to assume this word, since 'light-heartedly' gives satisfactory sense.

811. Kemble$_2$ first inserted *wæs* after *hē*, and was followed by almost all editors except Wülker. This appears to be a distinct enfeeblement of the MS. reading. *Fāg* comes at the beginning of a line in the MS., and Heyne says it cannot be settled whether or no *wæs* stood before it. But the facsimile shows 'there was no room for *wæs* before *fag*' (Zupitza).

inwid-sorȝe, þe hīe ǣr druȝon
ond for þrēa-nȳdum þolian scoldon,
torn unlȳtel. Þæt wæs tācen sweotol,
syþðan hilde-dēor hond āleȝde,
835 earm ond eaxle —þǣr wæs eal ȝeador
ȝrendles ȝrāpe— under ȝēapne hr[ōf].
XIII ÐĀ wæs on morȝen, mīne ȝefrǣȝe,
ymb þā ȝif-healle ȝūð-rinc moniȝ;
fērdon folc-toȝan feorran ond nêan
840 ȝeond wīd-weȝas wundor scēawian,
lāþes lāstas. Nō his līf-ȝedāl
sārlīc þūhte secȝa ǣneȝum,
þāra þe tīr-lēases trode scēawode,
hū hē wēriȝ-mōd on weȝ þanon,
845 nīða ofercumen on nicera mere,
fǣȝe ond ȝeflȳmed, feorh-lāstas bær.
Ðǣr wæs on blōde brim weallende,
atol ȳða ȝeswinȝ eal ȝemenȝed
hāton heolfre, |heoro-drēore wēol Fol. 148b.
850 dēað-fǣȝe dēoȝ siððan drēama lēas

836. MS. defective: *hr[ōf]*, Grundtvig[279] [an emendation often attributed to Rask, but Grundtvig does not say so]. The reading *hr[ōf]* is confirmed by l. 926. There is no contradiction with l. 983, if we suppose that the arm is placed outside the hall, reaches over the door, and towers to the roof. For such a use of *under*, not necessarily implying that the hand is within the house, cf. l. 211. [See T. Miller, 'The position of Grendel's arm in Heorot,' *Anglia*, xii. 396, *etc.*; and cf. Cosijn[14].]

845. *nīða ofercumen.* Unmetrical: cf. ll. 954, 2150. Holthausen emends *nīða genǣged.*

846. *feorh-lāstas*, 'tracks of failing life.' [Heyne: cf. Klaeber, *Anglia*, xxviii. 445.]

849. *hāton.* MS. *hat on heolfre*, and so Grein$_2$, Wülker. Grein$_1$ rightly read *hat on* as one word, *hātan* (unnecessarily altering *on* to *an*, for which see l. 788). The reading *hāton* is much easier than *hāt on*, and l. 1423 turns the probability in its favour. No weight can be attached to the spacing of words in the MS.

850. The MS. reading *deog* has been explained as 'dyed' (Grein) or 'concealed himself' (Heyne after Leo), but no verb *dēagan* with either meaning is recorded in O.E.

Sievers [*P.B.B.* ix. 138] *heoro-drēore wēol dēað-fǣge dēop* 'the deadly abyss welled with gore'; Bugge[89], *dēað-fǣges dēop* 'the abyss of the death-doomed one.' Cosijn[15], whilst supporting Sievers, suggests tentatively that the MS. may be right, and that *dēog* is a noun = *dēag*, 'dye.' Kemble$_2$ had already suggested *dēag*. Considerations of O.E. style favour our taking *dēað-fǣge dēog* or *dēop* as parallel to *brim weallende*, etc.

However *dēof*, the Northern form for *dēaf*, from *dūfan*, 'dive,' an emendation of Zupitza [*Archiv*, lxxxiv. 124–5] and, independently, of Trautmann[172], has been accepted by all recent edd.

in fen-freoðo feorh ālegde,
hæþene sāwle; þǣr him hel onfēng.
Þanon eft gewiton eald-gesīðas,
swylce geong manig of gomen-wāþe,
855 fram mere mōdge mēarum rīdan,
beornas on blancum. Ðǣr wæs Bēowulfes
mǣrðo mǣned; monig oft gecwæð,
þætte sūð ne norð be sǣm twēonum
ofer eormen-grund ōþer nǣnig
860 under swegles begong sēlra nǣre
rond-hæbbendra, rīces wyrðra.
Ne hīe hūru wine-drihten wiht ne lōgon,
glædne Hrōðgār, ac þæt wæs gōd cyning.
Hwīlum heaþo-rōfe hlēapan lēton,
865 on geflit faran, fealwe mēaras,
ðǣr him fold-wegas fǣgere þūhton,
cystum cūðe. Hwīlum cyninges þegn,
guma gilp-hlæden, gidda gemyndig,
sē ðe eal-fela eald-gesegena
870 worn gemunde, word ōþer fand
sōðe gebunden. Secg eft ongan
sīð Bēowulfes snyttrum |styrian, **Fol. 149ᵃ.**
ond on spēd wrecan spel gerāde,
wordum wrixlan; wel-hwylc gecwæð,
875 þæt hē fram Sigemunde secgan hȳrde

868. *guma gilp-hlæden.* Certainly not 'bombastic groom,' as Earle: *gilp* has not necessarily in O.E. any such evil signification: cf. ll. 640, 1749. Translate 'laden with glorious words'; or perhaps simply 'proud' or 'covered with glory' (as Klaeber[456], who compares *gylp-georn est* [Bede i. 34], translating *gloriae cupidissimus*).

870–1. *word ōþer fand sōðe gebunden,* 'framed a new story founded upon fact' [Clark-Hall]. But it is possible, as Rieger[390] and Bugge [*Z.f.d.Ph.* iv. 203] thought, that ll. 867–874 are all one sentence, and that these words form a parenthesis ('word followed word by the bond of truth,' Earle). Cf. *Hávamál: orð mér af orði orðs leitaði,* 'word from word found me word.'

Yet, though we may delete the stop in l. 871, we need not therefore, with Rieger and Bugge, alter *secg* to *secgan*: for *cyninges þegn, guma gilp-hlæden,* and *secg* would all be parallel, subject of *ongan styrian*: *eft* (l. 871) would go with *hwīlum* (l. 867), echoing the *hwīlum* of l. 864, just as in ll. 2107–11 *hwīlum......hwīlum...hwīlum eft.* [Klaeber[456].]

For *styrian* in the sense of 'treat of,' a parallel has been quoted from Byrhtferth's *Handbōc*: *Ne gelyst ūs þās þing leng styrian.*

875. 'Concerning Sigemund, concerning his deeds of valour.' Grein's emendation *Sigemunde[s]* is the more probable in that the next word begins with *s*; but, since it is not absolutely necessary, I refrain.

ellen-dǣdum, uncūþes fela,
Wælsinȝes ȝewin, wīde sīðas,
þāra þe ȝumena bearn ȝearwe ne wiston,
fǣhðe ond fyrena, būton Fitela mid hine,
880 þonne hē swulces hwæt secȝan wolde,
êam his nefan, swā hīe ā wǣron
æt nīða ȝehwām nȳd-ȝesteallan;
hæfdon eal-fela eotena cynnes
sweordum ȝesǣȝed. Siȝemunde ȝespronȝ
885 æfter dēað-dæȝe dōm unlȳtel,
syþðan wīȝes heard wyrm ācwealde,
hordes hyrde; hē under hārne stān,
æþelinȝes bearn, āna ȝenēðde
frēcne dǣde; ne wæs him Fitela mid;
890 hwæþre him ȝesǣlde, ðæt þæt swurd þurhwōd
wrǣtlīcne wyrm, þæt hit on wealle ætstōd,
dryhtlīc īren; draca morðre swealt.
Hæfde āȝlǣca elne ȝeȝonȝen,
þæt hē bēah-hordes brūcan mōste
895 selfes dōme; |sǣ-bāt ȝehlēod, Fol. 149b.
bær on bearm scipes beorhte frætwa
Wælses eafera; wyrm hāt ȝemealt.
Sē wæs wreccena wīde mǣrost
ofer wer-þēode, wīȝendra hlēo,
900 ellen-dǣdum, —hē þæs ǣr onðāh—

879. *fyrena* : MS. *fyrene* (a above).

Does *fyrena* relate to deeds of violence similar to those told of Sigemund in the *Volsunga Saga*, §§ 6–8?

Concerning Fitela, Sigemund's nephew, and companion in his outlawry, we learn much in the Old Norse sources. See *Index of Persons*.

881. The line is metrically deficient unless we take *ēam* as a disyllable. Cf. Germ. *Oheim* from a presumed Prim. Germ. **auhaimoz*.

895. *selfes dōme*, i.e., he was free to take as much as he liked; an old Germanic legal phrase, used when one party in a case is allowed to fix the amount due to him from the other. Cf. ll. 2147 (where see note), 2776.

gehlēod. Many editors normalise to *gehlōd*; *gehlēod* for *gehlōd* may be parallel to *wēox* for *wōx*; see Sievers$_3$ § 392, N. 5.

The loading of the boat with the plunder also follows the dragon fight of Frotho, in Saxo Grammaticus, Bk. II.

897. See *Index of Persons*: Wæls.

Earle adopts Scherer's emendation *hāt*[*e*], 'with heat.' [So Trautmann[174].] The alteration is unnecessary.

900. Cosijn's emendation *āron ðāh*, 'with honours throve,' is adopted by Holthausen, Trautmann, and Earle [cf. Sarrazin in *Engl. Stud.*, xxviii. 408]. For *āron* = *ārum* cf. *scypon*, l. 1154, and *hēafdon*, l. 1242, and, for the

siððan Heremōdes hild sweðrode,
*ea*foð ond ellen; hē mid eotenum wearð
on fēonda ȝeweald forð forlācen,
snūde forsended. Hine sorh-wylmas
905 lemede tō lanȝe; hē his lēodum wearð,
eallum æþellinȝum, tō aldor-ceare.
Swylce oft bemearn ǣrran mǣlum
swīð-ferhþes sīð snotor ceorl moniȝ,
sē þe him bealwa tō bōte ȝelȳfde,
910 þæt þæt ðēodnes bearn ȝeþēon scolde,
fæder-æþelum onfōn, folc ȝehealdan,
hord ond hlēo-burh, hæleþa rīce,
ēðel Scyldinȝa. Hē þǣr eallum wearð,
mǣȝ Hiȝelāces manna cynne,
915 frēondum ȝefæȝra; hine fyren onwōd.

phrase *āron ðāh*, cf. *weorð-myndum þāh*, l. 8. Nevertheless I cannot bring myself to abandon the clear reading of the MS., which makes at least as good sense as in many another passage.

901. It has been usual to begin a new paragraph with *siððan*: 'After Heremod's warring time had slackened off, he'......(Clark-Hall, Earle, *etc.*). The punctuation given above is strongly advocated by Klaeber[457]. So Gummere, who comments: 'Heremod, one is told, might have rivalled and surpassed Sigmund, but the former fell from grace, turned tyrant, and in fact was precisely what the aspiring hero should not be—quite the opposite, say, of this glorious Beowulf.' Sigemund is the greatest *wrecca* since Heremod.

In l. 902 *hē* must refer to Heremod [not to Sigemund, as Müllenhoff[119], Rieger[399] and others have taken it]. Heremod's story is continued; just as in the parallel passage, l. 1197, *etc.*, *syþðan Hāma ætwæg*, the story of Hama is continued in ll. 1200–1. In each case the poet drags in allusions rather forcibly. But that the connection between Heremod and Sigemund is not fortuitous, or the work of our poet, is shown by their being also mentioned together in the Old Norse. See *Index of Persons*: Heremod.

902. *eafoð*, Grimm [*Andreas u. Elene*, 101]: MS. *earfoð*, retained by Wülker; cf. l. 534. On the other hand see ll. 602, 2349.

eotenum. The word *eoten* has occurred several times in contexts where 'monster,' 'giant' was applicable. Here for the first time such meaning seems very doubtful, and we must assume either (1) that from 'giant' the generalized sense of 'enemy' has come into force [Rieger[399]: Holthausen] or (2) that the word here is a personal name distinct from the common noun, perhaps signifying 'Jutes.' [See Schücking for references.]

905. Note the false concord. Many edd. unnecessarily alter.

908, *etc.* The *sīð* (perhaps = 'going into exile') of Heremod is a disappointment to the wise, who had hoped that he would be a credit to his country.

909. 'Put their hope in him (Heremod) as a remedy against their evils' (*bealwa tō*). For other instances of *tō* following the noun it governs, see Glossary.

913, 915. *Hē*, l. 913, is Beowulf, 'the kinsman of Higelac': but *hine*, l. 915, is Heremod.

915. *gefægra*, 'more pleasing,' comparative of an otherwise unrecorded

Hwīlum flītende fealwe strǣte
mēarum mǣton. Ðā wæs morȝen-lēoht
scofen ond scynded. |Ēode scealc moniȝ Fol. 150a.
swīð-hicȝende tō sele þām hēan
920 searo-wundor sēon; swylce self cyninȝ
of brȳd-būre, bēah-horda weard,
tryddode tīr-fæst ȝetrume micle,
cystum ȝecȳþed, ond his cwēn mid him
medo-stiȝȝe mæt mæȝþa hōse.
XIV 925 Hrōðȝār maþelode; hē tō healle ȝēonȝ,
stōd on stapole, ȝeseah stēapne hrōf
ȝolde fāhne ond Ȝrendles hond:
"Ðisse ansȳne Al-wealdan þanc
lunȝre ȝelimpe. Fela ic lāþes ȝebād,
930 ȝrynna æt Ȝrendle; ā mæȝ Ȝod wyrcan

O.E. *gefæg* or *gefaga*, which can be postulated with some likelihood from the analogy of O.H.G. *gifag(o)*: M.H.G. *gevage*. [Cf. Sievers in *Z.f.d.Ph.* xxi. 356: Klaeber in *Anglia*, xxviii. 440.]

916. The story is resumed, with a repetition of incidents which, to the older critics, seemed the result of interpolation. Müllenhoff[120] compares ll. 916, *etc.* with 864, *etc.*; 917–8 with 837; 918 with 838; and 920 with 840.

'Fallow' seems more appropriate to horses than roads (cf. l. 865), and Cosijn[16] would accordingly emend to *fealwum*.

924. *medo-stigge*, see note to l. 1085.

926. *stapole*. The obvious meaning is 'column' (cf. l. 2718), and so Heyne took the word here: 'he stood beside the central (wooden) pillar of Heorot.' Heyne was thinking no doubt of the 'Branstock,' the central oak which plays its part in the story of the Volsung hall. Schücking and others still adhere to this interpretation, or to a parallel one which would make the *stapol* correspond to the 'high seat pillars' of Icelandic halls [Sarrazin, *Anglia*, xix. 370].

But (1) 'beside,' though possible (cf. l. 1117), is not the most obvious meaning of *on*, (2) we have no evidence for any great middle pillar or high seat pillars in Heorot, and, above all, (3) this would necessitate our supposing that Grendel's hand had been placed among the rafters, but it seems from l. 983 to have been outside the hall.

Miller [*Anglia*, xii. 398] therefore interpreted *stapol* as the steps leading up to the door or the landing at the top of them, his authorities being an O.E. gloss, and the Mid. Eng. use of the word: *þe steire of fiftene stoples*. In his annotated hand-copy of *Beowulf*, Miller further quotes instances from the O.E. translation of Bede of *stopol* = 'footstep,' 'step,' and notes the parallel of the *Odyssey* [iii. 404]: Nestor seated on the 'smooth stones' before his door. The same interpretation has been arrived at independently by Earle[139].

Rask's emendation *on staþole* = 'foundation,' 'base,' has been revived by Bugge[90] and Trautmann, but is unnecessary: and unsatisfactory too, for 'he stood on the floor or ground' seems but a feeble remark.

930. *grynna* has been variously interpreted as 'snares' (= O.E. *grin*) or 'sorrows' (= O.E. *gyrn*). The latter interpretation is probably correct, for

wunder æfter wundre, wuldres Hyrde.
Ðæt wæs unʒēara, þæt ic ǣniʒra mē
wēana ne wēnde tō wīdan feore
bōte ʒebīdan, þonne blōde fāh
935 hūsa sēlest heoro-drēoriʒ stōd;
wēa wīd-scofen witena ʒehwylc*um*,
ðāra þe ne wēndon, þæt hīe wīde-ferhð
lēoda land-ʒeweorc lāþum beweredon
|scuccum ond scinnum. Nū scealc hafað Fol. 150b.
940 þurh Drihtnes miht dǣd ʒefremede,
ðe wē ealle ǣr ne meahton
snyttrum besyrwan. Hwæt! þæt secʒan mæʒ
efne swā hwylc mæʒþa, swā ðone maʒan cende
æfter ʒum-cynnum, ʒyf hēo ʒȳt lyfað,
945 þæt hyre eald Metod ēste wǣre
bearn-ʒebyrdo. Nū ic, Bēowulf, þec,
secʒ[*a*] betsta, mē for sunu wylle
frēoʒan on ferhþe; heald forð tela
nīwe sibbe. Ne bið þē [*n*]ǣniʒr*a* ʒād
950 worolde wilna, þe ic ʒeweald hæbbe.
Ful oft ic for lǣssan lēan teohhode,
hord-weorþunʒe, hnāhran rince,

grin, 'snare,' is concrete, meaning 'halter' or 'net': the abstract sense, 'capturing,' given to it here by Earle, can hardly be demonstrated.

936. *gehwylcum.* This very slight change [Kemble$_3$] from MS. *gehwylcne*, though necessary, has been overlooked by most commentators. Klaeber [*Engl. Stud.* xlii. 326] argues strongly in its favour: 'a far-reaching woe unto every councillor' is supported by the comparison of l. 170, *etc.* Schücking in his last edition [1913] also adopts *gehwylcum*; so Holthausen$_3$.

If we retain the MS. reading we must interpret it to mean that the court had been scattered by Grendel's attacks, which is clearly not the case (cf. l. 171, and *passim*). And apart from this the passage presents serious difficulties.

Unless *wēa wīd-scofen* is construed as a nominative absolute, 'fear having driven far and wide' [Grein, Schücking, 1910], *hæfde* must be understood [Bugge[90]] or supplied [Trautmann and Holthausen$_2$—text], 'woe (had) scattered each councillor.' Trautmann and Holthausen$_2$ further adopt the emendation [of Grein$_2$], *wiðscofen*, which they interpret 'driven away.'

Holthausen$_2$, in a note, suggested *wēan wīde scufon*, 'woes scattered each of the councillors': so Sedgefield$_2$: already in 1820 Grundtvig[281] came very near this: *wēan wīdscufon.* Similarly Sedgefield$_1$, *wēa wīde scēaf.*

942, *etc.* Perhaps a biblical reminiscence.

947. *secg*[*a*]. The alteration is necessary here, and in l. 1759, for metrical reasons. [Cf. Sievers in *P.B.B.* x. 312.]

949. [*n*]*ǣnigra*, Grein$_1$: MS. *ænigre.* Grein afterwards abandoned this emendation; Grein$_2$ *nǣnigre.* [Cf. Bugge in *Z.f.d.Ph.* iv. 203.]

sǣmran æt sæcce. Þū þē self hafast
[*mid*] dǣdum ʒefremed, þæt þīn [*dōm*] lyfað
955 āwa tō aldre. Al-walda þec
ʒōde forʒylde, swā hē nū ʒȳt dyde!"
Bēowulf maþelode, bearn Ecþēowes:
"Wē þæt ellen-weorc ēstum miclum,
feohtan fremedon, frēcne ʒenēðdon
960 eafoð uncūþes; ūþe ic swīþor,
þæt ðū hine selfne ʒesēon mōste,
fēond on frætewum fyl-wēriʒne.
Ic hi*ne* hrædlīce |heardan clammum Fol. 151ᵃ.
on wæl-bedde wrīþan þōhte,
965 þæt hē for *mu*nd-ʒripe mīnum scolde
licʒean līf-bysiʒ, būtan his līc swice;
ic hine ne mihte, þā Metod nolde,
ʒanʒes ʒetwǣman; nō ic him þæs ʒeorne ætfealh.
feorh-ʒenīðlan; wæs tō fore-mihtiʒ
970 fēond on fēþe. Hwæþere hē his folme forlēt
tō līf-wraþe lāst weardian,
earm ond eaxle; nō þǣr ǣniʒe swā þēah
fēa-sceaft ʒuma frōfre ʒebohte;
nō þȳ lenʒ leofað lāð-ʒetēona
975 synnum ʒeswenced; ac hyne sār hafað
in *nȳ*d-ʒripe nearwe befonʒen,
balwon bendum; ðǣr ābīdan sceal
maʒa māne fāh miclan dōmes,
hū him scīr Metod scrīfan wille."
980 Ðā wæs swīʒra secʒ sunu Eclāfes
on ʒylp-sprǣce ʒūð-ʒeweorca,
siþðan æþelinʒas eorles cræfte

954. No gap in MS. The metre demands [*mid*] before *dǣdum*, and this is supplied by Holthausen$_2$: so Sedgefield$_1$. Holthausen$_3$, *dǣdum gefremed*[*ne*]. [*dōm*] is supplied by Kemble$_2$.

962. *frætewum*. Grendel bore no armour; but the familiar formula, 'the foe in his trappings,' is used, probably not with any such grimly ironical reference as Trautmann[175] sees, to some fetters with which Beowulf hoped to deck him.

963. *hine*, Thorpe: MS. *him*.

965. *mund-gripe*, Kemble$_1$: MS. *hand gripe*. The emendation is demanded by the alliteration.

976. *nȳd-gripe*, Bugge [*Tidsskr*. viii. 49]: MS. *mid gripe*; Thorpe, *nið-gripe*, followed by Sedgefield; Schücking, *mid nȳd-gripe*.

ofer hēanne hrōf hand scēawedon,
fēondes finᵹras —foran ǣᵹhwylc wæs,
985 steda næᵹla ᵹehwylc stȳle ᵹelīcost—
hǣþenes hand-sporu, |hilde-rinces Fol. 151b.
eᵹl unhēoru; ǣᵹhwylc ᵹecwæð,
þæt him heardra nān hrīnan wolde
īren ǣr-ᵹōd, þæt ðæs āhlǣcan
990 blōdᵹe beadu-folme onberan wolde.
XV ÐĀ wæs hāten hreþe, Heort innan-weard
folmum ᵹefrætwod; fela þǣra wæs,
wera ond wīfa, þe þæt wīn-reced,
ᵹest-sele, ᵹyredon. ᵹold-fāᵹ scinon
995 web æfter wāᵹum, wundor-sīona fela
secᵹa ᵹehwylcum, þāra þe on swylc starað.
Wæs þæt beorhte bold tōbrocen swīðe,

983. 'Looked up over' or 'in the direction of the high roof, and saw....' [Cf. Klaeber[256].] See l. 836, *note*.

985. This line was first correctly divided from the preceding line by Sievers [*P.B.B.* ix. 138], who further proposed the emendation:

stīðra nægla stȳle gelīcost.

The details of Sievers' reading had been anticipated by earlier editors [Ettmüller$_3$, Thorpe]. His reconstruction is satisfactory, and is now generally adopted [e.g. by Holthausen, Trautmann, and with modification, *stīð-nægla gehwylc*, 'each of his sharp nails,' by Sedgefield]. But as the reading of the MS. seems possible, it is here retained in the text [as also by Schücking].

986. *hilde-rinces*: MS. *hilde hilde rinces*, the first *hilde* being the last word on the page, the second the first word overleaf. In such cases it seems needless to call attention to the alteration by italics in the text.

spora is elsewhere a weak masc.; Rieger[390] would read *speru*, 'spears'; so Holthausen, spelling *hand-speoru* (u-umlaut).

987. *egl* (more usually *egle*) is well authenticated in the sense of 'awn,' 'beard of barley': but nowhere else do we find it in the derived sense of 'talon,' 'claw.' Accordingly many take the word here as the adj. *egle*, 'hateful,' 'grievous' (Goth. *agls*, 'shameful,' *aglus*, 'difficult'), agreeing with *speru* or *sporu*, and either suppose the *u* of *eglu* to be elided, or else restore it: *egl'*, *unheoru*, Rieger[391], Schücking, Holthausen: *eglu*, Trautmann. For both words cf. *ail* in *New English Dictionary*.

988. *him* must refer to Grendel, whom everyone said no sword might injure—unless [with Sievers, *P.B.B.* ix. 139, Holthausen, and Sedgefield] we read *þe* for *þæt* (MS. ꝥ) in l. 989. In that case it refers to Beowulf, who, having torn off Grendel's claw, might be expected to be proof against anything.

Sievers and Holthausen further alter *onberan wolde* (l. 990) to *āberan mihte*.

991. Many emendations have been made to avoid the awkward construction *hāten hreþe*; Bugge [*Tidsskr.* viii. 50, following Grundtvig[282]], *hēatimbred*, referring to *Heort*; Trautmann, *handum hreþe*; Sedgefield, *hāton hreþre*, 'with fervid zeal' or *hāt on hreþre*, 'zeal in hearts'; [cf. also Trautmann[178], Kluge[189]]. Holthausen$_{1,2}$ assumed a gap in the MS.

eal inne-weard īren-bendum fæst,
heorras tōhlidene; hrōf āna ȝenæs
1000 ealles ansund, þē se āȝlǣca
fyren-dǣdum fāȝ on flēam ȝewand,
aldres orwēna. Nō þæt ȳðe byð
tō beflēonne, fremme sē þe wille;
ac ȝesēcan sceal sāwl-berendra,
1005 nȳde ȝenȳdde, niþða bearna,
ȝrund-būendra, ȝearwe stōwe,
þǣr his līc-homa leȝer-bedde fæst
swefeþ æfter symle. Þā wæs sǣl ond mǣl,
þæt tō healle ȝanȝ Healfdenes sunu; Fol. 152a.
1010 wolde self cyninȝ symbel þicȝan.
Ne ȝefræȝen ic þā mǣȝþe māran weorode
ymb hyra sinc-ȝyfan sēl ȝebǣran.
Buȝon þā tō bence blǣd-āȝande,
fylle ȝefǣȝon, fǣȝere ȝeþǣȝon
1015 medo-ful maniȝ; māȝas *wāra[n]*
swīð-hicȝende on sele þām hēan,

1000. MS. *þe*: emended by Ettmüller$_2$ and almost all editors to *þā*. It does not seem clear that this is necessary: for *þē* without antecedent can mean 'where,' 'when,' cf. l. 2468. [Cf. Schücking, *Satzverknüpfung*, 1904, pp. 7, 57–8.]

1004. *gesēc(e)an*, Kemble$_2$: MS. *gesacan*. If we keep the MS. reading we must render either 'gain by strife...' (cf. *geslēan*), or, with Schücking and Bosworth-Toller, 'strive against the inevitable prepared place of the children of men.' Neither of these meanings gives very satisfactory sense: *gesacan* seems otherwise unrecorded, and is unmetrical [Sievers in *P.B.B.* x. 291].

Kemble's *gesēcean* has accordingly been generally accepted. 'Though a man would flee it, he must seek the grave' is one of those truisms which lend themselves to the hypothesis of a didactic interpolator. [Cf. Mullenhoff[121].]

sāwl-berendra, *bearna* and *grund-būendra* are all parallel [Klaeber[241]] and depend upon *gearwe stōwe* [Bugge[368]].

For another interpretation see Sedgefield.

Trautmann, in part following Ettmüller$_2$, reads, *ǣghwylc sēcan sceal sāwl-berendra nīðe genȳded...*, 'each of living souls compelled by distress must seek....'

1008. *swefeð æfter symle.* Cf. l. 119. Cook [*M.L.N.* ix. 474] quotes many parallels for the metaphor of 'life's feast.'

1009. *gang.* This form, which occurs here, in l. 1295 and in l. 1316, for the normal *gēong*, *giong* may perhaps be a dialectal peculiarity of a former copyist of this section of the poem. [Cf. Brandl[991].]

1013. Thorkelin's transcripts, A '*blæd agande*,' B '*blædagande*.' The MS. now has only *blæd* left, and *de* on the next line.

1015. *wāran.* Ten Brink[73] and Klaeber [*Anglia*, xxviii. 442] suggested *wǣron*: MS. *þara*. All recent editors have adopted this emendation, except Trautmann[180], who reads *māgas þwǣre*, 'the gentle kinsmen.' Earlier

Hrōðȝār ond Hrōþulf. Heorot innan wæs
frēondum āfylled; nalles fācen-stafas
Þēod-Scyldinȝas þenden fremedon.
1020 Forȝeaf þā Bēowulfe *bearn* Healfdenes
seȝen ȝyldenne siȝores tō lēane,
hroden hilte-cumbor, helm ond byrnan;
mǣre māðþum-sweord maniȝe ȝesāwon
beforan beorn beran. Bēowulf ȝeþah
1025 ful on flette. Nō hē þǣre feoh-ȝyfte
for sc[*ē*]oten[*d*]um scamiȝan ðorfte;
ne ȝefræȝn ic frēondlīcor fēower mādmas
ȝolde ȝeȝyrede ȝum-manna fela
in ealo-bence ōðrum ȝesellan.

editors retained the MS. reading, and attempted to remedy the obscurity by devices of punctuation. Wyatt in 1894 read:

> Bugon þā tō bence blǣd-āgende,
> fylle gefǣgon; fǣgere geþǣgon
> medo-ful manig māgas þāra...

and commented "What is to hinder the antecedent of *þāra* being implied in *blǣd-āgende*, in speaking of a court where everyone was doubtless related to everyone else, as in a Scotch clan?" With this interpretation the *blǣd-āgende*, who take their places on the mead-bench, are the Danish nobility generally: their kinsmen, who empty many a cup, are Hrothgar and Hrothulf. But it may be objected (1) that the task of emptying the cups would not be confined to Hrothgar and Hrothulf; (2) that the point of the allusion is not that Hrothgar and Hrothulf are akin to the Danish nobility (*blǣd-agande*), but that they are akin to *each other*, and are, *as yet*, true to the ties which kinship imposes (cf. ll. 1164–5).

The alteration is a very slight one, 'paꞃā' (i.e. *wāran*) might easily be misread 'þaꞃa' (i.e. *þāra*), and the gain in sense is very great. The poet has been speaking of rejoicing: then, with the tragic irony which he loves, he continues, beginning a new period, 'The kinsmen too were in the hall—*not yet* was wrong being plotted.' See *Index of Persons*: Hrothulf.

1020. *bearn*, Grundtvig[282]: MS. *brand.*

1022. *hilte-cumbor*. Ettmüller$_2$ *hilde-*, followed by Rieger[391], Holthausen, Trautmann and Schücking (1913): *hilte-cumbor* perhaps gives satisfactory sense, 'banner with a handle' [cf. Cosijn[18]], but it is very difficult to account for *hilte* instead of *hilt*. [Cf. Sievers in *P.B.B.* xxxvi. 420.]

Cosijn[18] justifies the punctuation, as given above. There is something of a pause before *mǣre māðþum-sweord*, the final gift, is mentioned. We might almost render '*and finally* a glorious sword.'

1026. *scēotendum*, Kemble$_3$: MS. *scotenum.* Kemble's emendation has been generally followed, especially by recent editors. Grein$_2$, *scoterum.* Heyne$_{1-3}$ retained the MS. reading, and, when he abandoned it, Kluge [*P.B.B.* viii. 533] took up the defence, deriving from *scota*, 'shooter,' and quoting *oxenum, nefenum*, as examples of similar weak dat. pls. But the alteration is necessary on metrical grounds [cf. Sievers in *P.B.B.* x. 312]: and see, too, ll. 703, 1154.

1028. *fela.* Kölbing would read *frēan*, on the ground that such costly gifts are naturally not given by 'many men,' but by 'kings of men' (*Engl. Stud.* xxii. 325).

1030 Ymb þæs helmes hrōf hēafod-beorʒe
wīrum bewunden wal*a* ūtan hēold,
þæt him fēla |lāf frēcne ne meahton — Fol. 152^b.
scūr-heard sceþðan, þonne scyld-freca
onʒēan ʒramum ʒanʒan scolde.
1035 Heht ðā eorla hlēo eahta mēaras
fǣted-hlēore on flet têon,
in under eoderas; þāra ānum stōd
sadol searwum fāh, since ʒewurþad;
þæt wæs hilde-setl hēah-cyninʒes,
1040 ðonne sweorda ʒelāc sunu Healfdenes
efnan wolde; nǣfre on ōre læʒ
wīd-cūþes wīʒ, ðonne walu fēollon.
Ond ðā Bēowulfe bēʒa ʒehwæþres
eodor Inʒwina onweald ʒetēah,
1045 wicʒa ond wǣpna; hēt hine wel brūcan.
Swā manlīce mǣre þēoden,

1030–1. *wala*, emendation of Ettmüller$_2$ adopted by Grein: MS. *heafod beorge wirum be wunden walan uian heold*. If we leave the MS. reading unaltered there is a choice of difficulties. Either we must take *walan* as subject and *hēafod-beorge* as object, with a striking violation of grammatical concord in the verb *hēold*; or we must (with Heyne and Socin) take *hēafod-beorge* as a weak fem. noun in the nom. and *walan* as object, with considerable loss to the sense. The nom. pl. *scūr-beorge* (*Ruin*, 5) also tells against the latter view, which has no support from analogy. The emendation has accordingly of late been generally adopted. Sievers, Bugge^{369}, Trautmann and Sedgefield prefer the more archaic form *walu* (Goth, *walus*, 'staff'). The change is slight, as in many scripts *u* and *a* can hardly be distinguished.

1032. *fēla*. Holthausen$_{1,2}$ and Sedgefield [following Rieger, *Lesebuch*] normalize to *fēola*: unnecessarily. See Bülbring, 199 *b*.

lāf...meahton. So the MS. Since *lāf* is collective, it may quite conceivably be the subject of a plural verb *meahton*. But almost all editors feel bound to correct what they regard as a false concord. Earlier editors chose to emend *lāf* to *lāfe*, because *lāf* is not now in the MS.: our authorities for it being merely Thorkelin's two transcripts. But, from the position of the word, it must have been perfectly clear, when these transcripts were made, whether the reading was *lāf* or *lāfe*. Therefore to write *lāfe* to agree with *meahton* is practically as violent a departure from MS. authority as to write *meahte* to agree with *lāf*: and since the former change lands us in metrical difficulties [cf. Sievers in *P.B.B.* x. 273–4], it is best, if we make any alteration, to write *lāf...meahte* [following Thorpe].

1033. *scūr-heard*. Cf. *Judith*, 79: *scūrum heardne*. Various interpretations are offered: 'tempered in water' (cf. 'the ice-brook's temper,' *Othello*, v. ii. 253); 'hard or sharp in the storm of battle,' 'cutting like a storm.' [Cf. *M.L.N.* vii. 193; viii. 61; xix. 234.] But I doubt if *scūr* does more than intensify: 'mighty hard.' Cf. Minot, x. 43: *Full swith redy seruis fand þai þare a schowre*, i.e. 'a great quantity, abundance.'

1037. *under eoderas*. The same expression is used in the *Heliand* (of the court of the High Priest, into which the 'earls' led Christ: *thar lêddun ina...erlos undar ederos*, 4943).

hord-weard hæleþa, heaþo-rǣsas ʒeald
mēarum ond mādmum, swā hȳ nǣfre man lyhð,
sē þe secʒan wile sōð æfter rihte.

XVI 1050 ÐĀ ʒȳt ǣʒhwylcum eorla drihten,
þāra þe mid Bēowulfe brim-lāde tēah,
on þǣre medu-bence māþðum ʒesealde,
yr|fe-lāfe; ond þone ǣnne heht Fol. 153ᵃ.
ʒolde forʒyldan, þone ðe ʒrendel ǣr
1055 māne ācwealde, swā hē hyra mā wolde,
nefne him wītiʒ ʒod wyrd forstōde,
ond ðæs mannes mōd. Metod eallum wēold
ʒumena cynnes, swā hē nū ʒīt dêð;
forþan bið andʒit ǣʒhwǣr sēlest,
1060 ferhðes fore-þanc. Fela sceal ʒebīdan
lēofes ond lāþes, sē þe lonʒe hēr
on ðyssum win-daʒum worolde brūceð.
Þǣr wæs sanʒ ond swēʒ samod ætʒædere
fore Healfdenes hilde-wīsan,
1065 ʒomen-wudu ʒrēted, ʒid oft wrecen,
ðonne heal-ʒamen Hrōþʒāres scop
æfter medo-bence mǣnan scolde:
"Finnes eaferum, ðā hīe se fǣr beʒeat,

1048. *lyhð*. Metre demands two syllables: either *ne lyhð* or the older form *lehið*.

1051. *-lāde*, Kemble₁: MS. *leade*.

1056. Ettmüller takes *wyrd* as in apposition with *God*: so Sedgefield₁, who objects to the usual construction of *wyrd* as object of *forstōde* (see Glossary), because *wyrd* cannot be hindered or averted. But this seems open to dispute, both grammatically (since if, with Sedgefield, we render *forstōde* 'help, defend,' we should expect *hie* not *him*) and theologically (since God is *wyrda waldend*, *Exodus*, 432; *Andreas*, 1056; *Elene*, 80).

1064. *fore*, 'in the presence of': cf. l. 1215, and *Widsith*, 55, 140, where the phrase is used, as here also, in connection with a minstrel's song. 'Healfdene's war-leader,' in whose presence the song is sung, should then be Hrothgar. Or possibly we may take *hildewīsan* as dat. *pl.*, referring to the old captains who had fought under Healfdene. The phrase would then be equivalent to *for duguþe*, 'before the veterans' (l. 2020). Trautmann suggests *Healfdena*. [Cf. also Klaeber in *Anglia*, xxviii. 449, note; Trautmann[183]; Cosijn[18–19].]

To interpret *fore* as 'concerning' [Grein, *Jahrbuch f. rom. u. engl. Literatur*, 1862, p. 269, note; Earle] is exceedingly forced, if not impossible: the *hildewīsa* would then be Hnæf. Grein cites as a parallel *Panther*, 34, *þe ic ǣr fore sægde*, which he takes as 'concerning which I spoke before.' But this is extremely doubtful. [Cf. too Lübke in *A.f.d.A.* xix. 342.]

1068. Recent editors make the lay begin with l. 1069: Schücking [*Engl. Stud.* xxxix. 106] even with l. 1071. In both cases we must adopt

hæleð Healf-Dena, Hnæf Scyldinȝa,
1070 in Frēs-wæle feallan scolde.
Nē hūru Hildeburh herian þorfte
Eotena trēowe; unsynnum wearð
beloren lēofum æt þām *lin*d-pleȝan,
bearnum ond brōðrum; hīe on ȝebyrd hruron
1075 ȝāre |wunde; þæt wæs ȝeōmuru ides. **Fol. 153b.**
Nalles hōlinȝa Hōces dohtor
meotod-sceaft bemearn, syþðan morȝen cōm,
ðā hēo under sweȝle ȝesēon meahte
morþor-bealo māȝa. þǣr hē ǣr mǣste hēold
1080 worolde wynne, wīȝ ealle fornam
Finnes þeȝnas, nemne fēaum ānum,
þæt hē ne mehte on þǣm meðel-stede
wīȝ Henȝeste wiht ȝefeohtan,
ne þā wēa-lāfe wīȝe forþrinȝan

the emendation of Trautmann[183] *eaferan* for *eaferum*: rendering 'made mention of the children of Finn, when the sudden attack fell upon them, a tale which was a hall-joy adown the mead-bench.'...It is less satisfactory from the point of view of style to make the lay begin, as in the text, with l. 1068; but it enables us to keep *eaferum*, which we must take as instrumental: 'At the hands of the children of Finn...the hero of the Healfdene, Hnæf, was doomed to fall.' [See Klaeber in *Anglia*, xxviii. 443.]

The emendation *Healfdenes* [Grundtvig[283], Kemble$_2$], usual in editions up to and including Wülker, is unnecessary and misleading, since *Healfdene* is presumably a tribal name. [See Bugge[29] and *Index of Persons*.]

1070. MS. *infr es wæle*: '*r* altered from some other letter' [perhaps], 'after it a letter erased, then *es* on an erasure: that *fres* is all that the scribe intended to write, is shown by a line connecting *r* and *e*.' [Zupitza.]

1072. *Eotena*. Most of the problems of the Finnsburh story depend upon one another, and therefore must be considered together. See *Index of Persons*, and *Introduction to Beowulf*. Only the more isolated problems are dealt with in the notes which follow.

1073. *lind-*, Kemble$_1$ for the alliteration: MS. *hild*.

1074. Apparently Hildeburh lost only one brother. It seems unnecessary to see, with Möller, a survival in *brōðrum* of an ancient dual construction, parallel to *wit Scilling*, 'Scilling and I' [*V.E.* 59]. Cf. note to l. 565.

1079. All editors follow Ettmüller$_2$ in altering *hē* to *hēo*, making *þǣr hē*[*o*] *ǣr mǣste hēold worolde wynne* refer to Hildeburh. This is not necessary. Finn lost his thanes where he had had the greatest joy in the world, i.e. in and around his mead hall.

1081. *fēaum*. The original form must have been *fēam*; the *u* has been inserted on the analogy of other datives.

1083. *gefeohtan*. Klaeber [*Anglia*, xxviii. 443], followed by Holthausen$_2$, suggests *gebēodan*, 'offer fight' (cf. l. 603), on the ground that *wiht gefeohtan*, with a dat. of the hostile person, is not a permissible construction. Rieger (*Lesebuch*), Holthausen$_{1,3}$, *wiþ gefeohtan*. See also *Introduction to Beowulf: Finnsburh*.

1085 þēodnes ðeȝne; ac hiȝ him ȝeþinȝo budon,
þæt hīe him ōðer flet eal ȝerȳmdon,
healle ond hēah-setl, þæt hīe healfre ȝeweald
wið Eotena bearn āȝan mōston,
ond æt feoh-ȝyftum Folcwaldan sunu
1090 dōȝra ȝehwylce Dene weorþode,
Henȝestes hēap hrinȝum wenede,
efne swā swīðe sinc-ȝestrēonum
fǣttan ȝoldes, swā hē Frēsena cyn
on bēor-sele byldan wolde.
1095 Ðā hīe ȝetrūwedon on twā healfa
fæste frioðu-wǣre; Fin Henȝeste
elne unflitme āðum |benemde, Fol. 154a.
þæt hē þā wēa-lāfe weotena dōme
ārum hēolde, þæt ðǣr ǣniȝ mon
1100 wordum ne worcum wǣre ne brǣce,
ne þurh inwit-searo ǣfre ȝemǣnden,

1085. *hig*, the Frisians: *him*, Hengest's men.

The *g* of *hig* simply marks that the *i* is long, precisely as in M.E. and other scripts *ij*=ī. Other examples are *hig*, ll. 1596, 1770; *wigge*=*wīge*, 1656, 1770, 1783; *sig*=*sī*, 1778; *medostigge*=*medostīge*, 924; *wigtig* =*wītig*, 1841 (wrongly 'corrected' by many editors into *wittig*); *ligge*=*līge*, 727; *Scedenigge*=*Scedenīge*, 1686. See Sievers, § 24, N., and for pronunciation of *g*, § 211, *etc.*; [also Cosijn in *P.B.B.* viii. 571].

1087. *healfre.* Unless, with Ettmüller, and Thorpe (followed by Trautmann, Holthausen, Sedgefield), we read *healfne*, we must take this as a gen. dependent upon *geweald*, 'control of half the hall.'

1097. With *elne unflitme*, *Guthlac*, 923, *elne unslāwe*, has been compared: *unflitme* or *unhlitme* (l. 1129) is obviously an adv., but its form, meaning, and derivation are doubtful. It may mean 'indisputably,' from *flītan*, 'dispute,' or 'immovably,' from *flēotan*, 'float'; or, if *unhlitme* be the correct form, it may mean 'by evil lot' and be connected with *hlytm* (l. 3126). It is, of course, conceivable that both forms, *unhlitme* here and *unflitme* below, are correct, and represent different words. [Cf. Bugge[30], Trautmann[185], von Grienberger in *Z.f.ö.G.* 1905, 748–9.]

1101. *gemǣnden.* This may mean 'nor should they ever break the treaty,' and be parallel in meaning to *wǣre ne brǣce.* No such verb *gemǣnan* 'to violate an oath' is recorded, but the phrase *mǣne āþ* 'a perjured oath' (cf. *mān*, wickedness, and 'mansworn' in the *Heart of Midlothian*) is very common. (So Grein, Bosworth-Toller, *etc.*)

More probably, however, this is either the verb *mǣnan* 'to mention' or *mǣnan* 'to bemoan,' and we may render (1) 'they (i.e. people in general, and particularly the Frisians) should not mention it although the Danes were following the slayer of their lord,' i.e. the Danes are not to be taunted [Heinzel in *A.f.d.A.* xv. 192], or (2) 'they (the Danes) should not bemoan, although....' If we adopt (2) we must (since it is Finn's oath we are considering) render *þæt* 'upon condition that,' and *þonne* 'then on the other hand.' [Cf. Klaeber in *Anglia*, xxviii. 444.]

ðēah hīe hira bēaȝ-ȝyfan banan folȝedon
ðēoden-lēase, þā him swā ȝeþearfod wæs;
ȝyf þonne Frȳsna hwylc frēcnan sprǣce
1105 ðæs morþor-hetes myndȝiend wǣre,
þonne hit sweordes ecȝ syððan scolde.
Að wæs ȝeæfned, ond icȝe ȝold
āhæfen of horde. Here-Scyldinȝa
betst beado-rinca wæs on bǣl ȝearu;
1110 æt þǣm āde wæs ēþ-ȝesȳne
swāt-fāh syrce, swȳn eal-ȝylden,
eofer īren-heard, æþelinȝ maniȝ
wundum āwyrded; sume on wæle crunȝon.
Hēt ðā Hildeburh æt Hnæfes āde
1115 hire selfre sunu sweoloðe befæstan,
bān-fatu bærnan ond on bǣl dôn;
earme on eaxle ides ȝnornode,

1102. *bana* must mean 'slayer,' not merely 'foe,' as Heinzel takes it [*A.f.d.A.* xv. 192]. It does not follow that Finn slew Hnæf with his own hand. The achievements of the retainers are attributed to the chief, as Tacitus tells us.

1104. *frēcnan*, Thorpe: MS. *frecnen*.

1106. Unless we are to understand some word like 'decide'—a rather violent proceeding—something must, as Sievers supposes, be missing here; or perhaps the necessary infinitive to *scolde* is concealed in the word *syððan*. Holthausen suggests *snyððan*, 'restrain,' or *swȳðan*, 'confirm': Trautmann, and, independently, Sedgefield, *sehtan*, 'settle': Klaeber [*J.E.G.Ph.* viii. 255] *sēman*, 'reconcile,' or *sēðan*, 'declare the truth,' 'prove,' 'settle.'

1107. *Āð*. The emendation *ād*, 'the pyre' [Grundtvig[283]], has had its supporters in recent times. As Klaeber points out [*J.E.G.Ph.* viii. 256], it is more natural that the gold should be fetched from the hoard in order to deck the funeral pile of Hnæf than for any other purpose.

icge. The meaning 'costly' or 'massive' which has been suggested for this word is, of course, pure guess-work. It has been proposed to emend *i*[*n*]*cge-gold*, on the analogy of *incge-lāfe*, l. 2577, where see note [Singer in *P.B.B.* xii. 213; so already Rieger, *Lesebuch*]; or *ītge*, 'bright,' not found in O.E., but cf. Icel. *ītr*, 'glorious' [Holthausen$_2$; but cf. also *Anglia, Beiblatt*, xiii. 364]; or *ǣce* (a word found once on a runic inscription and supposed to mean 'one's own,' hence, 'domestic wealth') [Klaeber in *J.E.G.Ph.* viii. 256]; or to write *ondicge* as one word = 'exciting envy' [von Grienberger in *Anglia*, xxvii. 331: but cf. Sievers in *P.B.B.* xxxvi. 421]; or *ondiege* 'openly,' not elsewhere recorded, but cf. *andǣges*, l. 1935, and Goth. *andáugjō*, 'openly' [Bugge[30], Sedgefield$_1$]. Holthausen$_3$ takes *icge* = *īdge* 'eager.'

1114–7. The emendations here, mostly quite uncertain, are too numerous to record. Holthausen's *ēame on eaxle* is very probable: Hildeburh commanded her sons to be placed on the pyre 'by their uncle's (Hnæf's) side.' The tragedy of *Finnsburh* lies in the slaughter among kinsfolk. The relation of uncle to sister's son was the most sacred of Germanic ties (see below, l. 1186, note), and that the poet should emphasize this is natural. *sunu* is probably an Anglian pl. which the W.S. transcriber has omitted to alter. [Cf. Cosijn in *P.B.B.* viii. 569.]

ȝeōmrode ȝiddum. ȝūð-rinc āstāh.
Wand |tō wolcnum wæl-fȳra mǣst, Fol. 154b.
1120 hlynode for hlāwe; hafelan multon,
ben-ȝeato burston, ðonne blōd ætspranc
lāð-bite līces. Līȝ ealle forswealȝ,
ȝǣsta ȝīfrost, þāra ðe þǣr ȝūð fornam
bēȝa folces; wæs hira blǣd scacen.
XVII 1125 GEwiton him ðā wīȝend wīca nēosian
frēondum befeallen, Frȳsland ȝesēon,
hāmas ond hēa-burh. Henȝest ðā ȝȳt
wæl-fāȝne winter wunode mid Finne
[*e*]l[*ne*] unhlitme; eard ȝemunde,
1130 þēah þe hē [*ne*] meahte on mere drīfan
hrinȝed-stefnan; holm storme wēol,
won wið winde; winter ȳþe belēac
īs-ȝebinde, oþ ðæt ōþer cōm
ȝēar in ȝeardas, swā nū ȝȳt dêð,
1135 þā ðe synȝāles sēle bewitiað,
wuldor-torhtan weder. Ðā wæs winter scacen,
fǣȝer foldan bearm; fundode wrecca,

1118. Grundtvig[284] and Rieger[395] emend to *gūð-rēc.* Skeat supports this reading by l. 3144, and *Elene* 795, *rēc āstigan*, and compares *gūð-rēc* with the compound *wæl-fȳr* in the next line. But there is no necessity for any change. *āstāh*='ascended' (i.e. 'was placed on') the pyre. The same expression is found in O.N. (*áðr á bál stigi*, of Balder's funeral). [Cf. Bugge in *Tidsskr.* viii. 51.]

1120. *for hlāwe*, 'in front of the mound.' It has been objected that this would not yet have been raised, and emendations have been suggested. [Cf. Klaeber in *Engl. Stud.* xxxix. 463.] But no change is necessary. Bodies were frequently burnt at the burial place, beside mounds which had been previously raised. See *Introduction to Beowulf: Archaeology: Burials.*

1125. Finn's army breaks up and his warriors return home [cf. Klaeber in *J.E.G.Ph.* vi. 193].

nēosian. Metre favours *nēosan*, which is the more usual form in *Beowulf*: cf. l. 115 (note), ll. 125, 1786, 1791, *etc.* [and Sievers, *P.B.B.* x. 233].

1128–9. The reading in the text is that of Kemble$_{2,3}$. MS. *mid finnel unhlitme*; Heyne, *mid Finne* [*ealles*] *unhlitme* (='unitedly'); [cf. Rieger[397] and Trautmann[187]].

1130. [*ne*] added by Grundtvig[284]. Grein read *ne* in place of *hē*. Cf. l. 648.

1134–6. Cosijn[20] emends *dēð* to *dōað*, followed by Schücking, who with Boer [*Z.f.d.A.* xlvii. 138] interprets 'as men do at the present day,' alluding to Hengest's waiting for the return of spring. Much the same meaning is produced by Sedgefield's emendation, *þām* for *þā*: 'until a second year came to dwellings (i.e. to men) as it (the year) still does come to those who are continually watching the seasons.' But see *Glossary: weotian.* That *sele* means 'time' 'season' is pointed out by Cosijn[19].

ȝist of ȝeardum; hē tō ȝyrn-wræce
swīðor |þōhte, þonne tō sǣ-lāde, Fol. 155a.
1140 ȝif hē torn-ȝemōt þurhtēon mihte,
þæt hē Eotena bearn inne ȝemunde.
Swā hē ne forwyrnde worold-rǣdenne,
þonne him Hūnlāfinȝ hilde-lēoman,
billa sēlest, on bearm dyde;
1145 þæs wǣron mid Eotenum ecȝe cūðe.
Swylce ferhð-frecan Fin eft beȝeat
sweord-bealo slīðen æt his selfes hām,
siþðan ȝrimne ȝripe ȝūðlāf ond Ōslāf
æfter sǣ-sīðe sorȝe mǣndon,
1150 ætwiton wēana dǣl; ne meahte wǣfre mōd
forhabban in hreþre. Ðā wæs heal ⟨h⟩roden
fēonda fēorum, swilce Fin slæȝen,
cyninȝ on corþre, ond sēo cwēn numen.

1141. Apparently *þæt inne* must be taken together (= *þe*...*inne*), 'in which he would show his remembrance of the children of the Eotenas' (cf. Kock, *Eng. Rel. Pron.*, § 102). Sievers [*P.B.B.* xii. 193] would read *þǣr*...*inne* 'where, he knew, the heroes were.' Cf. Holthausen's note.

1142. *worold-rǣdenne.* How does Hengest 'not refuse the way of the world'? The current explanation has been that it means 'he died' [e.g. Grein: cf. Heinzel in *A.f.d.A.* x. 226].

Clark-Hall [*M.L.N.* xxv. 113] suggests 'he did not run counter to the way of the world,' i.e. he fell into temptation, and broke his oath to Finn. [Cf. Klaeber, *Christ. Elementen*, in *Anglia*, xxxv. 136.]

Those who suppose that Hengest entered Finn's service with treacherous intent (Bugge, Earle, *etc.*) favour the emendation *worod-rǣdenne* (not elsewhere found: taken as signifying 'allegiance' from *weorod*, 'retinue').

Schücking puts comma after *gemunde*, and renders *swā*... 'in such wise that,...' i.e., without breaking his allegiance.

1143. *hilde-lēoma* is probably the *name* of the sword which Hunlafing places in Hengest's bosom. See *Introduction to Beowulf: Finnsburh.*

1150. *wēana dǣl*, 'their manifold woes'; *dǣl* signifying 'a large part,' as in Mod. Eng. 'a deal of trouble.' [Cf. Kock in *Anglia*, xxvii. 228.]

ne meahte...*hreþre.* This is generally interpreted as referring to Finn: e.g. by Clark-Hall: 'His flickering spirit could not keep its footing in his breast'; that is 'he died.' For *wǣfre* of a spirit about to depart, cf. l. 2420. But it is more in accordance with O.E. style that ll. 1150–1 should be parallel to ll. 1149–50. Hence Bugge [*Tidsskr.* viii. 295], following Ettmüller, 'the spirit (of the attacking party, Guthlaf and Oslaf) could no longer restrain itself.'

1151. *roden*, 'reddened,' 'stained by the life-blood of foes,' Bugge [*Tidsskr.* viii. 64, 295]: MS. *hroden* 'covered.' Bugge's emendation [supported by Sievers, in *P.B.B.* ix. 139, xxxvi. 407 and Klaeber, in *Anglia*, xxviii. 445] is made for metrical reasons (cf. l. 2916), to prevent the superfluous double alliteration in the second half line, and is almost certainly correct: he compares *Andreas*, 1005, *dēað-wang rudon.*

1152. *fēorum*, 'bodies': cf. note to l. 1210.

Scēotend Scyldinʒa tō scypon feredon
1155 eal in-ʒesteald eorð-cyninʒes
swylce hīe æt Finnes hām findan meahton
siʒla, searo-ʒimma. Hīe on sǣ-lāde
drihtlīce wīf tō Denum feredon,
lǣddon |tō lēodum." Lēoð wæs āsunʒen, Fol. 155b.
1160 ʒlēo-mannes ʒyd. ʒamen eft āstāh,
beorhtode benc-swēʒ; byrelas sealdon
wīn of wunder-fatum. Þā cwōm Wealhþēo forð
ʒān under ʒyldnum bēaʒe, þǣr þā ʒōdan twēʒen
sǣton suhter-ʒefæderan; þā ʒȳt wæs hiera sib
ætʒædere,
1165 ǣʒhwylc ōðrum trȳwe. Swylce þǣr (H)unferþ þyle
æt fōtum sæt frēan Scyldinʒa; ʒehwylc hiora his
ferhþe trēowde,
þæt hē hæfde mōd micel, þēah þe hē his māʒum
nǣre
ār-fæst æt ecʒa ʒelācum. Spræc ðā ides Scyldinʒa:
"Onfōh þissum fulle, frēo-drihten mīn,
1170 sinces brytta; þū on sǣlum wes,
ʒold-wine ʒumena, ond tō ʒēatum spræc
mildum wordum, swā sceal man dôn.
Bēo wið ʒēatas ʒlæd, ʒeofena ʒemyndiʒ,
nēan ond feorran þū nū hafast.
1175 Mē man sæʒde, þæt |þū ðē for sunu wolde Fol. 156a.
here-ri[*n*]c habban. Heorot is ʒefǣlsod,

1158. *wīf*=Hildeburh.

1161. For *beorhtian*, 'to brighten,' used of sound, cf. *heaðotorht*, of a clear loud sound, l. 2553. Sedgefield reads *beorhtmode* (*beorhtm* 'sound').

1163, *etc*. Note the expanded lines. Cf. ll. 2173 *a*, 2995.

1164. *suhter-gefæderan*. See *Index of Persons*: Hrothulf, Unferth, and cf. note to l. 84, *āþum-swerian*.

1165. *Unferþ*: MS. *hun ferþ*.

1174. We must either understand (with Holthausen) or read (with Sedgefield) [*þe*] *þū nū hafast*: 'Be mindful of gifts; you have plenty of them.'

Ettmüller$_2$ suggested *þū nū* [*friðu*] *hafast*, and the reading *friðu* or *freoðo* has been widely accepted. But metrically it is unsatisfactory [cf. Sievers in *P.B.B.* x. 248; but see also xii. 196]. Also the alliteration should run on *n* not *f*.

[See also Bugge[92]; Klaeber in *J.E.G.Ph.* viii. 256–7.]

1176. *here-rinc*, Kemble$_2$: MS. *here ric*. The omission of the *n* (written as a mere stroke above the vowel) is a not uncommon scribal error. Cf.

bēah-sele beorhta; brūc þenden þū mōte
maniȝra mēdo, ond þīnum māȝum lǣf
folc ond rīce, þonne ðū forð scyle
1180 metod-sceaft sêon. Ic mīnne can
ȝlædne Hrōþulf, þæt hē þā ȝeoȝoðe wile
ārum healdan, ȝyf þū ǣr þonne hē,
wine Scildinȝa, worold oflǣtest;
wēne ic, þæt hē mid ȝōde ȝyldan wille
1185 uncran eaferan, ȝif hē þæt eal ȝemon,
hwæt wit tō willan ond tō worð-myndum
umbor-wesendum ǣr ārna ȝefremedon."
Hwearf þā bī bence, þǣr hyre byre wǣron,
Hrēðrīc ond Hrōðmund, ond hæleþa bearn,
1190 ȝioȝoð ætȝædere; þǣr se ȝōda sæt,
Bēowulf Ȝēata, be þǣm ȝebrōðrum twǣm.
XVIII Him wæs ful boren, ond frēond-laþu
wordum bewæȝned, ond wunden ȝold
ēstum ȝeēawed, earm-rēade twā,
1195 hræȝl ond hrin|ȝas, heals-bēaȝa mǣst, Fol. 156b.
þāra þe ic on foldan ȝefræȝen hæbbe.
Nǣniȝne ic under sweȝle sēlran hȳrde
hord-mādm hæleþa, syþðan Hāma ætwæȝ

ll. 60, 1510, 1883, 2307. Beowulf is meant, who has been adopted by Hrothgar (ll. 946 *etc.*) [cf. Klaeber[244]]. The letter should be compared in which Theodoric the Great adopts a king of the Eruli as his son in arms, sending him gifts of horses, swords, shields, and other war-trappings, and instructing him in the duties of his new relationship. [Cassiodorus, *Variae* iv. 2.]

1178. *mēdo.* Both Thorkelin's transcripts, A and B, read *medo*: MS. defective at edge. Editors have usually normalized to *mēda*, but we have already had a gen. pl. in *o* (see l. 70). Such gen. pls. are most usually found in masc. and neut. nouns: but cf. *þāra mīnra ondswaro* in *Epist. Alexand.* 423 [*Anglia*, iv. 155]; *hȳnðo* in l. 475 is perhaps also a gen. pl.

1186–7. Holthausen compares Tacitus [*Germania*, xx.]: *sororum filiis idem apud avunculum qui apud patrem honor*: and this close tie between the *maternal* uncle and his sister's sons is of course a feature of many primitive tribes (see note to ll. 1114–7, above). But Hrothulf is son, not of a sister, but of the brother Halga, himself a mighty sea-king: he has claims to the succession which the queen justly fears. See *Index of Persons*: Hrothulf.

1194. *earm-rēade*: so MS.; Grein_1 *earm-[h]rēade.* For the occasional absence of initial *h*, especially in the second element of compounds, see Sievers_3 § 217, Bülbring § 526.

1198. *hord-mādm*: MS. *hord madmum.* Almost all editors have emended to *māððum* [Grein_1] or *māðm* [Grundtvig, 1861]. The emendation is here adopted (though the spelling *mādm* is retained) because (1) a dat. *mādmum* can only be construed with difficulty, (2) *māðm* is metrically superior, and (3) a scribe, having in his original the archaic form *maðm* or *madm*, and

tō *þǣre* byrhtan byriȝ   Brōsinȝa mene,
1200 siȝle ond sinc-fæt;   searo-nīðas *flēah*
Eormenrīces,   ȝecēas ēcne rǣd.
Þone hrinȝ hæfde   Hiȝelāc ȝēata,
nefa Swertinȝes,   nȳhstan sīðe,
siðþan hē under seȝne   sinc ealȝode,
1205 wæl-rēaf werede;   hyne wyrd fornam,
syþðan hē for wlenco   wēan āhsode,
fǣhðe tō Frȳsum.   Hē þā frætwe wæȝ,
eorclan-stānas,   ofer ȳða ful,
rīce þēoden;   hē under rande ȝecranc.
1210 ȝehwearf þā in Francna fæþm   feorh cyninȝes,
brēost-ȝewǣdu   ond se bēah somod;
wyrsan wīȝ-frecan   wæl rēafed*on*

intending to modernize this to *maððum*, might very easily have miswritten *madmum*. [Cf. also Trautmann[192].]

1199. *þǣre*, Ettmüller$_2$: MS. *here*. Apart from difficulties of meaning, a compound *here-beorhtan* would be impossible here for the alliteration; cf. note to l. 707.

1200. *sinc-fæt*. On the analogy of *gold-fæt* (*Phœnix*, 302) the meaning 'precious setting' has been proposed [Klaeber, *J.E.G.Ph.* vi. 194].

flēah, Leo, Grundtvig (1861), Cosijn [*P.B.B.* viii. 569], Bugge[69]: MS. *fealh*. "*Flēah* gives an easier construction and is confirmed by the fact that, according to the saga, Hama in reality 'fled from the enmity of Eormenric.'" The emendation is accepted by recent editors. See *Index of Persons*: Hama.

1201. Two explanations of 'he chose the eternal counsel, welfare' have been suggested. (1) 'He went into the cloister,' as Hama does in the *Thidreks saga*. This, it is objected, is hardly a likely interpretation in so early a poem as *Beowulf*. The retirement of the hero to a monastery seems indeed to be a motive found most frequently in French Romance. Yet, since we know of early Anglo-Saxon chiefs, e.g. King Ethelred of Mercia and Eadberht of Northumbria, who *did* end their days in the cloister, it may have been a motive also in O.E. poetry. (2) The meaning 'he died' is suggested: similar euphemisms for death are common. Bugge[70] and Klaeber [*Christ. Elementen*, in *Anglia*, xxxv. 456] combine both meanings: 'he went into the monastery, and there ended piously.'

But in l. 1760, and in *Exodus*, 515, the phrase *ēce rǣdas* seems rather to mean 'counsel such as will lead to eternal benefit,' without any connotation of either the monastery or the grave. Professor Priebsch suggests to me that the pious *ēcne rǣd*, *ēce rǣdas* has in both places in *Beowulf* been substituted by a monkish copyist for some other phrase. This seems very possible.

1206. *wēan āhsode*, 'he went in search of trouble.' [Cf. Klaeber in *M.L.N.* xvi. 30.]

1210. *feorh*, 'the body': cf. l. 1152. That Hygelac's body passed into the possession of his foes is confirmed by the fact that his bones were shown, much later, near the mouth of the Rhine, presumably in the neighbourhood of this last fight. There seems no necessity to alter, with Sievers, to *feoh* [*P.B.B.* ix. 139; cf. Bugge[92]].

1212. *rēafedon*, Ettmüller$_2$: MS. *reafeden*; the pl. indic. in *en* does occur in O.E. dialects, but so rarely as to make it probable that here it is only the late scribe's error.

æfter ʒūð-sceare; Ʒēata lēode
hrēa-wīc hēoldon. Heal swēʒe onfēnʒ.
1215 Wealhðēo maþelode, hēo fore þǣm werede spræc:
"Brūc ðisses bēaʒes, Bēowulf lēofa,
hyse, mid hǣle, |ond þisses hræʒles nēot, Fol. 157ᵃ.
þēo[*d*]-ʒestrēona, ond ʒeþēoh tela;
cen þec mid cræfte, ond þyssum cnyhtum wes
1220 lāra līðe; ic þē þæs lēan ʒeman.
Hafast þū ʒefēred, þæt ðē feor ond nēah
ealne wīde-ferhþ weras ehtiʒað,
efne swā sīde swā sǣ bebūʒeð
windʒeard, weallas. Wes, þenden þū lifiʒe,
1225 æþelinʒ ēadiʒ; ic þē an tela
sinc-ʒestrēona. Bēo þū suna mīnum
dǣdum ʒedēfe, drēam healdende.
Hēr is ǣʒhwylc eorl ōþrum ʒetrȳwe,
mōdes milde, man-drihtne hol[*d*];
1230 þeʒnas syndon ʒeþwǣre, þēod eal ʒearo,
druncne dryht-ʒuman, dōð swā ic bidde."
Ēode þā tō setle. Þǣr wæs symbla cyst,
druncon wīn weras; wyrd ne cūþon,
ʒeō-sceaft ʒrim*me*, swā hit āʒanʒen wearð

1213. *gūð-sceare.* On the analogy of *inwitscear* (l. 2478) it seems that the 'cutting' or 'shearing' implied by *scear* is that of the sword of the foe, not the metaphorical dividing of Fate. Translate then 'after the carnage' rather than [with Earle, Clark-Hall] 'by the fortune of war.'

1214. Cosijn[21] would read *Halsbēge onfēng Wealhðēo maþelode*, 'Wealhtheow took the necklet and spake': he objects that 'noise' is out of place here: we should expect silence for the speech of Wealhtheow (cf. ll. 1698–9).

1218. *þēo*[*d*], Grundtvig[285], Kemble$_2$: MS. *þeo ge streona.*

1223. MS. *side* corrected from *wide.*

1224. *windgeard, weallas*: MS. *wind geard weallas.* The suggestion of Kemble$_1$, *windge eardweallas*, has been very generally adopted, and is still retained by Sedgefield. But such an instance of the alliteration being borne by the second element in a compound seems unprecedented. [Cf. Krackow in *Archiv*, cxi. 171.] So it is best either, with Schücking and Holthausen$_3$, to retain the MS. reading, interpreting 'the home of the winds, the cliffs' (cf. l. 229), or to emend with Holthausen$_{1,2}$, following Ettmüller$_2$, *windge weallas*, on the analogy of l. 572.

1225. Most recent editors put a comma after *æþeling*, making it a vocative. It seems to me that such breaks in the half-line are to be avoided wherever possible. Cf. ll. 130, 2188, 2342. But see Klaeber[457].

1229. *hol*[*d*], Thorkelin, Kemble$_1$: MS. *hol.*

1234. *geo-sceaft* seems to be written for *geasceaft* = **gæsceaft*, another form of *gesceaft*, 'that which is shaped, creation, fate.' [Cf. Kluge in *P.B.B.* viii.

1235 eorla maneȝum. Syþðan ǣfen cwōm,
ond him Hrōþȝār ȝewāt tō hofe sīnum,
rīce tō ræste, reced weardode
unrīm eorla, swā hīe oft ǣr dydon.
Benc-þelu beredon; hit ȝeond-brǣded wearð
1240 beddum ond bolstrum. Bēor-scealca sum
fūs ond fǣȝe flet-ræste ȝe|bēaȝ. **Fol. 157b.**
Setton him tō hēafdon hilde-randas,
bord-wudu beorhtan; þǣr on bence wæs
ofer æþelinȝe ȳþ-ȝesēne
1245 heaþo-stēapa helm, hrinȝed byrne,
þrec-wudu þrymlīc. Wæs þēaw hyra,
þæt hīe oft wǣron ānwīȝ-ȝearwe
ȝe æt hām ȝe on herȝe, ȝe ȝehwæþer þāra
efne swylce mǣla, swylce hira man-dryhtne
1250 þearf ȝesǣlde; wæs sēo þēod tilu.
XIX Sīȝon þā tō slǣpe. Sum sāre anȝeald
ǣfen-ræste, swā him ful oft ȝelamp,
siþðan ȝold-sele Ȝrendel warode,
unriht æfnde, oþ þæt ende becwōm,
1255 swylt æfter synnum. Þæt ȝesȳne wearþ,
wīd-cūþ werum, þætte wrecend þā ȝȳt
lifde æfter lāþum, lanȝe þrāȝe
æfter ȝūð-ceare; Ȝrendles mōdor,
ides, āȝlǣc-wīf, yrmþe ȝemunde,
1260 sē þe wæter-eȝesan wunian scolde,

533.] This *eó* for *ea* may be Anglian; yet it is also possible that *geō* is correct as the first element: 'fate ordained of old.'

grimme, Ettmüller$_2$: MS. *grimne*.

1242. *hēafdon*: *on* for *um* in dat. pl. Cf. l. 1154, and note to l. 900.

1247. The older edd. followed the MS., *an wig gearwe*: but *ānwīg-gearwe*, 'prepared for single combat,' or *an*[*d*]*wīg-gearwe*, 'prepared for attack,' involve the alliteration running on the vowel instead of on the *w* of *wīg*, and so make it easier to scan *þæt hīe oft wǣron*. [But cf. Klaeber[458] and Schücking.]

1250. The manners depicted are those of Tacitus' *Germania* [cf. especially cap. XXII.].

1253. *warode*: MS., as well as Thorkelin's transcripts, A and B; "the parchment under *wa* is rather thin, and besides there is a blot on the two letters" (Zupitza). Hence the word has several times been misread *farode*.

1257. *lange þrāge*. The 'higher critics' point out that there is a discrepancy between this 'long time' and the shortness of the time which does, in fact, elapse before Grendel's mother executes her vengeance.

1260. *sē* might here refer to Grendel: but there is no reason for so interpreting it, since below (ll. 1392, 1394, 1497) the masc. pronoun is used of

cealde strēamas, siþðan Câin wearð
tō ecʒ-banan ānʒan brēþer,
fæderen-mǣʒe; hē þā fāʒ ʒewāt,
morþre ʒemearcod, |man-drēam flêon, Fol. 158a.
1265 wēsten warode. Þanon wōc fela
ʒeō-sceaft-ʒāsta; wæs þǣra ʒrendel sum,
heoro-wearh hetelīc, sē æt Heorote fand
wæccendne wer wīʒes bīdan.
Þǣr him āʒlǣca ætʒrǣpe wearð;
1270 hwæþre hē ʒemunde mæʒenes strenʒe,
ʒim-fæste ʒife, ðe him ʒod sealde,
ond him tō Anwaldan āre ʒelȳfde,
frōfre ond fultum; ðȳ hē þone fēond ofercwōm,
ʒehnǣʒde helle-ʒāst. Þā hē hēan ʒewāt,
1275 drēame bedǣled, dēaþ-wīc sêon,
man-cynnes fēond. Ond his mōdor þā ʒȳt
ʒīfre ond ʒalʒ-mōd ʒeʒān wolde
sorh-fulne sīð, sunu *dēað* wrecan;
cōm þā tō Heorote, ðǣr Hrinʒ-Dene
1280 ʒeond þæt sæld swǣfun. Þā ðǣr sōna wearð
ed-hwyrft eorlum, siþðan inne fealh
ʒrendles mōdor. Wæs se ʒryre lǣssa
efne swā micle, swā bið mæʒþa cræft,
wīʒ-ʒryre wīfes, be wǣpned-men,
1285 þonne heoru bunden, hamere ʒeþ*rūe*n

Grendel's mother: and even should we, with Thorpe, Grein$_1$ and Holthausen, emend to *hē*[*o*], *sē*[*o*], there remain passages like l. 1379, where Grendel's mother is called *fela-sinnigne secg*. The poet is inconsistent, thinking sometimes of the female sex, sometimes of the daemonic power, of the monster. Ten Brink[97, 110] saw in this confusion traces of an earlier version in which Beowulf fought under the water with *two* monsters, one female, and one male—Grendel's mother and Grendel.

1261. *Cāin*, Grundtvig[286], Kemble$_1$, *etc.*: MS. *camp.*

1266. See note to l. 1234.

1271. Kemble$_3$, *etc.*, *gin-fæste*: an unnecessary emendation. For the change of *n* to *m* before labials, cf. *hlimbed*, l. 3034, and see Sievers$_3$ § 188.

1278. *sunu dēað*: MS. *sunu þeod.* Ettmüller$_2$ conjectured *suna dēað*; *dēað*, written *dēoð* by a Northern scribe, might easily be confused with *ðēod*; probably the mistake originally arose through the wrong *d* being crossed by a scribe.

Gen. *sunu* for W.S. *suna* is also Northern, cf. l. 344.

1280. *sōna*. Holthausen reads *sō*[*c*]*na*, 'a recurrence of attacks.'

1285. *geþrūen*, Grein$_1$: MS. *geþuren.* This isolated past part., meaning apparently 'pressed,' 'compact,' occurs in Boethius, *Metra*, xx. 134. Metre demands its restoration here, and in *Riddles*, lxxxix. [xci.] 1, though the MS. has *homere, hamere, geþuren.* [Cf. Sievers in *P.B.B.* ix. 282, 294; x. 458.]

sweord swāte fāh, swīn ofer helme
ecʒum |dyhtiʒ andweard scireð. **Fol. 158b.**
Ðā wæs on healle heard-ecʒ toʒen
sweord ofer setlum, sīd-rand maniʒ
1290 hafen handa fæst; helm ne ʒemunde,
byrnan sīde, þā hine se brōʒa anʒeat.
Hēo wæs on ofste, wolde ūt þanon
fēore beorʒan, þā hēo onfunden wæs;
hraðe hēo æþelinʒa ānne hæfde
1295 fæste befanʒen; þā hēo tō fenne ʒanʒ.
Sē wæs Hrōþʒāre hæleþa lēofost
on ʒesīðes hād be sǣm twēonum,
rīce rand-wiʒa, þone ðe hēo on ræste ābrēat,
blǣd-fæstne beorn. Næs Bēowulf ðǣr,
1300 ac wæs ōþer in ǣr ʒeteohhod
æfter māþðum-ʒife mǣrum ʒēate.
Hrēam wearð in Heorote; hēo under heolfre ʒenam
cūþe folme; cearu wæs ʒenīwod,
ʒeworden in wīcun. Ne wæs þæt ʒewrixle til,
1305 þæt hīe on bā healfa bicʒan scoldon
frēonda fēorum. Þā wæs frōd cyninʒ,
hār hilde-rinc, on hrēon |mōde, Fol. 159a.
syðþan hē aldor-þeʒn unlyfiʒendne,
þone dēorestan dēadne wisse.
1310 Hraþe wæs tō būre Bēowulf fetod,
siʒor-ēadiʒ secʒ; samod ǣr-dæʒe
ēode eorla sum, æþele cempa
self mid ʒesīðum, þǣr se snotera bād,
hwæþre him Al-walda ǣfre wille

1290–1. We must understand 'any one' as subject to *gemunde*.

þe hine, 'whom,' for *þā hine*, was suggested by Grein, (followed by Heyne, Sweet, *etc.*) and is ingenious but not necessary. [Cf. Pogatscher, *Unausgedrücktes Subjekt im Altenglischen, Anglia*, xxiii. 296.]

1302. *under heolfre*, 'amid the gore,' 'blood-stained.'

1304–6. 'The exchange was not a good one which they had to buy, to pay for, with the lives of their friends.' A typical description of a blood-feud, where, as in the Icelandic sagas, the lives on each side are set off, one against the other. *On bā healfa*, not, as often taken, the Danes and the Geatas, but the monster brood on the one side, and the Danes and Geatas on the other.

1314. *Alwealda*, Thorkelin; *Al-walda*, Thorpe: MS. *alf walda*. Cf. ll. 316, 955.

wille. For the tense *wille*, not *wolde*, Klaeber[260] compares ll. 381, 1928, 2495.

1315 æfter wēa-spelle wyrpe ȝefremman.
Ȝanȝ ðā æfter flōre fyrd-wyrðe man
mid his hand-scale —heal-wudu dynede—
þæt hē þone wīsan wordum *nǣ*ȝde
frēan Inȝwina, fræȝn ȝif him wǣre
1320 æfter nēod-laðu niht ȝetǣse.
XX Hrōðȝār maþelode, helm Scyldinȝa:
"Ne frīn þū æfter sǣlum; sorh is ȝenīwod
Deniȝea lēodum. Dēad is Æschere,
Yrmenlāfes yldra brōþor,
1325 mīn rūn-wita ond mīn rǣd-bora,
eaxl-ȝestealla, ðonne wē on orleȝe
hafelan weredon, þonne hniton fēþan,
eoferas cnysedan. |Swy[lc] scolde eorl wesan, Fol. 159b.
[*æþelinȝ*] ǣr-ȝōd, swylc Æschere wæs.
1330 Wearð him on Heorote tō hand-banan
wæl-ȝǣst wǣfre; ic ne wāt hwæ*d*er

1317. Some editors alter to the normal form *hand-scole*, cf. l. 1963. There is no other certain instance of the spelling *scale* (*sceal*=*scolu* in the *Lament of the Fallen Angels*, 268, is doubtful). The interchange of *a* and *o* is, however, not unprecedented [cf. parallels quoted by Kluge in Kuhn's *Z.f.v.S.* xxvi. 101, note: *rador* and *rodor*, *etc.*].

1318. *nǣgde*, Grein: Thorkelin's transcripts A and B, *hnægde*; now *de* gone. The *h* is a mere parasitic prefix. *Wordum nǣgan* (*nēgan*) occurs in *Elene*, 287, 559; *Exodus*, 23, *etc.*

1320. *nēod-laðu*. Sweet, *nēod-laðe*, Ettmüller$_3$, *etc.*, Holthausen, *nēod-laðu*[*m*]; but see Sievers$_3$ § 253, N. 2. Since *word-laðu* (*Crist*, 664; *Andreas*, 635)=not 'invitation,' but 'eloquence,' and *frēondlaðu* above (l. 1192) would be better suited by 'friendship' than 'friendly invitation,' it seems possible that *nēod-laðu* here='desire' (*nēod*), rather than 'pressing invitation' (*nēod*=*nīed*, 'necessity'). [Cf. Klaeber in *Archiv*, cxv. 179.]

1328. *swy*[*lc*], Thorkelin's emendation: MS. defective at corner. Thorkelin's transcripts A and B, *swy scolde*.

1329. No gap in MS. Grundtvig's emendation [1861, *ædeling*].

1331. *wæl-gǣst*. See note to l. 102.

hwæder: MS. *hwæþer*. Ten Brink[96] [cf. Möller, *V.E.*, 136] saw in *hwæþer*, 'which of the two,' a confirmation of his view that there had been a version representing Beowulf fighting under the water with both Grendel and his mother, and that what Hrothgar here states is that he does not know which of the two is the assailant [cf. Schücking$_1$]. But unless we are prepared, with ten Brink, to regard ll. 1330–1 as an isolated fragment of such a version, out of harmony with its present context, we must read not 'I know not *which*' but 'whither': since it appears from the context that Hrothgar has no doubt as to the personality of the assailant, but does not know her *exact* retreat (cf. ll. 1333, 1339).

We may therefore (1) retain *hwæþer*, attributing to it the meaning of *hwider* [Heyne$_1$, Holthausen], for which no precedent can be found; (2) emend to *hwæder*, a form of *hwider*, of which examples *are* elsewhere found, see Bosworth-Toller [Grein$_2$, Heyne$_2$, Cosijn[22–3], Sedgefield, Schücking$_2$, *etc.*]; or (3) emend to *hwider* [Sweet$_1$, Grein-Wülker, *etc.*]. The *via media* (2) seems preferable.

atol ǣse wlanc eft-sīðas tēah,
fylle ʒefrǣʒnod. Hēo þā fǣhðe wræc,
þē þū ʒystran niht ʒrendel cwealdest
1335 þurh hǣstne hād heardum clammum,
forþan hē tō lanʒe lēode mīne
wanode ond wyrde. Hē æt wīʒe ʒecranʒ
ealdres scyldiʒ, ond nū ōþer cwōm
mihtiʒ mān-scaða, wolde hyre mǣʒ wrecan,
1340 ʒe feor hafað fǣhðe ʒestǣled,
þæs þe þincean mæʒ þeʒne moneʒum,
sē þe æfter sinc-ʒyfan on sefan ʒrēoteþ,
hreþer-bealo hearde; nū sēo hand liʒeð,
sē þe ēow wel-hwylcra wilna dohte.
1345 Ic þæt lond-būend, lēode mīne,
sele-rǣdende, secʒan hȳrde,
þæt hīe ʒesāwon swylce twēʒen
micle mearc-stapan mōras healdan,
ellor-ʒǣstas; ðǣra ōðer wæs,
1350 þæs þe hīe ʒewislīcost ʒewitan meahton,
idese onlīcn*es*; ōðer earm-sceapen
on weres wæstmum wrǣc-lāstas |træd, Fol. 160a.
næfne hē wæs māra þonne ǣniʒ man ōðer,
þone on ʒeār-daʒum ʒrendel nemdo*n*
1355 fold-būende; nō hīe fæder cunnon,
hwæþer him ǣniʒ wæs ǣr ācenned
dyrnra ʒāsta. Hīe dȳʒel lond
wariʒeað, wulf-hleoþu, windiʒe næssas,
frēcne fen-ʒelād, ðǣr fyrʒen-strēam
1360 under næssa ʒenipu niþer ʒewīteð,

1333. The emendation of Kemble$_3$, *gefægnod*, 'made glad,' has been widely accepted: *fylle* would be from *fyllo*, 'feast,' rather than *fyll*, 'fall,' 'death' [of Æschere]: cf. ll. 562, 1014.

1342. *sinc-gyfa* should signify 'a ruling (not necessarily independent) chief': Æschere may have been, like Wulfgar, a tributary prince. Or perhaps, with Holthausen, we can take the word as a fem. abstract noun: 'after the giving of treasure' by Hrothgar: joyful occasions when the absence of Æschere would be remembered.

1344. Ettmüller$_2$, *etc.*, *sēo þe*; but cf. ll. 1887, 2685.

1351. *onlīcnes*, Kemble$_1$: MS. *onlic næs*; Sweet, *onlic*, *wæs*...; Holthausen, following Grundtvig [287 but cf. his edit. of 1861], omits *næs*.

1354. MS. defective; Thorkelin's transcripts A and B, *nemdod*; Kemble$_1$, *nem*[*nodon*]; Kemble$_2$, *nem*[*don*].

flōd under foldan. Nis þæt feor heonon
mīl-ȝemearces, þæt se mere standeð,
ofer þǣm honȝiað hrinde bearwas,
wudu wyrtum fæst wæter oferhelmað.
1365 Þǣr mæȝ nihta ȝehwǣm nīð-wundor sēon,
fȳr on flōde. Nō þæs frōd leofað
ȝumena bearna, þæt þone ȝrund wite.
Ðēah þe hǣð-stapa hundum ȝeswenced,
heorot hornum trum, holt-wudu sēce,
1370 feorran ȝeflȳmed, ǣr hē feorh seleð,
aldor on ōfre, ǣr hē in wille,
hafelan [*hȳdan*]. Nis þæt hēoru stōw;
þonon ȳð-ȝeblond ūp āstīȝeð
won tō wolcnum, þonne wind styreþ
1375 lāð ȝewidru, oð ðæt lyft drysmaþ,
roderas rēotað. Nū is se rǣd ȝelanȝ
eft æt |þē ānum. Eard ȝīt ne const, Fol. 160b.
frēcne stōwe, ðǣr þū findan miht
⟨fela⟩-sinniȝne secȝ; sēc ȝif þū dyrre.
1380 Ic þē þā fǣhðe fēo lēaniȝe,
eald-ȝestrēonum, swā ic ǣr dyde,
wundini ȝolde, ȝyf þū on weȝ cymest."

1362. *standeð*, Thorkelin's correction: MS. *stanðeð*.

1363. Many unsuccessful attempts were made to explain *hrinde* till Morris, editing the *Blickling Homilies*, found there, in a passage (p. 209) which he supposed to be imitated from these lines in *Beowulf*, the expression *hrīmige bearwas*, 'trees covered with frost.' The restoration of *hrīmige* in the text here was generally accepted.

But the *English Dialect Dictionary* drew attention to the fact that the word *rind*, meaning 'hoar-frost,' was still current in the North of England; *hrinde* is then presumably correct, and is a shortened form of **hrindede*, meaning 'covered with frost,' as was pointed out independently by Mrs Wright [*Engl. Stud.* xxx. 341] and by Skeat. *Hrinde* would be connected with *hrīm*, 'hoar-frost,' as *sund* with *swimman*: a new example for the transition from *md* to *nd* [cf. Holthausen in *I.F.* xiv. 339].

1372. *hȳdan*, supplied by $Kemble_3$. No gap in MS., but a mark like a colon shows that the scribe realized that something had been omitted.

1379. MS. *fela sinnigne*: *fela* is best omitted, as otherwise it should take the alliteration.

1380. *fēo*, instrumental.

1382. It is strange that whilst recent editors frequently restore into the text ancient forms which the later scribes refused to admit, yet here, when the scribe, by a curious oversight, seems to have copied the early 8th century form *wundini*, 'with twisted gold,' most editors refuse to accept it, and modernize to *wundnum*.

Wundini is instrumental, parallel to *binumini* and similar forms in the

XXI Bēowulf maþelode, bearn Ecȝþēowes:
"Ne sorȝa, snotor ȝuma; sēlre bið ǣȝhwǣm,
1385 þæt hē his frēond wrece, þonne hē fela murne.
Ūre ǣȝhwylc sceal ende ȝebīdan
worolde līfes; wyrce sē þe mōte
dōmes ǣr dēaþe; þæt bið driht-ȝuman
unlifȝendum æfter sēlest.
1390 Ārīs, rīces weard; uton hraþe fēran
ȝrendles māȝan ȝanȝ scēawiȝan.
Ic hit þē ȝehāte: nō hē on helm losaþ,
ne on foldan fæþm, ne on fyrȝen-holt,
ne on ȝyfenes ȝrund, ȝā þǣr hē wille.
1395 Ðȳs dōȝor þū ȝeþyld hafa
wēana ȝehwylces, swā ic þē wēne tō."
Āhlēop ðā se ȝomela, ȝode þancode,
mihtiȝan Drihtne, þæs se man ȝe|spræc. **Fol. 161ᵃ.**
Þā wæs Hrōðȝāre hors ȝebǣted,
1400 wicȝ wunden-feax; wīsa fenȝel
ȝeatolīc ȝende; ȝum-fēþa stōp

early *Glosses*. [Cf. Sievers, *Der ags. Instrumental*, in *P.B.B.* viii. 324, *etc.*] That a 10th or 11th century scribe should have written an 8th century form here is strange, but that he did so must be clear to anyone who will look at the MS.: the *d* is now covered, but the next letters are either *mi* or *ini*, certainly not *um*. (This was noted by Zupitza, and before him by Holder; Thorkelin's transcript A has *rundmi*; B, *wundini*.) The scribe in any case would hardly have copied the old form except through momentary inadvertence. But surely to suppose, with Bugge[93], that he wrote this *mi* or *ini* by error for *num* is less reasonable than to suppose that he wrote it because *ini* (often not distinguishable from *mi*) was in the MS. which he was copying.

In that case *Beowulf* must have been already written down in the 8th century and our MS. must be derived (no doubt with many intermediate stages) from this early MS. In any case it is surely no duty of an editor to remove from the text an interesting old form, from which important conclusions can possibly be drawn.

1390. Sweet, *raþe*, for the sake of the alliteration; but see Sievers$_3$ § 217, N. 1.

1391. *gang*: the second *g* has been added above the line in the MS.

1392. See note to l. 1260, above.

helm can mean 'protection,' 'refuge,' 'covering' [cf. Schröer in *Anglia*, xiii. 335], but is in that case usually followed by a gen., as in *helm Scyldinga*, *etc.* Hence the old emendation *holm*, 'sea,' is defended by Cosijn[23]. An example of *helm* without the gen. dependent on it appears in one of the *Hymns* [Grein$_1$, ii. 294; Grein-Wülker, ii. 280] *helme gedygled*.

1395. Heyne, *ðys dōgor*, acc. of duration; so also Schücking. But it seems better to read *ðȳs dōgor*, 'on this day' (instrumental). [See Sievers$_3$ § 289, and *P.B.B.* x. 312.]

1401. *gende*. Ettmüller$_2$ emended to *gen*[*g*]*de*, and has been followed by the editors. The emendation is probably correct (cf. l. 1412), but *gende*

lind-hæbbendra. Lāstas wǣron
æfter wald-swaþum wīde ʒesȳne,
ʒanʒ ofer ʒrundas; [*þǣr hēo*] ʒeʒnum fōr
1405 ofer myrcan mōr, maʒo-þeʒna bær
þone sēlestan sāwol-lēasne,
þāra þe mid Hrōðʒāre hām eahtode.
Oferēode þā æþelinʒa bearn
stēap stān-hliðo, stīʒe nearwe,
1410 enʒe ān-paðas, uncūð ʒelād,
neowle næssas, nicor-hūsa fela;
hē fēara sum beforan ʒenʒde
wīsra monna wonʒ scēawian,
oþ þæt hē fǣrinʒa fyrʒen-bēamas
1415 ofer hārne stān hleonian funde,
wyn-lēasne wudu; wæter under stōd
drēoriʒ ond ʒedrēfed. Denum eallum wæs,
winum Scyldinʒa, weorce on mōde
tō ʒeþolianne, ðeʒne moneʒum,
1420 oncȳð eorla ʒehwǣm, syðþan Æscheres
on þām holm-clife hafelan mētton.
Flōd blōde wēol —folc tō sǣʒon—
|hātan heolfre. Horn stundum sonʒ Fol. 161ᵇ.
fūslīc f[yrd]-lēoð. Fēþa eal ʒesæt;
1425 ʒesāwon ðā æfter wætere wyrm-cynnes fela,

is retained in the text, as it is a conceivable Kentish form [cf. Sievers, § 215, N. 1].

1404. [*þǣr hēo*] was suggested by Sievers [*P.B.B.* ix. 140] to supply the metrical deficiency. It has been generally adopted. [Other possible stop-gaps are enumerated by Klaeber, *J.E.G.Ph.* vi. 195.]

1405–6. *mago-þegna...þone sēlestan*: Æschere.

1408. *bearn* presumably refers to Hrothgar or Beowulf. Yet it may be pl.; for sg. verb with pl. noun, Klaeber[259] compares ll. 904, 2164, 2718.
Some classical parallels for the scenery of the episode of Grendel's mother are discussed by Cook (*M.L.N.* xvii. 418).

1410. This line occurs also in *Exodus*, 58.

1414. *fǣringa*. As with *semninga* (l. 644, q.v.) the meaning must not be pressed.

1418. *winum Scyldinga*. The expression is more usual in the sg., referring to the king alone (ll. 30, 148, 170, *etc.*), but that it can also be used of the more distinguished retainers seems to follow from l. 2567. See also note to l. 1342 [and cf. Klaeber in *J.E.G.Ph.* vi. 195].

1423. *hātan*. Cf. l. 849.

1424. MS. defective at edge. Thorkelin's transcript B gives *f*...; *f*[*yrd*]- is an emendation of Bouterwek [1859: *Z.f.d.A.*, xi. 92].

sellice sǣ-dracan, sund cunnian,
swylce on næs-hleoðum nicras licȝean,
ðā on undern-mǣl oft bewitiȝað
sorh-fulne sīð on seȝl-rāde,
1430 wyrmas ond wil-dēor; hīe on weȝ hruron
bitere ond ȝebolȝne, bearhtm onȝēaton,
ȝūð-horn ȝalan. Sumne Ȝēata lēod
of flān-boȝan fēores ȝetwǣfde,
ȳð-ȝewinnes, þæt him on aldre stōd
1435 here-strǣl hearda; hē on holme wæs
sundes þē sǣnra, ðē hyne swylt fornam.
Hræþe wearð on ȳðum mid eofer-sprēotum
heoro-hōcyhtum hearde ȝenearwod,
nīða ȝenǣȝed ond on næs toȝen,
1440 wundorlīc wǣȝ-bora; weras scēawedon
ȝryrelīcne ȝist. Ȝyrede hine Bēowulf
eorl-ȝewǣdum, nalles for ealdre mearn;
scolde here-byrne hondum ȝebrōden,
sīd ond searo-fāh, sund cunnian,
1445 sēo ðe bān-cofan beorȝan cūþe,
þæt him hilde-ȝrāp hreþre ne mihte,
eorres inwit-fenȝ aldre ȝesceþðan;
ac se hwīta helm |hafelan werede, Fol. 162a.
sē þe mere-ȝrundas menȝan scolde,

1426. The syllable *lic* in words like *sellic* is probably sometimes long, sometimes short. Metrical considerations make it likely that it is here short. Cf. ll. 232, 641 [and Sievers in *P.B.B.* x. 504; xxix. 568].

1428. It seems more reasonable to suppose that the nickers 'look after,' or 'undertake,' journeys of their own fraught with trouble, than that they 'look at' those of others. See *Glossary*: *(be)weotian*.

1439. *genǣged*: Sweet, *ge*[*h*]*nǣged*. But see l. 2206.

1440. *wǣg-bora* has been variously interpreted: 'bearer of the waves' [Grein, *etc.*], 'wave tosser' [cf. Holthausen in *Anglia*, Beiblatt xiv. 49], 'traveller through the waves' [Cosijn[24]; also in *M.L.N.* ii. 7, 1887], 'offspring of the waves' [von Grienberger, *P.B.B.* xxxvi. 99: cf. Sievers in *P.B.B.* xxxvi. 431], or 'piercer of the waves,' from *borian*, 'to bore' [an old interpretation adopted recently by Sedgefield$_1$: but cf. Sievers, *Anglia*, xiv. 135].

The emendation *wǣg-fara*, 'the wave-farer,' has been suggested [Trautmann, followed by Holthausen$_{1,2}$]: *wǣg-fara* is not recorded, but *wǣg-faru* is. The word *wǣg-dēor*, tentatively suggested by Klaeber [*Engl. Stud.* xxxix. 463], occurs in *Crist*, 988.

1447. *eorres*. Non-W.S. form, corresponding to W.S. *ierres*, *yrres*.

1449. *mengan* may possibly mean '|mingle with, visit,' as usually interpreted: but 'mingle together, stir up' seems a more likely rendering, in view of the common use of *gemenged* = 'disturbed' (cf. ll. 848, 1593). [Cf. Klaeber in *M.L.N.* xvi. 16.]

1450 sēcan sund-ʒebland since ʒeweorðad,
befonʒen frēa-wrāsnum, swā hine fyrn-daʒum
worhte wǣpna smið, wundrum tēode,
besette swīn-līcum, þæt hine syðþan nō
brond ne beado-mēcas bītan ne meahton.
1455 Næs þæt þonne mǣtost mæʒen-fultuma,
þæt him on ðearfe lāh ðyle Hrōðʒāres;
wæs þǣm hæft-mēce Hruntinʒ nama;
þæt wæs ān foran eald-ʒestrēona;
ecʒ wæs īren, āter-tānum fāh,
1460 āhyrded heaþo-swāte; nǣfre hit æt hilde ne swāc
manna ǣnʒum, þāra þe hit mid mundum bewand,
sē ðe ʒryre-sīðas ʒeʒān dorste,
folc-stede fāra; næs þæt forma sīð,
þæt hit ellen-weorc æfnan scolde.
1465 Hūru ne ʒemunde maʒo Ecʒlāfes
eafoþes cræftiʒ, þæt hē ǣr ʒespræc
wīne druncen, þā hē þæs wǣpnes onlāh
sēlran sweord-frecan; selfa ne dorste
under ȳða ʒewin aldre ʒenēþan,
1470 driht-scype drēoʒan; þǣr hē dōme forlēas,
ellen-|mǣrðum. Ne wæs þǣm ōðrum swā, Fol. 162[b].
syðþan hē hine tō ʒūðe ʒeʒyred hæfde.

1454. *brond* in the sense of 'sword' is found, though rarely, in O.E.: *brandr* with this meaning is common in O.N. Critics who object to the parallelism of *brond* and *beado-mēcas* have suggested *brogdne beado-mēcas*, 'brandished battle-knives' [cf. Cosijn[24]: so, too, Trautmann, Holthausen, Sedgefield].

1456. *ðyle Hrōðgāres*: Unferth.

1457. *hæft-mēce.* The weapon used by Grettir's adversary in the *Grettis saga* is called a *hepti-sax*. See *Introduction to Beowulf.*

1459. *āter-tānum*, 'twigs of venom,' referring to the wavy damasked pattern produced on the sword by the use of some corrosive. The term 'treed,' applied in Mod. Eng. to the pattern similarly produced on calf-bound books, might be compared. Some have taken the words literally, and supposed the sword to have been actually poisoned.

The emendation of Cosijn [*P.B.B.* viii. 571], *āter-tǣrum* for *āter-tēarum*, 'poison drops,' has been supported by *Andreas*, 1333, *earh āttre gemǣl*, 'the poison-stained arrow' [Cosijn[24]], and by a close O.N. parallel often instanced [first by Bugge, *Tidsskr.* viii. 66], *eldi vóro eggjar útan gǫrvar, enn eitrdropom innan fáþar*: 'the edges were tempered with fire and the blade between was painted with drops of venom,' *Brot af Sig.* 20, 3. But see note to l. 1489.

1471. *mǣrðum*: Thorkelin's transcripts A and B, *mærdam*; Thorpe, *mærðum*; Zupitza: '*mærðum*: *um* at the end of the word is still distinct, and before *um* I think I see a considerable part of *rð*': *um* is still clear, but *rð* is not now visible, to me.

XXII BĒOWVLF maþelode, bearn Ecȝþēowes:
"ȝeþenc nū, se mǣra maȝa Healfdenes,
1475 snottra fenȝel, nū ic eom sīðes fūs,
ȝold-wine ȝumena, hwæt wit ȝeō sprǣcon:
ȝif ic æt þearfe þīnre scolde
aldre linnan, þæt ðū mē ā wǣre
forð ȝewitenum on fæder stǣle.
1480 Wes þū mund-bora mīnum maȝo-þeȝnum,
hond-ȝesellum, ȝif mec hild nime;
swylce þū ðā mādmas, þe þū mē sealdest,
Hrōðȝār lēofa, Hiȝelāce onsend.
Mæȝ þonne on þǣm ȝolde onȝitan ȝēata dryhten,
1485 ȝesēon sunu Hrǣdles, þonne hē on þæt sinc starað,
þæt ic ȝum-cystum ȝōdne funde
bēaȝa bryttan, brēac þonne mōste.
Ond þū ⟨H⟩unferð lǣt ealde lāfe,
wrǣtlic wǣȝ-sweord, wīd-cūðne man
1490 heard-ecȝ habban; ic mē mid Hruntinȝe
dōm ȝewyrce, |oþðe mec dēað nimeð." Fol. 163a.
Ǣfter þǣm wordum Weder-ȝēata lēod
efste mid elne, nalas ondsware
bīdan wolde; brim-wylm onfēnȝ
1495 hilde-rince. Đā wæs hwīl dæȝes,
ǣr hē þone ȝrund-wonȝ onȝytan mehte.
Sōna þæt onfunde, sē ðe flōda beȝonȝ
heoro-ȝīfre behēold hund missēra,
ȝrim ond ȝrǣdiȝ, þæt þǣr ȝumena sum

1474. For this use of *se* with the vocative, which does not occur elsewhere in *Beowulf*, cf. *hæleþ min se lēofa*, *Rood*, 72.

1481. *hond-gesellum*. As this word does not occur elsewhere, Holthausen follows Grundtvig (1861, p. 51) in reading *hond-gesteallum*.

1485. *Hrǣdles*. Many editors normalize to *Hrēðles*: unnecessarily; see notes to ll. 445 and 454.

1488. *Unferð*: MS. *hunferð*.

1489. *wǣg-sweord*. The many emendations suggested are not satisfactory, nor necessary, for 'sword with wavy pattern' seems to explain the word adequately, although an exact parallel is nowhere found. [Reproductions of weapons, with wavy (and also twig-like—cf. l. 1459—) patterns will be found in Gustafson, *Norges Oldtid*, pp. 102–3.]

1495. *hwīl dæges*, 'a main while of the day' (Earle): not, as sometimes interpreted, 'a day.' [Cf. Earle's note and Müllenhoff[127].] For *hwīl*, 'a long time,' cf. ll. 105, 152.

1497. *sē*, of Grendel's mother: contrast *hēo* in l. 1504. Cf. note to l. 1260.

1500 æl-wihta eard ufan cunnode.
ʒrāp þā tōʒēanes, ʒūð-rinc ʒefēnʒ
atolan clommum; nō þȳ ǣr in ʒescōd
hālan līce; hrinʒ ūtan ymbbearh,
þæt hēo þone fyrd-hom ðurhfōn ne mihte,
1505 locene leoðo-syrcan, lāþan finʒrum.
Bær þā sēo brim-wyl[*f*], þā hēo tō botme cōm,
hrinʒa þenʒel tō hofe sīnum,
swā hē ne mihte nō (hē *þēah* mōdiʒ wæs)
wǣpna ʒewealdan; ac hine wundra þæs fela
1510 swe[*n*]cte on sunde, sǣ-dēor moniʒ
hilde-tūxum here-syrcan bræc,
ēhton āʒlǣcan. Ðā se eorl onʒeat,
þæt hē [*in*] nīð-sele nāt-hwylcum wæs,
þǣr him nǣniʒ wæter wihte ne sceþede,
1515 ne him for hrōf-sele hrīnan ne mehte
fǣr-ʒripe flōdes; |fȳr-lēoht ʒeseah, **Fol. 163^b.**
blācne lēoman beorhte scīnan.
Onʒeat þā se ʒōda ʒrund-wyrʒenne,

1502–3. 'No whit the sooner did she harm his body, but it remained whole.'

1506. *brim-wyl*[*f*], Kemble$_2$: MS. *brim wyl.*

1508. *þēah*, Grein: MS. *þæm.* Grein's emendation makes good sense. The majority of editors follow Grundtvig (1861, p. 52), reading *þæs*, but are not agreed whether to take *nō* with *hē þæs mōdig wæs* or not: and neither rendering, 'he was,' or 'he was not, brave enough to wield his weapons,' gives a very satisfactory sense. Schücking and Sedgefield$_2$ read *þǣr*.

1510. *swe*[*n*]*cte*, Kemble$_3$: MS. *swecte*: the *n*, which probably in an older MS. was signified simply by a stroke over the *e*, has been omitted: cf. l. 1176.

1511. *bræc*, probably 'sought to pierce,' like *wehte*, 'tried to awake,' l. 2854. [Cf. Klaeber[261].]

1512. It is not clear whether *āglǣcan* is nom. pl., 'the adversaries annoyed him,' or sg. (gen. or acc.), 'they annoyed their adversary.'

1513. [*in*], Thorpe.

nīð-sele, 'hostile hall.' Grein, followed by Heyne and Bugge[362], reads *nið-sele*, 'hall in the deep.'

1518. *Ongeat.* Here the discrepancy is a more real one than usual. The monster has seized Beowulf at the bottom of the sea, and carried him to her hall, powerless to use his weapons. Yet ll. 1518–22 give the impression that Beowulf enters the hall, able to fight, and there, by the light of the fire, sees Grendel's mother for the first time.

Gummere, following Jellinek and Kraus [*Z.f.d.A.* xxxv. 273], denies that the course of the action is hopelessly confused: 'Beowulf, overwhelmed by the first onset of Grendel's mother, is dragged to her lair, and on the way is beset by monsters of every kind. Managing to extricate himself from the coil, he finds he is in a great arched hall, free of the water, and has only the mother of Grendel before him. He takes good heed of her, and prepares his attack.'

But the difficulty of this explanation is that nothing is said in *Beowulf*

mere-wīf mihtiȝ; mæȝen-rǣs forȝeaf
1520 hilde-bille, hon*d* swenȝe ne oftēah,
þæt hire on hafelan hrinȝ-mǣl āȝōl
ȝrǣdiȝ ȝūð-lēoð. Ðā se ȝist onfand,
þæt se beado-lēoma bītan nolde,
aldre sceþðan, ac sēo ecȝ ȝeswāc
1525 ðēodne æt þearfe; ðolode ǣr fela
hond-ȝemōta, helm oft ȝescær,
fǣȝes fyrd-hræȝl; ðā wæs forma sīð
dēorum mādme, þæt his dōm ālæȝ.
Eft wæs ān-rǣd, nalas elnes læt,
1530 mǣrða ȝemyndiȝ, mǣȝ Hȳlāces.
Wearp ðā wunde*n*-mǣl wrǣttum ȝebunden
yrre ōretta, þæt hit on eorðan læȝ,
stīð ond stȳl-ecȝ; strenȝe ȝetrūwode,
mund-ȝripe mæȝenes. Swā sceal man dôn,
1535 þonne hē æt ȝūðe ȝeȝān þenceð
lonȝsumne lof, nā ymb his līf cearað.
Ȝefēnȝ þā be [*f*]eax*e* —nalas for fǣhðe mearn—
Ȝūð-Ȝēata lēod Ȝrendles mōdor,
bræȝd þā beadwe heard, þā hē ȝebolȝen wæs,

about the hero 'extricating himself from the coil.' The language of l. 1518 would rather lead us to suppose that the hero meets his adversary for the first time within the cave. This is certainly the case in the *Grettis saga*, and is probably the original form of the story.

1520. *hond*, Bouterwek [*Z.f.d.A.* xi. 92], Grein$_1$: MS. *hord*. Sweet, *swenge hond*, without explanation. The dat. *swenge* seems strange: we should expect the acc., and many editors accordingly alter to *sweng* here.

1522. *gist*. The 'stranger' is Beowulf.

1529. *ān-rǣd*. Here, and in l. 1575, it does not seem certain whether we should read *ānrǣd*, 'resolute,' or (with Holthausen and Schücking) *anrǣd* =*onrǣd*, 'brave.'

1530. *Hȳlāces*. On metrical grounds it is to be presumed that the original *Beowulf* had the Northern form of the name, *Hyglāc* [cf. Sievers in *P.B.B.* x. 463]. This has nearly everywhere been altered by the scribes to *Hygelāc*. We have here a survival of the older spelling: *Hȳlāc* standing for *Hyglāc* as *Wilaf* for *Wiglaf* (l. 2852). [Cf. Klaeber[458].]

1531. *wunden-mǣl*, Kemble$_2$: MS. *wundel mǣl*. Cf. note to l. 1616.

1534. *dōn* for *dōan*, disyllabic. Cf. *gān* (=*gāan* or *gangan*) below, l. 1644.

1537. [*f*]*eaxe*, Rieger: MS. *eaxle*. Rieger's emendation betters the alliteration, and has been adopted by Sweet, and by recent editors. Those who retain the reading *gōda* in l. 758 would however be justified in quoting that line as a parallel to *gefēng þā be eaxle*. To me *feaxe* appears also to give better sense: but this may be disputed. Mr Wyatt writes: 'William Morris agreed with me that it debased Beowulf's character, turning a wrestle into an Old Bailey brawl. Hair-pulling is a hag's weapon.'

1540 feorh-ȝenīðlan, þæt hēo on flet ȝebēah.
Hēo him eft hraþe ⟨h⟩and-lēan forȝeald
ȝrim|man ȝrāpum, ond him tōȝēanes fēnȝ; Fol. 164a.
oferwearp þā wēriȝ-mōd wiȝena strenȝest,
fēþe-cempa, þæt hē on fylle wearð.
1545 Ofsæt þā þone sele-ȝyst, ond hyre sea*x* ȝetēah
brād [*ond*] brūn-ecȝ, wolde hire bearn wrecan,
ānȝan eaferan. Him on eaxle læȝ
brēost-net brōden; þæt ȝebearh fēore,
wið ord ond wið ecȝe inȝanȝ forstōd.
1550 Hæfde ðā forsīðod sunu Ecȝþēowes
under ȝynne ȝrund, ȝēata cempa,
nemne him heaðo-byrne helpe ȝefremede,
here-net hearde, ond hāliȝ ȝod
ȝewēold wīȝ-siȝor, wītiȝ Drihten,
1555 rodera Rǣdend hit on ryht ȝescēd
ȳðelīce, syþðan hē eft āstōd.
XXIII GEseah ðā on searwum siȝe-ēadiȝ bil,

1541. *and-lēan*, Rieger[414]: MS. *hand lean*. Rieger's emendation has been accepted by recent editors, to allow of the word alliterating with *eft*.

The same scribal blunder appears in l. 2094, where again the alliteration demands the vowel: *ondlēan*. Cf. also ll. 2929, 2972.

1543. *oferwearp*: if we retain the MS. reading, with the nominatives *strengest* and *fēþe-cempa* referring to Beowulf, we must translate *oferwearp*, 'stumbled.' But no other instance is to be found of this intransitive use of *oferweorpan*. Hence the emendation of Ettmüller$_2$, *fēþe-cempan*: and of Cosijn[24], *wigena strengel*: 'she overthrew the prince of warriors, the champion' (cf. l. 3115). The added *n* is the slightest of alterations (see note to *rǣswan*, l. 60), but even this is not essential, since *fēþe-cempa* might refer to Grendel's mother.

[For a defence of *oferwearp*='stumbled,' see Schücking in *Engl. Stud.* xxxix. 98.]

1545. *seax*, Ettmüller$_2$, followed by all recent editors except Schücking: MS. *seaxe*. The emendation is not absolutely necessitated by the accusatives *brād, brūn-ecg*, which follow, for such a false concord as an apposition in the acc. following a noun in the dat. can be paralleled. Cf. l. 2703 [and Klaeber[259]]. It is more conclusive that *getēon* seems elsewhere always to take an acc.

1546. *brād* [*ond*] *brūn-ecg*, Heyne, on metrical and syntactical grounds: cf. *Maldon*, 163. Schücking shows that, whereas the conj. may be omitted when the two adjs. are synonymous, or nearly so (e.g. l. 1874), it cannot be omitted when the adjs., as here, signify distinct and independent qualities.

1550. *Hæfde*, optative: 'would have.'

1551. *under gynne grund*, 'under the earth.'

1556. Whether *ȳðelice* should be taken with *gescēd* or with *āstōd* has been much disputed, and does not seem to admit of final decision. The comparison of l. 478, *God ēaþe mæg*, favours the punctuation of the text.

[Cf. Klaeber in *Eng. Stud.* xxxix. 431.]

1557. *on searwum*, 'among other arms' rather than 'during the struggle.

eald sweord eotenisc, ecȝum þyhtiȝ,
wiȝena weorð-mynd; þæt [*wæs*] wǣpna cyst,
1560 būton hit wæs māre ðonne ǣniȝ mon ōðer
tō beadu-lāce ætberan meahte,
ȝōd ond ȝeatolīc, ȝīȝanta ȝeweorc.
Hē ȝefēnȝ þā fetel-hilt, freca Scyldinȝa
hrēoh ond heoro-ȝrim hrinȝ-mǣl ȝebræȝd,
1565 aldres orwēna yrrinȝa |slōh, Fol. 164b.
þæt hire wið halse heard ȝrāpode,
bān-hrinȝas bræc; bil eal ðurhwōd
fǣȝne flǣsc-homan; hēo on flet ȝecronȝ.
Sweord wæs swātiȝ; secȝ weorce ȝefeh.
1570 Līxte se lēoma, lēoht inne stōd,
efne swā of hefene hādre scīneð
rodores candel. Hē æfter recede wlāt,
hwearf þā be wealle; wǣpen hafenade
heard be hiltum Hiȝelāces ðeȝn
1575 yrre ond ān-rǣd —næs sēo ecȝ fracod
hilde-rince, ac hē hraþe wolde
Grendle forȝyldan ȝūð-rǣsa fela,
ðāra þe hē ȝeworhte tō West-Denum
oftor micle ðonne on ǣnne sīð,
1580 þonne hē Hrōðȝāres heorð-ȝenēatas
slōh on sweofote, slǣpende frǣt
folces Deniȝea fȳf-tȳne men,
ond ōðer swylc ūt offerede,
lāðlicu lāc; hē him þæs lēan forȝeald,
1585 rēþe cempa— tō ðæs þe hē on ræste ȝeseah
ȝūð-wēriȝne Grendel licȝan,

1559. [*wæs*] supplied by Grundtvig[290] and Kemble$_1$.

1570. The light, mentioned in ll. 1516–17 (as also in the *Grettis saga*), flashes up when Beowulf slays the monster. But *lēoma* has been taken as 'the flashing sword' [cf. Meissner, *Z.f.d.A.* xlvii. 407], and, since the 'sword of light' is common in story, this seems not unlikely.

1575. *ān-rǣd.* Holthausen, Schücking and Sievers [*Z.f.d.Ph.* xxi. 362] read *an-rǣd*, 'with forward thought,' 'pushing,' 'brave.' Cf. note to l. 1529.

1585. We may take *tō þæs þe* as 'until,' referring back to ll. 1572, *etc.*; or we may take it with *forgeald*, though in the latter case the exact force of *tō þæs þe* is difficult to define: 'he had paid him recompense for that;... insomuch that he now beheld him...' [Earle]; 'he paid him back...to that degree that...' [Clark-Hall]; 'paid him back...where he saw him lying' [Schücking: cf. *Satzverknüpfung*, 58].

aldor-lēasne, swā him ǣr ȝescōd
hild æt Heorote. Hrā wīde spronȝ,
syþðan hē æfter dēaðe drepe þrōwade,
1590 heoro-swenȝ heardne; ond hine þā hēafde becearf.
Sōna þæt ȝesāwon snottre |ceorlas, **Fol. 165a.**
þā ðe mid Hrōðȝāre on holm wliton,
þæt wæs ȳð-ȝeblond eal ȝemenȝed,
brim blōde fāh. Blonden-feaxe
1595 ȝomele ymb ȝōdne on ȝeador sprǣcon,
þæt hiȝ þæs æðelinȝes eft ne wēndon,
þæt hē siȝe-hrēðiȝ sēcean cōme
mǣrne þēoden, þā ðæs moniȝe ȝewearð,
þæt hine sēo brim-wylf ābroten hæfde.
1600 Ðā cōm nōn dæȝes; næs ofȝēafon
hwate Scyldinȝas; ȝewāt him hām þonon
ȝold-wine ȝumena. ȝistas sē*t*an
mōdes sēoce, ond on mere staredon;
wīston ond ne wēndon, þæt hīe heora wine-drihten
1605 selfne ȝesāwon. Þā þæt sweord onȝan

1589. *hē* refers to Grendel.

1590. The subject of *becearf* is Beowulf: *hine* refers to Grendel. Though Grendel, according to ll. 801–3, 987–90, cannot be wounded by the sword of Beowulf or his companions, there is no inconsistency here, since this is a magic sword. [Cf. Jellinek and Kraus in *Z.f.d.A.* xxxv. 278, *etc.*] The decapitation of a corpse is frequent in the Icelandic sagas: it prevents the ghost from 'walking' and doing mischief; and such a motive may, as Gering supposes, be present here also.

1591, *etc.* An attempt has been made to make the story run better by postulating a misplaced leaf, and suggesting that ll. 1591–1605 originally followed l. 1622. [See F. A. Blackburn in *Mod. Phil.* ix. 555–566.] But the story really runs quite well, and the order is the same as in the *Grettis saga.*

1599. *ābroten*, Kemble$_3$: MS. *abreoten.*

1602. *sētan*, Grein$_2$, following Grundtvig[290] *sǣton*: MS. *secan.* A very slight and quite certain correction.

1604. Cosijn [*P.B.B.* viii. 571] praises the 'common sense' of the English editors for having taken *wiston* as = *wȳscton*, 'wished.' So Kemble$_2$ *wiscton*; Sweet *wȳscton.* Recent editors make no alteration in the text, but regard *wiston* as = *wȳscton.* Cf. Sievers$_3$ § 405, N. 8. [Some parallel cases for the disappearance of the *c* are quoted in *Engl. Stud.* xxvii. 218: cf. also *A.f.d.A.* xxiv. 21.] That *wiston* is to be interpreted 'wished' is confirmed by the fact, pointed out by Klaeber[458], that *wȳscað ond wēnað* is a formula found in *Guthlac*, 47.

To interpret *wiston* as 'knew' would necessitate a blending of two constructions: *wiston* would require *ne gesāwon*: *ne wēndon* requires *gesāwon* only. Of course we might assume that the two constructions *had* been confused—confused syntax is common in *Beowulf*: or we might assume that *ne* had dropped out after the *ne* of *selfne*—'they knew, and did not merely expect, that they should not see their lord himself again.' But this gives, after all, only a feeble sense. For why, in that case, did they wait?

æfter heaþo-swāte hilde-ȝicelum,
wīȝ-bil wanian; þæt wæs wundra sum,
þæt hit eal ȝemealt īse ȝelīcost,
ðonne forstes bend Fæder onlǣteð,
1610 onwindeð wǣl-rāpas, sē ȝeweald hafað
sǣla ond mǣla; þæt is sōð Metod.
Ne nōm hē in þǣm wīcum, Weder-ȝēata lēod,
māðm-ǣhta mā, þēh hē þǣr moniȝe ȝeseah,
būton þone hafelan ond þā hilt somod
1615 since fāȝe; sweord ǣr ȝemealt,
forbarn brōden mǣl; wæs þæt blōd |tō þæs hāt,
Fol. 165b.
ǣttren ellor-ȝǣst, sē þǣr inne swealt.
Sōna wæs on sunde, sē þe ǣr æt sæcce ȝebād
wīȝ-hryre wrāðra, wæter ūp þurhdēaf;
1620 wǣron ȳð-ȝebland eal ȝefǣlsod,
ēacne eardas, þā se ellor-ȝāst
oflēt līf-daȝas ond þās lǣnan ȝesceaft.
Cōm þā tō lande lid-manna helm
swīð-mōd swymman, sǣ-lāce ȝefeah,
1625 mæȝen-byrþenne þāra þe hē him mid hæfde.
Eodon him þā tōȝēanes, ȝode þancodon,
ðrȳðlīc þeȝna hēap, þēodnes ȝefēȝon,
þæs þe hī hyne ȝesundne ȝesēon mōston.
Ðā wæs of þǣm hrōran helm ond byrne

1610. *wǣl-rāpas.* Grundtvig[291], not understanding *wǣl*, conjectured *wǣg-rāpas*, which would have the same meaning: 'wave-ropes, ice, icicles.' This was followed by many of the older editors, and was even adopted by Sweet (*Reader*). It is unnecessary, for *wǣl*, 'a deep pool,' occurs not infrequently, the best-known instance being in the *Cottonian Gnomic Verses*, 39: *leax sceal on wǣle mid scēote scrīðan*, 'the salmon must go darting in the pool.' The word is also found in other Germanic dialects, in Scotch ('whyles in a wiel it dimpl't,' Burns, *Halloween*), and in the North of England.

1616. *brōden* for *brogden.* The application of this term to a coat of mail (ll. 552, 1548) shows that the meaning must be 'woven,' 'intertwined': and the analogy of *wunden-mǣl* (l. 1531) or *hring-mǣl* (ll. 1521, 1564, 2037) shows that this is applicable to a sword. It must refer to the damasked, intertwined patterns on the blade, or possibly to the adornment of the hilt. [Cf. Sievers, in *Anglia*, i. 580.]

1616–17. *tō þæs* goes with both *hāt* and *ǣttren*: 'so hot was that blood, and so venomous the strange goblin' (Earle).

1622. *þās lǣnan gesceaft*, 'this transitory world.'

1624–5. To avoid a harsh construction, Bugge[95] would alter *þāra* to *þǣre*: Holthausen *sǣ-lāce* to *sǣ-lāca*.

1630 lunȝre ālȳsed. Laȝu drūsade,
wæter under wolcnum, wæl-drēore fāȝ.
Fērdon forð þonon fēþe-lāstum
ferhþum fæȝne, fold-weȝ mǣton,
cūþe strǣte, cyninȝ-balde men;
1635 from þǣm holm-clife hafelan bǣron
earfoðlīce heora ǣȝhwæþrum
fela-mōdiȝra; fēower scoldon
on þǣm wæl-stenȝe weorcum ȝeferian
tō þǣm ȝold-sele ȝrendles hēafod,
1640 oþ ðæt |semninȝa tō sele cōmon **Fol. 166a.**
frome, fyrd-hwate, fēower-tȳne
ȝēata ȝonȝan; ȝum-dryhten mid,
mōdiȝ on ȝemonȝe, meodo-wonȝas træd.
Ðā cōm in ȝân ealdor ðeȝna,
1645 dǣd-cēne mon dōme ȝewurþad,
hæle, hilde-dēor, Hrōðȝār ȝrētan.
Þā wæs be feaxe on flet boren
ȝrendles hēafod, þǣr ȝuman druncon,
eȝeslīc for eorlum ond þǣre idese mid,
1650 wlite-sēon wrǣtlīc; weras on sāwon.
XXIV BĒOwulf maþelode, bearn Ecȝþēowes:
"Hwæt! wē þē þās sǣ-lāc, sunu Healfdenes,
lēod Scyldinȝa, lustum brōhton
tīres tō tācne, þe þū hēr tō lōcast.
1655 Ic þæt unsōfte ealdre ȝedīȝde,
wiȝȝe under wætere weorc ȝenēþde
earfoðlīce; ætrihte wæs
ȝūð ȝetwǣfed, nymðe mec ȝod scylde.

1634. For *cyning-balde* Grein$_1$, followed by Holthausen$_{1,2}$ and Sedgefield [so Cosijn[25]], reads *cyne-balde*; the meaning is the same, 'royally bold': but the form is more easy to parallel: cf. *cire-* [obviously miswritten for *cine-*] *bald, Andreas*, 171.

1637. All recent editors seem agreed on the punctuation: yet *fela-mōdigra* might well go with *fēower*.

1640. *semninga*: cf. l. 644.

1649. *þǣre idese*, Wealhtheow.

1650. Some editors read *onsāwon*, and make it govern *wlite-sēon*.

1656. Cosijn[25] [partly following Thorpe] suggests *wig under wætere weorce genēbde*, 'with difficulty did I endure the warfare under the water.' Klaeber [*Engl. Stud.* xxxix. 463] tentatively supports *wig*, retaining *weorc*.

1657–8. Grundtvig [1861, p. 152], followed by Bugge [*Tidsskr.* viii. 52] and Sedgefield, takes *wæs* as 1st pers. and reads *gūðe*, 'I was almost

Ne meahte ic æt hilde mid Hruntinȝe
1660 wiht ȝewyrcan, þēah þæt wǣpen duȝe;
ac mē ȝeūðe ylda Waldend,
þæt ic on wāȝe ȝeseah wlitiȝ |hanȝian Fol. 166b.
eald sweord ēacen —oftost wīsode
winiȝea lēasum—, þæt ic ðȳ wǣpne ȝebrǣd.
1665 Ofslōh ðā æt þǣre sæcce, þā mē sǣl āȝeald,
hūses hyrdas. þā þæt hilde-bil
forbarn, broȝden mǣl, swā þæt blōd ȝesprанȝ,
hātost heaþo-swāta. Ic þæt hilt þanan
fēondum ætferede, fyren-dǣda wræc,
1670 dēað-cwealm Deniȝea, swā hit ȝedēfe wæs.
Ic hit þē þonne ȝehāte, þæt þū on Heorote mōst
sorh-lēas swefan mid þīnra secȝa ȝedryht,
ond þeȝna ȝehwylc þīnra lēoda,
duȝuðe ond ioȝoþe; þæt þū him ondrǣdan ne þearft,
1675 þēoden Scyldinȝa, on þā healfe
aldor-bealu eorlum, swā þū ǣr dydest."
Ðā wæs ȝylden hilt ȝamelum rince,
hārum hild-fruman, on hand ȝyfen,
enta ǣr-ȝeweorc; hit on ǣht ȝehwearf,
1680 æfter dēofla hryre, Deniȝea frêan,
wundor-smiþa ȝeweorc; ond þā þās worold ofȝeaf
ȝrom-heort ȝuma, ȝodes ondsaca,

deprived of my fighting power.' But the change is unnecessary: the words mean 'almost was my power of fighting ended.' [See Cosijn[25], who compares *Genesis*, 53.]

1663. The subject of *wīsode* is, of course, *hē* understood, referring to *Waldend*, 1661. Holthausen and Sedgefield, following Sievers, read *oft wīsode*.

1666. *hyrdas*. Pl. for sg.: cf. note to l. 565. Those who hold that in the earliest version of the story both Grendel and his mother were slain in the cave under the water may possibly derive some small support from this pl. form here.

1675. *on þā healfe*, 'from that quarter' (from Grendel and his mother).

1677. *gylden hilt*. It has been suggested tentatively [Kluge in *Engl. Stud.* xxii. 145] that this is a proper noun—the name of the sword: the same name is borne by Rolf's sword *Gullinhjalti* in the *Saga of Rolf Kraki*. But there is no question here of a complete sword, but only of the hilt: cf. ll. 1614, 1668. [See also Sarrazin in *Engl. Stud.* xxxv. 19: Lawrence in *Pub. Mod. Lang. Assoc. Amer.* xxiv. 2, 242–4.]

1681. Müllenhoff[130] and Bugge reject *ond* as superfluous [so Schröer, *Anglia*, xiii. 336; Holthausen and Sedgefield]. It is certainly very unusual at the beginning of a sentence which is only a parallel expansion of what precedes [cf. Schücking in *Satzverk.* p. 83].

morðres scyldiȝ, ond his mōdor ēac,
on ȝeweald ȝehwearf worold-cyninȝa
1685 ðǣm sēlestan be |sǣm twēonum, Fol. 167a.
ðāra þe on Sceden-iȝȝe sceattas dǣlde.
Hrōðȝār maðelode, hylt scēawode,
ealde lāfe, on ðǣm wæs ōr writen
fyrn-ȝewinnes, syðþan flōd ofslōh,
1690 ȝifen ȝēotende, ȝīȝanta cyn;
frēcne ȝefērdon; þæt wæs fremde þēod
ēcean Dryhtne; him þæs ende-lēan
þurh wæteres wylm Waldend sealde.
Swā wæs on ðǣm scennum scīran ȝoldes
1695 þurh rūn-stafas rihte ȝemearcod,
ȝeseted ond ȝesǣd, hwām þæt sweord ȝeworht,
īrena cyst, ǣrest wǣre,
wreoþen-hilt ond wyrm-fāh. Ðā se wīsa spræc

1686. *Sceden-igge*: MS. *scedenigge* in one word. It refers to Schonen (Skåne), now the southernmost province of Sweden, but at this date, and indeed much later, an integral part of Denmark: *Sconia est pulcherrima visu Daniae provincia*—Adam of Bremen. It seems to be used here as a name for the whole Danish realm.

1688, *etc.* Müllenhoff[130] was doubtless right in seeing in these lines a reference to the flood, in which the race of giants and descendants of Cain was destroyed. Cf. *Wisdom*, xiv. 6, 'For in the old time also, when the proud giants perished, the hope of the world, governed by thy hand, escaped in a weak vessel.' Cf. ll. 113, *etc.*, 1562. It is rather fanciful to suppose (as is often done) that there is any reference to that struggle between Gods and Giants which we find in Teutonic mythology.

How Grendel's kin lived through the deluge we need not enquire: surely they were sufficiently aquatic in their habits. Likewise it is too rationalistic to see any discrepancy (as does Müllenhoff[130]) between ll. 1688–9 and ll. 1696–8. The sword bears the names of ancient giants, Grendel's forerunners, of the time of the flood. Swords bearing inscriptions on hilt or blade, either in runic or Roman characters, are not uncommon. A good example is depicted in Clark-Hall (p. 231). Such writing of spells on swords is mentioned in *Salomon and Saturn*, 161, *etc.* and in the *Elder Edda*. Names may also betoken sometimes the owner, sometimes apparently the smith. The name of one smith, *Ulfbern*, is thus known from his swords. [For a representation of two of these, see Gustafson, *Norges Oldtid*, p. 102; cf. too Gering in *Z.f.d.Ph.* xxxviii. 138.]

1691. *frēcne gefērdon* might mean 'they bore themselves overweeningly,' or 'they suffered direly.'

1694. No final explanation of *scennum* is forthcoming. We do not even know whether we should read *on ðǣm, scennum*, 'on it (the sword) by means of wire-work, filigree work,' or *on ðǣm scennum*, 'on the sword guard,' or 'on the metal plates' (with which the hilt was often covered). [This last suggestion is that of Cosijn, *Taalkundige Bijdragen*, I, 286, 1877. He compares Dutch *scheen*, 'an iron band.']

1697. *irena*. See note to l. 673.

1698. *wyrm-fāh*. Intertwined serpent figures were a favourite form of Germanic ornament.

sunu Healfdenes: —swīȝedon ealle—
1700 "Þæt, lā! mæȝ secȝan, sē þe sōð ond riht
fremeð on folce, feor eal ȝemon,
eald ēðel-weard, þæt ðes eorl wǣre
ȝeboren betera. Blǣd is ārǣred
ȝeond wīd-weȝas, wine mīn Bēowulf,
1705 ðīn ofer þēoda ȝehwylce. Eal þū hit ȝeþyldum healdest,
mæȝen mid mōdes snyttrum. Ic þē sceal mīne ȝelǣstan
frēode, swā wit furðum sprǣcon; ðū scealt tō frōfre weorþan
eal lanȝ-twīdiȝ lēodum þīnum,
|hæleðum tō helpe. Ne wearð Heremōd swā Fol. 167b.
1710 eaforum Ecȝwelan, Ār-Scyldinȝum;
ne ȝewēox hē him tō willan, ac tō wæl-fealle
ond tō dēað-cwalum Deniȝa lēodum;
brēat bolȝen-mōd bēod-ȝenēatas,
eaxl-ȝesteallan, oþ þæt hē āna hwearf,
1715 mǣre þēoden, mon-drēamum from.
Ðēah þe hine mihtiȝ ȝod mæȝenes wynnum,
eafeþum stēpte ofer ealle men,

1700. This 'sermon' of Hrothgar (ll. 1700–1768), in which the Christian influence is exceptionally clear (cf. ll. 1745–7 with *Ephesians* vi. 16), was naturally attributed by Müllenhoff[130] to his Interpolator B, whom he regarded as a person at once theologically minded, and yet learned in tradition. [For an eloquent defence of the passage, see Earle, pp. 166–7.]

1702. Bugge [*Tidsskr.* viii. 53] suggests *þæt ðē eorl nǣre.* But the change is unnecessary. In OE. the comparative sometimes appears in a context where, according to our ideas, no real comparison takes place. Cf. ll. 134, 2555 [and see Klaeber[251]].

1707. *freoðe*, 'protection,' is supposed to be the reading of the MS. here. All recent editors read *frēode*, 'friendship' [Grundtvig[292]], which betters the sense. But I think there is no doubt that Thorkelin, Thorpe, and Wülker were right in reading the MS. itself as *freode.* That the contrary view has latterly prevailed is due to Zupitza, who says: 'I think the MS. has *freoðe*, not *freode*; although the left half of the stroke in *ð* has entirely faded, yet the place where it was is discernible, and the right half of it is left.' But the alleged trace of the left half is due only to a crease in the parchment, and of the right half to a mere dot, apparently accidental.

1710. *Ecgwela* is unknown. He is presumably an ancient king of the Danes (*Ār-Scyldingas*), who are thus named the children, or perhaps retainers (cf. l. 1068), of their national hero. Müllenhoff[50] wished to alter to *eafora*, and thus to make Heremod the son of Ecgwela: a change which, after all, leaves us little wiser about either. Cf. l. 901, *etc.*

1714–15. May refer, as Bugge[38] thought, to Heremod's lonely death.

forð ȝefremede, hwæþere him on ferhþe ȝrēow
brēost-hord blōd-rēow; nallas bēaȝas ȝeaf
1720 Denum æfter dōme; drēam-lēas ȝebād,
þæt hē þæs ȝewinnes weorc þrōwade,
lēod-bealo lonȝsum. Ðū þē lǣr be þon,
ȝum-cyste onȝit; ic þis ȝid be þē
āwræc wintrum frōd. Wundor is tō secȝanne
1725 hū mihtiȝ ȝod manna cynne
þurh sīdne sefan snyttru bryttað,
eard ond eorl-scipe; hē āh ealra ȝeweald.
Hwīlum hē on lufan lǣteð hworfan
monnes mōd-ȝeþonc mǣran cynnes,
1730 seleð him on ēþle eorþan wynne,
tō healdanne hlēo-burh wera,
|ȝedēð him swā ȝewealdene worolde dǣlas, Fol. 168a.
sīde rīce, þæt hē his selfa ne mæȝ
his unsnyttrum ende ȝeþencean.
1735 Wunað hē on wiste; nō hine wiht dweleð
ādl ne yldo, ne him inwit-sorh
on sefa[n] sweorceð, ne ȝesacu ōhwǣr,
ecȝ-hete, ēoweð, ac him eal worold

1722. Bugge[38] [following Müllenhoff in *A.f.d.A.* iii. 182] interpreted *lēod-bealo longsum* as the 'eternal pain' which Heremod had to suffer for his evil deeds. But a comparison of l. 1946, where the word is used to signify the 'national evils' of a wicked queen, favours Clark-Hall's translation: 'he suffered misery for his violence, the long-continued trouble of his folk.'

1724. *secganne*. See note to l. 473.

1726. *þurh sīdne sefan*, 'God in his wisdom.'

1728. *on lufan*, apparently 'allows to wander *in delight*,' but there are difficulties both as to this interpretation and also as to the alliteration. Holthausen$_2$ conjectures *on hyhte*, Holthausen$_3$, *on luston* with much the same meaning; Sedgefield$_1$ adopts the conjecture *on hēahlufan* (cf. l. 1954), Sedgefield$_2$, *on hlīsan*, 'in glory.' Grundtvig [1861, p. 59] had suggested *on luste*.

1733. Klaeber [*Archiv*, cxv. 180] takes *his* as referring to *rīce*: 'the proud ruler can conceive no end to his rule.' The same result is achieved by Trautmann's conjecture *sēlþa*, 'prosperity,' for the rather otiose *selfa*.

1734. Thorkelin reads *for his unsnyttrum*, but *for* is not in his transcripts. Kemble omits, Thorpe retains, *for*. There would perhaps have been room for the word in the MS., but in view of the conflicting evidence it seems impossible to decide whether it ever stood there or no. Cf. *Elene*, 947.

1737. MS. defective at edge: *sefa*[*n*], Grundtvig[292], Kemble$_1$.

Grein$_2$, *ne gesaca ōhwǣr ecg-hete ēoweð*, 'nor doth the adversary anywhere manifest deadly hate.' So Sedgefield, and, with slight variation, Holthausen.

wendeð on willan. Hē þæt wyrse ne con,
XXV 1740 oð þæt him on innan ofer-hyȝda dǣl
weaxeð ond wrīdað, þonne se weard swefeð,
sāwele hyrde —bið se slǣp tō fæst—
bisȝum ȝebunden, bona swīðe nēah,
sē þe of flān-boȝan fyrenum scēoteð.
1745 Þonne bið on hreþre under helm drepen
biteran strǣle —him bebeorȝan ne con—
wōm wundor-bebodum werȝan ȝāstes;
þinceð him tō lȳtel, þæt hē lanȝe hēold;
ȝȳtsað ȝrom-hȳdiȝ, nallas on ȝylp seleð
1750 fǣtte bēaȝas, ond hē þā forð-ȝesceaft
forȝyteð ond forȝȳmeð, þæs þe him ǣr ȝod sealde,
wuldres |Waldend, weorð-mynda dǣl. Fol. 168b.
Hit on ende-stæf eft ȝelimpeð,
þæt se līc-homa lǣne ȝedrēoseð,
1755 fǣȝe ȝefealleð; fēhð ōþer tō,
sē þe unmurnlīce mādmas dǣleþ,
eorles ǣr-ȝestrēon, eȝesan ne ȝȳmeð.
Bebeorh þē ðone bealo-nīð, Bēowulf lēofa,
secȝ[*a*] betsta, ond þē þæt sēlre ȝecēos,
1760 ēce rǣdas; oferhȳda ne ȝȳm,
mǣre cempa. Nū is þīnes mæȝnes blǣd

1739. The MS. has a stop after *con*, the usual space with the number xxv, and then a large capital *O*. But it seems impossible to begin a fresh sentence with *oð þæt*, 'until,' as Earle does. Grundtvig [1861, p. 60] and Grein$_2$ make the break in the middle of l. 1739, Heyne after l. 1744.

1740. *ofer-hygda dǣl*, 'a deal of presumption, excessive pride.' Cf. l. 1150, note; and l. 1752 below.

1741. *weard* is apparently 'the conscience' [cf. Schücking, *Satzverk.* 121], hardly, as Sarrazin[103] suggests, 'the guardian angel.'

1746. *him bebeorgan ne con* is apparently a parenthesis and *wōm wundor-bebodum* parallel to *biteran strǣle*. [Cf. Klaeber in *Archiv*, cviii. 369, and Holthausen in *Anglia, Beiblatt*, xiii. 364.]

1747. *wōm* = *wōum*.

1748. Zupitza: '*to* imperfectly erased between *he* and *lange*.'

1750. *fǣtte*, Thorpe: MS. *fædde*.

1756. So in the O.N. *Bjarkamál*, as preserved by Saxo, the niggardly spirit of Röricus (*Hrēðric*) is contrasted with the generosity of Roluo (*Hrōðulf*) who succeeded to his throne, and distributed to his followers all the hoarded treasures of Röricus.

unmurnlīce. It is exceptional for *un* not to take the alliteration (in *Beowulf* only here and in l. 2000). [Cf. Schröder in *Z.f.d.A.* xliii. 377.]

1757. *egesan ne gȳmeð* echoes the idea of recklessness implied in *unmurnlīce*. There is no necessity for emendation.

1759. *secg*[*a*], Sievers [*P.B.B.* x. 312]: MS. *secg*, cf. l. 947.

āne hwīle; eft sōna bið,
þæt þec ādl oððe ecȝ eafoþes ȝetwǣfeð,
oððe fȳres fenȝ, oððe flōdes wylm,
1765 oððe ȝripe mēces, oððe ȝāres fliht,
oððe atol yldo; oððe ēaȝena bearhtm
forsiteð ond forsworceð; semninȝa bið,
þæt ðec, dryht-ȝuma, dēað oferswȳðeð.
Swā ic Hrinȝ-Dena hund missēra
1770 wēold under wolcnum, ond hiȝ wiȝȝe belēac
maniȝum mǣȝþa ȝeond þysne middan-ȝeard
æscum ond ecȝum, þæt ic mē ǣniȝne
under sweȝles beȝonȝ ȝesacan ne tealde.
Hwæt! mē þæs on ēþle edwenden cwōm,
1775 ȝyrn æfter ȝomene, seoþðan Ȝrendel wearð,
eald ȝewinna, inȝenȝa mīn;
|ic þǣre sōcne sinȝāles wæȝ Fol. 169ᵃ.
mōd-ceare micle. Þæs siȝ Metode þanc,
ēcean Dryhtne, þæs ðe ic on aldre ȝebād,
1780 þæt ic on þone hafelan heoro-drēoriȝne
ofer eald ȝewin ēaȝum stariȝe.
Ȝā nū tō setle, symbel-wynne drēoh,
wiȝȝe weorþad; unc sceal worn fela
māþma ȝemǣnra, siþðan morȝen bið."
1785 Ȝēat wæs ȝlæd-mōd, ȝēonȝ sōna tō,

1766–7. Earle and Clark-Hall translate 'glance of eyes will mar and darken all': an allusion to the evil eye. But the verbs seem to be intransitive: translate then 'the light of thine eyes shall fail.'

1767. *semninga*. Cf. l. 644.

1770. *wigge belēac*. It is not clear whether this means that Hrothgar protected his people 'from war' [Klaeber in *Engl. Stud.* xxxix. 464] or 'in war,' 'by his warlike valour.'

The spelling *ig*=*ī* is particularly frequent in this part of the poem: *hig*=*hī* (1596); *wigge*=*wīge* (1656, 1783); *Scedenigge*=*Scedenige* (1686); *sig*=*sī* (1778); *wigtig*=*wītig* (1841). See note to l. 1085.

1774. *edwenden*, Grein: MS. *ed wendan*. Cf. ll. 280, 2188.

1776. Most editors read *eald-gewinna*. I have avoided such compounds except where clearly indicated by the absence of inflection in the adj. Cf. ll. 373, 945, 1781 (where no editor makes a compound of *eald gewin*) with ll. 853, 1381, 2778.

1781. *ofer*, 'after' (cf. l. 2394, note), or possibly 'in spite of' (cf. l. 2409). It seems unnecessary, with Holthausen, to alter to *eald-gewinnan*, on the analogy of l. 1776.

1783. Wülker, *wig-geweorþad*; Holthausen and Sedgefield, partly following Cosijn [*P.B.B.* viii. 571], who compares *Elene*, 150, *wige* [*ge*]*weorþad*. I have followed the MS., for which cf. *Elene*, 1195.

setles nēosan, swā se snottra heht.
Þā wæs eft swā ǣr ellen-rōfum
flet-sittendum fǣʒere ʒereorded
nīowan stefne. Niht-helm ʒeswearc
1790 deorc ofer dryht-ʒumum. Duʒuð eal ārās;
wolde blonden-feax beddes nēosan,
ʒamela Scyldinʒ. Ʒēat uniʒmetes wel,
rōfne rand-wiʒan, restan lyste;
sōna him sele-þeʒn sīðes wērʒum,
1795 feorran-cundum, forð wīsade,
sē for andrysnum ealle beweote*d*e
þeʒnes þearfe, swylce þȳ dōʒore
heaþo-līðende habban scoldon.
Reste hine þā rūm-heort; reced hlīuade
1800 ʒēap ond ʒold-fāh; ʒæst inne swæf,
oþ þæt hrefn blaca heofones wynne
blīð-heort bodode; |ðā cōm beorht scacan Fol. 169b.
[*scīma æfter sceadwe*]. Scaþan ōnetton,
wǣron æþelinʒas eft tō lēodum
1805 fūse tō faren*ne*; wolde feor þanon
cuma collen-ferhð cēoles nēosan.
Heht þā se hearda Hruntinʒ beran
sunu Ecʒlāfes, heht his sweord niman,

1792. *unigmetes*. Most edd. have followed Grundtvig[293] in normalizing *ig* to *ge*. But for the spelling see Sievers$_3$ § 212, N. 1. It shows the beginning of the development of *ge* to *i*, which is commonest after *un*: cf. *unilīc*=*ungelīc*. Holthausen, on the other hand, wishes to write *unigmete* in ll. 2420, 2721, 2728.

1796. *beweotede*, Grundtvig[293], Kemble$_2$: MS. *beweotene*.

1798. *heaþo-līðende*. See note to l. 1862.

1799. For *hlīuade*=*hlīfade*, see Sievers$_3$ § 194.

1803. There is no gap in the MS., but metre and sense both demand some supplement: *scīma æfter sceadwe* was suggested by Sievers [*Anglia*, xiv. 137]. It is satisfactory, and has been generally adopted.

Sedgefield proposes: *scīma scyndan*, 'the gleam hastening.'

Grein$_2$:

ðā cōm beorht [*lēoma*]
scacan [*ofer scadu*].

Heyne:

ðā cōm beorht [*sunne*]
scacan [*ofer grundas*].

The objection to both these last emendations is that they suppose two lacunae instead of one.

1805. *farenne*: MS. *farene ne*.

1808, *etc.* Grundtvig [1861, p. 62] suggested the change of *sunu* to *suna*, and the addition of *hine* after *heht*: Müllenhoff[132] the substitution of *lǣnes* for *lēanes*. With these alterations the meaning would be: *se hearda*

lēoflīc īren; sæᵹde him þæs lēanes þanc,
1810 cwæð, hē þone ᵹūð-wine ᵹōdne tealde,
wīᵹ-cræftiᵹne; nales wordum lōᵹ
mēces eċᵹe. Þæt wæs mōdiᵹ seċᵹ.
Ond þā sīð-frome, searwum ᵹearwe,
wīᵹend wǣron, ēode weorð Denum
1815 æþelinᵹ tō yppan, þǣr se ōþer wæs,
hǣle hilde-dēor Hrōðᵹār ᵹrētte.
XXVI Bēowulf maþelode, bearn Eċᵹþēowes:
"Nū wē sǣ-līðend seċᵹan wyllað
feorran cumene, þæt wē fundiaþ
1820 Hiᵹelāc sēcan; wǣron hēr tela
willum bewenede; þū ūs wel dohtest.
Ᵹif ic þonne on eorþan ōwihte mæᵹ
þīnre mōd-lufan māran tilian,
ᵹumena dryhten, ðonne ic ᵹȳt dyde,
1825 ᵹūð-ᵹeweorca ic bēo ᵹearo sōna.
Ᵹif ic þæt ᵹe|friċᵹe ofer flōda beᵹanᵹ, Fol. 170ᵃ.
þæt þec ymb-sittend eᵹesan þȳwað,
swā þec hetende hwīlum dydon,
ic ðē þūsenda þeᵹna brinᵹe
1830 hæleþa tō helpe. Ic on Hiᵹelāce wā*t*,
Ᵹēata dryhten, þēah ðe hē ᵹeonᵹ sȳ,

(Beowulf) orders Hrunting to be borne to Unferth, bids him take his sword, thanks him for the loan, and courteously speaks well of it.

But the text can be interpreted as it stands. We may render: 'Then the brave one (Beowulf) bade the son of Ecglaf bear Hrunting, bade him take his sword.' Or we may suppose that Beowulf has already returned the sword lent by Unferth. Then *se hearda* (Unferth) presents the sword to Beowulf, who courteously thanks him for the gift. The adj. *hearda* can well be applied to Unferth, whose spirit no one doubts (ll. 1166–7), though admittedly he is inferior to Beowulf, to whom the term *hearda* is even more appropriate (ll. 401, 1963). The change of subject (Unferth subject of *heht*, Beowulf of *sægde*) though harsh, can also be paralleled. That a parting gift should be given to Beowulf by so important an official as Unferth seems quite natural. The relations of Beowulf and Unferth would, with this interpretation, be curiously like those of Odysseus and Euryalus (*Odyssey*, viii. 408, *etc.*). [See Klaeber[460]. Other interpretations have been suggested by Jellinek and Kraus, *Z.f.d.A.* xxxv. 280.]

1816. *hǣle*, Kemble$_2$: MS. *helle.*

1828. Most editors follow Grein in normalizing to *hettende.*

dydon. Metre demands *dǣdon* [Sievers] or *dēdon* [Holthausen].

1830. *wāt*, Kemble$_2$: MS. *wac.*

1831. *dryhten.* We might expect *dryhtne*, in apposition with *Higelāce.* Is this inexact spelling or inexact syntax?

sȳ. See note to l. 435.

folces hyrde, þæt hē mec fremman wile
wordum ond w*eo*rcum, þæt ic þē wel heriȝe,
ond þē tō ȝēoce ȝār-holt bere,
1835 mæȝenes fultum, þǣr ðē bið manna þearf.
Ȝif him þonne Hrēþrīc tō hofum Ȝēata
ȝeþinȝeð, þēodnes bearn, hē mæȝ þǣr fela
frēonda findan; feor-cȳþðe bēoð
sēlran ȝesōhte, þǣm þe him selfa dēah."
1840 Hrōðȝār maþelode him on ondsware:
"Þē þā word-cwydas wiȝtiȝ Drihten
on sefan sende; ne hȳrde ic snotorlīcor
on swā ȝeonȝum feore ȝuman þinȝian;
þū eart mæȝenes stranȝ ond on mōde frōd,
1845 wīs word-cwida. Wēn ic taliȝe,
ȝif þæt ȝeȝanȝeð, þæt ðe ȝār nymeð,
hild heoru-ȝrimme, Hrēþles eaferan,
ādl oþðe īren ealdor ðīnne,
folces hyrde, ond þū þīn feorh hafast,
1850 þæt þē |Sǣ-Ȝēatas sēlran næbben Fol. 170ᵇ.
tō ȝecēosenne cyninȝ ǣniȝne,
hord-weard hæleþa, ȝyf þū healdan wylt
māȝa rīce. Mē þīn mōd-sefa
līcað lenȝ swā wel, lēofa Bēowulf.

1833. *wordum ond weorcum*, Thorpe: MS. *weordum* ⁊ *worcum*. Such interchange of *eo* and *o* was encouraged by the fact that in L.W.S. *weorc* often became *worc*: cf. Sievers$_3$ § 72.

herige, apparently from *herian*, 'praise': 'I will honour thee': but this sense of *herian* is hard to parallel: the comparison of *weorðode* in l. 2096 is hardly sufficient. The difficulty is, however, even greater if we take the verb as *hergian*, 'harry,' and interpret, with Leo and Schücking, 'supply with an army,' or, with Cosijn[27], 'snatch away.' If the symbol ꝥ is sometimes used for *þā* (see note to l. 15) it might be so interpreted here: *þā ic þē wel herige*, i.e. 'when I have so much to report in thy praise,' Hygelac will gladly send help.

1836. *Hrēþrīc*, Grundtvig[294]: MS. *hreþrinc*. Cf. l. 1189.

1837. *geþingeð*, Grein$_2$, partially following Kemble$_2$: MS. *geþinged*.

1840. Since *him* seems hardly sufficient to bear a full stress, Holthausen supposes a lacuna, which he fills thus:

Hrōðgār maþelode, [helm Scyldinga,
eorl æðelum gōd] him on ondsware.

1841. *wigtig*. Kemble$_2$, following Thorpe and followed by most editors, altered to *wittig*. But no change is necessary: *wigtig*=*wītig*. See notes to ll. 1085 and 1770.

1854. Grein (*Sprachschatz*, under *swā*) and Bugge[96], followed by most subsequent editors, *leng swā sēl*, 'the longer the better'—a tempting emendation. But if one finds gross anomalies in accidence in the *Beowulf*, why should one look for a flawless syntax?

1855 Hafast þū ȝefēred, þæt þām folcum sceal,
Ȝēata lēodum ond Ȝār-Denum,
sib ȝemǣne, ond sacu restan,
inwit-nīþas, þe hīe ǣr druȝon;
wesan, þenden ic wealde wīdan rīces,
1860 māþmas ȝemǣne; maniȝ ōþerne
ȝōdum ȝeȝrēttan ofer ȝanotes bæð;
sceal hrinȝ-naca ofer hea*f*u brinȝan
lāc ond luf-tācen. Ic þā lēode wāt
ȝe wið fēond ȝe wið frēond fæste ȝeworhte,
1865 ǣȝhwæs untǣle ealde wīsan."
Đā ȝīt him eorla hlēo inne ȝesealde,
maȝo Healfdenes, māþmas twelfe,
hēt [*h*]ine mid þǣm lācum lēode swǣse
sēcean on ȝesyntum, snūde eft cuman.
1870 Ȝecyste þā cyninȝ æþelum ȝōd,
þēoden Scyldinȝa, ðeȝn[*a*] betstan,
ond be healse ȝenam; hruron him tēaras
blonden-feaxum. Him wæs bēȝa wēn,
ealdum, in-|frōdum, ōþres swīðor, Fol. 171a.
1875 þæt h[*ī*]e seoðða[n nā] ȝesēon mōston,

1857. *gemǣne*, Sievers [*P.B.B.* ix. 140]: MS. *ge mænum.* The scribal error arises naturally from the three preceding datives.

1859–61. Holthausen regards *wesan* and *gegrēttan* as optatives for *wesen, etc.*, 'let there be'.... This compels us to take a pl. *gegrētten* with the sg. *manig.* Such syntax is possible, but it is surely simpler to take *wesan* and *gegrēttan* as infinitives depending on *sceal, sculon*, supplied from l. 1855.

1862. *heafu*, Kluge[190]: MS. *heaþu. Hēaþu* was retained by the older editors, who attributed to it the meaning 'sea' [from *hēah*: *altum, mare*, Grein; cf. also Cosijn, *P.B.B.* xxi. 10]. This would necessitate long *ēa*: which would give us a line, not indeed quite unprecedented, but of an exceedingly unusual type [cf. Sievers in *P.B.B.* x. 235, 245]. In view of this difficulty, and of the fact that no certain instance of *hēaþu*='sea' is forthcoming, it seems best to adopt the conjecture of Kluge[190], *ofer heafu*; especially as that phrase occurs later (l. 2477).

If we could substantiate a word *hēaþu* meaning 'sea,' it would certainly help to explain the compounds *heaþo-līðende* (*Beowulf*, 1798, 2955; *Andreas*, 426) and *heaþo-sigel* (*Riddles*, lxxii. [lxxiii.] 19). We *can* explain these as 'warlike travellers,' *etc.*, but it would be easier if we could take the first element in the compound as meaning 'sea.' For this, however, there seems insufficient evidence.

Sarrazin would retain *ofer heaþu*, 'after the fight' (cf. ll. 1857–8).

1867. *twelfe*: MS. xii.

1868. *hine*, Thorpe: MS. *inne.*

1871. *ðegn*[*a*], Kemble$_1$: MS. *ðegn.*

1875. *h*[*ī*]*e*, Grundtvig[294]: MS. *he.*

seoðða[*n nā*]. Bugge[96] supplied [*nā*] in order to give Hrothgar cause for

mōdiȝe on meþle. Wæs him se man tō þon lēof,
þæt hē þone brēost-wylm forberan ne mehte,
ac him on hreþre hyȝe-bendum fæst
æfter dēorum men dyrne lanȝað
1880 be*a*rn wið blōde. Him Bēowulf þanan,
ȝūð-rinc ȝold-wlanc, ȝræs-moldan træd
since hrēmiȝ; sǣ-ȝenȝa bād
āȝe[*n*]d-frêan, sē þe on ancre rād.
Þā wæs on ȝanȝe ȝifu Hrōðȝāres
1885 oft ȝeæhted. Þæt wæs ān cyninȝ
ǣȝhwæs orleahtre, oþ þæt hine yldo benam
mæȝenes wynnum, sē þe oft maneȝum scōd.
XXVII CWŌM þā tō flōde fela-mōdiȝra
hæȝ-stealdra [*hēap*]; hrinȝ-net bǣron,

his tears. The corner of the parchment is here broken away, and, on palæographical grounds alone, it is likely that a short word has been lost, though, when Thorkelin's transcripts were made, only *seoðða* was to be seen, as now. Bugge's conjecture is therefore almost certain, and has been supported by Sievers [*Anglia*, xiv. 141] and adopted by Trautmann, Holthausen and Sedgefield.

gesēon, 'see each other.' For a parallel usage of *gesēon* see *Andreas*, 1012: also *gedǣlan* in the sense of 'parting from each other' is found in Wulfstan. [Cf. Kluge[190]; Pogatscher in *Anglia*, xxiii. 273, 299.]

1879-80. *bearn*, Grein: MS. *beorn*. The meaning must be 'a secret longing burnt.' *Beorn* is an unexampled form of the pret. of *beornan* [cf. Sievers$_3$ § 386, N. 2], so that it is necessary to make the slight change to either *born* [Thorpe and recent edd.], or *bearn* [Grein], with identical meaning: 'the longing burnt to his blood,' i.e. right into him. So Cosijn[33], comparing, for similar use of *wið*, l. 2673. [Cf. also Sievers, *Z.f.d.Ph.* xxi. 363.] Heinzel [*A.f.d.A.* xv. 190] would interpret *bearn* as in l. 67 (from *be-iernan*, 'to run, occur'): but the alliteration is against this.

To avoid the unusual construction in the second half of this line Sedgefield would read *Gewāt him Bēowulf þanan*. Cf. l. 1601.

1883. *āge*[*n*]*d-frēan*, Kemble$_3$: MS. *agedfrean*.

1885. A colon is usually placed after *geæhted*, and Earle remarks that what follows is 'the gist of their talk as they went.' I take it to be a reflection of the scop.

1887. For *sē*, Grein$_1$ [followed by Holthausen] reads *sēo*, 'old age which has marred so many.' Cf. ll. 1344, 2685.

1889. We should expect *hæg-stealda*, not *hæg-stealdra*, and the reading of the text may well be only a misspelling resulting from the preceding *mōdigra*. It is conceivable, however, that the form is here used adjectivally.

The addition of [*hēap*], a conjecture of Grein$_1$ and Grundtvig [1861, p. 65], is metrically essential.

bǣron. In this type of half-line (A) the second accented syllable is almost always short if preceded by a compound (e.g. l. 838, *gūð-rinc monig*). Sievers [*P.B.B.* x. 224] would accordingly alter to the infinitive here, and in this he is followed by Trautmann (*beran*) and Holthausen (*beron*=*beran*). As Sievers points out, it is possible that the MS. should be read *beron*, as there is a dot under the first part of the diphthong *æ*, which perhaps is intended to cancel it.

1890 locene leoðo-syrcan. Land-weard onfand
eft-sīð eorla, swā hē ǣr dyde;
nō hē mid hearme of hliðes nōsan
|ȝæs[tas] ȝrētte, ac him tōȝēanes rād, Fol. 171b.
cwæð þæt wilcuman Wedera lēodum
1895 scaþan scīr-hame tō scipe fōron.
Þā wæs on sande sǣ-ȝēap naca
hladen here-wǣdum, hrinȝed-stefna
mēarum ond māðmum; mæst hlīfade
ofer Hrōðȝāres hord-ȝestrēonum.
1900 Hē þǣm bāt-wearde bunden ȝolde
swurd ȝesealde, þæt hē syðþan wæs
on meodu-bence *māþme þȳ weorþra*,
yrfe-lāfe. ȝewāt him on *naca*
drēfan dēop wæter, Dena land ofȝeaf.
1905 Þā wæs be mæste mere-hræȝla sum,
seȝl sāle fæst; sund-wudu þunede;
nō þǣr wēȝ-flotan wind ofer ȳðum
sīðes ȝetwǣfde; sǣ-ȝenȝa fōr,
flēat fāmiȝ-heals forð ofer ȳðe,
1910 bunden-stefna ofer brim-strēamas,
þæt hīe ȝēata clifu onȝitan meahton,
cūþe næssas; cēol ūp ȝeþranȝ
lyft-ȝeswenced, on lande stōd.
Hraþe wæs æt |holme hȳð-weard ȝeara, Fol. 172a.
1915 sē þe ǣr lanȝe tīd lēofra manna
fūs æt faroðe feor wlātode;

1893. MS. defective. Thorkelin's transcript A *gæs* (followed by a blank space); Grundtvig[294], *gæs[tas]*.

1895. MS. defective. Thorkelin's transcripts, A *scawan*; B *scaþan*.

1902. *māþme þȳ weorþra*, Thorpe: MS. *maþma þy weorþre*.

1903. *naca*: MS. *nacan*. Grein suggested [*ȳð*]-*nacan* for the alliteration. Rieger[402] suggested *gewāt him on naca*, 'the ship went on': *on* being then an adv., emphatic, and therefore capable of alliterating, as in l. 2523. The alteration is very slight, for elsewhere (ll. 375, 2769) the scribe adds a similar superfluous *n*.

Bugge[97] supposed two half-lines to have been lost.

1913. Sievers [*P.B.B.* ix. 141] would supply [*þæt hē*] *on lande stōd*, comparing l. 404. [So Holthausen and Sedgefield.]

1914. *geara* for *gearu* is probably not a scribal error: *a* for *u* in final unaccented syllables can be paralleled. [Cf. Bugge in *Z.f.d.Ph.* iv. 194; Klaeber, *Anglia*, xxvii. 419.]

1915. *lēofra manna* may depend upon *fūs* or upon *wlātode*, perhaps upon both: 'looked for the beloved men, longing for them.'

sǣlde tō sande sīd-fæþme scip
oncer-bendum fæst, þȳ lǣs hym ȳþa ðrym
wudu wynsuman forwrecan meahte.
1920 Hēt þā ūp beran æþelinȝa ȝestrēon,
frætwe ond fǣt-ȝold; næs him feor þanon
tō ȝesēcanne sinces bryttan,
Hiȝelāc Hrēþlinȝ, þǣr æt hām wunað
selfa' mid ȝesīðum sǣ-wealle nēah.
1925 Bold wæs betlīc, breȝo rōf cyninȝ,
hêa healle, Hyȝd swīðe ȝeonȝ,
wīs, wel þunȝen, þēah ðe wintra lȳt
under burh-locan ȝebiden hæbbe
Hæreþes dohtor; næs hīo hnāh swā þēah,
1930 ne tō ȝnēað ȝifa ȝēata lēodum,
māþm-ȝestrēona. Mōd þrȳðe [*ne*] wæȝ,
fremu folces cwēn, firen ondrysne;

1918. *oncer-bendum*, Grundtvig[295]: MS. *oncear-bendum*.

1923. Trautmann and Holthausen$_2$, *wunade*, following Thorpe and Grein. Sievers [*P.B.B.* ix. 141] regards this and the next line as *oratio recta*. But cf. the present tenses in ll. 1314, 1928, 2495.

Sievers would add *hē* after *þǣr*. [So Holthausen.]

1925. Kemble, *brego-rōf*, 'the king was a famous chieftain' [so Grundtvig 1861, p. 66], but the hyphen is unnecessary. Holthausen$_2$ suggests: *brēc rōf cyning hēan healle*, 'the brave king enjoyed his high hall': *brēc* being an Anglian form for W.S. *brēac*.

1926. Either we must interpret 'high were the halls' (an unusual use of the plural), or (as an instrumental-locative sg.) 'in the high hall'; von Grienberger and Schücking, *hēahealle*, 'in the royal hall'; Sedgefield, *on hēahealle*, with the same meaning; *on hēan healle* has also been suggested [Kluge, Holthausen$_3$].

1928. *hæbbe*. See note to l. 1923, above.

1931. *Mōd þrȳðe* [*ne*] *wæg*, Schücking: 'She [Hygd], brave queen of the folk, had not the mood, the pride of Thryth': MS. *þryðo wæg*. The alteration is essential, for *þrȳðo* is hardly a possible form, whether we take it as a common or a proper noun: the *u* would be dropped after the long syllable, as in *Ōsþrȳþ*, *Cyneþrȳþ* [cf. J. M. Hart in *M.L.N.* xviii. 118; Holthausen[118]]. Yet *þrȳþo* is perhaps conceivable as a diminutive of some form like *þrȳþ-gifu*, as *Ēadu* for *Ēadgifu* [cf. Klaeber in *Anglia*, xxviii. 452]. Both scribes frequently omit *ne*: cf. ll. 44, 1129, 1130, 2006, 2911.

Moreover the emendation explains *fremu folces cwēn*, which seems not very applicable to Thryth: also it explains the otherwise unintelligibly abrupt transition from Hygd to Thryth. Schücking's emendation has been adopted by Holthausen, and is much the best explanation of a difficult passage.

Hygd and Thryth are contrasted, like Sigmund and Heremod.

The violent introduction of this episode from the Offa-cycle points probably to an Anglian origin for our poem. See *Introduction to Beowulf* and *Index of Persons*: Thryth.

1932. Suchier [*P.B.B.* iv. 501] *firen-ondrysne*. We have elision of final

næniȝ þæt dorste dēor ȝenēþan
swǣsra ȝesīða, nefne sīn frêa,
1935 þæt hire an dæȝes ēaȝum starede;
ac him wæl-bende |weotode tealde Fol. 172b.
hand-ȝewriþene; hraþe seoþðan wæs
æfter mund-ȝripe mēce ȝeþinȝed,
þæt hit sceāden-mǣl scȳran mōste,
1940 cwealm-bealu cȳðan. Ne bið swylc cwēnlīc þēaw
idese tō efnanne, þēah ðe hīo ǣnlicu sȳ,
þætte freoðu-webbe fēores onsæce

e before a vowel in ll. 338 and 442. But perhaps the true explanation of the forms *frōfor* in l. 698 and *firen* here will be found in Sievers, § 251, N.

1933. *þæt* anticipates the clause *þæt...starede* (l. 1935).

1934. The MS. may be read either as *sinfrēa*, 'the great lord,' or as *sīn frēa*, 'her lord.' It has been urged that metrically the first is preferable: yet instances enough can be found of the possessive bearing the alliteration. Cf. note to l. 262.

Thryth is the perilous maiden of legend, who slays her wooers, till the destined husband arrives. Her cruel acts are prior to her marriage, and therefore *sinfrēa*, 'the great lord,' i.e. her father, gives good sense. Yet *sīn frēa* is possible—none save Offa, her destined husband, could gaze upon her as a wooer without paying the penalty. [See Cosijn in *P.B.B.* xix. 454; Klaeber in *Anglia*, xxviii. 449; and *Introduction to Beowulf*: Thryth.]

1935. *hire an dæges ēagum starede.* (1) This has been interpreted 'gazed on her by the eyes of day' [Grein, *etc.*]. But *hire an*, 'upon her,' is difficult, for *starian on* takes the *acc.* (cf. ll. 996, 1485). (2) If we read *ān-dæges*, the rendering 'gazed upon her by day,' or 'the whole day,' has been proposed [Leo]: but here again the construction, *starian hire*, 'to gaze upon her,' is inexplicable. The substitution of *hie* for *hire* has therefore been proposed. (3) The MS. certainly divides *an dæges.* But, since little importance can be attached to this spacing, Bugge [*Tidsskr.* viii. 296], following a suggestion of P. A. Munch, supposed *and-ǣges*=*and-ēges*='in the presence of' (cf. Goth. *and-áugjō*), governing *hire*, 'that gazed with his eyes in her presence.' Suchier [*P.B.B.* iv. 502] rendered 'eye to eye,' 'into her face,' apparently following Bugge's etymology.

1938. *æfter mund-gripe*, 'after the arrest' of the presumptuous *gesīð*. [So Bugge in *Z.f.d.Ph.* iv. 207; Suchier in *P.B.B.* iv. 502.] Sedgefield interprets *mund-gripe* as 'strangling,' but this surely would have rendered the subsequent use of the sword (l. 1939) superfluous.

1939. 'That the adorned sword might make it clear,' or 'decide it' [cf. Holthausen in *Anglia*, *Beiblatt*, x. 273] 'and make the death known': *sceāden-mǣl* is undoubtedly a compound, 'a sword adorned with diverse or distinct patterns' (*sceādan*, 'to divide' or 'decide'). [Cf. Sievers in *P.B.B.* x. 313: in xxxvi. 429 he compares *wunden-mǣl*, l. 1531.] The older critics took *sceāden* as a distinct word, qualifying *hit*: 'might make manifest (*scȳran*) the matter when it had been decided,' or 'that it should be decided.' [So Suchier in *P.B.B.* iv. 502, and (with unnecessary emendation, *scyrian*, after Thorpe's glossary) Bugge in *Z.f.d.Ph.* iv. 207.] But these renderings are forced and unnecessary.

The second hand in the MS. begins with *mōste.*

1941. *efnanne.* Cf. note to l. 473.

1942. Kemble$_3$, *onsēce* [so Rieger[403], Schücking and Holthausen]. The emendation is supported by *Juliana*, 679, *fēores onsōhte*, 'deprived of life.'

æfter liʒe-torne   lēofne mannan.
Hūru þæt onhōhsnod[*e*]   Hem*m*inʒes mǣʒ.
1945 Ealo-drincende   ōðer sǣdan,
þæt hīo lēod-bealewa   lǣs ʒefremede.
inwit-nīða,   syððan ǣrest wearð
ʒyfen ʒold-hroden   ʒeonʒum cempan,
æðelum dīore,   syððan hīo Offan flet
1950 ofer fealone flōd   be fæder lāre
sīðe ʒesōhte;   ðǣr hīo syððan well
in ʒum-stōle,   ʒōde mǣre,
līf-ʒesceafta   lifiʒende brēac,
hīold hēah-lufan   wið hæleþa breʒo,
1955 ealles mon-cynnes,   mīne ʒefrǣʒe,
þ*one* sēlestan   bī sǣm twēonum,
eormen-cynnes.   Forðam Offa |wæs,   Fol. 173ᵃ.
ʒeofum ond ʒūðum   ʒār-cēne man,
wīde ʒeweorðod;   wīsdōme hēold
1960 ēðel sīnne.   Þonon *Eomǣr* wōc
hæleðum tō helpe,   Hem[*m*]inʒes mǣʒ,
nefa ʒārmundes,   nīða cræftiʒ.
XXVIII GEwāt him ðā se hearda   mid his hond-scole
sylf æfter sande   sǣ-wonʒ tredan,

1944. *onhōhsnod*[*e*], Thorpe: MS. *on hohsnod*: *onhōhsnian* does not occur elsewhere. Dietrich [*Z.f.d.A.* xi. 413–5] proposed a derivation from *hōsc*=*hūsc*, 'contempt': 'Hemming's kinsman scorned this.' But the best suggestion is that of Bugge [*Tidsskr.* viii. 302] who took *onhōhsnian* as 'hamstring' [cf. O.E. *hōhsinu*: Mod. Eng. *hock*, *hough*: M.H.G. (*ent*) *hāhsenen*]. Bugge interpreted the word in a figurative sense, 'stop' 'hinder.'

Hemminges, $Kemble_1$: MS. *hem ninges*; in l. 1961 the name is written *heminges*. A comparison of the many passages where this name (or its cognates) appears seems to show that the correct form is *Hemming* [cf. Müllenhoff[159]; Sievers in *P.B.B.* x. 501; Binz in *P.B.B.* xx. 172]. The 'kinsman of Hemming' who 'put a stop to' Thryth's cruel dealings is presumably Offa.

1945. *ōðer sǣdan*, 'said yet another thing,' i.e. 'said further'; not 'said otherwise.' The words do not imply contradiction with what was said before. [Cf. Cosijn[28]; Klaeber in *Anglia*, xxviii. 448.]

1956. If we retained the MS. reading *þæs*, we should have to take *brego* also as a *gen.*, which is unparalleled, the word being elsewhere extant only in *nom. voc.* and *acc.* Hence almost all editors follow Thorpe in altering to *þone*.

1960. For the MS. *geomor*, which fails to alliterate, Thorpe read *Ēomēr*; so, simultaneously and independently, Bachlechner [*Germ.* i. 298] *Ēomǣr*. Eomær, in the Mercian genealogies, is grandson of Offa (see *Index of Persons*). The emendation seems fairly certain, though a skilful attempt to defend *geōmor*, as referring to Offa's dulness in his youth, has been made by Miss Rickert [*Mod. Phil.* ii. 54–8].

1965 wīde waroðas; woruld-candel scān,
sigel sūðan fūs; hī sīð drugon,
elne geēodon, tō ðæs ðe eorla hlēo,
bonan Ongenþēoes burgum in innan,
geongne gūð-cyning gōdne gefrunon
1970 hringas dǣlan. Higelāce wæs
sīð Bēowulfes snūde gecȳðed,
þæt ðǣr on worðig wīgendra hlēo,
lind-gestealla, lifigende cwōm,
heaðo-lāces hāl tō hofe gongan.
1975 Hraðe wæs gerȳmed, swā se rīca bebēad,
fēðe-gestum flet innan-weard.
Gesæt þā wið sylfne, sē ðā sæcce genæs,
mǣg wið mǣge, |syððan man-dryhten Fol. 178ᵇ.
þurh hlēoðor-cwyde holdne gegrētte
1980 meaglum wordum. Meodu-scencum hwearf
geond þæt *heal*-reced Hæreðes dohtor,
lufode ðā lēode, līð-wǣge bær
Hǣnum tō handa. Higelāc ongan

1968. The actual 'slayer of Ongentheow' was Eofor: but, according to Germanic custom, the retainer's achievement is attributed to the chief.

1975. *Hraðe* alliterates here with *r*. [Cf. Sievers in *P.B.B.* x. 272.]

1978–80. Ambiguous. [Cf. Klaeber[461].] Does Beowulf greet his 'gracious lord,' or the lord his 'faithful [thane]'?

1981. *heal-reced*, $Kemble_1$: MS. *þæt side ręced.* Zupitza: '*side* added over the line in the same hand I think, but with another ink.' Unless two half lines have been omitted [as Holthausen supposes] the emendation is necessary for the alliteration.

The meaning of the mark in the MS. under the first *e* of *ręced* is uncertain. Zupitza thinks it may be a mere flourish here, whilst it is used to convert *e* into *æ* in *bęl* (l. 2126). In *fæðmię* (l. 2652) also it is ambiguous; the older form of the optative would have been *fæðmiæ* [cf. $Sievers_3$ § 361]. Under the *æ* of *sæcce* (l. 1989) it seems to be meaningless.

1983. *Hǣnum*: MS. *hæ nū.* Zupitza writes: 'between *æ* and *n* a letter (I think *ð*) erased.' There seems to me no doubt as to the erased letter having been *ð*.

Hǣ(ð)num may be a proper name signifying the Geatas, or some tribe associated with them. So Bugge[10], who interprets 'dwellers of the heath' (of Jutland) in accordance with his theory of the Geatas being Jutes. But the evidence for any name corresponding to *Hǣ(ð)nas* in Jutland is not satisfactory. The *Hǣ(ð)nas* would rather be identical with the O.N. *Hei(ð)nir*, the dwellers in *Heiðmǫrk*, Hedemarken, in central Scandinavia. Warriors from this district might well have been in the service of Hygelac; or the poet may be using loosely a familiar epic name. That those *Hǣðnas* were known in O.E. tradition seems clear from *Widsith*, 81. The last transcriber of *Beowulf*, not understanding the name, and taking it for the adj. 'heathen,' may then (as Bugge supposes) have deleted the *ð*, not liking to apply such an epithet as 'heathen' to Hygelac's men.

sīnne ʒeseldan in sele þām hēan
1985 fæʒre fricʒcean, hyne fyrwet bræc,
hwylce Sǣ-ʒēata sīðas wǣron:
"Hū lomp ēow on lāde, lēofa Bīowulf,
þā ðū fǣrinʒa feorr ʒehoʒodest
sæcce sēcean ofer sealt wæter,
1990 hilde tō Hiorote? Ac ðū Hrōðʒāre
wīd-cūðne wēan wihte ʒebēttest,
mǣrum ðēodne? Ic ðæs mōd-ceare
sorh-wylmum sēað, sīðe ne trūwode
lēofes mannes. Ic ðē lanʒe bæd,
1995 þæt ðū þone wæl-ʒǣst wihte ne ʒrētte,
lēte Sūð-Dene sylfe ʒeweorðan
ʒūðe wið ʒrendel. ʒode ic þanc secʒe,
þæs ðe ic ðē ʒesundne ʒesēon mōste."
Bīowulf maðelode, bearn Ecʒðīoes:
2000 |"Þæt is undyrne, dryhten Hiʒelāc, **Fol. 174a.**
[mǣre] ʒemētinʒ, moneʒum fīra,
hwylc [orleʒ-]hwīl uncer ʒrendles
wearð on ðām wanʒe, þǣr hē worna fela
Siʒe-Scyldinʒum sorʒe ʒefremede,
2005 yrmðe tō aldre; ic ðæt eall ʒewræc,
swā [be]ʒylpan [*ne*] þearf ʒrendeles māʒa

Grein$_1$, followed by Sedgefield, conjectured *hælum*, i.e. dat. pl. of *hæle(þ)*, 'man, hero.' But although the *ð* is often dropped in the nom. *hæle* for *hæleþ*, a dat. pl. *hælum* is not paralleled, and if we wish to interpret the passage so, it is probably best, with Holthausen, to alter to *hæleðum*, the only recognised form (cf. l. 2024).

1985. Grein$_2$ puts into parenthesis (*hyne fyrwet bræc*); but ll. 232, 2784, show that these words form a satisfactory parallel to *fricgcean*, and can govern a following interrogative clause.

1989. MS. *sæcce*. See note to l. 1981.

1991. *wīd-*, Thorkelin, Thorpe: MS. *wið*.

1994, *etc.* The 'discrepancy' with ll. 415, *etc.*, 435, *etc.*, is not one which need trouble us much.

1995. *wæl-gǣst*. See note to l. 102.

2001. MS. defective (more than usually) here, and in l. 2002: [*mǣre*], Grein$_1$.

2002. [*orleg-*], Thorpe.

2006. MS. defective, here and in ll. 2007, 2009. Many editors (including recently Sedgefield) follow the reading of Grundtvig[296]: *swā* [*ne*] *gylpan þearf*: *ne* certainly is demanded by the sense, but that *ne* was not the word missing before *gylpan* is implied by Thorkelin's transcripts: A has *swabe*, B *swal*, which seems to show that a portion of a letter involving a long upright stroke could be read.

Against the reading of the text it may be urged that *begielpan* is other-

[ǣniʒ] ofer eorðan   ūht-hlem þone,
sē þe lenʒest leofað   lāðan cynnes
f[ācne] bifonʒen.   Ic ðǣr furðum cwōm
2010 tō ðām hrinʒ-sele   Hrōðʒār ʒrētan;
sōna' mē se mǣra   maʒo Healfdenes,
syððan hē mōd-sefan   mīnne cūðe,
wið his sylfes sunu   setl ʒetǣhte.
Weorod wæs on wynne;   ne seah ic wīdan feorh
2015 under heofones hwealf   heal-sittendra
medu-drēam māran.   Hwīlum mǣru cwēn,
friðu-sibb folca,   flet eall ʒeond-hwearf,
bǣdde byre ʒeonʒe;   oft hīo bēah-wriðan
secʒe |[sealde],   ǣr hīe tō setle ʒēonʒ.   Fol. 174ᵇ.
2020 Hwīlum for [d]uʒuðe   dohtor Hrōðʒāres
eorlum on ende   ealu-wǣʒe bær,
þā ic Frēaware   flet-sittende

wise unknown, and that it assumes an omission of *ne* where there is no gap in the MS. But the reading *ne gylpan þearf* involves difficulties at least as serious: for *gielpan* with an acc. can hardly be paralleled, and we should expect *gylpan ne þearf* (*nē gylpan þearf* would mean 'nor need he boast'). With difficulties thus on both sides there seems no justification for deserting the reading of Thorkelin's transcripts [cf. Klaeber in *Engl. Stud.* xxxix. 431].

2007. [*ǣnig*], Kemble$_1$.

ūht-hlem refers to the crash between Beowulf and Grendel rather than (as Gummere thinks) to the lamentation caused of old by Grendel (ll. 128–9) which is now no longer to be a cause of boasting to his kin: *hlem* signifies 'crash' rather than 'lamentation.'

2009. *f[ācne] bifongen* [so Schücking and Sedgefield] was first suggested by Bugge[97], and is supported by *Juliana*, 350, where the devil is so described.

Thorkelin's transcripts read: A *fæ* and a blank; B *fer*...; Kemble$_{1,2}$ reads *fǣr-bifongen* [so Wülker]; Kemble$_3$, *fen-bifongen*; Grundtvig [1861, p. 69] *fenne bifongen*; *flǣsce bifongen*, 'enveloped in flesh' [Trautmann, Holthausen] is good in itself, but seems incompatible with the (certainly very conflicting) evidence of Thorkelin's transcripts. These leave us in doubt what was the letter following *f*, but make it clear that it was not *l*.

2018. The MS. reading, *bædde*, must mean 'constrained, urged them to be merry.' But the conjecture of Klaeber[461] seems likely: *bǣlde* from *bieldan*, 'encouraged, cheered' [so Holthausen$_{2,3}$, Schücking]. Cf. l. 1094.

2019. MS. defective at corner: Thorpe, [*sealde*]. Many editors have normalized to *hīo*: but the spelling *hīe*=*hēo* can be paralleled. See Sievers$_3$ § 334.

gēong. Note the exceptional indicative here, after *ǣr*.

2020. MS. defective: [*d*]*uguðe*, Grundtvig[296].

2021. *eorlum on ende*. This is often interpreted 'to the earls at the end of the high table,' i.e. 'the nobles.' But the noblest did not sit at the end, but in the middle of the table. [Cf. Clark-Hall.] So the meaning must rather be 'from one end to the other.' Cosijn[29] would alter to *on handa*.

nemnan hȳrde, þǣr hīo [næ]ȝled sinc
hæleðum sealde. Sīo ȝehāten [is],
2025 ȝeonȝ, ȝold-hroden, ȝladum suna Frōdan;
[h]afað þæs ȝeworden wine Scyldinȝa,
rīces hyrde, ond þæt rǣd talað,
þæt hē mid ðȳ wīfe wæl-fǣhða dǣl,
sæcca ȝesette. Oft seldan hwǣr
2030 æfter lēod-hryre lȳtle hwīle
bon-ȝār būȝeð, þēah sēo brȳd duȝe.
Mæȝ þæs þonne ofþyncan ðēoden Heaðobeardna
ond þeȝna ȝehwām þāra lēoda,
þonne hē mid fǣmnan on flett ȝǣð,

2023. MS. defective at edge. [*næ*]*gled*, Grein's emendation, is confirmed by the *næglede bēagas* of the *Husband's Message*, l. 34.

2024. MS. defective at edge, here and in l. 2026: [*is*] supplied by Kluge. So all recent editors. That some such short word has been lost at the edge of the page is clear from the present condition of the MS. and also from Thorkelin's transcripts.

2026. [*h*]*afað*. MS. defective at edge: emendation of Kemble$_1$.

2028. *wæl-fǣhða dǣl*, 'the manifold murderous feuds.' Cf. ll. 1150, 1740, *etc.*, and 2068 below.

2029. *Oft* ends a line in the MS., which is defective at the beginning of the next line, the *s* of *seldan* being gone. In this gap Heyne proposed to insert the negative: *oft* [*nō*] *seldan hwǣr*. For the tautology of 'often, not seldom' cf. l. 3019, and *Psalm* lxxiv. 4. [Other parallels quoted by Bugge, *Tidsskr*. viii. 54.]

Zupitza's view, however, with which I agree, is that there is not room enough for *nō* to have stood before *seldan*, though Kölbing and Wülker think there is. *Oft seldan* has been defended by Kock [*Anglia*, XXVII. 233] as meaning 'as a rule there is seldom a place where the spear rests, when some time has elapsed....' Kock compares l. 3062. [See also Klaeber in *Engl. Stud.* xliv. 125: he would interpret, 'As a rule it is only in rare instances and for a short time that the spear rests....']

Sedgefield suggests *Oft sēlð* (=*sǣlð*) *onhwearf æfter lēodhryre*, 'often has fortune changed after the fall of a prince.' But this hardly gives a satisfactory sense. Fortune did not change. Ingeld was defeated, like his father before him. Better is the conjecture of Holthausen$_2$, *Oft* [*bið*] *sēl and wǣr*, 'often is there prosperity and peace....'

2032. Kemble$_1$, *etc.*, read *ðēodne*. In favour of this it can be urged that *ofðyncan* always takes a dat. of the person, and that *ðēoden* is not a defensible dat. form. But *ðeoden* is the clear reading of the MS., and he would be a bold man who should correct all its grammatical anomalies. [Cf. Klaeber[259].]

2033. *þāra* is emphatic, and hence can take the alliteration.

2034, *etc.* The general drift of what follows is perfectly clear. The Danish warriors, who escort Freawaru into the hall of the Heathobeard king, Ingeld (see *Index of Persons:* Heathobeardan, Ingeld), carry weapons which have been taken from slaughtered Heathobeard champions during the war now ended. An old Heathobeard warrior urges on a younger man (apparently not, in this version, Ingeld himself) to revenge, and in the end this Heathobeard youth slays the Dane, the *fǣmnan þegn* of l. 2059, who wears his father's sword; the slayer (*se ōðer*, l. 2061) takes to flight. Thus the feud breaks out again.

2035 dryht-bearn Dena duȝuða bi werede;
on him ȝladiað ȝomelra lāfe
heard ond hrinȝ-mǣl, Heaðabearna ȝestrēon,
þenden hīe ðām wǣpnum wealdan mōston,
[XXIX] oð ðæt hīe forlǣddan tō ðām lind-pleȝan
2040 swǣse ȝesīðas ond hyra sylfra feorh.
þonne cwið æt bēore, sē ðe bēah |ȝesyhð, Fol. 175ᵃ.

2035. *bi werede*, Grein$_1$: MS. *biwenede.* The alteration is exceedingly slight, since the difference between *n* and *r* in O.E. script is often imperceptible, and may well have been so here in the original from which our *Beowulf* MS. was copied; cf. *urder* for *under*, l. 2755.

Several interpretations of this passage are possible, (1) *hē* refers, not to Ingeld, but proleptically to the *dryht-bearn Dena*: 'when he [viz. the noble scion of the Danes] moves in the hall amid the chivalry [of the Heathobeardan] then doth it displease Ingeld and all his men.'

The repeated *þonne* seems to demand this interpretation. The Heathobeardan have consented to bury the feud, but *when* they see, *then* they can no longer control their fury.

But in spite of this, and of the slightness of the emendation *bi werede*, which it almost necessitates, most critics retain *biwenede.* We may then suppose that (2) *hē* refers to Ingeld, the *ðēoden Heaðobeardna*, and that the conjunction *þæt* has to be understood before *dryht-bearn*: it displeases Ingeld, 'when he goes with his lady into hall, that his high lords should entertain a noble scion of the Danes' [Clark-Hall, following Wyatt]. This interpretation compels us to assume a pl. subject with a sg. verb (*duguða biwenede*), but in subordinate clauses such false concords can be paralleled: cf. ll. 1051, 2130, 2164, 2251, *etc.* For the omission of *þæt* cf. l. 801 and note to l. 2206.

In both (1) and (2) the *dryht-bearn Dena* is a young Danish warrior escorting the queen. Some editors alter to *dryht-beorn*, 'noble warrior.'

(3) Sedgefield takes *dryht-bearn Dena* to mean the young queen herself: 'it displeases Ingeld when he treads the floor with his wife, that noble child of the Danes, attended by her chivalry.' With this interpretation it is, of course, to the *duguð*, and not to the *dryht-bearn*, that the mischief-causing weapons belong.

(4) Klaeber [*Engl. Stud.* xxxix. 465] would take *duguða biwenede* as a parenthesis: 'the heroes are being feasted.' (For the omission of the verb 'to be' Klaeber compares ll. 811, 1559.)

2037. *Heaðabearna.* Thorpe normalized to *Heaðobeardna*, and has been followed by most editors. It is not easy to say whether the omission of the *d* is an error of the scribe, due to confusion with *bearn*, 'child,' or whether it represents the omission of the middle consonant, which frequently occurs when three consonants come together. [Cf. Bülbring, § 533.] The *d* is omitted also below (l. 2067) and was likewise omitted by the scribe of the *Exeter Book* (*Widsith*, 49) who, however, corrected himself.

2038–9. *hie...hie*: the Heathobeard warriors.

2039. The MS. has a large capital *O* at the beginning of this line, such as one finds elsewhere only at the beginning of a new section (cf. l. 1740). But the number XXIX [XXVIIII] is wanting, and the next break is at l. 2144, where the number is XXXI. There are signs of confusion and erasure in the numbering from the twenty-fourth section (l. 1651) up to this point.

2041. *bēah* is strange, for it is a sword, not an armlet, which is the cause of strife. If *bēah* can mean simply 'treasure,' it may be applied to a sword, like *māþðum* (ll. 2055, 1528). [Cf. Klaeber[462].]

Bugge[98] would read *bā*: the old warrior gazes upon both Freawaru and her escort.

eald æsc-wiʒa, sē ðe eall ʒem[an],
ʒār-cwealm ʒumena —him bið ʒrim sefa—,
onʒinneð ʒeōmor-mōd ʒeonʒ[um] cempan
2045 þurh hreðra ʒehyʒd hiʒes cunnian,
wīʒ-bealu weccean, ond þæt word ācwyð.
'Meaht ðū, mīn wine, mēce ʒecnāwan,
þone þīn fæder tō ʒefeohte bær
under here-ʒrīman hindeman sīðe,
2050 dȳre īren, þǣr hyne Dene slōʒon,
wēoldon wæl-stōwe, syððan Wiðerʒyld læʒ,
æfter hæleþa hryre, hwate Scyldunʒas?
Nū hēr þāra banena byre nāt-hwylces
frætwum hrēmiʒ on flet ʒǣð,
2055 morðres ʒylpe[ð], ond þone māðþum byreð,
þone þe ðū mid rihte rǣdan sceoldest.'
Manað swā ond myndʒað mǣla ʒehwylce
sārum wordum, oð ðæt sǣl cymeð,
þæt se fǣmnan þeʒn fore fæder dǣdum
2060 æfter billes bite blōd-fāʒ swefeð,
ealdres scyldiʒ; him se ōðer þonan
losað ||[li]fiʒende, con him land ʒeare. **Fol. 175b.**
Þonne bīoð [ā]brocene on bā healfe

Holthausen's conjecture, *beorn*, referring to the Danish warrior who carries the sword (the *fǣmnan þegn* of l. 2059), has been adopted by Sedgefield, but abandoned by Holthausen himself.

2042. MS. defective at corner and edge: *gem*[*on*], Grundtvig[296].

2044. MS. defective: Kemble_1 and Grein_1 supply *geong*[*um*]. Schücking follows Kemble_2, *geong*[*ne*].

2048. The alliteration is improved by the addition of *frōd* before *fæder* [Holthausen_2, so Sedgefield_2] or of *fǣge* after [Holthausen_3].

2051. *Wiðergyld.* Some of the older editors take the word as a common noun: so Heyne_5, *syððan wiðer-gyld læg*, 'when vengeance failed.' But a hero of this name is mentioned in *Widsith*, 124, although not in a context which would connect him with this story.

2052. *Scyldungas*, in apposition with *Dene*.

2055. MS. defective at edge: *gylpeð*, Kemble_1. For *māðþum* referring to a sword, cf. l. 1528 and *māðþum-sweord*, l. 1023.

2062. MS. defective at corner and edge here and in two following lines. Thorkelin's transcripts, A *figende*, B *eigende*; Thorkelin's edition, *wigende* (so older editors); Heyne, [*li*]*figende*, followed by all recent editors.

him is a kind of 'ethic dative' or 'dative of advantage,' which cannot be rendered in modern English.

2063. Thorkelin's transcripts A and B *orocene* (B with a stop before it); Kemble_1, [*ā*]*brocene* [so Zupitza, Holthausen, Sedgefield]; Schücking, *brocene*. The space indisputably fits *ābrocene* best.

āð-sweord eorla, [syð]ðan Inȝelde
2065 weallað wæl-nīðas, ond him wīf-lufan
æfter cear-wælmum cōlran weorðað.
Þȳ ic Heaðobearna hyldo ne telȝe,
dryht-sibbe dǣl, Denum unfǣcne,
frēond-scipe fæstne. Ic sceal forð sprecan
2070 ȝēn ymbe Ȝrendel, þæt ðū ȝeare cunne,
sinces brytta, tō hwan syððan wearð
hond-rǣs hæleða. Syððan heofones ȝim
ȝlād ofer ȝrundas, ȝæst yrre cwōm,
eatol ǣfen-ȝrom, ūser nēosan,
2075 ðǣr wē ȝesunde sæl weardodon.
Þǣr wæs Hondsciô hil*d* onsǣȝe,
feorh-bealu fǣȝum; hē fyrmest læȝ,
ȝyrded cempa; him Ȝrendel wearð,
mǣrum maȝ*u*-þeȝne, tō mūð-bonan,
2080 lēofes mannes līc eall forswealȝ.
Nō ðȳ ǣr ūt ðā ȝēn īdel-hende
bona blōdiȝ-tōð, bealewa ȝemyndiȝ,
of ðām ȝold-sele ȝonȝan wolde;
ac hē mæȝnes rōf mīn costode,
2085 |ȝrāpode ȝearo-folm. Ȝlōf hanȝode **Fol. 176a.**
sīd ond syllīc, searo-bendum fæst;
sīo wæs orðoncum eall ȝeȝyrwed
dēofles cræftum ond dracan fellum.

2064. *āð-sweord*, Thorkelin's correction: MS. *að-sweorð*.
[*syð*]*ðan*, Kemble$_1$: MS. defective at edge.
2067. *Heaðobearna*. Cf. note to l. 2037.
2076. *Hondsciō* = *Hondsciōe* (dat.): presumably the name of the Geat slain by Grendel (ll. 740, *etc.*). Hondscio is naturally first mentioned by name to the people who know him. Cf. the delay in mentioning the name of Beowulf (l. 343).

Some editors have been unwilling to follow Grundtvig and Holtzmann [*Germ.* VIII. 496] in taking this as a proper name, and have seen in it a reference to Grendel's 'glove' (cf. l. 2085). But a comparison of ll. 2482–3 (*Hǣðcynne wearð...gūð onsǣge*), and the fact that place names postulating a proper name *Hondsciō* are found in both English and German charters (*Andscōheshām*, *Handschuchsheim*) seems to place the matter beyond doubt.

It is necessary, with Holtzmann and Rieger[405], to alter the *hilde* of the MS. to *hild*. [Cf. also Bugge, in *Z.f.d.Ph.* iv. 209.]

2079. *magu*, Kemble$_2$: MS. *mǣrū magū* (i.e. *magum*) *þegne*. But see ll. 293, 408, *etc.* The mistake is due to 'repetition,' *magū* being written, incorrectly, through the influence of *mǣrū*. In l. 158 we have the opposite error of 'anticipation.'

2085. *gearo*, Thorkelin's correction: MS. *geareo*.

Hē mec þǣr on innan unsynniᵹne,
2090 dīor dǣd-fruma, ᵹedōn wolde
maniᵹra sumne; hyt ne mihte swā,
syððan ic on yrre upp-riht āstōd.
Tō lanᵹ ys tō reccenne, hū i[c ð]ām lēod-sceaðan
yfla ᵹehwylces ⟨h⟩ond-lēan forᵹeald;
2095 þǣr ic, þēoden mīn, þīne lēode
weorðode weorcum. Hē on weᵹ losade,
lȳtle hwīle līf-wynna br[ēa]c;
hwæþre him sīo swīðre swaðe weardade
hand on Hiorte, ond hē hēan ðonan,
2100 mōdes ᵹeōmor, mere-ᵹrund ᵹefēoll.
Mē þone wæl-rǣs wine Scildunᵹa
fǣttan ᵹolde fela lēanode,
maneᵹum māðmum, syððan merᵹen cōm,
ond wē tō symble ᵹeseten hæfdon.
2105 Þǣr wæs ᵹidd ond ᵹlēo. ᵹomela |Scildinᵹ, Fol. 176ᵇ.
fela fricᵹende, feorran rehte;
hwīlum hilde-dēor hearpan wynne,
ᵹomen-wudu ᵹrētte, hwīlum ᵹyd āwræc

2093. *reccenne*. See note to l. 473.
MS. defective at edge here and in l. 2097. Thorkelin's transcript A has *huiedam*; *hū i*[*c ð*]*ām* is a conjecture of Grundtvig[297].
2094. *ond-lēan*, Grein$_1$: MS. *hond lean*. The alliteration demands *ond-lēan*, since in the first half-line the alliterating word is certainly *yfla*, not *gehwylces*. See note to l. 1541, where *hand-lēan* has been similarly mis-written.
2097. *br*[*ēa*]*c*. The evidence of Thorkelin's transcripts is confused (*bræc* A; *brene* altered to *brec* B). Probably the MS. had *breac*; it was so read, conjecturally, by Kemble$_1$.
2100. Cf. *eorðan gefēoll*, l. 2834, and *næs gerād*, l. 2898.
2107. Since it is Hrothgar who speaks in ll. 2105–6, and again in ll. 2109–10, it seems natural to assume that he is the *hilde-dēor* who plays the harp in l. 2107; rather than [with Earle, Clark-Hall and others] to assume an abrupt transition from Hrothgar to some anonymous warrior, and back to Hrothgar again. 'The poem gives us no ground,' says Clark-Hall, for attributing to Hrothgar 'the versatility of some modern monarchs.' But surely the burden of proof must lie with those who adopt a confused syntax in order to deny musical talent to Hrothgar. The ideal Germanic monarch was a skilled harper: Gunnar could even play with his toes [*Volsunga saga*, cap. 37]. And, as a matter of history, the last king of the Vandals, driven to the mountains, craved three boons from his conquerors: one was a harp, with which he might bewail his lot. [Procopius, *Bell. Vand.* II. 6.]
2108. *gomen*, Grundtvig[297]: Thorkelin's transcripts A and B *gomel*: *mel* not now visible in MS.

sōð ond sārlīc; hwīlum syllīc spell
2110 rehte æfter rihte rūm-heort cyninȝ;
hwīlum eft onȝan eldo ȝebunden,
ȝomel ȝūð-wiȝa ȝioȝuðe cwīðan
hilde-strenȝo; hreðer inne wēoll,
þonne hē wintrum frōd worn ȝemunde.
2115 Swā wē þǣr inne ondlanȝne dæȝ
nīode nāman, oð ðæt niht becwōm
ōðer tō yldum. Þā wæs eft hraðe
ȝearo ȝyrn-wræce Ȝrendeles mōdor,
sīðode sorh-full; sunu dēað fornam,
2120 wīȝ-hete Wedra. Wīf unhȳre
hyre bearn ȝewræc, beorn ācwealde
ellenlīce; þǣr wæs Æschere,
frōdan fyrn-witan, feorh ūð-ȝenȝe.
Nōðer hȳ hine ne mōston, syððan merȝen cwōm,
2125 dēað-wēriȝne Denia lēode,
bronde forbærnan, ne on bę̄l hladan
lēofne mannan; |hīo þæt līc ætbær Fol. 177a.
fēondes fæð[mum un]der firȝen-strēam.
Þæt wæs Hrōðȝāre hrēowa tornost,
2130 þāra þe lēod-fruman lanȝe beȝēate.
Þā se ðēoden mec ðīne līfe
healsode hrēoh-mōd, þæt ic on holma ȝeþrinȝ
eorl-scipe efnde, ealdre ȝenēðde,
mǣrðo fremede; hē mē mēde ȝehēt.
2135 Ic ðā ðæs wælmes, þe is wīde cūð,
ȝrimne, ȝryrelīcne ȝrund-hyrde fond.

2109. *sārlīc*. Grein$_1$, followed by Holthausen$_{2,3}$, *searolic*, 'cunning.' But note that the song is of an elegiac type. [Cf. Schücking in *Engl. Stud.* xxxix. 12.]

2126. MS. *bę̄l* (= *bæl*). See note to l. 1981.

2128. *fæð[mum]*, Grein$_2$: MS. torn. Grein's emendation probably represents what was actually written in the MS. Zupitza gives the MS. reading as *fæðrunga*, but *unga* rests only upon a conjecture of Thorkelin, and the torn letter, which Thorkelin read as *r*, may well have been part of an *m*.

[*un*]*der*. Kemble$_1$ conjectured [*þǣr un*]*der*.

2131. *ðīne līfe*, 'conjured me by thy life': certainly not, as Earle translates it, 'with thy leave.' For 'leave' is *lēaf*; also, how could Hygelac's leave be obtained?

2136. *grimne*, Thorpe: MS. *grimme*.

þǣr unc hwīle wæs hand-ȝemǣne;
holm heolfre wēoll, ond ic hēafde becearf
in ðām [*ȝrund*-]sele ȝrendeles mōdor
2140 ēacnum ecȝum; unsōfte þonan
feorh oðferede; næs ic fǣȝe þā ȝȳt;
ac mē eorla hlēo eft ȝesealde
māðma meniȝeo, maȝa Healfdenes.
XXXI Swā se ðēod-kyninȝ þēawum lyfde;
2145 nealles ic ðām lēanum forloren hæfde,
mæȝnes mēde, ac hē mē ||[māðma]s ȝeaf, Fol. 177ᵇ.
sunu Healfdenes, on [mīn]ne sylfes dōm,
ðā ic ðē, beorn-cyninȝ, brinȝan wylle,
ēstum ȝeȳwan. ȝēn is eall æt ðē
2150 [*mīnra*] lissa ȝelonȝ; ic lȳt hafo
hēafod-māȝa nefne, Hyȝelāc, ðec."
Hēt ðā in beran eafor, hēafod-seȝn,
heaðo-stēapne helm, hāre byrnan,

2137. All recent editors read *hand gemǣne*, but cf. German *handgemein werden*, 'to fight hand to hand.'

2139. No gap in MS. [*grund-*] was conjectured independently by Grundtvig[297] and Bouterwek (*Z.f.d.A.* xi. 97]; [*gūð-*]*sele*, Thorpe [followed by Holthausen and Sedgefield].

2146. MS. defective in corner here and in next line. Thorkelin's transcripts A and B give ...*is*: Grundtvig[297] and Kemble$_1$ conjecture [*māðma*]*s*.

2147. [*mīn*]*ne*, Kemble$_1$: [*sīn*]*ne*, the emendation of Grundtvig [1861, p. 73], gives inferior sense. With *on* [*mīn*]*ne sylfes dōm* cf. *on hyra sylfra dōm* (*Maldon*, 38), 'at my, their own choice.' Exactly parallel is the old Icelandic legal expression *sjalfdœmi*, 'self-doom,' the right of one party to settle for himself the extent of the compensation he shall receive from the other. So, too, in the 'Cynewulf and Cyneheard' episode in the *A. S. Chronicle*, the pretender offers to the retainers of the fallen king *hiera āgenne dōm*, 'as much as they wished': and in *Beowulf*, 2964, Ongentheow had to abide *Eafores ānne dōm*, 'Eofor did as he chose with him.' [See Kock in *Anglia*, xxvii. 235.] Cf. the Old Saxon phrase *an is selƀēs dōm* [*Heliand*, 4488, where Sievers' note should be compared].

2149–50. Does this mean 'From now on I look to you only for my reward: I have done with foreign service'?

2150. MS. *lissa gelong* is unmetrical [Sievers]: emendations suggested are *lissa gelenge* or *gelongra*: but a simpler remedy is to transpose the words [Holthausen, *Litteraturblatt*, xxi. 61] or to supply *mīnra* before *lissa gelong* [Klaeber, in *J.E.G.Ph.* viii. 257: so Holthausen$_3$].

hafo. For this old form of the 1st pers. sg. cf. ll. 2668, 3000.

2152. Most editors read *eafor-hēafod-segn.* For the triple compound Cosijn[31] compares *wulf-hēafod-trēo.* But, as compounds of three words are as rare in O.E. poetry as compounds of two words are common, it seems better to make two parallels, like *wudu, wæl-sceaftas* (l. 398).

But what is this boar ensign? A helmet, or an ensign with a boar-figure upon it? The last alternative is supported by l. 1021 [Klaeber[462]]. The *eoforcumbul* of *Elene*, 259, hardly helps us, being similarly ambiguous.

ȝūð-sweord ȝeatolīc, ȝyd æfter wræc:
2155 "Mē ðis hilde-sceorp Hrōðȝār sealde,
snotra fenȝel; sume worde hēt,
þæt ic his ǣrest ðē ēst ȝesæȝde;
cwæð þæt hyt hæfde Hioroȝār cyninȝ,
lēod Scyldunȝa, lanȝe hwīle;
2160 nō ðȳ ǣr suna sīnum syllan wolde,
hwatum Heorowearde, þēah hē him hold wǣre,
brēost-ȝewǣdu. Brūc ealles well."
Hȳrde ic, þæt þām frætwum fēower mēaras
lunȝre ȝelīce lāst weardode,
2165 æppel-fealuwe; hē him ēst ȝetēah
mēara ond māðma. Swā sceal |mǣȝ dôn, **Fol. 178ᵃ.**
nealles inwit-net ōðrum breȝdon,
dyrnum cræfte dēað rēn[ian]
hond-ȝesteallan. Hyȝelāce wæs
2170 nīða heardum nefa swȳðe hold,
ond ȝehwæðer ōðrum hrōþra ȝemyndiȝ.
Hȳrde ic, þæt hē ðone heals-bēah Hyȝde ȝesealde,
wrǣtlīcne wundur-māððum, ðone þe him Wealhðēo
ȝeaf,
ðēod[nes] dohtor, þrīo wicȝ somod
2175 swancor ond sadol-beorht; hyre syððan wæs,
æfter bēah-ðeȝe, br[*ē*]ost ȝeweorðod.

2157. The obvious interpretation is: 'that I should first give thee his (Hrothgar's) good wishes.' So Schröer [*Anglia*, xiii. 342], Clark-Hall, Sedgefield. Yet, according to the general rules of O.E. style, we should expect l. 2157 to be parallel to ll. 2158–9. Hence Klaeber[462] [followed by Holthausen] suggests that *ēst* may mean 'bequest,' 'transmission,' "so that the meaning would ultimately come near to Grein's old rendering 'that I the pedigree thereof should report to thee' [Earle]." Note, however, that this old rendering, if right, was so by accident. For the older editors misread *est* as *eft*; and having thus turned a noun into an adv., they were compelled to find a new object by turning the adv. *ǣrest* into a noun, to which they gave the quite unprecedented meaning of 'origin,' 'pedigree.' The separation of *his* from the noun *ēst* with which it goes is unusual.

2164. Sg. verb with pl. noun. Cf. l. 1408 (note). Kemble, *etc.*, *weardodon.*

lungre gelīce. It is not very clear here which is the adv. and which the adj.; are the horses 'quite alike' ('quite' is a rather forced use of *lungre*), or 'alike swift'?

2167. *bregdon* = *bregdan.*
2168. MS. defective at edge: *rēn*[*ian*], Kemble$_3$.
2174. MS. defective at edge: *ðēod*[*nes*], Kemble$_1$.
2175. *sadol-beorht.* Cf. l. 1038.
2176. *br*[*ē*]*ost*, Thorpe, Grundtvig [1861, p. 74]: MS. *brost.*

Swā bealdode bearn Ecȝðēowes,
ȝuma ȝūðum cūð, ȝōdum dǣdum,
drēah æfter dōme, nealles druncne slōȝ
2180 heorð-ȝenēatas; næs him hrēoh sefa,
ac hē man-cynnes mǣste cræfte
ȝin-fæstan ȝife, þe him ȝod sealde,
hēold hilde-dēor. Hēan wæs lanȝe,
swā hyne ȝēata bearn ȝōdne ne tealdon,
2185 ne hyne on medo-bence micles wyrðne
|drihten We*dera* ȝedōn wolde; Fol. 178b.
swȳðe [wēn]don, þæt hē sleac wǣre,
æðelinȝ unfrom. Edwenden cwōm
tīr-ēadiȝum menn torna ȝehwylces.
2190 Hēt ðā eorla hlēo in ȝefetian,
heaðo-rōf cyninȝ, Hrēðles lāfe
ȝolde ȝeȝyrede; næs mid ȝēatum ðā
sinc-māðþum sēlra on sweordes hād
þæt hē on Bīowulfes bearm āleȝde,
2195 ond him ȝesealde seofan þūsendo,
bold ond breȝo-stōl. Him wæs bām samod
on ðām lēod-scipe lond ȝecynde,
eard, ēðel-riht, ōðrum swīðor
sīde rīce, þām ðǣr sēlra wæs.

2200 Eft þæt ȝeīode ufaran dōȝrum
hilde-hlæmmum, syððan Hyȝelāc læȝ,
ond Hear[*dr*]ēde hilde-mēceas
under bord-hrēoðan tō bonan wurdon,

2186. The MS. has *drihten wereda*, which means 'Lord of Hosts' [cf. Rankin in *J.E.G.Ph.* viii. 405]. *Drihten Wedera*, 'lord of the Weder-Geatas,' the emendation of Cosijn[31], seems exceedingly probable [so Holthausen and Sedgefield].

2187. MS. defective at edge: [*wēn*]*don* is Grein's emendation. Cf. *Crist*, 310.

2195. Probably 'seven thousand hides of land,' which would be an earldom of the size of an English county. [Cf. Kluge in *P.B.B.* ix. 191 and 2994.]

2198. *ōðrum*, Hygelac, as being higher in rank (*sēlra*). [Cf. Cosijn[31].]

2202. *Hear*[*dr*]*ēde*, Grundtvig[298]: MS. *hearede*. See l. 2375.

ðā hyne ʒesōhtan on siʒe-þēode
2205 hearde hilde-frecan, Heaðo-Scilfinʒas,
nīða ʒenǣʒdan nefan Hererīces—
syððan |Bēowulfe brāde rīce Fol. 179a.
on hand ʒehwearf. Hē ʒehēold tela
fīftiʒ wintra —wæs ðā frōd cyninʒ,
2210 eald ēþel-weard—, oð ðæt ān onʒan
deorcum nihtum draca rīcs[*i*]an,
sē ðe on hēa[um hǣþe] hord beweotode,

2205. *hilde-frecan*. Many editors follow Grundtvig [1861, p. 75] in altering to *hildfrecan*.

2206. Most editors put a full stop or semicolon at the close of this line, leaving the sense of *þæt geiode, etc.* very lame or very obscure. I take the construction of the passage to be as follows: *þæt* (l. 2200), as in many other passages in the poem (cf. ll. 1846, 1591), has a forward reference like modern 'this,' and is anticipatory of a substantive clause, which usually begins with a correlative *þæt*; this substantive clause is contained in ll. 2207–8 (first half), but the conjunction *þæt* is omitted here, as in l. 2035, perhaps because *syððan* (l. 2207) is correlative with *syððan* (l. 2201).

2207. The folio that begins here (179a), with the word *beowulfe*, is the most defective and illegible in the MS. Moreover, it has been freshened up by a later hand, often inaccurately, so that most of what can be read cannot be depended upon (e.g. in l. 2209 the later hand seems to have changed *wintra* to *wintru*). Zupitza transliterates the readings of the later hand, and gives in footnotes what he can decipher of the original. I reproduce the more important of these notes: but in many cases I have not been able to make out as much of the first hand as Zupitza thought could be seen. All such cases I have noted: whenever Zupitza is quoted *without comment* it may be taken that I agree.

2209. Many editors follow Thorpe in altering *ðā* to *þæt*.

2210. *án* altered to *ón* by later hand. Cf. l. 100.

2211. *rīcs[i]an*, Kemble$_1$: Thorkelin's transcripts A and B *ricsan*: now gone in MS.

2212. MS. very indistinct; nothing in Thorkelin's transcripts A and B between *hea* and *hord*. Zupitza, *hea[ðo]-hlæwe*, and in a foot-note: 'what is left of the two letters after *hea* justifies us in reading them *ðo*.' Zupitza's reading is followed by Holthausen and Schücking. But it gives unsatisfactory sense: what is a 'war-mound'? 'A burial mound about which a fight is going to take place,' says Schücking: this however seems at best a far-fetched explanation.

Further, there is no evidence that the two missing letters were *ðo*: they look much more like *um*. And it is clear that the following word was not *hlæwe*, for the second letter of the word was not *l*. The word might be *hǣþe* or *hope*. Sedgefield reads *hēaum hǣþe*, 'on the high heath.' Indeed *hǣþe* was also read by Sievers in 1870–1 [*P.B.B.* xxxvi. 418], so this is probably to be taken as the MS. reading. However to me it looks more like *hēaum hope*, 'on the high hollow.' The word *hop* survives in Northern English *hope*, 'a hollow among the hills,' as, for example, in Forsyth, *Beauties of Scotland*: 'The hills are everywhere intersected by small streams called *burns*. These, flowing in a deep bed, form glens or hollows, provincially called *hopes*.'

Although by the sea, the mound may have stood in such a hollow or *hope*.

stān-beorh stēapne; stīȝ under læȝ
eldum uncūð. Þǣr on innan ȝīonȝ
2215 niða nāt-hwylc :::::: h ȝefēnȝ
hǣðnum horde hond ::::::::::
since fāhne hē þæt syððan ::::
þ[ēah] ð[e hē] slǣpende besyre[d wur]de
þēofes cræfte; þæt sīo ðīod [onfand]

2213. Later hand *stearne.*

2214–2220. Grein's attempt, in his *Beowulf*, to reconstruct the passage is too remote from the extant indications to need recording. That of Bugge[99–100] is important:

þǣr on innan giong
2215 *niððа nāt-hwylc, nēode tō gefēng*
hǣðnum horde; hond ætgenam
sele-ful since fāh; ne hē þæt syððan āgeaf,
þēah ðe hē slǣpende besyrede hyrde
þēofes cræfte: þæt se ðioden onfand,
2220 *bȳ-folc beorna, þæt hē gebolgen wæs.*

2214. *þǣr on innan giong niða nāt-hwylc* can be made out fairly clearly from the MS. and Thorkelin, and there can be little doubt of the correctness of the emendation to *niðða*, made by Kluge.

But what follows forms one of the severest cruces in *Beowulf.* Holthausen, in part following earlier editors, reads:

[*nēadbys*]*ge feng*
hǣðnum horde; hond [*āfeorde*
seleful] *sincfāh: ne hē þæt syððan* [*ādrēg*]...

'In dire need he (the fugitive) received the heathen hoard; his hand removed the jewelled goblet; nor did he (the dragon) endure it patiently.'...

This may be accepted as giving the general sense correctly, and the words supplied by Holthausen fit exactly into the gaps indicated in Zupitza's transliteration. But a glance at the MS. shows Holthausen's restoration to be impossible: (1) immediately preceding *gefeng* was a letter involving a long upright stroke; i.e. either *b, h, l,* or *þ*: (2) there is not room for [*āfeorde seleful*]; the space allows, according to Sedgefield's reckoning, only 8 or 9 letters, according to mine 10 or 11, but certainly not 13 (as Zupitza thought) or 14: (3) [*ādrēg*] cannot be right, for here again the first letter was *b, h, l,* or *þ*.

The suggestion of Klaeber [*Anglia*, xxviii. 446], *ne hē þæt syððan bemāþ*, seems likely, 'nor did he (the dragon) afterwards conceal it,' i.e. he showed evident tokens of his anger.

Sedgefield reads *sē* [*þe*] *n*[*ē*]*h geþ*[*ra*]*ng* in l. 2215, and does not attempt to fill the gap in l. 2216: *sē þe nēh* is probably right, but the space does not allow of *geþrang*.

2217. Zupitza: '*fah* originally *fac*, but *h* written over *c*.' Heyne-Schücking, *fācne* (cf. l. 2009).

2218. Grein and Heyne make two lines of this, and have been unaccountably followed by their modern editors, Wülker and Schücking. In compensation, however, they make one line of ll. 2228, 2229, so that their reckoning comes right again.

þ[*ēah*] *ð*[*e hē*] was made out with fair probability by Zupitza.

besyre[*d wur*]*de* partly read, partly conjectured, by Kluge.

2219. *sio*, Kluge. According to Thorkelin's transcripts, the MS. had *sie.* The *e* has now gone; *sie* is a possible dialectical form for *sio* (Sievers$_3$ § 337, N. 4), but, as the *e* was almost certainly in the later hand, which has here freshened everything up, we need not hesitate to alter it to *o*.

onfand, Grein$_2$.

2220 [bū-]folc beorna þæt hē ȝebolȝe[n] wæs.
XXXII Nealles mid ȝewealdum wyrm-hord ā*b*ræc
sylfes willum, sē ðe him sāre ȝesceōd;
ac for þrēa-nēdlan þ[ēow] nāt-hwylces
hæleða bearna hete-swenȝeas flēah,
2225 [ærnes] þearfa, ond ðǣr inne feal*h*,
secȝ syn-bysiȝ. Sōna inw[*l*]at*o*de
þæt : : : : ðām ȝyst[e ȝryre-]brōȝa stōd;
hwæðre [earm-]sceapen . . . .
. . . . . . |. . . . . [earm-]sceapen Fol. 179b.
2230 . . . . [þā hyne] se fǣr beȝeat,

2220. *bu-folc* or *by-folc* seems to be the MS. reading, and has been adopted by Bugge and Sedgefield. Holthausen follows Kluge, *burh-folc*: but the faint traces of letters in the MS. certainly favour *by* or *bu*, not *burh*: and there is not room for the longer word. Bugge[100] compares the prose *bifylc*, 'neighbouring people, province': Sedgefield renders *bū-folc*, 'nation, people.'

gebolge[*n*], Grein$_1$.

2221. '*weoldum* the later hand instead of *wealdum*, the *a* being still recognisable.' (Zupitza.)

The later hand reads *wyrm horda cræft*, which makes no sense. Kaluza's *wyrmhord abræc*, 'broke into the dragon's hoard,' has been adopted by Holthausen (q.v.), Schücking, and Sedgefield.

2223. Zupitza, *þ*[*egn*], and in a foot-note: 'the traces of three letters between *þ* and *nat* justify us in reading *egn* (*þegn*, Kemble.)' [So Holthausen and Schücking.] But the last three letters are now quite illegible, and even Thorpe, who made a careful collation of the MS. in 1830, three years before Kemble's first edition, leaves a blank. As *þegn* seems from the whole context to be an unlikely term for the *feā-sceaftum men* (l. 2285), I read *þēow*, following Grundtvig [1861, p. 76]. [So Sedgefield.]

2224. Later hand *fleoh.*

2225. *ærnes* is not clear, but 'to judge from what is left' (Zupitza), and that is exceedingly little, it seems to be correct.

fealh, Grein$_1$: Thorkelin's transcripts A and B *weall.* 'Now only *weal* left, but *w* stands on an original *f*, which is still recognisable' [perhaps]; 'and what seemed to be another *l* in Thorkelin's time may have been the remnant of an original *h*.' (Zupitza.)

2226. The second hand has traced over the obscured letters *sona mwatide*, which, of course, is nonsense. But what does it misrepresent? Thorpe [followed by Schücking: cf. Bugge[101]], *sōna inwlātode*, 'soon he gazed in': Holthausen, *sōna hē wagode*, 'soon he (the dragon) bestirred himself': Sedgefield, *sōna hē þā ēode.*

2227. Grein$_2$ [followed by Holthausen] suggests *þǣr* to fill the gap. But probably more than 3 letters are missing: Sedgefield thinks 4, Zupitza 5; it is difficult to say exactly, as the gap comes at the end of a line in the MS.

'The indistinct letter after *gyst* seems to have been *e*. The traces of the third word allow us to read [with Grein] *gryre*.' (Zupitza.)

2228. 'According to the traces left, the first word [i.e. in the MS. line] may have been *earm*.' (Zupitza.) Kemble gives it as *earm.*

2230. Zupitza reads, with some doubt, '*þa hine* before *se*.' The extant traces seem to me to bear this out with fair certainty.

fǣr; Wülker reads this as *fǣs*; Zupitza: '*fǣs* freshened up, but *s* seems to stand on an original *r*.' There can be little doubt that this is so.

sinc-fæt [ʒeseah]. þǣr wæs swylcra fela
in ðām eorð-[hū]se ǣr-ʒestrēona,
swā hȳ on ʒēar-daʒum ʒumena nāt-hwylc,
eormen-lāfe æþelan cynnes,
2235 þanc-hycʒende þǣr ʒehȳdde,
dēore māðmas. Ealle hīe dēað fornam
ǣrran mǣlum, ond sē ān ðā ʒēn
lēoda duʒuðe, sē ðǣr lenʒest hwearf,
weard wine-ʒeōmor, wēnde þæs ylcan,
2240 þæt hē lȳtel fæc lonʒ-ʒestrēona
brūcan mōste. Beorh eall ʒearo
wunode on wonʒe wæter-ȳðum nēah,
nīwe be næsse, nearo-cræftum fæst;
þǣr on innan bær eorl-ʒestrēona
2245 hrinʒa hyrde hord-wyrðne dǣl,
fǣttan ʒoldes, fēa worda cwæð:
"Heald þū nū, hrūse, nū hæleð ne mōstan,

2231. After the first line of the new folio, the illegibility is confined to the edges of the next three lines.

geseah is Heyne's emendation, but I doubt if there is room either for that or for *genōm*, Holthausen$_{2,3}$. Yet the metre demands two syllables: *funde* might fit in.

2232. [*hū*]*se*, Zupitza's conjecture.

2237. '*Si* the later hand, but *i* seems to stand on an original *e*.' (Zupitza.) I cannot see this.

2239. *wearð* or *weard*: both make sense. 'The last letter of the first word was originally *ð*, although the later hand has not freshened up the stroke through the *d*.' (Zupitza.) I cannot detect traces of this stroke: and *weard* gives the better sense. [Schücking reads *weard* as an emendation.]

'*rihde* the later hand, but *wende* the first.' (Zupitza.) Here again I cannot share this certainty as to the first hand.

Sedgefield was the first to note that the MS. reading *yldan* has been clumsily altered from *ylcan*. Both readings seem to be the work of the second hand. This is 'a genuine little find to rejoice at' [Klaeber in *Engl. Stud.* xliv. 122], as it gives us a simple and intelligible text:—the survivor 'expected the same fate as his friends,' viz. that his tenure of the hoard would be a transitory one.

2244. '*innon* the later hand, but *o* stands on an original *a*.' (Zupitza.) Not clear to me.

2245. Zupitza, *hard-wyrðne*, and in a foot-note: '*w* (or *f*?) and the stroke through *d* in *wyrðne* not freshened up.' The form *hard* occurs nowhere else in *Beowulf*. Klaeber [*Engl. Stud.* xxxix. 431] suggested *hord-wyrðne*, 'worthy of being hoarded,' and this was independently adopted by Sedgefield (both adapting Schücking's *hord, wyrðne dǣl*). The emendation to *hord* had already been made by Bouterwek [*Z.f.d.A.* xi. 98].

2246. '*fec* later hand, but originally *fea*.' (Zupitza.)

2247. '*mæstan* later hand, but I think I see an original *o* under the *æ*; *a* also seems to stand on another vowel, *u* or *o*'? (Zupitza.) All very obscure.

eorla ǣhte. Hwæt, hyt ǣr on ðā
ʒōde beʒēaton; ʒūð-dēað fornam,
2250 feorh-bealo frēcne, fȳra ʒehwylcne
lēoda mīnra, þāra ðe þis [*līf*] ofʒeaf;
ʒesāwon sele-drēam. ||[Ic] nāh hwā sweord weʒe,
oððe fe[o]r[mie] fǣted wǣʒe, [Fol. 180ᵃ.
drync-fæt dēore; duʒ[uð] ellor scōc.
2255 Sceal se hearda helm [hyr]sted ʒolde
fǣtum befeallen; feormynd swefað,
þā ðe beado-ʒrīman bȳwan sceoldon;
ʒe swylce sēo here-pād, sīo æt hilde ʒebād
ofer borda ʒebræc bite īrena,
2260 brosnað æfter beorne; ne mæʒ byrnan hrinʒ
æfter wīʒ-fruman wīde fēran

2250. '*reorh bealc* later hand, but the first *r* stands on an original *f*, and *c* on an original *o*.' (Zupitza.) Not clear to me.

fȳra, Kemble$_3$ [*fira*]: MS. *fyrena*.

2251. *þara*: the later hand has *þana*; 'nor do I see any sign of the third letter having originally been *r*.' (Zupitza.)

[*līf*] supplied by Kemble$_3$: [*lēoht*], Holthausen.

2252. *gesiþa sele-drēam*, a conjecture of Rieger[408], is adopted by Holthausen. Similar in meaning is (*ge*)*secga sele-drēam* [Trautmann: and independently Klaeber, in *J.E.G.Ph.* vi. 193, *Engl. Stud.* xxxix. 465]. This is supported by *Andreas*, 1656, *secga sele-drēam*; a support which is all the more weighty because the writer of the *Andreas* seems to have imitated the *Beowulf*. The change from *gesāwon* to *gesecga* is not as violent as it looks: for *gesāwon* in the Anglian original of *Beowulf* may have been written *gesega*(*n*), which might easily have been miswritten for *gesecga* or *secga*. In support of the text, however, can be quoted *Exod.* 36, *geswǣfon sele-drēamas*.

Holthausen supplies *ic*, as there is a gap in the MS. sufficient for two letters.

2253. MS. defective here and in ll. 2254, 2255, and 2268; *fe*[*o*]*r*[*mie*], the emendation of Grein$_1$, is supported by Zupitza, who shows that the remaining traces of the word in the MS. make *fetige* impossible. A trace of the tail of an *r* certainly seems to be visible. Cf. l. 2256.

A C-line: scan *oððe féormiè*.

2254. *dug*[*uð*], Kemble$_3$.

scōc, Grein$_1$: MS. *seoc*.

2255. *hyr* in [*hyr*]*sted* comes at the end of the line and is now lost. It is recorded by Kemble, after having been conjectured by Grundtvig[299].

2256. Many editors have normalized to *feormiend* or *feormend* (cf. l. 2761) but the change is unnecessary.

2259. *īrena*: Sievers would emend to *īren*[*n*]*a* [*P.B.B.* x. 253]. Cf. note to l. 673.

2260. *æfter beorne*: *æfter* is here certainly temporal: 'after the death of the warrior.' The same interpretation is often given to *æfter wīg-fruman* in the next line. But the two phrases are, in spite of appearances, not parallel: and it is very likely that *æfter wīg-fruman* means 'behind,' 'following,' 'along with,' the warrior. [Cf. Klaeber in *J.E.G.Ph.* vi. 197.] This is certainly the meaning of *hæleðum be healfe*, 'by the heroes' side.'

hæleðum be healfe. N*is* hearpan wyn,
ʒomen ʒlēo-bēames, ne ʒōd hafoc
ʒeond sæl swinʒeð, ne se swifta mearh
2265 burh-stede bēateð. Bealo-cwealm hafað
fela feorh-cynna forð onsended."
Swā ʒiōmor-mōd ʒiohðo mǣnde
ān æfter eallum, unblīðe hwe[arf]
dæʒes ond nihtes, oð ðæt dēaðes wylm
2270 hrān æt heortan. Hord-wynne fond
eald ūht-sceaða opene standan,
sē ðe byrnende biorʒas sēceð,
nacod nīð-draca, nihtes flēoʒeð
fȳre befanʒen; hyne fold-būend
2275 |[swīðe ondrǣ]da[ð]. Hē ʒesēcean sceall Fol. 180b.
[ho]r[d on] hrūsan, þǣr hē hǣðen ʒold
warað wintrum frōd; ne byð him wihte ðȳ sēl.
Swā se ðēod-sceaða þrēo hund wintra
hēold on hrūsa*n* hord-ærna sum
2280 ēacen-cræftiʒ, oð ðæt hyne ān ābealch
mon on mōde; man-dryhtne bær

2262. *Nis*, Thorpe's correction. [Cf. Bugge, *Z.f.d.Ph.* iv. 212.] The MS. has *næs*. Cf. ll. 1923, 2486, where I have kept the MS. reading. But here the change of tense is too harsh.

2266. *forð*: Thorkelin's transcripts A and B, *feorð*; Zupitza reads it as *forð*. He says: 'There is a dot under *e*, which is besides very indistinct.' Underdotting is equivalent to erasure.

2268. *hwe*[*arf*]. Kemble gives the MS. reading as *hweop*, but the confusion of Thorkelin and the evidence of Thorpe make it very doubtful whether the last two letters were clear in Kemble's time; and *hwēop*, which can only mean 'threatened,' makes no sense. It is possible either that *hwēop* was miswritten for *wēop*, 'wept,' or that we should read *hwearf*, 'wandered.' Both suggestions were made by Grein: the first is followed by Holthausen$_2$ and Schücking, the second by Holthausen$_3$ and Sedgefield. It seems on the whole less violent to alter the *op*, which may be a mere guess of Kemble's, than the *h*, which stands clearly in the MS.

2275. MS. defective and illegible. Zupitza's emendation. Cf. *Cottonian Gnomic Verses*, 26: *draca sceal on hlǣwe* | *frōd, frætwum wlanc.*

2276. [*ho*]*r*[*d on*] *hrūsan* was conjectured by Zupitza. *on* had been conjectured by Ettmüller$_3$, *hrūsan* read by Kemble$_1$.

2279. *hrūsan*, Thorkelin's correction: so Kemble, *etc.*: MS. *hrusam*.

2280. Most editors follow Grundtvig[300], and alter to the normal form *ābealh*. Such normalizations would not be tolerated in a Middle English text: why should they be allowed in an Old English one? The spelling *ch* is interesting here; see Sievers$_3$ § 223, N. 1.

2281. Müllenhoff[141] thinks that the lord (*man-dryhten*) to whom the treasure was carried, and who in return gave the fugitive his protection, must be Beowulf. This does not however seem certain. All we know is that the treasure *ultimately* came to Beowulf (l. 2404).

fǣted wǣȝe, frioðo-wǣre bæd
hlāford sīnne. Ðā wæs hord rāsod,
onboren bēaȝa hord; bēne ȝetīðad
2285 fēa-sceaftum men. Frēa scēawode
fīra fyrn-ȝeweorc forman sīðe.
Þā se wyrm onwōc, wrōht wæs ȝenīwad;
stonc ðā æfter stāne, stearc-heort onfand
fēondes fōt-lāst; hē tō forð ȝestōp
2290 dyrnan cræfte dracan hēafde nēah.
Swā mæȝ unfǣȝe ēaðe ȝedīȝan
wēan ond wrǣc-sīð, sē ðe Waldendes
hyldo ȝehealdeþ. Hord-weard sōhte
ȝeorne æfter ȝrunde, wolde ȝuman findan,
2295 þone þe him on sweofote sāre ȝetēode;
hāt ond hrēoh-mǭd |hlǣ*w* oft ymbehwearf Fol. 181a.
ealne ūtan-weardne; n*æs* ðǣr ǣniȝ mon
on þǣre wēstenne. Hwæðre *wīȝes* ȝefeh,

2283–4. The repetition of *hord* may perhaps be an error of the scribe. Holthausen$_1$ [followed by Sedgefield] suggests that the first *hord* is miswritten for *hlæw*, Bugge [*Z.f.d.Ph.* iv. 212] that the second *hord* is miswritten for *dǣl*.

2287. *wrōht wæs genīwad*, 'a new, unheard of, strife arose.' Cf. use of *nīwe* in l. 783. [See Klaeber[463].]

2295. Cosijn[33], followed by recent editors, reads *sār*. But cf. l. 2526.

2296. *hlǣw*, Kemble$_2$. Thorkelin's transcripts A and B have *hlæwum*. Grundtvig (ed. 1861, p. 79) *hlǣw nū*.

ymbehwearf. The *e* of *ymbe* has probably been inserted by a scribe. [Cf. Sievers in *P.B.B.* x. 258, and ll. 2618, 2691, 2734, *Finnsburg*, 35.]

2297. *ealne ūtan-weardne* is unmetrical. Holthausen and Klaeber [*Engl. Stud.* xxxix. 465], following Sievers [*P.B.B.* x. 306; *Metrik*, § 85], propose *eal ūtanweard*; Schücking, *ealne ūtweardne*. Cf. l. 2803.

2297–8. The MS. has: *ne ðær ænig mon on þære westenne hwæðre hilde gefeh.* This gives a sentence without a verb, and a line which fails to alliterate. The reading of the text is that of Schücking's edition [adopted by Holthausen$_2$, vol. II. p. 170]: *næs* is a conjecture of Cosijn[34]. It makes sense and gives a metrical line with the least possible disturbance of the text. Grein reads *ne* [*wæs*] *þǣr*...; Heyne [*wæs*] *on þǣre wēstenne.* Rieger[408] and Sedgefield assume two half-lines to be lost. Sedgefield$_2$ reconstructs the passage thus:

ealne ūtan ne wear[*ð*] *ðǣr ǣnig mon*
on þǣre wēstenne [*wiht gesȳne*].
Hwæðre hilde gefeh [......]
bea[*du*]-*weorces* [*georn*];

þǣre, Thorkelin's transcript B. A has a blank: in the MS. itself nothing is now left but the lower part of the perpendicular stroke of *þ*. Normally *wēsten* is masc. or neut., and many editors accordingly alter *þǣre* to *þǣm*. Considering how corrupt the passage is, little weight can be attached to *wēsten* being treated here as fem.

Grein has *hǣðe*, for the alliteration.

bea[du*we*] weorces; hwīlum on beorh æthwearf,
2300 sinc-fæt sōhte; hē þæt sōna onfand,
ðæt hæfde ʒumena sum ʒoldes ʒefandod,
hēah-ʒestrēona. Hord-weard onbād
earfoðlīce, oð ðæt ǣfen cwōm:
wæs ðā ʒebolʒen beorʒes hyrde,
2305 wolde *se* lāða līʒe forʒyldan
drinc-fæt dȳre. Þā wæs dæʒ sceacen
wyrme on willan; nō on wealle læ[*n*]ʒ
bīdan wolde, ac mid bǣle fōr,
fȳre ʒefȳsed. Wæs se fruma eʒeslīc
2310 lēodum on lande, swā hyt lunʒre wearð
on hyra sinc-ʒifan sāre ʒeendod.
XXXIII ÐĀ se ʒæst onʒan ʒlēdum spīwan,
beorht hofu bærnan; bryne-lēoma stōd
eldum on andan; nō ðǣr āht cwices
2315 lāð lyft-floʒa lǣfan |wolde. **Fol. 181b.**
Wæs þæs wyrmes wīʒ wīde ʒesȳne,
nearo-fāʒes nīð nēan ond feorran,
hū se ʒūð-sceaða ʒēata lēode
hatode ond hȳnde. Hord eft ʒescēat,
2320 dryht-sele dyrnne, ǣr dæʒes hwīle;
hæfde land-wara līʒe befanʒen,
bǣle ond bronde; beorʒes ʒetrūwode,
wīʒes ond wealles; him sēo wēn ʒelēah.
Þā wæs Bīowulfe brōʒa ʒecȳðed
2325 snūde tō sōðe, þæt his sylfes hām,
bolda sēlest, bryne-wylmum mealt,

2299. MS. mutilated: *bea*[*du*]*-weorces*, which was probably the MS. reading, gives a defective line. Holthausen [*Anglia*, xxi. 366] suggests *bea*[*du-*]*weorces* [*georn*]: Klaeber [*J.E.G.Ph.* viii. 257] *beaduwe weorces*, comparing l. 2626 (*gūðe rǣs* for *gūðrǣs*) and for the form *fealuwe*, l. 2165, *bealuwa*, l. 281, *bealewa*, ll. 1946, 2082. The *we* might easily, as Klaeber points out, have been written once only instead of twice (haplography). [So Schücking and Holthausen$_3$.]

2305. *se lāða*, Bugge [*Z.f.d.Ph.* iv. 212], *etc.*: MS. *fela ða.*

2307. *læ*[*n*]*g*: MS. *læg.* Grundtvig[300] [and Kemble$_2$, following Thorpe's suggestion], *leng.* But by adopting the old form *læng* we can keep nearer to the MS. See Sievers$_3$ § 89, N. 5.

2312. *gæst.* See note to l. 102.

2325. *hām.* The MS., by an obvious scribal error, has *him.* Curiously enough Conybeare (p. 150) read the MS. as *hām*, but the credit of making the emendation goes to Grundtvig[301] and Kemble$_2$.

ʒif-stōl ʒēata. Þæt ðām ʒōdan wæs
hrēow on hreðre, hyʒe-sorʒa mǣst;
wēnde se wīsa, þæt hē Wealdende
2330 ofer ealde riht, ēcean Dryhtne,
bitre ʒebulʒe; brēost innan wēoll
þēostrum ʒeþoncum, swā him ʒeþȳwe ne wæs.
Hæfde līʒ-draca lēoda fæsten,
ēa-lond ūtan, eorð-weard ðone,
2335 ʒlēdum forʒrunden; him ðæs ʒūð-kyninʒ,
Wedera þīoden, wræce leornode.
Heht him þā ʒewyrcean wīʒendra hlēo
eall-īrenne, eorla dryhten,
wīʒ-bord wrǣtlīc; |wisse hē ʒearwe, Fol. 182a.
2340 þæt him holt-wudu he[lpan] ne meahte,
lind wið līʒe. Sceolde *lǣn*-daʒa
æþelinʒ ǣr-ʒōd ende ʒebīdan,
worulde līfes, ond se wyrm somod,

2332. The 'dark thoughts' are presumably a foreboding of evil, rather than any rebellion against divine decree, and their unwonted character (*swā him geþȳwe ne wæs*) represents rather a lapse from Beowulf's customary optimism [Cosijn[34]] than from his 'high standard of piety' [Earle].

2334. Arguments as to the home of the Geatas have been based upon interpretations of *ēa-lond* as 'island.' But it seems clear that *ēa-lond* need mean no more than 'water-land,' 'land that is bordered (not of necessity completely) by water,' as first interpreted by Bugge [*Tidsskr.* viii. 68. For other examples, cf. Krapp in *Mod. Phil.* ii. 403 and *N.E.D.*: 'Norway is a great Ilond compassed abowt almost wyth the See'].

ūtan, 'from without,' marks the direction of the dragon's attack.

eorð-weard is parallel to *lēoda fæsten* and *ēa-lond*.

Sedgefield$_2$ reads *ðon[n]e*, comparing for position of *ðonne*, l. 3062; and for *ðone* written for *ðonne*, l. 70.

2336. *leornode*, 'studied, gave his mind to vengeance.' Cf. *Cura Pastoralis*, p. 435, l. 23, *geleornað ðæt hē dēð ðæt yfel*, 'gives his mind to evil.'

2338. *eall-īrenne* (masc.) forms, of course, a false concord with *wīg-bord* (neut.). Hence many editors [Holthausen$_{1,2}$, Schücking, 1910] have adopted the emendation *īrenne scyld* proposed by Bugge [*Tidsskr.* viii. 56]. Bugge subsequently withdrew his suggestion, in favour of the less probable explanation that there was a form *īrenne* standing to *īren* as *ǣtterne* to *ǣtren* [*Z.f.d.Ph.* iv. 213]. But syntax is often confused in *Beowulf*: *scyld* may have been in the author's mind when he wrote *eall-īrenne* [cf. Klaeber in *Engl. Stud.* xxxix. 465]. Holthausen$_3$ reads:

Heht him þā gewyrcean wigena hlēo [*scyld*]
eall-īrenne...

Mr Grattan suggests that *īrenne* is the *weak* neuter; 'that thing all of iron.'

This shield all of iron is, of course, as fictitious as the shield with which Achilles was equipped for his greatest struggle.

2340. MS. defective at corner: *helpan* is Thorkelin's emendation.

2341. *lǣn*, Grundtvig[301], Kemble$_2$: MS. *þend*. Cf. l. 2591.

þēah ðe hord-welan hēolde lange.
2345 Oferhogode ðā hringa fengel,
þæt hē þone wīd-flogan weorode gesōhte,
sīdan herge; nō hē him *þā* sæcce ondrēd,
ne him þæs wyrmes wīg for wiht dyde,
eafoð ond ellen, forðon hē ǣr fela,
2350 nearo nēðende, nīða gedīgde,
hilde-hlemma, syððan hē Hrōðgāres,
sigor-ēadig secg, sele fǣlsode,
ond æt gūðe forgrāp Grendeles mǣgum
lāðan cynnes. Nō þæt lǣsest wæs
2355 hond-gemōt[*a*], þǣr mon Hygelāc slōh,
syððan Gēata cyning gūðe rǣsum,
frēa-wine folca Frēs-londum on,
Hrēðles eafora, hioro-dryncum swealt
bille gebēaten; þonan Bīowulf cōm
2360 sylfes cræfte, sund-nytte drēah;
hæfde him on earme |[āna] þrittig **Fol. 182b.**
hilde geatwa, þā hē tō holme [st]āg.
Nealles Hetware hrēmge þorf[t]on
fēðe-wīges, þe him foran ongēan
2365 linde bǣron; lȳt eft becwōm
fram þām hild-frecan hāmes nīosan.
Oferswam ðā sioleða bigong sunu Ecgðēowes,

2347. *þā*, Kemble$_3$: MS. *þā* (=*þam*). *Sæcc* is fem. (Sievers$_3$ § 258, 1). The scribe, by a natural error, has repeated the stroke (signifying *m*) over the *a*, which he rightly wrote over the *i* in the preceding *hī* (=*him*).

2353. *mægum*. See note to l. 565.

2355. *hond-gemōt*[*a*], Kemble$_1$: MS. *hond gemot*.

2358. 'Died by the thirsty sword' [Earle, Cosijn[35]]. The metaphor is an obvious one. But it is not so easy to say which, of many interpretations, was in the poet's mind. [Cf. Krüger in *P.B.B.* ix. 574: Rickert in *Mod. Phil.* ii. 67.]

2361. MS. defective at corner, here and in two following lines. Before *þrittig*, written xxx in the MS., there seems to be space for some three letters. Grein$_1$ supplied [*āna*].

2362. [*st*]*āg*, Kemble$_2$.

2363. *þorf*[*t*]*on*, Kemble$_1$. *hrēmge þorfton*, 'needed to be exultant.'

2366. Holthausen and Sedgefield take *hild-frecan* as a dat. pl. =*Hetwarum*. But surely it refers to Beowulf: 'few got them back again from that war-wolf to see their homes' [Clark-Hall: so also Earle].

2367. *sioleða bigong*='expanse of still waters,' if the conjecture of Bugge [*Z.f.d.Ph.* iv. 214] be correct, and *sioloð* is to be connected with the Goth. *anasilan*, 'to sink to rest.' [Dietrich in *Z.f.d.A.* xi. 416 would connect with *sol*. But we have seen that the apparent occurrence of this word

earm ān-haʒa, eft tō lēodum,
þǣr him Hyʒd ʒebēad hord ond rīce,
2370 bēaʒas ond breʒo-stōl; bearne ne trūwode,
þæt hē wið æl-fylcum ēþel-stōlas
healdan cūðe, ðā wæs Hyʒelāc dēad.
Nō ðȳ ǣr fēa-sceafte findan meahton
æt ðām æðelinʒe ǣniʒe ðinʒa,
2375 þæt hē Heardrēde hlāford wǣre,
oððe þone cynedōm cīosan wolde;
hwæðre hē hi*ne* on folce frēond-lārum hēold,
ēstum mid āre, oð ðæt hē yldra wearð,
Weder-ʒēatum wēold. Hyne wrǣc-mæcʒas
2380 ofer sǣ sōhtan, suna Ōhteres;
hæfdon hȳ forhealden helm Scylfinʒa,
þone sēlestan sǣ-cyninʒa,
þāra ðe in Swīo-rīce sinc brytnade,
mǣrne |þēoden. Him þæt tō mearce wearð; Fol. 183a.
2385 hē þǣr [*f*]or feorme feorh-wunde hlēat
sweordes swenʒum, sunu Hyʒelāces.
Ond him eft ʒewāt Onʒenðīoes bearn
hāmes nīosan, syððan Heardrēd læʒ,
lēt ðone breʒo-stōl Bīowulf healdan,
2390 ʒēatum wealdan; þæt wæs ʒōd cyninʒ.
XXXIV SĒ ðæs lēod-hryres lēan ʒemunde
uferan dōʒrum; Ēadʒilse wearð

in l. 302 with the meaning of 'sea' is due to a scribal error: and the meaning of 'muddy pool' is equally unsatisfactory here.]

2370–3. *bearn, hē* refer to Heardred: *fēa-sceafte* to the Geatas.

2377. *hine*, Thorpe: MS. *hī* (=*him*).

2379. See *Index of Persons*: Onela, Eadgils.

2383. MS. *ðe ðe*, the first *ðe* at the end of a line, the second at the beginning of the next.

2384. With the punctuation given above, *Him* refers, of course, to Hygelac's son Heardred: 'that was his life's limit.' (For *mearc* in temporal sense cf. *Genesis*, 1719.) Sedgefield takes *him þæt tō mearce wearð* with the preceding lines, interprets *him* as referring to Onela, the *helm Scylfinga*, and *mearc* as meaning 'territory': 'Sweden had become his land,' i.e. Onela had succeeded Ohthere.

2385. *for feorme*. The MS. has *orfeorme*, 'forsaken,' which does not give very satisfactory sense. Grein's *on feorme*, 'at a banquet,' is an improvement. Better still is *for feorme*, 'on account of his hospitality.' This was suggested by Möller [*V.E.* 111], and has been adopted by most recent editors and translators.

2387. *Ongenðioes bearn*, i.e. Onela.

fēa-sceaftum frēond, folce ʒestēpte
ofer sǣ sīde sunu Ōhteres,
2395 wiʒum ond wǣpnum; hē ʒewræc syððan
cealdum cear-sīðum, cyninʒ ealdre bineat.
Swā hē nīða ʒehwane ʒenesen hæfde,
slīðra ʒeslyhta, sunu Ecʒðīowes,
ellen-weorca, oð ðone ānne dæʒ,
2400 þē hē wið þām wyrme ʒeweʒan sceolde.
Ʒewāt þā twelfa sum, torne ʒebolʒen,
dryhten Ʒēata dracan scēawian;
hæfde þā ʒefrunen, hwanan sīo fǣhð ārās,
bealo-nīð biorna; him tō bearme |cwōm Fol. 183b.
2405 māðþum-fæt mǣre þurh ðæs meldan hond.
Sē wæs on ðām ðrēate þreottēoþa secʒ,
sē ðæs orleʒes ōr onstealde;
hæft hyʒe-ʒiōmor sceolde hēan ðonon
wonʒ wīsian. Hē ofer willan ʒīonʒ,
2410 tō ðæs ðe hē eorð-sele ānne wisse,
hlǣw under hrūsan holm-wylme nēh,
ȳð-ʒewinne, sē wæs innan full
wrǣtta ond wīra. Weard unhīore,
ʒearo ʒūð-freca, ʒold-māðmas hēold,
2415 eald under eorðan; næs þæt ȳðe cēap
tō ʒeʒanʒenne ʒumena ǣniʒum.
Ʒesæt ðā on næsse nīð-heard cyninʒ,
þenden hǣlo ābēad heorð-ʒenēatum,
ʒold-wine Ʒēata. Him wæs ʒeōmor sefa,
2420 wǣfre ond wæl-fūs, wyrd unʒemete nēah,

2393. By supporting the exiled Eadgils against Onela, Beowulf obtains his revenge on the Swedes. [Cf. Bugge[13], *etc.*] See note to l. 2603 and *Index of Persons*: Eadgils.

2394. Schücking adopts the emendation of Schröder [*Z.f.d.A.* xliii. 366–7] *ofer sǣ-siðe*, 'after a journey by water.' *Sǣ sīde* means the same as the *wīd wæter* of l. 2473: the lakes which separate Swedes and Geatas.

2395. *hē*, Beowulf: *cyning*, Onela.

2396. *cealdum*: the battle between Eadgils and Onela took place on the ice of Lake Wener; nevertheless, *ceald* may mean nothing more than 'bitter, hostile.'

2401. *twelfa*: MS. XII.

2409. *wong wīsian*. Not merely 'to show,' but 'to lead the way.' Cf. l. 208.

sē ðone ʒomelan ʒrētan sceolde,
sēcean sāwle hord, sundur ʒedǣlan
līf wið līce; nō þon lanʒe wæs
feorh æþelinʒes flǣsce bewunden.
2425 Bīowulf maþelade, bearn Ecʒðēowes:
"Fela ic on ʒioʒoðe ʒūð-rǣsa ʒenæs,
orleʒ-hwīla; ic þæt eall ʒemon.
|Ic wæs syfan-wintre, þā mec sinca baldor, Fol. 184a.
frēa-wine folca, æt mīnum fæder ʒenam;
2430 hēold mec ond hæfde Hrēðel cyninʒ,
ʒeaf mē sinc ond symbel, sibbe ʒemunde;
næs ic him tō līfe lāðra ōwihte
beorn in burʒum þonne his bearna hwylc,
Herebeald ond Hæðcyn, oððe Hyʒelāc mīn.
2435 Wæs þām yldestan unʒedēfe⟨līce⟩
mǣʒes dǣdum morþor-bed strêd,
syððan hyne Hæðcyn of horn-boʒan,
his frēa-wine, flāne ʒeswencte,
miste mercelses ond his mǣʒ ofscēt,
2440 brōðor ōðerne, blōdiʒan ʒāre.
Þæt wæs feoh-lēas ʒefeoht, fyrenum ʒesynʒad,
hreðre hyʒe-mēðe; sceolde hwæðre swā þēah

2421. Many editors follow Grundtvig (ed. 1861, p. 83) and read *sēo*. *Wyrd* is fem. elsewhere, but cf. ll. 1344, 1887, 2685.

2423. *þon lange.* Sedgefield suggests that *þon* may be miswritten for *þon̄* (=*þonne*), which would then be interpreted, as in l. 435, *etc.* 'therefore, and so.' Keeping *þon*, we must interpret 'it was not long from that time.'

2430. Holthausen$_1$ and Sedgefield read

geaf me Hrēðel cyning
sinc ond symbel...

Hrēðel cyning alone is certainly a light line. Holthausen$_{2,3}$ avoids the difficulty by reading *Hrēðel cyning geaf* as the half-line.

2432. *ōwihte.* Sievers [*P.B.B.* x. 256] would read *wihte* for metrical reasons [so Schücking and Holthausen].

2435. *ungedēfelīce* is hypermetrical, and is probably miswritten for *ungedēfe*. [So Holthausen and Schücking: cf. Sievers, *P.B.B.* x. 234: *Metrik*, § 85.]

2438. Bugge[103], thinking *frēa-wine* 'lord' inapplicable, conjectured *frēo-wine* (='noble brother,' Earle), comparing *Genesis* 983, *frēomǣg ofslōh, brōþor sinne.* Keeping *frēa-wine*: 'smote him who should have been his lord.'

2439. *ofscēt*=*ofscēat*.

2441. *fyrenum* in l. 1744 perhaps means 'maliciously,' 'treacherously': but here it has only an intensifying force, 'exceedingly': no malicious intent is attributed to Hæthcyn. [Cf. Klaeber[459].]

2442. Holthausen, in part following Grein$_1$, reads *Hrēðle hygemēðo*, 'a heart sorrow for Hrethel.'

æðelinȝ unwrecen ealdres linnan.
Swā bið ȝeōmorlīc ȝomelum ceorle
2445 tō ȝebīdanne, þæt his byre rīde
ȝionȝ on ȝalȝan; þonne hē ȝyd wrece,
sāriȝne sanȝ, þonne his sunu hanȝað
hrefne tō hrōðre, ond hē him helpan ne mæȝ,
eald ond in-frōd, ǣniȝe ȝefremman.
2450 Symble bið ȝemyndȝad morna ȝehwylce
|eaforan ellor-sīð; ōðres ne ȝȳmeð **Fol. 184b.**
tō ȝebīdanne burȝum in innan
yrfe-weardas, þonne se ān hafað
þurh dēaðes nȳd dǣda ȝefondad.
2455 ȝesyhð sorh-ceariȝ on his suna būre
wīn-sele wēstne, wind-ȝereste
rēote berofene; rīdend swefað,
hæleð in hoðman; nis þǣr hearpan swēȝ,
ȝomen in ȝeardum, swylce ðǣr iū wǣron.
XXXV 2460 GEwīteð þonne on sealman, sorh-lēoð ȝæleð

2444. *Swā*, 'in such wise,' a comparison of Hrethel's woe to that which an old man might feel, if his son were hanged. Gering has seen in the grief of this man a reference to Ermanaric, who (in legend) hanged his son: but the likeness seems remote. Ermanaric was not credited with taking the death of his kin so much to heart.

2445. Cf. *galgan rīdan* in the *Fates of Men*, 33, and the Scandinavian 'kenning' for the gallows, 'Odin's horse.'

2446. MS. *wrece*. Grein *wreceð*, followed by many editors, including Holthausen and Sedgefield. But the change is unnecessary. [Cf. Bugge in *Tidsskr*. viii. 56.]

2448. *helpan*. Kemble$_2$ emended to *helpe*. There is no other certain instance of the weak noun. Possibly the scribe wrote *helpan* for *helpe*, thinking of the infinitive. [Cf. Sievers in *Z.f.d.Ph.* xxi. 357.] Indeed it would be possible to take *helpan* and *fremman* as two parallel infinitives, 'cannot help him, or in any wise support him' (understanding *hine*), as suggested by Kock [*Anglia*, xxvii. 220–1]. But *ǣnige*='in any wise' lacks analogy. [Cf. Klaeber[463] and Sedgefield's note.]

2453. For gen. sg. in *-as* see Sievers$_3$ § 237, N. 1. Cf. ll. 63, 2921.

2454. The alteration of Grundtvig (ed. 1861, p. 84) and Müllenhoff[149], who transposed *dǣda* and *dēaðes*, is not necessary.

2456. Holthausen's *windge reste*, 'windy resting place,' alters the form, but not the meaning.

2457. *rēote*. The best explanation seems to be that of Holthausen, that this is a mistranscription for *rōete* or *rǣte* (see Sievers$_3$ § 27, N.), the old spelling of *rēte* (dat. of **rētu*, 'joy,' from *rōt*, 'cheerful'; cf. *rētan*, 'cheer'). Holthausen's conjecture is supported by such spellings as *beoc* for *bǣc* in the *Codex Aureus Inscription*. An earlier explanation was that of Bugge [*Z.f.d.Ph.* iv. 215], who interpreted *rēot* as 'rest.'

swefað. Klaeber [*Anglia*, xxviii. 446] adopts Grein's emendation *swefeð*, and interprets *rīdend* as 'the rider on the gallows' (cf. l. 2445); *swefað* might be a Northern singular: see Sievers$_3$ § 358, N. 2.

ān æfter ānum; þūhte him eall tō rūm,
wonȝas ond wīc-stede. Swā Wedra helm
æfter Herebealde heortan sorȝe
weallinde wæȝ; wihte ne meahte
2465 on ðām feorh-bonan fǣȝhðe ȝebētan;
nō ðȳ ǣr hē þone heaðorinc hatian ne meahte
lāðum dǣdum, þēah him lēof ne wæs.
Hē ðā mid þǣre sorhȝe, þē him sīo sār belamp,
ȝum-drēam ofȝeaf, Ȝodes lēoht ȝecēas;
2470 eaferum lǣfde, swā dēð ēadiȝ mon,
lond ond lēod-byriȝ, þā hē of līfe ȝewāt.
Þā |wæs synn ond sacu Swēona ond Ȝēata, Fol. 185a.
ofer [w]īd wæter wrōht ȝemǣne,
here-nīð hearda, syððan Hrēðel swealt,
2475 oððe him Onȝenðēowes eaferan wǣran
frome, fyrd-hwate, frēode ne woldon
ofer heafo healdan, ac ymb Hreosnabeorh
eatolne inwit-scear oft ȝefremedon.
Þæt mǣȝ-wine mīne ȝewrǣcan,
2480 fǣhðe ond fyrene, swā hyt ȝefrǣȝe wæs,
þēah ðe ōðer his ealdre ȝebohte,

2466. *heaðorinc* = Hæthcyn.
hatian, 'pursue with hatred.' [Cf. Klaeber in *Archiv*, cix. 305.]

2468. Holthausen$_{1, 2}$ adopts the reading of Rieger (*Lesebuch*), *þe him swā sār belamp*, 'which befel him so sorely': Schücking omits *sīo*, on the ground that an article beginning with *s* is avoided before a substantive so beginning. Holthausen$_3$ accordingly reads *þe him gīo sār belamp.*

2473. MS. defective at corner: [*w*]*īd*, Grundtvig[303]. Thorkelin's transcript B has a blank, but A has *rid*: a mutilated O.E. *w* might easily be mistaken for *r*.

2475. For *oððe* = *ond*, see note to ll. 648–9.
Sedgefield's conjectures, *seoððe* (= *siððan*), or *oð ðæ*[*t*], do not seem necessary. War broke out after Hrethel died, and after Ongentheow's sons had grown to be valiant warriors.
him may be an 'ethic dative' referring to Ongentheow's sons [Bugge in *Tidsskr.* viii. 57], in which case it need not be translated, or it might refer to the Geatas: 'valiant against them.'
Holthausen, following Sievers, spells *Ongenðēos.*

2477. *Hreosnabeorh* is unknown. Sedgefield, following Bugge, reads *Hrefna beorh* (cf. ll. 2925, 2935). But the engagements and the localities seem to have been distinct; *Hreosnabeorh* in the land of the Geatas, *Hrefna wudu* in the land of the Swedes, as Bugge[11] admits.

2478. MS. *ge ge fremedon.* Cf. ll. 986 (see note), 2383.

2479. *mǣg-wine mīne*, i.e. Hæthcyn and Hygelac.

2481. *his. hit*, the emendation of Grein$_1$ [adopted by Schücking and Sedgefield], is certainly an improvement.

heardan cēape; Hæðcynne wearð,
ʒēata dryhtne, ʒūð onsǣʒe.
Þā ic on morʒne ʒefræʒn mǣʒ ōðerne
2485 billes ecʒum on bonan stǣlan,
þǣr Onʒenþēow Eofores nīosað;
ʒūð-helm tōʒlād, ʒomela Scylfinʒ
hrēas [*hilde-*]blāc; hond ʒemunde
fǣhðo ʒenōʒe, feorh-swenʒ ne ofteah.
2490 Ic him þā māðmas, þe hē mē sealde,
ʒeald æt ʒūðe, swā mē ʒifeðe wæs,
lēohtan sweorde; hē mē lond forʒeaf,
eard, ēðel-wyn. Næs him ǣniʒ þearf,
þæt hē tō ʒifðum, oððe tō ʒār-Denum,
2495 oððe in Swīo-rīce, sēcean þurfe
|wyrsan wīʒ-frecan, weorðe ʒecȳpan; Fol. 185b.
symle ic him on fēðan beforan wolde,
āna on orde, ond swā tō aldre sceall
sæcce fremman, þenden þis sweord þolað,
2500 þæt mec ǣr ond sīð oft ʒelǣste,
syððan ic for duʒeðum Dæʒhrefne wearð
tō hand-bonan, Hūʒa cempan.

2484–5. Rightly rendered by Bosworth-Toller: 'One kinsman with the edge of the sword brought home to the slayer the death of the other': but the kinsmen are not Eofor and Wulf, as there explained (since Wulf is not slain), but Hygelac and Hæthcyn. [See Kock in *Anglia*, xxvii. 232: Cosijn[23].]
The episode is narrated more fully later (ll. 2949–2998).

2486. Grein, *nīosade*; but cf. ll. 1923, 1928, *etc.*

2488. No gap in MS: [*hilde-*]*blāc*, Holthausen's conjecture [*Anglia*, xxi. 366], is followed by recent editors. The word is not extant, but cf. *wig-blāc*, *Exodus*, 204.

Bugge [*Tidsskr.* viii. 297] suggested *hrēa-blāc*, 'corpse-pale,' since the repetition *hrēas hrēa-* would have accounted for the scribal blunder; and Grein *heoro-blāc*; but both these stop-gaps are metrically objectionable [the first obviously; for the second cf. Sievers in *P.B.B.* x. 300].

2489. *feorh-sweng.* We should expect the gen. with *oftēon* (see l. 5). We also find the dat. (see l. 1520), and accordingly Holthausen, followed by Sedgefield[1], would write *feorh-swenge* here. [Cf. Sievers in *P.B.B.* xxix. 307.] Yet the change is unnecessary, for the acc. construction is also found.

2490. The episode is ended: *him* refers to Beowulf's lord, Hygelac.

2495. For the present *þurfe*, cf. *hæbbe* (l. 1928).

2500. *Ǣr ond sīð*, 'early and late.'

2501. It is not clear whether *for dugeðum* means 'by reason of my valour' (cf. l. 1206 *for wlenco*), or whether it means 'in the presence of the doughty' (cf. l. 2020 *for duguðe*).

2501–2. Beowulf praises his sword, which has done him good service, early and late, since the time when he slew Dæghrefn. But the following lines show that in this feat Beowulf did not use his sword. Hence some

Nalles hē ðā frætwe Frēs-cyninʒ[*e*],
brēost-weorðunʒe, brinʒan mōste,
2505 ac in *campe* ʒecronʒ cumbles hyrde,
æþelinʒ on elne; ne wæs ecʒ bona,
ac him hilde-ʒrāp heortan wylmas,
bān-hūs ʒebræc. Nū sceall billes ecʒ,
hond ond heard sweord, ymb hord wīʒan."
2510 Bēowulf maðelode, bēot-wordum spræc,
nīehstan sīðe: "Ic ʒenēðde fela
ʒūða on ʒeoʒoðe; ʒȳt ic wylle,
frōd folces weard, fǣhðe sēcan,
mǣrðum fremman, ʒif mec se mān-sceaða
2515 of eorð-sele ūt ʒesēceð."
ʒeʒrētte ðā ʒumena ʒehwylcne,
hwate helm-berend, hindeman sīðe,
swǣse ʒesīðas: "Nolde ic sweord beran,
wǣpen tō wyrme, |ʒif ic wiste hū   Fol. 186a.

editors [e.g. Schücking and Sedgefield$_2$] separate the two sentences by a full stop after *gelǣste*, and take *syððan*, not as a conj., but as an adv.

Yet the sword may have been taken by Beowulf from the dead Dæghrefn: in which case the connection is close enough between ll. 2499 and 2501. [So Rieger[414]; Klaeber in *Archiv*, cxv. 181.]

2503. *ðā frætwe*, 'those famous spoils,' clearly the necklet of ll. 1195, *etc.*, won by Beowulf at Heorot. This had naturally passed to his liege lord. (But note that in ll. 2172, *etc.*, this necklet is said to have been given, not to Hygelac, but to Hygd.) Dæghrefn must be the slayer of Hygelac: as such he would, had he lived, have presented the spoils he had won to his chief. But Beowulf avenged his lord, though the body of Hygelac (*Lib. Monst.*) and his arms (l. 1211) remained with the Frankish foe.

Frēs-cyning[*e*], Grundtvig[304], Kemble$_1$: MS. *frescyning*.

Who is the Frisian king? Does it refer to some tributary prince, or is it a title of the Frankish overlord? Since Dæghrefn is presumably a Frank (*Hūga cempa*) he would present the spoils to his own king, Theodoric the Frank, or to his son Theodobert, who was actually in command. Ll. 1210, 2921 also support the interpretation of *Frēs-cyning* as a reference to the Frankish overlord. But the writer of Beowulf may well have been using traditional names which he himself did not clearly understand.

2505. *Compe* (*campe*), Kemble$_1$: MS. *cempan*. If we keep the MS. reading, we shall have to interpret *cempan*=*cempum*, and render 'among the warriors' [von Grienberger, Schücking, 1908: cf. *Engl. Stud.* xlii. 110]. But *in* in this sense of 'among' seems unprecedented [Sievers in *P.B.B.* xxxvi. 409–10, as Schücking now admits].

2505–6. *cumbles hyrde*, *æþeling*, refer to Dæghrefn.

2509. Morgan [*P.B.B.* xxxiii. 105] and Holthausen suggest *heard-sweord*, for the metre.

2514. Kemble$_2$, *mǣrðo*, supported by Bugge[104], and all recent editors, on the analogy of ll. 2134, 2645. But the argument from analogy may be pushed too far, and it is even possible that *fremman* is intrans., as in l. 1003.

2520 wið ðām āȝlǣcean elles meahte
ȝylpe wiðȝrīpan, swā ic ȝiō wið ȝrendle dyde;
ac ic ðǣr heaðu-fȳres hātes wēne,
[*o*]reðes ond *ā*ttres; forðon ic mē on hafu
bord ond byrnan. Nelle ic beorȝes weard
2525 oferflēon fōtes trem, ac unc [*furður*] sceal
weorðan æt wealle, swā unc wyrd ȝetēoð,
metod manna ȝehwæs. Ic eom on mōde from,
þæt ic wið þone ȝūð-floȝan ȝylp ofersitte.
ȝebīde ȝē on beorȝe byrnum werede,
2530 secȝas on searwum, hwæðer sēl mæȝe
æfter wæl-rǣse wunde ȝedȳȝan
uncer twēȝa. Nis þæt ēower sīð,
ne ȝemet mannes nefn[e] mīn ānes,
þæt hē wið āȝlǣcean eofoðo dǣle,
2535 eorl-scype efne. Ic mid elne sceall
ȝold ȝeȝanȝan, oððe ȝūð nimeð,
feorh-bealu frēcne, frēan ēowerne."
Ārās ðā bī ronde rōf ōretta,
heard under helme, hioro-sercean bær
2540 under stān-cleofu, strenȝo ȝetrūwode
ānes mannes; ne bið swylc earȝes sīð.

2520–1. Sievers [*P.B.B.* ix. 141] suggests *þæs āglǣcean gylpe*, 'against the boast of the adversary.' Schröer [*Anglia*, xiii. 345] suggests *gūþe* for *gylpe*, 'come to grips with the adversary in war.' I take *gylpe*='with boast,' i.e. 'in such a manner as to fulfil my boast.'

2523. [*o*]*reðes*, Grein$_1$, *āttres* Kemble$_2$: MS. *reðes* 7 *hattres*. Cf. ll. 2557, 2839. There is a dot over the *h* of *hattres*, which Sievers [*Z.f.d.Ph.* xxi. 355] regards as intended by the scribe to signify that *h* is cancelled. I should rather regard the dot as accidental.

2525. The second half-line is metrically deficient: *furðor* is Klaeber's emendation [*Archiv*, cxv. 181] adopted by Holthausen. Holthausen's earlier suggestion, *feohte* [*Litteraturblatt für germ. u. rom. Philologie*, 1900, p. 61], is adopted by Schücking. Bugge[104] had also suggested *feohte*.

In view of the rarity of a 'prelude' of two syllables with this type of line [cf. Sievers in *P.B.B.* x. 302] Bugge[104] would omit *ofer*, comparing *Maldon*, 247, *flēon fōtes trym*. [So Sedgefield[288].]

Holthausen$_3$ reads *ferflēon* (=*forflēon*).

2528. *þæt*='so that.' Sievers' emendation [*P.B.B.* ix. 141] *þæs*, 'therefore,' is unnecessary. [Cf. Klaeber[463], Schücking, *Satzverk.*, 25.] 'The conj. *þæt* is found to denote the relation between two facts in the vaguest possible manner' (Klaeber).

2529. Note that, where the pronoun follows the imperative of the verb, the normal inflection of the verb is dropped.

2533. MS. defective at edge: *nefn*[*e*], Grundtvig[304].

2534. *þæt*, Grundtvig[304], Kemble$_1$: MS. *wat*.

ȝeseah ðā be wealle, |sē ðe worna fela, Fol. 186b.
ȝum-cystum ȝōd, ȝūða ȝedīȝde,
hilde-hlemma, þonne hnitan fēðan,
2545 sto[*n*]dan stān-boȝan, strēam ūt þonan
brecan of beorȝe; wæs þǣre burnan wælm
heaðo-fȳrum hāt; ne meahte horde nēah
unbyrnende ǣniȝe hwīle
dēop ȝedȳȝan for dracan lēȝe.
2550 Lēt ðā of brēostum, ðā hē ȝebolȝen wæs,
Weder-ȝēata lēod word ūt faran,
stearc-heort styrmde; stefn in becōm
heaðo-torht hlynnan under hārne stān;
hete wæs onhrēred, hord-weard oncnīow
2555 mannes reorde; næs ðǣr māra fyrst
frēode tō friclan. From ǣrest cwōm
oruð āȝlǣcean ūt of stāne,
hāt hilde-swāt; hrūse dynede.
Biorn under beorȝe bord-rand onswāf
2560 wið ðām ȝryre-ȝieste, ȝēata dryhten;
ðā wæs hrinȝ-boȝan heorte ȝefȳsed
sæcce tō sēceanne. Sweord ǣr ȝebrǣd
ȝōd ȝūð-cyninȝ, ȝomele lāfe,
ecȝum un*s*lāw; ǣȝhwæðrum wæs
2565 bealo-hycȝendra |brōȝa fram ōðrum. Fol. 187a.

2545. *sto[n]dan*, Thorpe: MS. *stodan*. Thorpe's emendation is confirmed by a passage in the *Andreas*, 1492, *etc.*, where these lines seem to be imitated.

2547. *ne meahte...dēop gedȳgan*, 'could not endure the depths of the cave.' Grundtvig[305] reads *dēor*; so Bugge [*Tidsskr.* viii. 297], but this was with the belief that the MS. could so be read, whereas the reading is clearly *deop*, not *deor*. *Dēor* has, however, been adopted by Earle and Sedgefield: 'nigh to the hoard could not the hero unscorched any while survive.'

2556. *frēode*. Sedgefield reads *freoðo*.

2559. *Biorn* refers to Beowulf. Sedgefield reads *born*, and puts the stop after *beorge*, making l. 2559a a continuation of ll. 2556–8: 'the earth resounded and burned under the hill.' For *biorn, beorn*=*born, bearn* he compares l. 1880.

2562. *sēceanne*. See note to l. 473.

ǣr gebrǣd, 'had already drawn his sword.'

2564. MS. *un* | *glaw*. 'A letter erased between *l* and *a* in *glaw*: that it was *e* is not quite certain' (Zupitza). As there is all the appearance of an uncompleted alteration, I have adopted the emendation of Bugge[104] (following Thorpe). Klaeber [*Anglia*, xxix. 380] defends *unglēaw*, which he takes to mean 'very sharp,' with *un* intensifying, as in *unhār* (l. 357). But this use of *un* appears to be very problematical.

Stīð-mōd ʒestōd wið stēapne rond
winia bealdor, ðā se wyrm ʒebēah
snūde tōsomne; hē on searwum bād.
Ʒewāt ðā byrnende ʒeboʒen scrīðan,
2570 tō ʒescipe scyndan. Scyld wel ʒebearʒ
līfe ond līce lǣssan hwīle
mǣrum þēodne, þonne his myne sōhte;
ðǣr hē þȳ fyrste forman dōʒore
wealdan mōste, swā him wyrd ne ʒescrāf
2575 hrēð æt hilde. Hond ūp ābrǣd
Ʒēata dryhten, ʒryre-fāhne slōh
incʒe lāfe, þæt sīo ecʒ ʒewāc
brūn on bāne, bāt unswīðor,
þonne his ðīod-cyninʒ þearfe hæfde,
2580 bysiʒum ʒebǣded. Þā wæs beorʒes weard
æfter heaðu-sweŋʒe on hrēoum mōde,
wearp wæl-fȳre; wīde spruŋʒon
hilde-lēoman. Hrēð-siʒora ne ʒealp
ʒold-wine Ʒēata; ʒūð-bill ʒeswāc
2585 nacod æt nīðe, swā hyt nō sceolde,
īren ǣr-ʒōd. Nẹ wæs þæt ēðe sīð,
þæt se mǣra maʒa Ecʒðēowes

2567. *winia.* Cf. note to l. 1418.

2570. MS. *ḡscipe.* Heyne emended *gescīfe*, 'headlong,' basing his conjecture upon an O.E. gloss in a MS. of Aldhelm's *de Virginitate*, now at Brussels, in which *per preceps* is rendered *niðerscife*, with the further explanation *niðersceotende* in the margin. [Cf. *Z.f.d.A.* ix. 468 and *scyfe* in Bosworth-Toller.] Heyne's emendation has been adopted by Holthausen and Sedgefield.

2573. *dōgore*: Sievers, followed by Holthausen, would read *dōgor* (uninflected instrumental, cf. Sievers$_3$ § 289) which improves the metre.

2573, *etc.* 'For the first time (literally, the first day) he had to spend his time in a struggle devoid of victory.' [But cf. Klaeber[464].]

2577. MS. *incgelafe.* The word *incge* is otherwise unrecorded (but cf. note to l. 1107). It has been conjectured that it means 'valuable' or 'weighty.' Thorpe conjectured *Incges lāfe* [so Holthausen$_{1,2}$, abandoning an earlier conjecture, *Anglia, Beiblatt*, xiii. 78, and Sedgefield], believing the word 'to be a corruption of some proper name.' If Thorpe's reading is correct, Ing would presumably be identical with the primaeval hero from whom the sea-tribes, the Ingaevones, were said to derive their name (see *Index of Persons*: Ingwine). Ing is recorded in the O.E. *Runic Song*, 67, as a hero of the East Danes. Some have identified Ing and Sceaf.

Holthausen$_3$, *Ing*[*win*]*e*[*s*] *lāfe*, a tempting conjecture, 'with the sword which Hrothgar had given him.'

2579. *his þearfe*, probably 'need of it.'

2581. *hrēoum.* See note to *fēaum*, l. 1081.

ʒrund-wonʒ þone ofʒyfan wolde;
sceolde [*ofer*] willan wīc eardian
2590 elles hwerʒen, swā |sceal ǣʒhwylc mon Fol. 187b.
ālǣtan lǣn-daʒas. Næs ðā lonʒ tō ðon,
þæt ðā āʒlǣcean hȳ eft ʒemētton.
Hyrte hyne hord-weard, hreðer ǣðme wēoll,
nīwan stefne; nearo ðrōwode
2595 fȳre befonʒen, sē ðe ǣr folce wēold.
Nealles him on hēape h*a*nd-ʒesteallan,
æðelinʒa bearn, ymbe ʒestōdon
hilde-cystum, ac hȳ on holt buʒon,
ealdre burʒan. Hiora in ānum wēoll
2600 sefa wið sorʒum; sibb ǣfre ne mæʒ
wiht onwendan, þām ðe wel þenceð.
XXXVI Wīʒlāf wæs hāten, Wēoxstānes sunu,
lēoflīc lind-wiʒa, lēod Scylfinʒa,

2588. *grund-wong* was taken by the older editors to mean 'the earth': hence *grund-wong ofgyfan*, 'to die' [so Clark-Hall]. This interpretation of *grund-wong* has recently been defended by Klaeber [*Engl. Stud.* xxxix. 466].

Since Bugge [*Tidsskr.* viii. 298], it has been more usual to interpret *grund-wong* as the ground in front of the barrow [so Cosijn[36]] or the floor of the dragon's den. Beowulf has hardly got so far as the floor: but a concrete, local interpretation is supported by l. 2770 (cf. too l. 1496).

Beowulf has to retreat (ll. 2586–8): the poet alludes to the issue of the combat (ll. 2589-91): then returns to his description again.

2589. No gap in MS. Rieger[410] emends [*ofer*] *willan* (cf. l. 2409); Grein$_2$, [*wyrmes*] *willan* (cf. l. 3077); Cosijn[35], [*wyrme tō*] *willan*.

2595. *sē ðe ǣr folce wēold*: Beowulf, 'who had long ruled over his folk.' [Cf. Cosijn[36]; Bugge in *Z.f.d.Ph.* iv. 216.]

2596. *hand*, Kemble$_2$: MS. *heand*.

2603. Wiglaf is called *lēod Scylfinga* because his father, Weoxstan (though apparently by origin a Geat), had once been a chief in the service of the Swedish (Scylfing) king Onela. Weoxstan may well have married into the family of his king, like Ecgtheow, Eofor, or Bothvar Bjarki: such a supposition would make the title *lēod Scylfinga* more appropriate to Wiglaf, and might perhaps explain *his māgum* (l. 2614, but see note there). Ælfhere, whose name begins with a vowel, would then be a member of the Swedish royal family (since in Germanic heroic tradition princes of the same family commonly have names which alliterate together) rather than one of the Wægmundingas (whose names run on *W*).

When Eadgils and Eanmund rebel against their uncle Onela, and take refuge among the Geatas, Onela smites them (see ll. 2379–90). Weoxstan, serving under Onela, slays Eanmund, and, according to Germanic custom, presents the spoils of his slain foe to his king. But, contrary to custom, Onela does not accept them (for to do so would be publicly to approve the slaying of his own nephew); yet he rewards the slayer with the spoils, and hushes up the matter: 'Onela spake not of the feud, though Weoxstan had slain his (Onela's) brother's son' (i.e. Eanmund, son of Ohthere), ll. 2618–9.

Yet Weoxstan belongs to the Wægmundingas (l. 2607), a family of the Geatas to which Beowulf is related (l. 2814). Why he was serving with

mǣȝ Ælfheres; ȝeseah his mon-dryhten
2605 under here-ȝrīman hāt þrōwian;
ȝemunde ðā ðā āre, þe hē him ǣr forȝeaf,
wīc-stede weliȝne Wǣȝmundinȝa,
folc-rihta ȝehwylc, swā his fæder āhte;
ne mihte ðā forhabban, hond rond ȝefēnȝ,
2610 ȝeolwe linde, ȝomel swyrd ȝetēah.
Þæt wæs mid eldum Ēanmundes lāf,
|suna Ōhtere[*s*], þām æt sæcce wearð, Fol. 188a.
wræcca[n] wine-lēasum, Wēohstā*n* bana
mēces ecȝum, ond his māȝum ætbær
2615 brūn-fāȝne helm, hrinȝde byrnan,
eald sweord etonisc, þæt him Onela forȝeaf,
his ȝædelinȝes ȝūð-ȝewǣdu,
fyrd-searo fūslīc; nō ymbe ðā fǣhðe spræc,
þēah ðe hē his brōðor bearn ābredwade.
2620 Hē frætwe ȝehēold fela missēra,
bill ond byrnan, oð ðæt his byre mihte
eorl-scipe efnan swā his ǣr-fæder;
ȝeaf him ðā mid Ȝēatum ȝūð-ȝewǣda
ǣȝhwæs unrīm, þā hē of ealdre ȝewāt
2625 frōd on forð-weȝ. Þā wæs forma sīð
ȝeonȝan cempan, þæt hē ȝūðe rǣs

the national enemy, or why, in spite of this, his own people ultimately received him back, we do not know. [Cf. Chadwick, *Origin of the English Nation*, p. 173.] The re-grant (l. 2606) of Weoxstan's fief to Wiglaf must not be taken as signifying that the fief had been forfeited by Weoxstan: a formal re-grant is in every case necessitated by the death of the father. [See *Widsith*, 95–6, and cf. Chadwick, p. 169.]

[The difficulties are well explained by Müllenhoff in *A.f.d.A.* iii. 176–8.]

2612. *Ōhtere*[*s*], Grundtvig[305], Kemble$_1$: MS. *ohtere* (partially corrected by Thorkelin).

2613. MS. defective at corner: *wrecca*[*n*], Ettmüller$_2$: *Wēohstān*, Grundtvig[306], Kemble$_1$: MS. *weohstanes.*

2614. *māgum* probably means Onela: pl. for sg., as in l. 2353: cf. note to l. 565.

his may refer to Weoxstan (see l. 2603, above) or, more probably, to Eanmund.

2615. The alliteration is improved if, with Rieger, followed by Holthausen, we read *byrnan hringde.*

2620. *Hē*, i.e. Weoxstan.

Grundtvig [1861, p. 89], followed by Holthausen, supplies *þā* before *frætwe.*

2623. We must understand *Wēoxstān* as subject to *geaf.*

mid his frēo-dryhtne fremman sceolde;
ne ʒemealt him se mōd-sefa, ne his mǣʒ*es* lāf
ʒewāc æt wīʒe; *þæt* se wyrm onfand,
2630 syððan hīe tōʒædre ʒeʒān hæfdon.
Wīʒlāf maðelode, word-rihta fela,
sæʒde ʒesīðum —him wæs sefa ʒeōmor—
"Ic ðæt |mǣl ʒeman, þǣr wē medu þēʒun, Fol. 188b.
þonne wē ʒehēton ūssum hlāforde
2635 in bīor-sele, ðe ūs ðās bēaʒas ʒeaf,
þæt wē him ðā ʒūð-ʒetāwa ʒyldan woldon,
ʒif him þyslicu þearf ʒelumpe,
helmas ond heard sweord. Ðē hē ūsic on herʒe ʒecēas
tō ðyssum sīð-fate sylfes willum,
2640 onmunde ūsic mǣrða, ond mē þās māðmas ʒeaf,
þē hē ūsic ʒār-wīʒend ʒōde tealde,
hwate helm-berend, þēah ðe hlāford ūs
þis ellen-weorc āna āðōhte
tō ʒefremmanne, folces hyrde,
2645 forðam hē manna mǣst mǣrða ʒefremede,
dǣda dollīcra. Nū is se dæʒ cumen,
þæt ūre man-dryhten mæʒenes behōfað
ʒōdra ʒūð-rinca; wutun ʒonʒan tō,
helpan hild-fruman, þenden hyt sȳ,
2650 ʒlēd-eʒesa ʒrim. ʒod wāt on mec,
þæt mē is micle lēofre, þæt mīnne līc-haman

2628. *mǣges*, Ettmüller$_2$: MS. *mægenes*.
his mǣges lāf, 'his father's sword.'
2629. *þæt*, Thorpe: MS. *þa*.
2633. To this appeal to the *gesīðas* to make good their boast there are two close parallels: *Maldon* (212–15) and the *Bjarka mál*, as recorded in the Latin paraphrase of Saxo Grammaticus (*Hist. Dan.*, Bk II.). It is a commonplace of Old Germanic poetry: and indeed of heroic poetry generally.
2636. See note to l. 368.
2642. Bugge [*Z.f.d.Ph.* iv. 216] suggested *hlāford ūser* instead of *hlāford ūs*: Cosijn[36], *hlāford ūr*.
2645. *forðam*: MS. *forðā*; Zupitza transliterates *forðan*. So also l. 2741.
2649. *þenden hit hāt sȳ* or *þenden hāt sȳ* are alternative suggestions of Kemble$_3$: *hāt* is supported by Bugge[105], who compares l. 2605, and is adopted by Earle and Sedgefield.

mid mīnne ȝold-ȝyfan ȝlēd fæðmię.
Ne þynceð mē ȝerysne, þæt wē rondas beren
eft tō earde, nemne wē ǣror mæȝen
2655 fāne ȝefyllan, feorh ealȝian Fol. 197a.
Wedra ðēodnes. Ic wāt ȝeare,
þæt nǣron eald ȝewyrht, þæt hē āna scyle
Ȝēata duȝuðe ȝnorn þrōwian,
ȝesīȝan æt sæcce; ūrum sceal sweord ond helm,
2660 byrne ond *bea*du-scrūd, bām ȝemǣne."
Wōd þā þurh þone wæl-rēc, wīȝ-heafolan bær
frēan on fultum, fēa worda cwæð:
"Lēofa Bīowulf, lǣst eall tela,
swā ðū on ȝeoȝuð-fēore ȝēara ȝecwǣde,
2665 þæt ðū ne ālǣte be ðē lifiȝendum
dōm ȝedrēosan; scealt nū dǣdum rōf,
æðelinȝ an-hȳdiȝ, ealle mæȝene
feorh ealȝian; ic ðē ful-lǣstu."

2652. MS. *fæðmię*, optative sing. I take ę here to signify *æ*, which is the oldest form of the optative ending. [Cf. $Sievers_2$ § 361.] See note to l. 1981.

2657. Most editors make a compound *eald-gewyrht*, which they generally [Holthausen, Sedgefield, Earle] render 'ancient custom,' etc.

eald-gewyrhtum occurs in the *Dream of the Rood*, 100, where it means 'deeds done of old,' with thought of the deserts therefrom resulting. 'Ties through deeds done' seems to be the meaning of *gewyrht* here.

2659. In the MS. a colon, a comma, and a ð are placed after *urum*, thus: *urū* ⁏ð. The colon signifies that something has been omitted, and the ð [signifying 'it is wanting': Lat. *deest*] corresponds to another ð in the margin, which is followed by the word *sceal*, between dots, thus: ð · sceal ·. This device, to signify that the word *sceal* has been omitted after *urum*, has often been misunderstood, and the line misread in consequence.

ūrum bām seems a strange way of expressing *unc bām*. Bugge [*Tidsskr.* viii. 58; *Z.f.d.Ph.* iv. 216] supposes a gap. So Rieger[410] and Earle. Parallels can, however, be found: Cosijn quotes examples of *nǣniges ūres, ūres nānes, etc.*, for *nǣniges ūre, ūre nānes* [*P.B.B.* viii. 573] and *iowra selfra* is found in *Orosius* [ed. Sweet, 48, 21] for *iower selfra.*

Sedgefield[288] conjectures *huru* for *urum*: 'surely sword and helmet...must be common to both.'

2660. *beadu-scrūd*, $Ettmüller_2$ (so Thorpe); MS. *byrdu scrūd*. The word *byrdu*, which is unknown, is defended by von Grienberger [*P.B.B.* xxxvi. 83] and *byrdu-scrūd* interpreted to mean 'coat of mail.' Yet it is possible that *beadu* has (not unnaturally) been written *byrdu* through the influence of the preceding *byrne*. Holthausen's further alteration [following Cosijn[36]], *bord ond beadu-scrūd*, does not seem essential, though it certainly improves the reading of the text, in which the shield is not mentioned, and the coat of mail enumerated twice.

Bugge [*Tidsskr.* viii. 55 *etc.*] suggested *bȳwdu scrūd*, 'adorned vestment'; *bȳwan*, to adorn, occurs in l. 2257.

Æfter ðām wordum wyrm yrre cwōm,
2670 atol inwit-ȝæst, ōðre sīðe
fȳr-wylmum fāh fīonda nīos[i]an,
lāðra manna. Līȝ-ȳðum forborn
bord wið rond[*e*]; byrne ne meahte
ȝeonȝum ȝār-wiȝan ȝēoce ȝefremman;
2675 ac se maȝa ȝeonȝa under his mǣȝes scyld
elne ȝeēode, þā his āȝen w[æs]
ȝlēdum forȝrunden. Þā ȝēn ȝūð-cyninȝ
m[ǣrða] ȝemunde, mæȝen-strenȝo slōh
hilde-bille, þæt hyt on heafolan stōd
2680 nīþe ȝenȳded; Næȝlinȝ forbærst,
ȝeswāc æt sæcce sweord Bīowulfes,| Fol. 197b.
ȝomol ond ȝrǣȝ-mǣl. Him þæt ȝifeðe ne wæs,
þæt him īrenna ecȝe mihton
helpan æt hilde —wæs sīo hond tō stronȝ—
2685 sē ðe mēca ȝehwane, mīne ȝefrǣȝe,
swenȝe ofersōhte, þonne hē tō sæcce bær
wǣpen wund[*r*]um heard; næs him wihte ðē sēl.
Þā wæs þēod-sceaða þriddan sīðe,
frēcne fȳr-draca, fǣhða ȝemyndiȝ,
2690 rǣsde on ðone rōfan, þā him rūm āȝeald,
hāt ond heaðo-ȝrim, heals ealne ymbefēnȝ

2671. MS. defective, here and in ll. 2676, 2678. Though evidence points to *niosian* having stood in the MS. here, it must have been a mere scribal variant of the form *niosan*, which the metre supports, and which is also found in *Beowulf*. See note to ll. 115, 1125.

2673. *rond*[*e*], Kemble₁: MS. *rond*. The emendation is metrically necessary; cf. l. 3027. *Wið ronde*='as far as to the *rond*.' [Cf. Klaeber in *M.L.N.* xx. 86.]

2675. In the *Iliad* (VIII. 267, *etc.*) Teucer fights under the shield of Ajax. For other remarkable coincidences with Homer cf. ll. 2806, 3169.

2676. MS. defective at edge: *w*[*æs*], Grundtvig[306], Kemble₁.

2678. MS. defective at edge: *m*[*ǣrða*], Grundtvig[306], Kemble₁.

2682. That a warrior should have been too strong for his sword seems to have been quite possible in the Germanic heroic age. It is told of Offa that he broke the swords offered him for his duel by simply brandishing them in the air [Saxo, *Hist. Dan.*, Bk II: ed. Holder, p. 115]. The Icelandic sagas, with their greater sobriety, tell of a hero, who, in his last fight, had to keep straightening out his sword under his foot [*Laxdæla Saga*, cap. 49].

2686. *þonne*. Bugge[105], followed by Holthausen, reads *þone*.

2687. *wund*[*r*]*um*, Thorpe: MS. *wundū*. A convincing emendation; cf. *wundrum wrætlīce*, *Phœnix*, 63; *wundrum hēah*, *Wanderer*, 98.

2691. *ymbefēng*. The *e* is probably a scribal insertion [cf. Sievers in *P.B.B.* x. 260]: the line runs better when it is deleted.

biteran bānum; hē ȝeblōdeȝod wearð
sāwul-drīore; swāt ȳðum wēoll.

XXXVII ÐĀ ic æt þearfe [*ȝefræȝn*] þēod-cyninȝes
2695 andlonȝne eorl ellen cȳðan,
cræft ond cēnðu, swā him ȝecynde wæs;
ne hēdde hē þæs heafolan —ac sīo hand ȝebarn
mōdiȝes mannes, þǣr hē his mǣ*ȝes* healp—,
þæt hē þone nīð-ȝæst nioðor hwēne slōh,
2700 secȝ on searwum, þæt ðæt sweord ȝedēaf
fāh ond fǣted, þæt ðæt fȳr onȝon
sweðrian syððan. Þā ȝēn sylf cyninȝ
ȝewēold his ȝewitte, wæll-seaxe ȝebrǣd
biter ond beadu-scearp, þæt hē on byrnan wæȝ;
2705 forwrāt Wedra |helm wyrm on middan. Fol. 189a.
Fēond ȝefyldan —ferh ellen wræc—,
ond hī hyne þā bēȝen ābroten hæfdon,
sib-æðelinȝas; swylc sceolde secȝ wesan,
þeȝn æt ðearfe. Þæt ðām þēodne wæs
2710 sīðas[*t*] siȝe-hwī*l* sylfes dǣdum,

2694. No gap in MS.: [*gefrægn*], Kemble$_1$. See ll. 2484, 2752, *etc.*

2697. It is not clear whether it was his own head or the dragon's which Wiglaf did not heed. [For the former interpretation see Cosijn[37]; for the latter Bugge[105], who compares l. 2679.]

Wiglaf attacks what he knows to be the more vulnerable part of the dragon; both Frotho and Fridlevus in Saxo [Bk II., ed. Holder, p. 39; Bk VI., p. 181] learn a similar discrimination: the parallels between these dragon fights in Saxo and those in our text are close. Sigurd also attacked Fafnir from below, but in a more practical and less heroic manner.

2698. *mǣges*, Kemble$_2$: MS. *mægenes* (so Grein-Wülker); cf. l. 2628, and foot-note. See also l. 2879.

2699. See note to l. 102.

2701. *þæt ðæt.* Sievers, objecting to this awkward collocation of *þæt*, proposed *þā ðæt* [*P.B.B.* ix. 141]. But Grundtvig had already suggested that the first *þæt* (which is written ꝥ) should be read *þā*. See note to l. 15, where this problem of the interpretation of ꝥ first meets us. Sedgefield reads *þā*; *þæt* can, however, be defended here. [Cf. Schücking, *Satzverk.*, 25.]

2704. It seems best, in spite of strict grammatical concord, to take *biter ond beadu-scearp* as referring to *wæll-seaxe.*

2706. *gefyldan.* Ettmüller$_2$ and Thorpe proposed to read *gefylde*, parallel to *forwrāt*: Sievers [*P.B.B.* ix. 141] argues for this reading, which has been adopted by Sedgefield.

ellen. Cosijn[37] suggested *ellor* [so Holthausen$_{1,2}$: but Holthausen$_3$, *ellen*]: cf. ll. 55, 2254. The meaning would be 'drove his life elsewhere,' i.e. to Hell. With much the same meaning Kluge[192] reads *feorh ealne wræc*, 'drove out all his life,' comparing *Genesis*, 1385.

2710. *sīðas*[*t*], Grein$_1$: MS. *siðas.* Grundtvig[307] suggested *sīþest.* Yet it is possible to defend *sīðas* here as gen. of *sīð*, parallel to *worlde geweorces*:

worlde ʒeweorces. Ðā sīo wund onʒon,
þe him se eorð-draca ǣr ʒeworhte,
swelan ond swellan; hē þæt sōna onfand,
þæt him on brēostum bealo-nīð[e] wēoll,
2715 āttor on innan. Ðā se æðelinʒ ʒionʒ,
þæt hē bī wealle wīs-hycʒende
ʒesæt on sesse, seah on enta ʒeweorc,
hū ðā stān-boʒan stapulum fæste
ēce eorð-reced innan healde.
2720 Hyne þā mid handa heoro-drēoriʒne,
þēoden mǣrne, þeʒn unʒemete till,
wine-dryhten his, wætere ʒelafede
hilde-sædne, ond his hel[m] onspēon.
Bīowulf maþelode: hē ofer benne spræc,
2725 wunde wæl-blēate; wisse hē ʒearwe,
þæt hē dæʒ-hwīla ʒedroʒen hæfde,
eorðan wynn[e]; ðā wæs eall sceacen
dōʒor-ʒerīmes, dēað unʒemete nēah:
"Nū ic suna mīnum syllan wolde
2730 ʒūð-ʒewǣdu, þǣr mē ʒifeðe swā

'That was to the chieftain a victorious moment of his allotted span, of his life-work.'

sige-hwil, Kemble$_2$: MS. *sigehwile*. After *sige*, *hwile* might easily be written in error for *hwil*. Grein$_1$, *sige-hwila*.

2714. The older editors read *bealo-nið*, so also Sedgefield$_1$: but the word comes at the end of the line, and evidence points to a letter having been lost. (Thorkelin's transcripts: A *bealomð*, B *bealo niði*: now only *beal* left.) *Bealo-niðe* is essential on metrical grounds [cf. Sievers in *P.B.B.* x. 269], and is probably to be regarded as the MS. reading.

2715. *giong*, 'went.'

2719. *ēce*. Holthausen would read *ēcne*=*ēacne*, 'mighty.'

Ettmüller$_2$, Rieger[411] [in an excellent note], Heyne, Holthausen, *etc.*, read *hēoldon*. But no change is necessary. For the tense cf. ll. 1923, 1928, 2486; and for the sg. verb with pl. subject in a subordinate clause cf. l. 2164, and see the note to ll. 1408 and 2035. Further I do not see why *eorð-reced* should not be the subject: 'How the earth-hall contained within itself the arches....'

2723. MS. defective: *hel*[*m*], Grein$_1$, *etc.*, following Grimm.

2724. Beowulf speaks *ofer benne*, 'over his wound,' 'wounded as he was,' just as the warriors boast *ofer ealowǣge*, 'over their cups' (l. 481). [Cf. Cosijn[37], and Klaeber, *Archiv*, civ. 287, where the passage is elaborately discussed. Corson's rendering, 'beyond (i.e. concerning other things than) his wound,' *M.L.N.*, iii. 193, seems impossible.]

2725. *wæl-blēate*. Holthausen, following Grein [*Sprachschatz*], reads *wæl-blāte*, 'deadly pale.' Cf. *Crist*, 771, *blātast benna*.

2727. *wynn*[*e*], Thorkelin's correction: MS. defective.

ǣniȝ yrfe-|weard æfter wurde Fol. 189[b].
līce ȝelenȝe. Ic ðās lēode hēold
fīftiȝ wintra; næs se folc-cyninȝ
ymbe-sittendra ǣniȝ ðāra,
2735 þe mec ȝūð-winum ȝrētan dorste,
eȝesan ðêon. Ic on earde bād
mǣl-ȝesceafta, hēold mīn tela,
ne sōhte searo-nīðas, ne mē swōr fela
āða on unriht. Ic ðæs ealles mæȝ
2740 feorh-bennum sēoc ȝefēan habban;
forðam mē wītan ne ðearf Waldend fīra
morðor-bealo māȝa, þonne mīn sceaceð
līf of līce. Nū ðū lunȝre ȝeonȝ
hord scēawian under hārne stān,
2745 Wīȝlāf lēofa, nū se wyrm liȝeð,
swefeð sāre wund, since berēafod.
Bīo nū on ofoste, þæt ic ǣr-welan,
ȝold-ǣht onȝite, ȝearo scēawiȝe
sweȝle searo-ȝimmas, þæt ic ðȳ sēft mæȝe
2750 æfter māððum-welan mīn ālǣtan
līf ond lēod-scipe, þone ic lonȝe hēold."
XXXVIII ĐĀ ic snūde ȝefræȝn sunu Wīhstānes
æfter word-cwydum wundum dryhtne
hȳran heaðo-sīocum, hrinȝ-net beran,
2755 broȝdne beadu-sercean, u*n*der beorȝes hrōf.
ȝeseah ðā siȝe-hrēðiȝ, þā hē bī sesse ȝēonȝ,
maȝo-þeȝn |mōdiȝ māððum-siȝla fealo, Fol. 190[a].
ȝold ȝlitinian ȝrunde ȝetenȝe,
wundur on wealle, ond þæs wyrmes denn,

2738. *fela.* A typical example of that understatement so common in O.E. poetry. We must not, of course, suppose (as some have done) that Beowulf admits to having sworn some false oaths, but not many. Cf. l. 203.

2749. Rieger[411–2] saw in *swegle* a corruption of *sigle*, 'brooch,' comparing the parallel passage, l. 1157. Holthausen and Sedgefield$_1$ read pl. *siglu*; Klaeber[250] defends the sg. form *sigle*, quoting parallels for such collocation of sg. and pl.

2755. *under*, Thorkelin's correction: MS. *urder*.

2757. Most editors normalise to *fela* or *feola*. But see Sievers, § 275, and cf. § 150, 3; Bülbring § 236.

2759. *ond.* Trautmann, followed by Holthausen and Sedgefield, reads *geond.*

2760 ealdes ūht-floʒan, orcas stondan,
fyrn-manna fatu, feormend-lēase,
hyrstum behrorene. Þǣr wæs helm moniʒ
eald ond ōmiʒ, earm-bēaʒa fela
searwum ʒesǣled. Sinc ēaðe mæʒ,
2765 ʒold on ʒrund[e], ʒum-cynnes ʒehwone
oferhīʒian, hȳde sē ðe wylle.
Swylce hē siomian ʒeseah seʒn eall-ʒylden
hēah ofer horde, hond-wundra mǣst,
ʒelocen leoðo-cræftum; of ðām lēom*a* stōd,
2770 þæt hē þone ʒrund-wonʒ onʒitan meahte,
wrǣ*te* ʒiondwlītan. Næs ðæs wyrmes þǣr
onsȳn ǣniʒ, ac hyne ecʒ fornam.
Ðā ic on hlǣwe ʒefræʒn hord rēafian,
eald enta ʒeweorc, ānne mannan,
2775 him on bearm hl*a*don bunan ond discas
sylfes dōme; seʒn ēac ʒenōm,
bēacna beorhtost. Bill ǣr ʒescōd
—ecʒ wæs īren— eald-hlāfordes

2760. *stondan*: Holthausen, following Ettmüller$_3$, reads *stōdan.*
2765. MS. defective at edge. *grund*[*e*], Grundtvig[307], Kemble$_1$.
2766. No satisfactory explanation of *oferhīgian* is forthcoming. The general drift is that gold gets the better of man, 'hide the gold whoso will.' But how? Because, in spite of all, the gold is discovered again? Or because, when found, it carries a curse with it? *Ofer-hīgian* may possibly be a compound of *hīgian*, 'to strive' (Mod. Eng. 'hie'), and so mean 'to over-reach.' An interpretation very widely accepted is 'to make proud, vain': hence 'deceive.' In this connection it has been proposed to connect *oferhīgian* with *hēah*, 'high,' and with Goth. *ufarháuhids*, 'puffed up, vain' [Bugge, in *Tidsskr.* viii. 60, 298; Klaeber in *Engl. Stud.* xxxix. 466]; or with *oferhȳd* (*oferhygd*), *oferhȳdig*, 'proud' [Kluge[192], followed by Schücking, who spells *oferhīdgian*, and others]. Against the last it is objected [Holthausen] that a derivative from the adj. *oferhȳdig* must preserve the accent on the first syllable, and so cannot alliterate with *h*. Sedgefield[288] suggests *oferhīwian* (not elsewhere recorded, but assumed to mean 'deceive': *hīwian* means 'to assume a false appearance,' 'to feign'): Sedgefield$_2$, *ofer hig*[*e h*]*ēan*, 'raise him above his (usual) mind, render presumptuous.'
2769. Earle follows Thorpe in reading *lēoðo-cræftum* (with *ēo*), 'locked by spells of song.' This seems forced and unnecessary.
lēoma, Kemble$_2$: MS. *leoman*. For the opposite mistake cf. l. 60.
2771. *wrǣte*, Thorpe, here and in l. 3060: MS. *wræce* in both places.
2775. *hladon*: MS. *hlodon*. Grundtvig[308] emended to *hladan*, but it is not necessary to alter the second *a*. For infin. in *-on* cf. ll. 308, *etc.*, and see Sievers$_3$ § 363, N. 1.
2777. *ǣr gescōd*: MS. *ærge scod*. Kemble *ǣr-gescōd*, 'sheathed in brass.' This has the support of Thorpe and Grein, but lacks analogy; for the reading in the text cf. l. 1587, and ll. 1615, 2562, and 2973.
2778. *Bill...eald-hlāfordes*, the MS. reading, is understood by Bugge

þām ðāra māðma mund-bora wæs
2780 lonȝe hwīle, līȝ-eȝesan wæȝ
hātne for horde, hioro-weallende
middel-nihtum, |oð þæt hē morðre swealt. Fol. 190b.
Ār wæs on ofoste, eft-sīðes ȝeorn,
frætwum ȝefyrðred; hyne fyrwet bræc,
2785 hwæðer collen-ferð cwicne ȝemētte
in ðām wonȝ-stede Wedra þēoden,
ellen-sīocne, þǣr hē hine ǣr forlēt.
Hē ðā mid þām māðmum mǣrne þīoden,
dryhten sīnne, drīoriȝne fand
2790 ealdres æt ende; hē hine eft onȝon
wæteres weorpan, oð þæt wordes ord
brēost-hord þurhbræc. [*Bīowulf reordode,*]
ȝomel on ȝio*h*ðe ȝold scēawode:
"Ic ðāra frætwa Frēan ealles ðanc,
2795 Wuldur-cyninȝe, wordum secȝe,
ēcum Dryhtne, þe ic hēr on starie,
þæs ðe ic mōste mīnum lēodum
ǣr swylt-dæȝe swylc ȝestrȳnan.
Nū ic on māðma hord mīn*e* bebohte

[*Tidsskr.* viii. 300], Holthausen, and Schücking to mean the sword of Beowulf, by Müllenhoff[152] the sword of the former possessor of the hoard.

It is obvious that ll. 2779–2782 refer to the dragon. Whether *eald-hlāfordes* be taken to mean Beowulf or the former owner will probably depend on the interpretation of l. 2777. If we read *ǣr gescōd*, we shall interpret 'the sword of the lord of old time [Beowulf] with iron edge had slain the guardian of the treasure.' If, with Kemble, we read *bill ǣr-gescōd*, this will be object of *genōm* in l. 2776, and we must accordingly delete the full stop.

Rieger[412] and Cosijn[37] read *eald-hlāforde* (=the dragon) in apposition with *þām*. [This is adopted by Earle and Sedgefield.]

2791. *wæteres*. Kemble$_3$, *etc.* emended to *wætere*: but the instrumental gen. seems possible enough [Bugge in *Z.f.d.Ph.* iv. 218; Cosijn[38]]. Cf. *gūð-geweorca*, l. 1825.

2792. No gap in MS. *Bēowulf maðelode* was suggested by Grundtvig[308] and Kemble$_2$ [so Sedgefield]. But since *maðelode* is never found in the second half-line, other suggestions have been made: *Bīowulf reordode* [Holthausen] or *þā sē beorn gespræc* [Schücking: the repetition of the letters *ræc* would account for the scribe's omission].

2793. *giohðe*, Thorpe (following Kemble$_1$, *gehðo*): MS. *giogoðe*. Cf. l. 3095.

2799. Instances of *in*, *on*='in exchange for,' are quoted by Klaeber [*Anglia*, xxvii. 258]: *hē bebohte bearn wealdendes on seolfres sinc*, *Crist and Satan*, 577.

mine, Ettmüller$_2$: MS. *minne*.

2800 frōde feorh-leȝe, fremmað ȝēna
lēoda þearfe; ne mæȝ ic hēr lenȝ wesan.
Hātað heaðo-mǣre hlǣw ȝewyrcean
beorhtne æfter bǣle æt brimes nōsan
sē scel tō ȝemyndum mīnum lēodum
2805 hēah hlīfian on Hrones-næsse,
þæt hit sǣ-līðend syððan hātan
Bīowulfes biorh, ðā ðe brentinȝas
ofer |flōda ȝenipu feorran drīfað." Fol. 191a.
Dyde him of healse hrinȝ ȝyldenne
2810 þīoden þrīst-hȳdiȝ; þeȝne ȝesealde,
ȝeonȝum ȝār-wiȝan, ȝold-fāhne helm,
bēah ond byrnan, hēt hyne brūcan well.
"Þū eart ende-lāf ūsses cynnes,
Wǣȝmundinȝa; ealle wyrd fors*w*ēo*p*
2815 mīne māȝas tō metod-sceafte,
eorlas on elne; ic him æfter sceal."
Þæt wæs þām ȝomelan ȝinȝæste word
brēost-ȝehyȝdum, ǣr hē bǣl cure,
hāte heaðo-wylmas; him of h*r*æðre ȝewāt
2820 sāwol sēcean sōð-fæstra dōm.
[XXXIX] Ðā wæs ȝeȝonȝen ȝum*an* unfrōdum
earfoðlīce, þæt hē on eorðan ȝeseah
þone lēofestan līfes æt ende

2800. *gēna.* Thorpe, *gē nū*; and this emendation has been adopted by most recent editors. It does not appear necessary.

2803. Holthausen and Klaeber [*Engl. Stud.* xxxix. 465], following Sievers, read *beorht* (see note to l. 2297), and similarly *þæt* for *sē* in the next line.

2806. Cf. *Odyssey*, xxiv. 80, *etc.*: 'Then around them [the bones of Achilles] did we, the holy host of Argive warriors, pile a great and glorious tomb, on a jutting headland above the broad Hellespont, that it might be seen afar from off the sea by men, both by those who now are, and by those who shall be hereafter.'

2814. *forswēop*, Kemble$_3$: MS. *for speof* (*speof* at the beginning of the next line).

2819. *hræðre*: MS. *hwæðre*, which might very easily have been miswritten for *hræðre*. Kemble$_1$ emended *hreðre*.

2820. There is no number in the MS. after this line to indicate the beginning of a new section, but there is a space, and l. 2821 begins with a large capital. The next 'fitte-'number (l. 2892) is xl.

2821. *guman*, Grein$_2$: MS. *gumū unfrodū*, doubtless another instance of 'anticipation.' Cf. l. 158, where the MS. has *banū folmū*, and see note.

bleate ȝebǣran. Bona swylce læȝ,
2825 eȝeslic eorð-draca ealdre berēafod,
bealwe ȝebǣded. Bēah-hordum lenȝ
wyrm wōh-boȝen wealdan ne mōste,
ac him īrenna ecȝa fornāmon,
hearde, heaðo-scearde, homera lāfe,
2830 þæt se wīd-floȝa wundum stille
hrēas on hrūsan hord-ærne nēah;
nalles |æfter lyfte lācende hwearf   Fol. 191b.
middel-nihtum, māðm-ǣhta wlonc
ansȳn ȳwde, ac hē eorðan ȝefēoll
2835 for ðæs hild-fruman hond-ȝeweorce.
Hūru þæt on lande lȳt manna ðāh
mæȝen-āȝendra, mīne ȝefrǣȝe,
þēah ðe hē dǣda ȝehwæs dyrstiȝ wǣre,
þæt hē wið attor-sceaðan oreðe ȝerǣsde,
2840 oððe hrinȝ-sele hondum styrede,
ȝif hē wæccende weard onfunde
būon on beorȝe. Bīowulfe wearð
dryht-māðma dǣl dēaðe forȝolden;
hæfde ǣȝhwæð*er* ende ȝefēred
2845 lǣnan līfes. Næs ðā lanȝ tō ðon,

2828. Grein$_1$ emended to *hine*: so Schücking and Sedgefield, on the ground that in other instances *forniman* governs the acc. But see Klaeber [*Engl. Stud.* xlii. 323] who instances *forgrīpan* with the dat., *Beowulf*, 2353; *Genesis*, 1275.

2829. Thorpe's emendation *heaðo-scearpe*, 'battle sharp,' has been followed by many editors, and, indeed, it seems very probable that *scearpe* might have been miswritten *scearde*, through the influence of the preceding *hearde*. Yet *scearde* can be defended [Schücking in *Engl. Stud.* xxxix. 110].

2834. *eorðan gefēoll*, 'fell to the earth.' Cf. ll. 2100, and 2898, *næs gerād*.

2836. *on lande*, 'in the world.'

lȳt is probably dat. after *ðāh*, 'has prospered with few.' Klaeber[465] takes *lȳt* as nom., translating 'few have attained or achieved': for this meaning of *ðēon* he compares *Cottonian Gnomic Verses*, 44, *gif hēo nelle on folce geþēon*, 'if she will not attain among the people that...' and a number of examples from the O.E. version of Bede's *History*, *etc.* [cf. *Anglia*, xxvii. 282].

2841. *wæccende*. Thorpe altered to *wæccendne*. But *wæccende* as acc. sing. masc. can be paralleled: cf. l. 46, *umbor-wesende*.

2842. *būon*=*būan*.

2844. *ǣghwæðer*, Kemble$_3$: MS. *æghwæðre*. Grein$_1$, *æghwæðre* (acc. pl.), *ende* (nom.). But cf. l. 3063; besides, *ǣghwæðer* is found nowhere else in the pl.

þæt ðā hild-latan holt ofȝēfan,
tȳdre trēow-loȝan tȳne ætsomne,
ðā ne dorston ǣr dareðum lācan
on hyra man-dryhtnes miclan þearfe;
2850 ac hȳ scamiende scyldas bǣran,
ȝūð-ȝewǣdu, þǣr se ȝomela læȝ;
wlitan on Wīlāf. Hē ȝewērȝad sæt,
fēðe-cempa, frēan eaxlum nēah,
wehte hyne wætre; him wiht ne spēo*w*.
2855 Ne meahte hē on eorðan, ðēah hē ūðe wel,
on ðām frum-ȝāre feorh ȝehealdan,
ne ðæs Wealdendes wiht oncirran.
Wolde dōm |ȝodes dǣdum rǣdan Fol. 192a.
ȝumena ȝehwylcum, swā hē nū ȝēn dêð.
2860 þā wæs æt ðām ȝeonȝum ȝrim ondswaru
ēð-beȝēte, þām ðe ǣr his elne forlēas.
Wīȝlāf maðelode, Wēohstānes sunu,
sec[*ȝ*] sāriȝ-ferð seah on unlēofe:
"þæt lā! mæȝ secȝan, sē ðe wyle sōð specan,
2865 þæt se mon-dryhten, sē ēow ðā māðmas ȝeaf,
ēored-ȝeatwe, þe ȝē þǣr on standað,
—þonne hē on ealu-bence oft ȝesealde
heal-sittendum helm ond byrnan,
þēoden his þeȝnum, swylce hē þrȳdlīcost

2852. It is possible that *wlitan*=*wlītan* (infin.), in which case only a comma should be placed after *læg*. [So Sedgefield.] Most editors have followed Thorkelin in normalizing to *Wīglāf*. See note to ll. 218 and 1530.

2854. *wehte*, 'tried to awake him' [Klaeber[261]]. Cf. *bræc* (l. 1511). Sedgefield[288] suggests *wēte*=*wǣtte*, 'wetted.'

spēow, Thorkelin: MS. *speop*.

2857. The reading of the text would mean 'change aught ordained of God.' Most editors follow Thorpe in substituting *willan* for *wiht* [so Holthausen and Schücking]. Klaeber suggests *weorold-endes wiht*, 'anything of the end of his life'; i.e. 'he could not avert his death at all' [*J.E.G.Ph.* viii. 258].

2860. The strong form *geongum* after *ðām* is, of course, exceptional, and is probably only a scribal error for *geongan*. Holthausen and Schücking alter to *geongan*. See note to l. 158.

2863. *sec*[*g*], Thorkelin's correction: MS. *sec*.

2869. *þrȳdlīcost*. From *þrȳþ*. Thorkelin[218] corrected to *þrȳþlīcost* here, and this spelling with *ð* has been retained down to the present day. The scribe is sometimes careless in crossing his *d*'s, but in the only other passage I know where the word occurs [Byrhtferth's *Handboc*, ed. Kluge in *Anglia*, viii. 302, l. 14] the same spelling with *d* occurs. Under the circumstances *d* for *ð* is quite a normal phonetic development (cf. Sievers, § 201, 3) and this spelling should surely be retained in the text.

2870 ōwēr feor oððe nēah findan meahte—,
þæt hē ʒēnunʒa ʒūð-ʒewǣdu
wrāðe forwurpe, ðā hyne wīʒ beʒet.
Nealles folc-cyninʒ fyrd-ʒesteallum
ʒylpan þorfte; hwæðre him ʒod ūðe,
2875 siʒora Waldend, þæt hē hyne sylfne ʒewræc
āna mid ecʒe, þā him wæs elnes þearf.
Ic him līf-wraðe lȳtle meahte
ætʒifan æt ʒūðe, ond onʒan swā þēah
ofer mīn ʒemet mǣʒes helpan.
2880 Symle wæs þȳ sǣmra, þonne ic sweorde drep
ferhð-ʒenīðlan; fȳr unswīðor
wēoll of ʒewitte. *W*erʒendra tō lȳt
þronʒ ymbe þēoden, þā hyne sīo |þrāʒ becwōm. Fol. 192b.
Hū sceal sinc-þeʒo ond swyrd-ʒifu,
2885 eall ēðel-wyn, ēowrum cynne
lufen āliċʒean! Lond-rihtes mōt,
þǣre mǣʒ-burʒe monna ǣʒhwylc
īdel hweorfan, syððan æðelinʒas
feorran ʒefricʒean flēam ēowerne,
2890 dōm-lēasan dǣd. Dēað bið sēlla
eorla ʒehwylcum þonne edwīt-līf."

2881. *fȳr unswīðor*. This was defended by Rieger[413] as a conjectural emendation, and an exact scrutiny of the MS. shows it to be the actual reading, except for the negligible discrepancy in the division of the letters: *fyrun* (*u* altered from *a*) *swiðor*. Grein conjectured *fȳr ran swīðor*. Since this is inconsistent with *wæs þȳ sǣmra* (l. 2880) we should then have to make Beowulf, instead of the dragon, the subject of *wæs*. Some [e.g. Cosijn[38] and Sedgefield] take Beowulf, in any case, as the subject of *wæs*: but it seems better to make the dragon the subject. This is clearer if, with Sievers [*P.B.B.* ix. 142] and Holthausen, we alter *ferhð-geniðlan* to *ferhð-geniðla*, putting a comma after *drep*.

2882. *Wergendra*, Grundtvig[309], $Kemble_1$: MS. *fergendra*, which is unmeaning, and does not alliterate. ƿ and ꝼ are easily confused.

2883. *þrāg*, 'time of terror.' Cf. note to l. 87.

2884. *Hū*. This was altered by $Kemble_2$ to *nū*, and almost all editors have followed. Yet, as Holthausen tentatively suggests, *hū* makes good sense as introducing an exclamatory clause. Cf. *Wanderer*, 95: *Hu sēo þrāg gewāt...!*

2886. If *lufen* means 'love,' it certainly forms an unsatisfactory parallel to *ēðelwyn*. [Cf. Sievers in *P.B.B.* xxxvi. 427.]

2890. MS. *dæd* corrected from *dæl*.

2890–1. Does Wiglaf mean 'you had better go and hang yourselves'? Tacitus [*Germ.* vi] mentions suicide as the last refuge from such disgrace: *multique superstites bellorum infamiam laqueo finierunt*. [Cf. Scherer, *Kleinere Schriften*, I. 490, for a comparison of this passage with other

XL Heht ðā þæt heaðo-weorc tō haȝan bīodan
ūp ofer ēȝ-clif, þǣr þæt eorl-weorod
morȝen-lonȝne dæȝ mōd-ȝiōmor sæt
2895 bord-hæbbende, bēȝa on wēnum,
ende-dōȝores ond eft-cymes
lēofes monnes. Lȳt swīȝode
nīwra spella, sē ðe næs ȝerād,
ac hē sōðlīce sæȝde ofer ealle:
2900 "Nū is wil-ȝeofa Wedra lēoda,
dryhten Ȝēata, dēað-bedde fæst,
wunað wæl-reste wyrmes dǣdum.
Him on efn liȝeð ealdor-ȝewinna
siex-bennum sēoc; sweorde ne meahte
2905 on ðām āȝlǣcean ǣniȝe þinȝa
wunde ȝewyrcean. Wīȝlāf siteð
ofer Bīowulfe, byre Wīhstānes,
eorl ofer ōðrum unlifiȝendum,
healdeð hiȝe-mǣðum |hēafod-wearde Fol. 193ᵃ.
2910 lēofes ond lāðes. Nū ys lēodum wēn
orleȝ-hwīle, syððan under[*ne*]
Froncum ond Frȳsum fyll cyninȝes
wīde weorðeð. Wæs sīo wrōht scepen

documents showing the punishment of the unfaithful retainer, and Bouterwek in *Z.f.d.A.* xi. 108 for a comparison with other formulas of solemn denunciation.]

2893. *ēg-clif*, Kemble_3: MS. *ecg clif.* Kemble's emendation is supported by l. 577, and has been adopted by almost all later editors, it being urged that '*ecg* is used only of weapons in O.E.' This however is far from being the case: *ecg*, 'verge, brink of high ground,' occurs very frequently in the charters. Nevertheless, since *næs* in l. 2898 makes it probable that the army was stationed on a sea-cliff, I adopt Kemble's emendation, though with hesitation.

2898. See note to l. 2834.

2904. *siex-bennum.* Holthausen and Sedgefield spell *sex-bennum* [from *seax*]. Cf. Sievers_3 § 108, 2.

2909. Kemble_2 and Rieger[413] read *hige-mēðum*, 'holds watch over the spirit-wearied, i.e. the dead.' This is not, in reality, a textual alteration, since in the Anglian original *mēðum* and *mǣðum* would have coincided in form; but we should rather have expected *hige-mēðra*, agreeing with *lēofes ond lāðes.* Sievers [*P.B.B.* ix. 142; but cf. *P.B.B.* xxxvi. 419] and, tentatively, Bugge[106] would read *hige-mēðe*, 'weary of soul,' qualifying Wiglaf, to whom similar epithets are applied, ll. 2852, 2863: *hyge-mēðe* occurs in l. 2442, where, however, it seems to mean 'wearying the mind.' Bugge also suggests *hige-mēðum*, from a presumed *hige-mēðu*, 'weariness of spirit' [so Holthausen].

2911. *under[ne]*, Grein_1: MS. *under.* Cf. l. 127, and, for omission of *ne*, l. 1931.

heard wið Hūȝas, syððan Hiȝelāc cwōm
2915 faran flot-herȝe on Frēsna land,
þǣr hyne Hetware hilde ȝe(h)nǣȝdon,
elne ȝeēodon mid ofer-mæȝene,
þæt se byrn-wiȝa būȝan sceolde,
fēoll on fēðan; nalles frætwe ȝeaf
2920 ealdor duȝoðe. Ūs wæs ā syððan
Merewīoinȝas milts unȝyfeðe.
Ne ic te Swēo-ðēode sibbe oððe trēowe
wihte ne wēne; ac wæs wīde cūð,
þætte Onȝenðīo ealdre besnyðede
2925 Hæðcen Hrēþlinȝ wið Hrefna-wudu,
þā for onmēdlan ǣrest ȝesōhton
Ȝēata lēode Ȝūð-Scilfinȝas.
Sōna him se frōda fæder Ōhtheres,
eald ond eȝes-full, (h)ondslyht āȝeaf,
2930 ābrēot brim-wīsan, brȳd āheorde,
ȝomela iō-mēowlan ȝolde berofene,
Onelan mōdor ond Ōhtheres,
ond ðā folȝode feorh-ȝenīðlan,

2916. MS. *gehnægdon*: *genǣgdon*, 'assailed,' Grein$_1$ and Bugge [*Tidsskr.* viii. 64] followed by Holthausen and Sedgefield: cf. l. 2206. This has the advantage of avoiding double alliteration in the second half-line: cf. l. 1151 and note.

2919. 'The prince gave no treasures to his retainers' (as he would have done had he been victorious). [So Bugge[106].]

2921. Grein$_1$, etc., *Merewīoinga*, following Thorpe (Grundtvig[309] had suggested *mere-wicinga*). But correction is unnecessary: *Merewīoingas* is gen. sg., 'of the Merovingian king.' See note to l. 2453. [So Bugge in *Tidsskr.* viii. 300.]

2922. *te* is the unaccented subsidiary form of *tō*. Instances occur both in E.W.S. (*Cura Pastoralis*) and in early glosses. Cf. O.S. *ti-*, *te-*; O.H.G. *zi*, *ze*. See Bosworth-Toller, and Napier's *O.E. Glosses*.

2929. *ondslyht*, a correction of Grein$_1$: MS. *hond slyht*, here and in l. 2972. The change is necessary for the alliteration. Cf. l. 1541 (and note), and see Sievers$_3$ § 217, N. 1.

2930. *ābrēot*. Some editors follow Kemble$_2$ in normalizing to *ābrēat*. But confusion of *ĕo* and *ĕa* is common in the non-W. S. dialects, and traces of it are abundant in *Beowulf*. Further, in this type of strong verb, *ēo* is found in place of *ēa*, even in W.S. See Sievers$_3$ § 384, N. 2.

brim-wīsan refers to Hæthcyn, who must have carried off the wife of Ongentheow.

brȳd āheorde. The MS. has *bryda heorde*. No importance can be attached to the spacing of the MS.: yet the verb *āheordan*, 'to release from guardianship' (*heord*) is not elsewhere recorded, and is doubtful. Holthausen$_{1,2}$ *āfeorde*, 'removed': so Sedgefeld; Holthausen$_3$ follows Bugge[107], *ahredde*, 'saved.'

oð ðæt hī oðēodon earfoðlīce
2935 in Hrefnes-holt hlāford-lēase.
Besæt ðā sin-herȝe sweorda lāfe
wundum wērȝe; |wēan oft ȝehēt Fol. 193b.
earmre teohhe ondlonȝe niht;
cwæð, hē on merȝenne mēces ecȝum
2940 ȝētan wolde, sum[*e*] on ȝalȝ-trēowu[*m*]
[*fuȝlum*] tō ȝamene. Frōfor eft ȝelamp
sāriȝ-mōdum somod ǣr-dæȝe,
syððan hīe Hyȝelāces horn ond bȳman,
ȝealdor onȝēaton, þā se ȝōda cōm
2945 lēoda duȝoðe on lāst faran.
XLI Wæs sīo swāt-swaðu Sw[*ē*]ona ond Ȝēata,
wæl-rǣs weora, wīde ȝesȳne,
hū ðā folc mid him fǣhðe tōwehton.
Ȝewāt him ðā se ȝōda mid his ȝædelinȝum,
2950 frōd, fela-ȝeōmor, fæsten sēcean,
eorl Onȝenþīo ufor oncirde;
hæfde Hiȝelāces hilde ȝefrunen,
wlonces wīȝ-cræft; wiðres ne trūwode,
þæt hē sǣ-mannum onsacan mihte,
2955 heaðo-līðendum, hord forstandan,
bearn ond brȳde; bēah eft þonan

2940–1. Sedgefield, following Thorpe, reads *grētan*: but the change is unnecessary; *gētan*, 'to destroy,' is not uncommon in the compound *āgētan*. [For the etymology cf. *I.F.* xx. 327, where Holthausen adduces Lithuanian and Lettish cognates.]

The MS. has *sum on galg treowu to gamene*: Thorpe corrected *sum*[*e*] and supplied [*fuglum*], comparing *Judith*, 297, *fuglum tō frōfre*: Kemble$_2$ had emended to *trēowu*[*m*].

Bugge[107] [cf. *Tidsskr.* viii. 60], Holthausen, and Sievers [*P.B.B.* ix. 143] suppose a gap here of a line or more, and this is borne out by the fact that, even after making the three corrections in the text in ll. 2940–1, the construction is not very satisfactory.

2943. *horn ond bȳman* are to be taken together in apposition with *gealdor* [with Holthausen], rather than *bȳman* construed as a gen. dependent on *gealdor* [with Schücking, *etc.*].

2946. *Sw*[*ē*]*ona*, Thorkelin's correction: MS. *swona*.

2949. *se gōda* is Ongentheow. Bugge[372] proposed *gomela* (cf. l. 2968), because he thought so complimentary a word inapplicable to the Swedish king in the mouth of the Geat who is here speaking. An unnecessary scruple; cf. l. 2382 for praise of a Swedish king.

2951. It is difficult to say whether *ufor* means 'on higher ground' or 'further away.' [Cf. Kock in *Anglia*, xxvii. 236.]

2955. *heaðo-līðendum*. See note to l. 1862.

eald under eorð-weall. Þā wæs ǣht boden
Swēona lēodum, segn Higelāce;
freoðo-wong þone forð oferēodon,
2960 syððan Hrēðlingas tō hagan þrungon.
Þǣr wearð Ongenðīow ecgum sweorda.
blonden-fexa, on bid wrecen,
þæt se þēod-cyning ðafian sceolde
Eafores |ānne dōm. Hyne yrringa Fol. 194a.
2965 Wulf Wonrēding wǣpne geræhte,
þæt him for swenge swāt ǣdrum sprong
forð under fexe. Næs hē forht swā ðēh,
gomela Scilfing, ac forgeald hraðe
wyrsan wrixle wæl-hlem þone,
2970 syððan ðēod-cyning þyder oncirde.
Ne meahte se snella sunu Wonrēdes
ealdum ceorle ⟨h⟩ondslyht giofan,
ac hē him on hēafde helm ǣr gescer,
þæt hē blōde fāh būgan sceolde,
2975 fēoll on foldan; næs hē fǣge þā gīt,

2957–9. If we retain the MS. reading, we must interpret: 'Pursuit was offered to the Swedes and a captured banner [was] offered to Hygelac.' Thus many editors, and lately Schücking, who quotes parallels for the importance attached in Germanic times to the capture of the enemy's banner. [Cf. Cosijn[33].] This reading compels us to take *boden* with two widely different nouns, but l. 653 may be quoted as a parallel to this [Klaeber[240]]; and, though the construction is harsh, none of the emendations are sufficiently convincing to justify our deserting the MS.

Schröer [*Anglia*, xiii. 347] takes *ǣht* as 'treasure,' and alters *lēodum* to *lēoda*: 'the treasure of the Swedes and a banner were offered [as ransom] to Hygelac.' So, too, Sedgefield, but without altering the text: 'were offered by the people of the Swedes to Hygelac.' Bugge[107] [and in *Tidsskr.* viii. 61], following Kemble$_2$ and Thorpe, read *Hygelāces*, and explained: 'the banner of Hygelac was raised as a sign of pursuit.' But this also involves a forced construction: therefore if we read *Hygelāces* it is better to delete the semicolon, and construe with Holthausen: 'the banners of Hygelac overran the fastness' [so Clark-Hall]. Sievers, *sæcc Hygelāces*, 'the battle of Hygelac,' parallel to *ǣht*.

Holthausen, *ōht*, 'pursuit,' for *ǣht*.

2959. *forð*, Thorkelin's correction: MS. *ford*.

2960. Is the *haga* ('enclosure') equivalent here to the *wī-haga* ('phalanx') of *Maldon*, 102? [Cf. Cosijn[39].]

2961. *sweorda*, Kemble$_2$: MS. *sweordū*. Cf. l. 158.

2964. Grundtvig[310], *Eofores*. But see l. 2757 (note), and cf. *eafor*, l. 2152.

ānne dōm. See note to l. 2147.

2972. See note on l. 2929.

2973. *hē*, Ongentheow; *him*, Wulf.

2974–5. *hē*, Wulf.

ac hē hyne ȝewyrpte, þēah ðe him wund hrine.
Lēt se hearda Hiȝelāces þeȝn
brād[*n*]e mēce, þā his brōðor læȝ,
eald sweord eotonisc, entiscne helm
2980 brecan ofer bord-weal; ðā ȝebēah cyninȝ,
folces hyrde, wæs in feorh dropen.
Đā wǣron moniȝe, þe his mǣȝ wriðon,
ricone ārǣrdon, ðā him ȝerȳmed wearð,
þæt hīe wæl-stōwe wealdan mōston.
2985 Þenden rēafode rinc ōðerne,
nam on Onȝenðīo īren-byrnan,
heard swyrd hilted ond his helm somod;
hāres hyrste Hiȝelāce bær.
Hē ð[ām] frætwum fēnȝ, ond him fǣȝre ȝehēt
2990 lēana [mid] |lēodum, ond ȝelǣst*e* swā; Fol. 194ᵇ.
ȝeald þone ȝūð-rǣs ȝēata dryhten,
Hrēðles eafora, þā hē tō hām becōm,
Iofore ond Wulfe mid ofer-māðmum,
sealde hiora ȝehwæðrum hund þūsenda
2995 landes ond locenra bēaȝa; ne ðorfte him ðā lēan
oðwītan
mon on middan-ȝearde, syðða[*n*] hīe ðā mǣrða
ȝeslōȝon;

2977. Holthausen and Sedgefield, following Sievers, insert *þā* after *lēt*. *þegn*, Eofor.
2978. *brād[n]e*, Thorpe : MS. *brade*.
2982. *his mǣg*, Eofor's brother, Wulf.
2985. *rinc*, Eofor : *ōðerne*, Ongentheow.
2989. MS. defective at corner : *ð[ām]*, Grundtvig[310].
2990. MS. defective at corner: room for either two or three letters. Kemble$_1$, [*on*]; Grundtvig (1861, p. 102), [*mid*]. Bugge[108] compares ll. 2611, 2623.
gelǣste, Kemble$_2$: MS. *gelæsta*.
2994. *þūsenda*. According to Plummer [*Anglo-Saxon Chronicle*, II, 23] and Kluge [*P.B.B.* ix. 191], 'hides' must be understood. But an earldom of 100,000 hides would have been about the size of the whole land of the Geatas: Sussex contained only 7,000: see l. 2195. Again, how, in this case, are we to construe *locenra bēaga*? I should rather, with Rieger[415] and Schücking, understand some money denomination: 'the value of 100,000 sceattas in land and rings': a great, but not inconceivable, reward.
2995. The typical O.E. figure of understatement. It is not clear, however, whether *him* is sg. or pl., whether it is the generosity of Hygelac which is being celebrated (in which case *ne ðorfte...middan-gearde* must be taken as a parenthesis), or the valour of Eofor and Wulf.
2996. *syðða[n]*, Grundtvig[310] : MS. *syðða*. Cf. note to l. 60.

ond ðā Iofore forȝeaf ānȝan dohtor,
hām-weorðunȝe, hyldo tō wedde.
Þæt ys sīo fǣhðo ond se fēond-scipe,
3000 wæl-nīð wera, ðæs ðe ic [*wēn*] hafo,
þe ūs sēceað tō Swēona lēoda,
syððan hīe ȝefricȝeað frēan ūserne
ealdor-lēasne, þone ðe ǣr ȝehēold
wið hettendum hord ond rīce
3005 æfter hæleða hryre, hwate Scildinȝas,
folc-rēd fremede, oððe furður ȝēn
eorl-scipe efnde. *Nū* is ofost betost,
þæt wē þēod-cyninȝ þǣr scēawian,
ond þone ȝebrinȝan, þe ūs bēaȝas ȝeaf,
3010 on ād-fære. Ne scel ānes hwæt
meltan mid þām mōdiȝan, ac þǣr is māðma hord,
ȝold unrīme, ȝrimme ȝecēa[po]d,
ond nū æt sīðestan sylfes fēore

3000. No gap in MS.: [*wēn*], Kemble_1. Cf. l. 383.

3001. For the pl. *lēoda* see Wulfstan (ed. Napier), p. 106, l. 23 and *Psalms* lxxi. 10. [Cf. Sievers § 264 and Royster in *M.L.N.* xxiii. 122.]

3005. Müllenhoff[155] considered this line a careless repetition of l. 2052, and this is the easiest way out of the difficulty. Thorpe explained: 'It would appear that Beowulf, in consequence of the fall of Hrothgar's race [*hæleþa hryre*] was called to rule also over the Danes (Scyldings).' Klaeber calls this an 'extraordinary assumption,' but we may note that, according to Saxo (Book III), the throne of Denmark *was* thus left vacant after the fall of Hrothulf, and was taken by a Swedish prince, who ruled jointly over both kingdoms. Since Saxo does not recognise any kingdom of the Geatas apart from the Swedes, this might reasonably be interpreted as a reminiscence of such a tradition as Thorpe assumes. The Geatic kingdom was at this date nearing its fall. It is accordingly exceedingly improbable that any such rule existed as a historic fact: for its existence in tradition cf. the empire attributed to king Arthur.

Most editors follow Grein_2 and alter to *Scylfingas*, and this can be taken (1) in apposition with *hīe* in l. 3002, which is intolerably forced; (2) parallel with *hord ond rīce* in l. 3004, in which case we can only suppose that the term *Scylfingas* could be applied equally, on the ground of common ancestry, to both Swedes and Geatas; compare l. 2603, where Wiglaf is called *lēod Scylfinga*; (3) l. 3005 might be taken as a parenthesis: 'After the fall of the heroes, the Scylfingas were bold'; or (4) it can be transposed to follow l. 3001 [Ettmüller_2: so Holthausen and Sedgefield].

But, since so little relief is gained by altering the text to *Scylfingas*, it is better to let *Scildingas* stand, unless we have the courage to make the satisfactory alteration to *Sǣ-Gēatas* [with Klaeber, whose discussion of the subject in *J.E.G.Ph.* viii. 258–9 should be consulted].

3007. *Nū is*, Kemble_2: MS. *meis*. *Mē is* is a possible reading: 'As for me,' 'as it seems to me.'

3012. MS. defective at corner: *gecēa*[*po*]*d*, Kemble_1.

bēaȝas [ȝeboh]te; þā sceall brond fretan,
3015 ǣled þeccean, |nalles eorl weȝan Fol. 195a.
māððum tō ȝemyndum, ne mæȝð scȳne
habban on healse hrinȝ-weorðunȝe,
ac sceal ȝeōmor-mōd, ȝolde berēafod,
oft, nalles ǣne, el-land tredan,
3020 nū se here-wīsa hleahtor āleȝde,
ȝamen ond ȝlēo-drēam. Forðon sceall ȝār wesan,
moniȝ morȝen-ceald, mundum bewunden,
hæfen on handa, nalles hearpan swēȝ
wīȝend weccean, ac se wonna hrefn
3025 fūs ofer fǣȝum fela reordian,
earne secȝan hū him æt ǣte spēow,
þenden hē wið wulf[*e*] wæl rēafode."
Swā se secȝ hwata secȝȝende wæs
lāðra spella; hē ne lēaȝ fela
3030 wyrda ne worda. Weorod eall ārās;
ēodon unblīðe under Earna-næs,
wollen-tēare, wundur scēawian.
Fundon ðā on sande sāwul-lēasne
hlim-bed healdan, þone þe him hrinȝas ȝeaf
3035 ǣrran mǣlum; þā wæs ende-dæȝ
ȝōdum ȝeȝonȝen, þæt se ȝūð-cyninȝ,
Wedra þēoden, wundor-dēaðe swealt.
Ǣr hī þǣr ȝesēȝan syllīcran wiht,

3014. [*geboh*]*te*: MS. defective, Grundtvig[311] suggested *bebohte*. We may interpret *gebohte* as a pret. sing., with *Bīowulf* understood as subject: or as pl. of the past part., agreeing with *bēagas*. [Cf. Lawrence in *J.E.G.Ph.* x. 638.]

3027. *wulf*[*e*], Grundtvig[311]: MS. *wulf*. Correction metrically necessary. Cf. l. 2673. [See Martin in *Engl. Stud.* xx. 295.]

3028. Grein$_2$, *secg-hwata* (i.e. 'sword-brave'), a quite unnecessary compound: *se secg hwata* is paralleled by *se maga geonga* (l. 2675). [Cf. Bugge, *Tidsskr.* viii. 61.]

For *secggende* see Sievers$_3$ § 216, N. 1.

3034. See note on l. 1271.

3035. According to Zupitza the MS. has *ærrun* ('*u* altered from *a* by erasure'). But I should read this as *ærran*, and attribute the partial obliteration to accident.

See Sievers$_3$ § 304, N. 3.

3038. 'But first they saw a stranger being there' [Clark-Hall]. Many attempts have been made to improve this sentence: [*þ*]*ǣr hī þā gesēgan*, Sievers' emendation, is followed by Holthausen and Sedgefield. But, though somewhat awkwardly phrased, the meaning seems clear. [Cf. Klaeber in

wyrm on wonȝe wiðer-ræhtes þǣr
3040 lāðne licȝean; wæs se lēȝ-draca,
ȝrimlīc ȝry[re-fāh], |ȝlēdum beswǣled. **Fol. 195b.**
Sē wæs fīftiȝes fōt-ȝemearces
lanȝ on leȝere; lyft-wynne hēold
nihtes hwīlum, nyðer eft ȝewāt
3045 dennes nīosian; wæs ðā dēaðe fæst,
hæfde eorð-scrafa ende ȝenyttod.
Him biȝ stōdan bunan ond orcas,
discas lāȝon ond dȳre swyrd,
ōmiȝe, þurhetone, swā hīe wið eorðan fæðm
3050 þūsend wintra þǣr eardodon;
þonne wæs þæt yrfe ēacen-cræftiȝ,
iū-monna ȝold, ȝaldre bewunden,
þæt ðām hrinȝ-sęle hrīnan ne mōste
ȝumena ǣniȝ, nefne ȝod sylfa,
3055 siȝora Sōð-cyninȝ, sealde þām ðe hē wolde
—hē is manna ȝehyld— hord openian,

Engl. Stud. xxxix. 427.] The fifty-foot-long dragon would naturally be the first thing to attract the gaze of those approaching.

3041. MS. defective at corner: *gry[re]*, Thorkelin; Heyne's *gryre-gæst* (cf. l. 2560) was based on Kölbing's statement that there is room for from four to six letters on the missing corner. [So Holthausen and Schücking.] Zupitza, on the other hand, reads *gryr[e]* simply. Yet an examination of the other side of the leaf, where several letters have been lost, makes it probable that more than one letter has been lost on this side also. On the other hand, there is hardly room for *gry[re-gæst]*: but *gry[re-fāh]* [Bugge in *Tidsskr.* viii. 52] fills the gap well, and has the support of l. 2576.

3043–4. It is not clear whether *lyft-wynne* means 'joy in the air, pleasure of flying,' or is equivalent to *wynsumne lyft*, 'the joyous air,' abstract for concrete, like *eard-lufan* (l. 692). [For this last rendering cf. Cosijn[39].]

Equally it is uncertain whether we should construe *nihtes hwīlum* as 'by night, at times' [cf. Bugge[373]] or 'in the time of night' [Cosijn[39]].

3045. *nīosian.* See note to l. 115.

3049. It is unnecessary to follow Kemble$_2$ and normalize *þurhetone* to *þurhetene.*

The emendation *ōme þurhetone*, 'eaten through with rust' [Scheinert in *P.B.B.* xxx. 377], is one of those improvements of the MS. which are hardly legitimate.

3050. *þūsend wintra.* Müllenhoff draws attention to the discrepancy with l. 2278, according to which the time was 300 years. Krüger [*P.B.B.* ix. 577] tries to reconcile the passages by interpreting *swā* here 'as if,' 'as though.' But the discrepancy is immaterial. [Cf. Cosijn[40].]

3051. *þonne*, i.e. when the gold was laid in the earth [Bugge[374]].

3056. Bugge[109] [followed by Holthausen and Schücking] would read *hæleþa* for *manna* [so Morgan in *P.B.B.* xxxiii. 110], so as to get the alliterating syllable in the right place. The same improvement can be made more simply by transposing the words: *hē is gehyld manna* [Sedgefield$_2$].

Grein$_2$ reads *hēlsmanna gehyld* in apposition to *hord*; so Earle: 'to open the hoard, the sorcerers' hold.'

efne swā hwylcum manna, swā him ʒemet ðūhte.

XLII Þā wæs ʒesȳne, þæt se sīð ne ðāh

þām ðe unrihte ınne ʒehȳdde

3060 wrǣ*te* under wealle. Weard ǣr ofslōh

fēara sumne; þā sio fǣhð ʒewearð

ʒewrecen wrāðlīce. Wundur hwār þonne

eorl ellen-rōf ende ʒefēre

līf-ʒesceafta, þonne lenʒ ne mæʒ

3065 mon mid his [mā]ʒum medu-seld būan.

Swā wæs Bīowulfe, |þā hē biorʒes weard Fol. 196a.

sōhte, searo-nīðas; seolfa ne cūðe,

þurh hwæt his worulde ʒedāl weorðan sceolde.

Swā hit oð dōmes dæʒ dīope benemdon

3070 þēodnas mǣre, þā ðæt þǣr dydon,

þæt se secʒ wǣre synnum scildiʒ,

herʒum ʒeheaðerod, hell-bendum fæst,

3058, *etc.*, mean, apparently, that the issue was a bad one for the dragon. Bugge[109, 375] attempts a re-arrangement of ll. 3051–76, and makes ll. 3058–60 refer to the fugitive who originally stole the treasure.

3060. *wrǣte*, Thorpe: MS. *wræce*. Cf. l. 2771.

3061. *fēara sumne* means Beowulf, being 'one of a few' (cf. l. 1412), i.e. Beowulf with few companions. But, by the usual understatement, 'few' here probably means 'none.' Cosijn[40] compares *Rood*, 69, *mǣte weorode*, interpreting 'with a small company,' as meaning 'quite alone.'

3062 ff. The meaning seems to be 'It is a subject for wonder [i.e. it is uncertain] where a man will end his life, when he may no longer dwell on this earth. Even so was it with Beowulf—*he* knew not...'; *þonne* in l. 3062 is parallel with *þonne* in l. 3064. [See Kock in *Anglia*, xxvii. 233; Sievers in *P.B.B.* ix. 143; Nader in *Anglia*, x. 544–5; Cosijn[40], who compares Alfred's *Cura Pastoralis*, Preface (ed. Sweet, p. 8), *uncūð hū longe*, 'it is uncertain how long.']

On the other hand we might take the *swā* in l. 3066 and *swā* in l. 3069 as correlative, with *seolfa...sceolde* forming a parenthesis. The meaning would then be: 'It happened unto Beowulf in such wise as the *þēodnas mǣre* had laid the spell.'

3065. MS. defective at corner: [*mā*]*gum*, Kemble$_1$.

3067. *sōhte* governs both *biorges weard* and *searo-nīðas*.

Sedgefield reads *searo-nīða*, comparing for the adverbial gen. pl. ll. 845, 1439.

3068. *þurh hwæt*, 'by what.' This is explained in the following lines (3069–3073); Beowulf's death is really caused by the curse which, unknown to him, had been placed upon the gold by the great chiefs (*þēodnas mǣre*) who had it in olden time. [Cf. Klaeber in *Engl. Stud.* xxxix. 432.] So feared were these curses that forms of prayer are extant for purifying *vasa reperta in locis antiquis*. [See *Rituale Eccl. Dunelmensis*, Surtees Society, 97, *etc.*, and Bouterwek in *Z.f.d.A.* xi. 109.] The curse on the Niblung hoard may be compared.

3069. *dīope*. Holthausen$_1$, *dīore*: so Sedgefield.

3072. *hergum*. Holthausen$_{1,2}$ conjectures *hefgum*, 'confined by cares.' The change (ƞ to ƿ) is a slight one, but hardly for the better: *hergum* makes a good parallel to *hellbendum*.

wommum ȝewītnad, sē ðone wonȝ str*u*de;
næs hē ȝold-hwæte ȝearwor hæfde
3075 Āȝendes ēst ǣr ȝescēawod.
Wīȝlāf maðelode, Wihstānes sunu:
"Oft sceall eorl moniȝ ānes willan
wrǣc ādrēoȝ*an*, swā ūs ȝeworden is.
Ne meahton wē ȝelǣran lēofne þēoden,
3080 rīces hyrde, rǣd ǣniȝne,
þæt hē ne ȝrētte ȝold-weard þone,
lēte hyne licȝean, þǣr hē lonȝe wæs,
wīcum wunian oð woruld-ende;
hēold on hēah ȝesceap. Hord ys ȝescēawod,

3073. *strude*, Grundtvig[311]: MS. *strade*. [Cf. Bugge[374].] See ll. 581 and 3126: *a* and *u* are in many scripts hardly distinguishable.

3074–5. The MS. reading is difficult, but admits of interpretation, if we take *næs* as the adv. of negation (cf. l. 562): 'Not before had he (Beowulf) beheld more fully the gold-abounding grace of the Lord': i.e. this was the biggest prize of gold which God had ever granted to him. [So Bugge in *Tidsskr.* viii. 62, *etc.*] The MS. is also tentatively defended by Cosijn[41], but with a different explanation: 'he (Beowulf) had by no means in gold-greedy wise (*gold-hwæte*) accurately surveyed (*gearwor gescēawod*, cf. l. 2748) the owner's inheritance (the dragon's hoard).' [For *ēst*='inheritance,' cf. also Klaeber[264].] This would mean that, although Wiglaf had shown him some of the spoils, Beowulf had not been able to survey the hoard closely. Müllenhoff [*Z.f.d.A.* xiv. 241] also retains the MS. reading.

Holthausen's objection that *gold-hwæte* must be wrong, because *hwæt* is only compounded with abstract nouns, seems invalid: *blēd-hwat*, 'flower or fruit abounding' (*Riddles*, I. [II.] 9), is an exact parallel, and Holthausen$_2$ returns to *gold-hwæte* as an adv.

Neither Bugge's rendering nor Cosijn's gives very good sense, but neither are any of the suggested emendations satisfactory. Sievers [*P.B.B.* ix. 143] reads *næs hē goldhwætes gearwor hæfde, etc.*, 'Beowulf had not experienced the favour of the gold-greedy owner (the dragon)'; Rieger[416] and Cosijn[41], *næs hē gold hwæðre gearwor hæfde* [*ofer*] *āgendes ēst ǣr gescēawod*, 'Beowulf had never looked more eagerly upon gold which he had gained against the will of its owner'; ten Brink[145] and Wyatt, *næs* [i.e. *ne wæs*] *hē gold-hwæt*; *gearwor hæfde*...'Beowulf was not avaricious; rather he had experienced the grace of the Lord' (and therefore was endowed with the virtues); Holthausen$_2$, Schücking, and Sedgefield read *goldǣhte* or *goldfrætwe*, 'never before had Beowulf gazed more eagerly upon gold adornments, the delight [or inheritance] of their owner'; or we might interpret the same reading, with Schücking [*Engl. Stud.* xxxix. 111], partly following Trautmann, 'rather would he [*se secg* of l. 3071] not have gazed upon the gold adornments...'

If the text is to be altered at all it would probably be best to read *hie...hæfdon* for *hē...hæfde*: 'in no wise had these avaricious lords known the grace of the Creator,' i.e. the authors of the spell were heathen. Cf. note to l. 3068 and ll. 175–188.

3078. *ādrēogan*, Kemble$_1$: MS. *a dreogeð*.

3084. 'We could not dissuade him; he held (on)to his high fate,' *or* 'he held on (adv.) his high fate.' Grein and Toller give several instances of the intrans. use of *healdan*, and of *on* used adverbially. See also Mätzner's *O.E. Dict.*, p. 405, col. 1; among other passages there quoted is: *hald hardiliche o þat tu haues bigunnen*, *St. Kath.*, 676.

3085 ʒrimme ʒeʒonʒen; wæs þæt ʒifeðe tō swīð,
þe ðone [*þēod-cyning*] þyder ontyhte.
Ic wæs þǣr inne ond þæt eall ʒeondseh,
recedes ʒeatwa, þā mē ʒerȳmed wæs
nealles swǣslīce, sīð ālȳfed
3090 inn under eorð-weall. Ic on ofoste ʒefēnʒ
micle mid mundum mæʒen-byrðenne
hord-ʒestrēona, hider ūt ætbær Fol. 196b.
cyninʒe mīnum; cwico wæs þā ʒēna,
wīs ond ʒewittiʒ. Worn eall ʒespræc
3095 ʒomol on ʒehðo, ond ēowic ʒrētan hēt,
bæd þæt ʒē ʒeworhton æfter wines dǣdum
in bǣl-stede beorh þone hêan,
micelne ond mǣrne, swā hē manna wæs
wīʒend weorðfullost wīde ʒeond eorðan,
3100 þenden hē burh-welan brūcan mōste.
Uton nū efstan ōðre [*sīðe*]
sēon ond sēcean searo[-*ʒimma*] ʒeþræc,
wundur under wealle; ic ēow wīsiʒe,
þæt ʒē ʒenōʒe nēon scēawiað

Reading *hēoldon* [Heyne-Schücking, Holder], we must render 'we have gotten a hard destiny,' or, perhaps, 'fate appointed from on high'; reading *healdan* [Kemble$_2$ *etc.*], 'leave him (the dragon) to fulfil his high destiny' [Earle, Sedgefield]; or we might read *heoldon*=*healdan* [Bugge in *Z.f.d.Ph.* iv. 220-2, q.v. for further suggestions].

gescēawod. Sarrazin [*Engl. Stud.* xxviii. 410] suggests *gecēapod*, 'purchased.'

3085. *gifeðe*, 'Fate,' rather than, with Bugge[109], 'that which enticed the king (i.e. the treasure) was granted (*gifeðe*) in manner too overpowering, i.e. at too great a price, bought too dear.'

3086. No gap in MS.: [*þēod-cyning*], Grein$_2$; Grundtvig[311] had suggested *þēoden*.

3094. *wīs ond gewittig*, either 'the prudent and wise king' [Scheinert in *P.B.B.* xxx. 381, footnote] or 'still alert and conscious' [Klaeber in *Anglia*, xxix. 382]. This last interpretation is supported by the use of *gewittig* in Ælfric's *Homilies*, e.g. II. p. 24, l. 12: *hēo þærrihte wearð gewittig*, 'she forthwith became of sound mind.'

3096. *æfter wines dǣdum*, 'in memory of the deeds of our king,' is defended by Cosijn[41] against the conjecture of Bugge [*Tidsskr.* viii. 300], *æfter wine dēadum*, 'in memory of your dead king.'

3101. No gap in MS.: [*sīðe*], Grundtvig[312], Kemble$_2$.

3102. Line defective both in sense and metre. Bugge[109] supplied [*gimma*], comparing ll. 1157, 2749.

3103-4. Sievers [*P.B.B.* ix. 144] suggests *þǣr* for *þæt*, with *ic ēow wīsige* in parentheses; so too Holthausen. [But see Schücking, *Satzverk.* 26.]

Grundtvig[312] normalized *nēon* to *nēan*, but unnecessarily. [See Sievers$_3$ § 150, 3, and Bugge in *Tidsskr.* viii. 63.]

3105 bēaᵹas ond brād ᵹold. Sie sīo bǣr ᵹearo
ǣdre ᵹeæfned, þonne wē ūt cymen,
ond þonne ᵹeferian frēan ūserne,
lēofne mannan, þǣr hē lonᵹe sceal
on ðæs Waldendes wǣre ᵹeþolian."
3110 Hēt ðā ᵹebēodan byre Wīhstānes,
hæle hilde-dīor, hæleða moneᵹum,
bold-āᵹendra, þæt hīe bǣl-wudu
feorran feredon, folc-āᵹende,
ᵹōdum tōᵹēnes: "Nū sceal ᵹlēd fretan
3115 —weaxan wonna lēᵹ— wiᵹena strenᵹel,
þone ðe oft ᵹebād īsern-scūre,
þonne strǣla storm strenᵹum ᵹebǣded
scōc ofer scild-weall, sceft nytte hēold,
feðer-ᵹearwum fūs flāne full-ēode."
3120 Hūru se snotra sunu Wīhstānes
ācīᵹde of corðre |cyniᵹes þeᵹnas Fol. 198ᵃ.
syfone [æt]somne, þā sēlestan,
ēode eahta sum under inwit-hrōf
hilde-rinc[*a*]; sum on handa bær
3125 ǣled-lēoman, sē ðe on orde ᵹēonᵹ.
Næs ðā on hlytme, hwā þæt hord strude,

3113. *folc-āgende* may be nom. pl. [Cosijn[41]] or dat. sg. [Bugge[109]].

3115. The introduction of a parenthesis between the verb *fretan* and its object *strengel* is certainly strange. Consequently many editors take *weaxan*, not as the intrans. verb 'to grow,' but as a trans. verb, meaning 'to devour,' parallel to *fretan* and, with it, governing *strengel*. Various cognates and derivations have been suggested. Cosijn connects with Lat. *vesci*, Earle and Sedgefield with *wascan* 'to bathe, envelope,' Holthausen with Goth. *fra-wisan*, 'to spend, exhaust.'

3119. *feðer-gearwum*, Kemble$_1$, partly following an emendation of Thorkelin: MS. *fæder gearwū*.

3121. This folio, the last, is very badly mutilated.

cyniges. Thorkelin corrected to *cyni*[*n*]*ges*. But *cynig* is a recognized form in the late 10th and 11th centuries.

3122. All recent editors read [*tō*]*-somne*, following Zupitza, who however admits: 'now *to* entirely gone.' But there seems to be no evidence that it existed even in Thorkelin's time: its occurrence in Kemble$_2$ seems to be due to conjecture. In the absence of evidence in its favour, I read [*æt*]*somne* with Grein$_2$; cf. l. 2847.

3124. *hilde-rinc*[*a*]. Style and metre necessitate this emendation, made independently by Ettmüller$_2$ and Sievers [*P.B.B.* ix. 144]: cf. l. 1412. [For a defence of the MS. reading, see Cosijn[41].]

3126. 'It was not decided by lot who should...' means, by the usual under-statement, that all pressed to take part. [Klaeber in *Engl. Stud.* xxxix. 432.]

syððan orwearde ǣniʒne dǣl
secʒas ʒesēʒon on sele wunian,
lǣne licʒan; lȳt ǣniʒ mearn,
3130 þæt hī ofostlīc[e] ūt ʒeferedon
dȳre māðmas. Dracan ēc scufun,
wyrm ofer weall-clif, lēton wēʒ niman,
flōd fæðmian, frætwa hyrde.
Þā wæs wunden ʒold on wǣn hladen,
3135 ǣʒhwæs unrīm; æþelinʒ boren,
hār hilde[-*rinc*], tō Hrones-næsse.
XLIII Him ðā ʒeʒiredan Ʒēata lēode
ād on eorðan unwāclīcne,
helm[*um*] behonʒen, hilde-bordum,
3140 beorhtum byrnum, swā hē bēna wæs;
āleʒdon ðā tōmiddes mǣrne þēoden
hæleð hīofende, hlāford lēofne.
Onʒunnon þā on beorʒe bǣl-fȳra mǣst
wīʒend weccan; wud[u]-rēc āstāh
3145 sweart ofer swio*ð*ole, swōʒende lēʒ
wōpe bewunden —wind-blond ʒelæʒ—,
oð þæt hē ðā bān-hūs ʒebrocen hæfde,
hāt on hreðre. Hiʒum unrōte
mōd-ceare mǣndon mon-dryhtnes cw[e]alm;
3150 swylce ʒiōmor ʒyd ||[s]īa ʒ[eō-]mēowle Fol. 198b.

3130. *ofostlīc*[*e*]: MS. defective at edge, emended by Ettmüller$_2$.
3134. MS. ꝥ, which should stand for *þæt* (but see note to l. 15): *þā*, Thorkelin's emendation, so Kemble$_2$: *þǣr*, Kemble$_3$.
3135. *æþeling*, Kemble$_2$: MS. *æþelinge*. Probably the original MS. had *æþelingc* [Bugge[109]]. See Sievers$_3$ § 215.
3136. MS. *hilde to*. 'I am unable to decide whether there is an erasure of one letter after *hilde* or an original blank' (Zupitza): [*rinc*] is an emendation of Ettmüller$_2$: cf. ll. 1307 and 3124.
3139. *helm*[*um*], Grein: MS. *helm*.
Sedgefield reads *helmum behēngon*, to avoid the discrepancy between *unwāclīcne* (inflected) and *behongen* (uninflected).
3144. Hole in MS.: *wud*[*u*], Kemble$_1$.
3145. MS. *swicðole*; *swioðole* is Thorpe's conjecture, though he gave an impossible interpretation of it. See note to l. 782.
lēg, Thorpe: MS. *let*.
3147. *hē* refers to *lēg* (l. 3145).
3149. MS. torn at foot: *cw*[*e*]*alm*, Kemble$_1$.
3150, *etc.* All that can either be made out at present, or for which we have adequate evidence in Thorkelin's transcripts or elsewhere, is given in the text. It seems clear that the mutilated passage occupies six lines (not seven, as was unaccountably supposed by Heyne and Wülker, and still is by Schücking).

. . . . [b]unden-heorde
. . . sorȝ-cearïȝ sǣlðe ȝeneahhe,
þæt hīo hyre : : : : : : : ȝas hearde on : : ēde
wæl-fylla wonn : : : : des eȝesan
3155 hyðo : h : : : : : d. Heofon rēce swe[a]lȝ.
ȝeworhton ðā Wedra lēode
hl[ǣw] on [*h*]liðe, sē wæs hēah ond brād,
[wǣ]ȝ-līðendum wīde ȝ[e]sȳne,

It must be remembered that this page has been almost entirely freshened up in a later hand, and, in part, erroneously. Thus in ll. 3150, 3155, though only [*s*]*ia*, *hyðo* can now be read, no doubt *sio*, *hynðo* were the original readings. Bugge's restoration is therefore not to be discredited merely because a letter does not agree with what is now visible in the MS.

The reconstruction of ll. 3150–55 made by Bugge[110–11] is, apart from the last half-line, not to be improved upon:

3150 *swylce giōmor-gyd sīo geō-mēowle*
æfter Bēowulfe bunden-heorde
song sorg-cearig, sǣde geneahhe,
þæt hīo hyre hearm-dagas hearde ondrēde
wǣl-fylla worn wīgendes egesan
3155 *hȳnðo ond hæft-nȳd hēof on rīce wealg.*

geō (l. 3150) had been conjectured by Ettmüller, and *sio geo-meowle*, partly conjectured, partly deciphered, by Zupitza, who pointed out that this reading was confirmed by the Latin gloss *anus* written above. Under an exceptionally good light, Zupitza had also read, or 'thought he had been able to read,' first *metodes*, and later [*w*]*igendes* (l. 3154). The *b* of *bunden-heorde* (l. 3151) was conjectured by Grein$_2$. All the remainder of this excellent restoration is due to Bugge.

But Bugge's last half-line, *hēof on rīce wealg*, 'lamentation in a strange land,' is a wanton departure from the MS., and is certainly wrong. The MS. reading is clearly *heofon rece swealg*, 'heaven swallowed the smoke' [*swealg* was conjectured by Ettmüller$_2$: on further examination it proved to be the MS. reading].

Bugge comments upon his reconstruction: 'For the whole passage cf. ll. 3016–20. Beowulf's aged widow (*geō-mēowle*) was perhaps Hygd; cf. ll. 2369 ff.'

A close parallel is provided by the *Fates of Men*, 46–7, 'the lady laments, seeing the flames consume her son.' [For the O.E. song of lament over the dead, cf. Schücking in *Engl. Stud.* xxxix. 1, *etc.*] Compare too the lament of Andromache over Hector [*Iliad* xxiv. 725–45], which has the same governing motive: the fear that, now the tribal hero is dead, nothing but captivity awaits the defenceless folk. See also ll. 2999, *etc.*, 3016, *etc.*

3153. 'The first two letters after *hearde* look like *on* or *an*, the letter before *de* may have been *e*, as the stroke that generally connects *e* with a following letter is preserved' (Zupitza).

3157. Zupitza, *leode hl* : : *on liðe*, and in a foot-note: 'I am unable to make out *hlæw* after *leode*: the two last letters seem to me to be rather *eo*' [certainly]; *hlæw* is recorded by Kemble$_1$ as the MS. reading. See l. 3169. Thorpe, *hliðe*.

Holthausen [followed by Schücking] reads, for the sake of the metre, *hl*[*ǣw*] *on* [*h*]*liðe*[*s nōsan*].

3158. The remainder of this page of the MS. is frequently illegible or defective, both at the edges and elsewhere.

wǣg is Kemble's conjecture.

ond betimbredon on tȳn daʒum
3160 beadu-rōfes bēcn; bronda lāfe
wealle beworhton, swā hyt weorðlīcost
fore-snotre men findan mihton.
Hī on beorʒ dydon bēʒ ond siʒlu,
eall swylce hyrsta, swylce on horde ǣr
3165 nīð-hēdiʒe men ʒenumen hæfdon;
forlēton eorla ʒestrēon eorðan healdan,
ʒold on ʒrēote, þǣr hit nū ʒēn lifað
eldum swā unnyt, swā hi[t ǣro]r wæs.
Þā ymbe hlǣw riodan hilde-dēore
3170 æþelinʒa bearn ealra twelfa,
woldon [ceare] cwīðan, kyninʒ mǣnan,
word-ʒyd wrecan, ond ymb w[er] sprecan;
eahtodan eorl-scipe, ond his ellen-weorc
duʒuðum dēmdon, swā hit ʒedē[fe] bið,
3175 þæt mon his wine-dryhten wordum herʒe,
ferhðum frēoʒe, þonne hē forð scile
of līc-haman [lǣded] weorðan.
Swā beʒnornodon ʒēata lēode
hlāfordes [hry]re, heorð-ʒenēatas;
3180 cwǣdon þæt hē wǣre wyruld-cyninʒ,
manna mildust ond mon-[ðw]ǣrust,
lēodum līðost, ond lof-ʒeornost.

3163. *bēg.* Thorpe, *bēagas* [so Holthausen, *bēgas*].
3168. Zupitza, *hi* : : : : *r*; *h*[*it ǣro*]*r*, Kemble$_2$.
3169. So when Attila was buried (doubtless according to Gothic rites) mounted horsemen rode round the body as it lay in state. The account of the burial of Achilles (*Odyssey*, xxiv. 68–70) may also be compared: 'And many heroes of the Achaeans moved in armour around thy pyre as thou wast burning, both foot and horse.'
3170. *twelfa* may be a gen., attracted to *ealra*, but more probably it is miswritten for *twelfe*, 'twelve of the entire body' [Ettmüller$_2$. So Klaeber in *M.L.N.* xvi. 17, Holthausen, Schücking, Sedgefield. Cf. also Einenkel in *Anglia*, xxvii. 5, 51].
3171. Zupitza, : : : : ; *ceare*, Grein; *hīe*, Sedgefield.
3172. Zupitza, *w* : : ; *wer*, Grein.
3174. Hole in MS.: *gedē*[*fe*], Kemble$_2$.
3177. Zupitza: '*lachaman* MS., but there can be little doubt that *lac* instead of *lic* is owing only to the late hand.'
Zupitza, : : : : ; Kemble, *lǣne*, so Schücking. Kluge, Trautmann, Sedgefield, *lȳsed*. But the reading *lǣded* is supported by a comparison of the *Speech of the Soul*, 21, *syððan of lichoman lǣded wǣre* [Jacobsen, so Holthausen].
3179. Zupitza, : : : *re*; Thorpe, *hryre*.
3180. *wyruld-cyning.* Kemble, *etc.*, *cyning*[*a*].
3181. MS. torn at foot: [*ðw*]*ǣrust*, Grundtvig[312].

APPENDIX

THE FIGHT AT FINNSBURG

George Hickes first printed the fragment of the *Fight at Finnsburg* in his *Thesaurus* (1705: vol. I. p. 192). He mentions that he had found it written on a single leaf in a MS. of 'Semi-Saxon' Homilies in the Lambeth Library. Repeated search has failed to discover this leaf, and we have nothing to depend on but Hickes' very inaccurate transcript [quoted as 'Hickes' in the notes below].

* * * [hor]nas byrnað nǣfre?'
Hlēoþrode ðā heaþo-ȝeonȝ cyninȝ:
"Ne ðis ne daȝað ēastan, ne hēr draca ne flēoȝeð,
ne hēr ðisse healle hornas ne byrnað,
5 ac hēr forþ berað, ...
. . . . fuȝelas sinȝað,

1\. The first three words belong to a watcher (possibly Hengest), who is answered by the 'war-young king' (Hnæf).

[*hor*]*nas*, supplied by Rieger, *Lesebuch*.

2\. Trautmann and Holthausen would write, for the sake of the metre, *ðā hlēoþrode*.

heaþo-geong, Grundtvig's correction; Hickes, *hearo geong*.

3\. *ðis*, 'this light': *ēastan*, Grundtvig: Hickes, *eastun*; *a* and *u* are easily and often confused, cf. l. 27 below and *Beowulf*, 158, 581, *etc.*

5–6. The two half-lines make sense individually, but do not combine. Hence it has been generally supposed that between them two half-lines have been lost, though there is no gap indicated by Hickes. Bugge [*Tidsskr.* viii. 305, *P.B.B.* xii. 23], following in part a suggestion of Rieger [*Lesebuch*, cf. *Z.f.d.A.* xlviii. 9], proposed:

ac hēr forþ berað [*fyrd-searu rincas,*
flacre flānbogan] *fugelas singað,*

'But here champions bear forward their battle array: the flickering birds of the bow [i.e. arrows] sing.'

Another suggestion is to make the two recorded half-lines fit each other either by altering *hēr* to *fēr* [=*fǣr*], 'they bring forward the sudden assault' [Grein, so Heyne, and, though abandoned by Grein, the conjecture was long-lived], or *berað* to *fērað*, 'they, i.e. the foes, press forward' [Grundtvig, followed by Holthausen]. In this case the *fugelas* will be birds: either carrion birds [ten Brink, *Pauls Grdr.* II. i. 545] or the birds of the morning [Klaeber in *Anglia*, xxviii. 447]; this last interpretation is supported by a parallel in the *Bjarkamál*, the opening call to arms of which has struck many students as resembling *Finnsburh*.

ȝylleð ȝrǣȝ-hama, ȝūð-wudu hlynneð,
scyld scefte oncwyð. Nū scȳneð þes mōna
waðol under wolcnum; nū ārīsað wēa-dǣda
10 ðe ðisne folces nīð fremman willað.
Ac onwacniȝeað nū, wīȝend mīne,
habbað ēowre [*h*]lenca[*n*], hicȝeaþ on ellen,
winnað on orde, wesað onmōde."
14, 15 Ðā ārās mæniȝ ȝold-hladen ðeȝn, ȝyrde hine his swurde;
Ðā tō dura ēodon drihtlīce cempan,
Siȝeferð and Eaha, hyra sword ȝetuȝon,
and æt ōþrum durum Ordlāf and ȝūþlāf,
and Henȝest sylf hwearf him on lāste.

7. *grǣg-hama*, 'the grey coat,' may refer equally well to the wolf or to a coat of mail.

8. *þes mōna*, 'the moon,' is quite idiomatic. [Cf. Klaeber in *Archiv*, cxv. 181.]

9. *waðol*. Exact meaning unknown. Suggestions, 'full (moon)' [so Holthausen and Schücking]; 'inconstant' [Boer, *Z.f.d.A.* xlvii. 143]; 'half covered' [von Grienberger, *P.B.B.* xxxvi. 100]. The M.H.G. 'wadel' has often been quoted in illustration; but as this term is ambiguous, denoting sometimes the full, sometimes the new moon, it does not help much. Cf. Grimm's *Mythology*, trans. Stallybrass, III. 711.

12. [*h*]*lenca*[*n*]: *landa*, which Hickes gives, is unintelligible. The obvious correction *habbað ēowre linda* [Bugge in *Tidsskr.* viii. 305], 'seize your shields,' is unsatisfactory from the point of view of alliteration, and *habbað* or *hebbað ēowre handa* [Ettmüller, Grein, Heyne, Sedgefield], 'raise your hands,' does not give very satisfactory sense; *hlencan* was suggested, but not adopted, by Bugge [*P.B.B.* xii. 23], and has been adopted by Holthausen and Trautmann. *Exodus*, 215, *etc.*, *Moyses bebēad eorlas...habban heora hlencan, hycgan on ellen*, seems to be connected with the *Finnsburg* passage, and it seems probable therefore that *hlencan* should be restored here.

hicgeað is Grundtvig's obviously successful correction of Hickes' *hie geað*.

13. *winnað on orde*. Hickes reads *windað*, 'fly, spring.' Sedgefield retains this, but most editors alter to *winnað*. The old characters used by Hickes have been read by Trautmann [*B.B.* vii. 41] and others as *þindað*, 'show your temper': but, as Mr Dickins has shown, this is an error.

14. Metrically this line seems rather overweighted, and it is likely enough that two lines have here been telescoped into one. Holthausen [in part following Trautmann] reads

Ðā ārās [of ræste rūm-heort] mænig
goldhladen [gum-]ðegn gyrde hine his swurde.

'Then arose from his couch many a valiant and gold-bedecked thane.'

17. *Sigeferth*, prince of the Secgan (l. 25), is clearly identical with the Sæferth, prince of the Sycgan, mentioned in *Widsith*, 31.

Eaha. Most editors emend to *Eawa*, a form for which there is more authority, as it occurs in the Mercian *Genealogy*.

18. *durum*. Pl. for sg.

Ordlāf: Ordlaf and Guthlaf are no doubt identical with the Guthlaf and Oslaf of *Beowulf*, 1148.

20 Đā ȝȳt ȝārulf[*e*] ȝūðere stȳrde,
ðæt hē swā frēolīc feorh forman sīþe
tō ðǣre healle durum hyrsta ne bǣr*e*,
nū hyt nīþa heard ānyman wolde;
ac hē fræȝn ofer eal undearninȝa,
25 dēor-mōd hæleþ, hwā ðā duru hēolde.
"Siȝeferþ is mīn nama ⟨cweþ hē⟩, ic eom Secȝena lēod,
wrecce*a* wīde cūð. Fæla ic wē*a*na ȝebād,
heardra hilda; ðē is ȝȳt hēr witod,
swæþer ðū sylf tō mē sēcean wylle."
30 Đā wæs on *w*ealle wæl-slihta ȝehlyn,
sceolde cel*lod* bor*d* cēnum on handa,

20. *þā gȳt*, as in *Maldon*, 273, serves to introduce a new incident in the chain of events. [Klaeber in *Engl. Stud.* xxxix. 307.]

stȳrde, Ettmüller's emendation. Hickes, *styrode*; but the sense demands 'restrained' rather than 'incited.'

Guthere is apparently the speaker and Garulf the person who is being restrained. For it is Garulf who, neglecting the advice, falls.

Gārulfe, Trautmann: *Gārulf*, Hickes, followed by most recent editors. But *stȳran* should take a dat. of the person and the metre of the line is improved by reading *Gārulfe*. [Cf. Klaeber in *Engl. Stud.* xxxix. 307.]

21–22. Hickes has *he...bæran*. We must alter either to *hīe bǣran* [Grein, Heyne] or to *hē...bǣre* [Kemble]. The context emphatically favours the sg. because the advice to hold back from the attack can obviously be given to a special person for a special reason, but cannot be recommended generally. [Rieger in *Z.f.d.A.* xlviii. 11.]

forman siþe, 'in the first brunt,' or perhaps 'in his first battle.' Guthere is probably, as Klaeber points out [*Engl. Stud.* xxxix. 307], the uncle of Garulf. It is essentially the part of the uncle, in heroic poetry, to watch over and advise the nephew. Guthlaf and Guthere would then be brothers.

The parallel examples quoted by Klaeber from the *Waltarius* and the *Nibelungen Lied*, where the uncle restrains the nephew, are not quite apposite, as in those cases the uncle has personal reasons for not wishing the nephew to join in the fight. Hygelac restraining Beowulf (ll. 1994, *etc.*) is more appropriate.

23, *etc.* *niþa heard* refers to Sigeferth; *hē...dēor-mōd hæleþ* to Garulf.

24. *eal*: Trautmann, *ealle*, for metrical reasons, followed by Holthausen.

26. *cweþ hē* is hypermetrical, and doubtless the insertion of some copyist.

27. *wreccea*. Hickes, *wrecten*. Grundtvig emended *t* to *c*.

Fæla. There is no necessity, either here or in l. 35, to normalize, as many editors have done, to *fela*.

wēana. Conybeare's emendation. Hickes, *weuna*.

28. *heardra*, Kemble's emendation. Hickes, *heordra*.

29. *swæþer*, probably 'thou canst have from me what thou wilt, good or evil,' rather than, as ten Brink thinks [*Pauls Grdr.* II. i. 546], a bitter jest, 'thou canst have from me which thou wilt, either "woes" or "sharp contests."'

30. *on wealle*, Ettmüller: Hickes, *on healle*. The alliteration demands the change.

31. *cellod*, Grein; *bord*, Kemble: Hickes, *Celæs borð*. A comparison

bān-helm berstan. Buruh-ðelu dynede,
oð æt ðǣre ʒūðe ʒārulf ʒecranʒ,
ealra ǣrest eorð-būendra,
35 ʒūðlāfes sunu, ymbe hyne ʒōdra fæla.
Hwearf [*f*]lacra hrǣ*w* hræfen, wandrode
sweart and sealo-brūn; swurd-lēoma stōd
swylce eal Finns-buruh fȳrenu wǣre.
Ne ʒefræʒn ic nǣfre wurþlīcor æt wera hilde
40 sixtiʒ siʒe-beorna sēl ʒebǣrann,
ne n*ǣ*fre swān*as* swētne medo sēl forʒyldan,
ðonne Hnæfe ʒuldan his hæʒ-stealdas.
Hiʒ fuhton fīf daʒas, swā hyra nān ne fēol

with *Maldon*, 283, leaves little doubt as to the correctness of the restoration; the meaning of *cellod* is a more difficult matter. Suggestions are: 'keel-shaped' [Grein]: 'vaulted' [Lat *celatus*, Kluge]; 'chilled, cold' [Jellinek in *P.B.B.* xv. 431]; 'leather-covered = *cyllod*' [Trautmann in *B.B.* vii. 46]: 'having a boss or beak, *cele*' [Bosworth-Toller].

Holthausen$_2$ proposed *ce*[*or*]*læs*, 'the man's, warrior's, shield,' the sg. used collectively: Holthausen$_3$, *clǣne*.

32. *bān-helm* means either (1) 'bone-protector,' 'shield,' parallel to *bord*, or (2) *bān-hūs*, 'body,' object to *brecan*, the shield being used in the last resort as a weapon of *offence*, as it was by Hereward the Wake.

34. *eorð-būendra*, perhaps 'first of all the dwellers in that land,' i.e. of the natives, Eotenas or Frisians, who are attacking Hnæf and his men.

35. The Guthlaf here, father of one of the assailants, can hardly be identical with the Guthlaf of l. 18, who is one of the besieged. It is probably not a case of the tragic meeting of father and son on opposite sides, for, if so, more would surely have been made of it. It is possible that we are dealing with two heroes of the same name [Klaeber in *Engl. Stud.* xxxix. 308] or that *Gūðlaf* here is a corrupt reading [Trautmann, *B.B.* vii. 48].

36. *Hwearf* [*f*]*lacra hrǣw hræfen*, 'the quickly moving raven hovered over the corpses,' an emendation hazarded by Bugge [*P.B.B.* xii. 27: Conybeare had already conjectured *hrǣw*], for Hickes' *Hwearflacra hrær*. But, as Bugge recognized, the sense does not fit the metre. Grundtvig, followed by Grein$_2$, had suggested *hwearflīcra hrǣw*, 'the corpses of the swift,' a phrase explaining *gōdra fæla* above. [So Sedgefield.] Jellinek suggests *hwearf lāðra hrēas*, 'a crowd of foemen fell' [*P.B.B.* xv. 431]; Holthausen, *hwearf* [*b*]*lācra hrēas*, 'a company of pale [corpses] fell'; Trautmann, *hrǣwblācra hwearf* [noun] *hræfen wundrode*, 'the raven gazed in astonishment at the mass of the corpse-pale [slain].'

40, *etc.* Cf. *Beowulf*, 2633 ff.

41. *nǣfre*, Grundtvig: Hickes, *nefre*.

swānas swētne medo, Grein, partly following Ettmüller: Hickes, *swa noc hwitne medo*.

43. This line, with the alliteration on the fourth accented syllable, is unmetrical. Hence Rieger and Grein postulated a gap of two half-lines, and suggested various stop-gaps which Möller finally improved into

hig fuhton fīf dagas [*forðgerīmed*
ond nihta ōðer swylc] *swā hyra...*,

and Trautmann

hig fuhton fīf dagas [*ferhð-grimme hæleð*
ond niht eal-]*swā*: *hyra....*

driht-ʒesīðа, ac hiʒ ðā duru hēoldon.
45 Ðā ʒewāt him wund hæleð on wæʒ ʒanʒan,
sǣde þæt his byrne ābrocen wǣre,
here-sceorp u*n*hrōr, and ēac wæs his helm ðȳrl.
Ðā hine sōna fræʒn folces hyrde,
hū ðā wiʒend hyra wunda ʒenǣson,
50 oððe hwæþer ðǣra hyssa * * *

44. *duru* must be pl., and is very probably an error for *dura*. Similar miswritings of *u* for *a* occur in ll. 3 and 27.

46, *etc.* It seems impossible to decide who is the wounded champion or whether the king who enquires is Hnæf or Finn. Is it possible that the speaker is Hnæf, who enquires why the *wīgend*, the opposing warriors, seem to recover miraculously from the blows which his men give them? The position would then be identical with that in *Heimskringla* [ed. Jónsson, I. 449], when King Olaf Tryggvason 'looked forward on the ship and saw his men swinging their swords and smiting fast, but that the swords bit ill, and he shouted, "Is it because ye raise your swords so dully that I see they bite not?" A man answered, "Our swords are blunted and broken"....'

47. Hickes has *here-sceorpum hrōr*, 'the brave one in his battle array,' which can be construed as in apposition to *wund hæleð*. Thorpe, followed by Bugge and Schücking, *here-sceorp unhrōr*, in apposition with *byrne*, an exceedingly tempting emendation. The interpretation of *unhrōr* is, however, not clear. Is it 'not stirring' in the sense of 'firm,' 'trusty,' 'his byrnie was broken, his trusty war gear,' or is it 'not stirring,' 'inactive,' 'useless,' 'his byrnie was broken and his war gear useless'? So Hialto exclaims in the *Bjarka mál*, as translated by Saxo [Bk. II, p. 65],

Iam dure acies et spicula scutum
Frustratim secuere meum, partesque minutim
Avulsas absumpsit edax per prelia ferrum...
Rupti etenim clypei retinacula sola supersunt.

48. Holthausen, transposes, for the metre; *þā fræʒn hine sōna.*

50. Rieger [*Z.f.d.A.* xlviii. 12] suggests that the struggle probably ended by the hall being fired, Hnæf and his sixty men being driven into the open, and Hnæf there slain by Finn. This is improbable, for in that case we may presume that they would have all been overwhelmed, whilst we gather from *Beowulf*, 1082–5, that after Hnæf's death they were able, under Hengest's leadership, to hold out against Finn successfully to the end.

GENEALOGICAL TABLES

The names of the corresponding characters in Scandinavian legend are added in italics; first the Icelandic forms, then the Latinized names as recorded by Saxo Grammaticus.

(1) THE DANISH ROYAL FAMILY.

Scyld Scēfing [*Skjǫldr, Scioldus*]

Bēowulf [not the hero of the poem]

Healfdene [*Halfdan, Haldanus*]

- Heorogār [*no Scandinavian parallel*]
  - Heoroweard [*Hjǫrvarðr, Hiarwarus: but not recognized as belonging to this family*]
- Hrōðgār [*Hroarr, Roe*], *mar.* Wealhþēow
  - Hrēðrīc [*Hrærekr, Røricus: not recognized as a son of Hroarr*]
  - Hrōðmund
  - Frēawaru *mar.* Ingeld
- Hālga [*Helgi, Helgo*]
  - Hrōðulf [*Hrolfr Kraki, Roluo*]
- a daughter [*Signy*]

(2) THE GEAT ROYAL FAMILY.

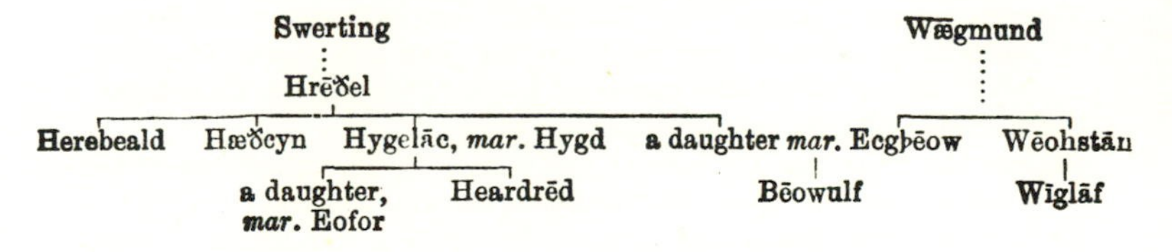

(3) THE SWEDISH ROYAL FAMILY.

Ongenþēow

- Onela [*Āli, not recognized as belonging to this family*]
- Ōhthere [*Ōttarr*]
  - Ēanmund
  - Ēadgils [*Aðils, Athislus*]

PERSONS AND PLACES

The student will find particulars of many of the persons and places mentioned in *Beowulf* in the following books (among others):

Chadwick, *Origin of the English Nation*, 1907.

Clark, *Sidelights on Teutonic History during the Migration Period*, 1911.

Chadwick, *The Heroic Age*, 1912.

The *Introduction to the study of Beowulf*, supplementary to the present volume, will include a discussion of the origin of the legends most prominent in *Beowulf*.

Many of the characters mentioned in *Beowulf* are also referred to in *Widsith*. The references are to my edition (Cambridge Press, 1912).

Ābel, slain by Cain (q.v.), 108.

Ælfhere. Wiglaf is called 'kinsman of Ælfhere,' 2604.

Æschere, Hrothgar's counsellor and comrade in arms, slain and carried off by Grendel's dam in revenge for her son, 1288–1344, 2120–2130.

Ār-Scyldingas, 464, Honour-Scyldings, a name of the Danes; see **Scyldingas.**

Bēanstān, Breca's father, 524. Müllenhoff[2] has suggested that the first element in the name may be connected with O.N. *bauni*, 'dog-fish,' thus echoing the aquatic names of Breca (q.v.) and the Brondingas.

Beorht-Dene, 427, 609, Bright-Danes; see **Dene.**

Bēowulf the Dane (not the hero of the poem), 18, 53, an ancestor of the Danish king Hrothgar. Cf. Chadwick, *Origin*, 273, 291.

Bēowulf the Geat (the second scribe, who begins in the MS. in l. 1939, preserves the spelling 'Bīowulf,' 1987, 1999, *etc.*), the hero of the poem, first mentioned as 'Hygelac's thane' in l. 194, first named in l. 343. He is the son of Ecgtheow (263, *etc.*); his mother's name is not given, but she was the daughter of Hrethel, king of the Geatas, and therefore sister of Hygelac (371–5). After his seventh year Beowulf was brought up at the court of his grandfather, Hrethel (2428–34). In his youth (like many other heroes of legend) he was despised as slothful (2183–9), but when he grew up his hand had the strength of thirty other men's (379, cf. 2361). He gained glory in a swimming match with Breca (506–581), voyaged to Heorot, the hall of Hrothgar, king of the Danes, and purged it from the ravages of Grendel and Grendel's mother (q.v.), with both of whom he wrestled successfully. It is as a 'hand-slayer' (2502) that he attains his chiefest fame (2684 ff.).

He accompanied Hygelac in his fatal expedition against the Hetware, and saved his own life, after the fall of his king, by swimming (2359 ff.). He refused the throne, offered him by Hygelac's widow (2369 ff.); acted as guardian and protector to Hygelac's son Heardred (2377), and on the death of the latter became king of the Geatas, whom he ruled for fifty years (2209). Finally he slew, and was slain by, a fiery dragon (2210, *etc.*).

The setting against which Beowulf's exploits are depicted is historic: Hygelac was undoubtedly ruling the Geatas in the years following 500 A.D., and there is no reason to doubt that the other sovereigns mentioned are equally authentic. The contrast in tone between this historic setting and the fanciful character of Beowulf's chief exploits is obvious, and has led to the widely prevalent theory that our hero is a compound of a historic prince (Beowulf of the Geatas) and a mythical monster-quelling Beowa, who would be identical with the Beow, son of Sceldwea (Scyld), found in the Anglo-Saxon genealogies. The theory of double origin derives some support from the fact that our poem recognizes two Beowulfs, one the son of Scyld and the other the prince of the Geatas. Presumably the monster-slaying exploits have been transferred from the one to the other; but this theory does not admit of proof. For further details see *Introduction to Beowulf*: and for theories as to the etymology of the name *Beowulf* see (*inter alia*) Cosijn[42]; Bugge in *Tidsskr.* viii. 287; Binz in *P.B.B.* xx. 153, 159; Sarrazin in *Engl. Stud.* xlii. 19.

Breca, son of Beanstan (524), and a chief of the Brondingas (521). Unferth taunts Beowulf with his unsuccessful swimming-match with Breca. Beowulf asserts that he was the better swimmer, and could have outpaced Breca, but did not wish to do so (543).

Breca probably had a place in Old English legend, quite independently of Beowulf: he is mentioned as prince of the Brondingas, and a famous ruler, in *Widsith*, l. 25. The names are suggestive of a sea-story: *brecan* is used in O.E. of a ship dashing over the waves (*Elene*, 244, *Andreas*, 223, 513), and *branding* has for centuries been in use among the sailors of the North Sea to signify 'breakers,' 'surge.' But we need not therefore regard Breca as a mythological abstraction of the sea, which Beowulf conquers. A swimming contest between young men is a favourite episode in Germanic story. Cf. Bugge[51].

Brondingas, 521, see Breca.

Brōsinga mene (Icel. *Brisinga men*), the famous Brising necklace. The collar given to Beowulf is compared with it (l. 1197 ff.). Incidentally we are told that Hama carried off the *Brōsinga mene* from Eormenric. In Scandinavian poetry the *Brisinga men* is the adornment of the goddess Freyja; but although Eormenric (q.v.) is a well-known figure in this Old Norse poetry, he is there in no way connected with the necklet. Elaborate theories have been invented, especially by Müllenhoff, to connect the Scandinavian references to the necklet with the English and German references to Eormenric, but these theories are necessarily hazardous. See *Widsith*, Introduction, p. 30, *etc.*

Cāin is the ancestor of Grendel (107 ff., 1261 ff.), as of monsters and giants generally: see Emerson, "Legends of Cain, especially in Old and Middle English," in *Pub. Mod. Lang. Assoc. Amer.* 1906, xxi. 831, particularly § vi., on "Cain's descendants." Such a theological view of Grendel is not an isolated one, limited to the two passages where Cain's name occurs, but runs through the whole earlier portion of the poem. Contrast the dread (but not hellish) fire drake. For further notes on Cain's kin, cf. Bugge[81-2]; Kittredge, *P.B.B.* xiii. 210.

Dæghrefn (*dat.* 2501), a warrior of the Hugas, seems to have killed Hygelac (cf. 1207–14 with 2503–4). Beowulf was his 'hand-slayer' (2501–8).

Dene (*gen.* Dena 242, Deniga 271, Denia 2125), the Danes, the subjects of Hrothgar. Their head-place is Heorot (q.v.), and their territory includes what is now the southern extremity of Sweden (Skaane), which is, indeed, the only portion of their kingdom specifically mentioned by name in our poem (*Scede-landum*, 19; *Sceden-īg*, 1686). They are called by various names: *Beorht-Dene*, *Gār-Dene*, *Hring-Dene*, in allusion to their warlike character; *Ēast-Dene*, *Norð-Dene*, *Sūð-Dene*, *West-Dene*, in allusion to their wide distribution; *Scyldingas*, *Ingwine*, and *Hrēðmen*, all of which see.

Ēadgils, son of Ohthere.

What is told of the brothers Eadgils and Eanmund in the poem, as in the case of the other allusions and episodes, must have been originally intended for hearers who were supposed to know all about them. For us, the order and nature of the events referred to are often by no means clear. In this particular instance, however, it is not difficult to put together a complete story, as we have the Scandinavian accounts to help us.

Eanmund and Eadgils are banished from Sweden for rebellion against their uncle, king Onela (2379 ff.), and take refuge at the court of the Geat king, Heardred. The fact of their finding an asylum with his hereditary foes (see Ongentheow) causes Onela to invade the land of the Geatas (2202 ff.) and to slay Heardred (2384 ff.); but Beowulf succeeds to the throne (2389–90). Beowulf at a later time (2392) balances the feud by supporting Eadgils in the invasion of Sweden, in which Eadgils slays the king, his uncle Onela (2391 ff.), and takes the throne. This version of the story is confirmed by reference to the Norse accounts, in which Aðils (=Eadgils) slays Āli (=Onela) on the ice of Lake Wener (see l. 2396). Cf. Clark, *Sidelights*, 149, *etc.*; and *Introduction to Beowulf.*

Eafor (*gen.* 2964). See **Eofor.**

Ēanmund, 2611, son of Ohthere; see **Ēadgils.** Fighting, together with his brother Eadgils, against his uncle Onela, he was slain by Weohstan, who was at that time obviously a retainer of Onela. See note to l. 2603.

Earna-næs, 3031, Eagles'-ness, near the scene of Beowulf's fight with the dragon.

Ēast-Dene, 392, 616, East-Danes; see **Dene.**

Ecglāf, 499, father of Unferth.

Ecgþēow (Ecgþēo, 373; *gen.* Ecgþīoes, 1999), father of Beowulf the Geat;

married the only daughter of Hrethel, king of the Geatas and father of Hygelac (373–5). Having slain Heatholaf, the Wylfing, Ecgtheow seeks protection at the court of Hrothgar in the early days of his kingship; Hrothgar accepts his fealty, and settles the feud by a money-payment (459 ff.).

Ecgwela, 1710 (see note), apparently an ancient king of the Danes.

Eofor (*dat.* Iofore, 2993, 2997), a warrior of the Geatas, son of Wonred and brother of Wulf. He comes to the aid of Wulf in his combat with Ongentheow, whom he slays. Hygelac liberally rewards both the brothers, and gives his only daughter to Eofor (2484 ff., 2961 ff.). [Weyhe, in *Engl. Stud.* xxxix. 14, *etc.*, seeks to connect this episode with several Scandinavian tales presenting similar features.]

Eomǣr (MS. *geomor*), 1960, son of Offa and Thryth (q.v.).

Eormenric, 1201; see **Brōsinga** mene. The existence of Eormenric, king of the Goths, is certified by the contemporary evidence of Ammianus Marcellinus (xxxi. 3, 1), who records how Ermenrichus (=O.E. Eormenric) warred victoriously against his neighbours, till the Huns broke in upon his extensive empire, after which he slew himself (about the year 375 A.D.). Eormenric was remembered in the traditions of all the Germanic peoples as the type of a tyrant: he was supposed to have slain his wife Swanhild and his nephews the Harlungen (O.E. *Herelingas*), and to have persecuted and exiled a third nephew, Theodoric of Verona. This last evil deed is chronologically impossible, the supposed nephew not having been born till eighty years after the death of the supposed uncle. The story of the murder of Swanhild is based on a cruel vengeance which the king is stated to have executed upon the wife of a traitor who had escaped him (Jordanes, xxiv.). Of the origin of the tale of the murder of the Harlungen we know nothing. By a series of most hazardous conjectures it has been argued that it was through this murder that Eormenric became possessed of the *Brōsinga mene*, which Hama in turn stole from him.

How well-known Eormenric was in Old English tradition is proved from the references to him in *Widsith* and *Deor*. See Clark, *Sidelights*, 232, *etc.*; *Widsith*, Introduction, pp. 15–36.

Eotenas, 1072, 1088, 1141, 1145; see **Finn**.

Finn (Fin, 1096, 1146, 1152; *gen.* Finnes, 1068, *etc.*), king of the Frisians, in some way comes to blows with Hnæf, the brother of his wife Hildeburh. Hnæf is the son of Hoc and lord of the Hocingas (*Widsith*, l. 29), who are a Danish, or at least half-Danish, clan (and are therefore called *Healf-Dene*, q.v.). Hnæf is slain, but ultimately vengeance for his death is taken upon Finn.

The story has to be pieced together from the short fragment of the *Lay of Finnsburg*, and from the references in the *Finn-Episode* in *Beowulf* (1068–1159), which are allusive and obviously intended for people who knew the story quite well. Agreement has not been reached as to the relation of these two versions. According to Möller, Hnæf attacks Finn, in vengeance for an old quarrel, in which Finn had carried off his sister Hildeburh by force and slain his father Hoc. [For all this there is no evidence whatever.] Hnæf is slain, and peace made between Finn and Hengest, the successor of Hnæf and captain of the Danish survivors. But the Frisians, Möller assumes, break the truce and attack Hengest. This, according to him, is the night attack described in the *Fragment*.

Möller's view is open to at least half a dozen objections, of which the most serious are (1) that it forces us to suppose that the 'war-young king' who is attacked by night in the *Fragment* is Hengest, whilst the evidence would lead us to suppose it to be Hnæf; and (2) that it forces us to assume a stirring night attack to have taken place between ll. 1145 and 1146 of the *Episode*, although there is no mention of it there.

This theory is, therefore, now generally discredited, and most recent scholars follow in the main the view of Bugge: that Finn attacked Hnæf by night, and that this is the night attack narrated in the *Fragment*; and that it is also the struggle which is alluded to in the *Episode* as preceding those further events which the *Episode* then narrates more at length.

Bugge's theory, though much more satisfactory than that of Möller, involves a very serious difficulty: it forces us to suppose that the Danish survivors ultimately entered the service of the Frisian king, *in spite of the fact that he had slain their lord by treachery*. Such conduct would be contrary to all the ties of Germanic honour, and cannot be reconciled with the praise which, in the *Fragment*, is given to the bearing of the Danish thanes.

The responsibility for the attack is placed, in *Beowulf*, upon a people called the *Eotenas*, whom critics have identified either with the Frisians [so Bugge, *etc.*] or with the Danes [so Möller] according to the view taken as to the beginning of the fight. Neither identification is very satisfactory, and a better solution is, I think, to be found by supposing the *Eotenas* to be a distinct tribe, possibly identical with the *Ēote* or *Ȳte*, whom modern historians know as Jutes.

Archæological and historic evidence points to the Frisians having been a great nation, whilst the other tribes mentioned as taking part in the struggle—the *Hōcingas* or *Healfdene*, the *Secgan*, and the *Eotenas*—are small and obscure clans. For it is clear that the *Hōcingas* or *Healfdene*, though Danish, are not identical with the Danish nation proper, which was never ruled by kings named *Hōc* or *Hnæf*.

Finn, king of the Frisians, probably called a meeting of chieftains of subordinate clans subject to or allied with him, such as we read of in the Norse sagas. At this meeting a night attack was made upon Hnæf and the Hocingas by Garulf, presumably prince of the Eotenas. It may be assumed that the supreme chief, Finn, had no share in this treachery, though he had to interfere in order to end the conflict, and to avenge his son, who had fallen in the struggle. It is quite possible that Finn slew Hnæf with his own hands, but this does not necessarily follow from his being called the 'slayer of Hnæf' (l. 1102) since the chief is responsible for the acts of his followers. So Hygelac is called 'slayer of Ongentheow' (l. 1968).

Such a succession of events would explain allusions in the poem not explicable on other hypotheses, and the action of the Danish survivors, in making peace with Finn, becomes less unintelligible if Finn had no hand in the original treachery, and interfered only to avenge a slain son. That, nevertheless, this peace should have been broken, and Finn in the end slain, is quite in accordance with the usual development of a Germanic feud. Compare the story of Ingeld, and other tales where the tragic interest lies not merely in the actual fighting, but in the struggle in the minds of the heroes, who have to harmonize the duty of revenge with other conflicting claims.

Cf. Clark, *Sidelights*, 177, *etc.*; Möller, *V.E.*, 46–99; Bugge[20], *etc.*; Boer in *Z.f.d.A.* xlvii. 125, *etc.*; *Introduction to Beowulf.*

Finnas, 580, the Finns. The sea washed Beowulf up on their land at the end of his swimming-match with Breca.

Fitela, 879, 889, nephew and comrade of the outlaw Sigemund (q.v.). Their adventures are told at length in the Icelandic *Vǫlsunga Saga*. Vǫlsung (= *O.E.* Wæls), the father of Sigmund and Signy, is treacherously slain, with his retinue, by the husband of Signy, on a visit. Sigmund alone escapes, and becomes an outlaw. Signy sends him as helper her son Sinfjǫtli (=Fitela), who is also Sigmund's own son. They take their vengeance, and Sigmund regains his father's throne. But Sinfjǫtli is at last slain through the wiles of Sigmund's wife, whose kin he has slain. Sigmund takes the corpse of Sinfjǫtli to the sea, and places it in a small boat to be ferried across a fiord: whereupon both the boat and the boatman, who is doubtless Odin, vanish.

Folcwalda, 1089, the father of Finn.

Francan, 1210, see **Froncan**.

Frēawaru (*acc.* Freaware 2022), daughter of Hrothgar and Wealhtheow, and wife of Ingeld. See **Ingeld**.

Frēsan, 1093, 2915, see **Frȳsan**.

Frēs-cyning, 2503, the king of the [West] Frisians; see **Frȳsan**.

Frēs-lond (pl.), 2357, the land of the [West] Frisians; see **Frȳsan**.

Frēs-wæl, 1070, the Frisian field or place of battle, where Hnæf fell; see **Finn**.

Frōda, 2025, father of Ingeld (q.v.).

Froncan (*gen.* Francna 1210), the Franks. Hygelac was defeated and slain, in his historic invasion of the Netherlands, by a combined army of Frisians and Franks (1202 ff., 2910 ff.).

Frȳsan (*gen.* Frēsena 1093, Frȳsna 1104, Frēsna 2915), the Frisians. The Frisians are alluded to in two connections, (1) as the people of Finn (q.v.; 1068 ff.), who are apparently the main body of the Frisians, dwelling east and north of what is now the Zuyder Zee; (2) as the [West] Frisians, who combined with the Franks against Hygelac (1202 ff., 2912 ff.). The land of the former is called 'Frȳs-land' in l. 1126, that of the latter 'Frēs-lond' (pl.) in l. 2357, 'Frēsna land' in l. 2915; but that this is a purely accidental distinction is clear from *Widsith*, where the *e* and *y* are reversed (ll. 27, 68).

Frȳs-land, 1126, the land of the Frisians. See **Frȳsan**.

Gār-Dene, 1, 601, 1856, 2494, Spear-Danes; see **Dene**.

Gārmund, 1962. Eomær is said to be 'nefa Gārmundes.' Garmund is presumably the Wærmund of the Mercian genealogy of the Anglo-Saxon Chronicle, in which Offa and Eomær also appear.

Gēat, 640, 1301, 1785, 1792, the Geat (i.e. Beowulf). Used in the gen. pl., *Bēowulf Gēata*, 'Beowulf of the Geatas,' 374, 1191, 1202, *etc.* [Cf. Sievers in *P.B.B.* xxix. 309–11.]

Gēatas (*gen.* Gēotena 443), the people to whom Beowulf belonged. They are also called *Gūð-Gēatas*, *Hrēðlingas*, *Sǣ-Gēatas*, *Weder-Gēatas*, and *Wederas*. Evidence both etymological and historical is in favour of the identification of the Geatas with the inhabitants of what is now Southern Sweden, south of the great lakes (the Swedish *Götar*, O.N. *Gautar*). We have references in Greek writers to these *Gautoi* as an independent nation in the second century, and again in the sixth; and though at a later date they were absorbed in Sweden, the title of the king of Sweden, *rex Sveorum Gothorumque*, commemorates to the present day the old distinction.

Another theory (the warmest advocates of which have been Fahlbeck, Bugge, and Schütte) identifies the Geatas with the Jutes. But the arguments in favour of this view are not conclusive.

Cf. Bugge[1], *etc.*; ten Brink[194], *etc.*; Schück, *Folknamnet Geatas*, Upsala, 1907; Schütte in *J.E.G.Ph.* xi. 574, *etc.*; *Introduction to Beowulf.*

Gēat-mecgas (*dat.* Gēat-mæcgum 491, *gen.* Gēat-mecga 829), Geat men, referring to the fourteen Geatas (207) who accompanied Beowulf to Heorot.

Gifðas (2494), probably the Gepidae, a people closely akin to the Goths, and originally their neighbours, dwelling near the mouth of the Vistula. They migrated south in the third century, and founded a kingdom in what is now S.E. Hungary, which was overthrown by the Langobardi in the sixth century. After this the Gepidae disappear from history, though their mention here and in *Widsith* (l. 60) points to the name having survived in tradition.

Grendel (*gen.* Grendles 127, 195, 2002, *etc.*, Grendeles 2006, 2118, 2139, 2353; *dat.* Grendle 666, 930, 1577, 2521, *etc.*), the famous monster, slain by Beowulf. He is of the kindred of Cain (1265 ff.). His father is unknown (1355).

Grendles mōdor (Grendeles mōdor 2118, 2139), Grendel's dam, the slaying of whom is Beowulf's second great exploit. She is sometimes spoken of as a male, sometimes as a female; cf. ll. 1260, 1379, 1392, 1394, 1497, 2136 with 1292 ff., 1339, 1504 ff., 1541 ff.

Gūð-Gēatas, 1538, War-Geatas; see **Gēatas**.

Gūðlāf, 1148, a Danish warrior under Hnæf and Hengest. Since it was customary to give brothers names in which the same element occurred, it is probable, on *a priori* grounds alone, that the Ordlaf who is associated with Guthlaf (F. 18) is his brother, and that Hunlaf, who would be the father of Hunlafing, is a third brother. This is confirmed by the discovery of Chadwick, that, in the Latin summary of the *Skjǫl-*

dunga Saga, a Danish king named *Leifus* is mentioned, who had seven sons, three of whom were called *Hunleifus*, *Oddleifus*, and *Gunnleifus*, names which correspond exactly to Hunlaf, Ordlaf, and Guthlaf.

Gūð-Scilfingas, 2927, War-Scylfings; see **Scylfingas**.

Hæreð, 1929, 1981, the father of Hygd, Hygelac's wife. [Cf. Binz, *P.B.B.* xx. 162.]

Hæðcyn (Hæðcen 2925, *dat.* Hæðcynne 2482), second son of Hrethel, king of the Geatas. He accidentally kills his elder brother Herebeald with an arrow during his father's lifetime (2435 ff.); succeeds to the throne at his father's death, but falls in battle at Ravenswood fighting against the Swedish king Ongentheow (2923 ff.).

Hǣ(ð)nas. See note to l. 1983.

Hālga, 61, 'the good' (*til*), younger brother of Hrothgar. He is the father of Hrothulf (1017, *etc.*), for he corresponds to the Scandinavian Helgi, the father of Rolf Kraki (=Hrothulf).

Hāma, 1198; see **Brōsinga** mene. Hama is the *Heime* of continental German tradition, the comrade of Wittich (O.E. *Wudga*, *Widia*), with whom he is also associated in Old English story (*Widsith*, ll. 124, 130). In German, just as in Old English legend, Hama harries and robs the tyrant Eormenric (*Ermrich*, *Erminrek*).

Cf. Bugge[69], *Widsith*, Introduction, pp. 48–57.

Healfdene, 57, king of the Danes, son of Beowulf the Scylding. As father of Hrothgar and Halga (=Hroarr and Helgi), he is known to us from Scandinavian sources.

Healf-Dene, Half-Danes, the tribe to which Hnæf belongs; see l. 1069. The name may perhaps signify a tribe akin to the Danes, but independent, or half independent, of the central Danish power at Leire (Heorot).

Heardrēd, son of Hygelac and Hygd. While still under age (2370) he succeeds his father as king of the Geatas, so that Beowulf for a time acts as his counsellor and protector (2377). He is slain by the Swedes under Onela (2200 ff., 2379 ff.).

Heaðo-Beardan (2032, *etc.*), the tribe to which Ingeld (q.v.) belongs. They have been identified with the Langobardi, the tribe from whom the Lombards are descended; and with the Heruli, who are known to have been at feud with the Danes. But evidence for either identification is insufficient, though early kinship with the Langobardi is probable enough. Cf. *Widsith*, ed. Chambers, pp. 205–6.

Heaðolāf, 460, a warrior of the Wylfings, slain by Ecgtheow, the father of Beowulf.

Heaðo-Rǣmas, 519, the people on whose shores Breca is cast after his swimming-match with Beowulf. The name is given more correctly in *Widsith* (l. 63) as *Heaðo-Rēamas*: they are the Old Norse *Raumar*, and have given their name to Romerike in Southern Norway, near the modern Christiania.

Heaðo-Scilfingas (*gen. sg.* Heaðo-Scilfingas 63), 2205, Battle-Scylfings; see **Scylfingas**.

Helmingas, 620. Hrothgar's queen, Wealhtheow, is 'a woman of the

Helmings,' but we have no satisfactory information as to the clan. [Cf. Binz, *P.B.B.* xx. 177.]

Hemming, 1944*, 1961*. 'Kinsman of Hemming' describes both Offa (q.v.) and his son Eomær.

Hengest, 1083, 1091, 1096, 1127, took command of the Danes after Hnæf's fall; see **Finn.**

Heorogār (Heregār 467, Hiorogār 2158), 61, eldest son of Healfdene, and elder brother of Hrothgar (468). His arms are given by Hrothgar to Beowulf, and Beowulf gives them to Hygelac (2155 ff.).

Heorot (Heort 78, *dat.* Heorute 766, Hiorte 2099), the hall Heorot or Hart, which Hrothgar built (67 ff.). The site of Heorot can almost certainly be identified with Leire in Seeland, which, according to Scandinavian tradition, was the capital of the kings whose names correspond to *Hrothgar* and *Hrothulf.*

Heoroweard, 2161, son of Heorogar; see **Hrothulf.**

Herebeald, 2434, 2463, eldest son of the Geat king Hrethel, accidentally killed with an arrow by his brother Hæthcyn (2435 ff.).

Heremōd, 901, 1709, a Danish king, is twice introduced as a kind of stock example of a bad and cruel king. In the end he is betrayed into the hands of his foes (903). He would seem to have preceded Scyld, and it must have been after his fall that the Danes suffered owing to lack of a lord (cf. l. 15). See Chadwick, *Origin*, 148 ff., 272 f., 291 ff.; Bugge[87], *etc.*

Hererīc, 2206. Heardred is called 'Hererīces nefa.' Probably Hereric was the brother of Hygd; the tie with the uncle on the *mother's* side was always peculiarly close.

Here-Scyldingas, 1108, the Army-Scyldings; see **Scyldingas.**

Hetware, 2363, 2916, the Hattuarii, the tribe against whom Hygelac made the raid in which he met his death. They were a Frankish people, and seem, in classical times, when they are first mentioned as submitting to Tiberius, to have been dwelling between the Rhine and the present Zuyder Zee. Subsequently they spread higher up the Rhine, to the neighbourhood of the modern Cleves, and it was no doubt here that Hygelac attacked the '*Attoarios*,' as they are called in the account of this attack given in the *Liber Historiæ Francorum* (see **Hygelac**).

Hildeburh, 1071, 1114, daughter of Hoc (1076), and wife of Finn; see **Finn.**

Hnæf, 1069, 1114, fell in the fight with Finn on the 'Frēs-wæl' (1070); see **Finn.**

Hōc, father of Hildeburh (1076); see **Finn.**

Hondscīo, 2076, the one of Beowulf's fourteen comrades, in his expedition to the Danish kingdom, whom Grendel devoured before attacking Beowulf (740 ff., 2076 ff.).

Hrefna-wudu, 2925, Ravenswood, where Ongentheow slew Hæthcyn. Also called

Hrefnes-holt, 2935. See above.

Hreosna-beorh, 2477, the scene of the marauding invasions of Geatland made by Onela and Ohthere after the death of Hrethel.

Hrēðel (*gen. weak form* Hrǣdlan 454, *gen.* Hrǣdles 1485), king of the

Geatas; he was 'nefa' to Swerting (1203), father of Hygelac, and grandfather of Beowulf (373 ff.), to whom he left his coat of mail (454). He died of grief at the loss of his eldest son Herebeald (2435 ff.), who was accidentally shot by his own brother Hæthcyn.

Hrēðling, son of Hrethel; applied in l. 1923 to Hygelac, and in l. 2925 to Hæthcyn.

Hrēðlingas, 2960, the people of Hrethel, the Geatas; see **Gēatas**.

Hrēð-men, 445, a name of the Danes; see **Dene**.

Hrēðrīc, 1189, 1836*, son of Hrothgar.

Hring-Dene, 116, 1279, Ring-Danes; see **Dene**.

Hrones-næs, 2805, 3136, 'Whale's Ness.' Beowulf, in his dying speech, names this place as the site of the barrow which is to hold his ashes and perpetuate his name.

Hrōðgār, 61, *etc.*, king of the Danes, and builder of Heorot. The Scandinavian records (*Saga of Rolf Kraki*, Saxo Grammaticus) know him as 'Hroarr' or 'Roe.'

Hrōðmund, 1189, son of Hrothgar.

Hrōðulf, 1017, 1181, the son of Hrothgar's younger brother Halga (q.v.). He lived at the Danish court. Wealhtheow expresses the hope that he will be good to their children in return for their kindness to him, if he survives Hrothgar (1180 ff.). It would seem that this hope was not destined to be fulfilled (1164–5). We know from Scandinavian sources that Roluo (Hrothulf) deposed and slew Røricus (Hrethric) and that finally his hall was burnt over his head and he himself slain by Hiarwarus (Heoroweard).

Cf. Chadwick, *Origin*, 146, *etc.*; *Widsith*, Introduction, pp. 81, *etc.*; *Introduction to Beowulf*; Clark, *Sidelights*, 63, *etc.*

Hrunting, 1457, 1490, 1659, 1807, the sword of Unferth (q.v.), which he lends to Beowulf for his fight with Grendel's mother.

Hūgas, 2502, 2914. A name for the Franks current in Germanic epic poetry.

Cf. the *Quedlinburg Annals*, "olim omnes Franci Hugones vocabantur a suo quodam duce Hugone" (*Monumenta Germ.*, folio, *SS.* III. 31).

Hunferð, see **Unferð**.

Hūnlāfing, 1143, the son of Hunlaf. Hunlaf is almost certainly a brother of Guthlaf and Ordlaf, and therefore a warrior on the Danish side. When the son of Hunlaf places a sword in Hengest's bosom, this signifies that Hengest enters his service. It may be that Hunlaf was slain by Finn's men in the fighting at Finnsburg, and that, by doing allegiance to his son, Hengest undertakes to help to avenge him, and thus to break his oath to Finn and the Eotenas.

Hygd, 1926, 2172, 2369, daughter of Hæreth (1929), wife of Hygelac (q.v.), and mother of Heardred; see 1926 ff., and **Hygelāc**.

Hygelāc (*usually spelt* Higelāc, 435, *etc.*; Hygelāc 2151, *etc.*; *gen.* Hygelāces 2386, 2943, Higelāces 194, *etc.*, Hȳlāces 1530; *dat.* Hygelāce 2169, Higelāce 452, *etc.*), the reigning king of the Geatas during the greater part of the action of the poem. He is the third son of Hrethel, and uncle to Beowulf; see genealogical tables.

When his brother Hæthcyn was defeated and slain by Ongentheow at Ravenswood (2924), Hygelac came quickly in pursuit (2943) and put Ongentheow to flight (2949); but though, as the leader of the attack, he is called 'Ongentheow's banesman' (1968), the actual slayer was Eofor (q.v.), whom Hygelac rewards with the hand of his only daughter (2977 ff.). At the later time of Beowulf's return from his expedition against Grendel, Hygelac, who is still young (1831), is married to Hygd, who is herself 'very young' and has not long been queen (1926–8); she would seem then to have been his second wife.

Hygelac came by his death in his historical invasion of the Netherlands, which is four times referred to in the poem (1202 ff., 2354 ff., 2501 ff., 2913 ff.), and occurred between 512 and 520 A.D. We have an account of this raid of 'Chlochilaicus' (*sic*) in the *History* of Gregory of Tours, who wrote in the same century in which it took place; and in the anonymous *Liber Historiæ Francorum*, which, though much later, preserves original features which are wanting in the earlier account.

Cf. Clark, *Sidelights*, 42, *etc.*; and *Introduction to Beowulf.*

Ingeld, 2064, son of Froda (2025), and prince of the Heathobeardan. Beowulf tells Hygelac that Hrothgar's daughter Freawaru is promised in marriage to Ingeld, and that the Danish king hopes thereby to terminate the feud between the two peoples (2024 ff.). Beowulf goes on to foretell that these hopes will prove vain (2067–9). That this was actually the case we learn from *Widsith*, ll. 45–49, which tells how Ingeld made an unsuccessful attack upon Hrothwulf and Hrothgar at Heorot:

> "Hrōþwulf and Hrōðgār hēoldon lengest
> sibbe ætsomne suhtorfædran,
> siþþan hȳ forwrǣcon Wīcinga cynn
> and Ingeldes ord forbīgdan,
> forhēowan æt Heorote Heaðobeardna þrym."

The story of Ingeld (Ingellus) is also told by Saxo Grammaticus, though with some essential variations.

Cf. Clark, *Sidelights*, 103, *etc.*; *Widsith*, Introduction, pp. 79–81.

Ingwine is used in *Beowulf*, 1044, 1319, as synonymous with 'Danes.' It is obviously connected with the term 'Ingævones,' which, according to Tacitus, was the name of those Germanic peoples who dwelt *proximi Oceano.* Ing, the eponymous hero from whom the Ingwine claimed to derive their name, is referred to in the *Runic Poem*, 67–8: 'Ing was first seen among the East Danish folk.'

Cf. Chadwick, *Origin*, 209, 287–90, 295–6.

Iofor, 2993, 2997; see **Eofor.**

Merewīoing (*gen.* Merewīoingas 2921), the Merwing or Merovingian king of the Franks.

Nægling, 2680, the name of the sword which Beowulf used in his encounter with the dragon.

Norð-Dene, 783, North-Danes; see **Dene.**

Offa, 1949, 1957, king of the Angles ('Offa wēold Ongle,' *Widsith*, l. 35). The reference to Offa as a descendant of Garmund and ancestor of Eomær [MS. *geomor*] identifies him with Offa son of Wærmund, whose name occurs in the Mercian pedigree twelve generations above that of Offa II, the historic king of Mercia. Offa the First must, if this pedigree is accurate, have ruled over the Angles towards the end of the fourth century, whilst they were still dwelling on the Continent; and there is very little doubt that he actually did so. His warlike exploits are alluded to in *Widsith* (ll. 35–44), and much later we have a detailed account of them in the Danish History of Saxo Grammaticus, and in the *Life of Offa I*, written at St Albans (both documents belonging to about the year 1200).

The *Beowulf* poet gives no details of these warlike exploits, but speaks at some length of Thryth, the fierce queen of Offa. In the *Lives of the Two Offas*, Thryth has been confused with Cynethryth, the historic wife of Offa II, and the story of the fierce wife is attributed in an altered form to the later king. There is little doubt, however, that the tale really belongs to Offa I, and that Thryth is a type of the perilous maiden, known to Germanic and classical story, who causes her wooers to be slain, till at length she meets with her destined lover.

See Suchier in *P.B.B.* iv. 500; Chadwick, *Origin*, 118-145; *Widsith*, Introduction, pp. 84–92; *Introduction to Beowulf*; and especially Rickert in *Mod. Phil.* ii. 29–76, 321-376.

Ōhthere (*gen.* Ōhteres 2380, 2394, 2612, Ōhtheres 2928, 2932), son of the Swedish king Ongentheow, and father of Eanmund and Eadgils.

Onela, 2616, 2932, brother of Ohthere, and king of Sweden at the time of the rebellion of Eanmund and Eadgils. He invades the land of the Geatas, and slays Heardred (2387). At a later time Beowulf avenges his late king by supporting Eadgils in an invasion of Sweden, in which Onela is slain (2391 ff.). See **Ēadgils**.

Ongenþēow (*nom.* Ongenþēow 2486, Ongenþīo 2924, 2951, Ongenþīow 2961; *gen.* Ongenþēowes 2475, Ongenþēoes 1968, Ongenþīoes 2387; *dat.* Ongenþīo 2986), king of the Swedes, and father of Onela and Ohthere. The early strife between the Swedes and the Geatas, in which he plays the leading part, is told in ll. 2472 ff., and more fully in ll. 2910-98. In retaliation for the marauding invasions of Onela and Ohthere (2475), Hæthcyn invades Sweden, and captures Ongentheow's queen. Ongentheow then invades the land of her captor, whom he slays, and rescues his wife; but in his hour of triumph he is attacked in his turn by Hygelac near Ravenswood, and falls by the hand of Eofor (q.v.).

Ordlāf, a Danish warrior engaged against the Frisians (*Finnsburg*, 18). In the Finnesburh episode in *Beowulf* (1148) he is called Oslaf, but that Ordlaf is the more correct form is clear from the Danish form of the name in the *Skjǫldunga Saga*—Oddleif. See **Guðlāf**.

Ōslāf, 1148; see **Ordlāf**.

Sǣ-Gēatas, 1850, 1986, Sea-Geatas; see **Gēatas**.

Scede-land (pl.), 19, = **Sceden-Ig** (q.v.).

Sceden-Ig (*dat.* Sceden-igge 1686; *O. Norse* Skāney), the most southern portion of the Scandinavian peninsula. See note to l. 1686.

Scēfing, 4; see **Scyld**.

Scyld Scēfing, 4, 19, 26, the mythical founder of the Danish Scylding dynasty. He comes as a child across the sea, and, after a glorious reign, his body is sent back in a funeral ship over the ocean. His mysterious advent rather precludes the idea of his parentage being known. We may then interpret Scyld Scēfing not as 'son of Sceaf' but as 'Scyld with the sheaf,' for according to one version the child was found in the boat with his head resting on a sheaf of corn. Or we may suppose that the story was originally told of Sceaf, and has been transferred to Scyld. The names of both Scyld and Sceaf occur in the West Saxon genealogy, and two Anglo-Latin historians, Ethelwerd and William of Malmesbury, tell the tale, but make the hero Sceaf, not Scyld.

See Chadwick, *Origin*, 274–285; *Widsith*, Introduction, pp. 117–121; *Introduction to Beowulf.*

Scylding (Scilding 2105), 1792, the Scylding, i.e. Hrothgar.

Scyldingas (Scyldungas 2052; *gen.* Scildunga 2101, Scyldunga 2159, Scyldinga 30, *etc.*), 58, *etc.*, the Scyldings, descendants of Scyld (q.v.), the name of the reigning Danish dynasty, commonly extended to include the Danish people. They are also called *Ār-Scyldingas*, *Here-Scyldingas*, *Sige-Scyldingas*, and *þēod-Scyldingas* (q.v.). Cf. Chadwick, *Origin*, 284, and see **Dene**.

Scylfing (Scilfing 2968), 2487, the Scylfing, i.e. Ongentheow.

Scylfingas, 2381, the Scylfings, the name of the reigning Swedish dynasty, extended to the Swedish people in the same way as 'Scyldings' to the Danes. They are also called *Gūð-Scylfingas*, *Heaðo-Scylfingas* (q.v.). Cf. Chadwick, *Origin*, 250.

If the MS. reading of l. 2603 is correct, Beowulf's kinsman Wiglaf belongs to the family of the Scylfings as well as to that of the Wægmundings (2814). Wiglaf may have been related to the Swedish house through his mother; Wiglaf's father Weohstan had been in the service of the Swedish king, and may well have wedded a Swedish princess.

Sigemund, 875, 884, son of Wæls, and uncle of Fitela. In our poem Sigemund slays the dragon; in the *Vǫlsunga Saga* and the *Nibelungenlied*, it is Sigemund's son, Sigurd or Siegfried, who does the deed. See ll. 874–900. Cf. Chadwick, *Origin*, 148, 299; Binz in *P.B.B.* xx. 191.

Sige-Scyldingas, 597, 2004, Victory-Scyldings, a name of the Danes; see **Scyldingas**.

Sūð-Dene, 463, 1996, South-Danes; see **Dene**.

Swēon, 2472, 2946*, 2958, 3001, the Swedes, called also 'Swēo-þēod,' and their country 'Swīo-rīce.' They are ruled by the Scylfing dynasty. Their home was in Sweden, north of the Geatas.

Swēo-þeod, 2922, = **Swēon** (q.v.).

Swerting, 1203. Hygelac is called his 'nefa.'

Swīo-rīce, 2383, 2495, the land of the Swedes, modern Svea Rike; see **Swēon**.

þēod-Scyldingas, 1019, 'the mighty nation of the Scyldings,' a name of the Danes; see **Scyldingas**.

Þrȳð, 1931, wife of the Angle king Offa (q.v.), is introduced in contrast to Hygd, in much the same way as Heremod is a foil to Beowulf. She is at first the type of cruelty. But by her marriage with Offa she is subdued and changed. See ll. 1931–62.

Unferð, 499, 530, 1165, 1488 (his name is always 'Hunferð' in the MS., but alliterates with vowels), son of Ecglaf, and spokesman (1165, 1456) of Hrothgar, at whose feet he sits (500, 1166). He is of a jealous disposition (503–5), and is twice spoken of as the murderer of his own brothers (587, 1167). For his 'flyting' with Beowulf see ll. 506–606. He afterwards lends his sword Hrunting for Beowulf's encounter with Grendel's mother (1455), but it fails the hero at need (1522, 1659). The sword is returned to Unferth, and according to one interpretation finally given by Unferth to Beowulf (1807).

It has been conjectured that Unferth is the evil counsellor, through whose advice trouble arose between Hrothgar and Hrothulf (q.v.).

Wǣgmundingas, 2607, 2814, Wægmundings, the family to which both Beowulf and Wiglaf belong; see **Scylfingas**.

Wæls, 897, father of Sigemund; see also **Fitela**.

Wælsing, 877, son of Wæls, i.e. Sigemund.

Wealhþēow, 612 (Wealhþēo, 664, 1162, 1215; *dat.* Wealhþēon, 629), of the family of the Helmings (620), Hrothgar's queen. Mention is made of her queenly hospitality to Beowulf (612 ff., 1188 ff., 1215 ff.).

Wederas (*gen.* Wedera 225, *etc.*; but the second scribe uses the contracted *gen.* 'Wedra' everywhere but in l. 2336; see ll. 2120, 2462, *etc.*), = Weder-Gēatas, a name of the Gēatas (q.v.).

Weder-Gēatas, 1492, 1612, 2379, 2551; see **Wederas**.

Weder-mearc, 298, Wedermark, apparently a name for the land of the Wederas or Weder-Geatas, i.e. the Geatas.

Wēland, 455 (the *Vǫlundr* of the Edda), the famous smith of Germanic legend, the maker of Beowulf's coat of mail. (See the Franks casket in the British Museum, and cf. Wayland Smith's forge in Berkshire.) The best account of Weland will be found in Jiriczek, *Die Deutsche Heldensage*, 1898, pp. 1–54.

Wendlas, 348. Wulfgar (q.v.) is a 'chief of the Wendlas.' They are probably the inhabitants of Vendill, the modern Vendsyssel in the north of Jutland. We have evidence that the northern portion of Jutland was, at the time of Hrothgar, inhabited by a Danish folk: the Wendlas are therefore probably to be regarded as a Danish clan, subject to Hrothgar.

It is just possible, however, that the Wendlas are the Vandals of history, whose name was long remembered, though at this date they had migrated far south. If so, Wulfgar would be a wandering champion who has settled at the court of Hrothgar. [So Müllenhoff[89–90], Bugge[7].]

There was also a famous Vendil, north of Upsala, but it is not very probable that the Wendlas here referred to are connected with it. See *Widsith*, l. 59, and the note there given.

Wēohstān, 2613 (*gen.* Wēohstānes 2862, Wēoxstānes 2602, Wihstānes 2752, *etc.*), father of Wiglaf, and slayer of Eanmund (q.v.).

West-Dene, 383, 1578, West-Danes; see **Dene.**

Wīglāf, son of Weohstan. He is a kinsman of Beowulf (2813), a Wægmunding (2814), and a 'chief of the Scylfings' (2603). He was chosen with ten others (2401, 2847) to accompany Beowulf on his expedition against the dragon (2638 ff.), and he alone justified the choice. Taking shelter under Beowulf's shield (2675), he showed the utmost valour, and was the first to wound the dragon (2694 ff.). To him alone Beowulf made his dying speech, and gave his dying bequests (2809 ff.). He upbraids the coward thanes (2886), and gives orders for the burial of the hero in accordance with his dying instructions (2802, 3094 ad fin.).

Wiðergyld, 2051 (see note), the name of a Heathobeard warrior.

Wonrēd, 2971, father of Wulf and Eofor (q.v.).

Wonrēding, 2965, son of Wonred, i.e. Wulf (q.v.).

Wulf, 2965, 2993, son of Wonred and brother of Eofor (q.v.). Wulf attacks Ongentheow and is disabled by him, but his brother Eofor comes to his aid and slays Ongentheow single-handed (2964 ff.).

Wulfgār, 348, 360, 390*, a chief of the Wendlas (q.v.); an official of Hrothgar's court, who is the first to greet the Geatas (331 ff.), and introduces them to Hrothgar.

Wylfingas (*dat.* Wilfingum 461, Wylfingum 471). Heatholaf, who was slain by Beowulf's father, was a warrior of this tribe. They are probably identical with the *Wulfingas* mentioned in *Widsith*, 29, and with the *Wülfinge* who in High German story are the faithful retainers of Theodoric of Verona (Dietrich von Bern). This last identification derives some support from the fact that in both cases members of the family form their names by compounds in *heaðo*: e.g. *Heatholaf, Hadubrant.*

Yrmenlāf, 1324, younger brother of Æschere (q.v.).

PLAN OF GLOSSARY

The order of words is strictly alphabetical, except in the case of compound verbs, which will be found under their simple verbs.

Past participles compounded with *ge-* are usually glossed under the simple verb (Sievers$_3$ § 366), but occasionally an infinitive also compounded with *ge-* is assumed.

æ comes between **ad** and **af.**

ð and **þ** are treated as identical, and come after **t.**

Numerous cross references are given, especially for unusual forms, but not as a rule for mere flexional forms, such as parts of verbs, which a knowledge of grammar should suffice to trace.

All words are glossed under forms which actually occur in the poem, not under normalised forms. When divergent forms of the same word occur and cross references are not given,

io (both initial and medial) should be sought under		**eo,**
y	"	**i,**
a (before nasals)	"	**o.**

Dative and Instrumental are not distinguished, except when they have different forms, as in the singular of adjectives and of some pronouns.

Where the Modern English word is directly connected with the given Old English equivalent it is printed in small capitals. But the student must remember that in 'Beowulf' we normally find the word in its West Saxon form, which often differs from that Anglian form from which the modern word is derived. Where the Modern English word is descended from a related word, whether in O.E. or belonging to some other Germanic dialect, it is printed in small italic capitals. Such related words may naturally show umlaut changes or a different ablaut-grade.

Of course the Modern English etymological equivalent is often quite unsatisfactory as a translation. See Preface, p. xxxiv.

Gothic cognates have been given in cases where it appeared that they would be helpful, but not in cases where the Gothic parallel, without further details, might mislead a student (e.g. Goth. *qēns*, O.E. *cwēn*). When doubtful whether or not to insert a Gothic cognate, I have quoted it if it occurs in parts of the Gothic Bible usually read by students, but have avoided exceptional words.

An Asterisk is placed after the reference in cases where the word is not found in the MS., but is conjecturally restored.

The following abbreviations alone require explanation:

st.	strong	pl.	plural
w.	weak	subj.	subjunctive
m.	masculine	part.	participle
f.	feminine	pp.	past participle
neut.	neuter	conj.	conjunction
n.	noun	esp.	especially
v.	verb	obl.	oblique
sg.	singular		

GLOSSARY

***N.B.* All compound verbs must be sought under their simple verbs.**

A

ā, *adv.*, AY, ever, always, 283, etc. [*Cf. Goth.* áiw.]

ac, *conj.*, but, 109, etc. [*Cf. Goth.* ak.]

ac, *adv.*, *interr.*, = Lat. nonne, *used to mark a question*, 1990.

ād, *st. m.*, funeral pile, pyre, 1110, etc.

ād-faru, *st. f.*, [pyre-FARing] way on to the funeral pile, 3010.

ādl, *st. f.*, burning-fever, *hence* sickness, 1736, etc.

ǣder, *st. f.*, stream, channel, vein; *dat. pl.* blōd ēdrum dranc, 'drank blood in streams,' or 'from his veins,' 742; *cf.* 2966.

ǣdre, *adv.*, quickly, 77, etc.

ǣfen, *st. m. and neut.*, EVEN, evening, 1235, 2303.

ǣfen-grom, *adj.*, [EVENing-angry] fierce in the evening, 2074.

ǣfen-lēoht, *st. neut.*, EVENING-LIGHT, 413.

ǣfen-ræst, *st. f.*, EVENING-REST, 646, 1252.

ǣfen-sprǣc, *st. f.*, EVENING-SPEECH, 759.

æfnan, see **efnan**.

ǣfre, *adv.*, EVER, at any time, 70, etc.

æfter, *prep.*, AFTER (1) *time*; 85, 117, etc. (2) *relation*: concerning, according to, 332, 944, etc. (3) *position*: along, on the side of, 140, 995, etc. Æfter beorne, 'after (the death of) the warrior,' 2260; æfter māððum-welan, 'after obtaining wealth of treasure,' 2750; æfter faroðe, 'with the tide,' 580, 3096 (see note). [*Cf. Goth.* aftra.]

æfter, *adv.*, AFTER, afterwards, 1389, 315 (thereupon), etc.; eafera æfter cenned, 'a son born coming after him,' 12; so 2731.

æf-þunca, *w. m.*, vexation, 502.

ǣg-hwā, **ǣg-hwæt**, *pron.*, each, every one, every man, etc., 1384.

ǣg-hwæs, *gen. neut. used adverbially*, in every respect, altogether, 1865, 1886, 2624, 3135.

ǣg-hwǣr, *adv.*, everyWHERE, 1059.

ǣg-hwæðer, *pron.*, EITHER, each (*usu.* of two), 2564, 2844: Ǣghwæðres sceal scearp scyldwiga gescād witan, worda ond worca, 'a sharp shield-warrior must know the difference between words and works,' 287; earfoðlīce heora ǣghwæðrum, 'with difficulty for each one of them,' 1636.

ǣg-hwylc,
(1) *pron.*, each, everyone, 984, etc.; *with gen.*, 9, 1050, etc.;
(2) *adj.*, each, every, 621, etc.

ǣglǣca, see **āglǣca**.

ǣg-weard, *st. f.*, sea-WARD, watch by the sea-coast, 241.

ǣht, *st. f.*, owning, possession, power, 42, 516, etc. [*Cf. Goth.* áihts *and O.E.* āgan.]

ǣht, *st. f.*, pursuit, chase, 2957 (see note).

-æhted, see **eahtian**.

ǣled, *st. m.*, fire, 3015.

ǣled-lēoma, *w. m.*, fire-gleam, torch, 3125.

æl-fylce, *st. neut.*, alien FOLK, foreign nation, 2371. [æl, *cf. Goth.* aljis: fylce, *cf.* folc.]

æl-mihtig, *adj.* [*cf.* eall], ALMIGHTY; *weak*, se Ælmihtiga, 92.

æl-wiht, *st. f.*, [alien-WIGHT] strange monster, 1500.

ǣne, *adv.*, ONCE, once only, 3019.

ǣnig, *adj.-pron.*, ANY, anyone, 474, 503, etc.; *nom.* næs se folc-cyning ymbe-sittendra ǣnig ðāra þe, 'among neighbouring folk-kings there was not one that,' 2734. *For* ǣnige þinga *see* þing.

ǣn-līc, *adj.*, [ONE-LIKE] unique, peerless, 251, 1941.

ǣnne, see **ān**.

æppel-fealu, *adj.*, APPLE-FALLOW, apple *or* reddish yellow, 2165.

ǣr, *adv.*, ERE, erst, before, formerly, 15, etc.; earlier, 2500; first, 3038. nō þȳ ǣr, 'none the sooner,' 754, etc.; ǣr hē feorh seleð...ǣr hē..., 'he will sooner give up life than he...,' 1370. [*Cf. Goth.* áiris.]

ǣr *is often used simply to mark that the verb is pluperfect*: sweord ǣr gemealt, 'the sword had melted,' 1615. *Cf.* 2562, 2777, 3060.

ǣror, *compar.*, before, formerly, first, 809, etc.

ǣrest, *superl.*, [ERST] first, 6, etc.

ǣr, *prep.*, *with dat.*, ERE, before, 1388, etc.

ǣr, *conj.*, ERE, before: *usu. with subj.* 252, etc.; *with indic.* 2019. *Correl. with* ǣr *adv.* (q. v.), 1371.

ǣr þon, *conj.*, ERE, 731.

ǣr-dæg, *st. m.*, [ERE-DAY] morning twilight, day-break, 126, etc.

ǣrende, *st. neut.*, ERRAND, 270, 345.

ǣrest, see **ǣr**.

ǣr-fæder, *st. m.*, [ERE-FATHER] father, 2622.

ǣr-gestrēon, *st. neut.*, [ERE-treasure] ancient treasure, former gain, 1757, 2232.

ǣr-geweorc, *st. neut.*, [ERE-WORK] ancient work, 1679.

ǣr-gōd, *adj.*, [ERE-GOOD] good before others, very good, 130, 989, etc.

ǣrn, *st. neut.*, house, 2225*. [*Cf. Goth.* razn, *and O.E.* renweardas, l. 770.]

ǣrra, *compar. adj.* (*formed from adv.* ǣr), earlier, former: *dat. pl.* ǣrran mǣlum, 'in former times,' 907, 2237, 3035.

ǣr-wela, *w. m.*, [ERE-WEAL] ancient wealth, 2747.

ǣs, *st. neut.*, carrion, carcase, corpse: *dat.* atol ǣse wlanc, 'the dire creature carrion-proud' (Grendel's mother exulting over Æschere's corpse), 1332.

æsc, *st. m.*, [ASH] spear, 1772.

æsc-holt, *st. neut.*, [ASH-wood] spear, 330.

æsc-wiga, *w. m.*, [ASH-warrior] spear-warrior, 2042.

æt, *prep. with dat.*, AT, in, *of time, place and circumstance*, 32, etc.; at the hands of, from, 629, etc.: nū is se rǣd gelang eft æt þē ānum, 'now is the rede again along of thee alone,' 1377.

ǣt, *st. n.*, EATing, meal, 3026.

æt-gædere, *adv.*, TOGETHER, 321, etc.; *after* samod, 'all together,' 329, etc.

æt-grǣpe, *adj.*, AT GRIPS with, 1269.

æt-rihte, *adv.*, almost, 1657.

æt-somne, *adv.*, together, 307, etc.

ǣttren, *adj.*, poisonous, 1617.

æþele, *adj.*, noble, 198, etc.

æþeling, *st. m.*, ATHELING, noble, prince, 3, etc.

æþelu, *st. neut.* (*always pl. in 'Beowulf'*), noble descent, lineage, 332*, 392: æþelum gōd, dīore, 'good, dear, by virtue of lineage,' 1870, 1949.

ǣðm, *st. m.*, breath, 2593.

āgan, *pret. pres. v.*, *pres.* āh, *pret.* āhte (OUGHT): *OWN*, possess, have, 487, etc.; *absolutely*, 31 (but see note). *Neg. form* nāh = ne + āh, 2252. [*Cf. Goth.* áigan.]

āgen, *adj.* (*pp.* of āgan), OWN, 2676.

Āgend, *st. m.* (*pres. part.*), *OWN*er, perhaps = God, 3075 (see note to ll. 3074–5).

āgend-frēa, *w. m.*, *OWN*ing lord, owner, 1883*.

āglǣca, **ǣglǣca**, *w. m.*: adversary *hence*: (1) monster, 159, 425, 433, 556, 592, 732, 739, 816, 1000, 1269, 2520, 2534, 2557, 2905, ahlǣcan, 646, 989; (2) champion, 893, perhaps 1512 (see note); both meanings combined, 2592.

āglǣc-wīf, *st. neut.*, monster-WIFE; *nom.* Grendles mōdor, ides, āglǣc-wīf, 1259.

āh, **āhte**, see **āgan**.

āhsian, (āscian), *w. v.*, learn by ASKing, 423, 433, 1206. [Sievers$_3$ § 204. 3.]

āht (= ā-wiht), *st. neut.*, AUGHT; *with gen.* āht cwices, 'aught living,' 2314; see also **ō-wiht**.

aldor, see **ealdor**.

Al-walda, **Alwealda**, *w. m.*, the ALL-*WIELD*er, God, 316, 928, 955, 1314.

an, 1225, *pres. sg.* 1*st of* unnan, *q. v.*

an, *prep.*, see on.

ān, *num.* (*adj. and pron.*), *acc. sg. m.* ānne *and* ǣnne:

(1) ONE, AN, A, 46, 100, 135, etc.; *with the def. art.* 1053, 2237; *emphatic*, *sometimes perhaps de-*

monstrative, 1458, 1885, 2410, 2774: *weak masc.* āna, ONLY, ALONE, 145, etc.: on ǣnne sīð, 'once,' 1579; *gen. pl.* ānra gehwylces, gehwylcum, 'of, to, each one,' 732, 784; (=Lat. *alter*) ān æfter ānum, 'the one for the other,' 2461.
(2) ONLY, ALONE, 46, 1377, 2964 (sole); *gen.* ānes hwæt, 'a part only,' 3010. [*Cf. Goth.* áins.]

ancor, *st. m.*, ANCHOR, 303, 1883. [*From Lat.* ancora.]

and, see **ond**.

anda, *w. m.*, indignation, evil intent, mischief, 2314; *dat.* wrāþum on andan, 'meaning mischief to the foe,' 708. [*Cf. Goth.* us-anan, 'breathe out.']

and-git, *st. neut.*, understanding, intelligence, 1059.

and-lēan, see **ond-lēan**.

and-long, see **ond-long**.

and-rysno, *st. f.*, etiquette, courtesy, attention due, 1796.

and-weard, *adj.*: *acc. neut.*, sweord swāte fāh swin ofer helme...andweard scireð, 'the blood-stained sword cuts the opposed boar,' *i.e.* the boar standing on the opposed (foe's) helmet, 1287.

and-wlita, *w. m.*, face, countenance, 689.

ān-feald, *adj.*, ONEFOLD, plain, frank, 256. [*Cf. Goth.* áinfalþs.]

ānga, *w. adj.*, ONLY, sole, 375, 1262, 1547, 2997. [*Cf. Goth.* áinaha.]

āngeng(e)a, *w. m.*, [ONE-*GO*er] one who goes alone (of Grendel), 165, 449.

ān-haga, *w. m.*, a solitary, 2368.

an-hār, *adj.*, HOARY, 357* (see note).

an-hȳdig, *adj.*, resolute, 2667.

an-mōd, *adj.*, resolute, F. 13.

ān-pæð, *st. m.*, [ONE-PATH] lonesome path, *or* single track, 1410.

ān-rǣd, *adj.*, resolute, 1529 (see note), 1575.

an-sund, *adj.*, SOUND, 1000.

an-sȳn, see **on-sȳn**.

an-tīd, *st. f.*, 219 (see note).

ānunga, *adv.*, ONCE for all, utterly, 634.

An-walda, *w. m.*, [ON-*WIELD*er] God, 1272.

ānwīg-gearu, *adj.*, prepared for single combat, 1247 (see note).

ār, *st. m.*, messenger, 336, 2783. [*Cf. Goth.* áirus.]

ār, *st. f.*, honour, kindness, benefit, favour, grace, 2378, 1272; *in concrete sense*, estate, 2606; *gen. pl.* ārna, 1187; *dat. pl.* ārum healdan, 'hold in (with) honour, hold safe,' 296, 1099, 1182.

ār-fæst, *adj.*, [kindness-FAST] merciful [*cf.* Klaeber[249]] 1168.

ārian, *w. v.*, *with dat.*, respect, spare, 598.

-arn, see **-iernan**.

ār-stafas, *st. m. pl. only*, favour, mercy, kindness, 317, 382, 458.

atelic, *adj.*, horrible, dire, 784.

āter-tān, *st. m.*, poison-twig, 1459 (see note). [*Cf. Goth.* táins, *and Mod. Eng.* TOE *in* mistletoe.]

atol, eatol, *adj.*, dire, horrible, 159*, etc.; *dat. pl.* atolan, 1502.

āttor, *st. neut.*, poison, venom, 2715; *gen. sg.* āttres, 2523*.

āttor-sceaða, *w. m.*, [poison-*SCATH*er] poisonous foe, 2839.

āð, *st. m.*, OATH, 472, etc. [*Cf. Goth.* áiþs.]

āð-sweord, *st. n.*, OATH-SWEARing, oath, 2064.

āðum-swerian, *w. m. pl.*, father-in-law and son-in-law; *dat.* āðum-swerian, 84 (but see note).

āwa, *adv.*, aye, ever; *in* āwa tō aldre, 'for ever and ever,' 955; see also **ā**.

B

bā, bām, see **bēgen**.

bǣdan, *w. v.*, constrain, oppress, urge, encourage, 2018 (see note); *pp.* gebǣded, 2580, 2826, 3117. [*Cf. Goth.* báidjan.]

bǣl, *st. neut.*, fire, burning, 2308, 2322; bęl, 2126 (see note); the fire of the funeral pile, pyre, 1109, etc.

bǣl-fȳr, *st. neut.*, FIRE of the funeral pile, 3143.

bǣl-stede, *st. m.*, pyre-STEAD, place of the funeral pile, 3097.

bǣl-wudu, *st. m.*, pyre-WOOD, wood for the funeral pile, 3112.

bǣr, *st. f.*, BIER, 3105.

-bǣran, *w. v.*
ge-bǣran, *w. v.*, *BEAR* oneself, behave, fare, 2824; *with two comparatives*, ne gefrægen ic þā mǣgþe māran weorode...sēl gebǣran, 'I heard not that that people in greater numbers ever bore themselves better,' 1012; *cf.* F. 40.

bærnan, *w. v.*, *trans.*, *BURN*, 1116, 2313. [*Cf. Goth.* -gabrannjan.]
forbærnan, *w. v.*, *trans.*, burn up, 2126.

bǣtan, *w. v.*, bridle, bit; *pp.* gebǣted, 1399.

bæð, *st. neut.*, BATH, 1861.

baldor, see **bealdor**.

balu, *adj.*, BALEful; *dat. pl.*, balwon, 977.

bān, *st. neut.*, BONE, 2578 (of the dragon's teeth), 2692.

bana, see **bona**.

bān-cofa, *w. m.*, [BONE-COVE] body, 1445.

bān-fæt, *st. neut.*, [BONE-VAT] body; *acc. pl.* bān-fatu, 1116.

bān-fāg, *adj.*, BONE-dight, adorned with antlers, 780.

bān-helm, *st. m.*, F. 32 (see note).

bān-hring, *st. m.*, BONE-RING, vertebra, 1567.

bān-hūs, *st. neut.*, BONE-HOUSE, body, 2508, 3147.

bān-loca, *w. m.*, BONE-*LOCK*, joint, 818; BONE-*LOCK*er, body, 742.

bannan, *st. v.* [*cf.* BAN *in sense of* 'summon'].

ge-bannan, *st. v.*, order; *inf.* ðā ic wīde gefrægn weorc gebannan manigre mǣgþe, 'then I learnt that orders for the work were given widely to many a tribe,' 74.

bāt, *st. m.*, BOAT, 211.

bāt-weard, *st. m.*, BOAT-WARD, 1900.

be, **bī**, *prep.*, *with dat.*, BY *in its various meanings, originally and usu.* local, *more rarely* instrumental (*nearer in meaning to German* bei *than Eng.* by): BEside, near, by, 36, 814, 1191, 1537, 1722, 1872, 1905, 1950, 2243, 2538, 2716, 2756; by, along, 566 (rest), 1188 (motion), 1573; by (in 'I'll do my duty *by* you'), in connexion with, 1723. *Following its case*, him big, 3047. Wǣpen hafenade heard be hiltum, 'raised the sharp weapon by the hilt,' 1574; be ðē lifigendum, 'during thy life,' 2665; wæs se gryre lǣssa efne swā micle, swā bið mægþa cræft...be wǣpned-men, 'the terror was less even by so much, as is women's power beside (in comparison with) a man,' 1284.

be (**bī**) **sǣm twēonum** = be-twēonum sǣm, 'BETWEEN the seas,' 858, 1297, 1685, 1956.

bēacen, *st. neut.*, BEACON, 570, 2777; *nom.* bēcn, 3160.

bēacnian, *w. v.*, [BECKON] indicate; *pp.* gebēacnod, 140.

beado, **beadu**, *st. f.*, battle, war, 709; *gen.* beaduwe, 2299*, beadwe, 1539.

beado-grīma, *w. m.*, battle-mask, helmet, 2257.

beado-hrægl, *st. neut.*, [battle-RAIL] coat of mail, 552.

beado-lēoma, *w. m.*, [battle-ray] sword, 1523.

beado-mēce, *st. m.*, battle-sword, 1454.

beado-rinc, *st. m.*, [battle-]warrior, 1109.

beadu-folm, *st. f.*, battle-hand, 990.

beadu-lāc, *st. neut.*, battle-play, battle, war, 1561.

beadu-rōf, *adj.*, battle-strong, 3160.

beadu-rūn, *st. f.*, [battle-*RUNE*] quarrel, 501.

beadu-scearp, *adj.*, battle-SHARP, 2704.

beadu-scrūd, *st. neut.*, [battle-SHROUD] coat of mail, 453, 2660* (see note).

beadu-serce, *w. f.*, battle-SARK, coat of mail; *acc. sg.* beadu-sercean, 2755. [Sievers$_3$ § 159, 1, 2.]

beadu-weorc, *st. neut.*, battle-WORK, battle, 2299* (but see note).

bēag, **bēah**, *st. m.*, ring, circlet (armlet, necklace, etc.), money, treasure, 35, 80, etc.; *acc. sing. used collectively*, bēg, 3163. [*Cf. O.E.* būgan.]

bēag-gyfa, *w. m.*, ring-GIVER, 1102.

bēag-hroden, [*O.E.** hrēoðan, 'adorn'] *adj.* (*pp.*), ring-adorned, 623.

bēah-hord, *st. neut.*, ring-HOARD, 894, etc.

bēah-sele, *st. m.*, ring-hall, hall in which rings were given, 1177.

bēah-þegu, *st. f.*, ring-receiving, 2176 (referring to Hygd's receiving from Beowulf the necklace which Wealhtheow gave him).

bēah-wriða, *w. m.*, ring-*WREATH*, circlet, 2018.

bealdian, *w. v.*, bear oneself BOLDly, 2177.

bealdor, **baldor**, *st. m.*, prince, lord, 2428, 2567. [*Cf. O.N.* Baldr.]

bealo, **bealu**, *st. neut.*, BALE, evil, ruin, 2826; *gen. pl.* bealwa, 909, bealuwa, 281, bealewa, 2082.

bealo, **bealu**, *adj.*, see **balu**.

bealo-cwealm, *st. m.*, BALEful *or* violent death, 2265.

bealo-hycgende, *adj.* (*pres. part.*), [BALE-thinking] intending evil, 2565.

bealo-hȳdig, *adj.*, [BALE-minded] intending evil, 723.

bealo-nīð, *st. m.*, [BALE-envy, -hate, -mischief] baleful envy, malicious hatred, 1758, 2404, 2714.

bearhtm, *st. m.*
(1) brightness, 1766 (see note).
(2) sound, 1431.

bearm, *st. m.*, [BARM] lap, bosom, 35, etc., 21*, 2404 (possession). [*Cf. Goth.* barms.]

bearn, *st. neut.*, BAIRN, child, son, 59, etc.; *pl.* ylda bearn, 605, gumena bearn, 878, niðða bearn(a), 1005, 'the children of men.' [*Cf. Goth.* barn.]

bearn-gebyrdo, *st. f.*, BAIRN-*BIR*th, child-bearing; *gen.* 946.

bearu, *st. m.*, grove, wood, 1363.

bēatan, *st. v.*, BEAT, smite, paw, 2265; *pp.* gebēaten, 2359.

bēcn, see **bēacen.**

bed(d), *st. neut.*, BED, 140, etc. [*Cf. Goth.* badi.]

be-foran, *adv.*, BEFORE; *of place*, 1412, *of time*, 2497.

be-foran, *prep., with acc.*, BEFORE, 1024.

bēg, see **bēag.**

bēgen, *m.*, **bā**, *f. and neut.*, *num. and adj.-pron.*, both, 536, etc.; *gen.* bēga folces, 'of the folk of both [peoples],' 1124; bēga wēn, 'expectation of both things,' 1873.

be-gong, **be-gang**, *st. m.*, extent, expanse, compass, circuit, 362, 860, etc.; *acc.* bigong, 2367.

belgan, *st. v.*, swell with anger, anger oneself; *pp.* gebolgen 'swollen,' 2401, 'swollen with anger, enraged,' 723* (see note), 1539, 2220*, etc.; *pl.* gebolgne, 1431.

ā-belgan, *st. v.*, anger; *pret.* ābealch, 2280.

ge-belgan, *st. v.*, *with dat.*, anger; *pret. subj.* gebulge, 2331.

bēn, *st. f.*, [BENE] *BOON*, request, 428, 2284.

bēna, *w. m.*, suppliant, 352, 364; *nom.* swā hē bēna wæs, 'as he had begged,' 3140.

benc, *st. f.*, BENCH, 327, etc.

benc-swēg, *st. m.*, BENCH-sound, noise from the benches, 1161.

benc-þel, *st. neut.*, [BENCH-THEAL] bench-board, bench, 486, 1239.

bend, *st. m. f.*, *BAND*, *BOND*, 977, 1609. [*Cf. Goth.* bandi.]

ben-geat, *st. neut.*, wound-GATE, opening of a wound, 1121.

benn, *st. f.*, wound, 2724. [*Cf. Goth.* banja.]

bēodan, **bīodan**, *st. v.*
(1) announce, 2892.
(2) offer, give, 385, 1085, 2957. [*Cf. Goth.* -biudan.]

ā-bēodan, *st. v.*, announce, 390; offer, 668; *pret.* him hǣl ābēad, 'bade him hail, wished him health,' 653; hǣlo ābēad, 'bade farewell,' 2418.

be-bēodan, *st. v.*, bid, command, order, 401, 1975.

ge-bēodan, *st. v.*, proclaim, offer, give, 603, 2369; *inf.* hēt þā gebēodan byre Wīhstānes...hæleða monegum, 'then the son of Weohstan ordered that it should be proclaimed to many heroes,' 3110.

bēod-genēat, *st. m.*, board-comrade, table-companion, 343, 1713.

bēon, *irreg. v.*, BE, *pres. sg.* 3*rd* bið, 183, etc., byð, 1002, 2277; *pl.* bēoð, 1838, bīoð, 2063; *imperat. sg.* bēo, 386, etc., bīo, 2747.

bēor, *st. neut.*, BEER, beer-drinking, 480, 531, 2041.

beorgan, *st. v.*, *with dat.*, defend, protect, save, 1293, 1445; *pret. pl.* burgan, 2599. [*Cf. Goth.* baírgan.]

be-beorgan, *st. v.*, ward (a danger) from oneself: *construed* (1) *with refl. dat. of the person*, him bebeorgan ne con, 'he cannot save himself,' 1746; (2) *with dat. of the person and acc. of the thing*, 1758.

ge-beorgan, *st. v.*, *with dat.*, protect, save; *pret.* gebearg, 2570, gebearh, 1548.

ymb-beorgan, *st. v.*, [about-protect] surround and protect, 1503.

beorh, **biorh**, **beorg**, *st. m.*, BARROW, hill, mountain, grave-mound, 211, etc.

beorht, *adj.*, BRIGHT, light, shining, splendid, 158, 231, etc.; *weak forms*, beorhte, 997, byrhtan, 1199, etc. [*Cf. Goth.* baírhts.]

beorhtost, *superl.*, BRIGHTEST, 2777.

beorhte, *adv.*, BRIGHTly, 1517.

beorhtian, *w. v.*, *intrans.*, BRIGHTEN, sound clearly, 1161 (see note).

beorn, **biorn**, *st. m.*, hero, warrior, 211, 856, 1024, etc.

beornan, see **byrnan.**

beorn-cyning, *st. m.*, warrior-KING, 2148.

bēor-scealc, *st. m.*, [BEER-sene*SCHAL*] drinker, comrade, 1240.

bēor-sele, **bīor-sele**, *st. m.*, BEER-hall, 482, 2635, etc.

bēor-þegu, *st. f.*, [BEER-taking] beer-drinking, 117, 617.

bēot, *st. neut.*, vow, boast, 80, 523. [*Cf. Goth.* biháit, 'strife.']
bēotian, *w. v.*
ge-bēotian, *w. v.*, vow, boast, 480, 536.
bēot-word, *st. neut.*, [boast-WORD] boastful word, 2510.
beran, *st. v.*
(1) BEAR, carry, wear, 48, 437, 2055, 2281, etc.; *pres. sg. 3rd*, byreð, 296, etc.; *pret. pl.* bǣron, 213, etc., bǣran, 2850.
(2) BEAR, give birth to; *pp.* geboren, BORN, 1703.
æt-beran, *st. v.*, BEAR to, carry to, bear, 28, 519, etc.
for-beran, *st. v.*, FORBEAR, restrain, 1877.
on-beran, *st. v.*, BEAR off, rifle, impair, diminish, 990, 2284.
oþ-beran, *st. v.*, BEAR to, bear, 579.
berian, *w. v.*, *BARE*, clear, 1239.
berstan, *st. v.*, *intrans.*, BURST, 760 (crack), 818, 1121, F. 32.
for-berstan, *st. v.*, *intrans.*, BURST, break in pieces, snap, 2680.
bētan, *w. v.* [*Cf. Goth.* bōtjan.]
ge-bētan, *w. v.*, amend, make good, requite, 1991, 2465; *pp. pl.* gebētte, 830.
betera, *adj. compar.* (*of* gōd), BETTER, 469, 1703. [*Cf. Goth.* batiza.]
betost, betst, *superl.*, BEST, 453, 3007, etc.; *weak forms* betsta, 947, betstan, 1871.
betlīc, *adj.*, excellent, splendid, 780*, 1925.
bī, see **be**.
bī-, see **be-**.
bicgan, see **bycgan**.
bid, *st. neut.*, *BID*ing; on bid wrecen, 'brought to bay,' 2962.
bīdan, *st. v.*, *with gen. or absolutely*, BIDE, abide, wait for, 82, 87, etc.
ā-bīdan, *st. v.*, *with gen.*, ABIDE, await, 977.
ge-bīdan, *st. v.*
(1) *usu. with acc. or governed clause*, BIDE, abide, endure, experience, 7, 264, 638, etc.; *pp.* gebiden, 1928; *imperat. absolutely*, gebīde gē, 2529. (2) *with gen.*, wait for; *dat. inf.* ōðres...tō gebīdanne...yrfeweardas, 'to wait for another heir,' 2452.
on-bīdan, *st. v.*, *with gen.*, ABIDE, await; 2302, *inf.* lætað hildebord hēr onbīdan...worda geþinges, 'let your battle-boards here abide the issue of words,' 397.
biddan, *st. v.*, [BID] ask, beg, pray, 29, 176, 1994, etc.; *pret. sg.* bæd hine blīðne, 'begged him to be blithe,' 617; *with acc. pers. and gen. rei*, ic þē...biddan wille... ānre bēne, 'I will ask of thee one boon,' 427; frioðo-wǣre bæd hlāford sīnne, 'asked peace of his lord,' 2282. [*Cf. Goth.* bidjan.]
big, see **bī**.
bigong, see **begong**.
bil(l), *st. neut.*, BILL, sword, 40, etc.
bindan, *st. v.*, BIND: *pp.* bunden, 216 (see note), 1285, 1900; gebunden, 871, 1531, 1743, 2111.
ge-bindan, *st. v.*, BIND, 420.
on-bindan, *st. v.*, UNBIND; *pret. sg.* onband beadu-rūne, 'opened a quarrel,' 501.
bisgu, bisigu, see **bysigu**.
bītan, *st. v.*, BITE, cut, 742, 1454, etc.
bite, *st. m.*, *BITE*, 2060, 2259.
biter, *adj.*, BITTER, cutting, sharp, furious, 1431, 1746, 2704; *dat. pl.* biteran, 2692.
bitre, *adv.*, BITTERly, 2331.
blāc, *adj.*, *BLEAK*, bright, brilliant, 1517.
blæc, *adj.*, BLACK, 1801.
blǣd, *st. m.*, breath, life, prosperity, renown, 18, 1124, 1703, 1761.
blǣd-āgande, *adj.* (*pres. part.*), success-*OWN*ing, prosperous, 1013.
blǣd-fæst, *adj.*, prosperous, renowned, 1299.
blanca, *w. m.*, a white horse, 856.
blēate, *adv.*, miserably, pitifully, 2824.
blīcan, *st. v.*, shine, gleam, 222.
blīðe, *adj.*, BLITHE, joyous, 617; gracious, *with gen.*, 436. [*Cf. Goth.* bleiþs.]
blīð-heort, *adj.*, BLITHE-HEARTed, 1802.
blōd, *st. neut.*, BLOOD, 486, 742, etc.
blōdegian, *w. v.*, make BLOODY; *pp.* geblōdegod, 2692.
blōd-fāg, *adj.*, BLOOD-stained, 2060.
blōdig, *adj.*, BLOODY, 2440, etc.
blōdig-tōð, *adj.*, BLOODY-TOOTHed, 2082.
blōd-rēow, *adj.*, BLOOD-fierce, bloodthirsty, 1719.
blonden-feax, *adj.*, [*BLEND*ed-haired] gray-haired, 1594, 1791, 1873; *weak nom. sg.* blonden-fexa, 2962.
bodian, *w. v.*, [BODE] announce, 1802.
bolca, *w. m.*, gangway, 231.
bold, *st. neut.*, *BUILD*ing, 997, 1925, etc.

bold-āgend, *st. m. (pres. part.)*, house-OWNer, 3112.
bolgen-mōd, *adj.*, swollen in MOOD, enraged, 709, 1713.
bolster, *st. m.*, BOLSTER, 1240.
bona, bana, *w. m.*, BANE, banesman, slayer, 158*, 587, etc.
bon-gār, *st. m.*, BANE-spear, deadly spear, 2031.
bord, *st. neut.*, [BOARD] shield, 2259, 2524, 2673, F. 31*.
bord-hæbbend, *adj. (pres. part.)*, [BOARD-HAVing] shield-bearing, 2895.
bord-hrēoða, *w. m.*, [BOARD-cover] shield, 2203. [*Cf. O.E.* hrēoðan.]
bord-rand, *st. m.*, [BOARD-]shield, 2559.
bord-weal, *st. m.*, BOARD-WALL, shield, 2980.
bord-wudu, *st. m.*, [BOARD-WOOD] shield; *acc. pl.* 1243.
bōt, *st. f.*, BOOT, remedy, help, compensation, 158, 281, etc. [*Cf. Goth.* bōta.]
botm, *st. m.*, BOTTOM, 1506.
brād, *adj.*, BROAD, wide, ample, 1546, 2207, 2978*, 3105, etc. [*Cf. Goth.* bráiþs.]
brǣdan, *w. v.*, *BROAD*en. [*Cf. Goth.* bráidjan.]
geond-**brǣdan,** *w. v.*, overspread, 1239.
brecan, *st. v.*
(1) *trans.*, BREAK, 1100, 1511 (see note), 2980; hine fyrwyt bræc, 'curiosity tormented him (as to),' 232, 1985, 2784.
(2) *intrans.*, BREAK, 2546.
ā-**brecan**, *st. v.*, BREAK into, spoil, 2063*, 2221*, F. 46.
ge-**brecan,** *st. v.*, BREAK, crush, shatter, 2508, 3147.
tō-**brecan,** *st. v.*, BREAK to pieces, knock about, 780, 997.
þurh-**brecan,** *st. v.*, BREAK THROUGH, 2792.
brecþa, *w. m.*, grief, 171. [*Cf.* brecan.]
-bredwian, *w. v.*
ā-**bredwian,** *w. v.*, prostrate, slay, 2619.
bregdan, *st. v.*, *with acc. or dat.*
(1) brandish, whirl, pull, draw, 707, 794, 1539 (throw); *pret. pl.* mundum brugdon, 'brandished your hands,' 514; *pp.* brōden, brogden mǣl, 'sword,' 1616 (see note), 1667.
(2) BRAID, weave; *inf.* bregdon, 2167; *pp.* brōden, 552, 1548; *acc. sg. f.* brogdne, 2755.
ā-**bregdan,** *st. v.*, swing, lift; *pret. sg.* ābrǣd, 2575.
ge-**bregdan,** *st. v.*, *with acc. or dat.*
(1) draw; *pret.* gebrægd, gebrǣd, 1564, 1664, 2562, 2703.
(2) BRAID, weave; *pp.* gebrōden, 1443.
on-**bregdan,** *st. v.*, burst open; *pret. sg.* onbrǣd, 723.
brego, *st. m.*, prince, lord, king, 427, 1954 (see note to l. 1956), etc.; *nom.* brego rōf cyning, 'the prince [was] a brave king,' 1925.
brego-stōl, *st. m.*, [prince-STOOL] throne, dominion, 2196, 2370, 2389.
brēme, *adj.*, [BREME, BRIM] renowned, 18.
brenting, *st. m.*, high ship, 2807. [*Cf. O.E.* bront.]
brēost, *st. f. and neut.*, BREAST, 2176*, etc.; *pl.* 453, etc.
brēost-gehygd, *st. f. and neut.*, BREAST-thought, thought of the heart, 2818.
brēost-gewǣdu, *st. neut. pl.*, [BREAST-WEEDS] coat of mail, 1211, 2162.
brēost-hord, *st. neut.*, [BREAST-HOARD] breast's treasure, mind, thought, 1719, 2792.
brēost-net, *st. neut.*, BREAST-NET, coat of chain-mail, 1548.
brēost-weorðung, *st. f.*, BREAST-adornment, 2504 (*see* ll. 1202 ff.).
brēost-wylm, *st. m.*, [BREAST-*WELL*ing] heaving of the breast, grief, 1877.
brēotan, *st. v.*, break, kill, 1713.
ā-**brēotan,** *st. v.*, break up, destroy, kill, 1298, 1599*, 2707, 2930 (see note).
brim, *st. neut.*, [BRIM] surge, billow, sea, mere, 28, 570, 847, 1594, 2803.
brim-clif, *st. neut.*, [BRIM-CLIFF] sea-cliff, 222.
brim-lād, *st. f.*, ocean-way, 1051*.
brim-līðend, *st. m. (pres. part.)*, sea-farer, 568.
brim-strēam, *st. m.*, sea-STREAM, 1910.
brim-wīsa, *w. m.*, [sea-WISE] sea-leader, sea-king, 2930.
brim-wylf, *st. f.*, she mere-*WOLF*, 1506*, 1599.
brim-wylm, *st. m.*, mere-*WELL*ing, surge, 1494.
bringan, *st. and w. v.*, BRING, 1829, etc.
ge-**bringan,** *st. and w. v.*, BRING; *subj. pres. pl.* gebringan, 3009.

brōden, see **bregdan.**
brōga, *w. m.*, terror, 1291, etc.; *gen. sg.* 583.
brond, *st. m.*, BRAND, burning, fire, sword, 1454, 2126, 2322, 3014, 3160.
bront, *adj.*, high, steep, towering, 238, 568 (see note).
brosnian, *w. v.*, crumble, perish, 2260.
brōþor, *st. m.*, BROTHER, 587, 1074, etc.; *gen.* brōðor, 2619.
brūcan, *st. v.*, *with gen.*, BROOK, use, enjoy, 894, etc.; *without expressed object*, 1045, 1487, etc.
brūn, *adj.*, BROWN, 2578. [For 'brown' applied to metal objects *cf.* Mod. Eng. 'BURNish.']
brūn-ecg, *adj.*, BROWN-EDGed, 1546.
brūn-fāg, *adj.*, BROWN-coloured, of brown hue, 2615.
brȳd, *st. f.*, BRIDE, wife, 2031; *acc. sg.* brȳd, 2930, brȳde, 2956. [*Cf. Goth.* brūþs.]
brȳd-būr, *st. neut.*, BRIDE-BOWER, woman's room, 921.
bryne-lēoma, *w. m.*, BURNing-ray (the dragon's vomit of fire), 2313.
bryne-wylm, *st. m.*, [*BURN*ing-*WELL*ing] surge of fire, 2326.
brytnian, *w. v.*, distribute; *pret. sg.* brytnade, 2383.
brytta, *w. m.*, distributer, giver, 35, 352, etc. [*Cf. O.E.* brēotan.]
bryttian, *w. v.*, distribute, bestow, 1726.
būan, *v.* [*both strong and weak*].
(1) *intrans.*, dwell; *inf.* būon, 2842.
(2) *trans.*, dwell in, inhabit, occupy, 3065; *pp.* gebūn, 117.
bū-folc, *st. n.*, nation, 2220* (see note).
būgan, *st. v.*, BOW, bend, stoop, 327, 2031, 2598, 2918, etc.; *pret. sg.* bēah, 2956; *pp.* gebogen, 2569.
ā-būgan, *st. v.*, [BOW **away**] give **way**, start, 775.
be-būgan, *st. v.*, [BOW about] **encompass**, 93, 1223.
ge-būgan, *st. v.*, *pret.* gebēag, gebēah:
(1) *intrans.*, BOW, bend, fall, 1540, 2567, 2980.
(2) *trans.*, BOW to; *pret. sg.* selereste gebēah, 'lay down on his bed in the hall,' 690; *so* 1241.
bunden-heord, *adj.*, with tresses BOUND, 3151* (see note).
bunden-stefna, *w. m.*, BOUND-STEM, bound-prow, ship, 1910.
bune, *w. f.*, cup, drinking-vessel, 2775, 3047.
būr, *st. neut.*, BOWER, room, 140, etc.
burg, **burh**, *st. f.*, BURGH, BOROUGH, fortified place, castle, city, 53, 523, 1968, 2433, 2452; *dat.* byrig, 1199.
burh-loca, *w. m.*, BURGH-*LOCK*, castle-lock, town-precincts, 1928.
burh-stede, *st. m.*, BURGH-STEAD, courtyard, 2265.
burh-þelu, *st. f.*, castle floor, buruh-þelu, F. 32.
burh-wela, *w. m.*, [BURGH-WEAL] wealth of a castle *or* city, 3100.
burne, *w. f.*, BURN, stream, 2546. [*Cf. Goth.* brunna.]
buruh, see **burh.**
būton, *prep.*, *with dat.*, BUT, except, 73, 657, 705.
būton, **būtan**, *conj.* [=be-ūtan].
(1) *with subj.*, unless, 966.
(2) *with indic.*, withOUT, BUT that, except, 1560; *in elliptical sentences*, 879, 1614.
bycgan, **bicgan**, *w. v.*, BUY, 1305. [*Cf. Goth.* bugjan.]
be-bycgan, *w. v.*, sell, 2799.
ge-bycgan, *w. v.*, BUY, obtain, 973; *pret.* his ealdre gebohte, 'paid for [it] with his life,' 2481; *pp. pl.* 3014*.
byldan, *w. v.*, encourage, 1094. [*From* beald.]
bȳme, *w. f.*, trumpet, 2943. [*From* bēam.]
byrdu-scrūd, *st. neut.*, 2660 (see note).
byre, *st. m.*, son, boy, youth, 1188, etc.
byrele, *st. m.*, cup-*BEAR*er, 1161.
byreð, see **beran.**
byrgean, *w. v.*, taste, 448.
byrht, see **beorht.**
byrig, see **burg.**
byrnan, *st. v.*, *intrans.*, BURN, 1880 (see note); *pres. part.* byrnende, 2272, 2569. [*Cf. Goth.* brinnan.]
for-byrnan, *st. v.*, *intrans.*, *pret.* forbarn, forborn: BURN up, 1616, 1667, 2672.
ge-byrnan, *st. v.*, *intrans.*, BURN, be burnt, 2697.
byrne, *w. f.*, *BYRNY*, coat of mail, 40, 238, 405, etc. [*Cf. Goth.* brunjō.]
byrn-wiga, *w. m.*, *BYRNY*-warrior, mailed warrior, 2918.

bysigu, *st. f.*, [BUSINESS] trouble, affliction; *nom.* bisigu, 281; *dat. pl.* bisgum, 1743, bysigum, 2580.
byð, see **bēon**.
bȳwan, *w. v.*, prepare, adorn, 2257.

C

camp, *st. m.*, *or neut.*, battle, 2505*.
can, see cunnan.
candel, *st. f.*, CANDLE, 1572 (of the sun). [*From Lat.* candela.]
ceald, *adj.*, COLD, 1261, 2396 (see note). [*Cf. Goth.* kalds.]
cealdost, *superl.*, COLDEST, 546.
cēap, *st. m.*, [CHEAP] bargain, purchase, 2415, 2482.
cēapian, *w. v.*, [CHEAPen] purchase; *pp.* gecēapod, 3012*. [*Cf. Goth.* káupōn.]
cearian, *w. v.*, CARE, take care, 1536. [*Cf. Goth.* karōn.]
cear-sīð, *st. m.*, [CARE-journey] expedition bringing sorrow, 2396.
cearu, *st. f.*, CARE, sorrow, 1303, 3171*. [*Cf. Goth.* kara.]
cear-wylm, -wælm, *st. m.*, [CARE-WELLing] surge of care, wave of sorrow, extreme grief, 282, 2066. [Sievers$_3$ § 159, 3.]
ceaster-būend, *st. m.* (*pres. part.*), denizen of a city, 768. [*Lat.* castra.]
cellod, *adj.*, F. 31* (see note).
cempa, *w. m.*, champion, fighter, 206, 1312, etc. [*From* camp.]
cēne, *adj.*, KEEN, bold, brave, 768, F. 31.
cēnost, *superl.*, KEENEST, boldest, 206.
cennan, *w. v.* [*Cf. Goth.* kannjan.]
(1) beget, bear, bring forth, 12, 943.
(2) declare; *imperat. sg. refl.* cen þec, 1219.
ā-cennan, *w. v.*, beget, bear, 1356.
cēnðu, *st. f.*, KEENness, boldness, 2696.
cēol, *st. m.*, ship, 38, etc. [cēol survives in Northern dialectal form KEEL, 'a flat bottomed vessel, a lighter,' but is distinct from Mod. Eng. 'keel,' which is from the Norse.]
ceorfan, *st. v.*, CARVE.
be-ceorfan, *st. v.*, *with acc. pers. and dat. rei*, cut off, 1590, 2138.
ceorl, *st. m.*, CHURL, man, 202, etc.
cēosan, **clīosan**, *st. v.*, CHOOSE, accept, 2376, 2818; *pp. pl.* gecorone, 206. [*Cf. Goth.* kiusan.]
ge-cēosan, *st. v.*, CHOOSE, 1201 (see note), 1759, 2469, 2638; *dat. inf.* gecēosenne, 1851.
cīgan, *w. v.*
ā-cīgan, *w. v.*, call, summon, 3121.
cirran, *w. v.*
on-cirran, *w. v.*
(1) *trans.*, turn, change, 2857 (see note).
(2) *intrans.*, turn, return, 2951, 2970.
clif, *st. neut.*, CLIFF, 1911.
clomm, clamm, *st. m.*, clasp, grip, 963, 1335, 1502.
cnāwan, *st. v.*
ge-cnāwan, *st. v.*, KNOW, recognise, 2047.
on-cnāwan, *st. v.*, KNOW, recognise, 2554.
cniht, *st. m.*, [KNIGHT] boy, 1219.
cniht-wesende, *adj.* (*pres. part.*), being a boy *or* youth, 372, 535.
cnyssan, *w. v.*, crash, clash; *pret. pl.* cnysedan, 1328. [*Cf. Goth.* knussjan.]
cōl, *adj.*, COOL.
cōlra, *compar.*, COOLER, 282, 2066.
collen-ferhð, -ferð, *adj.*, [swollen-minded] of excited spirit, bold-minded, 1806, 2785.
con, **const**, see cunnan.
corðer, *st. neut.*, troop, guard, crowd, 1153, 3121.
costian, *w. v.*, *with gen.*, try, prove, 2084.
cræft, *st. m.*, might, strength; skill, CRAFT; 418, 699, etc.; *dat. pl.* dēofles cræftum, 'with devil's devices,' 2088.
cræftig, *adj.*, [CRAFTY] strong, powerful, 1466, 1962.
cringan, *st. v.*, CRINGE, fall, 635, 1113.
ge-cringan, *st. v.*, CRINGE, fall; *pret. sg.* gecrong, 1568, 2505, gecrang, 1337, gecranc, 1209, F. 33.
cuma, *w. m.*, COMER, 1806 (see also note to l. 244).
cuman, *st. v.*, *pret.* c(w)ōm: COME, 23, etc.; *subj. pres. pl.* cymen, 3106; *pret. pl.* cwōmon, 239, etc., cwōman, 650; *pp. pl.* cumene, 361. *Often with foll. inf.* (*which is sometimes best translated by a pres. part.*), 268, 710, etc. [*Cf. Goth.* quiman.]
be-cuman, *st. v.*, *pret.* bec(w)ōm: (1) COME, 115, 192, etc.

(2) *with acc. pers.*, befall, 2883.
  ofer-cuman, *st.v.* OVERCOME; *pret. sg.* oferc wōm, 1273; *pret. pl.* ofercōmon, 699; *pp.* 845.
cumbol, *st. m.*, standard, banner, 2505.
cunnan, *pret.-pres. v.*, *pres. sg.* 1*st*, 3*rd*, con, can, 2*nd*, const:
  (1) *with acc. or clause*, know, be acquainted with, 359, 372, 392, 418, 1180, 1377, 1739, etc.; *with acc. and clause*, 1355.
  (2) *with inf.*, know how to, be able to, 50, 90, 182, etc.
cunnian, *w. v.*, *with acc. or gen.*, try, make trial of, explore, 508, 1426, 1444, 1500, 2045.
cūð, *adj.* (*pp. of* cunnan, *cf. Goth.* kunþs), known, well known, famous, 150, etc.
cūð-līce, *adv.*, openly.
  cūð-līcor, *compar.*, more openly, 244.
cwealm, *st. m.*, [QUELLing] murder, death, 107, 3149*.
cwealm-bealu, *st. neut.*, death-BALE, deadly evil, 1940.
cwealm-cuma, *w. m.*, murderous COMer, 792.
cweccan, *w. v.*, [cause to QUAKE] brandish, 235.
cwellan, *w. v.*, QUELL, kill, 1334.
  ā-cwellan, *w. v.*, QUELL, kill, 886, 1055, 2121.
cwēn, *st. f.*, QUEEN, wife, 62, etc.
cwēn-līc, *adj.*, QUEENLY, womanly, 1940.
cweðan, *st. v.*, say, speak, 2041; *pret.* cwæð, 'QUOTH,' 92, etc.; cweð, F. 26. [*Cf. Goth.* qiþan.]
  ā-cweðan, *st. v.*, say, speak; *pres. sg.* ācwyð, 2046; *pret. sg.* ācwæð, 'QUOTH,' 654.
  ge-cweðan, *st. v.*, say, agree, 535, 2664; *pret. sg.* gecwæð, 'QUOTH,' 857, etc.
  on-cweðan, *st. v.*, answer, F. 8.
cwic, **cwico**, *adj.*, QUICK, living, alive, 98, etc.
cwīðan, *w. v.*, *with acc.*, lament, mourn, 2112, 3171.
-cwyð, see **-cweðan**.
cyme, *st. m.*, COMing; *pl.* 257.
cymen, see **cuman**.
cȳm-līce, *adv.*
  cȳm-līcor, *compar.*, in more COMELY fashion, more fitly, 38.
cyn(n), *st. neut.*, KIN, race, 98, 107, 421, etc. [*Cf. Goth.* kuni.]
cyn(n), *adj. and noun*, ('AKIN, suitable'), customs, courtesies, etiquette, 613.
cyne-dōm, *st. m.*, KINGDOM, 2376.
cyning, **kyning**, *st. m.*, KING, 11, 619, 3171, etc.
cyning-bald, *adj.*, [KING-BOLD] royally bold, 1634.
  Kyning-wuldor, *st. m.*, KINGly glory, King of glory, God, 665.
cȳpan, *w. v.*, sell. [*Cf.* cēap.]
  ge-cȳpan, *w. v.*, buy, purchase, hire, 2496.
cyssan, *w. v.*
  ge-cyssan, *w. v.*, KISS, 1870.
cyst, *st. f.*, [CHOOSing] choice, choice quality, excellence, pick, 673, 802, 867, 923, etc.: wǣpna cyst, 'choicest of weapons,' 1559. [*Cf.* cēosan.]
cȳðan, *w. v.*, make known, show, 659, etc.; *pp.* gecȳðed, 'made known, famed,' 262, etc. [*From* cūð, *cf. Goth.* kunþjan.]
  ge-cȳðan, *w. v.*, make known, 257, 354.

D

dǣd, *st. f.*, DEED, act, 181, etc.; *acc.* dǣd, 585, etc., dǣde, 889; *gen. pl.* hafað...dǣde gefondad, 'has experienced deeds (of violence),' 2454.
dǣd-cēne, *adj.*, [DEED-KEEN] bold in act, 1645.
dǣd-fruma, *w. m.*, [DEED-chief] doer of deeds, 2090.
dǣd-hata, *w. m.*, [DEED-HATer] one who shows his hatred in deeds, persecutor, 275 (see note).
dæg, *st. m.*, DAY, 197, 485, etc. [*Cf. Goth.* dags.]
  dæges, *gen. of* dæg *used adverbially*, by day, 2269.
dæg-hwīl, *st. f.*, DAY-WHILE, day; *acc. pl.*, 2726.
dæg-rīm, *st. neut.*, [DAY-RIME] number of days; *nom.* dōgera dægrīm, 'the number of his days,' 823.
dǣl, *st. m.*, DEAL, part, portion, share, 621, etc.; a large part, great deal, 1150, 1740, 1752, 2028, 2068, 2245, 2843.
dǣlan, *w. v.*, DEAL, divide, distribute, share, 80, 2534, etc. [*Cf. Goth.* dáiljan.]
  be-dǣlan, *w. v.*, *with dat. rei*, deprive, bereave, 721, 1275.
  ge-dǣlan, *w. v.*, DEAL out, 71; divide, part, 731, 2422.
dagian, *w. v.*, dawn, F. 3.
daroð, *st. m.*, DART, javelin, 2848.

dēad, *adj.*, DEAD, 467, etc. [*Cf. Goth.* dáuþs.]

***dēagan**, *st. v.*, *DYE*; but see note to l. 850.

dēah, see **dugan**.

deall, *adj.*, proud of, adorned by, 494.

dear, **dearst**, see **durran**.

dēað, *st. m.*, DEATH, 441, etc.

dēað-bedd, *st. neut.*, DEATH-BED, 2901.

dēað-cwalu, *st. f.*, [DEATH-*QUELL*-ing] violent death, slaughter, 1712.

dēað-cwealm, *st. m.*, [DEATH-*QUELL*-ing] violent death, slaughter, 1670.

dēað-dæg, *st. m.*, DEATH-DAY, 187, 885.

dēað-fǣge, *adj.*, [DEATH-FEY] doomed to death, 850.

dēað-scūa, *w. m.*, DEATH-shadow, deadly sprite, 160.

dēað-wērig, *adj.*, DEATH-WEARY, dead, 2125.

dēað-wīc, *st. neut.*, [DEATH-WICK] dwelling of the dead, 1275.

dēman, *w. v.*, DEEM; adjudge, 687; extol, 3174. [*From* dōm, *cf. Goth.* dōmjan.]

dēmend, *st. m.* (*pres. part.*), judge, 181.

denn, *st. neut.*, DEN, 2759, 3045.

dēofol, *st. m. and neut.*, DEVIL, 756, 1680, 2088. [*From Greek, through Lat.* diabolus.]

dēogol, see **dȳgel**.

dēop, *st. neut.*, DEEP, 2549 (see note).

dēop, *adj.*, DEEP, 509, 1904. [*Cf. Goth.* diups.]

dēor, **dīor**, *adj.*, bold, brave, fierce, 1933, 2090. [*Cf. Goth.* dius.]

deorc, *adj.*, DARK, 160, 275, etc.

dēore, see **dȳre**.

dēor-līc, *adj.*, bold, 585.

dēor-mōd, *adj.*, valiant, F. 25.

dēð, see **dōn**.

-dīgan, see **-dȳgan**.

dīope, *adv.*, DEEPly, 3069.

dīore, see **dȳre**.

disc, *st. m.*, DISH, 2775, 3048. [*From Greek through Lat.* discus.]

dōgor, *st. neut.*, day, 219, 2573 (see note), etc.; *inst. sg.* dōgore, 1797, dōgor, 1395 (see note); *gen. pl.* dōgora, 88, dōgera, 823, dōgra, 1090.

dōgor-gerīm, *st. neut.*, number of days, 2728.

dohtor, *st. f.*, DAUGHTER, 375, etc.

dol-gilp, *st. m. and neut.*, [*DOL*tish YELP] foolhardiness, 509.

dol-līc, *adj.*, rash, desperate, audacious, 2646.

dol-sceaða, *w. m.*, *DOL*tish *SCATH*er, foolish *or* rash foe, 479.

dōm, *st. m.*, DOOM, judgment, 441, etc.; free-will, choice, 895, 2147, etc.; glory, 885, 2666, etc.: æfter dōme, 'according to right custom,' 1720; drēah æfter dōme, 'lived, employed himself, according to right, *or* honour,' 2179.

dōm-lēas, *adj.*, [glory-LESS] inglorious, 2890.

dōn, *irreg. v.*, DO, make, take, esteem, put, lay, 444, etc.; *pres. sg.* dēð, 1058; *pret. sg.* dyde, etc., 44, 1676, 2809, etc.: him Hūnlāfing hildelēoman...on bearm dyde, 'the son of Hunlaf gave the sword into his [Hengest's] bosom,' 1144; ne him þæs wyrmes wīg for wiht dyde, eafoð ond ellen, 'he esteemed the worm's warfare as naught, its strength and courage,' 2348.

gē-dōn, *st. v.*, DO, make, put, esteem, 2090, 2186; *pres. sg.* gedēð, 1732.

dorste, pret. of **durran**.

draca, *w. m.*, DRAKE, dragon, 892, 2088, 2211, etc., F. 3. [*From Lat.* draco.]

-drǣdan, *st. v.*

on-drǣdan, *st. v.*, DREAD, 1674, 2275*, *pret.* ondrēd, 2347.

The alliteration of l. 1674 *shows that this was regarded as a compound of a verb* **drǣdan**: *whether this is so, or whether it is from* **ond-rǣdan** *is disputed.* [See Pogatscher in *Anglia*, *Beiblatt*, XIV. 182.]

drēah, see **drēogan**.

drēam, *st. m.*, joy, mirth, 88, 99, etc.

drēam-lēas, *adj.*, joyLESS, 1720.

drēfan, *w. v.*, trouble, stir, 1904; *pp.* gedrēfed, 1417. [*Cf. Goth.* drōbjan.]

drēogan, *st. v.*, [DREE] go through, experience, suffer, enjoy, 589, 1470, 2179 (*see* dōm), etc.; *imperat. sg.* drēoh, 1782; *pret. sg.* drēah, 131; *pret. pl.* drugon, 798, 1966; *pp.* gedrogen, 'spent,' 2726: sund-nytte drēah, 'did a feat of swimming,' 2360. [*Cf. Goth.* driugan.]

ā-drēogan, *st. v.*, endure, 3078*.

drēor, *st. m. or neut.*, blood, 447*. [*Cf. O.E.* drēosan.]

drēor-fāh, *adj.*, blood-stained, 485.

drēorig, **drīorig**, *adj.*, [DREARY] bloody, 1417, 2789.

drēosan, *st. v.* [*Cf. Goth.* driusan.]
 ge-drēosan, *st. v.*, fall, sink, fail, decline, 1754, 2666.
drepan, *st. v.*, strike, hit; *pret. sg.* drep, 2880; *pp.* drepen, 1745, dropen, 2981.
drepe, *st. m.*, stroke, blow, 1589.
drīfan, *st. v.*, DRIVE, 1130, 2808.
 tō-drīfan, *st. v.*, DRIVE asunder, 545.
driht-, see **dryht-.**
drihten, see **dryhten.**
drincan, *st. v.*, DRINK, 742, 1233, etc.; *pp.* druncen, 'drunk, having drunk (not *necessarily* to intoxication),' 531, etc.; *pl.* druncne, 480, etc.
drinc-fæt, see **drync-fæt.**
drohtoð, *st. m.*, way of life, faring, 756. [*Cf. O.E.* drēogan.]
dropen, see **drepan.**
drūsian, *w. v.*, subside, 1630 [perhaps DROWSE].
dryht-bearn, *st. neut.*, [noble BAIRN] noble youth, noble scion; *acc.* 2035.
dryhten, drihten, *st. m.*
 (1) lord, chieftain, 1050, 1484, etc.; *dat.* dryhtne, 2483, etc., dryhten, 1831 (see note).
 (2) Lord (of the Deity), 108, etc.
dryht-gesīð, *st. m.*, man at arms, F. 44.
dryht-guma, driht-guma, *w. m.*, warrior, noble warrior, 99, 1790, etc.
dryht-līc, driht-līc, *adj.*, lordly, courtly, royal, noble, excellent, 892, F. 16; *weak neut.* drihtlīce wīf, 1158.
dryht-māðum, *st. m.*, lordly treasure, 2843.
dryht-scype, driht-scype, *st. m.*, [warrior-SHIP] heroic deed, bravery, 1470.
dryht-sele, driht-sele, *st. m.*, lordly hall, warrior-hall, 485, etc.
dryht-sibb, *st. f.*, troop-peace, peace between bands of warriors, 2068.
drync-fæt, drinc-fæt, *st. n.*, [DRINK-VAT] drinking vessel, 2254, 2306.
drysmian, *w. v.*, darken, grow dark, 1375.
dūfan, *st. v.*, *DIVE* (see note to l. 850).
 ge-dūfan, *st. v.*, *DIVE* into, sink into; *pret. sg.* gedēaf, 2700.
 þurh-dūfan, *st. v.*, *DIVE* THROUGH, swim through; *pret. sg.* þurhdēaf, 1619.
dugan, *pret.-pres. v.*, *pres. sg. indic.* dēah, 369, etc.; *pres. sg. subj.* duge, 589, etc.; *pret. sg.* dohte, 526, 1344, etc.: be *DOUGH*ty, avail, 369, 573, etc., *with gen.* 526; treat well (with dat.), 1821.
duguð, *st. f.*, (1) *DOUGH*tiness; (2) the *DOUGH*ty, tried warriors, *often contrasted with* geogoð, 'the youthful,' 160, etc. *In 'Beowulf' the meaning is usually concrete, the abstract meaning 'doughtiness' is rare; it occurs in* duguðum, 'doughtily,' 3174, *and* (*perhaps*) for duguðum, 2501 (see note). [*Cf. Germ.* Tugend.]
***durran,** *pret.-pres. v.*, DARE; *pres. sg.* dear, dearst, 684, 527; *pres. subj.* dyrre, 1379; *pret. sg.* dorste, 1462, etc. [*Cf. Goth.* gadaúrsan.]
duru, *st. f.*, DOOR, 389*, 721, F. 14, etc.
dwellan, *w. v.*, [DWELL] mislead, deceive, hinder; *pres. sg.* dweleð, 1735. [*Cf. Goth.* dwals, 'foolish.']
dyde, dydon, see **dōn.**
dȳgan, *w. v.*
 ge-dȳgan, ge-dīgan, *w. v.*, survive, escape, endure, 300, 578, 661, etc.
dȳgel, dēogol, *adj.*, secret, hidden, 275, 1357.
dyhtig, *adj.*, *DOUGHTY*, 1287.
dynnan, *w. v.*, DIN, resound; *pret. sg.* dynede, 767, etc.
dȳre, dēore, *adj.*, DEAR, *in both senses*, costly *and* beloved, 561, 1528, 1879, etc.; *nom.* dīore, 1949; *gen. sg. f.* dēorre, 488.
 dēorest, *superl.*, DEAREST, 1309.
dyrne, *adj.*, secret, hidden, 271, 1879, etc.
dyrre, see **durran.**
dyrstig, *adj.*, daring, bold; *with gen.* 2838. [*Cf.* *durran.]

E

ēac, *adv.*, EKE, also, 97, etc.; *once* ēc, 3131. [*Cf. Goth.* áuk.]
ēacen, *adj.* [*pp.* of *ēacan: *cf. Goth.* áukan], [EKEd] great, extensive, mighty, powerful, 198, 1621, 1663, 2140.
ēacen-cræftig, *adj.*, enormously strong, immense, 2280, 3051.
ēadig, *adj.*, rich, prosperous, 1225, 2470. [*Cf. Goth.* áudags.]
ēadig-līce, *adv.*, happily, 100.
eafor, see **eofor.**
eafora, eafera, *w. m.*, child, son, 12, etc.; *dat. pl.* eaferan, 1185.
eafoð, *st. neut.*, strength, might, 902*, etc.; *acc. pl.* eofoðo, 2534;

dat. pl. eafeðum, 1717: ic him Gēata sceal eafoð ond ellen...gūþe gebēodan, 'I shall proclaim to him the strength, courage and warfare of the Geatas,' 602 (see note to l. 601).

ēage, *w. neut.*, EYE, 726, etc. [*Cf. Goth.* áugō.]

ēagor-strēam, *st. m.*, water-STREAM, 513.

eahta, *num.*, EIGHT, 1035; *gen.* eahta sum, 'one of eight, with seven others,' 3123. [*Cf. Goth.* ahtáu.]

eahtian, *w. v.*, consider, deliberate about, esteem, praise, watch over: *pres. pl.* ehtigað, 1222; *pret. sg.* eahtode, 1407; *pret. pl.* eahtedon, 172, eahtodan, 3173; *pp.* geæhted, 'esteemed, praised,' 1885.

eal(l), *adj.*, ALL, 71, etc.; *nom. sg. f.* eal, 1738; *neut. pl.* eal, 486. *In some instances it is impossible to say certainly whether the word is an adj. or an adv.*: 77, 1230, 1567, 1620, 2241. *Substantively, sg. and pl.*: 145, 649, 2162, 2794, 1727 (all things), 2461 (everything); *gen. pl.* ealra, 'in all,' 3170; *with gen.* 744, 835, 1057, 1122, 2149, 2727. [*Cf. Goth.* alls.]

eal, *adv.*, ALL, 680, 1708, 3164 (*see* þēah).

ealles, *adv.* (*gen. of* eall), ALL, altogether, 1000.

eald, *adj.*, OLD, 72, etc.; *acc. pl. neut.* ealde, 2330: eald Metod, 'our God of old,' 945; goldmāðmas hēold eald under eorðan, 'the old [dragon] held gold-treasures under the earth,' 2415. [*Cf. Goth.* alþeis.]

yldra, *compar.*, ELDER, older, 468, etc.

yldesta, *weak superl.*, ELDEST, senior, chief, 258, etc.

ealder-, see under **ealdor-**.

eald-gesegen, *st. f.*, OLD *SAGA*, old tradition, 869.

eald-gesīð, *st. m.*, OLD comrade, 853.

eald-gestrēon, *st. neut.*, old treasure, 1381, 1458.

eald-hlāford, *st. m.*, OLD LORD (Beowulf), 2778 (but see note).

ealdor, **aldor**, *st. m.*, [ALDER- *in* alderman] chief, lord, prince, sovereign, 56, etc.

aldor-lēas, *adj.*, princeLESS, without a chief, 15*.

aldor-þegn, *st. m.*, [prince-THANE] chief thane, 1308.

ealdor, **aldor**, *st. neut.*, life, 510, etc.; vitals, 1434: tō aldre, 'for life, for ever, always,' 2005, 2498; āwa tō aldre, 'for ever and ever,' 955.

aldor-bealu, *st. neut.*, life-BALE, death, 1676.

aldor-cearu, *st. f.*, life-CARE, 906.

aldor-dæg, **ealder-dæg**, *st. m.*, life-DAY, day of life, 718, 757.

aldor-gedāl, *st. neut.*, life-parting, death, 805.

ealdor-gewinna, *w. m.*, [life-WINNER] life-adversary, 2903.

ealdor-lēas, **aldor-lēas**, *adj.*, lifeLESS, 15, 1587, 3004.

eal-fela, *adj.*, [ALL-many] very many, *with gen.*, 883; *acc.* ealfela...worn, 'a very great number,' 869.

ealgian, *w. v.*, defend, protect, 796, 1204, etc. [*Cf. Goth.* alhs, 'temple.']

eall, see **eal**.

eal(l)-gylden, *adj.*, ALL-*GOLDEN*, 1111, 2767.

eall-īren, *adj.*, ALL-IRON, 2338 (see note).

ealo-benc, **ealu-benc**, *st. f.*, ALE-BENCH, 1029, 2867.

ealo-drincend, *st. m.* (*pres. part.*), ALE-DRINKER, 1945.

ēa-lond, *st. neut.*, water-LAND; *acc.* 2334 (see note). [*With* ēa, *cf. Goth.* ahwa.]

ealo-wǣge, **ealu-wǣge**, *st. neut.*, ALE-stoup, tankard of ale, 481, 495, 2021.

ealu-scerwen, *st. f.*, great terror, 769 (see note).

ēam, *st. m.*, [EME] uncle, mother's brother, 881.

eard, *st. m.*, country, estate, home, dwelling, 56, 104, 1621 (expanses), 1727, 2198, 2493, 2736, etc.

eardian, *w. v.*

(1) *intrans.*, dwell, rest, 3050.

(2) *trans.*, inhabit, 166; *inf.* wīc eardian, 'take up his abode,' 2589.

eard-lufu, *w. f.*, home-LOVE, dear home, 692. [Sievers$_3$ § 278, N. 1.]

earfoð, *st. neut.*, hardship, stress; *acc. pl.* earfeðo, 534. [*Cf. Goth.* arbáiþs, 'work.']

earfoð-līce, *adv.*, hardly, with difficulty, 86, etc.; with trouble, sorrowfully, 2822.

earfoð-þrāg, *st. f.*, time of stress, time of tribulation, 283. [See Sievers, *P.B.B.*, XVIII. 406.]

earg, *adj.*, cowardly; *gen. absolutely*, earges sīð, 'coward's way,' 2541.

earm, *st. m.*, ARM, 513, etc. [*Cf. Goth.* arms.]
earm, *adj.*, wretched, 2368, 2938; *weak fem.* earme, 1117. [*Cf. Goth.* arms.]
earmra, *compar.*, more wretched, 577.
earm-bēag, *st. m.*, ARM-ring, armlet, 2763.
earm-[h]rēad, *st. f.*, ARM-ornament, 1194 (see note).
earm-līc, *adj.*, wretched, miserable, 807.
earm-sceapen, *adj.* (*pp.*), wretched-SHAPEN, miscreated, miserable, 1351, 2228*, 2229*.
earn, *st. m.*, ERNE, eagle, 3026.
eart, ART, 352, 506, etc., *2nd sg. pres. indic. of* wesan (q. v.).
ēastan, *adv.*, from the EAST, 569, F. 3*.
eatol, see **atol**.
ēaðe, **ȳðe**, *adj.*, easy, pleasant, 228, 1002, etc.; *once* **ēðe**, 2586.
ēaðe, *adv.*, easily, 478, etc.
ēað-fynde, *adj.*, easy to *FIND*, 138.
ēawan, see **ȳwan**.
eaxl, *st. f.*, [*AXLE*] shoulder, 816, 835, etc.
eaxl-gestealla, *w. m.*, shoulder-comrade, bosom friend, 1326, 1714.
ēc, see **ēac**.
ēce, *adj.*, eternal, 108, etc.
ecg, *st. f.*, EDGE (of a weapon), sword, 1106, etc.; *gen. pl.* ecga, 483, etc.
ecg-bana, *w. m.*, [EDGE-BANE] sword-slayer, 1262.
ecg-hete, *st. m.*, EDGE-HATE, sword-hate, 84*, 1738.
ecg-þracu, *st. f.*, EDGE-onset, sword-onset, armed attack, 596.
ed-hwyrft, *st. m.*, return, change, reverse, 1281. [*Cf.* hweorfan.]
ēdre, see **ǣdre**.
ed-wenden, *st. f.*, return, change, 1774*, 2188.
edwīt-līf, *st. neut.*, LIFE of reproach, life of infamy, 2891.
efn, *adj.*, EVEN.
on efn, *with dat.*, EVEN with, beside, 2903.
efnan, **æfnan**, *w. v.*, achieve, accomplish, make, 1041, 1254, etc.; *pp.* geæfned, 3106; āð wæs geæfned, 'the oath was sworn,' 1107.
ge-æfnan, *w. v.*, perform, etc., 538.
efne, *adv.*, EVEN, 943, etc.
efstan, *w. v.*, hasten, 1493, 3101. [*P.B.B.* x. 506: *from* ofost.]
eft, *adv.*, *AFT*er, afterwards, again, back, 22, etc.
eft-cyme, *st. m.*, back-*COM*ing, return, 2896.
eft-sīð, *st. m.*, back-journey, return, 1332, etc.
ēg-clif, *st. neut.*, sea-CLIFF, 2893*.
egesa, *w. m.*, fear, terror, 784, etc.; *acc.* egsan, 276 (see note). [*Cf. Goth.* agis.]
eges-full, *adj.*, terrible, 2929.
eges-līc, *adj.*, terrible, 1649, etc.
egl, *st. f.*, [AIL=a spike or awn of barley] claw, 987 (see note).
egsa, see **egesa**.
egsian, *w. v.*, terrify; *pret.* 6 (see note).
ēg-strēam, *st. m.*, water-STREAM, ocean current, 577.
ēhtan, *w. v*, *with gen.*, pursue, persecute, 159, 1512.
ehtigað, see **eahtian**.
elde, see **ylde**.
eldo, see **yldo**.
el-land, *st. neut.*, alien LAND, strange land, 3019.
ellen, *st. neut.*, strength, courage, bravery, 3, 573, etc.; *dat. sg.* elne, *sometimes best rendered by an adv.*, 'courageously,' 2676; *sometimes with strictly adverbial force*, 'quickly,' 1967, 'absolutely,' 'altogether,' 1097, 1129. [*Cf. Goth.* aljan.]
ellen-dǣd, *st. f.*, [strength-DEED] deed of strength *or* courage, 876, 900.
ellen-gǣst, *st. m.*, [strength-GHOST] powerful sprite, 86 (see note to l. 102).
ellen-līce, *adv.*, mightily, courageously, 2122.
ellen-mǣrðu, *st. f.*, [might-renown] fame for strength *or* courage, feat of strength, 828, 1471.
ellen-rōf, *adj.*, courage-strong, famed for strength *or* courage, 340, 358, 1787, 3063.
ellen-sīoc, *adj.*, [strength-SICK] strengthless, 2787.
ellen-weorc, *st. neut.*, strength-WORK, deed of might *or* courage, 661, etc.
elles, *adv.*, ELSE, otherwise, 138, etc.
ellor, *adv.*, ELSEwhithER, 55, 2254.
ellor-gāst, **ellor-gǣst**, *st. m.*, [ELSE-whithER-GHOST] sprite living elsewhere, alien sprite, 807, 1349, 1617, 1621. (See note to l. 102.)
ellor-sīð, *st. m.*, journey elsewhither, death, 2451.
elne, see **ellen**.

elra, *adj.*, another, 752 [*compar. of* *el(l), *Goth.* aljis—*root found in* elles *and* ellor].

el-þēodig, *adj.*, of alien nation, foreign, 336.

ende, *st. m.*, END, 224, etc.; *acc.* hæfde eorð-scrafa ende genyttod, 'had had the last of his earth-caves,' 3046; *dat.* eorlum on ende, 2021 (see note). [*Cf. Goth.* andeis.]

ende-dæg, *st. m.*, END-DAY, day of death, 637, 3035.

ende-dōgor, *st. neut.*, END-*DAY*, day of death, 2896.

ende-lāf, *st. f.*, [END-*LEAV*ing] last remnant, 2813.

ende-lēan, *st. neut.*, END-reward, final reward, 1692.

ende-sǣta, *w. m.*, [END-*SIT*ter] coast-guard, 241.

ende-stæf, *st. m.*, [END-STAFF] end; *acc.* on ende-stæf, 'towards, in, the end,' 1753.

endian, *w. v.*

ge-endian, *w. v.*, END; *pp.* geendod, 2311.

enge, *adj.*, narrow, 1410.

ent, *st. m.*, giant, 1679, 2717, 2774.

entisc, *adj.*, gigantic, 2979.

ēode, ēodon, see **gān**.

eodor, *st. m.*

(1) fence, barrier; *acc. pl.* under eoderas, 'within the barriers, into the house,' 1037,

(2) protector, lord, prince, 428, 1044; *nom.* eodur, 663.

eofer, eofor, *st. m.*, boar, figure of a boar upon a helmet, 1112, 1328; *acc.* eafor, 2152.

eofer-sprēot, *st. m.*, boar-spear, 1437.

eofor-līc, *st. neut.*, boar-LIKEness, figure of a boar upon a helmet; *pl.* 303.

eofoð, see **eafoð**.

eolet, *st. m.* or *neut.*; *gen.* 224 (see note).

eom, AM, see **wesan**.

eorclan-stān, *st. m.*, precious STONE, 1208. [*Cf. O.N.* jarkna-steinn, *and Goth.* -aírkns, 'good, holy.']

ēored-geatwe, *st. f. pl.*, troop-trappings, military equipments, 2866. [ēored *from* *eoh-rād.]

eorl, *st. m.*, EARL, noble, warrior, 6, 248, etc.

eorl-gestrēon, *st. neut.*, EARLS' treasure, 2244.

eorl-gewǣde, *st. neut.*, [EARL-WEEDS] armour, 1442.

eorlīc (=eorl-līc), *adj.*, EARL-LIKE, noble, 637.

eorl-scipe, *st. m.*, EARLSHIP, courage, heroic deeds, 1727, 2133, etc.

eorl-weorod, *st. neut.*, [EARL-host] warrior-band, 2893.

eormen-cynn, *st. neut.*, [vast KIN] mankind, 1957.

eormen-grund, *st. m.*, [vast GROUND] the whole broad earth, 859.

eormen-lāf, *st. f.*, [vast *LEAV*ing] immense legacy, 2234.

eorre, see **yrre**.

eorð-būend, *st. m.* (*pres. part.*), dweller in the land, F. 34.

eorð-cyning, *st. m.*, EARTH-KING, earthly king, 1155.

eorð-draca, *w. m.*, EARTH-DRAKE, earth-dragon, 2712, 2825.

eorðe, *w. f.*, EARTH, world, 92, 2834 (see note), etc.

eorð-hūs, *st. neut.*, EARTH-HOUSE, 2232*.

eorð-reced, *st. neut.*, EARTH-house, earth-hall, 2719 (see note).

eorð-scræf, *st. neut.*, EARTH-cave; *gen. pl.* eorð-scrafa, 3046.

eorð-sele, *st. m.*, EARTH-hall, 2410, 2515.

eorð-weall, *st. m.*, EARTH-WALL, 2957, 3090.

eorð-weard, *st. m.*, EARTH-possession, land-property, locality, 2334.

eoten, eoton, *st. m.*, ETTIN, giant, monster, 112, 421, 761, 883, 902 (see note), etc.

eotenisc, eotonisc, *adj.*, gigantic, of a giant, 1558, 2979; *acc.* etonisc, 2616.

eoten-weard, *st. f.*, [ETTIN-WARD] ward *or* watch against a monster; *acc.* eoten-weard ābead, 'offered watch against Grendel,' 668 (see note).

ēow, *pers. pron., acc. and dat. pl.* (*of* þū), YOU, 391, 2865, etc.

ēowan, see **ȳwan**.

ēower, *pers. pron., gen. pl.* (*of* þū), of YOU, 248, etc.

ēower, *poss. adj.*, YOUR, 251, etc.

ēowic, *pers. pron., acc. pl.* (*of* þū), YOU, 317, 3095.

ēst, *st. f.*, favour, grace, 958, 2165, etc.; *acc.* 2157 (see note), 3075; *dat. pl.* ēstum, *with adverbial force*, 'graciously, gladly, kindly,' 1194, 2149, 2378. [*Cf. Goth.* ansts.]

ēste, *adj.*, gracious; *with gen.* hyre ...ēste wǣre bearn-gebyrdo, 'was gracious to her in her child-bearing,' 945.

etan, *st. v.*, EAT, 444, 449.
  þurh-etan, *st. v.*, EAT THROUGH; *pp. pl.* þurhetone, 3049.
etonisc, see **eotenisc.**
ēð-begēte, *adj.*, [easy-BEGOTten] easily got, 2861.
ēðe, see **ēaðe.**
ēðel, *st. m.*, native land, fatherland, land, estate, 520, etc.
ēðel-riht, *st. neut.*, land-RIGHT, 2198.
ēðel-stōl, *st. m.*, [fatherland-STOOL] native seat; *pl.* country, 2371.
ēðel-turf, *st. f.*, native TURF, native soil; *dat.* ēðel-tyrf, 410.
ēðel-weard, *st. m.*, fatherland-WARD, guardian of his country, 616, 1702, 2210.
ēðel-wyn, *st. f.*, home joy, joyful home, 2885; *acc.* ēðel-wyn, 2493.
ēð-gesȳne, ȳð-gesēne, *adj.*, [easy-] manifest, easily visible (*not* seen, *pp.*), 1110, 1244.

F

fācen, *st. neut.*, treachery, crime, 2009*.
fācen-stæf, *st. m.*, treachery, 1018.
fæc, *st. neut.*, period of time, 2240.
fæder, *st. m.*, FATHER, 55, 316 (of God), etc.; *gen.* fæder, 21, etc.
fæder-æþelu, *st. neut. pl.*, ancestral virtue, *dat. pl.* 911.
fæderen-mǣg, *st. m.*, kinsman on the FATHER's side, 1263. [*Cf. Goth.* fadrein, 'paternity.']
fǣge, *adj.*, FEY, doomed, 846, etc.
fægen, *adj.*, FAIN, glad, 1633.
fæger, *adj.*, FAIR, beautiful, 522, etc. [*Cf. Goth.* fagrs.]
fægere, fægre, *adv.*, FAIRly, becomingly, courteously, 1014, 1788, etc.
fæghð, see **fǣhð.**
-fǣgon, see **-fēon.**
fǣhð, fǣhðo, *st. f.*, FEUD, hostility, 2403, 2999; *acc.* fǣhðe, 137, etc., fæghðe, 2465, fǣhðo, 2489.
fæla, see **fela.**
fǣlsian, *w. v.*, cleanse, 432, etc.; *pp.* gefǣlsod, 825, etc.
fǣmne, *w. f.*, maid, lady, 2034, 2059.
fær, *st. neut.*, craft, vessel, 33.
fǣr, *st. m.*, [FEAR] sudden attack or danger, 1068, 2230*.
fǣr-gripe, *st. m.*, FEAR-GRIP, sudden grip, 738, 1516.
fǣr-gryre, *st. m.*, [FEAR-terror] sudden terror, terror of sudden danger, 174.
fǣringa, *adv.*, suddenly, 1414 (see note), 1988.
fǣr-nīð, *st. m.*, [FEAR-malice] sudden mischief, 476.
fæst, *adj.*, FAST, 137, etc.; *often with dat.* 1290, 1878, etc.
fæstan, *w. v.*, FASTEN.
  be-fæstan, *w. v.*, commit to, 1115.
fæste, *adv.*, FAST, 554, etc.
  fæstor, *compar.*, FASTER, 143.
fæsten, *st. neut.*, FASTNESS, stronghold, 104, 2333, 2950.
fæst-rǣd, *adj.*, [FAST-REDE] firm-purposed, steadfast, 610.
fæt, *st. neut.*, VAT, vessel, flagon, 2761.
fǣt, *st. neut.*, plating, gold-plate, 716, 2256.
fǣted, *adj.* (*pp.*), plated, gold-plated, 2253, etc.: *contracted forms* fǣtte, fǣttan, 333, 1093, 1750*.
fǣted-hlēor, *adj.*, with bridle covered with plates of gold, 1036.
fǣt-gold, *st. neut.*, plated GOLD, 1921.
fǣtte, fǣttan, see **fǣted.**
fæðm, *st. m.*, [FATHOM] embrace, bosom, lap, 185, 188, 1393, etc.; power, 1210.
fæðmian, *w. v.*, embrace, 2652, 3133.
fāg, fāh, *adj.*, stained, coloured, variegated, bright, shining, 305, 1615, 1631, 2701, 420 (blood-stained), 1038 (bedecked); *acc. sg. m.* fāgne, fāhne, 725, 447, 2217, etc.
fāh, fāg, *adj.*:
  (1) hostile, 554; *nom.* hē fāg wið God, 'he a foe to God,' 811. *Substantively*, FOE; *acc. sg. m.* fāne, 2655; *gen. pl.* fāra, 578, 1463.
  (2) guilty, outlawed, 978, 1001, 1263.
fāhne, see **fāg, fāh.**
fāmig-heals, *adj.*, FOAMY-necked, 1909; fāmī-heals, 218.
fandian, see **fondian.**
fāne, see **fāh, fāg.**
-fangen, see **-fōn.**
fāra, see **fāh, fāg.**
faran, *st. v.*, FARE, go, 124, etc.; *pret. sg.* fōr, 1404, etc.; *pl.* foron, 1895, *dat. inf.* farenne, 1805*.
  ge-faran, *st. v.*, FARE, 738.
faroð, *st. m.*, tide, stream, flood, 28, etc.
fēa, *pl. adj.*, FEW; *acc.* (*with gen.*) fēa worda, 2246, 2662; *gen.* fēara, 1412, 3061 (see note); *dat.* fēaum, 1081. [*Cf. Goth. pl.* fawái.]

-feah, see **-fēon.**
fealh, see **fēolan.**
feallan, *st. v.*, FALL, 1070, etc. *pret. sg.* fēol(l), 772, 2919, etc.
be-feallan; *pp.* befeallen, 'deprived, bereft,' 1126, 2256.
ge-feallan, *st. v.*
(1) *intrans.*, FALL, 1755.
(2) *trans.*, fall to, fall on to, 2100, 2834 (see note).
fealo, see **fela.**
fealu, *adj.*, FALLOW, yellow, dun; *acc. sg. m.* fealone, 1950; *f.* fealwe, 916; *acc. pl.* fealwe, 865.
fēa-sceaft, *adj.*, wretched, destitute, 7, 973, 2285, 2373, 2393.
feax, *st. neut.*, hair, hair of the head, *dat.* feaxe, 1537*, 1647, fexe, 2967.
fēdan, *w. v.*, FEED. [*Cf. Goth.* fōdjan.]
ā-fēdan, *w. v.*, bring up, 693.
-fēgon, see **-fēon.**
-feh, see **-fēon.**
fēhð, see **fōn.**
fēl (-fēol), *st. f.*, FILE; *gen. pl.* fēla lāf, 'leaving of files, i.e. sword,' 1032.
fela, *st. neut., indecl.*, much, many, 36, etc. [*Cf. Goth.* filu, *dat.* filáu.]
Usu. with gen. sg. or pl.; fealo, 2757; *see also* worn.
Used as an adj. qualifying worn (q. v.), 530, etc.
fela, *adv.*, much, greatly, 1385, etc.; fæla, F. 27, 35 (*see* micel).
fela-gēomor, *adj.*, very sad, 2950.
fela-hrōr, *adj.*, very vigorous, 27.
fela-mōdig, *adj.*, [very MOODY] very brave, 1637, 1888.
fela-synnig, *adj.*, very SINful, 1379 (but see note).
fell, *st. neut.*, FELL, skin, 2088.
fen(n), *st. neut.*, FEN, moor, 104, 1295. [*Cf. Goth.* fani, 'clay.']
fen-freoðo, *st. f.*, FEN-refuge, 851.
feng, *st. m.*, clutch, grasp, 578, 1764.
fēng, see **fōn.**
fengel, *st. m.*, prince, 1400, 1475, 2156, 2345.
fen-gelād, *st. neut.*, FEN-path, 1359.
fen-hlið, *st. neut.*, FEN-slope; *pl.* fen-hleoðu, 820.
fen-hop, *st. neut.*, FEN-retreat, 'sloping hollow with a fenny bottom' (Skeat), 764.
feoh, *st. neut.*, FEE, property, money; *dat. sg.*, fēo (fēa), 156 (see note), etc. [*Cf. Goth.* faihu.]
feoh-gift, -gyft, *st. f.*, FEE-GIFT, gift of money, valuable gift, 21, 1025, 1089.
feoh-lēas, *adj.*, FEE-LESS, not to be atoned for with money, 2441.
feohtan, *st. v.*, FIGHT, F. 43.
ge-feohtan, *st. v.*, FIGHT out, achieve, 1083.
feohte, *w. f.*, FIGHT, 576, 959.
fēolan, *st. v.*, penetrate; *pret. sg.* fealh, 1281, 2225*. [*Cf. Goth.* filhan.]
æt-fēolan, *st. v.*, cleave, stick; *pret.* ætfealh, 968.
-fēon, *st. v.*
ge-fēon, *st. v.*, rejoice; *pret. sg.* gefeah, 109, etc., gefeh, 827, etc.; *pret. pl.* gefǣgon, 1014, gefēgon, 1627.
fēond, *st. m.*, FIEND, foe, 101, 164, etc. [*Cf. Goth.* fijands.]
fēond-grāp, *st. f.*, FIEND-GRIP, foe's grasp, 636.
fēond-scaða, *w. m.*, [FIEND-*SCATH*er] dire foe, 554.
fēond-scipe, *st. m.*, FIENDSHIP, enmity, 2999.
feor, *adj.*, FAR, 1361, 1921.
feor, *adv.*, FAR, afar, 42, 109, 542, 808, 1221, 1340, etc.; *once* feorr, 1988; *of time*, 'far back,' 1701. [*Cf. Goth.* faírra, 'far.']
fyr, *compar.*, farther, 143, 252.
feor-būend, *st. m.* (*pres. part.*), FAR dweller, dweller afar; *pl.* 254.
feor-cȳðð, *st. f.*, FAR country; *pl.* feor-cȳþðe bēoð sēlran gesōhte þǣm þe him selfa dēah, 'distant lands are better sought by one who is himself a good man,' 1838.
feorh, *st. m. neut.*, life, 73, 439, 1152 (bodies), 1210 (see note), 2040, etc.; *gen.* feores, 1433, etc.; *dat.* feore, 1843, etc.; *acc.* ferh (*see* wrecan), 2706; wæs in feorh dropen, 'was mortally wounded,' 2981; wīdan feorh, 'ever,' 2014; *dat.* tō wīdan feore, 'ever,' 933. [*Cf. Goth.* fairhwus, 'world.']
feorh-bealu, -bealo, *strong neut.*, life-BALE, deadly evil, 156, 2077, 2250, 2537.
feorh-benn, *st. f.*, life-wound, deadly wound, 2740.
feorh-bona, *w. m.*, [life-BANE] murderer, 2465.
feorh-cynn, *st. neut.*, life-KIN, generation *or* race of men, 2266.
feorh-genīðla, *w. m.*, life-foe, deadly foe, 969, 1540, 2933.
feorh-lāst, *st. m.*, life-step, 846 (see note).

feorh-legu, *st. f.*, decreed term of life, *hence* conclusion of life, *acc.* nū ic on māðma hord mīne bebohte frōde feorh-lege, 'now that in exchange for the hoard of treasures I have sold my old life,' 2800.
feorh-sēoc, *adj.*, life-SICK, mortally wounded, 820.
feorh-sweng, *st. m.*, [life-*SWING*] deadly blow, 2489.
feorh-wund, *st. f.*, life-WOUND, deadly wound, 2385.
feorh-weard, *st. f.*, guard over life, 305 (see note).
feorm, *st. f.*, food, sustenance, 451 (see note), 2385* (see note).
feormend-lēas, *adj.*, polisher-LESS, wanting the furbisher, 2761.
feormian, *w. v.*
(1) polish; *subj. pres.* 2253*.
(2) eat, devour; *pp.* gefeormod, 744.
feormynd, *st. m.* (*pres. part.*), polisher; *pl.* 2256.
feorran, *w. v.*, banish, 156.
feorran, *adv.*, from AFAR,
(1) *of space*, 361, etc.
(2) *of time*, 91, 2106 (of old times).
feorran-cund, *adj.*, come from AFAR, 1795.
feor-weg, *st. m.*, FAR WAY, distant land, 37.
fēower, *num.*, FOUR, 59, 1027, 1637, 2163.
fēower-tȳne, *num.*, FOURTEEN, 1641.
fēran, *w. v.*, *FARE*, go, 27, etc.; *pret. pl.* fērdon, 839, 1632; *subj. pres. pl.*, fēran, 254.
ge-fēran, *w. v.*
(1) *trans.*, go to, reach, gain, bring about, 1221, 1855, 2844, 3063.
(2) *intrans.*, fare; *pret. pl.*, 1691 (see note).
ferh, 2706, see **feorh**.
ferh, *st. m.*, [FARROW] pig, 305 (see note).
ferh-weard, see **feorh-weard**.
ferhð, *st. m. or neut.*, heart, mind, 754, etc. [*connected with* feorh, 'life'].
ferhð-frec, *adj.*, bold-minded, 1146.
ferhð-genīðla, *w. m.*, life-foe, deadly foe, 2881.
ferian, *w. v.*, [FERRY] bear, carry, bring; *pres. pl.* ferigeað, 333; *pret. pl.* feredon, 1154, etc., fyredon, 378; *pp. pl.* geferede, 361. [*Cf. Goth.* farjan.]
æt-ferian, *w. v.*, bear off, 1669.
ge-ferian, *w. v.*, bear, bring, 1638, 3130; *imperat. pl.* 1*st*, ´geferian, 'let us bear,' 3107.
of-ferian, *w. v.*, bear off, 1583.
oð-ferian, *w. v.*, bear away, save, 2141.
fetel-hilt, *st. neut.*, belted HILT, 1563.
fetian, *w. v.*, FETCH; *pp.* fetod, 1310.
ge-fetian, *w. v.*, fetch, bring, 2190.
fēða, *w. m.*, troop on foot, troop, 1327, 1424, 2497, 2544, 2919.
fēðe, *st. neut.*, movement, pace, 970.
fēðe-cempa, *w. m.*, foot-champion, foot-warrior, 1544, 2853.
fēðe-gest, *st. m.*, foot-GUEST, 1976.
fēðe-lāst, *st. m.*, [movement-track] foot-track, 1632.
feðer-gearwa, *st. f. pl.*, FEATHER-GEAR, 3119*.
fēðe-wīg, *st. m.*, foot-war, battle on foot, 2364.
fex, see **feax**.
fīf, *num.*, FIVE, 545, F. 43; *inflected*, fīfe, 420. [*Cf. Goth.* fimf.]
fīfel-cynn, *st. neut.*, monster-KIN, race of monsters, 104.
fīf-tēne, *num.*, FIFTEEN; *acc.* fȳftȳne, 1582; *inflected gen.*, fīftēna sum, 'with fourteen others,' 207.
fīftig, *num.*, FIFTY; *as adj.* 2209; *with gen.* 2733; *inflected gen. sg.* fīftiges, 3042.
findan, *st. v.*, FIND, 7, 207, etc.; obtain, prevail, 2373: *pret.* fand, 118, etc.; funde, 1415, etc.; *inf.* swā hyt weorðlīcost fore-snotre men findan mihton, 'as very wise men could most worthily devise it,' 3162.
on-findan, *st. v.*, FIND out, perceive, 750, 1293, 1890, etc.
finger, *st. m.*, FINGER, 760, etc.
fīras, *st. m. pl.*, men, 91, etc.; *gen. pl.* fȳra, 2250*. [*P. B. B.* x. 487.]
firen, **fyren**, *st. f.*, crime, violence, 915, etc.; *acc.* fyrene, 101, 137, 153, etc., firen, 1932: *dat. pl.* fyrenum, 'by crimes, maliciously,' 1744. For 2441 see note. [*Cf. Goth.* faírina, 'accusation.']
fyren-dǣd, *st. f.*, crime-DEED, deed of violence, 1001, 1669.
fyren-ðearf, *st. f.*, [crime-need] dire distress, 14.
firgen-, see **fyrgen-**.
flǣsc, *st. neut.*, FLESH, 2424.

flǣsc-homa, *w. m.*, FLESH-covering, body, 1568.
flacor, *adj.*, flickering, quickly moving, F. 36*.
flān, *st. m.*, arrow, barb, 2438, 3119.
flān-boga, *w. m.*, arrow-BOW, 1433, 1744.
flēah, see **flēon**.
flēam, *st. m.*, flight, 1001, 2889.
flēogan, *st. v.*, FLY, 2273, F. 3.
flēon, *st. v.*, FLEE, 755, etc.; *pret. sg.*, *with acc.*, flēah, 1200* (see note), 2224.
be-flēon, *st. v.*, *with acc.*, FLEE, escape from; *dat. inf.* nō þæt ȳðe byð to beflēonne, 'that (fate *or* death) will not be easy to escape from,' 1003.
ofer-flēon, *st. v.*, FLEE from; *inf.* nelle ic beorges weard oferflēon fōtes trem, 'I will not flee from the barrow's warden a foot's space,' 2525.
flēotan, *st. v.*, [FLEET] *FLOAT*, swim, 542, 1909.
flet, *st. neut.*, floor, floor of a hall, hall, 1025, 1036, 1086, etc.
flet-ræst, *st. f.*, floor-REST, bed in a hall, 1241.
flet-sittend, *st. m.* (*pres. part.*), floor-SITTING, hall-sitter, 1788, 2022.
flet-werod, *st. neut.*, [floor-host] hall-troop, 476.
fliht, *st. m.*, FLIGHT, 1765.
flītan, *st. v.*, [*Sc.* FLITE] contend, strive, 916; *pret. sg. 2nd*, 507.
ofer-flītan, *st. v.*, OVERcome, 517.
flōd, *st. m.*, FLOOD, 42, 545, etc. [*Cf. Goth.* flōdus.]
flōd-ȳð, *st. f.*, FLOOD-wave, 542.
flōr, *st. m.*, FLOOR, 725, 1316.
flota, *w. m.*, [FLOATer] bark, ship, 210, etc.
flot-here, *st. m.*, [FLOAT-army] fleet, 2915.
flȳman, *w. v.*, put to flight; *pp.* geflȳmed, 846, 1370. [*Cf.* flēam.]
-fōh, see **-fōn**.
folc, *st. neut.*, FOLK, nation, people, warriors, army, 14, 55, 262, etc. *The plural is sometimes used with the same meaning as the singular*, 1422, etc.; *cf.* lēod, lēode.
folc-āgend, *st. m.* (*pres. part.*), [FOLK-*OWN*er] folk-leader, 3113 (see note).
folc-cwēn, *st. f.*, FOLK-QUEEN, 641.
folc-cyning, *st. m.*, FOLK-KING, 2733, 2873.
folc-rēd, *st. m.*, FOLK-REDE; *acc.* folc-rēd fremede, 'did what was for the public good,' 3006.
folc-riht, *st. neut.*, FOLK-RIGHT, public right, 2608.
folc-scaru, *st. f.*, FOLK-SHARE, (public) land, 73.
folc-stede, *st. m.*, FOLK-STEAD, 76 (Heorot); *acc.* folc-stede fāra, 'the field of battle,' 1463.
folc-toga, *w. m.*, FOLK-leader, 839.
fold-bold, *st. neut.*, earth-*BUILD*ing, hall on the earth, 773.
fold-būend, *st. m.* (*pres. part.*), earth-dweller, 309; *pl.* fold-būend, 2274, fold-būende, 1355.
folde, *w. f.*, earth, ground, world, 96, 1137, 1196, etc.
fold-weg, *st. m.*, earth-WAY, 866, 1633.
folgian, *w. v.*, FOLLOW, pursue, 1102, 2933.
folm, *st. f.*, hand, 158, etc.
fōn, *st. v.*, seize, take, receive, grapple, clutch, 439; *pres. 3rd*, fēhð ōðer tō, 'another inherits (the treasure),' 1755; *pret.* fēng, 1542, *with dat.* 2989. [*Cf. Goth.* fāhan.]
be-fōn, **bi-fōn**, *st. v.*, seize, seize on, embrace; *pp.* befongen, 976, 1451, 2274, etc., bifongen, 2009, befangen, 1295, etc.
ge-fōn, *st. v.*, *with acc.*, seize; *pret.* gefēng, 740, 1501, 1537, 1563, 2215, 2609, 3090.
on-fōn, *st. v.*, *usu. with dat.*, receive, take, seize, 911; *imperat. sg.* onfōh, 1169; *pret.* onfēng, 52, 1214, etc.; 748 (see note).
þurh-fōn, *st. v.*, *with acc.*, [seize THROUGH] penetrate, 1504.
wið-fōn, *st. v.*, *with dat.*, grapple WITH; *pret.* wið-fēng, 760.
ymbe-fōn, *st. v.*, *with acc.*, [seize about] encircle, enclose; *pret.* ymbefēng, 2691.
fondian, **fandian**, *w. v.*, *with gen.*, search out, prove, experience; *pp.* gefandod, 2301, hafað dǣda gefondad, 'has experienced deeds (of violence),' 2454.
for, *prep.*
(1) *with dat.*, before, 358, 1026, 1120, 1649, 2020, 2990; before *or* because of, 169, 2781; FOR, out of, from, through, because of, on account of, about, 110, 338-9, 385, 508, 832, 951, 965, 1442, 1515, 2501 (see note), 2549, 2926, 2966, etc.; for (purpose), 382, 458.

(2) *with acc.*, FOR, instead of, as, 947, 1175, 2348.
foran, *adv.*, BEFORE, to the fore, forwards, 984, 1458; þe him foran ongēan linde bǣron, 'who bare their linden-shields forwards against him,' 2364.
ford, *st. m.*, FORD, 568.
fore, *prep.*, *with dat.*, BEFORE, 1215, 1064 (see note); in the presence of, for, through, because of, 2059.
fore, *adv.*, therefore, for it, 136.
fore-mǣre, *adj.*, [FORE-great].
fore-mǣrost, *superl.*, most famous of all, 309.
fore-mihtig, *adj.*, [FORE-MIGHTY] over-powerful, 969.
fore-snotor, *adj.* [FORE-prudent] very wise, 3162.
fore-þanc, *st. m.*, FORETHOUGHt, 1060.
forht, *adj.*, fearful, afraid, 754, 2967.
forma, *adj. superl.* (*of* fore), first, 716, etc.
forst, *st. m.*, FROST, 1609.
forð, *adv.*, FORTH, forward(s), away, on, 45, 210, 2289 (*see* tō, *adv.*), etc.;
of time, henceforth, from now, 948, 2069.
for-ðam, **for-ðan**, **for-ðon**, *adv.*, FOR THAT, therefore, 149, 418, etc.
for-þon þe, *conj.*, because, 503.
forð-gesceaft, *st. f.*, [FORTH-creation] future world *or* destiny, 1750.
for-þon, see **for-ðam**.
forð-weg, *st. m.*, FORTH-WAY, way forth, 2625.
fōt, *st. m.*, FOOT, 500, 745, etc.
fōt-gemearc, *st. neut.*, FOOT-MARK, foot-length, foot; *gen. sg.* fīftiges fōt-gemearces lang, 'fifty feet long,' 3042.
fōt-lāst, *st. m.*, FOOT-track, 2289.
fracod, *adj.*, worthless, 1575. [*Cf. Goth.* frakunnan, 'despise.']
frægn, see **frignan**.
frǣgnian, *w. v.*
ge-frǣgnian, *w. v.*, make famous; *pp.* gefrǣgnod, 1333.
frætwa, **frætwe**, *st. f. pl.*, adornments, jewels, decorated armour, 37, etc.; *dat.* frætwum, 2054, etc., frætewum, 962.
frætw(i)an, *w. v.*, adorn, 76; *pp.* gefrætwod, 992. [*Cf. Goth.* -fratwjan.]
ge-frætw(i)an, *w. v.*, adorn; *pret. sg.* gefrætwade, 96.
fram, see **from**.
frēa, *w. m.*, lord, 271, etc., 1934 (see note); *of the Deity*, the Lord, 27, 2794. [*Cf. Goth.* fráuja.]
frēa-drihten, *st. m.*, lord and master, 796.
frēa-wine, *st. m.*, lord-friend, friendly ruler, 2357, 2429; *acc.* 2438.
frēa-wrāsn, *st. f.*, lordly chain (diadem surrounding the helmet), 1451.
freca, *w. m.*, [FRECK], bold man, warrior, 1563. [*Cf. Mod. Germ.* frech, 'audacious.']
frēcne, *adj.*, daring, audacious, 889, 1104, 2689; dangerous, dread, fearful, 1359, 1378, 2250, 2537. (See Förster in *Engl. Stud.* XXXIX. 327–39.)
frēcne, *adv.*, daringly, fiercely, terribly, 959, 1032, 1691 (see note).
fremde, *adj.*, foreign, 1691.
freme, *adj.*, brave, excellent, 1932.
fremman, *w. v.*, FRAME, do, accomplish, bring about, try, 3, 101*, 1003, 2514 (see note), etc.; further, support, 1832; *pret.* fremede, 3006, etc.; *pp.* gefremed, 954, etc., *acc. f.* gefremede, 940.
ge-fremman, *w. v.*, FRAME, do, work, etc., 174, etc.; *pret.* hine mihtig God...forð gefremede, 'him mighty God advanced,' 1718.
frēo-burh, *st. f.*, FREE BURGH, free city, noble city, 693.
frēod, *st. f.*, friendship, 1707 (see note), 2476, 2556.
frēo-dryhten, *st. m.*, noble lord, 1169, 2627.
frēogan, *w. v.*, love, show love, treat kindly, 948, 3176. [*Cf. Goth.* frijōn.]
frēo-līc, *adj.*, [FREE-LIKE] noble, 615, F. 21; *fem.* frēolicu, 641.
frēond, *st. m.*, FRIEND, 915, etc. [*Cf. Goth.* frijōnds.]
frēond-lār, *st. f.*, [FRIEND-LORE], friendly counsel, 2377.
frēond-laþu, *st. f.*, FRIENDLY cheer, 1192 (see note to l. 1320, nēodlaðu).
frēond-līce, *adv.*
frēondlīcor, *compar.*, in a more FRIENDLY way, 1027.
frēond-scipe, *st. m.*, FRIENDSHIP, 2069.
frēo-wine, *st. m.*, noble lord, 430.
freoðo, *st. f.*, protection, peace, 188.
freoðo-burh, *st. f.*, protecting BURGH, peaceful city, 522.
freoðo-wong, *st. m.*, peace-plain, place of refuge, 2959.

freoðu-webbe, *w. f.*, peace-WEAVer, lady, 1942.

frioðo-wǣr, frioðu-wǣr, *st. f.*, peace-compact, treaty of peace, 1096, 2282.

friðu-sibb, *st. f.*, peace-kin, peace-bringer, 2017.

fretan, *st. v.*, [FRET] devour, consume, 1581, 3014, 3114. [*Cf. Goth.* fra-itan.]

fricgean, *st. v.*, ask, learn; *inf.* fricgcean, 1985; *pres. part.* fela fricgende, 'learning much, experienced,' 2106.

ge-fricgean, *w. v.*, learn, 3002; *pres. subj.* 1826, 2889.

frician, *w. v.*, seek for, 2556.

frignan, frīnan, *st. v.*, ask, inquire, 351; *imperat. sg.* frīn, 1322; *pret. sg.* frægn, 236, etc. [*Cf. Goth.* fraíhnan.]

ge-frignan, *st. v.*, learn, hear of; *pret. sg.*, gefrægn, 74, 194, etc., gefrægen, 1011; *pret. pl.* gefrunon, 2, etc., gefrungon, 666; *pp.* gefrunen, 694, etc., gefrægen, 1196. *Often followed by acc. and inf.* 74, 1969, etc.

frīnan, see **frignan**.

frioðo-, frioðu-, friðu-, see **freoðo-**.

frōd, *adj.*, old, wise, 279, 1306, etc. [*Cf. Goth.* frōþs.]

frōfor, *st. f.*, solace, comfort, 14, etc.; *acc.* frōfre, 7, etc., frōfor, 698.

from, *adj.*, forward, keen, bold, 1641, 2476, 2527; splendid, 21.

from, fram, *prep.*, *with dat.*, FROM, away from, 194 (see note), 420, 541, 1635, 2565, etc.; of, concerning, 532, 581, etc. *Following its case*, 110, etc.

from, fram, *adv.*, away, forth, 754, 2556.

fruma, *w. m.*, beginning, 2309.

frum-cyn, *st. neut.*, [first KIN] lineage, origin, 252.

frum-gār, *st. m.*, [first-spear, *cf. Lat.* primipilus] chieftain, 2856.

frum-sceaft, *st. f.*, first creation, beginning, 45, 91.

-frunen, -frungon, -frunon, see **-frignan**.

fugol, *st. m.*, FOWL, bird; *dat. sg.* fugle, 218; *nom. pl.* fugelas, F. 6; *dat. pl.* 2941*. [*Cf. Goth.* fugls.]

ful, *adv.*, FULL, very, 480, 951, 1252.

ful(l), *st. neut.*, cup, beaker, 615, etc.; *acc.* ȳða ful, 'the cup of the waves, i.e. the sea,' 1208.

full, *adj.*, FULL, 2412.

fullǣstan, see under **lǣstan**.

fultum, *st. m.*, help, aid, 698, 1273, 1835, 2662.

funde, *pret.*, see **findan**.

fundian, *w. v.*, hasten, intend, strive to go, 1137, 1819.

furðum, *adv.*, first, 323, 465, 2009; at first, formerly, 1707.

furður, *adv.*, FURTHER, further forward, 254, 761, 2525*, 3006.

fūs, *adj.*, ready, eager, longing, 1241, 1475, etc.; hastening, inclined, 1916 (see note to l. 1915), 1966.

fūs-līc, *adj.*, ready, prepared, 1424, 2618; *neut. pl.* fūslicu, 232.

fȳf-tȳne, see **fīf-tēne**.

fyll, *st. m.*, FALL, 1544, 2912.

fyllan, *w. v.* [*From* full, *cf. Goth.* fulljan.]

ā-fyllan, *w. v.*, FILL up, fill, 1018.

fyllan, *w. v.* [*From* feall.]

ge-fyllan, *w. v.*, FELL, 2655; *pret. pl.* gefyldan, 2706.

fyllo, *st. f.*, FILL, 562, 1014, 1333.

fyl-wērig, *adj.*, FALL-WEARY, weary to the point of falling, 962.

fyr, see **feor**, *adv.*

fȳr, *st. neut.*, FIRE, 185, etc.

fȳras, see **fīras**.

fȳr-bend, *st. m. f.*, FIRE-BAND, band forged with fire, 722.

fyrd-gestealla, *w. m.*, army-comrade, 2873.

fyrd-hom, *st. m.*, army-coat, coat of mail, 1504.

fyrd-hrægl, *st. neut.*, [army-RAIL] armour, 1527.

fyrd-hwæt, *adj.*, [army-active] warlike, brave; *pl.* fyrd-hwate, 1641, 2476.

fyrd-lēoð, *st. neut.*, army-lay, war-song, 1424*.

fȳr-draca, *w. m.*, FIRE-DRAKE, fire-dragon, 2689.

fyrd-searu, *st. neut.*, [army-] armour, 2618; *pl.* 232.

fyrd-wyrðe, *adj.*, [army-WORTHy] war-worthy, distinguished in war, 1316.

fyren, see **firen**.

fȳren, *adj.*, AFIRE, F. 38.

fȳrgen-bēam, *st. m.*, [mountain-BEAM] mountain-tree, 1414. [*Cf. Goth.* fairguni.]

fyrgen-holt, *st. neut.*, mountain-HOLT, mountain-wood, 1393.

fyrgen-strēam, firgen-strēam, *st. m.*, mountain-STREAM, 1359, 2128.

fȳr-heard, *adj.*, FIRE-HARD, fire hardened, 305.

fyrian, see **ferian**.

fȳr-lēoht, *st. neut.*, FIRELIGHT, 1516.
fyrmest, *adv. superl.* (*of* fore), *FOREMOST*, first, 2077.
fyrn-dagas, *st. m. pl.*, former DAYS, days of old, 1451. [*Cf. Goth.* faírneis, 'old.']
fyrn-geweorc, *st. neut.*, former WORK, ancient work, 2286.
fyrn-gewinn, *st. neut.*, former strife, ancient strife, 1689.
fyrn-mann, *st. m.*, former MAN, man of old, 2761.
fyrn-wita, *w. m.*, former counsellor, old counsellor, 2123.
fyrst, *st. m.*, time, space of time, 76, 545, etc.
fyrðran, *w. v.*, FURTHER; *pp.* frætwum gefyrðred, 'furthered by, urged on by, the jewels' (hastening to show them to Beowulf), 2784. [*From* furðor.]
fyr-wet, -wyt, *st. neut.*, curiosity, 232, etc.
fȳr-wylm, *st. m.*, FIRE-*WELL*ing, surge of fire, 2671.
fȳsan, *w. v.*, make ready, incite; *pp.* gefȳsed, 630, 2309, 2561; winde gefȳsed, 'impelled by the wind,' 217. [*From* fūs.]

G

gād, *st. neut.*, lack, 660, etc. [*Cf. Goth.* gáidw.]
gædeling, *st. m.*, relative, comrade, 2617, 2949.
gæst, gæst, see note to l. 102.
gæð, see gān.
galan, *st. v.*, sing, sound, 786, 1432; *pres. sg.*, gæleð, 2460.
  ā-galan, *st. v.*, sing, ring; *pret.* āgōl, 1521.
galdor, see **gealdor.**
galga, *w. m.*, GALLOWS, 2446.
galg-mōd, *adj.*, [sad-MOOD] sad in mind, gloomy, 1277.
galg-trēow, *st. neut.*, GALLOWS-TREE, 2940.
gamen, gamol, see **gomen, gomol.**
gān, *irreg. v.*, GO; *pres. indic. 3rd*, gǣð, 455; *pres. subj.* gā, 1394; *pret.* ēode, 358, 493, etc.; *imperat.* gā, 1782; *pp.* syððan hīe tōgædre gegān hæfdon, 'after they had closed in strife,' 2630. (See also **gongan.**)
  full-gān, *st. v.*, *with dat.*, follow and aid; *pret.* sceft...flāne fulleode, 'the shaft followed and aided the barb,' 3119.
  ge-gān, *st. v.*, *pret.* geēode, geīode (2200):
  (1) GO (*intrans.*), 1967, 2676.
  (2) GO (*trans.*), make, venture, 1277, 1462.
  (3) gain (by going), obtain, 1535; *with dependent clause*, 2917.
  (4) happen, 2200.
  ofer-gān, *st. v.*, *with acc.*, GO OVER, 1408, 2959.
  oð-gān, *st. v.*, GO (to), 2934.
  ymb-gān, *st. v.*, *with acc.*, GO about, go around, 620.
gang, *st. m.*, *GO*ing, journey, 1884; power of going, 968; track, 1391, 1404.
gang, gangan, see **gongan.**
ganot, *st. m.*, GANNET, Solan goose, 1861.
gār, *st. m.*, spear, javelin, 328, etc.
gār-cēne, *adj.*, spear-KEEN, spear-bold, 1958.
gār-cwealm, *st. m.*, [spear-*QUELL*ing] death by the spear, 2043.
gār-holt, *st. neut.*, spear-HOLT, spear-shaft, spear, 1834.
gār-secg, *st. m.*, ocean, 49, 515, 537.
gār-wiga, *w. m.*, spear-warrior, 2674, 2811.
gār-wīgend, *st. m.* (*pres. part.*), spear-warrior, 2641.
gāst, gǣst, *st. m.*, GHOST, sprite, devil, 102 (see note), 133, etc.; *gen. pl.* gāsta, 1357, gǣsta, 1123.
gāst-bona, *w. m.*, [GHOST-BANE] soul-slayer, the devil, 177.
ge, *conj.*, and, 1340; *with* swylce, 2258; *correl.* ge...ge, 'both...and,' 1248, 1864.
gē, *pers. pron.* (*pl. of* þū), YE, you, 237, etc.
geador, *adv.*, TOGETHER, 835; *with* ætsomne, 491.
  on geador, TOGETHER, 1595.
ge-æhtle, *w. f.*, high esteem, 369.
geald, see **gyldan.**
gealdor, *st. neut.*:
  (1) sound, blast, 2944.
  (2) incantation; *dat.* galdre, 3052.
gealp, see **gilpan.**
gēap, *adj.*, spacious, extensive, roomy, 836, 1800.
gēar, *st. neut.*, YEAR, 1134. [*Cf. Goth.* jēr.]
  gēara, *gen. pl.* (in adverbial sense), of YORE, formerly, 2664.
geard, *st. m.*, YARD; *always pl. in* 'Beowulf,' courts, dwelling-place, 13, 265, 1134, 1138, 2459. [*Cf. Goth.* gards, 'house.']

gēar-dagas, *st. m. pl.*, YORE-DAYS, days of yore, 1, 1354, 2233.
geare, see **gearwe**.
gearo, gearu, once **geara**, *adj.*, YARE, ready, prepared, 77, 1109, 1914, etc.; *with gen.* 1825; *acc. sg. f.* gearwe, 1006; *pl.* gearwe, 211, etc.
gearo, *adv.*, well, 2748. See also **gearwe**.
gearo-folm, *adj.*, ready-handed, 2085*.
gearwe, geare, *adv.*, well, 265, 2656, etc.; *with* ne, 'not at all,' 246.
  gearwor, *compar.*, more readily, 3074.
  gearwost, *superl.*, most surely, 715.
-geat, see **-gitan**.
geato-līc, *adj.*, stately, splendid, 215, 308, 1401, 1562, 2154.
geatwa, *st. f. pl.*, garniture, 3088.
ge-bedda, *w. m. or f.*, BED-fellow, 665. [*Cf.* heals-gebedda.]
ge-bræc, *st. neut.*, crash, 2259. [*Cf.* brecan.]
ge-brōðor, ge-brōðru, *st. m. pl.*, BROTHERS, 1191.
ge-byrd, *st. f. or neut.*, order, established order, fate, 1074.
ge-cynde, *adj.*, [KIND] natural, hereditary, 2197, 2696.
ge-dāl, *st. neut.*, severance, parting, 3068. [*Cf. Goth.* dáils, 'division.']
ge-dēfe, *adj.*, meet, fitting, 561, 1670, 3174*; friendly, 1227.
ge-dræg, *st. neut.*, tumult, 756 (see note).
ge-dryht, ge-driht, *st. f.*, band, troop, 118, 431, etc.
ge-fægra, *compar. adj.*, more pleasing; *nom.* hē...wearð...frēondum gefægra; hine fyren onwōd, 'he (Beowulf) became more dear to his friends; him (Heremod) crime assailed,' 915 (see note).
-gēfan, see **-gifan**.
ge-fēa, *w. m.*, joy, 562, 2740.
ge-feoht, *st. neut.*, FIGHT, 2048, 2441.
ge-flit, *st. neut.*, 'FLITing,' contest, match, 586*, 865.
ge-frǣge, *adj.*, renowned, notorious, 55, 2480.
ge-frǣge, *st. neut.*, hearsay; *dat.* (*instr.*) *sg.* mīne gefrǣge, 'as I have heard *or* learned,' 776, 837, 1955, 2685, 2837.
ge-frǣgnian, *w. v.*, make famous; *pp.* gefrǣgnod, 1333.
gegn-cwide, *st. m.*, reply, 367.
gegnum, *adv.*, forwards, straight, direct, 314, 1404.
gehlyn, *st. n.*, noise, din, F. 30.
gehðo, see **giohðo**.
ge-hwā, *pron.*, *with gen.*, each, each one; *acc.* gehwone, gehwane, 294, 2397, etc.; *dat. m.* gehwām, gehwǣm, 88, 1420, etc.; *dat. f.* gehwǣre, 25. *Masc. form with dependent gen. of fem. or neut. n.* 800, 1365, 2838, 2765.
ge-hwǣr, *adv.*, everyWHERE, 526.
ge-hwæðer, *pron.*, eITHER, 584, etc.; *nom. neut.*, an wīg gearwe ge æt hām ge on herge, ge gehwæþer þāra efne swylce mǣla, 'ready for war both at home and in the field, and either (i.e. both) of them even at such times,' 1248.
ge-hwylc, ge-hwelc, *adj.-pron.*, *with gen.* each, 98, 148, etc.
ge-hygd, *st. f. and neut.*, thought, 2045.
ge-hyld, *st. neut.*, protection, 3056. [*From* healdan.]
ge-lāc, *st. neut.*, play, 1040, 1168.
ge-lād, *st. neut.*, [LODE] path, 1410.
ge-lang, see **ge-long**.
ge-lenge, *adj.*, beLONGing to, 2732.
ge-līc, *adj.*, LIKE, 2164 (but see note).
  ge-līcost, *superl.*, LIKEST, most like, 218, 727, 985, 1608.
ge-lōme, *adv.*, frequently, 559.
ge-long, ge-lang, *adj.*; gelong (gelang) æt þē, 'ALONG of, dependent on, thee,' 1376, 2150.
ge-mǣne, *adj.*, common, in common, 1784, etc. [*Cf. Goth.* gamáins.]
ge-mēde, *st. neut.*, consent, 247.
ge-met, *st. neut.*, measure, power, ability, 2533, 2879; mid gemete, 'in any wise,' 779 (see note).
ge-met, *adj.*, MEET, 687, 3057.
ge-mēting, *st. f.*, MEETING, 2001.
ge-mong, *st. neut.*, troop, 1643.
ge-mynd, *st. f. and neut.*, REMINDER, memorial, 2804, 3016. [*Cf. Goth.* gamunds.]
ge-myndig, *adj.*, MINDful, 613, etc.
gēn, *adv.*, AGAIN, yet, still, 734, 2070, 3006, etc.; *often with* þā, nū, 83, 2859, etc.
gēna, *adv.*, still, 2800, 3093.
ge-neahhe, *adv.*, enough, 783; frequently, 3152.
  genehost, *superl.*, very often: genehost brægd eorl Bēowulfes ealde lāfe, 'very abundantly did an earl of Beowulf draw...i.e. many an earl of Beowulf drew,' 794.

gengan, gengde, see **gongan.**
ge-nip, *st. neut.*, mist, 1360, 2808.
ge-nōg, *adj.*, ENOUGH, 2489, 3104.
gēnunga, *adv.*, wholly, utterly, 2871.
gēo, gīo, īu, *adv.*, formerly, 1476, 2459, 2521. [*Cf. Goth.* ju.]
gēoc, *st. f.*, help, 177, 608, 1834, 2674.
gēocor, *adj.*, dire, sad, 765.
geofon, gifen, gyfen, *st. neut.*, ocean, 362, 515, 1394, 1690.
geofu, see **gifu.**
geogoð, giogoð, *st. f.*, YOUTH, both abstract and concrete (=younger warriors), 66, etc.; *gen.* iogoðe, 1674.
geogoð-feorh, *st. m. and neut.*, YOUTH-life, days of youth, 537, 2664.
geolo, *adj.*, YELLOW, 2610.
geolo-rand, *st. m.*, YELLOW buckler, yellow shield, 438.
gēo-mann, see **īu-monn.**
gēo-mēowle, *w. f.*, former maiden, spouse, 3150*; *acc.* īo-mēowlan, 2931. [*Cf. Goth.* mawilō.]
gēomor, gīomor, *adj.*, sad, 49, 3150, etc.; *f.* gēomuru, 1075.
gēomore, *adv.*, sadly, 151.
gēomor-līc, *adj.*, [sad-LIKE] sad, 2444.
gēomor-mōd, gīomor-mōd, *adj.*, [sad-MOOD] sad-minded, sorrowful, 2044, 2267, 3018.
gēomrian, *w. v.*, lament, 1118.
gēomuru, see **gēomor.**
geond, *prep.*, *with acc.*, [YOND] throughout, 75, etc.
geong, giong, *adj.*, YOUNG, 13, etc.; *dat. sg.*, geongum, 2044*, etc., geongan, 2626.
  gingæst, *superl.*, YOUNGEST, last; *weak*, 2817.
geong, 2743, see **gongan.**
gēong, see **gongan.**
georn, *adj.*, YEARNing, eager, 2783. [*Cf. Germ.* gern.]
georne, *adv.*, eagerly, gladly, 66, etc.; well, 968.
  geornor, *compar.*, more surely, 821.
gēo-sceaft, *st. f.*, fate, 1234 (see note).
gēosceaft-gāst, *st. m.*, fated spirit, 1266.
gēotan, *st. v.*, pour, rush, 1690. [*Cf. Goth.* giutan.]
ge-rād, *adj.*, skilful, 873. [*Cf. Goth.* garáiþs, 'due.']
ge-rūm-līce, *adv.*, ROOMILY.
  ge-rūmlīcor, *compar.*, more roomily, further away, 139.
ge-rysne, *adj.*, befitting, 2653.
ge-saca, *w. m.*, adversary, 1773.
ge-sacu, *st. f.*, strife, 1737.
ge-scād, *st. neut.*, difference, 288.
gescæp-hwīl, *st. f.*, [SHAPEd WHILE] fated hour, 26.
ge-sceaft, *st. f.*, [what is SHAPED] creation, world, 1622. [*Cf.* scyppan *and Goth.* gaskafts.]
ge-sceap, *st. neut.*, SHAPE, 650; destiny, 3084 (see note).
ge-scipe, *st. neut.*, fate, 2570 (see note).
ge-selda, *w. m.*, hall-fellow, comrade, 1984.
ge-sīð, *st. m.*, retainer (*originally* comrade in a journey), 29, etc.
ge-slyht, *st. neut.*, slaying, encounter, 2398. [*Cf. O.E.* slēan.]
ge-strēon, *st. neut.*, possession, treasure, 1920, 2037, 3166.
gest-sele, *st. m.*, GUEST-hall, 994.
ge-sund, *adj.*, SOUND, safe and sound, 1628, 1988; *with gen.* sīða gesunde, 'safe and sound on your journeys,' 318.
ge-swing, *st. neut.*, SWING, eddy, 848.
ge-sȳne, *adj.*, evident, visible, 1255, etc.
ge-synto, *st. f.*, SOUNDness, health, 1869.
-get, see **-gitan.**
ge-tǣse, *adj.*, quiet, pleasant, 1320.
gētan, *w. v.*, slay, destroy, *inf.* cwæð, hē on mergenne mēces ecgum gētan wolde, sume on galgtrēowum fuglum tō gamene, 'quoth, he would destroy [them] in the morn with the edges of the sword, [hang] some on gallows-trees for a sport for birds,' 2940 (see note).
ge-tenge, *adj.*, lying on, 2758.
ge-trum, *st. neut.*, troop, 922.
ge-trȳwe, *adj.*, TRUE, faithful, 1228.
ge-þinge, *st. neut.*:
(1) terms, *pl.* 1085.
(2) issue, 398, 709; *gen. pl.* geþingea, 525 (see note).
ge-þōht, *st. m.*, THOUGHT, resolution, 256, 610.
ge-þonc, *st. m. and neut.*, THOUGHt, 2332.
ge-þræc, *st. neut.*, heap, 3102.
ge-þring, *st. neut.*, throng, eddy, 2132.
ge-þwǣre, *adj.*, gentle, 1230.
ge-þyld, *st. f.*, patience, 1395, etc.: geþyldum, *adverbially*, 'patiently, steadily,' 1705.
ge-þȳwe, *adj.*, [THEWy] wonted, customary, 2332.

ge-wǣde, *st. neut.*, WEEDS, armour 292.
ge-wealc, *st. neut.*, [*WALK*] rolling, 464.
ge-weald, *st. neut.*, *WIELD*ing, power, control, 79, 808, 2221 (*see* mid), etc.
ge-wealden, *adj.* (*pp.*), subject, 1732.
ge-weorc, *st. neut.*, WORK, 455, etc.
ge-wider, *st. neut.*, *WEATHER*, storm, tempest; *pl.* 1375.
ge-wif, *st. neut.*, *WEB*, of destiny, fortune; *pl.* gewiofu, 697. [*Cf. O.E.* wefan.]
ge-win(n), *st. neut.*, strife, struggle, 133, etc.
ge-winna, *w. m.*, striver, foe, 1776 (see note).
ge-wiofu, see **ge-wif**.
gewis-līce, *adv.*
gewis-līcost, *superl.*, most certainly, 1350.
ge-witt, *st. neut.*, WIT, senses, 2703; head, 2882.
ge-wittig, *adj.*, [WITTY] 3094 (see note).
ge-worht, see **wyrcan**.
ge-wrixle, *st. neut.*, exchange, 1304.
ge-wyrht, *st. neut.*, desert, 457* (see note); *pl.* 2657.
gid(d), **gyd(d)**, *st. neut.*, formal speech, song, dirge, 151, etc.
giest, **gist**, **gyst**, **gæst**, *GUEST*, stranger (often = hostile stranger), 1138, 1441, 1522, 2227: gæst, 1800, 1893; probably also, 2312 (see note to l. 102). [*Cf. Goth.* gasts.]
gif, **gyf**, *conj.*, IF, 442, 944, etc.; if = whether, 272, etc.
gifan, **giofan**, *st. v.*, *pret.* geaf, gēafon, *pp.* gyfen: GIVE, 49, 64, 1719, etc.
ā-gifan, *st. v.*, GIVE back, 355, 2929.
æt-gifan, *st. v.*, GIVE (to), render, 2878.
for-gifan, *st. v.*, GIVE, 17, etc.
of-gifan, **of-gyfan** *st. v.*, GIVE up, leave, 1600, 2251, 2588, etc.; *pret. pl.* ofgēfan, 2846.
gifen, see **geofon**.
gifeðe, **gyfeðe**, *adj.*, *GIV*en, granted, 299, 555, etc.
gifeðe, *neut. used as a noun*, thing granted, fate, 3085 (see note).
gif-heall, *st. f.*, GIFT-HALL, 838.
gifre, *adj.*, greedy, 1277.
gīfrost, *superl.*, greediest, 1123.
gif-sceatt, *st. m.*, gift of treasure, 378.
gif-stōl, *st. m.*, GIFT-STOOL, throne, 168, 2327.
gifu, *st. f.*, GIFT, 1173, 1271, etc.; *gen. pl.* gifa, 1930, geofena, 1173; *dat. pl.* geofum, 1958.
gīgant, *st. m.*, giant, 113, 1562, 1690. [*P.B.B.* x. 501. *From Greek, through Lat.* gigantem.]
gilp, **gylp**, *st. m. and neut.*, [YELP] boast, 829, 1749, 2521 (see note to ll. 2520–1), etc.; on gylp, 'proudly,' 1749.
gilpan, **gylpan**, *st. v.*, [YELP] boast, 536, 2583, etc.
be-gilpan, *st. v.*, boast of, 2006* (see note).
gilp-cwide, *st. m.*, [YELP-speech] boasting speech, 640.
gilp-hlæden, *adj.* (*pp.*), [YELP-LADEN] glory-laden, 868 (see note).
gylp-sprǣc, *st. f.*, [YELP-SPEECH] boasting-speech, 981.
gylp-word, *st. neut.*, [YELP-WORD] boastful word, 675.
gim, *st. m.*, gem, 2072. [*From Lat.* gemma, whence 'gem.']
gim-fæst, see **gin-fæst**.
gimme-rīce, *adj.*, gem-RICH, rich in jewels, 466 (see note).
gin-fæst, **gim-fæst**, *adj.*, [wide-FAST] ample, 1271 (see note), 2182.
gingæst, see **geong**.
-ginnan, *st. v.*
on-ginnan, *st. v.*, BEGIN, undertake, attempt, 244 (see note), 409, 2878, etc.; *pret. sg.* ongan, 100, etc.; ongon, 2790.
gīo, see **gēo**.
giofan, see **gifan**.
giogoð, see **geogoð**.
giohðo, *st. f.*, sorrow, care; *dat.* giohðo, 2267, giohðe, 2793*, gehðo, 3095.
gīomor, see **gēomor**.
giong, see **geong**.
-giredan, see **-gyrwan**.
gist, see **giest**.
git, *pers. pron.* (*dual of* þū), ye two, 508, etc.
gīt, **gȳt**, *adv.*, YET, still, 47, 536, 944, 956, etc.
-gitan, *st. v.*, *pret.* -geat, -gēaton.
an-gitan, see **on-gitan**.
be-gitan, *st. v.*, *GET*, obtain, seize, befall, 1068, 2249, etc.; *pret. sg.* beget, 2872; *pret. subj.* (*sg. for pl.*) begēate, 2130: ferhð-frecan Fin eft begeat sweord-bealo sliðen, 'dire sword-bale afterwards befell the bold-minded Finn,' 1146 (*cf.* 2230).

for-gytan, *st. v.*, FORGET, 1751.

on-gitan, on-gytan, *st. v.*
(1) GET hold of, seize; *pret. sg.* angeat, 1291.
(2) get hold of with the mind, perceive, 14, 1431, 1723, 2748, etc.; *inf.* ongyton, 308.

gladian, *w. v.*, shine triumphantly, 2036.

glæd, *adj.*, [GLAD] gracious, 58 (see note), etc.

glæd-man, *adj.*, cheerful, courteous, 367 (see note).

glæd-mōd, *adj.*, GLAD of MOOD, 1785.

glēd, *st. f.*, GLEED, ember, fire, 2312, etc.

glēd-egesa, *w. m.*, GLEED-terror, terror of fire, 2650.

glēo, *st. neut.*, GLEE, 2105.

glēo-bēam, *st. m.*, [GLEE-BEAM], glee-wood, harp, 2263.

glēo-drēam, *st. m.*, [GLEE-joy] mirth, 3021.

glēo-mann, *st. m.*, GLEEMAN, minstrel, 1160.

glīdan, *st. v.*, GLIDE, 515, etc.

tō-glīdan, *st. v.*, [GLIDE asunder] fall to pieces, 2487.

glitinian, *w. v.*, *GLIT*ter, glisten, gleam, 2758.

glōf, *st. f.*, GLOVE; pouch, bag, 2085 (see ten Brink, 123, footnote).

gnēað, *adj.*, niggardly, 1930.

gnorn, *st. m. or neut.*, sorrow, 2658.

gnornian, *w. v.*, mourn, 1117.

be-gnornian, *w. v.*, *with acc.*, bemoan, 3178.

God, *st. m.*, GOD, 13, etc.

gōd, *adj.*, GOOD, 11, etc.; *pl.* gōde, 'good men,' 2249.

gōd, *st. neut.*, GOOD, goodness, good thing, good gift, 20, 1952, etc.; *dat. pl.* manig ōþerne gōdum ge-grēttan, 'many a one [shall] greet another with good things,' 1861; *gen. pl.* gōda, 681 (see note).

gōd-fremmend, *st. m.* (*pres. part.*), [GOOD-*FRAM*ing] framer of good, one who acts well or bravely, 299.

gold, *st. neut.*, GOLD, 304, etc.

gold-æht, *st. f.*, treasure in GOLD, 2748.

gold-fāg, -**fāh**, *adj.*, GOLDen-hued, adorned with gold, gold-brocaded, 308, 994, 1800, 2811.

gold-gyfa, *w. m.*, GOLD-GIVER, 2652.

gold-hladen, *adj.* (*pp.*), GOLD-adorned, F. 15.

gold-hroden, *adj.* (*pp.*), GOLD-adorned, 614, etc.

gold-hwæt, *adj.*, [GOLD-active] greedy for gold, 3074 (see note).

gold-māðum, *st. m.*, GOLD-treasure, 2414.

gold-sele, *st. m.*, GOLD-hall, 715, 1253, 1639, 2083.

gold-weard, *st. m.*, [GOLD-WARD] guardian of gold, 3081.

gold-wine, *st. m.*, GOLD-friend, prince, 1171, etc.

gold-wlanc, *adj.*, GOLD proud, 1881.

gomban, *w. acc.*, tribute, 11. [*Only twice recorded: gender and exact form of nom. uncertain.*]

gomen, **gamen**, *st. neut.*, GAME, mirth, joy, 1160, 2459, etc.

gomen-wāð, *st. f.*, [GAME-path] joyous journey, 854.

gomen-wudu, *st. m.*, [GAME-WOOD] harp, 1065, etc.

gomol, **gomel**, **gamol**, *adj.*, old, gray, aged, ancient, 58, 2112, 3095, etc.; *weak* gomela, gamela, 1792, 2105, etc.; *gen. pl.* gomelra lāfe, 'the heirlooms of their fathers before them,' 2036.

gamol-feax, *adj.*, gray-haired, 608.

gongan, **gangan**, **gengan**, *st. v.*, GO, 314, 395, etc.; *imperat.* geong, 2743; *pret.* gēong, 925, etc., gīong, 2214, etc.; gang, 1009 (see note) 1295, 1316; gende, 1401 (see note); gengde, 1412; *pp.* gegongen, 822, 3036; *inf.* gangan cwōmon, 'came going, marching,' 324; *so* 711, 1642, 1974. (See also gān.)

ā-gangan, *st. v.*, GO forth, befall, 1234.

ge-gangan, ge-gongan, *st. v.*:
(1) gain (by GOing), obtain, 2536; *pp.* gegongen, 3085, *with dependent clause*, 893; *dat. inf.* gegannenne, 2416.
(2) come to pass, happen, 1846; *pp.* gegongen, 2821.

grǣdig, *adj.*, GREEDY, 121, etc. [*Cf. Goth.* grēdags, 'hungry.']

grǣg, *adj.*, GRAY, 330, etc.

grǣg-hama, *w. m.*, the GRAY-coated one, F. 7.

grǣg-mǣl, *adj.*, marked, *or* coloured GRAY, 2682.

græs-molde, *w. f.*, GRASS-MOULD, grass-plain, 1881.

gram, *adj.*, angry, hostile, 424, 765, 777, 1034.

grāp, *st. f.*, *GRIP*, clutch, 438, 836, etc.

grāpian, *w. v.*, GROPE, gripe, grasp, 1566, 2085.

grēot, *st. neut.*, GRIT, earth, 3167.
grēotan, *st. v.* [*Scotch* GREET] weep, 1342.
grētan, *w. v.*, *pret.* grētte: GREET: (1) salute, 347, etc.
(2) approach, seek out, attack, touch, 168, 803, 1995, 2735, 3081, etc.
ge-grētan, *w. v.*, GREET, 652*, 1979, 2516; *inf.* gegrēttan, 1861.
grim(m), *adj.*, GRIM, 121, etc.; *dat. pl.* grimman, 1542.
grīm-helm, *st. m.*, visored HELMet, 334.
grim-līc, *adj.*, GRIM[-LIKE], 3041.
grimman, *st. v.*, rage; *pret. pl.* grummon, 306 (but see note to ll. 303, etc.).
grimme, *adv.*, GRIMly, terribly, 3012, 3085.
grindan, *st. v.*
for-grindan, *st. v.*, GRIND down, grind to pieces, ruin, destroy; *with dat.*, 424; *with acc.* 2335, 2677.
grīpan, *st. v.*, GRIPE, grasp, seize, 1501.
for-grīpan, *st. v.*, *with dat.*, GRIP[E] to death, 2353.
wið-grīpan, *st. v.*, GRIPE at, grapple with, 2521.
gripe, *st. m.*, GRIP, 1148, etc.
grom-heort, *adj.*, fierce-HEARTed, hostile-hearted, 1682.
grom-hȳdig, *adj.*, angry-minded, hostile-minded, 1749.
grōwan, *st. v.*, GROW; *pret. sg.* grēow, 1718.
grund, *st. m.*, GROUND, earth, bottom, floor, 553, 1367, 1404, etc.
grund-būend, *st. m.* (*pres. part.*), [GROUND-dweller] inhabitant of earth, 1006.
grund-hyrde, *st. m.*, [GROUND-HERD] guardian of the bottom (of the mere), 2136.
grund-sele, *st. m.*, GROUND-hall, hall *or* cave at the bottom (of the mere), 2139* (see note).
grund-wong, *st. m.*, GROUND-plain, plain, floor (of a cave), bottom (of a mere), 1496, 2588 (see note), 2771.
grund-wyrgen, *st. f.*, [GROUND-hag] of Grendel's dam at the bottom of the mere, 1518. [*Cf.* wearg, 'accursed.']
gryn, see **gyrn**.
gryre, *st. m.*, terror, terrible deed, 384, 478, 483, 591.
gryre-brōga, *w. m.*, *GRI*sly terror, horror, 2227*.
gryre-fāh, *adj.*, [*GRI*sly-stained] horribly bright, 2576, 3041*.
gryre-gēatwa, *st. f. pl.*, *GRI*sly trappings, warlike trappings, 324.
gryre-giest, *st. m.*, *GRI*sly GUEST, terrible stranger, 2560.
gryre-lēoð, *st. neut.*, *GRI*sly lay, terrible song, 786.
gryre-līc, *adj.*, *GRISLY*, terrible, 1441, 2136.
gryre-sīð, *st. m.*, *GRI*sly journey, terrible expedition, 1462.
guma, *w. m.*, man, 20*, etc.
gum-cynn, *st. neut.*, [man-KIN] race, tribe, *or* nation of men, 260, 944, 2765.
gum-cyst, *st. f.*, manly virtue, 1723, etc.; *dat. pl.* gum-cystum gōd, 'excellently good,' 1486, 2543.
gum-drēam, *st. m.*, joy of men, 2469.
gum-dryhten, *st. m.*, lord of men, 1642.
gum-fēða, *w. m.*, troop of warriors on foot, 1401.
gum-mann, *st. m.*, MAN, 1028.
gum-stōl, *st. m.*, [man-STOOL] throne, 1952.
gūð, *st. f.*, war, battle, fighting-power, 438, etc.
gūð-beorn, *st. m.*, warrior, 314.
gūð-bill, *st. neut.*, war-BILL, 803, 2584.
gūð-byrne, *w. f.*, war-*BYRNY*, coat of mail, 321.
gūð-cearu, *st. f.*, war-CARE, war-sorrow, 1258.
gūð-cræft, *st. m.*, war-CRAFT, war-might, 127.
gūð-cyning, **-kyning**, *st. m.*, war-KING, 199, 1969, etc.
gūð-dēað, *st. m.*, war-DEATH, death in battle, 2249.
gūð-floga, *w. m.*, war-*FLI*er, 2528.
gūð-freca, *w. m.*, bold fighter, 2414.
gūð-fremmend, *st. m.* (*pres. part.*), war-FRAMER, warrior, 246.
gūð-geatwa, **-getāwa**, *st. f. pl.*, war-raiment, war-gear, war-equipments; *acc.* gūð-getāwa, 2636; *dat.* gūð-geatawum, 395. [See note to l. 368 (*wig-getāwum*) and Sievers$_3$ § 43, N. 4.]
gūð-gewǣde, *st. neut.*, war-WEED, armour; *nom. pl.* gūð-gewǣdu, -gewǣdo, 227, 2730, etc.; gūð-gewǣda, 2623, either *gen. pl.* or =gūð-gewǣdu.
gūð-geweorc, *st. neut.*, war-WORK, warlike deed, 678, 981, 1825.
gūð-helm, *st. m.*, war-HELM, 2487.

gūð-horn, *st. m.*, war-HORN, 1432.
gūð-hrēð, *st. m. or neut.*, war-fame, 819.
gūð-kyning, see **gūð-cyning**.
gūð-lēoð, *st. neut.*, war-lay, battle-song, 1522.
gūð-mōdig, *adj.*, [war-MOODY] of war-like mind, 306* (see note to ll. 303, etc.).
gūð-rǣs, *st. m.*, [war-*RACE*] attack in war, storm of battle, 1577, 2426, 2991.
gūð-rēo(u)w, *adj.*, war-fierce, 58.
gūð-rinc, *st. m.*, warrior, 838, 1501, 1881, 2648.
gūð-rōf, *adj.*, war-famed, 608.
gūð-scear, *st. m.*, [war-*SHEAR*ing] slaughter in battle, 1213.
gūð-sceaða, *w. m.*, war-*SCATH*er, battle-foe, 2318.
gūð-searo, *st. neut.*, war-armour, 215, 328.
gūð-sele, *st. m.*, war-hall, 443.
gūð-sweord, *st. neut.*, war-SWORD, 2154.
gūð-wērig, *adj.*, war-WEARY, dead, 1586.
gūð-wiga, *w. m.*, warrior, 2112.
gūð-wine, *st. m.*, war-friend, sword, 1810, 2735.
gūð-wudu, *st. m.*, war-WOOD, spear, F. 7.
gyd(d), see **gid(d)**.
gyddian, *w. v.*, speak, 630.
gyf, see **gif**.
gyfan, see **gifan**.
gyfen, *n.*, see **geofon**.
gyfen, *pp.*, see **gifan**.
gyfeðe, see **gifeðe**.
gyldan, *st. v.*, *pret.* geald: YIELD, pay, repay, 11, 1184, 2636, etc.
  ā-gyldan, *st. v.*, offer (oneself, itself); *pret.* þā mē sǣl āgeald, 'when the opportunity offered itself to me,' 1665; *so* 2690.
  an-gyldan, *st. v.*, pay for, 1251.
  for-gyldan, *st. v.*, repay, requite, atone for, 114, 956, 1054, etc.
gylden, *adj.*, *GOLDEN*, 47*, etc. [*Cf. Goth.* gulþeins.]
gyllan, *st. v.*, YELL, F. 7.
gylp, see **gilp**.
gylpan, see **gilpan**.
gȳman, *w. v.*, *with gen.*, heed, care, incline to, 1757, 1760, 2451. [*Cf. Goth.* gáumjan.]
  for-gȳman, *w. v.*, *with acc.*, neglect, despise, 1751.
gyn(n), *adj.*, wide, spacious; *acc. m. sg.* gynne, 1551.
gyrdan, *w. v.*, GIRD, 2078, F. 15.

gyrede, etc., see **gyrwan**.
gyrn, gryn, *st. masc. or fem.*, sorrow, 1775; gryn, 930 (see note).
gyrn-wracu, *st. f.*, revenge for harm, 1138, 2118.
gyrwan, *w. v.*, *pret.* gyrede, *pp.* gegyr(w)ed: *GEAR*, prepare, equip, adorn, 994, 1472, 2087, etc.; *pp. pl.* gegyrede, 1028, etc. [*From* gearo.]
  ge-gyrwan, *w. v.*, *GEAR*, prepare, 38, 199; *pret. pl.* gegiredan, 3137.
gyst, see **giest**.
gystra, *adj.*, YESTER, 1334.
gȳt, see **gīt**.
gȳtsian, *w. v.*, be greedy, covet, 1749.

H

habban, *w. v.*, *pret.* hæfde: HAVE, 383, etc.; *often as auxiliary*, 106, etc. *Pres. 1st*, hafu, 2523, hafo, 2150, 3000; *2nd*, hafast, 953, etc.; *3rd*, hafað, 474, etc. *Negative form of subj. pres. pl.* næbben, 1850.
  for-habban, *w. v.*, keep back, retain, refrain, 1151 (see note to l. 1150), 2609.
  wið-habban, *w. v.*, WITHstand, resist, 772.
hād, *st. m.*, [-HOOD] condition, quality, manner, wise, 1297, 1335, 2193. [*Cf. Goth.* háidus, 'manner.']
hador, *st. m.*, receptacle, 414 (see note).
hādor, *adj.*, clear-voiced, 497.
hādre, *adv.*, clearly, brightly, 1571.
hæf, *st. neut.*, sea, mere; *pl.* heafo, 1862*, 2477.
hæfen, see **hebban**.
hæft, *st. m.*, captive, 2408. [*Cf. Goth.* hafts.]
hæfta, *w. m.*, captive; *acc.* hæfton, 788 (see note).
hæft-mēce, *st. m.*, [HAFT-sword] hilted sword, 1457.
hæft-nȳd, *st. f.*, captivity, 3155*.
hæg-steald, *st. m.*, bachelor, liege-man, young warrior, 1889, F. 42.
hǣl, *st. f. and neut.*:
  (1) HEALth, good luck, greeting, 653, 1217.
  (2) omen, 204 (see note), 719.
hæle(ð), *st. m.*, man, hero, warrior, *nom. sing.* hæleð, 190, etc.; hæle, 1646, etc.; *nom. pl.* hæleð, 52, etc.; *gen.* hæleþa, 467, etc. (Cf. note to l. 1983.)

hǣlo, *st. f.*, HEALth, *HAIL*, farewell, 2418.

hærg-træf, *st. neut.*, idol-tent, heathen fane, 175*.

hǣste, *adj.*, violent, 1335.

hǣðen, *adj.*, HEATHEN, 179, 852, etc.

hǣðen, *st. m.*, HEATHEN, 986. [*Cf. Goth.* háiþnō.]

hǣð-stapa, *w. m.*, HEATH-STEPPER, stag, 1368.

hafa, *imperat. sg. of* habban.

hafela, hafala, heafola, *w. m.*, head, 446, 672, etc.

hafen, see hebban.

hafenian, *w. v.*, heave, uplift; *pret.* hafenade, 1573.

hafo, hafu, see habban.

hafoc, *st. m.*, HAWK, 2263.

haga, *w. m.*, [HAW] hedge, enclosure, entrenchment, 2892, 2960.

hāl, *adj.*, WHOLE, HALE, safe and sound, 300, 1503: wæs...hāl, 'hail,' 407; *with gen.* heaðo-lāces hāl, 'safe and sound from the strife,' 1974. [*Cf. Goth.* háils.]

hālig, *adj.*, HOLY, 381, 686, 1553.

hals, see heals.

hām, *st. m.*, HOME; hām, *uninflected dat. used with preps.*, 124, etc. [*Cf. Goth.* háims, 'village.']

hamer, see homer.

hām-weorðung, *st. f.*, HOME-adorning, that which graces a home, 2998.

hand, see hond.

hangian, see hongian.

hār, *adj.*, HOAR, hoary, gray, 887, etc.; *gen.* hāres hyrste, 'the old man's (Ongentheow's) harness,' 2988.

hāt, *adj.*, HOT, 1616, etc.; *dat. sg.* hāton (see note), 849; *nom.* wyrm hāt gemealt, 'the dragon melted in its heat,' 897.

  hātost, *superl.*, hottest, 1668.

hāt, *st. neut.*, *HEAT*, 2605.

hātan, *st. v.*:

(1) order, command, bid, 293, 386, etc.; *pret. sg.* heht, 1035, etc., hēt, 198, etc.; *pp.* ðā wæs hāten hreþe Heort innan-weard folmum gefrætwod, 'then was the order quickly given, and Heorot within was adorned by hands,' 991.

(2) name, call, 102, etc.; *subj. pres. pl.* hātan, 2806.

  ge-hātan, *st. v.*, *usu. with acc.*, promise, vow, 1392, 2024, etc.; *with gen.* 2989; *pret.* gehēt, 175, 2937, etc.

hatian, *w. v.*, *with acc.*, HATE, pursue with hatred, 2319, 2466.

hē, hēo, hit, *pers. pron.*, HE, she, IT, 7, etc.; *sing. nom. m.*, hē, *f.* hēo, 627, etc.; hīo, 455, etc.; *n.* hit, 77, etc.; hyt, 2091, etc.; *acc. m.*, hine, 22, etc., hyne, 28, etc., *f.* hie, *n.* hit, 116, etc., hyt, 2091, etc.; *gen. m. n.*, his, *f.* hire, 641, etc., hyre, 1188, etc.; *dat. m. n.*, him, *f.* hire, 626, etc., hyre, 945, etc. *Plur. m. f. n.*, *nom. acc.*, hie, 15, etc., hȳ, 307, etc., hī, 28, etc., hig, 1085, etc., *gen.*, hira, 1102, etc., hyra, 178, etc., hiera, 1164, heora, 691, etc., hiora, 1166, etc.; *dat.* him, 49, etc. *Used reflexively*, 26, 301, 2949, 2976, etc. *Alliterating*, hē, 505. *Possessive dat.* 40, etc.

hēa, see hēah.

hēa-burh, *st. f.*, HIGH BURGH, chief city, 1127.

heafo, see hæf.

hēafod, *st. neut.*, HEAD, 48, etc.; *dat. pl.* hēafdon, 1242. [*Cf. Goth.* háubiþ.]

hēafod-beorg, *st. f.*, HEAD-protection; *acc. sg.* 1030 (*see* wala).

hēafod-mǣg, *st. m.*, HEAD-kinsman, near relative, 588; *gen. pl.* hēafod-māga, 2151.

hēafod-segn, *st. m. neut.*, HEAD-sign, 2152 (see note).

hēafod-weard, *st. f.*, HEAD-WARD, guard over the head, 2909.

heafola, see hafela.

hēah, *adj.*, HIGH, 57, etc.; *acc. sg. m.* hēanne, 983; *gen. dat.* hēan, 116, 713; *dat. sg. m.* hēaum, 2212*; *pl.* hēa, 1926. *Denoting position*, hēah ofer horde, 'high above the hoard,' 2768. [*Cf. Goth.* háuhs.]

hēah-cyning, *st. m.*, HIGH KING, 1039.

hēah-gestrēon, *st. neut.*, HIGH treasure, splendid treasure, 2302.

hēah-lufu, *w. f.*, HIGH LOVE, 1954.

hēah-sele, *st. m.*, HIGH hall, 647.

hēah-setl, *st. neut.*, HIGH SETTLE, high seat, throne, 1087.

hēah-stede, *st. m.*, HIGH STEAD, high place, 285.

heal(1), *st. f.*, HALL, 89, etc.; *pl.* healle, 1926.

heal-ærn, *st. neut.*, HALL-house, 78.

healdan, *st. v.*, *with acc.*, *pret.* hēold, 2183, etc., hīold, 1954: HOLD, keep, protect, have, possess, inhabit, 230, etc.; rule, 57, 1852;

subj. sg. for pl. 2719, hold up (but see note). Gēata lēode hrēa-wīc hēoldon, 'the corpses of the Geatas covered the field,' 1214; 3084 (see note); sceft nytte hēold, 'the shaft did its duty,' 3118. [*Cf. Goth.* haldan.]

be-healdan, *st. v.*, *with acc.*, (1) HOLD, guard, (2) BEHOLD, 1498: (sundor-)nytte behēold, 'minded, attended to, the (special) service,' 494, 667; þrȳð-swȳð behēold mǣg Higelāces, 'Hygelac's mighty kinsman beheld,' 736.

for-healdan, *st. v.*, *with acc.*, come short in duty towards, set at nought, 2381.

ge-healdan, *st. v.*, *with acc.*, HOLD, have, keep, guard, rule, 317, 658, 674, 911, 2293, etc.; *pret.* hē gehēold tela, 'he ruled [it] well,' 2208.

healf, *st. f.*, HALF, side, 800, 1675 (see note), etc. [*Cf. Goth.* halbs.]

healf, *adj.*, HALF; *gen. sg. f.* healfre [healle], 1087.

heal-gamen, *st. neut.*, HALL-GAME, mirth in hall, 1066.

heal-reced, *st. neut.*, HALL-house, palace, 68, 1981* (see note).

heals, *st. m.*, neck, 1872, etc.; *dat. sg.* halse, 1566. [*Cf. Goth.* hals.]

heals-bēag, **-bēah**, *st. m.*, neck-ring, carcanet, 1195, 2172.

heals-gebedda, *w. m. f.*, beloved BED-fellow, wife, 63.

healsian, *w. v.*, entreat, 2132.

heal-sittend, *st. m.* (*pres. part.*), HALL-SITTER, 2015, 2868.

heal-þegn, *st. m.*, HALL-THANE, 142, 719.

heal-wudu, *st. m.*, HALL-WOOD, 1317.

hēan, *adj.*, abject, ignominious, despised, 1274, 2099, 2183, 2408.

hēan, **hēanne**, see **hēah**.

hēap, *st. m.*, HEAP, band, company, 335, 400, etc.

heard, *adj.*, HARD, hardy, strong, brave, cruel, severe, 166, 322, 342, 432, 540, 1574, 1807, etc.; *wk.* hearda, 401, etc.; *dat. pl.* heardan, 963. *With gen.* 'brave in,' 886, 1539, etc. *Adverbial usage:* þæt hire wið halse heard grāpode, 'so that [the sword] smote her sharply on the neck,' 1566. [*Cf. Goth.* hardus.]

heardra, *compar.*, HARDER, 576, 719.

hearde, *adv.*, HARD, 1438, 3153.

heard-ecg, *adj.*, HARD-EDGED, 1288, 1490.

heard-hicgende, *adj.* (*pres. part.*), [HARD-thinking] brave-minded, bold of purpose, 394, 799.

hearm, *st. m.*, HARM, insult, 1892.

hearm-dæg, *st. m.*, DAY of sorrow, 3153*.

hearm-scaða, *w. m.*, [HARM-*SCATH*-er] harmful foe, 766.

hearpe, *w. f.*, HARP, 89, etc.

heaðerian, *w. v.*, restrain, confine; *pp.* hergum geheaðerod, 'confined in idol-fanes (-groves), i.e. accursed,' 3072.

heaðo-byrne, *w. f.*, battle-*BYRNY*, coat of mail, 1552.

heaðo-dēor, *adj.*, battle-brave, bold in fight, 688, 772.

heaðo-fȳr, **heaðu-fȳr**, *st. neut.*, battle-FIRE, 2522, 2547.

heaðo-geong, *adj.*, battle-YOUNG, F.2*.

heaðo-grim, *adj.*, battle-GRIM, 548, 2691.

heaðo-lāc, *st. neut.*, battle-play, 584, 1974.

heaðo-līðend, *st.m.* (*pres. part.*), warlike-farers, warrior-sailors, 1798, 2955. See note to l. 1862.

heaðo-mǣre, *adj.*, battle-great, famous in war, 2802.

heaðo-rǣs, *st. m.*, [battle-*RACE*] rush of battle, 526, 557, 1047.

heaðo-rēaf, *st. neut.*, battle-dress, armour, 401.

heaðo-rinc, *st. m.*, warrior, 370, 2466.

heaðo-rōf, *adj.*, battle-strong, war-renowned, 381, 864, 2191.

heaðo-sceard, *adj.*, battle-notched, battle-gashed, 2829 (see note).

heaðo-sēoc, *adj.*, battle-SICK, wounded in battle, 2754.

heaðo-stēap, *adj.*, [battle-STEEP] towering *or* bright in battle, 1245, 2153.

heaðo-swāt, *st. m.*, battle-*SWEAT*, blood shed in battle, 1460, 1606, 1668.

heaðo-torht, *adj.*, battle-bright, clear in battle, 2553.

heaðo-wǣde, *st. neut.*, [battle-WEED] armour, 39.

heaðo-weorc, *st. neut.*, battle-WORK, 2892.

heaðo-wylm, *st. m.*, [battle-*WELL*-ing] flame-surge, surging of fire, 82, 2819.

heaðu-sweng, *st. m.*, [battle-*SWING*] battle-stroke, 2581.

hēawan, *st. v.*, HEW, 800.

ge-hēawan, *st. v.*, HEW, cleave, 682.
hebban, *st. v.*, *pp.* hafen, hæfen: HEAVE, raise, lift, 656, 1290, 3023. [*Cf. Goth.* hafjan.]
ā-hebban, *st. v.*, UPHEAVE, uplift, 128, 1108.
hēdan, *w. v.*, *with gen.*, HEED; *pret.* 2697 (see note).
ge-hēdan, *w. v.*, 505 (see note).
hefen, see **heofon.**
-hēgan, *w. v.*
ge-hēgan, *w. v.*, carry out, hold (a meeting, etc.); þing gehēgan, 'to hold a meeting,' 425: see also 505, note. [*Cf. O. N.* heyja, 'conduct a meeting, duel, etc.']
hēht, see **hātan.**
hel(l), *st. f.*, HELL, 101, etc.
helan, *st. v.*
be-helan, *st. v.*, hide; *pp.* beholen, 414.
hell-bend, *st. m. and f.*, HELL-*BOND*, 3072.
helle-gāst, *st. m.*, HELL-GHOST, 1274.
helm, *st. m.*, [HELM]:
(1) helmet, 672, etc.
(2) covert, protection, 1392 (see note).
(3) protector, king, 371, etc.; God, 182.
helm-berend, *st. m.* (*pres. part.*), [HELM-BEARing] helmet-wearer, 2517, 2642.
helmian, *w. v.*
ofer-helmian, *w. v.*, *with acc.*, OVERhang, overshadow, 1364.
help, *st. f.*, HELP, 551, etc.
helpan, *st. v.*, HELP, 2340*, etc.
helpe, *w. f.*, HELP, 2448 (an exceedingly doubtful form: see note).
hel-rūna, *w. m.*, (but see note), sorcerer, 163.
heofon, *st. m.*, HEAVEN, 52, etc.; *dat.* hefene, 1571.
heolfor, *st. m. or neut.*, gore, 849, 1302, 1423, 2138.
heolster, *st. m. or neut.*, place of concealment, darkness, 755. [*Cf. Mod. Eng.* HOLSTER of a pistol, and *O. E.* helan, 'hide.']
heonan, **heonon**, *adv.*, HENCE, 252, 1361.
heora, *gen. pl. of* hē (q. v.).
-heordan, *w. v.*
***ā-heordan**, *w. v.*, liberate, 2930 (see note).
heorde, see **bunden-heorde.**
hēore, *adj.*, canny, pleasant, 1372.
heoro, **heoru**, *st. m.*, sword, 1285. [*Cf. Goth.* hairus.]
heoro-blāc, *adj.*, [sword-*BLEAK*] sword-pale, 2488* (see note).
heoro-drēor, **heoru-drēor**, *st. m. or neut.*, sword-blood, 487, 849.
heoro-drēorig, *adj.*, [sword-DREARY] sword-gory, 935, 1780, 2720.
hioro-drync, *st. m.*, sword-DRINK, 2358 (see note).
heoro-gīfre, *adj.*, [sword-greedy] fiercely greedy, 1498.
heoro-grim, **heoru-grim**, *adj.*, [sword-GRIM] fiercely grim, 1564, 1847.
heoro-hōcyhte, *adj.*, [sword-HOOKED] savagely barbed, 1438.
hioro-serce, *w. f.*, [sword-SARK] shirt of mail; *acc.* hioro-sercean, 2539. [Sievers$_3$ § 159. 1, 2.]
heoro-sweng, *st. m.*, [sword-*SWING*] sword-stroke, 1590.
heorot, *st. m.*, HART, 1369.
hioro-weallende, *adj.* (*pres. part.*), [sword-] fiercely *WELL*ing; *acc. sg. m.* -weallende, 2781.
heoro-wearh, *st. m.*, [sword-felon] fierce monster, 1267.
heorr, *st. m.*, hinge, 999. [*Cf. Chaucerian* harre.]
heorte, *w. f.*, HEART, 2270, 2463, 2507, 2561. [*Cf. Goth.* haírtō.]
heoru, see **heoro.**
heorð-genēat, *st. m.*, HEARTH-comrade, 261, etc.
hēoð, *st. f.*, 404 (see note).
hēr, *adv.*, HERE, hither, 244, etc.
here, *st. m.*, army; *dat. sg.* herge, 2347, 2638; on herge, 'in the field,' 1248. [*Cf. Goth.* harjis.]
here-brōga, *w. m.*, army-terror, fear of war, 462.
here-byrne, *w. f.*, army-*BYRNY*, coat of mail, 1443.
here-grīma, *w. m.*, army-mask, visored helmet, 396, 2049, 2605.
here-net, *st. neut.*, army-NET, coat of ring-mail, 1553.
here-nīð, *st. m.*, army-hate, hostility, 2474.
here-pād, *st. f.*, army-coat, coat of mail, 2258.
here-rinc, *st. m.*, army-man, warrior, 1176*.
here-sceaft, *st. m.*, [army-SHAFT] spear, 335.
here-sceorp, *st. n.*, war-dress, F. 47.
here-spēd, *st. f.*, [army-SPEED] success in war, 64.
here-strǣl, *st. m.*, army-arrow, war-arrow, 1435.
here-syrce, *w. f.*, army-SARK, shirt of mail, 1511.

here-wǣde, *st. neut.*, [army-WEED] armour, 1897.

here-wǣstm, *st. m.*, army-might, prowess in war; *dat. pl.* here-wǣsmun, 677. [*See* Bülbring in *Anglia*, Beiblatt, xv, 160, note.]

here-wīsa, *w. m.*, [army-WISE] army-leader, 3020.

herg, *st. m.*, idol-grove, idol-fane, 3072 (*see* **heaðerian**).

herge, *n.*, see **here**.

herge, *v.*, see **herian**.

herian, *w. v.*, *with acc.*, praise, 182, 1071; *pres. subj.* herige, herge, 1833 (see note), 3175. [*Cf. Goth.* hazjan.]

hete, *st. m.*, HATE, 142, 2554. [*Cf. Goth.* hatis.]

hete-līc, *adj.*, full of hatred, HATEful, 1267.

hete-nīð, *st. m.*, HATE-enmity, bitter enmity, 152.

hete-sweng, *st. m.*, HATE-blow; *pl.* hete-swengeas, 2224.

hete-þanc, *st. m.*, HATE-*THOUGH*t, malice, 475.

hettend, *st. m.*, HATer, foe, 1828 (hetend), 3004.

hicgan, see **hycgan**.

hider, *adv.*, HITHER, 240, 370, 394, 3092.

hige, see **hyge**.

-hīgian, *w. v.*

  ofer-hīgian, *w. v.*, 2766 (see note).

hild, *st. f.*, battle, war, 452, etc.; prowess in battle, 901, 2952.

hilde-bil(l), *st. neut.*, battle-BILL, sword, 557, etc.

hilde-blāc, *adj.*, [war-*BLEAK*] war-pale, 2488* (see note).

hilde-bord, *st. neut.*, [battle-BOARD] shield, 397, 3139.

hilde-cyst, *st. f.*, [battle-virtue] bravery in battle, 2598.

hilde-dēor, **-dīor**, *adj.*, battle-brave, bold in battle, 312, etc.

hilde-freca, **hild-freca**, *w. m.*, battle-hero, 2205, 2366.

hilde-geatwe, *st. f. pl.*, battle-trappings, equipments for war, armour, 674, 2362.

hilde-gicel, *st. m.*, battle-ICICLE; *dat. pl.* ðā þæt sweord ongan æfter heaþo-swāte hilde-gicelum...wanian, 'then the sword began to dwindle in icicles of gore in consequence of the blood (of the monster),' 1606.

hilde-grāp, *st. f.*, battle-grasp, war-clutch, 1446, 2507.

hilde-hlemm, **-hlæmm**, *st. m.*, battle-crash, crash of battle, 2201, 2351, 2544.

hilde-lēoma, *w. m.*, battle-ray:
(1) battle-flame (of the dragon), 2583.
(2) flashing sword, 1143 (see note).

hilde-mēce, *st. m.*, battle-sword; *pl.* hilde-mēceas, 2202.

hilde-mecg, *st. m.*, battle-man, warrior, 799.

hilde-rǣs, *st. m.*, [battle-*RACE*] rush of battle, 300.

hilde-rand, *st. m.*, battle-shield, 1242.

hilde-rinc, *st. m.*, battle-man, warrior, 986, etc.

hilde-sæd, *adj.*, [SAD] battle-sated, 2723.

hilde-sceorp, *st. neut.*, battle-dress, armour, 2155.

hilde-setl, [battle-SETTLE] *st. neut.* battle-seat, saddle, 1039.

hilde-strengo, *st. f.*, battle-STRENGth, 2113.

hilde-swāt, *st. m.*, [battle-*SWEAT*] war-breath (of the dragon), 2558.

hilde-tūx (**hilde-tūsc**), *st. m.* battle-TUSK, 1511. [Sievers$_3$ § 204, 3.]

hilde-wǣpen, *st. neut.*, battle-WEAPON, 39.

hilde-wīsa, *w. m.*, [battle-WISE] battle-leader, 1064.

hild-freca, see **hilde-freca**.

hild-fruma, *w. m.*, battle-chief, 1678, 2649, 2835.

hild-lata, *w. m.*, [battle-LATE] laggard in battle, 2846.

hilt, *st. m. neut.*, HILT, sword-hilt, 1668, 1677 (see note), 1687; *pl.* (of a single weapon; cf. 'Julius Caesar' v. 3. 43) 1574, 1614.

hilte-cumbor, *st. neut.*, [HILT-banner] staff-banner, 1022 (but see note).

hilted, *adj.*, HILTED, 2987.

hindema, *superl. adj.*, HINDMost, last, 2049, 2517.

hin-fūs, *adj.*, [HENCE-ready] eager to be gone, 755.

hīo = hēo, *fem. of* hē (q. v.).

hīofan, *w. and st. v.*, lament; *pres. part.* 3142. [*Cf. Goth.* hiufan *and* Sievers, *P. B. B.* IX. 278.]

hīold, see **healdan**.

hīora, *gen. pl. of* hē (q. v.).

hīoro-, see **heoro-**.

hladan, *st. v.*, LADE, load, lay, 1897, 2126, 3134; *inf.* hladon, 2775*.

  ge-hladan, *st. v.*, LADE, load; *pret.* gehlēod, 895.

hlæst, *st. masc.*, [LAST] load, freight, 52.

hlǣw, hlāw, *st. m.*, [LOW, in place-names] mound, burial mound, 1120, 2411, 3157*, etc. [*Cf. Goth* hláiw.]
hlāford, *st. m.*, LORD, 267, etc.
hlāford-lēas, *adj.*, LORD-LESS, 2935.
hlāw, see hlǣw.
hleahtor, *st. m.*, LAUGHTER, 611, 3020.
hlēapan, *st. v.*, LEAP, gallop, 864.
ā-hlēapan, *st. v.*, LEAP up, 1397.
hlenca, **hlence**, *w. m. and f.*, LINK, coat of mail, F. 12*.
hlēo, *st. m.*, [LEE] refuge, protection, protector (used of a chieftain or king), 429, 791, etc.
hlēo-burh, *st. f.*, protecting BURGH or city, 912, 1731.
-hlēod, see -hladan.
hleonian, *w. v.*, LEAN, slope, 1415.
hlēor-berge, *w. f.*, cheek-guard, 304* (see note to ll. 303, etc.).
hlēor-bolster, *st. m.*, [cheek-] BOLSTER, 688.
hlēotan, *st. v.*, *with acc.*, get by LOT, 2385.
hlēoðor-cwyde, *st. m.*, [sound-speech] courtly speech, ceremonious speech, 1979.
hlēoðrian, *w. v.*, speak, F. 2.
hlīdan, *st. v.*
tō-hlīdan, *st. v.*, spring apart; *pp. pl.* tōhlidene, 999.
hliehhan, *st. v.* [*Cf. Goth.* hlahjan.]
ā-hliehhan, *st. v.*, LAUGH aloud; *pret. sg.*, āhlōg, 730.
hlīfian, *w. v.*, tower, 2805; *pret.* hlīfade, 81, 1898, hlīuade, 1799. [*P. B. B.* x. 502.]
hlim-bed, *st. neut.*, LEANing BED, (last) resting-place, 3034. [See note and cf. *O.E.* hlinian, hleonian, 'to recline.']
hlið, *st. neut.*, cliff, slope, 1892, 3157*.
hlūd, *adj.*, LOUD, 89.
hlyn, *st. m.*, din, noise, 611.
hlynnan, **hlynian**, *w. v.*, resound, roar, crackle, 2553, F. 7; *pret.* hlynode, 1120.
hlynsian, *w. v.*, resound, 770.
hlytm, *st. m.*, lot, 3126.
hnǣgan, *w. v.*
ge-hnǣgan, *w. v.*, *with acc.*, fell, vanquish, 1274, 2916 (but see note).
hnāh, *adj.*, mean, base, illiberal, 1929.
hnāgra, **hnāhra**, *compar.*, lower, inferior, 677, 952.
hnītan, *st. v.*, encounter, clash, 1327; *pret. pl.* hnitan, 2544.
hof, *st. neut.*, court, dwelling, mansion, 312*, 1236, etc.
hōfian, *w. v.*
be-hōfian, *w. v.*, *with gen.*, [BEHOVE] need, 2647.
hogode, see hycgan.
-hōhsnian, *w. v.*
***on-hōhsnian**, *w. v.*, check 1944 (but see note).
hold, *adj.*, friendly, gracious, 267, 290, 376, etc.; faithful, loyal, 487, 1229*, etc.
hōlinga, *adv.*, without reason, 1076.
holm, *st. m.*, ocean, sea, mere, 48, etc.
holm-clif, *st. neut.*, sea-CLIFF, 230, 1421, 1635.
holm-wylm, *st. m.*, [sea-WELLing] sea-surge, 2411.
holt, *st. neut.*, HOLT, wood, 2598, 2846, 2935.
holt-wudu, *st. m.*, HOLT-WOOD; wood, forest, 1369; wood (material), 2340.
homer, **hamer**, *st. m.*, HAMMER, 1285; *gen. pl.* homera lāfe, 'leavings of hammers, i.e. swords,' 2829.
hōn, *st. v.* [*Cf. Goth.* hāhan.]
be-hōn, *st. v.*, *trans.*, HANG with; *pp.* behongen, 3139.
hond, **hand**, *st. f.*, HAND, 558, 656, etc.
hand-bona, **-bana**, *w. m.*, [HAND-BANE] hand-slayer, 460, 1330, 2502.
hand-gemǣne, *adj.*, [HAND-MEAN] hand to hand; *nom. neut.* þǣr unc hwīle wæs hand-gemǣne, 'there we two engaged a while hand to hand,' 2137 (see note). [*Ger.* hand-gemein.]
hand-gewriðen, *adj.* (*pp.*), HAND-WREATHed, hand-twisted; *pl.* 1937.
hand-sporu, *st. f.*, HAND-SPUR, claw, 986 (see note).
hond-gemōt, *st. neut.*, HAND-MEETing, hand to hand fight, 1526, 2355.
hond-gesella, *w. m.*, HAND-comrade, 1481.
hond-gestealla, **hand-gestealla**, *w. m.*, HAND-to-hand-comrade, 2169, 2596*.
hond-geweorc, *st. neut.*, HANDIWORK, 2835.
hond-lēan, **hand-lēan**, see ondlēan.
hond-locen, *adj.* (*pp.*), HAND-LOCKed, 322, 551.
hond-rǣs, *st. m.*, [HAND-RACE] hand to hand fight, 2072.
hond-scolu, **hand-scalu**, *st. f.*, [HAND-SHOAL] hand-troop, followers, 1317 (see note), 1963.

hond-slyht, see **ondslyht**.
hond-wundor, *st. neut.*, [HAND-WONDER] wonderful handiwork, 2768.
-hongen, see **-hōn**.
hongian, **hangian**, *w. v.*, HANG, 1363, 1662, etc.
hop, *st. n.*, glen, 2212* (see note).
hord, *st. neut.*, HOARD, treasure, 887, 912, etc. [*Cf. Goth.* huzd.]
hord-ærn, *st. neut.*, HOARD-hall, treasure-cave, 2279, 2831.
hord-burh, *st. f.*, HOARD-BURGH, wealthy city, 467.
hord-gestrēon, *st. neut.*, HOARD-treasure, 1899, 3092.
hord-mādm, *st. m.*, HOARD-treasure, hoarded jewel, 1198* (see note).
hord-weard, *st. m.*, [HOARD-WARD] guardian of a hoard *or* treasure, 1047 (of the king), 2293 (of the dragon), etc.
hord-wela, *w. m.*, HOARD-WEAL, wealth of treasure, 2344.
hord-weorðung, *st. f.*, [HOARD-honouring] honouring by gifts, valuable reward, 952.
hord-wynn, *st. f.*, HOARD-joy, joy-giving hoard, 2270.
hord-wyrð, *adj.*, WORTHy of being hoarded, 2245*.
horn, *st. m.*, HORN, 1369, etc., gable of a hall, F. 1*, F. 4.
horn-boga, *w. m.*, HORN-BOW, 2437.
horn-gēap, *adj.*, with wide interval between (the HORNS on) the gables, 82 (see note to l. 78).
horn-reced, *st. neut.*, [HORN-house, i.e.] a house with horns on the gables, *or* a house with gables, 704.
hors, *st. neut.*, HORSE, 1399.
hōs, *st. f.*, bevy, 924. (*Cf. Goth.* hansa, 'company': *and* 'Hanseatic League.')
hoðma, *w. m.*, darkness, concealment, grave, 2458.
hrā, **hrǣw**, *st. neut.*, corpse, 1588, F. 36*. [*Cf. Goth.* hráiwa-.]
hrædlīce, *adv.*, hastily, quickly, 356, 963. [*Cf.* hraðe.]
hræfen, see **hrefn**.
hrægl, *st. neut.*, [RAIL] dress, armour, 454, 1195, 1217.
hræðre, see **hreðer**.
hrǣw, see **hrā**.
hrā-fyl, *st. m.*, fall of corpses, slaughter, havoc, 277.
hraðe, **hræðe**, *adv.*, [RATHE] quickly, hastily, 224, 740, etc.; hreðe, 991; raðe, 724.
  hraðor, *compar.*, [RATHER] more quickly, 543.
hrēam, *st. m.*, noise, clamour, 1302.
hrēa-wīc, *st. neut.*, [corpse-WICK] abode of corpses, 1214 (*see* healdan).
hrefn, **hræfen**, *st. m.*, RAVEN, 1801, etc., F. 36.
hrēmig, *adj.*, exultant, 124, etc.; *pl.* hrēmge, 2363.
***hrēodan**, *st. v.*, cover, clothe, adorn; *pp.* hroden, gehroden, 304, 495, 1022.
hrēoh, **hrēow**, *adj.*, rough, fierce, cruel, sad, 1564, 2180; *dat. sg.* hrēon, 1307, hrēoum, 2581; *pl.* hrēo, 548.
hrēoh-mōd, *adj.*, of fierce MOOD, of sad mood, 2132, 2296.
hrēosan, *st. v.*, fall, 1074, 1430, etc.
  be-hrēosan, *st. v.*, deprive; *pp. pl.* behrorene, 2762.
hrēow, *st. f.*, distress, grief, 2129, 2328.
hrēran, *w. v.*
  on-hrēran, *w. v.*, rouse, arouse, stir up, 549, 2554. [*Cf.* hrōr.]
hrēð, *st. m. or neut.*, glory, renown; *acc.* 2575 (see note to ll. 2573, etc.).
hreðe, see **hraðe**.
hreðer, *st. neut.*, breast, heart, 1151, 1446, etc.; *dat. sing.* hræðre, 2819*.
hreðer-bealo, *st. neut.*, heart-BALE; *nom.* þæs þe þincean mæg þegne monegum ... hreþer-bealo hearde, 'as it may seem, heavy heart-woe to many a thane,' 1343.
hrēð-sigor, *st. m. or neut.*, triumphant victory, 2583.
hrīmig, *adj.*, RIMY, covered with hoar-frost (see note to l. 1363).
hrīnan, *st. v.*, *usu. w. dat.*, touch, lay hold of, 988, 2270, etc.; *subj. pret. sg.* þēah ðe him wund hrine, 'though the wound touched him close,' 2976.
  æt-hrīnan, *st. v.*, *w. gen.*, touch, lay hold of, 722*.
hrinde, *adj.* (*pp.*), = **hrindede**, covered with RIND, frosty, 1363 (see note).
hring, *st. m.*, RING, ring-mail, 1202, 1503, etc.; *nom.* byrnan hring, 'ring-mail of the byrny, ringed byrny,' 2260.
hringan, *w. v.*, RING, rattle, 327.
hring-boga, *w. m.*, [RING-BOW] one that bends himself in the shape of a ring (the dragon), 2561.
hringed, *adj.* (*pp.*), RINGED, 1245; *inflected* 2615.
hringed-stefna, *w. m.*, ship with RINGED STEM, 32, etc.

hring-īren, *st. neut.*, RING-IRON; *nom.* hring-īren scīr song in searwum, 'the bright iron rings rang in the armour,' 322.
hring-mǣl, *adj.*, RING-adorned, 2037, *used as subst.*, RING-sword, 1521, 1564.
hring-naca, *w. m.*, [RING-bark] ship with a ringed prow, 1862.
hring-net, *st. neut.*, [RING-NET] shirt of mail made of rings, 1889, 2754.
hring-sele, *st. m.*, RING-hall, 2010, 2840, 3053, etc.
hring-weorðung, *st. f.*, RING-adornment, 3017.
hroden, see **hrēoðan**.
hrōf, *st. m.*, ROOF, 403, 836*, 926, 983, etc.
hrōf-sele, *st. m.*, ROOFed hall, 1515.
hron-fix (hron-fisc), *st. m.*, whale-FISH, whale, 540. [See Sievers, § 204, 3.]
hron-rād, *st. f.*, whale-ROAD, sea, 10.
hrōr, *adj.*, stirring, valorous, strong, 1629, F. 47 (but see note).
hrōðor, *st. m. or neut.*, benefit, joy, 2171, 2448. [*Cf.* hrēð.]
hrūse, *w. f.*, earth, 2247, etc.
hrycg, *st. m.*, RIDGE, back, 471.
hryre, *st. m.*, fall, destruction, 1680, etc. [*Cf. O.E.* hrēosan.]
hryssan, *w. v.*, shake, 226. [*Cf. Goth.* -hrisjan.]
hū, *adv.*, HOW, 3, etc. *In exclamation*, 2884.
hund, *st. m.*, HOUND, 1368.
hund, *num.*, *with gen.*, HUNDred, 1498, etc.
hūru, *adv.*, indeed, especially, at least, verily, 182, etc.
hūs, *st. neut.*, HOUSE, 116, etc.
hūð, *st. f.*, booty, plunder, 124. [*Cf. Goth.* hunþs, 'captivity.']
hwā, *m. and f.*, **hwæt**, *neut.*, *interr. and indef. pron.*, WHO, WHAT, any (one), somewhat, 52, 3126, etc. *With gen.* hwæt...hȳnðo, 'what humiliation,' 474; swulces hwæt, 'somewhat of such (matter),' 880; ānes hwæt, 'somewhat only, a part only,' 3010. Nāh hwā sweord wege, 'I have no one who may wear sword,' 2252; *dat.* hwām, 'for whom,' 1696; *instr.* tō hwan syððan wearð hond-rǣs hæleða, 'to what issue the hand-fight of heroes afterwards came,' 2071. [*Cf. Goth.* hwas.]
hwæder, see **hwyder**.
hwǣr, *adv.*, WHERE, anywhere, 2029, elles hwǣr, 'ELSEWHERE,' 138.
hwæt, *adj.*, active, keen, bold; *weak* hwata, 3028; *dat.* hwatum, 2161; *pl.* hwate, 1601, etc.
hwæt, *pron.*, see **hwā**.
hwæt, *interj.*, WHAT, lo, 1, 240*, 530, etc.
hwæðer, *adj.-pron.*, WHETHER, which of two; *nom.* gebīde gē...hwæðer sēl mæge...uncer twēga, 'await ye whether of us twain may the better,' 2530; *acc. f.* on swā hwæðere hond...swā him gemet þince, 'on whichsoever hand it may seem to him meet,' 686. [*Cf. Goth.* hwaþar.]
hwæðer, **hwæðre**, *conj.*, WHETHER, 1314, 1356, 2785.
hwæð(e)re, *adv.*, however, yet, 555, 578*, etc.; anyway, however that may be, 574 (see note); *with* swā þēah, 2442.
hwan, see **hwā**.
hwanan, **hwanon**, *adv.*, *WHEN*ce, 257, 333, etc.
hwār, see **hwǣr**.
hwata, **hwate**, **hwatum**, see **hwæt**, *adj.*
hwealf, *st. f.*, vault, 576, etc.
hwēne, *adv.*, a little, a trifle, 2699.
hweorfan, *st. v.*, turn, wander, go, 356, etc.; ellor hwearf, 'departed elsewhere, died,' 55.
  æt-hweorfan, *st. v.*, return, 2299.
  ge-hweorfan, *st. v.*, pass, go, 1210, 1679, 1684, 2208.
  geond-hweorfan, *st. v.*, traverse, 2017.
  ond-hweorfan, *st. v.*, turn against; *pret.* norðan wind...ond-hwearf, 'a wind from the north blew against [us],' 548.
  ymb(e)-hweorfan, *st. v.*, *with acc.*, turn about, go round, 2296 (see note).
hwergen, *adv.*, *in* elles hwergen, 'ELSE*WHERE*,' 2590.
hwettan, *w. v.*, WHET, urge, encourage, 204, 490. [*From* hwæt, 'keen,' *cf. Goth.* -hwatjan.]
hwīl, *st. f.*, WHILE, space of time, 146, 1495, etc.; *dat. pl.*, *used adverbially*, hwīlum, 'at whiles, sometimes, WHILOM, of old,' 175, 864, 867, etc.; 'at one time...at another,' 2107-8-9-11.
hwīt, *adj.*, WHITE, flashing, 1448.
hwōpan, *st. v.*, see note to 2268.
hworfan, see **hweorfan**.
hwyder, hwæder, *adv.*, WHITHER, 163, 1331* (see note).

hwylc, *adj.-pron.*, WHICH, what, any, 274 (*see* witan), 1986, 2002, etc.; *with gen.*, 1104, 2433. [*Cf. Goth.* hwileiks.]
  swā hwylc swā, see **swā**.
hwyrfan, *w. v.*, move, 98. [*Cf.* hweorfan.]
hwyrft, *st. m.*, going, turn; *dat. pl.* 'in their goings, *or* to and fro,' 163.
hycgan, **hicgan**, *w. v.*, think, resolve (upon); *pret.* hogode, 632, F. 12*. [*Cf. Goth.* hugjan.]
  for-hicgan, *w. v.*, FORGO, reject, despise, 435.
  ge-hycgan, *w. v.*, purpose, 1988.
  ofer-hycgan, *w. v.*, scorn, 2345.
hȳdan, *w. v.*, HIDE, 1372*, 2766; bury, 446.
  ge-hȳdan, *w.v.*, HIDE, 2235, 3059.
hyge, **hige**, *st. m.*, mind, soul, temper, purpose, 267, etc. [*Cf. Goth.* hugs.]
  hige-mǣð, *st. j.*, mind-honour, heart-reverence, 2909 (but see note).
  hige-mēðe, *adj.*, wearying the soul *or* mind, 2442.
  hige-þihtig, *adj.*, great-hearted, 746.
  hige-þrymm, *st. m.*, [mind-strength] magnanimity, 339.
hyge-bend, *st. m. f.*, mind-BOND; *dat. pl.*, hyge-bendum fæst...dyrne langað, 'a secret longing...fast in the bonds of his mind,' 1878.
hyge-gīomor, *adj.*, sad at heart, 2408.
hyge-rōf, **hige-rōf**, *adj.*, strong of mind *or* heart, valiant, 204*, 403*.
hyge-sorg, *st. f.*, SORROW of mind *or* heart, 2328.
hyht, *st. m.*, hope, 179. [*Cf.* hycgan.]
hyldan, *w. v.*, HEEL(D) over, incline (oneself), lie down; *pret.* 688.
hyldo, *st. f.*, favour, friendliness, 670, 2293, 2998; *acc.* hyldo ne telge...Denum unfǣcne, 'I reckon not their favour sincere towards the Danes,' 2067. [*Cf.* hold.]
hym, *dat. pl. of* hē (q. v.).
hȳnan, *w. v.*, humiliate, oppress, 2319. [*From* hēan.]
hyne, *acc. sg. m. of* hē (q. v.).
hȳnðo, **hȳnðu**, *st. f.*, humiliation, 166, 277, 475, 593, 3155*.
hyra, *gen. pl. of* hē (q. v.).
hȳran, *w. v.*, HEAR, learn, 38, 62, 273, 1197, etc.; *with dat. pers.*, obey, 10, etc. [*Cf. Goth.* háusjan.]
  ge-hȳran, *w. v.*, HEAR, learn, 255, 290, 785, etc.
hyrdan, *w. v.* [*From* heard, *cf. Goth.* hardjan.]
  ā-hyrdan, *w. v.*, *HARD*en, 1460.
hyrde, *st. m.*, [HERD] keeper, guardian, etc., 610, etc.; *nom.* wuldres Hyrde, 'the King of glory,' 931, fyrena hyrde, 'lord in the kingdom of crime,' 750. [*Cf. Goth.* hairdeis.]
hyre, *gen. and dat. sg. f. of* hē (q. v.).
hyrst, *st. f.*, harness, accoutrement, adornment, 2988, 3164, F. 22.
hyrstan, *w. v.*, adorn; *pp.* 'dight, jewelled,' 672, 2255*.
hyrtan, *w. v.*, HEARTen, embolden; *with refl. pron.*, 2593. [*From* heorte.]
hyse, **hysse**, *st. m.*, youth, 1217, F. 50.
hyt, (**hitt**) *st. f.*, *HEAT*, 2649.
hyt, *neut. of* hē (q. v.).
hȳð, *st. f.*, HYTHE, haven, 32.
hyðo, see note on ll. 3150, etc.
hȳð-weard, *st. m.*, [HYTHE-WARD] guard of the haven, 1914.

I

ic, *pers. pron.*, I, 38, etc.; *acc.* mē, 415, etc., mec, 447; *gen.* mīn, 2084, etc.; *dat.* mē, 316, etc.; *dual nom.* wit, 535, etc.; *acc.* unc, 540, etc.; *gen.* uncer, 2002, etc.; *dat.* unc, 1783, etc.; *pl. nom.* wē, 1, etc.; *acc.* ūsic, 458, etc.; *gen.* ūre, 1386, ūser, 2074; *dat.* ūs, 269.
icge, *adj.*, 1107 (see note).
īdel, *adj.*, IDLE, empty, 145, 413; deprived; *nom.* lond-rihtes...īdel, 'deprived of land-right,' 2888.
īdel-hende, *adj.*, IDLE-*HAND*ed, empty-handed, 2081.
ides, *st. f.*, woman, lady, 620, etc.
iernan, *st. v.* [*Cf. Goth.* rinnan.]
  be-iernan, *st. v.*, RUN, occur; *pret.* him on mōd bearn, 'it occurred to him,' 67.
  on-iernan, *st. v.*, spring open; *pret.* onarn, 721.
in, *prep.*, IN, *with dat.* (of rest) *and acc.* (of motion):
(1) *with. dat.*, in, on, 13, 25, 87, 89, 324, 443, 1029, 1952, 2505, 2599, 2635, 2786, 3097, etc.; *after its case*, 19; *of time*, 1.
(2) *with acc.*, into, 60, 185, 1210, 2935.
  in innan, see **innan**.

in, *adv.*, IN, 386, 1037, etc.; *once* inn, 3090.
in, *st. neut.*, INN, dwelling, 1300.
inc, *pers. pron.* (*dat. dual. of* þū), to you two, 510.
incer, *pers. pron.* (*gen. dual. of* þū), of you two, 584.
incge, *adj.*, 2577 (see note).
in-frōd, *adj.*, very old, 1874, 2449.
in-gang, *st. m.*, entrance, 1549.
in-genga, *w. m.*, IN-GOer, invader, 1776.
in-gesteald, *st. neut.*, house-property, 1155.
inn, see **in**, *adv.*
innan, *adv.*, withIN, inside, 774, etc.
in innan, within; *with preceding dat.* 1968, 2452.
on innan, within, 2715; *with preceding dat.* 1740.
þǣr on innan, therein, therewithin, in there, 71, 2089, etc.
innan-weard, *adj.*, INWARD, inside, interior, 991, 1976.
inne, *adv.*, INside, within, 390 (see note), 642, 1866, etc.; therein, 1141.
þǣr inne, THEREIN, 118, etc.
inne-weard, *adj.*, INWARD, interior, 998.
inwid-sorg, see **inwit-sorh**.
inwit-feng, *st. m.*, malicious grasp, 1447.
inwit-gæst, *st. m.*, malicious GUEST, foe, 2670 (see note to l. 102).
inwit-hrōf, *st. m.*, malicious ROOF, 3123.
inwit-net, *st. neut.*, treacherous NET, malicious snare, 2167.
inwit-nīð, *st. m.*, treacherous hate, malicious enmity, 1858, 1947.
inwit-scear, *st. m.*, malicious slaughter, inroad, 2478.
inwit-searo, *st. neut.*, malicious cunning, 1101.
inwit-sorh, **inwid-sorg**, *st. f.*, [hostile or malicious SORROW] sorrow caused by a foe, 831, 1736.
inwit-ðanc, *st. m.*, hostile *or* malicious *THOUGH*t, 749 (see note).
-iode, see **-gān**.
iogoð, see **geogoð**.
io-mēowle, see **gēo-mēowle**.
īren, *st. neut.*, IRON, sword, 892, etc.; *gen. pl.*, īrena, īrenna, 673, 802, etc.
īren, *adj.*, of IRON, 1459, 2778. [*Cf. O.E.* īsern.]
īren-bend, *st. m. f.*, IRON-*BAND*, 774, 998.
īren-byrne, *w. f.*, IRON-*BYRNY*, coat of iron mail, 2986.
īren-heard, *adj.*, IRON-HARD, 1112.
īren-þrēat, *st. m.*, IRON-band, troop of armed men, 330.
īs, *st. neut.*, ICE, 1608.
īsern-byrne, *w. f.*, *BYRNY* of *IRON*, coat of iron mail, 671. [*Cf. O.E.* īren.]
īsern-scūr, *st. f.*, *IRON*-SHOWER, 3116. [scūr *is elsewhere masc., but for use here cf. Goth.* skūra.]
īs-gebind, *st. neut.*, ICE-*BOND*, 1133.
īsig, *adj.*, ICY, covered with ice, 33.
īu, see **gēo**.
īu-monn, *st. m.*, former MAN, man of olden times, 3052.

K

kyning, 619, 3171; Kyning-wuldor, 665, see **cyning**.

L

lā, *interj.*, LO, 1700, 2864.
lāc, *st. neut.*, gift, offering, booty, prey, 43, 1584, etc.
lācan, *st. v.*, play, 2832, 2848. [*Cf. Goth.* láikan, 'to leap.']
for-lācan, *st. v.*, decoy, betray, 903.
lād, *st. f.*, [LODE] way, faring, journey, 569, 1987.
lǣdan, *w. v.*, LEAD, bring, 239, 1159, 3177*; *pp.* gelǣded, 37. [*Cf.* līðan, lād, 'go.']
for-lǣdan, *w. v.*, *w. acc.*, misLEAD; *pret. pl.*, forlǣddan, 2039.
lǣfan, *w. v.*, LEAVE, 1178, 2315, etc. [*From* lāf: *cf. Goth.* láibjan.]
lǣn, *st. neut.*, *LOAN* (see note to ll. 1808, etc.)
lǣn-dagas, *st. m.*, *LOAN*-DAYS, fleeting days, 2341*, 2591.
lǣne, *adj.*, fleeting, transitory, 1622, etc.
læng, see **longe**.
lǣran, *w. v.*, teach, 1722. [*Cf. Goth.* láisjan.]
ge-lǣran, *w. v.*, teach, persuade, give (advice), 278, 415, 3079.
lǣs, *compar. adv.*, LESS, 487, 1946 (*see* sē).
þȳ lǣs, *conj.*, LEST, 1918.
lǣssa, *compar. adj.*, LESS, lesser, fewer, 1282, 2571; *dat. pl.* lǣssan, 43. *Absolutely*, for lǣssan, 'for less,' 951.
lǣsest, *superl. adj.*, LEAST, 2354.
lǣstan, *w. v.:*
(1) *with dat.*, LAST, hold out, 812.

(2) *with acc.*, do, perform, 2663.
ful-lǣstan, *w. v.*, *with dat.*, help; *pres. sg. 1st* ful-lǣstu, 2668.
ge-lǣstan, *w. v.:*
(1) *with acc. or dat.*, help, serve, 24, 2500.
(2) *usu. with acc.*, do, perform, fulfil, etc., 1706, 2990*, etc.
ge-lǣsted, *pp. of* lǣstan *or* ge-lǣstan, 'performed,' 829.
læt, *adj.*, [LATE] slow; *with gen.* 1529. [*Cf. Goth.* lats, 'slothful.']
lǣtan, *st. v.*, LET, allow, 48, etc.
ā-lǣtan, *st. v.*, LET, 2665; let go, leave, 2591, 2750.
for-lǣtan, *st. v.*, LET, leave behind, 970, 2787, 3166; let go, 792.
of-lǣtan, *st. v.*, leave, 1183, 1622.
on-lǣtan, *st. v.*, loosen, 1609.
lāf, *st. f.*, LEAving, heirloom, bequest (often a sword), 454, etc. [*Cf. Goth.* láiba, 'remnant.']
lafian, *w. v.*
ge-lafian, *w. v.*, LAVE, refresh, 2722.
lagu, *st. m.*, lake, water, sea, 1630.
lagu-cræftig, *adj.*, [sea-CRAFTY] skilful as a sailor, 209.
lagu-strǣt, *st. f.*, [sea-STREET] way over the sea, 239.
lagu-strēam, *st. m.*, sea-STREAM, current, tide, 297.
lāh, see **lēon**.
land, see **lond**.
lang, see **long**.
langaþ, *st. m.*, LONGing, 1879.
lange, see **longe**.
lang-twīdig, see **long-twīdig**.
lār, *st. f.*, LORE, instruction, guidance, 1950; *gen. pl.* lāra, 1220, lārena, 269.
lāst, *st. m.*, track, trace, 132, etc. [*Cf. Goth.* láists.]
on lāst(e), *with preceding dat.*, in the tracks of, behind, 2945, F. 19.
lāð, *adj.*, [LOTH], LOATHly, LOATHsome, hated, hostile, 134, 511, 2315, 2467, etc.; *dat. pl.* lāðan, 1505.
Often used absolutely, foe, loathed foe, 550, 841, 1061; *gen. pl.* 242; *weak*, se lāða, 2305*; lāð wið lāþum, 'foe with foe,' 440; æfter lāðum, 'after the loathed foe,' 1257; *neut.* fela ic lāðes gebād, 'much hostility *or* evil I endured,' 929.
lāðra, *compar.*, more LOATHly, more hateful, 2432.
lāð-bite, *st. m.*, foe-BITE, wound, 1122.
lāð-getēona, *w. m.*, evil-doer, monster, 559, 974.
lāð-līc, *adj.*, LOATHLY, 1584.
lēaf, *st. neut.*, LEAF, 97.
lēafnes-word, *st. neut.*, LEAVE-WORD, permission, pass-word, 245.
-lēah, see **-lēogan**.
lēan, *st. neut.*, reward, 114, 951, 1021, etc. [*Cf. Goth.* láun.]
lēan, *st. v.*, *w. acc.*, blame; *pres. sg. 3rd* lyhð, 1048; *pret.* lōg, 203, etc.
be-lēan, *st. v.*, *with acc. rei and dat. pers.*, dissuade from, prohibit, 511.
lēanian, *w. v.*, *with acc. rei and dat. pers.*, pay for, repay, reward for, 1380, 2102.
lēas, *adj.*, [-LESS] *with gen.*, lacking, deprived of, 850, 1664. [*Cf. Goth.* láus, 'empty.']
lēas-scēawere, *st. m.*, spy, 253 (see note).
lecgan, *w. v.* [*Cf. Goth.* lagjan.]
ā-lecgan, *w. v.*, LAY, lay down, lay aside, 34, 834, etc.
lēg, see **līg**.
leger, *st. neut.*, [LAIR] lying, 3043. [*Cf. Goth.* ligrs, 'bed, couch.']
legerbedd, *st. neut.*, death-BED, grave, 1007.
-lēh, see **lēogan**.
lemian, **lemman**, *w. v.*, LAME, trouble; *pret. sg. with pl. nom.*, lemede, 905.
leng, see **longe**.
lenge, 83 (see note).
lengest, see **longe**.
lengra, see **long**.
lēod, *st. m.*, prince, chief, 341, etc.
lēod, *st. f.*, people, nation, 596, 599, etc.; *pl.* lēoda, 3001. [*See* lēode.]
lēod-bealo, *st. neut.*, [nation-BALE] national evil, 1722 (see note); *gen. pl.* -bealewa, 1946.
lēod-burg, *st. f.*, [nation-BURGH] chief city; *acc. pl.* -byrig, 2471.
lēod-cyning, *st. m.*, nation-KING, king of a people, 54.
lēode, *st. m. pl.*, people, 24, 362, etc. [*See* lēod, *st. f. and cf. Germ.* Leute.]
lēod-fruma, *w. m.*, nation-chief, prince of a people, 2130.
lēod-gebyrgea, *w. m.*, protector of a people, 269. [*Cf.* beorgan.]

lēod-hryre, *st. m.*, fall of a prince *or* people, 2030, 2391.
lēod-sceaða, *w. m.*, *SCATH*er of a people, national foe, 2093.
lēod-scipe, *st. m.*, [people-SHIP] nation, 2197, 2751.
lēof, *adj.*, LIEF, dear, 31, etc.
leofað, see **libban.**
lēof-līc, *adj.*, dear, beloved, precious, 1809, 2603.
lēogan, *st. v.*, LIE, belie, 250, 3029. [*Cf. Goth.* liugan.]
  ā-lēogan, *st. v.*, *with acc. rei*, beLIE, falsify; *pret.* ālēh, 80.
  ge-lēogan, *st. v.*, *with dat. pers.*, deceive; *pret.* gelēah, 2323.
lēoht, *st. neut.*, LIGHT, brilliance, 569, 727, etc. [*Cf. Goth.* liuhaþ.]
lēoht, *adj.*, LIGHT, bright, flashing, 2492.
lēoma, *w. m.*, gleam, ray, 311, 1570 (see note), etc.
leomum, see **lim.**
lēon, *st. v.*, *LE*nd; *pret.* **lāh**, 1456. [*Cf. Goth.* leihwan.]
  on-lēon, *st. v.*, *with gen. rei and dat. pers.*, *LE*nd; *pret.* onlāh, 1467.
leornian, *w. v.*, LEARN, study, devise, 2336 (see note).
lēosan, *st. v.*, *LOSE*. [*Cf. Goth.* (fra-)liusan.]
  be-lēosan, *st. v.*, deprive; *pp.* beloren, 1073.
  for-lēosan, *st. v.*, *with dat.*, LOSE, 1470, etc.
lēoð, *st. neut.*, lay, 1159.
leoðo-cræft, *st. m.*, [limb-CRAFT] hand-craft; *dat. pl.* segn...gelocen leoðo-cræftum, 'a banner woven by skill of hand,' 2769 (see note).
leoðo-syrce, *w. f.*, limb-SARK, shirt of mail, 1505, 1890.
lettan, *w. v.*, *with acc. pers. and gen. rei*, LET, hinder, 569. [*Cf. Goth.* latjan.]
libban, *w. v.*, *pres. sg.* lifað, lyfað, leofað; *subj.* lifige; *pret.* lifde, lyfde; *pres. part.* lifigende: LIVE, 57, etc.
līc, *st. n.*, [LYCH] body, 451, etc.; corpse, 1122, etc. [*Cf. Goth.* leik.]
licg(e)an, *st. v.*, LIE, lie down, lie low, lie dead, 40, etc.; fail, 1041.
  ā-licg(e)an, *st. v.*, fail, cease, 1528, 2886.
  ge-licg(e)an, *st. v.*, sink to rest, 3146.
līc-homa, līc-hama, *w. m.*, [LYCH-covering] body, 812, 1007, etc.
līcian, *w. v.*, *with dat.*, [LIKE] please, 639, 1854.
līc-sār, *st. neut.*, body-SORE, wound in the body, 815.
līc-syrce, *w. f.*, body-SARK, shirt of mail, 550.
lid-mann, *st. m.*, sea-MAN, 1623.
līf, *st. neut.*, LIFE, 97, etc.
lifað, etc., see **libban.**
līf-bysig, *adj.*, [LIFE-BUSY] in the throes of death, 966.
līf-dagas, *st. m. pl.*, LIFE-DAYS, 793, 1622.
Līf-frēa, *w. m.*, LIFE-lord, Lord of life, 16.
līf-gedāl, *st. neut.*, LIFE-parting, death, 841.
līf-gesceaft, *st. f.*, destiny, 1953, 3064.
līf-wraðu, *st. f.*, LIFE-protection, 971, 2877.
līf-wynn, *st. f.*, LIFE-joy, 2097.
līg, **lēg**, *st. m.*, flame, 83, 2549, etc.; *dat.* ligge, 727.
līg-draca, lēg-draca, *w. m.*, flame-DRAKE, flaming dragon, 2333, 3040.
līg-egesa, *w. m.*, flame-terror, 2780.
lige-torn, *st. neut.*, [LYing-anger] pretended insult, 1943. (See Bugge, *Z. f. d. Ph.*, IV. 208.)
ligge, see **līg.**
līg-ȳð, *st. f.*, flame-wave, 2672.
lim, *st. neut.*, LIMB, branch; *dat. pl.* leomum, 97.
limpan, *st. v.*, happen, befall; *pret.* lomp, 1987.
  ā-limpan, *st. v.*, befall, 622, 733.
  be-limpan, *st. v.*, befall, 2468.
  ge-limpan, *st. v.*, befall, happen, 76, 626 (be fulfilled), 929 (be given), etc.
  ge-lumpen, *pp. of* limpan *or* gelimpan, 'fulfilled,' 824.
lind, *st. f.*, LINDen, shield (made of linden), 2341, 2365, 2610.
lind-gestealla, *w. m.*, shield-comrade, comrade in arms, 1973.
lind-hæbbende, *st. m.* (*pres. part.*), [LINDEN-HAVing] shield-warriors, 245, 1402.
lind-plega, *w. m.*, LINDEN-PLAY, battle, 1073*, 2039.
lind-wiga, *w. m.*, LINDen-warrior, shield-warrior, 2603.
linnan, *st. v.*, *with gen. or dat.*, cease, depart, be deprived, 1478, 2443.
liss, *st. f.*, favour, 2150. [*From* *liðs, *cf.* līðe, 'gentle.']
list, *st. m. and f.*, cunning; *dat. pl adverbially*, 781.
līðan, *st. v.*, go; *pp.* liden, 'traversed,' 223 (see note to l. 224).

līðe, *adj.*, gentle, mild, 1220.
  līðost, *superl.*, gentlest, 3182.
līðend, *st. m.* (*pres. part.*), [going] sailor, 221.
līð-wǣge, *st. neut.*, stoup of drink, 1982. [*Cf. Goth.* leiþu, 'strong drink.']
līxan, *w. v.*, gleam, glisten; *pret.* līxte, 311, 485, 1570.
locen, see **lūcan**.
lōcian, *w. v.*, LOOK, 1654.
lof, *st. m.*, praise, 1536.
lof-dǣd, *st. f.*, praise-DEED, deed worthy of praise, 24.
lof-georn, *adj.*, YEARNing for praise.
  lof-geornost, *superl.*, most eager for praise, 3182.
lōg, see **lēan**.
lomp, see **limpan**.
lond, land, *st. neut.*, LAND, 221, 2197, 2836 (see note), etc.
  land-fruma, *w. m.*, LAND-chief, ruler of a land, 31.
  land-gemyrcu, *st. neut. pl.*, LAND-MARKS, boundaries, shore, 209. [*Cf. O.E.* mearc.]
  land-geweorc, *st. neut.*, LAND-WORK, stronghold, 938.
  land-waru, *st. f.*, LAND-people; *pl.* land-wara, 'people of the land,' 2321.
  land-weard, *st. m.*, [LAND-WARD] guardian of a country, 1890.
lond-būend, land-būend, *st. m.* (*pres. part.*), LAND-dweller, 95, 1345.
lond-riht, *st. neut.*, LAND-RIGHT, right of a citizen *or* freeholder, 2886.
long, lang, *adj.*, LONG, 16, 54, etc.
  lang-twīdig, *adj.*, LONG-granted, lasting, 1708.
  lengra, *compar.*, LONGER, 134.
longe, lange, *adv.*, LONG, 31, etc.
  leng, læng, *compar.*, LONGer, leng, 451, 974, etc.; læng, 2307.
  lengest, *superl.*, LONGEST, 2008, 2238.
long-gestrēon, *st. neut.*, [LONG-possession] treasure of long ago, 2240.
long-sum, *adj.*, [LONG-SOME] lasting long, 134, etc.
losian, *w. v.*, [LOSE oneself] escape, 1392, etc.
lūcan, *st. v.*, LOCK, interlock, weave; *pp.* locen, gelocen, 'LOCKED, of interlocked rings,' 1505, 1890, 2769, 2995.
  be-lūcan, *st. v.*, LOCK, secure; *pret.* belēac, 1132, 1770.
  on-lūcan, *st. v.*, UNLOCK; *pret.* onlēac, 259.
  tō-lūcan, *st. v.*, shatter, destroy, 781.
lufen, *st. f.*, hope, comfort, 2886 [occurs here only; *cf. Goth.* lubáins, 'hope,' but see note].
lufian, *w. v.*, LOVE, hence, show love, treat kindly, 1982.
luf-tācen, *st. neut.*, LOVE-TOKEN, 1863.
lufu, *w. f.*, LOVE, 1728 (see note).
lungre, *adv.*:
(1) quickly, hastily, 929, 1630, etc.
(2) quite, 2164 (but see note).
lust, *st. m.*, [LUST] pleasure, joy; *acc.* on lust, *dat. pl.* lustum, 'with joy, with pleasure,' 618, 1653.
lȳfan, *w. v.*
  ā-lȳfan, *w. v.*, entrust, permit, 655, 3089.
  ge-lȳfan, *w. v.*, beLIEVE in, trust for, rely on; *with dat. pers.* 909; *with dat. rei*, 440, 608; þæt hēo on ǣnigne eorl gelȳfde fyrena frōfre (*acc.*), 'that she believed in any earl for comfort from crime,' 627; him tō Anwaldan āre (*acc.*) gelȳfde, 'believed in favour from the Almighty for himself,' 1272. [*Cf. Goth.* galáubjan.]
lyfað, lyfde, see **libban**.
lyft, *st. m. f. neut.*, [LIFT] air, 1375, etc.
lyft-floga, *w. m.*, [LIFT-FLIer] flier in the air, 2315.
lyft-geswenced, *adj.* (*pp.*), wind-urged, driven by the wind, 1913.
lyft-wynn, *st. f.*, [LIFT-joy] air-joy, 3043 (see note).
lyhð, see **lēan**.
lȳsan, *w. v.* [*From* lēas, *cf. Goth.* láusjan.]
  ā-lȳsan, *w. v.*, LOOSE, loosen, 1630.
lystan, *w. v.*, *impers.*, *with acc. pers.*, LIST, please; *pret.* 1793. [*From* lust.]
lȳt, *neut. adj. or n.*, *indecl.*, few, 2365; *with gen.* 1927, 2150, 2882, 2836 (*dat.*) (see note).
lȳt, *adv.*, LITTle, but little, 2897, 3129.
lȳtel, *adj.*, LITTLE, 1748, 2097, etc.; *acc. f.* lȳtle hwīle, 'but a little while,' 2030.
lȳt-hwōn, *adv.*, LITTle, but little (see note), 203.

M

mā, *compar. adv.*, *with gen.*, MO, MORE, 504, etc. [*Cf. Goth.* máis.]

mādmas, etc., see **māð(ð)um.**
mæg, see **magan.**
mǣg, *st. m.*, kinsman, blood-relative, 408, etc.; *pl.* māgas, etc., 1015, etc.; *gen. pl.* māga, 2006; *dat. pl.* māgum, 1178, etc., 2614 (see note), mǣgum, 2353.
mǣg-burg, *st. f.*, [kin-BURGH] family; *gen.* mǣg-burge, 2887.
mæge, mægen, 2654, see **magan.**
mægen, *st. neut.*, MAIN, strength, force, army, 155, 445, etc.
mægen-āgende, *adj.* (*pres. part.*), [MAIN-*OWN*ing] mighty, 2837.
mægen-byrðen, *st. f.*, MAIN-BURTHEN, great BURDEN, 1625, etc.
mægen-cræft, *st. m.*, MAIN-CRAFT, mighty strength, 380.
mægen-ellen, *st. neut.*, MAIN-strength, great courage, 659.
mægen-fultum, *st. m.*, MAIN-aid, strong help, 1455.
mægen-rǣs, *st. m.*, [MAIN-*RACE*] mighty impetus, onset, 1519.
mægen-strengo, *st. f.*, MAIN-STRENGth; *dat.* 2678.
mægen-wudu, *st. m.*, [MAIN-WOOD] spear, 236.
mægð, *st. f.*, *MAID*, woman, 924, etc. [*Cf. Goth.* magaþs.]
mǣgð, *st. f.*, tribe, people, 5, etc.
mǣg-wine, *st. m.*, kinsman-friend; *pl.* 2479.
mǣl, *st. neut.*, [MEAL, *cf. Goth.* mēl, 'time.']
(1) time, occasion, 316, 1008, etc.
(2) sword with marks, 1616, 1667.
mǣl-cearu, *st. f.*, time-CARE, 189 (see note).
mǣl-gesceaft, *st. f.*, time appointed, 2737.
mǣnan, *w. v.*, [MEAN] *with acc.*, declare, proclaim, 857, 1067 (see note to l. 1101).
mǣnan, *w. v.*, *trans. and intrans.*, *MOAN*, bemoan, mourn, lament, 1149, 2267, 3149, 3171.
mænig, see **monig.**
mænigo, see **menigeo.**
mǣre, *adj.*, famous, notorious, 103, 762, 1301, etc. [*Cf. Goth.* -mēreis.]
mǣrost, *superl.*, 898.
mǣrðo, mǣrðu, *st. f.*, glory, fame, 504, 659, etc.; deed of glory, exploit, 408, 2134, 2645; *dat. pl. as adv.*, gloriously, 2514. [*Cf. Goth.* mēriþa.]
mæst, *st. m.*, MAST, 36, etc.
mǣst, see **māra.**
mǣte, *adj.*, small.
mǣtost, *superl.*, smallest, 1455.
maga, *w. m.*, son, man, 189, etc.
māga, see **mǣg.**
magan, *pret. pres. v.*, MAY, can, be able; *pres. sg. 1st and 3rd* mæg, 277, etc., *2nd* meaht, 2047, miht, 1378; *pres. subj. sg.* mæge, 2530, etc., *pl.* mægen, 2654; *pret.* meahte, 542, 648, etc., mihte, 190, 308, etc., mehte, 1082, etc. *With* gān *omitted*, 754.
māge, *w. f.*, kinswoman, 1391.
mago, *st. m.*, kinsman, son, man, 1465, etc. [*Cf. Goth.* magus, 'boy.']
mago-driht, *st. f.*, kindred-troop, band of warriors, 67.
mago-rinc, *st. m.*, retainer, warrior, 730.
mago-þegn, magu-þegn, *st. m.*, THANE, 293, 408, 1405, etc.
man(n), see **mon(n).**
manna, see **mon(n).**
mān, *st. neut.*, wickedness, crime, 110, 978, 1055.
mān-fordǣdla, *w. m.*, wicked destroyer, 563.
manian, *w. v.*, exhort, 2057.
manig, see **monig.**
man-līce, *adv.*, in a MANLY way, 1046.
mān-sc(e)aða, *w. m.*, wicked *SCATH*er, deadly foe, 712, 737, etc.
māra, *compar.*, *adj.* (*of* micel), greater, mightier, 247, 518, 533, etc.; *neut.*, *with gen.*, māre, MORE, 136. [*Cf. Goth.* máiza.]
mǣst, *superl.*, [*MOST*] greatest, 78, etc.; *neut.*, *with gen.*, 2645, etc.
maðelian, *w. v.*, harangue, discourse, speak, 286, etc. [*Cf. Goth.* maþljan.]
māðm-ǣht, *st. f.*, valuable possession, 1613, 2833. [*Cf.* āgan.]
māðm-gestrēon, *st. neut.*, jewel-treasure, 1931.
māð(ð)um, *st. m.*, thing of value, treasure, jewel, 169, etc.; mādme, 1528; *pl.* māðmas, mādmas, etc., 36, 41, 385, etc. [*Cf. Goth.* máiþms.]
māððum-fæt, *st. neut.*, treasure-VAT, costly vessel, 2405.
māððum-gifu, *st. f.*, treasure-GIFT, 1301.
māððum-sigle, *st. neut.*, treasure-jewel, costly sun-shaped ornament, 2757.
māððum-sweord, *st. neut.*, treasure-SWORD, sword inlaid with jewels, 1023.
māððum-wela, *w. m.*, [treasure-WEAL] wealth of treasure, 2750.

mē, *pers. pron.*, *acc. and dat. of* ic, ME, to me, 316, 415, etc.; *dat.* for myself, 2738.
meagol, *adj.*, forceful, earnest, solemn, 1980.
meahte, **meahton**, see **magan**.
mēaras, etc., see **mearh**.
mearc, *st. f.*, MARK, limit; *dat.* 2384 (see note). [*Cf. Goth.* marka.]
mearcian, *w. v.*, MARK, stain, engrave, 450; *pp.* gemearcod, 1264, 1695.
mearc-stapa, *w. m.*, MARK-*STEP*per, march-stalker, 103, 1348.
mearh, *st. m.*, [*MARE*] horse; *pl.* mēaras, etc., 865, etc.
mearn, see **murnan**.
mec, *pers. pron.*, *acc.* of ic, ME, 447, etc.
mēce, *st. m.*, sword, 565, etc. [*Cf. Goth.* mēkeis.]
mēd, *st. f.*, MEED, reward, 2134, etc.; *gen. pl.* medo, 1178.
medo, **medu**, *st. m.*, MEAD, 2633; F. 41, *dat.* 604.
medo-ærn, *st. neut.*, MEAD-hall, 69.
medo-benc, **medu-benc**, **meodu-benc**, *st. f.*, MEAD-BENCH, 776, 1052, 1067, 1902, 2185.
medo-ful, *st. neut.*, MEAD-cup, 624, 1015.
medo-heal, **meodu-heall**, *st. f.*, MEAD-HALL, 484, 638.
medo-stīg, *st. f.*, MEAD-path, path to the mead-hall, 924.
medu-drēam, *st. m.*, MEAD-joy, 2016.
medu-seld, *st. neut.*, MEAD-hall, 3065.
  meodo-setl, *st. neut.*, MEAD-SETTLE, 5.
  meodo-wong, *st. m.*, MEAD-plain, field where the mead-hall stood, 1643.
  meodu-scenc, *st. m.*, MEAD-draught, mead-cup, 1980.
mehte, see **magan**.
melda, *w. m.*, informer, finder, 2405.
meltan, *st. v.*, *intrans.*, MELT, 1120, etc.
  ge-meltan, *st. v.*, MELT, 897, etc.
mene, *st. m.*, collar, necklace, 1199.
mengan, *w. v.*: MINGle; *pp.* gemenged, 848, 1449 (see note), 1593.
menigeo, **mænigo**, *st. f.*, MANY, multitude, 41, 2143.
meodo-, **meodu-**, see under **medo-**.
meoto, see **met**, **metian**.
meotod-, see **metod-**.
mercels, *st. m.*, *MARK*, aim, 2439. [Sievers$_3$ § 159, 1, 2: *cf. O.E.* mearc.]
mere, *st. m.*, MERE, sea, 845, etc. [*Cf. Goth.* marei.]
mere-dēor, *st. neut.*, MERE-DEER, sea-monster, 558.
mere-fara, *w. m.*, MERE-FARer, seafarer, 502.
mere-fix (**mere-fisc**), *st. m.*, MERE-FISH, sea-fish, 549. [Sievers$_3$ § 204, 3.]
mere-grund, *st. m.*, [MERE-GROUND] bottom of a mere *or* sea, 1449, 2100.
mere-hrægl, *st. neut.*, [MERE-RAIL] sea-garment, sail, 1905.
mere-līðend, *st. m.* (*pres. part.*), [MERE-going] sailor, 255.
mere-strǣt, *st. f.*, [MERE-STREET] way over the sea, 514.
mere-strengo, *st. f.*, [MERE-STRENGth] strength in swimming, 533.
mere-wīf, *st. neut.*, [MERE-WIFE] mere-woman, 1519.
mergen, see **morgen**.
met, *st. neut.*, thought; *pl.* meoto, 489 (see note).
metan, *st. v.*, METE, measure, pass over, 514, 917, 924, 1633.
mētan, *w. v.*, MEET, find, 751, 1421.
  ge-mētan, *w. v.*, MEET, find, 757, 2785; *pret. pl.* hȳ (*acc.*) gemētton, 'met each other,' 2592. [*Cf. Goth.* gamōtjan.]
***metian**, *w. v.*, think; *imp.* meota (MS. meoto) 489 (see note).
Metod, *st. m.*, Creator, God, 110, etc.; fate, 2527.
metod-sceaft, **meotod-sceaft**, *st. f.*, appointed doom, 1077, 2815, 1180 (Creator's glory). [*Cf.* Klaeber in *Anglia*, xxxv., 465.]
meðel, *st. neut.*, council, 1876. [*Cf. Goth.* maþl, 'market-place.']
meðel-stede, *st. m.*, meeting-place, 1082.
meðel-word, *st. neut.*, council-WORD, formal word, 236.
micel, *adj.*, MICKLE, great, 67, etc.; *gen.* micles wyrðne, 'worthy of much,' 2185. [*Cf. Goth.* mikils.]
  micles, *gen. used adverbially*; tō fela micles, 'far too *MUCH*,' 694.
  micle, *instr. used adverbially*, by *MUCH*, much, 1579, 2651; *so* swā micle, 'by so much,' 1283.
mid, *prep.*, *with dat. and acc.*
(1) *with dat.*, with, among, 77, 195, 274, etc.; *following its case*, 41, 889, 1625; *of time*, 126; with, by means of, through, 317, 438, etc.: mid rihte, 'by right,' 2056;

mid gewealdum, 'of his own accord,' 2221; mid him, 'among themselves,' 2948.
(2) *with acc.*, with, among, 357, 879, 2652, etc. [*Cf. Goth.* miþ.]
mid, *adv.*, with them, withal, therewith, 1642, 1649.
middan-geard, *st. m.*, [MID-YARD] world, earth, 75, etc.; *gen.* 'in the world,' 504, etc. [*Cf. Goth.* midjungards.]
midde, *w. f.*, MIDDle, 2705.
middel-niht, *st. f.*, MIDDLE of the NIGHT, 2782, 2833.
miht, *st. f.*, MIGHT, 700, 940. [*Cf. Goth.* mahts.]
mihte, see **magan**.
mihtig, *adj.*, MIGHTY, 558, etc.
milde, *adj.*, MILD, kind, 1172, 1229.
mildust, *superl.*, MILDEST, kindest, 3181.
mīl-gemearc, *st. neut.*, MILE-MARK, measure by miles; *gen.* nis þæt feor heonon mīl-gemearces, 'that is not many miles away,' 1362. [*From Lat.* milia, millia.]
milts, *st. f.*, *MILD*ness, kindness, 2921.
mīn, *pers. pron.* (*gen. sg. of* ic), of me, 2084, 2533.
mīn, *poss. adj.* (*gen. sg. of* ic), MINE, my, 255, etc.
missan, *w. v.*, *w. gen.*, MISS, 2439.
missēre, *st. neut.*, half-year, 153, 1498, 1769, 2620.
mīst-hlið, *st. neut.*, MIST-slope, misty hill-side; *dat. pl.* mīsthleoþum, 710.
mīstig, *adj.*, MISTY, 162.
mōd, *st. neut.*:
(1) MOOD, mind, etc., 50, etc.
(2) courage, 1057, etc.
mōd-cearu, *st. f.*, MOOD-CARE, sorrow of mind *or* heart, 1778, 1992, 3149.
mōdega, mōdgan, etc., see **mōdig**.
mōd-gehygd, *st. f. and neut.*, mind-thought, 233.
mōd-geðonc, *st. m. and neut.*, mind-*THOUGH*t, 1729.
mōd-gīomor, *adj.*, sad in mind *or* heart, 2894.
mōdig, *adj.*, *weak* mōd(i)ga, mōdega; *gen. m.* mōd(i)ges; *pl.* mōd(i)ge: [MOODY] brave, proud, 312, 502, etc.
mōdig-līc, *adj.*, [MOODY-LIKE].
mōdig-līcra, *compar.*, braver, prouder, 337.
mōd-lufu, *w. f.*, [MOOD-LOVE] heart's love, 1823.
mōdor, *st. f.*, MOTHER, 1258, etc.
mōd-sefa, *w. m.*, [MOOD-mind] mind, courage, 180, 349, 1853, 2012, 2628.
mōd-þracu, *st. f.*, [MOOD-] daring, 385.
mon(n), man(n), *st. m.*, *weak* manna; *dat. sg.* men(n); *pl.* men: MAN, 25, etc.; *weak acc. sg.* mannan, 297 (see note), 1943, 2127, 2774, 3108; mannon, 577.
mon, man, *indef. pron.*, one, they, people, 1172, 1175, 2355.
mōna, *w. m.*, MOON, 94, F. 8. [*Cf. Goth.* mēna.]
mon-cynn, man-cynn, *st. neut.*, MANKIND, 110, 164, 196, 1276, 1955, 2181.
mon-drēam, man-drēam, *st. m.*, [MAN-DREAM] human joy, 1264, 1715.
mon-dryhten, -drihten, man-dryhten, -drihten, *st. m.*, [MAN-]lord, etc., 436, 1229, 1978, 2865, etc.
monig (moneg-), **manig** (maneg-), *adj.*, MANY, 5, 75, etc.; mænig, F. 14; *nom.* monig oft gesæt rīce tō rūne, 'many a mighty one oft sat in council,' 171. *Often absolutely*, 857, etc.; *and with dependent gen. pl.* 728, etc. [*Cf. Goth.* managa.]
mon-þwǣre, *adj.*, [MAN-]gentle, kind to men, 3181 *.
mōr, *st. m.*, MOOR, 103, etc.
morgen, mergen, *st. m.*, *dat.* morgne, mergenne: MORN, MORNing, MORROW, 565, 837, 2484, etc.; *gen. pl.* morna, 2450.
morgen-ceald, *adj.*, MORNing-COLD, cold in the morning, 3022.
morgen-lēoht, *st. neut.*, MORNing LIGHT, morning sun, 604, 917.
morgen-long, *adj.*, MORNing-LONG, 2894.
morgen-swēg, *st. m.*, [MORN-*SOUGH*] morning-clamour, 129.
morgen-tīd, *st. f.*, MORNing-TIDE, 484, 518.
mōr-hop, *st. neut.*, MOOR-hollow, 'sloping hollow on a moorside' (Skeat), 450.
morna, see **morgen**.
morð-bealu, *st. neut.*, MURDER-BALE, murder, 136.
morðor, *st. neut.*, MURDER, 892, etc. [*Cf. Goth.* maúrþr.]
morðor-bealo, *st. neut.*, MURDER-BALE, murder, 1079, 2742.
morðor-bed, *st. neut.*, MURDER-BED, 2436.
morðor-hete, *st. m.*, MURDEROUS HATE, 1105.

mōste, see **mōtan**.
***mōtan**, *pret. pres. v.*, may, be to, MUST, 186, 2886, etc.; *pret.* mōste, 168, 2574, etc.; *pret. pl.* mōstan, 2247*.
munan, *pret. pres. v.*
ge-munan, (*pret. pres.*) *v.*, have in *MIN*d, remember; *pres.* gemon, geman, 265, 1185, etc.; *pret.* gemundon, 179, etc.; *imp. sg.* gemyne, 659.
on-munan, *pret. pres. v.*, re*MIN*d; *pret.* onmunde ūsic mǣrða, 'reminded us of glory, urged us on to great deeds,' 2640.
mund, *st. f.*, hand, 236, etc.
mund-bora, *w. m.*, protector, 1480, 2779. [*Cf.* beran.]
mund-gripe, *st. m.*, hand-GRIP, 380, etc., 1938 (see note).
murnan, *st. v.*, MOURN, be anxious, reck, care, 50, 136, etc.
be-murnan, *st. v.*, *with acc.*, BEMOURN, mourn over, 907, 1077.
mūða, *w. m.*, MOUTH, 724. [*Cf. Goth.* munþs.]
mūð-bona, *w. m.*, MOUTH-BANE, one who slays by biting, 2079.
myndgian, *w. v.*, call to *MIND*:
(1) *with gen.*, remember, 1105.
(2) re*MIND*, 2057.
ge-myndgian, *w. v.*, bring to *MIND*, remember; *pp.* gemyndgad, 2450.
myne, *st. m.*: [*Cf. Goth.* muns.]
(1) wish, hope, 2572.
(2) love: *acc.* ne his myne wisse, 'nor did he know his mind,' 169 (see note).
-myne, see **munan**.
myntan, *w. v.*, be *MIN*ded, intend, 712, 731, 762.
myrce, *adj.*, MURKY, 1405.
myrð, *st. f.*, MIRTH; *dat.* mōdes myrðe, 810 (see note).

N

nā, *neg. adv.*, *N*ever, *N*ot at all, not, 445, 567, 1536, 1875*.
naca, *w. m.*, bark, craft, 214, 295, 1896, 1903.
nacod, *adj.*, NAKED, 539, 2585; bare, smooth, 2273.
næbben, 1850, = ne hæbben, see **habban**.
næfne, see **nefne**.
nǣfre, *adv.*, NEVER, 247, etc.
nǣgan, *w. v.*, greet, accost, 1318*.
ge-nǣgan, *w. v.*, assail; *pret. pl.* genǣgdan, 2206, 2916* (see note); *pp.* genǣged, 1439.
nægl, *st. m.*, NAIL, 985.
næglian, *w. v.*, NAIL; *pp.* nægled, 'nailed, riveted, studded,' 2023*.
nǣnig (= ne ǣnig), *adj.-pron.*, not ANY, none, no, 859, etc.; *with gen. pl.* 157, etc.
nǣre, nǣron, = ne wǣre, ne wǣron, see **wesan**.
næs, = ne wæs, see wesan.
næs, *neg. adv.*, not, not at all, 562, etc.
næs(s), *st. m.*, NESS, headland, 1358, etc.
næs-hlið, *st. neut.*, NESS-slope, headland-slope; *dat. pl.* næs-hleoðum, 1427.
nāh, = ne āh, see **āgan**.
nalas, nalæs, nales, nallas, nalles, see **nealles**.
nam, see **niman**.
nama, *w. m.*, NAME, 78, 343, 1457, F. 26.
nāman, -nāmon, see **niman**.
nān, (= ne ān), *adj.-pron.*, NONE, NO, 988; *with gen. pl.* 803, F. 43.
nāt, = ne wāt, see **witan**.
nāt-hwylc (= ne wāt hwylc; cf. l. 274), *adj.-pron.*, [WOT NOT WHICH] some, some one, a certain (one), 1513; *with gen. pl.* 2215, 2223, 2233, etc.
ne, nē, *neg. particle*, NOT, 38, 1384, etc.; *doubled*, ne...ne, 182, 245–6, etc.; nōðer...ne, 2124; ne...nō, 1508. *Often found in composition with verbs, e.g.* nāh, næbben, næs, nolde, nāt, etc., *for which see* āgan, habban, wesan, willan, witan; *in composition with* ā, ǣnig, etc., *it forms the words* nā, nǣnig, etc. (q. v.).
Correlated with ne *or another negative*, not...nor, neither...nor, etc., 511, 1082–4, etc.; ne...ne ...ne, 1100–1; nō...ne, 168–9, 575–7, etc.; nō...ne...ne...ne, 1392–4, 1735–7; nǣfre...ne, 583–4, 718; nalles...ne, 3015–6.
nē, *not preceded by another negative*, 'nor,' 510, 739 (see note), 1071.
Correlated with a doubled negative: ne...nǣnig...nǣre, 858–60.
nēah, *adj.*, NIGH, near, 1743, 2728, 2420. [*Cf. Goth.* nēhw.]
niehst, nȳhst, *superl.*, [NEXT] last, 1203, 2511.
nēah, *adv.*, NIGH, near, 1221, 2870; *with dat.* 564, 1924, 2242, etc.
nēar, *compar.*, NEARer, 745.

nealles, etc. (=ne ealles), *adv.*, NOT at ALL, by no means, 2145, etc.; nalles, 338, etc.; nallas, 1719, etc.; nales, 1811; nalas, 1493, etc.; nalæs, 43.

nēan, **nēon**, *adv.*, from near, near, 528 (at close quarters), 839, 3104, etc. [*Cf.* nēah.]

nearo, *st. neut.*, [NARROW] straits, distress, 2350, 2594.

nearo, *adj.*, NARROW, 1409.

nearo-cræft, *st. m.*, [NARROW-CRAFT] inaccessibility, 2243.

nearo-fāh, *st. m.*, [NARROW-FOE] foe causing distress; *gen.* nearo-fāges, 2317.

nearo-þearf, *st. f.*, [NARROW-need] dire distress, 422.

nearwe, *adv.*, NARROWly, 976.

nearwian, *w. v.*, [NARROW] straiten, press; *pp.* genearwod, 1438.

nefa, *w. m.*, nephew, 881, etc.; grandson, descendant, 1203, 1962.

nefne, **næfne**, **nemne**, *conj.*:
(1) unless, 250*, 1056, 1552, etc.; except that, 1353.
(2) *In elliptical sentences, with quasi-prepositional force*, unless, save, 1934, 2151, 2533.

nēh, see **nēah**, *adj.*

nelle, = ne wille, see **willan**.

nemnan, *w. v.*, *NAME*, call, 364, etc. [*Cf. Goth.* namnjan.]
  be-nemnan, *w. v.*, declare solemnly, 1097, 3069.

nemne, *prep.*, *with dat.*, except, 1081.

nemne, *conj.*, see **nefne**.

nēod-laðu, *st. f.*, pressing invitation, or desire, 1320 (see note).

nēon, see **nēan**.

nēos(i)an, **nīos(i)an**, *w. v.*, *with gen.*, visit, revisit, attack, 115, 125, 2388, 2671, etc.; *pres. 3rd* nīosað, 2486.

nēotan, *st. v.*, use, enjoy, 1217.
  be-nēotan, **bi-nēotan**, *st. v.*, *with acc. pers. and dat. rei*, deprive, 680, 2396.

neoðor, see **niðer**.

neowol, *adj.*, steep; *pl.* neowle, 1411.

nerian, *w. v.*, save, preserve, 572; *pp.* genered, 827. [*Cf. Goth.* nasjan.]

nesan, *st. v.*
  ge-nesan, *st. v.*:
(1) *intrans.* survive, escape, 999.
(2) *trans.* survive, escape (from), 1977, 2426, F. 49; *pp.* genesen, 2397.

nēðan, *w. v.*: [*Cf. Goth.* nanþjan.]
(1) *with acc.*, dare, encounter, 2350.
(2) *with dat.*, risk, 510, 538.
  ge-nēðan, *w. v.*:
(1) *with acc.* hazard, dare, venture on, brave, 888, 959, 1656, 1933, 2511.
(2) *with dat.* risk, 1469, 2133.

nicor, *st. m.*, NICKER (sea-monster), 422, etc.

nicor-hūs, *st. neut.*, NICKER-HOUSE, cavern of a sea-monster, 1411.

nīehst, see **nēah**, *adj.*

nigen, *num.*, NINE; *inflected*, 575. [*Cf. Goth.* niun.]

niht, *st. f.*, NIGHT, 115, etc. [*Cf. Goth.* nahts.]
  nihtes, *gen.* (*m.*) *used adverbially*, of a NIGHT, by night, 422, 2269, etc.

niht-bealu, *st. neut.*, NIGHT-BALE, evil at night, 193.

niht-helm, *st. m.*, NIGHT-HELM, night, 1789.

niht-long, *adj.*, NIGHT-LONG, 528.

niht-weorc, *st. neut.*, NIGHT-WORK, 827.

niman, *st. v.*, take, seize; *pres. 3rd*, nimeð, nymeð, 441, 598, etc.; *pret. sg.*, nam, nōm, 746, 1612, etc.; *pret. pl.* nāman, 2116; *pp.* (ge)numen, 1153, 3165.
  ā-niman, *st. v.*, take away, F. 23.
  be-niman, *st. v.*, deprive; *pret.* benam, 1886.
  for-niman, *st. v.*, carry off; *pret.* fornam, -nāmon, 488, 2828, etc.
  ge-niman, *st. v.*, take, seize, take away, clasp; *pret.* genam, genōm, 122, 2776, etc.

nīod, *st. f.*, desire, pleasure, 2116.

nīos(i)an, see **nēos(i)an**.

nioðor, see **niðer**.

nīowe, see **nīwe**.

nīpan, *st. v.*, darken, 547, 649.

nis, = ne is, see **wesan**.

nīð, *st. m.*, envy, hate, violence, war, struggle, 184, 827, etc.; affliction, 423.
Gen. pl. used instrumentally, in fight, in war, by force, 845, 1439, 1962, 2170, 2206.

niðas, see **niððas**.

nīð-draca, *w. m.*, [envy-DRAKE] malicious dragon, 2273.

niþer, **nyðer**, *adv.*, [NETHER] down, downwards, 1360, 3044; *compar.* **nioðor**, further down, 2699.

nīð-gæst, *st. m.*, [envy-GUEST] malicious guest, 2699. (See note to l. 102.)
nīð-geweorc, *st. neut.*, [envy-WORK] work of enmity, deed of violence, 683.
nīð-grim, *adj.*, [envy-GRIM] maliciously grim *or* terrible, 193.
nīð-heard, *adj.*, war-HARD, hardy in war, 2417.
nīð-hēdig, *adj.*, war-minded, 3165.
nīð-sele, *st. m.*, hostile hall, 1513 (see note).
niððas, niðas, *st. m. pl.*, men, 1005, 2215. [*Cf. Goth.* niþjōs, 'kinsmen.']
nīð-wundor, *st. neut.*, dread WONDER, 1365.
nīwe, *adj.*, NEW, 783 (startling), 949, etc.; *dat. weak* nīwan, nīowan, stefne, 'anew,' 1789, 2594. [*Cf. Goth.* niujis.]
nīwian, *w. v.*, RENEW; *pp.* genīwod, genīwad, 1303, 1322, 2287 (see note).
nīw-tyrwed, *adj.* (*pp.*), NEW-TARRED, 295.
nō, *adv.*, NOT at all, not, 136, 168 (*see* **ne**), 541, 543, 1508 (*see* **ne**), etc.
nolde, =ne wolde, see **willan.**
nōm, see **niman.**
nōn, *st. f.*, [NOON] ninth hour, 3 p.m., 1600. [*From Lat.* nōna.]
norð, *adv.*, NORTH, 858.
norðan, *adv.*, from the NORTH, 547.
nōse, *w. f.*, [NOSE] *NAZE*, cape, 1892, 2803.
nōðer (=**ne ō hwæðer**), *adv.*, NOR, 2124.
nū, *adv.*, NOW, 251, etc.
nū, *conj.*, NOW, now that, seeing that, 430, etc.; *correlative with* nū, *adv.*, 2743–5.
nȳd, *st. f.*, NEED, compulsion, 1005, 2454 (pangs). [*Cf. Goth.* náuþs.]
nȳdan, *w. v.*, force, compel; *pp.* genȳded, 2680; *inflected*, genȳdde, 1005 (*see* gesacan).
nȳd-bād, *st. f.*, [NEED-pledge] forced toll, 598.
nȳd-gestealla, *w. m.*, NEED-comrade, comrade in *or* at need, 882.
nȳd-gripe, *st. m.*, [NEED-GRIP] dire grip, 976*.
nȳd-wracu, *st. f.*, [NEED-*WRACK*] dire ruin, 193.
nȳhst, see **nēah**, *adj.*
nyman, see **niman.**
nymðe, *conj.*, unless, 781, 1658.
nyt, *adj.*, useful, of use, 794. [*Cf. Goth.* -nuts.]
nytt, *st. f.*, duty, office, service, 494, 3118.
nyttian, *w. v.*, *with gen.*
ge-nyttian, *w. v.*, *with acc.*, use, enjoy; *pp.* genyttod, 3046.
nyðer, see **niðer.**

O

of, *prep.*, *with dat.*, from, 37, etc.; OF (*after* ūt), 663, 2557; out of, 419; OFF, 672. *Following case:* ðā hē him of dyde, 'then he doFFed,' 671. [*Cf. Goth.* af.]
ofer, *prep.*, OVER, *with acc.* (of motion, etc.) *and dat.* (of rest): (1) *with acc.*, over, 10, 46, etc.; against, 2330, 2409, 2589*, 2724 (see note); above, beyond, 2879; without, 685; *of time*, after, 736, 1781 (but see note). Ofer eorðan, 'on earth,' 248, etc.; ofer werþeode, 'throughout the nations of men,' 899; ofer ealle, 'so that all could hear,' 2899; ofer eal, F. 24. (2) *with dat.*, over, 481, etc. [*Cf. Goth.* ufar.]
ōfer, *st. m.*, bank, shore, 1371.
ofer hygd, -hȳd, *st. f. neut.*, contempt, pride, 1740, 1760.
ofer-mægen, *st. neut.*, OVER-MAIN, superior force, 2917.
ofer-māðum, *st. m.*, [OVER-treasure] very rich treasure, 2993.
ofost, *st. f.*, haste, 256, 3007; *dat.* ofoste, ofeste, ofste, 386, 1292, 2747, etc. [*P. B. B.* x. 505.]
ofost-līce, *adv.*, hastily, 3130*.
oft, *adv.*, OFT, often, 4, etc.
oftor, *compar.*, OFTENER, 1579.
oftost, *superl.*, OFTENEST, 1663.
ō-hwǣr, **ō-wēr**, *adv.*, anyWHERE, 1737, 2870.
ombeht, ombiht, *st. m.*, servant, officer, messenger, 287, 336. [*Cf. Goth.* andbahts.]
ombiht-þegn, *st. m.*, attendant-THANE, 673.
ōmig, *adj.*, rusty, 2763, etc.
on, an (677, 1247, 1935), *prep.*, ON; *with dat. and acc.*, *usu. dat. of rest and acc. of motion, but instances of the acc. are common, as will be seen, in which there is no suggestion, or the merest suggestion, of motion:*
(1) *with dat.*, *of place and time*, on, in, 40, 53, 76, 409, 607, 609, 677, 702, 782, 847, 891, 926, 1041, 1292, 1352, 1544, 1581, 1618

(A-swimming), 1643, 1662, 1830 (with respect to), 1884, 2197, 2248, 2276, 2311 (upon), 2705, 3157, etc.; *after its case*, 1935 (but see note), 2357, 2866; in, among, 1557; at, 126, 303, 575, 683, 3148; by, 1484. (2) *with acc.*, onto, into, 35, 67, etc.; on, in, 507, 516, 627, 635, 708, 996, 1095, 1109, 1297, 1456, 1675, 2132, 2193, 2690, 2650 (with regard to; cf. 1830-1), etc.; *of time*, 484, 837, 1428, etc.; to, 2662, 1739 (according to);
873 (*see* spēd), 1579 (*see* ān), 1753 (*see* endestæf), 2799 (*see* feorh-legu), 2903 (*see* efn), 2962 (*see* wrecan); on gebyrd, 'by fate,' 1074; an wīg, 'for war,' 1247 (see note); on ryht, 'rightly,' 1555; on unriht, 'falsely,' 2739; on gylp, 'proudly,' 1749; on mīnne sylfes dōm, 'at my own disposal, choice,' 2147; þe ic hēr on starie, 'on which I am here gazing,' 2796.
[*Cf. Goth.* ana.]
on innan, see **innan.**
on weg, AWAY, 763, etc.

on, *adv.*, ON, 1650, 3084 (see note).

oncer-bend, *st. m. f.*, ANCHOR-*BAND*, anchor-chain, 1918*.

on-cȳð(ð), *st. f.*, distress, suffering, 830, 1420.

ond, *conj.*, AND, 39, etc.; *usually the symbol* ⁊ *is used in 'Beowulf'*: ond *occurs in* ll. 600, 1148, 2040. *In Hickes' transcript of 'Finnsburh'* and *is used exclusively.*

ondlēan, *st. m.*, requital, 1541*, 2094* (see notes: *in both cases miswritten in MS* hondlean).

ond-long, and-long, *adj.*, (1) live-LONG, 2115, 2938; (2) stretching or standing up to; andlongne eorl, 'the earl upstanding,' 2695.

on-drysne, *adj.*, terrible, 1932.

ond-saca, *w. m.*, adversary, 786, 1682.

ond-slyht, *st. m.*, back-stroke, return blow, 2929, 2972.

ond-swaru, *st. f.*, ANSWER, 354, 1493, 1840, 2860.

ōnettan, *w. v.*, hasten; *pret. pl.* 306, 1803. [*P. B. B.* x. 487.]

on-gēan, *prep.*, *with dat.*, AGAINst, towards, at, 1034; *after its case*, 681, 2364 (*see* foran).

onlīc-nes, *st. f.*, LIKENESS, 1351*.

on-mōd, see **an-mōd**.

on-mēdla, *w. m.*, arrogance, 2926.

on-sǣge, *adj.*, impending, attacking, fatal, 2483; *nom.* þǣr wæs Hondscīo hild onsǣge, 'there warfare assailed Hondscio,' 2076.

on-sȳn, an-sȳn, *st. f.*, sight, appearance, form, 251, 928, 2772, 2834.

on-weald, *st. m.*, [*WIELD*ing] control, possession, 1044.

open, *adj.*, OPEN, 2271.

openian, *w. v.*, OPEN, 3056.

ōr, *st. neut.*, beginning, origin, van, 1041, 1688, 2407.

orc, *st. m.*, flagon, 2760, etc. [*Cf. Goth.* aúrkeis. *From Lat.* urceus.]

orcnēas, *st. m. pl.*, monsters, 112 (see note).

ord, *st. m.*, point, front, van, 556, etc.

ord-fruma, *w. m.*, chief, prince, 263.

ōret-mecg, *st. m.*, warrior, 332, 363, 481.

ōretta, *w. m.*, warrior, 1532, 2538. [*Cf.* ōret, from orhāt, 'a calling out, challenge,' and see Sievers, § 43, N. 4.]

oreð-, see **oruð**.

or-feorme, *adj.*, devoid of, destitute, wretched (see note to l. 2385).

or-leahtre, *adj.*, blameless, 1886.

or-lege, *st. neut.*, battle, war, 1326, 2407.

orleg-hwīl, *st. f.*, battle-WHILE, time of battle *or* war, 2002*, 2427, 2911.

or-þonc, or-þanc, *st. m.*, [original *THOUGH*t] skill, 406; *dat. pl. adverbially*, skilfully, 2087.

oruð, *st. neut.*, breath, 2557; *gen.* oreðes, 2523*; *dat.* oreðe, 2839. [*From* or, 'out of,' *and* uð=ōð= *anþ, *cf. Goth.* us-anan, 'to breathe forth.']

or-wearde, *adj.*, WARDless, unguarded, 3127.

or-wēna, *adj.* (*weak form*), *with gen.*, [WEENless] hopeless, despairing, 1002, 1565. [*Cf. Goth.* us-wēna.]

oð, *prep.*, *w. acc.*, until, 2399, etc.
oð þæt, *conj.*, till, until, 9, etc.; oðð þæt, 66.

ōðer, *num. adj.-pron.*, OTHER, (the) one, (the) other, the second, another, 219 (see note), 503, 1583, (*see* swylc), etc.; *correl.* ōðer... ōðer, 'one...the other,' 1349–51; ōðer sǣdan, 'said further,' 1945 (see note). [*Cf. Goth.* anþar.]

oðð, see **oð**.

oððe, *conj.*:
(1) or, 283, etc.
(2) and, 649 (see note to l. 648), 2475.

ōwēr, see **ohwǣr**.

ō-wiht, *pron.*, AUGHT; *dat.* a WHIT, 1822, 2432. See also **āht**.

R

rǣcan, *w. v.*, *intrans.*, REACH; *pret.* rǣhte, 747.
  ge-rǣcan, *w. v.*, *trans.*, **REACH**; *pret.* gerǣhte, 556, 2965.
rǣd, *st. m.*, [REDE] advice, counsel, help, benefit, gain, 172, etc.
rǣdan, *st. and w. v.* [READ]:
  (1) *intrans.*, **REDE**, decide, decree, 2858.
  (2) *trans.*, possess, 2056.
rǣd-bora, *w. m.*, counsellor, 1325. [*Cf.* beran.]
Rǣdend, *st. m.* (*pres. part.*), Ruler (God), 1555.
rǣran, *w. v.* [*Cf. Goth.* (ur)ráisjan.]
  ā-rǣran, *w. v.*, REAR, *RAISE*, exalt, extol, 1703, 2983.
rǣs, *st. m.*, *RACE*, rush, storm, onslaught, 2356, 2626.
rǣsan, *w. v.*, *RACE*, rush, 2690.
  ge-rǣsan, *w. v.*, *RACE*, rush, 2839.
ræst, *st. f.*, REST, resting-place, bed, 122, etc.
rǣswa, *w. m.*, leader, 60.
rand, see **rond**.
rāsian, *w. v.*, explore; *pp.* **rāsod**, 2283.
raðe, see **hraðe**.
rēafian, *w. v.*, **REAVE**, rob, plunder; *pret.* rēafode, rēafedon, 1212, 2985, etc. [*Cf. Goth.* ráubōn.]
  be-rēafian, *w. v.*, **BEREAVE**; *pp.*, *with dat.*, bereft, 2746, etc.
rēc, *st. m.*, **REEK**, smoke, 3155.
reccan, *w. v.*, *with gen.*, **RECK**, care; *pres. 3rd*, recceð, 434.
reccan, *w. v.*, relate, tell, 91; *dat. inf.* reccenne, 2093; *pret.* rehte, 2106, 2110.
reced, *st. neut.*, house, building, hall, 310, 412, etc.
regn-heard, *adj.*, [mighty-HARD] wondrous hard, 326 (see note).
regnian, **rēnian**, *w. v.*, prepare, adorn, 2168*; *pp.* geregnad, 777.
ren-weard, *st. m.*, 770 (see note).
rēoc, fierce, 122.
rēodan, *st. v.*, make *RED*, 1151*.
rēofan, *st. v.*
  be-rēofan, *st. v.*, *BEREAVE*, deprive; *pp.*, *acc. sg. f.*, berofene, 2457, 2931.
rēon, see **rōwan**.
reord, *st. f.*, speech, 2555. [*Cf. Goth.* razda.]
reordian, *w. v.*, speak, 2792*, 3025.
  ge-reordian, *w. v.*, prepare a feast; *pp.* gereorded, 1788.
rēot, 2457 (see note).
rēotan, *st. v.*, weep, 1376.
restan, *w. v.*, **REST**, cease, 1793, etc.
rēþe, *adj.*, fierce, furious, 122, etc.
rīce, *st. neut.*, realm, 861, etc.
rīce, *adj.*, RICH, powerful, mighty, 172, etc.
rīcone, *adv.*, quickly, 2983.
rīcsian, **rīxian**, *w. v.*, reign, rule, domineer, 144, 2211*.
rīdan, *st. v.*, RIDE, 234, 1883, etc.; *pret. pl.* riodan, 3169.
  ge-rīdan, *st. v.*, *with acc.*, RIDE over, 2898.
rīdend, *st. m.* (*pres. part.*), RIDER; *pl.* rīdend, 2457.
riht, *st. neut.*, RIGHT, 144, 1700, etc.; *acc.* on riht, 'rightly,' 1555; *dat.* æfter rihte, 'in accordance with right,' 1049, etc.; *acc. pl.* ofer ealde riht, 'contrary to the ancient law' (*sing.*, ealde *being the weak form*), 2330.
rihte, *adv.*, RIGHTly, 1695.
rīman, *w. v.*, count, number; *pp.* gerīmed, 59.
rinc, *st. m.*, man, wight, warrior, 399, etc.
riodan, see **rīdan**.
rīsan, *st. v.*
  ā-rīsan, *st. v.*, ARISE, 399, etc.
rīxian, see **rīcsian**.
rodor, *st. m.*, sky, heaven, 310, 1376, 1555, 1572.
rōf, *adj.*, strong, brave, renowned, 1793, 1925, 2538, 2666, 2690; *with gen.* 682, 2084.
rond, **rand**, *st. m.*, shield, 231, 656, 2538, 2673 (boss), etc.
  rand-wiga, *w. m.*, shield-warrior, 1298, etc.
rond-hæbbend, *st. m.* (*pres. part.*), [shield-HAVing] shield-warrior, 861.
rōwan, *st. v.*, ROW, swim; *pret. pl.* rēon = rēowon, 512, 539.
rūm, *st. m.*, ROOM, space, 2690.
rūm, *adj.*, ROOMY, spacious, ample, great, 2461; þurh rūmne sefan, 'gladly and freely and with all good will,' 278.
rūm-heort, *adj.*, [ROOM-HEART] great-hearted, 1799, 2110.
rūn, *st. f.*, *RUNE*, council, 172.
rūn-stæf, *st. m.*, *RUNE*-STAVE, runic letter, 1695.
rūn-wita, *w. m.*, [*RUNE*-] wise man, councillor, 1325.
ryht, see **riht**.
rȳman, *w. v.* [*from* rūm]:
  (1) make *ROOMY*, prepare; *pp.* gerȳmed, 492, 1975.

(2) make *ROOM*, clear a way; *pp.* ðā him gerȳmed wearð, þæt hīe wæl-stōwe wealdan mōston, 'when the way was made clear for them so that they were masters of the field,' 2983; *so* 3088.

ge-rȳman, *w. v.*, make ROOMY, prepare, 1086.

S

sacan, *st. v.*, strive, 439. [*Cf. Goth.* sakan, 'rebuke, dispute.']

on-sacan, *st. v.*:

(1) *with acc. pers. and gen. rei*, attack: *pres. subj.* þætte freoðu-webbe fēores onsæce...lēofne mannan, 'that a peaceweaver should assail the life of a beloved man,' 1942.

(2) *with acc. rei and dat. pers.*, refuse, dispute, 2954.

sacu, *st. f.*, strife, 1857, 2472; *acc.* sæce, 154. [*Cf.* sæcc.]

sadol, *st. m.*, SADDLE, 1038.

sadol-beorht, *adj.*, SADDLE-BRIGHT, 2175.

sǣ, *st. m. f.*, SEA, 318, etc.; *dat. pl.* sǣm, 858, etc. [*Cf. Goth.* sáiws.]

sǣ-bāt, *st. m.*, SEA-BOAT, 633, 895.

sæcc, *st. f.*, strife, fight, contest, 953, 1977, 2029, etc.; *gen. sg.* secce, 600. [*Cf.* sacu, *and Goth.* sakjō.]

sæce, see **sacu**.

sǣ-cyning, *st. m.*, SEA-KING, 2382.

sǣdan, see **secgan**.

sǣ-dēor, *st. neut.*, SEA-DEER, sea-monster, 1510.

sǣ-draca, *w. m.*, SEA-DRAKE, sea-dragon, 1426.

sǣgan, *w. v.*, cause to sink, lay low; *pp.* gesǣged, 884. [*Cf.* sīgan, sāg.]

sǣ-gēap, *adj.*, SEA-wide, spacious, 1896.

sǣ-genga, *w. m.*, SEA-GOer, ship, 1882, 1908.

sǣgon, see **sēon**.

sǣ-grund, *st. m.*, SEA-GROUND, bottom of the sea, 564.

sæl, *st. neut.*, hall, 307*, etc.; *acc.* sel, 167.

sǣl, *st. m. f.* [*Cf. Goth.* sēls.]

(1) time, season, occasion, opportunity, 489 (see note), 622, 1008, etc.; *acc. sg.* sēle, 1135 (see note to ll. 1134–6).

(2) happiness, joyance, bliss, 643, etc.; *dat. pl.* sālum, 607.

sǣ-lāc, *st. neut.*, SEA-booty, 1624; *acc. pl.* sǣ-lāc, 'sea-spoils,' 1652.

sǣ-lād, *st. f.*, SEA-path, sea-voyage, 1139, 1157.

sǣlan, *w. v.*, bind, tie, secure, 226, 1917; *pp.* gesǣled, 'bound, twisted, interwoven,' 2764. [*From* sāl, *cf. Goth.* sáiljan.]

on-sǣlan, *w. v.*, unbind; see note to l. 489.

sǣlan, *w. v.*, happen. [*From* sǣl.]

ge-sǣlan, *w. v.*, *often impers.*, befall, chance, happen, 574, 890, 1250.

sæld, *st. neut.*, hall, 1280.

sǣ-līðend, *st. m.* (*pres. part.*), SEA-farer; *nom. pl.* sǣ-līðend, 411, 1818, 2806; sǣ-līðende, 377.

sǣlðe, 3152 (see note to ll. 3150, etc.).

sǣ-mann, *st. m.*, SEA-MAN, 329, 2954.

sǣ-mēðe, *adj.*, SEA-weary, 325.

sǣmra, *compar. adj.* (*without pos.*), worse, weaker, 953, 2880.

sǣ-næss, *st. m.*, SEA-NESS, headland, 223, 571.

sǣne, *adj.*

sǣnra, *compar.*, slower, 1436.

sǣ-rinc, *st. m.*, SEA-warrior, 690.

sǣ-sīð, *st. m.*, SEA-journey, 1149.

sǣ-weall, *st. m.*, SEA-WALL, 1924.

sǣ-wong, *st. m.*, SEA-plain, shore, 1964.

sǣ-wudu, *st. m.*, SEA-WOOD, ship, 226.

sǣ-wylm, *st. m.*, [SEA-*WELL*ing] sea-surge, 393.

-saga, see **-secgan**.

sāl, *st. m.*, rope, 302*, 1906.

sālum, see **sǣl**.

samod, see **somod**.

sand, *st. neut.*, SAND, 213, etc.

sang, *st. m.*, SONG, 90, etc.

sār, *st. neut.*, SORE, pain, wound, 787, 975; *nom.* sīo sār, 2468 (*gender extraordinary; see note*); *acc.* sāre, 'harm,' 2295. [*Cf. Goth.* sáir.]

sār, *adj.*, SORE, 2058.

sāre, *adv.*, SOREly, 1251, 2222, 2311, 2746.

sārig, *adj.*, SORRY, sad, 2447.

sārig-ferð, *adj.*, [SORRY-heart] sore at heart, 2863.

sārig-mōd, *adj.*, [SORRY-MOOD] in mournful mood, 2942.

sār-līc, *adj.*, [SORE-LIKE] painful, sad, 842, 2109.

sāwl-berend, *st. m.* (*pres. part.*), [SOUL-BEARing] being endowed with a soul, 1004.

sāwol, *st. f.*, SOUL, 2820, etc.; *acc.*, *gen.* sāwle, 184, 2422, etc.; *gen.* sāwele, 1742. [*Cf. Goth.* sáiwala.]

sāwol-lēas, sāwul-lēas, SOULLESS, lifeless, 1406, 3033.
sāwul-drīor, *st. m. or neut.*, [SOULgore] life's blood, 2693.
scacan, *st. v.*, *pres. sg.* sceaceð, 2742, *pp.* scacen, sceacen, 1124, 2306, etc.: SHAKE, go, depart, hasten, 1136, 2254*, etc., 1802; *pret.* strǣla storm strengum gebǣded scōc ofer scild-weall, 'the storm of arrows, sent by the strings, flew over the shield-wall,' 3118.
scādan, *st. v.*
  ge-scādan, *st. v.*, decide; *pret.* gescēd, 1555.
scadu-helm, *st. m.*, [SHADE-HELM] shadow-covering, cover of night; *gen. pl.* scadu-helma gesceapu, 'shapes of the shadows,' 650.
scami(g)an, *w. v.*, be ASHAMED, 1026, 2850.
scaþa, see sceaþa.
sceacen, sceaceð, see scacan.
scead, *st. neut.*, *SHADE*: *acc. pl.* under sceadu bregdan, 'draw under the shades, *i.e.* kill,' 707: see also note to l. 1803. [*Cf. Goth.* skadus.]
scēaden-mǣl, *adj.*, curiously inlaid sword, 1939.
sceadu-genga, *w. m.*, SHADE-*GO*er, prowler by night, 703.
sceal, etc., see sculan.
scealc, *st. m.*, mar*SHAL*, retainer, 918, 939. [*Cf. Goth.* skalks.]
scearp, *adj.*, SHARP, 288.
scēat, *st. m.*, [*SHEET*] corner, region, quarter, 96; *gen. pl.* scēatta, 752. [*Cf. Goth.* skáuts, 'hem of a garment.']
sceatt, *st. m.*, money, 1686. [*Cf. Goth.* skatts.]
sceaþa, scaþa, *w. m.*, *SCATH*er, foe, warrior: *nom. pl.* scaþan, 1803, 1895; *gen. pl.* sceaþena, 4, sceaðona, 274.
scēawi(g)an, *w. v. with acc.*, [SHOW, SHEW] espy, see, view, observe, 840, 843, 1391, etc.; *pres. pl. subj.* scēawian, 3008; *pret. pl.* scēawedon, 132, etc.; *pp.* gescēawod, 3075, 3084.
-scēd, see -scādan.
sceft, *st. m.*, SHAFT, 3118, F. 8.
scel, see sculan.
scencan, *w. v.*, *SKINK*, pour out; *pret. sg.* scencte, 496.
scennum, *dat. pl.*, 1694 (see note).
-scēod, see -sceððan.
sceolde, see sculan.
-scēop, see -scyppan.
scēotan, *st. v.*, SHOOT, 1744.
  ge-scēotan, *st. v.*, *with acc.*, SHOOT *or* dart into, hurry to; *pret. sg.* hord eft gescēat, 2319.
  of-scēotan, *st. v.*, *with acc.*, SHOOT OFF, lay low, kill; *pret. sg.*, ofscēt, 2439.
scēotend, *st. m.* (*pres. part.*), SHOOTER, warrior; *pl.* 703, 1026* (see note), 1154.
scepen, see scyppan.
sceran, *st. v.*, SHEAR, cut, 1287.
  ge-sceran, *st. v.*, SHEAR, cut in two, 1526; *pret. sg.* gescer, 2973.
-scēt, see -scēotan.
sceððan, *st. and w. v.*, *usu. with dat.*, *SCATHE*, injure, 1514, 1524, 1887, etc.; *absolutely*, 243. [*Cf. Goth.* skaþjan.]
  ge-sceððan, *w. v.*, *with dat.*, *SCATHE*, injure, 1447, 1502, 1587. *Pret. sg.* sē ðe him sāre gescēod, 'who injured himself sorely,' 2222, 2777 (see note).
scild-, see scyld-.
scile, see sculan.
scīma, *w. m.*, brightness, gleam, 1803* (see note).
scīnan, scȳnan, *st. v.*, SHINE, 1517, etc., F. 6; *pret. pl.* scinon, 994, scionon, 303 (see note).
scinna, *w. m.*, apparition, 939.
scionon, see scīnan.
scip, *st. neut.*, SHIP, 302, etc.; *dat. pl.* scypon, 1154.
scip-here, *st. m.*, SHIP-army, naval force; *dat.* scip-herge, 243.
scīr, *adj.*, *SHEER*, bright, 322, 496, 979; *weak gen.* 1694.
scīr-ham, *adj.*, bright-coated, with shining mail, 1895.
scōd, see sceððan.
scolde, etc., see sculan.
scop, *st. m.*, [*SHAP*er] maker, bard, etc., 90, 496, 1066.
scōp, see scyppan.
scota, *w. m.*, *SHOOT*er, warrior. See note to l. 1026.
scrīfan, *st. v.*, [SHRIVE] prescribe, pass sentence, 979. [*From Lat.* scrībo.]
  for-scrīfan, *st. v.*, *with dat. pers.*, proscribe, 106.
  ge-scrīfan, *st. v.*, prescribe: *pret. sg.* swā him wyrd ne gescrāf hrēð æt hilde, 'in such wise that weird did not assign to him triumph in battle,' 2574.
scrīðan, *st. v.*, stride, stalk, glide, wander, move, 163, 650, 703, 2569.
scucca, *w. m.*, devil; *dat. pl.* 939.

scūfan, *st. v., with acc.*, SHOVE, launch, 215, 918; *pret. pl.* scufun, 3131. [*Cf. Goth.* -skiuban.]

be-scūfan, *st. v., with acc.*, shove, cast, 184.

wīd-scūfan, *st. v.*, [WIDE-SHOVE] scatter, 936 (see note).

sculan, *pret. pres. v., pres. sg. 1st, 3rd* sceal, 20, etc., scel, 455, etc., sceall, 1862, etc.; *pres. subj.* scyle, 1179, 2657, scile, 3176; *pret.* scolde, 10, etc., sceolde, 2341, etc., *2nd sg.* sceoldest, 2056; *pl.* scoldon, 41, etc., sceoldon, 2257: SHALL, must, have as a duty, be obliged, ought, *pret.* SHOULD, was to, etc., 230, etc.; *sometimes expressing mere futurity*, 384, etc. Hē gesēcean sceall hord on hrūsan, 'it is his to seek the hoard in the earth,' 2275. *With foll. inf. omitted*: unc sceal worn fela māþma gemǣnra [wesan], 1783; ūrum sceal sweord ond helm ...bām gemǣne, 'to us both shall one sword and helmet [be] in common,' 2659; sceal se hearda helm ...fǣtum befeallen, 2255; þonne ðū forð scyle, 1179; *so*, 2816.

scūr-heard, *adj.*, [SHOWER-HARD] 1033 (see note).

scyld, *st. m.*, SHIELD, 325, etc.

scild-weall, *st. m.*, SHIELD-WALL, 3118.

scyldan, *w. v.*, *SHIELD*: *pret.* nymðe mec God scylde, 'unless God had shielded me,' 1658.

scyld-freca, *w. m.*, SHIELD-warrior, 1033.

scyldig, *adj.*, guilty; *with dat.*, synnum scildig, 3071; *with gen.* 1683; ealdres scyldig, 'having forfeited his life,' 1338, 2061.

scyld-wiga, *w. m.*, SHIELD-warrior, 288.

scyle, see **sculan**.

scȳnan, see **scīnan**.

scyndan, *w. v.*, hasten, 918, 2570.

scȳne, *adj.*, SHEEN, beauteous, 3016. [*Cf. Goth.* skáuns, 'beautiful.']

scyn-scaþa, *w. m.*, spectral-foe, 707* (see note).

scyp, see **scip**.

scyppan, *st. v.*, SHAPE, create, make, 78; wæs sīo wrōht scepen heard wið Hūgas, 'the strife was made hard against the Hugas,' 2913. [*Cf. Goth.* -skapjan.]

ge-scyppan, *st. v.*, SHAPE, create, 97.

Scyppend, *st. m.* (*pres. part.*), SHAPER, Creator, 106.

scȳran, *w. v.*, bring to light, *hence* decide, 1939. [*Cf.* scīr.]

se, sēo, þæt, *demonst. adj.*, the, THAT. *Sing.*: *nom. m.* se; *f.* sēo, 66, etc.; sīo, 2098, etc.; *n.* þæt; *acc. m.* þone; *f.* þā; *n.* þæt; *gen. m. n.* þæs; *f.* þǣre; *dat. m. n.* þǣm, 52, etc., þām, 425, etc.; *instr. m. n.* þȳ; *f.* þǣre.

Pl.: *nom. acc., m. f. n.*, þā; *gen. m. f. n.* þāra; *dat. m. f. n.* þǣm, 370, etc., þām, 1855, etc. *Following its noun: acc. m.* þone, 2007, etc.; *gen. pl.* ðāra, 2734. *Alliterating, dat. m.* þǣm, *in the phrase* 'on þǣm dæge, þisses līfes' 197, 790, 806; *acc. f. sg.* þā, 736, 1675; *instr. neut.* þȳ, 1797; *gen. pl.* þāra, 2033. *Correl. with* sē *used as a relative pron.*: se...sē, 2865, 3071–3; sēo...sīo, 2258. *See also* þe. [*Cf. Goth.* sa, sō, þata.]

sē, *m.*, **sēo, sīo**, *f.*, **þæt**, *neut.*, *pron.*

I. *Demonst. pron.*, THAT, that one, he, etc.: *sing. nom. m.* sē, *f.* sēo, sio, *n.* þæt; *acc. m.* þone, *f.* þā, *n.* þæt; *gen. m. n.* þæs, *f.* þǣre; *dat. m. n.* þǣm, 183, etc., þām 1957, *f.* þǣre; *instrum. m. n.* þȳ, 87, etc., þē, 821, etc., þon, 504, etc. *Immediately followed by the rel. particle* þe (q. v.): *nom.* sē þe, 90, etc.; *acc.* þone þe, *dat.* þām þe; *gen. pl.* þāra þe, 98, etc., 1625 ('of those *things* which'). *With* þe *omitted:* þām = þām þe, 2199, 2779. *Correl. with* sē *used as a rel. pron.:* sē...sē, 2406–7.

Special usages:

(1) *gen. neut.* **þæs**, of that, of this, thereof, for that, for this, therefor, 7, etc. *Correl. with* þæt, *conj.*, 2026–8, etc. See also **þæs**, *adv.*

(2) *instr. neut.* **þȳ**, **þē**, by that, therefore, 1273, 2067. *Correl. with* þē, *conj.* (q. v.), 487, 1436, 2638. *Often with comparatives*, THE: 821, etc., 2880; nō þȳ ǣr, 'none the sooner,' 754, etc.

(3) *instr. neut.* **þon**, 2423 (see note); þon mā, '(the) more,' 504; æfter þon, 'after that,' 724; ǣr þon, 'ere,' 731; be þon, 'by that,' 1722; tō þon, þæt, 'until,' 2591, 2845; tō þon, 'to that degree, so,' 1876. *See also under* tō.

II. *Rel. pron.*, THAT, who, which, what; *m.* sē, 143, etc.; sē *for* sēo, 2421 (*see also* **þe**); *neut.* þæt = 'what,' 15 (but see note), 1466, 1748, *m. acc.* þone, 13, etc.;

f. acc. þā, 2022; *gen. neut.* Gode þancode...þæs se man gespræc, 'thanked God for what the man spake,' 1398; þæs ic wēne, 'according to what I expect, as I ween,' 272; *so*, 383; *dat. sing. m. and neut.* þǣm, þām, 137, etc., *exclusively* þām *in portion of poem written by second scribe*; *pl.* þā, 41, etc. See also **þæs**, *adv.*

þæs þe, see under **þæs**.

sealde, etc., see **sellan**.

sealma, *w. m.*, sleeping-place, couch, chamber, 2460.

sealo-brūn, *adj.*, SALLOW-BROWN, dark-brown, F. 37.

sealt, *adj.*, SALT, 1989.

searo, *st. neut.*
(1) skill, device, cunning, *dat. pl. adverbially*, searwum, 'cunningly, curiously,' 1038, 2764;
(2) [cunningly devised] armour, 249, 323, 329, etc., 1557 (see note);
(3) ambush, straits, 419 (but the meaning may be: 'when I did off my armour').

searo-bend, *st. m. f.*, cunning *BAND*, 2086.

searo-fāh, *adj.*, cunningly coloured, variegated, 1444.

searo-gimm, *st. m.*, cunning gem, jewel of artistic workmanship, 1157, 2749, 3102*.

searo-grim, *adj.*, [cunning-GRIM] cunningly fierce, *or* fierce in battle, 594.

searo-hæbbend, *st. m.* (*pres. part.*), [armour-HAVing] warrior, 237.

searo-net, *st. neut.*, [cunning- *or* armour-NET] coat of mail, 406.

searo-nīð, *st. m.*, armour-strife, hostility, 582, 3067; cunning-hatred, wile, plot, 1200, 2738.

searo-þonc, *st. m.*, cunning *THOUGHt*, 775.

searo-wundor, *st. neut.*, [cunning-WONDER] rare wonder, 920.

seax, *st. neut.*, hip-sword, dagger, 1545.

sēcan, **sēcean**, *w. v.*, 664, 187, etc.; *dat. inf.* tō sēceanne, 2562; *pres. pl.* (*fut.*) sēceað, 3001; *pret. pl.* sōhton, 339, sōhtan, 2380: SEEK *in its various meanings;* visit, go to, strive after, 139*, 208, etc., 2380 (of a friendly visit). Sāwle sēcan, 'kill,' 801; *so*, sēcean sāwle hord, 2422. *Intrans.* 2293, 3001 (of a hostile attack); þonne his myne sōhte, 'than his wish (hope) SOUGHT,' 2572. [*Cf. Goth.* sōkjan.]

ge-sēc(e)an, *w. v.*, 684, 1004* (see note), etc.; *dat. inf.* tō gesēcanne, 1922; *pret. pl.* gesōhton, 2926, gesōhtan, 2204: SEEK, *in its various meanings as above*, 463, etc.; *often of hostile attack*, 2515, etc.

ofer-sēc(e)an, *w. v.*, OVERtax, test too severely; *pret. sg.* sē ðe mēca gehwane...swenge ofersōhte, 'which with its swing overtaxed every sword,' 2686.

secc, see **sæcc**.

secg, *st. m.*, man, etc., 208, 213, etc.; *of Grendel's mother*, 1379.

secg, *st. f.*, sword, 684.

secgan, *w. v.*, 51, etc.; SAY, speak, *dat. inf.* tō secganne, 473, 1724; *pret. sg.* sægde, 90, etc., sǣde, F. 46; *pret. pl.* sægdon, 377, etc., sǣdan, 1945; *pp.* gesægd, gesǣd, 'published, made manifest,' 141, 1696. *Imperf. with partitive gen.* secggende wæs lāðra spella, 'was telling dire tales,' 3028.

ā-secgan, *w. v.*, SAY out, declare, 344.

ge-secgan, *w. v.*, SAY, 2157; *imperat. sg.* gesaga, 388.

sefa, *w. m.*, mind, soul, heart, 49, etc.

sēft, *compar. adv.* (*of* sōfte), *SOFTer*, more easily, 2749.

-sēgan, see **-sēon**.

segen, see **segn**.

segl, *st. neut.*, SAIL, 1906.

segl-rād, *st. f.*, SAIL-ROAD, sea, 1429.

segn, *st. m. neut.*, banner, 1204; *acc.* segn, 2767, 2776, segen, 47, 1021, 2958 (see note to ll. 2957–9). [*From* L. signum, whence 'sign.']

-sēgon, see **-sēon**.

-seh, see **-sēon**.

sel, see **sæl**.

sēl, *compar. adv.* (*no positive*, cf. sēlra), better, 1012, 2277, 2530, 2687, F. 40, 41.

seldan, *adv.*, SELDOM, 2029 (see note).

seld-guma, *w. m.*, hall-man: *nom. sg.*, 249 (see note).

sele, *st. m.*, hall, 81, etc.; *of the dragon's lair*, 3128.

sēle, see **sǣl**.

sele-drēam, *st. m.*, hall-joy, 2252 (see note).

sele-ful, *st. neut.*, hall-beaker, hall-cup, 619.

sele-gyst, *st. m.*, hall-GUEST, 1545.

sele-rǣdend, *st. m.* (*pres. part.*), [hall-counsellor] hall-ruler, 51*, 1346.

sele-rest, *st. f.*, hall-REST, bed in a hall, 690.

sēlest, etc., see under **sēlra.**

sele-þegn, *st. m.*, hall-THANE, chamberlain, 1794.

sele-weard, *st. m.*, [hall-WARD] guardian of a hall, 667.

self, *reflex. adj.; nom. sg.* self, 594, 920, etc., sylf, 1964; *weak* selfa, 29, 1924, etc., seolfa, 3067, sylfa, 505, etc.; *acc. sg. m.* selfne, 961, etc., sylfne, 1977, 2875; *gen. sg. m.* selfes, 700, etc., sylfes, 2013, etc.; *f.* selfre, 1115; *nom. pl.* selfe, 419, sylfe, 1996; *gen. pl.* sylfra, 2040: SELF, etc. *Often absolutely* 419, 2222, etc.; on mīnne sylfes dōm, 2147. *Sometimes agreeing with the nom. instead of with the oblique case next to which it stands:* þū þē (dat.) self, 953; þǣm þe him selfa dēah, 1839.

sēlla, see **sēlra.**

sellan, syllan, *w. v.*, [SELL] give, give up, 72, etc. [*Cf. Goth.* saljan, 'to bring an offering.']

ge-sellan, *w. v.*, [SELL] give, 615, etc.

sel-līc, syl-līc (=seld-līc), *adj.*, rare, strange, 2086, 2109; *acc. pl.* sellice, 1426. [*Cf. Goth.* silda-leiks.]

syl-līcra, *compar.*, stranger, 3038.

sēlra, *compar. adj.* [no positive, but *cf. Goth.* sēls], better, 860, etc., 2198 (see note), *nom. sg. m.* sēlla, 2890. *Absolutely*, þæt sēlre, 1759.

sēlest, *superl.*, best, 146, etc. *Weak form*, reced sēlesta, 412; *and often after the def. art.* se, 1406, etc.

semninga, *adv.*, forthwith, presently, 644 (see note), 1640, 1767.

sendan, *w. v.*, SEND, 13, 471, 1842. [*Cf. Goth.* sandjan.]

for-sendan, *w. v.*, SEND away, 904.

on-sendan, *w. v.*, SEND away, send off, 382, 452, 1483; *with* forð, 45, 2266.

sendan, *w. v.*, 600 (see note).

sēo, see **se, sē.**

sēoc, *adj.*, SICK, 'sick unto death,' 1603, 2740, 2904. [*Cf. Goth.* siuks.]

seofon, SEVEN, 517; *acc.* seofan, 2195; *inflected* syfone, 3122. [*Cf. Goth.* sibun.]

seolfa, see **self.**

seomian, siomian, *w. v.*:
(1) rest, ride, lie, stand, 302, 2767. seomade ond syrede, 'he held himself in ambush, and entrapped them,' 161.

sēon, *st. v.*, SEE, look, 387, etc.; *inf.* þǣr mæg...sēon, 'there it is possible to see, there may one see,' 1365; *pret. pl.*, sǣgon, 1422. [*Cf. Goth.* saíhwan.]

ge-sēon, *st. v.*, SEE, 229, etc.; see one another, 1875; *pret. pl.* gesāwon, 221, etc., gesēgon, 3128, gesēgan, 3038; *subj. pret. pl.* gesāwon, 1605.

geond-sēon, *st. v.*, SEE throughout, see over; *pret. sg.* geondseh, 3087.

ofer-sēon, *st. v.*, OVERSEE, survey, look on, 419.

on-sēon, *st. v.*, look ON, look at, 1650 (but see note).

seonu, *st. f.*, SINEW; *nom. pl.* seonowe, 817.

sēoðan, *st. v.*, *with acc.*, SEETHE, brood over; *pret. sg.* mǣl-ceare, mōd-ceare...sēað, 190 (see note to l. 189), 1993.

seoððan, see **siððan.**

seowian, *w. v.*, SEW, link; *pp.* seowed (of a byrny), 406.

sess, *st. m.*, *SEAT*, 2717, 2756.

sētan, see **sittan.**

setl, *st. neut.*, SETTLE, seat, 1232, 1289, etc.

settan, *w. v.*, SET, set down, 325, 1242; *pp.* geseted, 1696. [*Cf. Goth.* satjan.]

ā-settan, *w. v.*, SET, set up, 47; *pp.* āseted, 667.

be-settan, *w. v.*, BESET, set about, 1453.

ge-settan, *w. v.*:
(1) SET, 94.
(2) set at rest, 2029.

sib(b), *st. f.*, peace, kinship, friendship, 949, etc.; *uninflected acc.* sibb, 154, 2600 (see note). [*Cf. Goth.* sibja.]

sib-æðeling, *st. m.*, kindred-ATHELING, 2708.

sibbe-gedriht, *st. f.*, kindred-band, band of kindred-warriors, 387 (see note), 729.

sīd, *adj.*, broad, ample, great, 149, 1291, 1726 (see note), etc.; *weak forms* 1733, 2199, 2347.

sīde, *adv.*, widely, 1223.

sīd-fæðme, *adj.*, [wide-FATHOMED] broad-bosomed, 1917.

sīd-fæðmed, *adj.* (*pp.*), [wide-FATHOMED] broad-bosomed, 302.

sīd-rand, *st. m.*, broad shield, 1289.

sie, see **wesan.**

siex-benn, *st. f.*, hipknife-wound, 2904. [*From* seax.]

sig, see **wesan**.
sīgan, *st. v.*, sink, march down, 307, 1251.
  ge-sīgan, *st. v.*, sink, fall, 2659.
sige-beorn, *st. m.*, victorious warrior, F. 40.
sige-drihten, *st. m.*, victory-lord, victorious prince, 391.
sige-ēadig, *adj.*, rich in victories, victorious, 1557.
sige-folc, *st. neut.*, victory-FOLK, victorious people, 644.
sige-hrēð, *st. m. neut.*, victory-fame, presage of victory, confidence *or* exultation in victory, 490.
sige-hrēðig, *adj.*, victory exultant, exulting in victory, 94, 1597, 2756.
sige-hwīl, *st. f.*, victory-WHILE, 2710 (see note).
sigel, *st. neut.*, sun, 1966.
sige-lēas, *adj.*, victory-LESS, of defeat, 787.
sige-rōf, *adj.*, victory-famed, victorious, 619.
sige-þēod, *st. f.*, victory-nation, victorious people, 2204.
sige-wǣpen, *st. neut.*, victory-WEAPON, 804.
sigle, *st. neut.*, sun-shaped ornament, jewel, 1157, 1200; *acc. pl.* siglu, 3163.
sigor, *st. m. or neut.*, victory, 1021, 2875, 3055.
sigor-ēadig, *adj.*, rich in victories, victorious, 1311, 2352.
sīn, *poss. adj.*, his, her, 1236, etc.
sinc, *st. neut.*, treasure, jewelry, gold, silver, prize, 81, etc.
sinc-fæt, *st. neut.*, treasure-VAT, costly vessel, casket, 1200 (but see note), 2231, 2300; *acc. pl.* sinc-fato sealde, 'passed the jewelled cup,' 622.
sinc-fāg, *adj.*, treasure-variegated, bedecked with treasure; *weak acc. sg. neut.* sinc-fāge, 167.
sinc-gestrēon, *st. neut.*, treasure-possession, costly treasure, 1092, 1226.
sinc-gifa, **sinc-gyfa**, *w. m.*, treasure-GIVer, 1012, 1342 (see note), 2311.
sinc-māðþum, *st. m.*, treasure-jewel (sword), 2193.
sinc-þego, *st. f.*, treasure-taking, receiving of treasure, 2884.
sin-frēa, *st. m.*, great lord, 1934.
sin-gāl, *adj.*, continuous, 154.
sin-gāla, *adv.*, continually, 190.
sin-gāles, **syn-gāles**, *adv.*, continually, always, 1135, 1777.
singan, *st. v.*, *pret.* song, sang: SING, sound, 496, 1423, F. 6; *pret. sg.* hring-īren scīr song in searwum, 'the bright iron rings rang in the armour,' 323.
  ā-singan, *st. v.*, SING, sing out, 1159.
sin-here, *st. m.*, [continuous army] army drawn out, very strong, immense; *dat.* sin-herge, 2936.
sin-niht, *st. f.*, long NIGHT; sin-nihte, 'during the long nights,' 161.
sin-snǣd, see **syn-snǣd**.
sint, see **wesan**.
sīo, see **se**, **sē**.
sioloð, *st.*, still water, 2367 (see note).
siomian, see **seomian**.
sittan, *st. v.*; *pret. pl.* sǣton, 1164, sētan, 1602*; *pp.* geseten, 2104: SIT, 130, etc.; *inf.* ēodon sittan, 'went and sat,' 493.
  be-sittan, *st. v.*, [SIT BY] besiege, 2936.
  for-sittan, *st. v.*, fail; *pres. sg. 3rd*, 1767 (see note to ll. 1766–7).
  ge-sittan, *st. v.*:
  (1) *intrans.* SIT, sit together, 171, 749 (see note), etc.
  (2) *trans.* sit down in, 633.
  ofer-sittan, *st. v.*, *with acc.*, abstain from, refrain from, 684, 2528.
  of-sittan, *st. v.*, *with acc.*, SIT upon, 1545.
  on-sittan, *st. v.*, *with acc.*, dread, 597.
  ymb-sittan, *st. v.*, *with acc.*, SIT about, sit round, 564.
sīð, *st. m.*: [*Cf. Goth.* sinþs.]
  (1) way, journey, adventure, 765, etc., 872 (exploit), 908 (way of life *or* exile—see note), 1971 (return), 2586 (course), 3089 (passage), etc.
  (2) time, repetition, 716, 1579, 2049, etc.
sīð, *compar. adv.* (*pos.* sīð); ǣr ond sīð, 'earlier and later,' 2500.
sīðest, **sīðast**, *superl. adj.* [no pos., except the adv., but *cf. Goth.* seiþus, 'late'], latest, last, 2710*, *absolutely*, æt sīðestan, 'at latest, at the last,' 3013.
sīð-fæt, *st. m.*, expedition, 202; *dat.* sīð-fate, 2639.
sīð-from, *adj.*, [journey-forward] ready for a journey, 1813.
sīðian, *w. v.*, journey, 720, 808, 2119.
  for-sīðian, *w. v.*, [journey amiss] perish, 1550.

siððan, **syððan**, **seoððan**, *adv.*, [SITHENCE] SINCE, after, afterwards, 142, etc. For 1106, see note: ǣr ne siððan, 'before nor since,' 718. *Correl. with* syððan, *conj.*, 2201–7.
siððan, syððan, **seoððan**, *conj.*, [SITHENCE] SINCE, after, when, 106, etc. *With pret.=pluperf.* 1978, etc. *With pret. and pluperf.* syððan mergen cōm, ond wē tō symble geseted hæfdon, 2103–4.
sixtig, *with gen.*, SIXTY, F. 40.
slǣp, *st. m.*, SLEEP, 1251, 1742.
slǣpan, *st. v.*, SLEEP; *pres. part.*, *acc. sg. m.* slǣpendne, 741, *uninflected*, 2218; *acc. pl.* 1581.
sleac, *adj.*, SLACK, 2187.
slēan, *st. v.*, *pret. sg.* slōh, slōg. [*Cf. Goth.* slahan.]
I. *intrans.* strike, 681, 1565, 2678.
II. *trans.*:
(1) strike, 2699.
(2) SLAY, 108, etc.
ge-slēan, *st. v.*, *with acc.*: gain, achieve by fighting, 459 (see note); *pret. pl.* hīe ðā mǣrða geslōgon, 'they gained glory by fighting,' 2996.
of-slēan, *st. v.*, SLAY, 574, 1665, 1689, 3060.
slītan, *st. v.*, *SLIT*, tear to pieces, 741.
slīðe, *adj.*, savage, hurtful, dangerous, 184, 2398.
slīðen, *adj.*, dire, deadly, 1147.
smið, *st. m.*, SMITH, 406; *nom.* wǣpna smið, 'weapon-smith,' 1452.
smiðian, *w. v.*
be-smiðian, *w. v.*, make firm by SMITH's work, 775.
snell, *adj.*, brisk, prompt, keen, bold; *weak nom. sg. m.* snella, 2971.
snel-līc, *adj.*, brisk, prompt, keen, bold, 690.
snotor, **snottor**, *adj.*, wise, prudent, 190, etc.; *pl.* snotere, 202, snottre, 1591; *weak nom. sg. m.* snottra, 1313, etc., snotra, 2156, etc.; *absolutely*, 1786, etc. [*Cf. Goth.* snutrs.]
snotor-līce, *adv.*
snotor-līcor, *compar.*, more wisely, more prudently, 1842.
snūde, *adv.*, quickly, 904, etc. [*Cf. Goth.* sniwan, 'hasten.']
snyrian, *w. v.*, hasten, 402.
snyttru, *st. f.*, wisdom, prudence, 942, 1706, 1726. [*Cf.* snotor.]
snyttrum, *dat. pl. used adverbially*, wisely, 872.
snyððan, *w. v.*
be-snyððan, *w. v.*, deprive, 2924.
sōcn, *st. f.*, persecution; *dat.* þǣre sōcne, 'from that persecution,' 1777. [*Cf. Goth.* sōkns, 'search, enquiry.']
somod, **samod**, *adv.*, together, 1211, 2196, etc.; *with* ætgædere, 329, 387, etc.
somod, **samod**, *prep.*, *with dat.*; somod (samod) ǣr-dæge, 'at dawn,' 1311, 2942.
sōna, *adv.*, SOON, 121, etc.
song, see **singan**.
sorg-, see **sorh-**.
sorgian, *w. v.*, SORROW, care, 451, 1384.
sorh, *st. f.*, SORROW, 473, etc.; *obl. sg.* sorge, 119, 2004, etc.; *dat.* sorhge, 2468.
sorh-cearig, **sorg-cearig**, *adj.*, [SORROW-CAREful] sorrowful, heartbroken, 2455, 3152.
sorh-ful(l), *adj.*, SORROWFUL, 512, 1278, 1429, 2119.
sorh-lēas, *adj.*, SORROWLESS, free from sorrow, 1672.
sorh-lēoð, *st. neut.*, SORROW-lay, lamentation, 2460.
sorh-wylm, *st. m.*, [SORROW-*WELL*ing] surge of sorrow *or* care, 904, 1993.
sōð, *st. neut.*, SOOTH, truth, 532, etc.; *dat.* tō sōðe, 'for sooth,' 51, etc.; *inst.* sōðe, *used adverbially*, 'truly, with truth,' 524, 871.
sōð, *adj.*, [SOOTH] true, 1611, 2109.
Sōð-cyning, *st. m.*, [SOOTH-KING] God, 3055.
sōð-fæst, *adj.*, SOOTHFAST, just, 2820.
sōð-līce, *adv.*, [SOOTHLY] truly, 141, 273, 2899.
specan, SPEAK, 2864, see **sprecan**.
spēd, *st. f.*, SPEED, success; *acc.* on spēd, 'with good speed, successfully,' 873.
spel(l), *st. neut.*, SPELL, story, tale, tidings, 2109, 2898, 3029; *acc. pl.* spel gerāde, 'skilful tales,' 873.
spīwan, *st. v.*, SPEW; *inf.* glēdum spīwan, 'to vomit forth gleeds,' 2312.
sponnan, *st. v.*
on-sponnan, *st. v.*, UNSPAN, loosen; *pret.* onspēon, 2723.
spōwan, *st. v.*, *impers.*, *with dat. pers.*, speed, succeed; *pret. sg.*

him wiht ne spēow, 'he had no success,' 2854*; hū him æt ǣte spēow, 'how he sped at the eating,' 3026.

sprǣc, *st. f.*, SPEECH, 1104.

sprecan, specan, *st. v.*, SPEAK, say, 341, 531, etc.; *imperat. sing.*, spræc, 1171; *with foll. clause*, gomele ymb gōdne on geador sprǣcon, þæt hig..., 'old men spake together about the hero, [saying] that they...,' 1595.

ge-sprecan, *st. v.*, SPEAK, 675, 1398, etc.

springan, *st. v.*, *pret.* sprong, sprang; SPRING, 18 (spread), 1588 (gape), 2582 (shoot), 2966 (spurt).

æt-springan, *st. v.*, SPRING forth; *pret. sg.* ætspranc, 1121.

ge-springan, *st. v.*, *pret.* gesprong, gesprang: SPRING forth, arise, 884, 1667.

on-springan, *st. v.*, SPRING apart, 817.

stǣl, *st. m.*, place, stead, 1479. [Sievers$_3$ § 201, N. 2.]

stǣlan, *w. v.*: to impute to, avenge upon, 2485 (see note); feor hafað fǣhðe gestǣled, 'she has gone far in avenging the feud,' 1340.

stān, *st. m.*, STONE, rock, 887, etc. [*Cf. Goth.* stáins.]

stān-beorh, *st. m.*, STONE-BARROW, barrow *or* cave of rock, 2213.

stān-boga, *w. m.*, [STONE-BOW] stone-arch, arch of rock; *acc. sg.* 2545, 2718 (see note to l. 2719).

stān-clif, *st. neut.*, STONE-CLIFF, cliff of rock; *acc. pl.* stān-cleofu, 2540.

standan, see **stondan**.

stān-fāh, *adj.*, [STONE-variegated] paved or inlaid with stones, 320.

stān-hlið, *st. neut.*, STONE-slope, rocky slope; *acc. pl.* stān-hliðo, 1409.

stapol, *st. m.*, [STAPLE]:
(1) column; *dat. pl.* ðā stānbogan stapulum fæste, 'the stone-arches firm on columns,' 2718.
(2) step, 926 (see note).

starian, *w. v.*, *pres. sg.* 1*st* starige, starie, 3*rd* starað, *pret.* starede, staredon: STARE, gaze, 996, 1485, etc.

stēap, *adj.*, STEEP, towering, tall, 222, etc.

stearc-heort, *adj.*, [STARK-HEART] stout-hearted, 2288, 2552.

stede, *st. m.*, STEAD, place; *gen. pl.* wæs steda nægla gehwylc stȳle gelīcost, 'each of the places of the nails was most like to steel,' 985 (see note).

stefn, *st. m.*, STEM (of a ship), 212.

stefn, *st. m.*, time, repetition; *dat. sg.* nīwan (nīowan) stefne, 'anew,' 1789, 2594.

stefn, *st. f.*, voice, 2552.

stellan, *w. v.*

on-stellan, *w. v.*, institute, set on foot, 2407.

stēpan, *w. v.*, exalt, 1717. [*From* stēap.]

ge-stēpan, *w. v.*, exalt; *pret. sg.* folce gestēpte...sunu Ōhteres, 'he advanced the son of Ohthere with an army,' 2393.

steppan, *st. v.*, STEP, march; *pret.* stōp, 761, 1401.

æt-steppan, *st. v.*, STEP forward; *pret.* forð nēar æstōp, 745.

ge-steppan, *st. v.*, STEP; *pret.* =*pluperf.* gestōp, 2289.

stīg, *st. f.*, path, 320, 2213; *acc. pl.* stīge, 1409.

stīgan, *st. v.*, ['to STY'—Spenser] go, ascend, descend, 212, 225, 676; *pret.* þā hē tō holme stāg, 'when he went down to the sea (to swim),' 2362*.

ā-stīgan, *st. v.*, ascend, arise, 1373; *pret.* āstāg, 782, āstāh, 1160, 3144; gūð-rinc āstāh, 1118 (see note).

ge-stīgan, *st. v.*, [STY] go; *pret.* þā ic on holm gestāh, 'when I went onto the sea (into the ship),' 632.

stille, *adj.*, STILL, 2830; *adv.*, 301.

stincan, *st. v.*, [STINK] sniff, snuff; *pret.* stonc ðā æfter stāne, 'he sniffed the scent along the rock,' 2288. [Yet this may very possibly be a distinct word **stincan**, 'to circle round,' cognate with *Goth.* stigquan and *Icel.* støkkva.]

stīð, *adj.*, stout, 1533, 985* (see note).

stīð-mōd, *adj.*, stout of mood, 2566.

stondan, standan, *st. v.*, STAND, 32, etc.; 726 (come), 783 (arise), 1037 (lie), etc.; *pret. pl.* stōdon, 328, stōdan, 3047: līxte se lēoma, lēoht inne stōd, 'the beam shone forth, light filled the place,' 1570 (see note); stōd eldum onandan, 'shone forth for a trouble to men,' 2313.

ā-stondan, *st. v.*, STAND, stand up, 759, 1556, 2092.

æt-stondan, *st. v.*, STAND (in), strike into, 891.

for-stondan, for-standan, *st. v.*,

withSTAND, avert, defend, 1549; *construed either with acc. of thing averted:* him wyrd forstōde, 'averted fate from them,' 1056; ingang forstōd, 'prevented entry,' 1549; *or acc. of person or thing defended:* hēaðolīðendum hord forstandan, 'defend his hoard against the ocean-farers,' 2955.

ge-stondan, *st. v.*, STAND, take up one's stand, 358, 404, 2566, 2597.

stōp, see **steppan**.

storm, *st. m.*, STORM, 1131, 3117.

stōw, *st. f.*, place, 1006, 1372, 1378.

strǣl, *st. m. f.*, arrow, shaft, 1746, 3117.

strǣt, *st. f.*, STREET, road, 320, 916, 1634. [*From Lat.* strāta.]

strang, see **strong**.

strēam, *st. m.*, STREAM, flood, 212, 1261, 2545.

strēgan, *w. v.*, *STREW*; *pp.* strēd, 2436. [*Cf. Goth.* stráujan.]

streng, *st. m.*, STRING, 3117.

strengel, *st. m.*, *STRONG* chief, 3115.

strengest, see **strong**.

strengo, *st. f.*, STRENGth; *acc. dat.* strenge, 1270, 1533, *dat.* strengo, 2540.

strong, **strang**, *adj.*, STRONG, 133, 2684; *with gen.* mægenes strang, 'strong in might,' 1844.

strengest, *superl.*, STRONGEST, 1543; *with gen. or dat.* mægenes, mægene, strengest, 196, 789.

strūdan, *st. v.*, spoil, plunder; *subj. pret.* strude, 3073*, 3126.

strȳnan, *w. v.* [*From* strēon.]

ge-strȳnan, *w. v.*, obtain, acquire, 2798.

stund, *st. f.*, time, hour; *dat. pl. adverbially*, stundum, 'from time to time,' 1423.

stȳle, *st. neut.*, STEEL; *dat.* 985.

stȳl-ecg, *adj.*, STEEL-EDGED, 1533.

stȳman, *w. v.*

be-stȳman, *w. v.*, wet, 486.

stȳran, *w. v.*, STEER, guide, restrain, F. 19*. [*Cf. Goth.* stiurjan, 'establish.']

styrian, *w. v.*, STIR, disturb, 1374, 2840; handle, treat, 872 (see note).

styrman, *w. v.*, *STORM*, 2552.

suhter-gefæderan, *w. m. pl.*, uncle and nephew, 1164.

sum, *adj.*, SOME, one, a certain, 2156. *Although* sum *always has the inflections of an adj.* (see l. 1432), *it is more often used substantively, or as an indef. pron.*, 400, 1251, 1432, etc.; *neut.* ne sceal þǣr dyrne sum wesan, 'there shall be naught secret,' 271. *Often with partitive gen.* 675, 713, 1499, etc.; *esp. with gen. of numerals and adjs. of quantity:* fīftēna sum, 'one of fifteen, *i.e.* with fourteen others,' 207; *so* 3123, 1412, 2091; sumne fēara, 'one of a few, *i.e.* some few,' 3061 (see note). *In a few cases* sum *appears to have a certain demonst. force*, 248, 314, 1312, 2279.

sund, *st. neut.*, *SWIM*ming, 507, 517, 1436, 1618; SOUND, channel, sea, 213, etc.

sund-gebland, *st. neut.*, [SOUND-*BLEND*], tumult of the waves, 1450.

sund-nytt, *st. f.*, [*SWIM*ming-use]; *acc.* sund-nytte drēah, 'achieved a feat of swimming,' 2360.

sundor-nytt, *st. f.*, special service, 667.

sundur, *adv.*, ASUNDER, 2422.

sund-wudu, *st. m.*, [SOUND-WOOD] ship, 208, 1906.

sunne, *w. f.*, SUN, 94, 606, 648.

sunu, *st. m.*, SON, 268, etc.; *dat.* suna, 1226, etc., sunu, 344.

sūð, *adv.*, SOUTH, southwards, 858.

sūðan, *adv.*, from the SOUTH, 606, 1966.

swā:

I. *adv. of manner and degree*, so, thus, 20, etc.: leng swā wel, 'the longer the better,' 1854.

II. *conjunctive adv.*, as *in its various meanings*, 29, 1667 (so soon as), 2184 (since), etc.; *in elliptical sentences*, 2622; eft swā ǣr, 642; *correl. with* swā I., 594, 1092–3, etc.: swā mē Higelāc sīe...mōdes blīðe, 'so may H. be gracious to me,' 435; swā hyra nān ne fēol, 'in such wise that none of them fell,' F. 43.

III. = *rel. pron.;* wlite-beorhtne wang, swā wæter bebūgeð, 'the beauteous-bright plain, which water encompasses,' 93.

IV. *conj.*, so that, 1508, 2006.

swā þēah, **swā ðēh**, however, 972, 2967, etc.; *redundant after* hwæðre, 2442.

swā hwæðere...swā, whichsoever, 686–7.

swā hwylc...swā, *with gen.*, WHICHSOEVER, 943, 3057.

swǣlan, *w. v.* [SWEAL]

be-swǣlan, *w. v.*, scorch, 3041.

swǣs, *adj.*, dear, own dear, 29, 520, etc.
swǣslīce, *adv.*, gently, 3089.
swæþer, *pron.*, whichever of two [=swā-hwæþer], F. 29.
swān, *st. m.*, young warrior, F. 41*. [*Cf.* SWAIN *from O.N.* sveinn.]
swancor, *adj.*, [SWANK] slender, 2175.
swan-rād, *st. f.*, SWAN-ROAD, sea, 200.
swāpan, *st. v.* [SWOOP]
  for-swāpan, *st. v.*, *SWEEP* away, sweep off, 477, 2814*.
swarian, *w. v.*
  ond-swarian, **and-swarian**, *w. v.*, ANSWER, 258, 340.
swāt, *st. m.*, [*SWEAT*] blood, 1286, 2693, 2966.
swāt-fāh, *adj.*, blood-stained, 1111.
swātig, *adj.*, bloody, 1569.
swāt-swaðu, *st. f.*, [*SWEAT*-SWATH] blood-track, 2946.
swaðrian, *w. v.*, subside; *pret. pl.* swaðredon, 570. See also **sweðrian.**
swaðu, [SWATH] *st. f.*, track, 2098; *acc.* him sīo swīðre swaðe weardade hand, 'his right hand showed where he had been,' 2098.
swaðul, *st. m. or neut.*, flame, 782 (see note).
sweart, *adj.*, SWART, black, dark, 167, 3145, F. 37. [*Cf. Goth.* swarts.]
swebban, *w. v.*, send to sleep, kill, 679; *pres. sg. 3rd*, swefeð, 600.
  ā-swebban, *w. v.*, put to sleep, kill; *pret. part. pl.* āswefede, 567.
swefan, *st. v.*, sleep, sleep the sleep of death, 119, 1008, etc.; *pret. pl.* swǣfon, 703, swǣfun, 1280.
-swefede, see **-swebban.**
swefeð, see **swebban.**
swēg, *st. m.*, sound, noise, 89, 644, etc.
swegel, *st. neut.*, sky, 860, 1078, etc.
swegel, *adj.*, bright, clear, 2749.
swegl-wered, *adj.*, ether-clad, radiant, 606.
swelan, *st. v.*, burn, 2713.
swelgan, *st. v.*, *SWALLOW*; *pret.*, *with dat.*, swealh, 743, swealg, 3155*; *pret. subj.*, *absolutely*, swulge, 782.
  for-swelgan, *st. v.*, *SWALLOW* up, 1122, 2080.
swellan, *st. v.*, SWELL, 2713.
sweltan, *st. v.*, [*SWELTER*] die, 1617, etc.; *with cognate dat.* morðre, -dēaðe, 892, 2782, 3037.
swencan, *w. v.*, molest, oppress, 1510*. [*Cf.* swincan.]
  ge-swencan, *st. v.*, strike, bring low, 2438.
  ge-swenced, *pp.* (*of* swencan *or* geswencan), made to toil, harassed, harried, pressed, 975, 1368.
sweng, *st. m.*, *SWING*, stroke, 1520 (see note), etc.
sweofot, *st. m. or neut.*, sleep, 1581, 2295.
sweoloð, *st. m. or neut.*, flame, 1115 (see note to l. 782).
-swēop, see **-swāpan.**
sweorcan, *st. v.*, grow dark, 1737.
  for-sw(e)orcan, *st. v.*, grow dim, 1767 (see note to ll. 1766–7).
  ge-sweorcan, *st. v.*, lour, 1789.
sweord, **swurd**, **swyrd**, **sword**, *st. neut.*, SWORD, 437, etc.; *pl.* sweord, 2638, swyrd, 3048, sword, F. 17.
sweord-bealo, *st. neut.*, SWORD-BALE, death by the sword, 1147.
sweord-freca, *w. m.*, SWORD-warrior, 1468.
swurd-lēoma, *w. m.*, SWORD-light, F. 37.
  swyrd-gifu, *st. f.*, SWORD-GIVING, 2884.
sweotol, *adj.*, clear, 833; *nom.* swutol, 90; *weak dat.* sweotolan, 141; wearð sweotol, 'became visible,' 817.
swerian, *st. v.*, SWEAR, 472, 2738.
  for-swerian, *st. v.*, *with dat.*, FORSWEAR, lay a spell upon, 804 (see note).
swēte, *adj.* SWEET, F. 41.
swēðrian, *w. v.*, wane, lessen, 901, 2702.
swīcan, *st. v.*, fail, disappear, escape, 966, 1460.
  ge-swīcan, *st. v.*, weaken, fail, 1524, 2584, 2681.
swīfan, *st. v.*
  on-swīfan, *st. v.*, swing forward, raise, 2559.
swift, *adj.*, SWIFT; *weak*, 2264.
swīge, *adj.*, silent.
  swīgra, *compar.*, more silent, 980.
swīgian, *w. v.*, be silent; *pret. sg.* swīgode, 2897, *pl.* swīgedon, 1699.
swilce, see **swylce.**
swimman, **swymman**, *st. v.*, SWIM, 1624.
  ofer-swimman, *st. v.*, OVER-SWIM, swim over; *pret.* oferswam, 2367.
swīn, **swȳn**, *st. neut.*, SWINE, image of a boar on a helmet, 1111, 1286.
swincan, *st. v.*, SWINK, toil, 517.
swingan, *st. v.*, SWING, 2264.

swīn-līc, *st. neut.*, SWINE-shape, image of a boar, 1453.

swioðol, *st. m. or neut.*, flame, 3145* (see note to l. 782).

swīð, swӯð, *adj.*, strong, severe, 191, 3085. [*Cf. Goth.* swinþs.]

swīðra, *compar.*, stronger; *nom. fem.* sīo swīðre hand, 'the right hand,' 2098.

swīðan, *st. and w. v.*

ofer-swӯðan, *st. and w. v.*, OVER-power, overcome, 279, 1768.

swīðe, swӯðe, *adv.*, strongly, greatly, very, 597, etc.

swīðor, *compar.*, more greatly, more, more especially, rather, 960, 1139, 1874, 2198.

swīð-ferhð, swӯð-ferhð, *adj.*, strong-souled, stout-hearted, 173, 493, 826, 908.

swīð-hicgende, *adj.* (*pres. part.*), [strong-thinking] stout-hearted, 919, 1016.

swīð-mōd, *adj.*, [strong-MOOD] stout-hearted, 1624.

swōgan, *st. v.*, sound; *pres. part.* 3145. [*Cf. Goth.* ga-swōgjan, 'to sigh,' *and O.E.* swēgan.]

swōr, see **swerian**.

-sworcan, see **-sweorcan**.

sword, see **sweord**.

swulces, see **swylc**.

swurd, see **sweord**.

swutol, see **sweotol**.

swylc, *adj.-pron.*, SUCH, such as, as. [*Cf. Goth.* swa-leiks.]

I. (=L. talis) such:

(1) *adj.* 582, 1347, etc.

(2) *pron.* 299 (*with gen.*), 996; *gen.* swulces, 880 (*see* **hwā**); *acc.* ōðer swylc ūt offerede, 'carried out and off another such [number],' 1583.

II. (=L. qualis) such as, 1156 (*with gen.*), 1797, 2869; *acc.* eall gedǣlan...swylc him God sealde, 'deal out all that God gave him,' 72.

III. (=L. talis...qualis) swylc... swylc, 'such...as,' 1249 (*with gen.*), 1328–9, 3164.

swylce:

I. *adv.*, as well as, likewise, 113, 293, etc.; *once* swilce, 1152.

II. *conjunctive adv.*, as, 757; as if, F. 38.

swylt, *st. m.*, death, 1255, 1436. [*Cf. Goth.* swulta-.]

swylt-dæg, *st. m.*, death-DAY, 2798. [*Cf.* sweltan.]

swymman, see **swimman**.

swӯn, see **swīn**.

swynsian, *w. v.*, resound, 611.

swyrd, see **sweord**.

swӯð, see **swīð**.

-swӯðan, see **-swīðan**.

swӯðe, see **swīðe**.

sӯ, see **wesan**.

syfan-wintre, *adj.*, SEVEN WINTERS old, 2428.

syfone, see **seofon**.

-syhð, see **-sēon**.

sylf(a), see **self**.

syll, *st. f.*, SILL, base, floor, 775.

syllan, see **sellan**.

syllīc, see **sellīc**.

symbel, *st. neut.*, feast, banquet, 564, etc.; *dat.* symble, 119, 2104, symle, 81, 489, 1008. [*From Greek through Lat.* symbola, 'a share'; *cf.* Holthausen, *Anglia*, Beiblatt XIII. 226.]

symbel-wynn, *st. f.*, feast-joy, joy in feasting, 1782.

sym(b)le, *adv.*, always, 2450, 2497, 2880. [*Cf. Goth.* simlē, 'once.']

symle, *n.*, see **symbel**.

syn-bysig, *adj.*, [SIN-BUSY] guilt-haunted, troubled by guilt, 2226.

syn-dolh, *st. neut.*, ceaseless wound, incurable wound, 817.

syndon, see **wesan**.

syngāles, see **singāles**.

syngian, *w. v.*, SIN; *pp.* gesyngad, 2441.

synn, *st. f.*, SIN, crime, injury, hatred, struggle, 975, 1255, 2472, 3071.

syn-scaða, *w. m.*, cruel *SCATH*er, 707 (see note), 801.

syn-snǣd, *st. f.*, [ceaseless piece] huge gulp, 743.

synt, see **wesan**.

syrce, *w. f.*, SARK, shirt of mail, 226, 334, 1111.

syrwan, *w. v.*, ensnare, 161. [*From* searu.]

be-syrwan, *w. v.*, ensnare, 713, etc.; contrive, 942; besyred, 2218*.

syððan, see **siððan**.

T

tācen, *st. neut.*, TOKEN, 833; *dat.* tācne, 141, 1654. [*Cf. Goth.* táikns.]

tǣcan, *w. v.*

ge-tǣcan, *w. v.*, TEACH, indicate, assign, 313, 2013.

talian, *w. v.*, reckon, claim, 532, 594, 677, 2027; *pres. sg. 1st* wēn ic talige, 'I reckon it a thing to be expected,' 1845.

te, *prep. with dat.*, TO, from, 2922 (see note).

tear, *st. m.*, TEAR, 1872. [*Cf. Goth.* tagr.]

tela, *adv.*, well, 948, etc.

telge, see **tellan**.

tellan, *w. v.*, TELL, reckon, deem, 794, etc.; *pres. sg. 1st* telge, 2067: ac him wæl-bende weotode tealde, 'but [if he did] he might reckon death-bands prepared for himself,' 1936.

teoh, *st. f.*, band, troop; *dat. sg.* teohhe, 2938.

teohhian, *w. v.*, assign, 951; *pp.* geteohhod, 1300.

tēon, *st. v.*, [*TOW*] *TUG*, draw, 553, 1036, 1288 (of a sword), 1439; *pret. sg.* brim-lāde tēah, 'took the ocean-way,' 1051; *so* eft-sīðas tēah, 1332. [*Cf. Goth.* tiuhan.]

ā-tēon, *st. v.*, [*TUG*] take; *pret. sg.* ātēah, 766 (see note to ll. 765–6).

ge-tēon, *st. v.*, *TUG*, draw, 1545, 2610, F. 17; deliver, 1044: *imperat. sg.* nō ðū him wearne getēoh ðīnra gegn-cwida, 'do not thou give them a refusal of thy replies,' 366; *pret. sg.* hē him ēst getēah mēara ond māðma, 'he presented to him the horses and treasures,' 2165.

of-tēon, *st. v.*, TUG OFF *or* away, withhold; *with gen. rei and dat. pers.*, 5; *with dat. rei*, 1520; *with acc. rei*, 2489. See **of-tēon**, below and note to l. 5.

þurh-tēon, *st. v.*, [*TUG* THROUGH] bring about, 1140.

tēon, *st. v.*, accuse. [*Cf. Goth.* teihan, 'show.']

of-tēon, deny, 5 (see note) and cf. **of-tēon**, *above*.

tēon, *w. v.*, *with acc.*, make, adorn, provide, 1452; *pret. pl.* tēodan, 43.

ge-tēon, *w. v.*, appoint, arrange, prepare, 2295, 2526.

tīd, *st. f.*, TIDE, *TIME*, 147, 1915.

til(1), *adj.*, good, 61, 1250, 1304, 2721.

tilian, *w. v.*, *with gen.*, [TILL] gain, 1823.

timbran, *w. v.*, TIMBER, build, 307.

be-timbran, *w. v.*, [BETIMBER] build; *pret. pl.*, betimbredon, 3159.

tīr, *st. m.*, glory, 1654.

tīr-ēadig, *adj.*, [glory-blessed] glorious, happy in fame, 2189.

tīr-fæst, *adj.*, [glory-FAST] glorious, 922.

tīr-lēas, *adj.*, glory-LESS; *gen. sg. absolutely*, 843.

tīðian, *w. v.*, *impers.*, *with gen.*, grant; *pp.* wæs...bēne getīðad, '(of) the boon (it) was granted,' 2284.

tō, *prep.*, *with dat.*, TO, towards, 28, etc.: for, as, *esp. in predicative dats.*, 14, tō sōðe, 'as a fact,' 51, etc.: *with verbs of asking, etc.* at the hands of, from, 158, 525, 601, *etc.*; at (*time*), 26.

Special usages:

(1) for, *in adverbial phrases of time:* tō aldre, 'for ever,' 955, 2005, 2498; tō līfe, 'in his lifetime, ever,' 2432; tō wīdan fēore, 'ever,' 933.

(2) to, *with gerundial infin.*, 316, 473 (see note), etc.

(3) weorðan tō, 'to become,' 460, 587, etc.

(4) *Following its case:* him tō, 'to it,' 313; 909 (see note); 1396 (*see* wēnan); þe þū hēr tō lōcast, 'on which thou lookest here,' 1654; ūs sēceað tō Swēona lēoda, 'the peoples of the Swedes will come against us,' 3001.

tō hwan, see **hwā**, **hwæt**.

tō þæs, *adv.*, so, 1616.

tō þæs þe, *conjunctive phrase*, TO (the point) where, thither whence, 714, 1967, 2410; to the point (degree) that, until, 1585 (see note).

tō þon, *adv.*, TO that degree, so, 1876.

tō þon, þæt, until, 2591, 2845; *see* **sē**.

tō, *adv.*:

(1) =*preposition without expressed object* (*cf. the particles of separable verbs in German*): thereTO, to him, to it, 1422, 1755, 1785, 2648.

(2) TOO, *before adjs. and advs.*, 133, 137, 191, etc.: tō fela micles, 'far too much,' 694; hē tō forð gestōp, 'he had stepped too far forward,' 2289.

tō-gædre, *adv.*, TOGETHER, 2630.

to-gēanes, **tō-gēnes**, *prep.*, *with dat.*, *following its case*, towards, AGAINST, 666, 747*, 1542, 1626 (to meet), 1893: gōdum tōgēnes, 'to where the good man lay,' 3114.

tō-gēanes, *adv.*: grāp þā togēanes, 'then she clutched at [him],' 1501.

tō-middes, *adv.*, in the MIDst, 3141.
torht, *adj.*, bright, clear, 313.
torn, *st. neut.*, anger, rage, 2401; insult, distress, 147, 833, 2189.
torn, *adj.*
  tornost, *superl.*, bitterest, 2129.
torn-gemōt, *st. neut.*, [wrath-*MEET*-ing] angry meeting, encounter, 1140.
tō-somne, *adv.*, together, 2568.
tredan, *st. v.*, *with acc.*, TREAD, 1352, 1964, etc.
treddian, **tryddian**, *w. v.*, *intrans.*, *TREAD*, go, 725, 922.
trem, *st. m. or neut.: acc. sg. adverbially*, fōtes trem, 'a foot's breadth *or* space,' 2525.
trēow, *st. f.*, TRoth, TRUth, good faith, 1072, 2922. [*Cf. Goth.* triggwa.]
trēowan, *w. v.*, *with dat.*, *TROW*, trust: *pret. sg.* gehwylc hiora his ferhþe trēowde, 'each of them trusted Unferth's mind,' 1166. (See also trūwian.)
trēow-loga, *w. m.*, TROth-LIar, troth-breaker, 2847.
trodu, *st. f.*, track, 843.
trum, *adj.*, strong, 1369.
trūwian, *w. v.*, *with gen. or dat.*, *TROW*, trust, believe, 669, 1993, etc.
  ge-trūwian, *w. v.*:
  (1) *with gen. or dat.*, trow, trust; *with gen.*, 2322, 2540; *with dat.*, 1533.
  (2) *with acc.*, confirm; *pret. pl.* getrūwedon, 1095.
tryddian, see **treddian**.
trȳwe, *adj.*, TRUE, 1165. [*Cf. Goth.* triggws.]
twā, see **twēgen**.
twǣfan, *w. v.*
  ge-twǣfan, *w. v.*, *usu. with acc. pers. and gen. rei*, divide, sever, separate, restrain, 479, etc.; *pp.* getwǣfed, 'ended,' 1658.
twǣman, *w. v.*
  ge-twǣman, *w. v.*, *with acc. pers. and gen. rei*, sever, cut off, 968.
twēgen, *m.*, **twā**, *f. and neut.*, *num.*, TWAIN, TWO, 1095, 1163, etc.; *gen.* twēga, 2532; *dat.* twǣm, 1191. [*Cf. Goth.* twái.]
twelf, *num.*, TWELVE; 147; twelfa, 3170 (see note). [*Cf. Goth.* twa-lif.]
twēonum, *dat. pl. of distrib. numeral:* be (bī) sǣm twēonum, 'by the *TWO* seas, *i.e.* BETWEEN the seas,' 858, 1297, 1685, 1956.
tȳdre, *adj.*, feeble, unwarlike, 2847.
tyhtan, *w. v.*
  on-tyhtan, *w. v.*, entice, 3086.
tȳn, TEN, 3159; *inflected* tȳne, 2847. [*Cf. Goth.* taíhun.]

Þ, Ð

þā:
  I. *adv.*, then, 26, etc.
  II. *rel. adv.* or *conj.*, *with indic.*, when, as, since, seeing, 201, etc.; *correl. with* þā *above*, 140, etc.
þā, *adj.-pron.*, see **se**, **sē**.
þǣm, THEM, see **se**, **sē**.
þǣr: [*Cf. Goth.* þar.]
  I. *adv.*, THERE, 32, etc.; *unemphatic* (*like mod.* there *with impers. verbs*) 271, 440, etc. *For* **ðǣr on innan**, 71, 2089, etc., *see* innan.
  II. *rel. adv.*, where, 286, etc.; (to) where, 356, etc.; if, 1835. *With* swā *following:* ðǣr...swā, 'if so be that,' 797, 2730. (Cf. note to l. 762.)
þǣra, **þǣre**, see **se**, **sē**.
þæs, *adj.-pron.*, see **se**, **sē**.
þæs, *adv.*:
  (1) therefore, 900, 1992, etc.; see **sē**.
  (2) so, 773, 968, etc.
  þæs þe, *conj.*:
  (1) as, 1341, 1350, 3000.
  (2) because, 108, 228, 626, 1628, 1751, 1998, 2797, etc.; *correl. with preceding* þæs, 1779.
  tō þæs þe, see **tō**.
þæt, *adj.-pron.*, see **se**, **sē**.
þæt, *conj.*, THAT, so that, 62, etc.; until, 84, 1911; in that, 3036; *often correl. with the demonst. neut. pron.* þæt *or* þæs (*see* **sē**), 778–9, 1591–3, 1598–9, etc.; *repeated*, 2864–5–71. See note to l. 765.
  þæt þe, *conj.*, THAT, 1846.
þætte (=þæt þe), *conj.*, THAT, 151, etc.
þafian, *w. v.*, *with acc.*, consent to, submit to, 2963.
-þah, see **-þicgan**.
þām, see **se**, **sē**.
þanan, see **þonan**.
þanc, *st. m.*:
  (1) *with gen. rei*, THANKS, 928, 1997, etc.
  (2) content, pleasure; *dat. sg.* þā ðe gif-sceattas Gēata fyredon þyder tō þance, 379.
þanc-hycgende, *adj.* (*pres. part.*), [*THOUGHt*-thinking], *THOUGHt*ful, 2235.

þancian, *w. v.*, THANK, 625, 1397; *pret. pl.*, þancodon, 1626, þancedon, 227.

þanon, see **þonan**.

þāra, see **se**, **sē**.

þās, see **þes**.

þĕ, *rel. particle, indecl.*, who, that, which, etc.

(1) *Alone*, 192, 500, etc.; *acc. sg.* 355, 2182; *dat. sg.* 2400, 3001; *nom. pl.* 45, etc.; *acc. pl.* 2490, 2796; *gen. pl.* 950; *dat. pl.* þe gē þǣr on standað, 'in which ye stand there,' 2866; *so* 1654: hēo þā fǣhðe wræc, þē þū gystran niht Grendel cwealdest, 'she avenged the feud, in which thou killedst Grendel yesternight,' 1334; mid þǣre sorhge, þē him sīo sār belamp, 'with the sorrow, wherewith that blow befell him (see sār),' 2468.

(2) *Immediately preceded by* sē, sēo, þæt, etc.; sē þe, 103, 1260, 1342, 1449, 1462 (*antec.* ǣngum); sē þe *for* sēo þe, 1344, 1887, 2685; sēo þe, 1445; ðone þe, 1054, 1298, 2056, 2173; *pl.* þā þe, 1592. *Correlatives:* se...sē þe, 506 (followed by verb in 2nd pers.); sēo hand ...sē þe, 1343–4; sīo hond...sē þe, 2684–5.

N.B. *After* þāra þe *the verb is often in the sg.*: 843, 996, 1051, 1461, 2130, 2251, 2383.

(3) *Followed by redundant* hē: *acc. sg. m.* þe hine dēað nimeð, 'whom death will take,' 441, cf. 1436, etc.

þæs þe, see **þæs**, *adv.*

þæt þe, see **þæt**, *conj.*

þēah þe, see **þēah**.

forðon þe, see **forþam**.

tō þæs þe, see **tō**.

þē, *pers. pron.* (*acc. and dat. of* þū), THEE, to thee, etc., 417, etc. *With a comparative*, than thou, 1850.

þē, *demonst. pron.*, see **sē**.

þē, *conj.:*

(1) because, *correl. with a preceding* þȳ, þē (*see* sē), 488, 1436. Đē hē ūsic...gecēas...þē, 'on this account he chose us, because,' 2638–41.

(2) that, so that, 242.

-þeah, see **-þicgan**.

þēah, *conj.*, *usu. with subj.*, *rarely indic.* (1102): THOUGH, although, 203, etc.; *once*, þēh, 1613; þēah ic eal mæge, 'although I may,' 680. [*Cf. Goth.* þáuh.]

þēah þe, *conj.*, *usu. with subj.*, THOUGH, although, 682, etc.

þēah, *adv.*, THOUGH, yet, however, 1508.

swā þēah, see **swā**.

þearf, *st. f.*, need, 201, etc.; *acc.* fremmað gēna lēoda þearfe, 'fulfil still the people's need,' 2801. [*Cf. Goth.* þarba.]

þearf, *v.*, see **þurfan**.

þearfa, *w. m.*, ærnes þearfa, 'shelterless,' 2225.

(*ge-*)**þearfian**, *w. v.*, necessitate, render necessary; *pp.* geþearfod, 1103.

þearle, *adv.*, severely, hard, 560.

þēaw, *st. m.*, [THEW] custom, 178, etc.; *dat. pl.* 'in good customs,' 2144.

þec, *pers. pron.* (*archaic acc. of* þū), thee, 946, etc.

þeccean, *w. v.*, [THATCH] cover, enfold, 3015; *pret. pl.* þehton, 513.

þegn, *st. m.*, THANE; used of Beowulf, 194, etc., Hengest, 1085, Wiglaf, 2721, etc.

þegn-sorg, *st. f.*, THANE-SORROW, sorrow for one's thanes, 131.

þēgon, **þēgun**, see **þicgan**.

þēh, see **þēah**.

þehton, see **þeccean**.

þenc(e)an, *w. v.*, THINK, intend: *usu. with following inf.*, 355, 448 (fut.), 739, etc.; *with dependent clause*, 691; *absolutely*, 289, 2601 (*see* onwendan).

ā-þenc(e)an, *w. v.*, THINK out, intend, 2643.

ge-þenc(e)an, *w. v.*, *with acc.*, THINK, think of, 1474, 1734.

þenden, *adv.*, then, 1019, 2985.

þenden, *conj.*, *with indic. or subj.*, while, whilst, 30, etc.

þengel, *st. m.*, prince, king, 1507.

þēnian (=þegnian), *w. v.*, *with dat.*, serve, 560.

þēod, *st. f.*, people, nation, 643, etc. [*Cf. Goth.* þiuda.]

þēod-cyning, **-kyning**, **þīod-cyning**, *st. m.*, nation-KING, king of a people, 2, 2144 (Hrothgar), 2579 (Beowulf), 2963 (Ongentheow), etc.

þēoden, **þīoden**, *st. m.*, prince, king, 34, etc.; *dat.* þēodne, 345, etc., þēoden, 2032; *pl.* þēodnas, 3070. [*Cf. Goth.* þiudans.]

þēoden-lēas, *adj.*, prince-LESS, without one's chief, 1103.

þēod-gestrēon, *st. neut.*, nation-treasure, national possession, 44, 1218*.

þēod-kyning, see **þēod-cyning**.
þēod-sceaða, *w. m.*, nation-SCATHer, national foe, 2278, 2688.
þēod-þrēa, *st. f. and w. m.*, national misery, 178.
þēof, *st. m.*, THIEF, 2219.
þēon, *st. v.*, thrive, succeed, 8; *pret. sg.* 2836 (see note). [*Cf. Goth.* þeihan.]
ge-þēon, *st. v.*, thrive, 25, 910; *imperat. sg.*, 1218.
on-þēon, *st. v.*, thrive; *pret. sg.* hē þæs ǣr onþāh, 'he therefore throve erewhile,' 900 (but see note).
þēon (=þȳwan), *w. v.*, oppress, 2736.
þeos, see **þes**.
þēostre, *adj.*, dark, 2332.
þēow, *st. m.*, slave, 2223*.
þēs, **þēos**, **þis**, *demonst. adj.*, THIS, *sing. nom. m.* þes, *f.* þēos, *n.* þis; *acc. m.* þisne, 75, þysne, 1771, *f.* þās, *n.* þis; *gen. m. n.* þisses, 1216, þysses, 197, etc., *f.* þisse; *dat. m. n.* þissum, 1169, ðyssum, 2639, *f.* þisse; *instrum. m. n.* ðȳs. *Plur. m. f. n. nom. acc.*, þās; *gen.* þissa, *dat.* þyssum, 1062, etc.
þicg(e)an, *st. v.*, *with acc.*, seize, take, partake of, eat, 736, 1010; *pret. pl. indic.* þēgun, 2633, *subj.* þēgon, 563.
ge-þicgan, *st. v.*, *with acc.*, take, receive, 1014; *pret. sg.* geþeah, 618, 628; geþah, 1024.
þīn, *poss. adj.*, THINE, thy, 267, etc.
þinc(e)an, see **þyncan**.
þindan, *st. v.*, swell with pride, anger, etc., see note to F. 13.
þing, *st. neut.*, THING, matter, affair, 409, 426; *gen. pl.* ǣnige þinga, 'by any means, in any way, on any condition, at all,' 791, 2374, 2905.
þingan, *w. v.*, determine, appoint, 1938; *pp.* wiste þǣm āhlǣcan... hilde geþinged, 'knew that battle was in store for the monster,' 647.
ge-þingan, *w. v.*, *with refl. dat.*, determine (to come, go, etc.); *pres.* gif him þonne Hrēþrīc to hofum Gēata geþingeð, 'if then Hrethric betakes him to the Geats' court,' 1836.
þingian, *w. v.:*
(1) address, speak, 1843.
(2) compound, settle, allay, 156, 470.
þīod-, see **þēod-**.
þīoden, see **þēoden**.
þis, *demonst. adj.*, see **þes**.
þolian, *w. v.*, [THOLE] endure: [*Cf. Goth.* þulan.]
(1) *trans.* 832, 1525, etc.
(2) *intrans.* 2499.
ge-þolian, *w. v.*, [THOLE]:
(1) *trans.*, endure, 87, 147; *dat. inf.* tō geþolianne, 1419.
(2) *intrans.*, wait patiently, 3109.
þon, *pron.*, see **sē**.
tō þon, *adv.*, to that degree, so, 1876; see **sē**.
tō þon, **þæt**, until, 2591, 2845; see **sē**.
þonan, **þonon**, **þanan**, **þanon**, *adv.*, THENCE, 819, 520, 1668, 111, etc.; *sometimes of personal origin*, 1960, etc.
þone, see **se**, **sē**.
þonne, *adv.*, THEN, 377, etc.; *repeated*, 1104–6. *See* **þonne**, *conj.*
þonne, *conj.:*
(1) when, while, *with indic. and subj.*, 23, 573, etc.; *in elliptical sentence*, brēac þonne mōste, 'enjoyed [him *or* them] while I might,' 1487. *Correl. with* þonne, *adv.*: 484–5, 2032–4; þonne hē gyd wrece...þonne his sunu hangað, '[that] he should then utter a dirge, when his son is hanging,' 2446–7.
(2) THAN, *after compars.:* 44*, etc. *With compar. omitted:* medo-ærn micel...þonne yldo bearn ǣfre gefrunon, 'a great mead-hall, [greater] than the children of men ever heard of,' 70* (but see note).
þonon, see **þonan**.
þorfte, see **þurfan**.
þrāg, *st. f.*, time; *acc. sg. of duration of time*, 54, 114, 1257; *nom. sg.* þā hyne sīo þrāg becwōm, 'when the time (of stress) came upon him,' 2883; cf. 87 (see note). [*Cf. Goth.* þragjan, 'to run.']
þrēa-nēdla, *w. m.*, dire NEED, 2223. [*Cf. O. E.* nȳd.]
þrēa-nȳd, *st. f.*, dire need, oppression, misery, 284; *dat. pl.* þe hīe ...for þrēa-nȳdum þolian scoldon, 'which they through dire compulsion had to endure,' 832.
þrēat, *st. m.*, troop, band, 4, 2406.
þrēatian, *w. v.*, THREATEN, press; *pret. pl.* mec...þrēatedon þearle, 'pressed me hard,' 560.
þrec-wudu, *st. m.*, [might-WOOD] spear, 1246.
þrēo, **þrīo**, *num. neut.* (*of* **þrīe**), THREE, 2278, 2174. [*Cf. Goth.* **þreis**.]

þreotteoþa, *ord. num.*, THIRTEENTH, 2406.

þridda, *ord. num.*, THIRD, 2688.

þringan, *st. v., intrans.*, *THRONG*, 2960; *pret. sg.* þrong, 2883.

 for-þringan, *st. v.*, snatch, rescue, 1084.

 ge-þringan, *st. v.*, *THRONG*, bound, 1912.

þrīo, see **þrēo**.

þrist-hȳdig, *adj.*, bold-minded, 2810.

þritig, **þrittig**, *st. neut.*, *with gen.*, THIRTY, 123, 2361; *gen. sg.* 379.

þrong, see **þringan**.

þrōwian, *w. v.*, suffer, 2605, etc.; *pret. sg.* þrōwode, 2594, þrōwade, 1589, 1721.

ge-**þrūen**, *pp.* (isolated: Sievers₃ § 385, N. 1), forged, 1285 (see note).

þrym(m), *st. m.*, might, force, 1918; glory, 2; *dat. pl. adverbially*, þrymmum, 'powerfully,' 235.

þrym-līc, *adj.*, mighty, glorious, 1246.

þrȳð, *st. f.*, strength; *dat. pl.* þrȳðum dealle, 'proud in their strength,' 494.

þrȳð-ærn, *st. neut.*, mighty house, noble hall, 657.

þrȳð-līc, *adj.*, excellent, 400, 1627.

 þrȳd-līcost, *superl.*, most excellent; *acc. pl.* 2869 (see note).

þrȳð-swȳð, *adj.*, strong in might, 131 (see note), 736.

þrȳð-word, *st. neut.*, choice *or* mighty WORD, excellent talk, 643.

þū, *pers. pron.*, THOU, 269, etc.; *acc. sg.* þec, þē (q. v.).

þungen, **ge-þungen**, *adj.* (*pp.*), [thriven] mature, distinguished, excellent, 624, 1927. [*Cf.* þēon *and see* Sievers₃ §§ 383, N. 3, 386, N. 2.]

þunian, *w. v.*, THUNder, resound, groan, hum; *pret.* þunede, 1906.

ge-**þuren**, see *ge*-**þrūen**.

þurfan, *pret. pres. v.*, need: *pres.* þearf, þearft, 445, 595, etc.; *subj.* þurfe, 2495; *pret.* þorfte, 157, etc.; *pret. pl.* 2363* (see note). [*Cf. Goth.* þaúrban.]

þurh, *prep.*, *with acc.*, THROUGH, *local, causal, instrumental or marking attendant circumstances* (see note to l. 276), 267, etc.

þus, *adv.*, THUS, 238, 337, 430.

þūsend, *st. neut.*, THOUSAND, 3050; *pl.* þūsenda, 1829. *Without following noun of measure: gen. pl.* hund þūsenda landes ond locenra bēaga, 2994 (see note). *Even without a dependent gen.: acc. pl.* ond him gesealde seofan þūsendo, 2195.

þȳ, see **se**, **sē**.

 þȳ lǣs, *conj.*, LEST, 1918.

þyder, *adv.*, THITHER, 379, 2970, 3086.

þyhtig, *adj.*, doughty, strong, 1558. [*Cf.* þēon.]

þyle, *st. m.*, spokesman, 1165, 1456.

þyncan, **þincean**, *w. v.*, *with dat. pers.*, seem, 368, 687, etc.; *sometimes impers.*, 2653.

 of-þyncan, *w. v.*, displease, 2032.

þȳrl, *adj.*, pierced, F. 47.

þyrs, *st. m.*, giant, 426.

þȳs, see **þes**.

þys-līc, *adj.*, [*THUS*LIKE] such; *nom. sg. f.*, þyslicu, 2637.

þysne, **þysses**, **þyssum**, see **þes**.

þȳstru, *st. f.*, darkness, 87. [*Cf.* þēostre.]

þȳwan, *w. v.*, oppress, 1827, see **þēon**. [*Cf.* þēow.]

U

ufan, *adv.*, from above, above, 330, 1500.

ufera, *compar. adj.*, later; *dat. pl.* uferan, 2392, ufaran, 2200.

ufor, *compar. adv.*, higher, upwards, on to higher ground, 2951 (but see note).

ūhte, *w. f.*, dawn, twilight, 126. [*Cf. Goth.* ūhtwō.]

ūht-floga, *w. m.*, dawn-*FLI*er, 2760.

ūht-hlem, *st. m.*, din *or* crash in the dawn, 2007.

ūht-sceaða, *w. m.*, dawn-*SCATH*er, dawn-foe, 2271.

umbor-wesende, *adj.* (*pres. part.*), being a child, 46, 1187.

un-blīðe, *adj.*, UNBLITHE, joyless, 130, 2268, 3031.

un-byrnende, *adj.* (*pres. part.*), UNBURNing, without being burnt; *nom. sg. absolutely*, 2548.

unc, *pers. pron.* (*dat. and acc. dual of* ic), to us two, us two, 540, 545, 2137, etc.

uncer, *pers. pron.* (*gen. dual of* ic), of us two, 2532; *coupled with the gen. of a proper name*, uncer Grendles, 'of Grendel and me,' 2002.

uncer, *poss. adj.* (see above), our (*dual*); *dat. pl.* uncran, 1185.

un-cūð, *adj.*, UNCOUTH, unknown, evil, 276, 1410, 2214; *gen. sg. absolutely*, 960 (Grendel); uncūþes fela, 'many a thing unknown,' 876.

under, *prep.*, UNDER:
(1) *with dat.* (of rest), 8, etc.; amid, 1302, 1928; (temporal) during, 738 (see note).
(2) *with acc.* (of motion, expressed or implied), 403, etc.; within, underneath, 1037. *To denote extent:* under swegles begong, 'under the sky's expanse,' 860, 1773; under heofones hwealf, 2015.

under, *adv.*, UNDER, beneath, 1416, 2213.

undern-mǣl, *st. neut.*, [UNDERN-MEAL] morning-time, 1428.

un-dearninga, *adv.*, openly, F. 24. [*Cf.* dyrne.]

un-dyrne, un-derne, *adj.*, UNsecret, manifest, 127, 2000, 2911 *.

un-dyrne, *adv.*, UNsecretly, openly, 150, 410.

un-fǣcne, *adj.*, UNguileful, sincere, 2068.

un-fǣge, *adj.*, [UNFEY] undoomed, not fated to die, 573, 2291.

un-fǣger, *adj.*, UNFAIR, 727.

un-flitme, *adv.*, incontestably, 1097 (see note).

un-forht, *adj.*, UNafraid, 287.

un-forhte, *adv.*, fearlessly, 444.

un-frōd, *adj.*, not old, young, 2821.

un-from, *adj.*, inert, not bold, UNwarlike, 2188.

un-gēara, *adv.*, not of YORE:
(1) but now, 932.
(2) erelong, 602.

un-gedēfelīce, *adv.*, unfittingly, unnaturally, 2435.

un-gemete, *adv.*, [UN*MEET*ly] immeasurably, 2420, 2721, 2728.

un-gemetes, *adv.* (*gen. of adj.* ungemet, UN*MEET*), immeasurably, unigmetes, 1792 (see note).

un-gyfeðe, *adj.*, not granted, 2921.

un-hǣlo, *st. f.*, [UNHEALth] destruction; *gen. sg.* wiht unhǣlo, 120 (see note).

un-hēore, un-hīore, un-hȳre, *adj.*, UNcanny, monstrous, 2120, 2413; *nom. sg. f.* unhēoru, 987.

unhlitme, *adv.* 1129 (see note to l. 1097).

unhror, *adj.*, not stirring, F. 47 (see note).

unigmetes, *adv.*, see **ungemetes**.

un-lēof, *adj.*, [UNLIEF] not dear, unloved; *acc. pl. absolutely*, 2863.

un-lifigende, un-lyfigende, *adj.* (*pres. part.*), UNLIVing, lifeless, dead, 468, 744, 1308, 2908; *dat. sg. m.* þæt bið driht-guman unlifgendum æfter sēlest, 'that will afterwards be best for the noble warrior when dead,' 1389.

un-lȳtel, *adj.*, [UNLITTLE] no little, 498, 833, 885.

un-murnlīce, *adv.*, UNMOURNfully, without hesitation, recklessly, 449, 1756.

unnan, *pret.-pres. v.*, grant, will, wish, OWN, 503, 2874; *pres. sg.* 1*st*, an, 1225; *subj. pret.* 1*st*, ūþe ic swīþor, þæt ðū hine selfne gesēon mōste, 'I would rather that thou mightst have seen himself,' 960; 3*rd*, þēah hē ūðe wel, 'how much soever he wished,' 2855.
ge-unnan, *pret.-pres. v.*, grant, 346, 1661.

un-nyt, *adj.*, useless, 413, 3168.

un-riht, *st. neut.*, UNRIGHT, wrong, 1254, 2739.

un-rihte, *adv.*, UNRIGHTly, wrongly, 3059.

un-rīm, *st. neut.*, countless number, 1238, 2624, 3135.

un-rīme, *adj.*, countless, 3012.

un-rōt, *adj.*, [UNglad] sad, 3148.

un-slāw, *adj.*, [UNSLOW] not slow; *nom. sg.* ecgum unslāw, 'not slow of edge,' 2564 * (see note).

un-snyttro, *st. f.*, UNwisdom; *dat. pl.* his unsnyttrum, 'in his folly,' 1734.

un-sōfte, *adv.*, [UNSOFTly] with difficulty, 1655, 2140.

un-swīðe, *adv.*
un-swīðor, *compar.*, less strongly, 2578, 2881.

un-synnig, *adj.*, UNSINning, guiltless, 2089.

un-synnum, *adv.* (*dat. pl. of* *unsynn), 'SINlessly,' 1072.

un-tǣle, *adj.*, blameless, 1865.

un-tȳdre, *st. m.*, evil progeny; *nom. pl.* untȳdras, 111.

un-wāclīc, *adj.*, [UN*WEAK*LIKE] firm, strong, 3138.

un-wearnum, *adv.*, without hindrance, 741.

un-wrecen, *adj.* (*pp.*), UN*WREAK*ed, unavenged, 2443.

ūp, *adv.*, UP, 128, 224, etc.

ūp-lang, *adj.*, [UPLONG] upright, 759.

uppe, *adv.*, UP, 566.

upp-riht, *adj.*, UPRIGHT, 2092.

ūre, *pers. pron.* (*gen. pl. of* ic), of us, 1386.

ūre, *poss. adj.* (see above), OUR, 2647.

ūrum, *pers. pron.* (*anom. form of the dat. pl. of* ic, *used here for* unc), to us, 2659 (see note).

ūs, *pers. pron.* (*dat. pl. of* ic), to us, 346, 382, etc.; for us, 2642.

ūser, *pers. pron.* (= ūre, *gen. pl. of* ic); ūser nēosan, 'to visit us,' 2074.

ūser, *poss. adj.* (see above), our; *acc. sg. m.* ūserne, 3002; *gen. sg. neut.* ūsses, 2813; *dat. sg. m.* ūssum, 2634.

ūsic, *pers. pron.* (*acc. pl. of* ic), US, 458, 2638, etc.

usses, ussum, see **ūser**, *poss. adj.*

ūt, *adv.*, OUT, 215, etc.

ūtan, *adv.*, from withOUT, without, 774, etc. [*Cf. Goth.* ūtana.]

ūtan-weard, *adj.*, OUTWARD, the outside of, 2297.

ūt-fūs, *adj.*, OUTward bound, ready to start, 33.

uton, see **wutun**.

ūt-weard, *adj.*, [OUTWARD] wæs ūtweard, 'was outward bound,' 761.

ūðe, see **unnan**.

ūð-genge, *adj.*, escaping, transitory; *nom. sg.* wæs Æschere...feorh ūðgenge, 'life departed from Æschere,' 2123.

W

wā, *interj.*, WOE: wā bið þǣm...wel bið þǣm..., 183, 186. [*Cf. Goth.* wái.]

wacian, *w. v.*, *WATCH*; *imperat. sg.* waca, 660. See **wæccan**.

wacnigean.

  on-wacnigean, *w. v.*, *intrans.* [AWAKEN], F. 10.

wadan, *st. v.*, WADE, go; *pret. sg.* wōd, 714, 2661; *pp.* gewaden, 220.

  on-wadan, *st. v.*, assail; *pret. sg.* hine fyren onwōd, 'him (Heremod) crime assailed,' 915.

  þurh-wadan, *st. v.*, WADE THROUGH, pierce, penetrate, 890, 1567.

wado, etc., see **wæd**.

wæccan, *w. v.*, *participle only found, except in North: for other parts* wacian *used*: cf. Sievers₃ § 416, 5; *WATCH*, keep a*WAKE*, *pres. part.*, *nom. sg. m.* wæccende, 708, *acc. sg. m.* wæccendne 1268, wæccende, 2841.

wæcnan, *st. v.*, *intrans.* [WAKEN], arise, spring, come, be born, 85, 1265, 1960; *pret. pl.* wōcun, 60. See Sievers₃ § 392, 2. [*Cf. Goth.* gawaknan.]

  on-wæcnan, [AWAKEN] 2287; be born, arise, spring, 56, 111.

wæd, *st. n.*, flood, sea, wave; *nom. pl.* wado, 546; wadu, 581*: *gen. pl.* wada, 508.

wǣfre, *adj.*, *WAVER*ing, about to die, expiring, 1150 (but see note), 2420; wandering, 1331.

wæg, see **weg**.

wǣg-bora, *w. m.*, 1440 (see note).

wǣge, *st. neut.*, stoup, flagon, tankard, 2253, 2282.

wǣg-holm, *st. m.*, the billowy sea, 217.

wǣg-līðend, *st. m.* (*pres. part.*), wave-farer, sea-farer, 3158*.

wægnan, *w. v.*

  be-wægnan, *w. v.*, offer, 1193.

wǣg-sweord, *st. neut.*, wave-SWORD, sword with a wavy pattern, 1489.

wæl, *st. neut.*, slaughter, the slain, corpse, 448, etc.; *nom. pl.* walu, 1042.

wæl-bedd, *st. neut.*, slaughter-BED, 964.

wæl-bend, *st. m. f.*, slaughter-*BOND*, death-*BAND*, 1936.

wæl-blēat, *adj.*, [slaughter-wretched]; *acc. f.* wunde wæl-blēate, 'his deathly pitiful wound,' 2725.

wæl-dēað, *st. m.*, slaughter-DEATH, death by violence, 695.

wæl-drēor, *st. m. or neut.*, slaughter-gore, 1631.

wæl-fǣhð, *st. f.*, slaughter-*FEUD*, deadly feud, 2028.

wæl-fāg, *adj.*, slaughter-stained, cruel, bitter, 1128.

wæl-feall, -fyll, *st. m.*, slaughter-FALL, violent death, 3154; *dat. sg.* geweōx hē...to wæl-fealle...Deniga lēodum, 'he waxed great for a slaughter to the Danish people,' 1711.

wæl-fūs, *adj.* [slaughter-ready] expecting death, 2420.

wæl-fyll, see **wæl-feall**.

wæl-fyllo, *st. f.*, slaughter-FILL, fill of slaughter, 125.

wæl-fȳr, *st. neut.*, slaughter-FIRE, death-bringing fire, 2582; corpse-fire, pyre, 1119.

wæl-gǣst, *st. m.*, slaughter-GHOST, 1331, 1995 (see note to l. 102).

wæl-hlem, *st. m.*, slaughter-crash, terrible blow, 2969.

wæll-seax, *st. neut.*, slaughter-knife, deadly short-sword; *dat. sg.* (*with uninflected adjs.*) wæll-seaxe gebrǣd biter ond beadu-scearp, 'drew his keen and battle-sharp knife,' 2703.

wælm, see **wylm**.

wæl-nīð, *st. m.*, deadly enmity, 85, 2065, 3000.

wæl-rǣs, *st. m.*, [slaughter-RACE] deadly strife, mortal combat, 824, 2531, 2947.

wǣl-rāp, *st. m.*, [pool-ROPE] icicle, 1610 (see note).

wæl-rēaf, *st. neut.*, slaughter-spoil, battle-booty, plunder, 1205.

wæl-rēc, *st. m.*, slaughter-REEK, deadly fumes, 2661.

wæl-rēow, *adj.*, slaughter-fierce, fierce in strife, 629.

wæl-rest, *st. f.*, [slaughter-REST] bed of (violent) death, 2902.

wæl-sceaft, *st. m.*, slaughter-SHAFT, deadly spear, 398.

wæl-slyht, *st. m.*, deadly slaughter, F. 30. [*Cf. O.E.* slean.]

wæl-steng, *st. m.*, slaughter-pole, spear, 1638.

wæl-stōw, *st. f.*, slaughter-place, battle-field, 2051, 2984.

wǣn, *st. m.*, WAIN, wagon; *acc. sg.* 3134.

wǣpen, *st. neut.*, WEAPON, 250, etc.; *acc. pl.* wǣpen, 292.

wǣpned-mon(n), *st. m.*, WEAPONED MAN, man, 1284.

wǣr, *st. f.*, compact, treaty, 1100; keeping, protection, 27, 3109. [*P.B.B.* x. 511.]

wǣran, etc., see **wesan**.

wæstm, *st. m.*, growth, form; *dat. pl.* on weres wæstmum, 'in man's form,' 1352.

wæter, *st. neut.*, WATER, the sea, 93, etc.; *dat.* wætere, 1425, 1656, 2722, wætre, 2854; *instrumental gen.* hē hine eft ongon wæteres weorpan, 'he began again to sprinkle him with water,' 2791.

wæter-egesa, *w. m.*, WATER-terror, the terrible mere, 1260.

wæter-ȳð, *st. f.*, WATER-wave, 2242.

wāg, *st. m.*, wall, 995, 1662.

wala, *w. m.*, WALE, 'wreath' (in heraldry), a protecting rim *or* roll on the outside of the helmet (Skeat); *nom. sg.* ymb þæs helmes hrōf hēafod-beorge wīrum bewunden wala ūtan hēold, 'round the helmet's crown the "wreath," wound about with wires, gave protection for the head from the outside,' 1031 (see note). [*Cf. Goth.* walus.]

Waldend, see **Wealdend**.

wald-swæð, *st. neut.*, *or*

wald-swaðu, *st. f.*, [WOLD-SWATH] forest-track, forest-path; *dat. pl.* wald-swaðum, 1403.

walu, see **wæl**.

wan, *v.*, see **winnan**.

wan, *adj.*, see **won**.

wandrian, *w. v.*, WANDER, F. 36.

wang, see **wong**.

wanian, *w. v.*:
(1) *intrans.*, WANE, diminish, 1607.
(2) *trans.*, diminish, curtail, decrease, 1337; *pp.* gewanod, 477.

wānigean, *w. v.*, bewail, lament; *inf.* gehȳrdon gryre-lēoð galan Godes ondsacan, sige-lēasne sang, sār wānigean helle hæfton, 'heard God's adversary singing his terror-lay, his song without victory hell's captive bewailing his sore,' 787.

wāran, see **wesan**.

warian, *w. v.*, GUARD, inhabit, 1253, 1265, 2277 (guards); *pres. pl.* warigeað, 1358.

waroð, *st. m.*, [WARTH] shore, 234, 1965.

wāt, etc., WOT, see **witan**.

waðol, *adj.*, F. 9 (see note).

wē, *pers. pron.* (*pl. of* ic), WE, 1, 260, etc.

wēa, *w. m.*, WOE, 191, etc.; *gen. pl.* wēana, 148, etc.

wēa-dǣd, *st. f.*, DEED of WOE, deed of evil, F. 9.

weal(l), *st. m.*, *gen.* wealles, *dat.* wealle, *acc.* weal, 326: WALL *in its various meanings;* rampart, burgh-wall, 785, etc.; wall of a building, 326, 1573; natural wall of rock, sometimes the side of a barrow or den, 2307, 2759, 3060, etc.; wall of cliff, 229, etc. [*From Lat.* vallum.]

wēa-lāf, *st. f.*, [WOE-LEAVing] wretched remnant (of either army after the fight in which Hnæf fell), 1084, 1098.

wealdan, *st. v.*, *with dat.*, *gen.*, *or absolutely*, WIELD, rule, rule over, govern, possess, control; prevail; 442, etc. þenden wordum wēold wine Scyldinga, 'while the friend of the Scyldings still had power of speech,' *or* 'ruled with his word,' 30; 2574 (see note to ll. 2573, etc.), wælstōwe wealdan, 'to be masters of the field,' 2984.

ge-wealdan, *st. v.*, *with gen.*, *dat.*, *or acc.*, WIELD, control, possess, bring about, 1509, 1554, 2703.

Wealdend, Waldend, *st. m.* (*pres. part.*), the WIELDer, God, 1693, etc.; *often with dependent gen.*, 17, etc.; *gen.* Wealdendes, 2857, Waldendes, 2292, 3109; *dat.* Wealdende, 2329.

weall, see **weal.**

weallan, *st. v.*, WELL, boil, be agitated, *literally and figuratively; pret.* wēoll, 2113, 2138, etc.; wēol, 515, etc.; *pres. part.* weallende, 847, weallinde, 2464; *nom. pl. neut.* weallende, 546, weallendu, 581. Ingelde weallað wæl-nīðas, 'in Ingeld's breast deadly hatred wells up,' 2065; hreðer ǣðme wēoll, 'his breast swelled with breath,' 2593.

weall-clif, *st. neut.*, WALL-CLIFF, sea-cliff, 3132.

weard, *st. m.*, [WARD], *GUARD*ian, owner, 229, 1741 (see note), etc.

weard, *st. f.*, WARD, watch, 305, 319.

weardian, *w. v.*, WARD, guard, indwell, 105, 1237, 2075. *Especially in the phrase* lāst *or* swaðe weardian: *inf.* hē his folme forlēt...lāst weardian, 'he left his hand behind to mark his track,' 971; *so pret.* weardade, 2098; *pret. sg. for pl. in subordinate clause,* þæt þām frætwum fēower mēaras...lāst weardode, 'that four horses followed the armour,' 2164.

wearn, *st. f.*, refusal, 366.

wēa-spell, *st. neut.*, *WOE*-SPELL, tidings of woe, 1315.

weaxan, *st. v.*, WAX, grow, 8, 1741; 3115 (see note).

ge-weaxan, *st. v.*, WAX, grow, become, 66, 1711.

web, *st. neut.*, WEB, tapestry; *nom. pl.* 995.

wecc(e)an, *w. v.*, *WAKE*, rouse, stir up, 2046, 3024; *pret.* wehte, 2854. Bǣl-fȳra mǣst...weccan, 'to kindle the greatest of funeral piles,' 3144. [*Cf. Goth.* (us)-wakjan.]

tō-weccan, *w. v.*, wake up, stir up; *pret. pl.* tō-wehton, 2948.

wedd, *st. neut.*, pledge, 2998.

weder, *st. neut.*, WEATHER, 546; *nom. pl.* weder, 1136.

weg, *st. m.*, WAY; *in* on weg, 'away,' 264, etc., on wæg, F. 45.

wēg, *st. m.*, wave, 3132. [*Cf.* wǣg-(bora).]

wegan, *st. v.*, bear, wear, wage, 3015, *pres. sg. 3rd* wigeð, 599; *pret.* wæg, 152, etc.; *subj. pres.* wege, 2252.

æt-wegan, *st. v.*, bear away, carry off, 1198.

wegan, *st. v.*

ge-wegan, *st. v.*, engage, fight, 2400.

wēg-flota, *w. m.*, wave-FLOATer, ship, 1907.

wehte, see **weccan.**

wel(l), *adv.*, WELL, rightly, much, 186, 289, etc.; *usual form* wel, *but* well, 2162, 2812.

wel-hwylc, *indef. adj. and pron.*

I. *Pron.: with gen.* wel-hwylc witena, 'every councillor,' 266; *neut. absolutely*, everything, 874.

II. *Adj.* every, 1344.

welig, *adj.*, WEALthy, rich, 2607.

wēn, *st. f.*, WEENing, expectation, 383, 734, etc.: wēn ic talige, 'I reckon it a thing to be expected,' 1845; *dat. pl.* bēga on wēnum, ende-dōgores ond eft-cymes lēofes monnes, 'in expectation of both, the day of death and the return of the dear man' (*i.e.* expecting one or the other), 2895.

wēnan, *w. v.*, *with gen.*, *infin.*, *clause, or absolutely:* WEEN, expect, hope, 157, etc.; *pres. sg. 1st* wēn, 338, 442: þæs ic wēne, 'as I hope,' 272; swā ic þē wēne tō, 'as I expect from thee,' 1396; similarly with 157–8 (see note), 525 (see note), 1272–3; *with inf.* ic ǣnigra mē wēana ne wēnde...bōte gebīdan, 'I expected not to abide the remedy of any of my woes,' 933; *with gen. and clause,* hig þæs æðelinges eft ne wēndon, þæt hē...cōme, 'they expected not the atheling again, that he would come,' 1596.

wendan, *w. v.*, *intrans.*, WEND, turn, 1739. [*Cf. Goth.* wandjan.]

ed-wendan, *w. v.*, *intrans.*, turn back, desist, cease, 280 (but see note).

ge-wendan, *w. v.*, *trans. and intrans.*, turn, change, 186, 315.

on-wendan, *w. v.*, *trans.*, turn aside, set aside, avert, 191: sibb ǣfre ne mæg wiht onwendan, þām ðe wel þenceð, 'naught can ever set aside kinship, to a right-minded man,' 2601.

wenian, *w. v.*, honour, 1091.

be-wenian, bi-wenian, *w. v.*, entertain, attend on; *pp. pl.* bewenede, 1821; see also note to l. 2035.

weorc, *st. neut.*, WORK, deed, trouble, 74, etc.; *gen. pl.* worda ond worca,

289; *dat. pl.* wordum ne worcum, 1100: he þæs gewinnes weorc þrōwade, 'he suffered trouble for that strife,' 1721; *dat. pl. adverbially*, weorcum, 'with difficulty,' 1638; *dat.* (*instr.*) *sg.* weorce, *used adverbially*, 'grievously,' 1418.

weorod, see **werod**.

weorpan, *st. v.*, [WARP]: [*Cf. Goth.* wairpan.]
(1) *with acc. rei*, throw, 1531.
(2) *with acc. pers. and gen. rei*, sprinkle, 2791.
(3) *with dat.*, cast forth, 2582.
for-weorpan, *st. v.*, throw away; *pret. subj.* forwurpe, 2872.
ofer-weorpan, *st. v.*, stumble, 1543 (but see note).

weorð, *st. neut.*, WORTH, price, pay, 2496.

weorð, *adj.*, WORTHY, honoured, dear; *nom. sg. m.* weorð Denum æþeling, 'the atheling dear to the Danes,' 1814. See also **wyrðe**. [*Cf. Goth.* -wairþs.]
weorþra, *compar.*, worthier, 1902*.

weorðan, *st. v.*, become, be, befall, happen, come, 6, etc.; *inf.* wurðan, 807; *pres. pl.* wurðað, 282; *pret. sg.* hē on fylle wearð, 'he fell,' 1544; *pp.* geworden, 'happened, arisen,' 1304, 3078. *Often with predicative dat. governed by* tō, *and dat. pers.:* ðū scealt tō frōfre weorðan...lēodum þīnum, hæleðum tō helpe, 'thou shalt be for a comfort to thy people, a help to the heroes,' 1707; *so also* 460, etc. [*Cf. Goth.* wairþan.]
ge-weorðan, *st. v.:*
(1) *intrans.*, become, be, happen, 3061.
(2) *trans.*, agree about, settle; *inf.* þæt ðū...lēte Sūð-Dene sylfe geweorðan gūðe wið Grendel, 'that thou wouldst let the South Danes themselves settle their war with Grendel,' 1996.
(3) *impers.*, *with gen.*, *and following clause in apposition*, appear, seem, seem good; *pret.* þā ðæs monige gewearð, þæt..., 'then it appeared to many that...,' 1598; *pp.* hafað þæs geworden wine Scyldinga...þæt..., 'this had seemed good to the friend of the Scyldings, that,' 2026.

weorð-full, *adj.*
weorð-fullost, *superl.*, [WORTHFULLEST], WORTHiest, 3099.

weorðian, *w. v.*, WORTHY ('Lear,' II. 2. 128), honour, adorn, 2096, 1090, etc.; *pp.* geweorðod, 2176; geweorðad, 250, 1450, 1959; gewurðad, 331, 1038, 1645; weorðad, 1783.

weorð-līce, *adv.*
wurðlīcor, *compar.*, more WORTHILY, F. 39.
weorð-līcost, *superl.*, most WORTHILY, 3161.

weorð-mynd, *st. m. f. and neut.*, WORship, honour, glory, 8, 65, 1559, 1752; *dat. pl.* tō worð-myndum, 'for (his) honour,' 1186.

weotena, see **wita**.

weotian, *w. v.*, prepare, etc.: *pp. acc. pl.* wælbende weotode, 'death-bands prepared, appointed, destined,' 1936; witod, F. 28. [*Cf. Goth.* witōþ, 'law.']
be-weotian, **be-witian**, *w. v.*, observe, etc.: *pres. pl.* þā ðe syngales sēle bewitiað, 'those [weathers, days] which continually observe the season,' 1135; bewitigað sorhfulne sīð, 'make a journey full of woe,' 1428 (see note); *pret. sg.* ealle beweotode þegnes þearfe, 'attended to all the thane's needs,' 1796*; hord beweotode, 'watched over a hoard,' 2212.

wer, *st. m.*, man, 105 (used of Grendel), etc.; *gen. pl.* wera, 120, etc.; weora, 2947. [*Cf. Goth.* waír.]

wered, *st. neut.*, beer, mead, 496.

werede, etc., see **werod**.

werga, *adj.*, cursed; *gen. sg.* wergan gāstes, 133 (Grendel: see note), 1747 (the devil).

wērge, etc., see **wērig**.

wergend, *st. m.* (*pres. part. of* werian), defender, 2882*.

wērgian, *w. v.*, WEARY; *pp.* gewērgad, 2852.

werhðo, *st. f.*, curse, damnation; *acc. sg.* werhðo, 589. [*Cf. Goth.* wargiþa.]

werian, *w. v.*, guard, defend, protect, 453, 1205, etc.; *reflex.*, 541; *pp. nom. pl.* 238, 2529. [*Cf. Goth.* warjan.]
be-werian, *w. v.*, defend; *pret. subj.* beweredon, 938.

wērig, *adj.*, *with gen. or dat.*, WEARY, 579; *dat. sg.* wērgum, 1794; *acc. f. sg. or pl.* wērge, 2937.

wērig-mōd, *adj.*, WEARY of MOOD, 844, 1543.

werod, **weorod**, *st. neut.*, troop, band, 290, 319, 651, etc.; *dat.* werede,

1215, 2035*; weorode, 1011, 2346; *gen. pl.* wereda, 2186; weoroda, 60. [*Cf. O.E.* wer.]

wer-þēod, *st. f.*, [man-nation] people; *acc. pl.* ofer wer-þēode, 'throughout the nations of men,' 899.

wesan, *irreg. v.*, be, 272, etc.; *pres. sg. 3rd* is, 256, 1761, etc.; ys, 2093, 2910, 2999, 3084; *pres. pl.* sint, 388; synt, 260, 342, 364; syndon, 237, 257, etc.; *pres. subj. sg.* sīe, 435, etc.; sȳ, 1831, etc.; sig, 1778, etc.; *pret. pl.* wǣron, 233, etc.; wǣran, 2475, wāran, 1015*; *imperat. sg.* wes, 269, etc., wæs, 407. *Negative forms: pres. sg. 3rd* nis, 249, etc.; *pret. sg. 1st and 3rd* næs, 134, etc.; *pret. pl.* nǣron, 2657; *pret. subj. sg.* nǣre, 860, etc.
Special usages:
(1) *Omission of infin.* 617, 1857, 2363, 2497, 2659; *also* 992, 2256.
(2) *Forming, with a pres. part., an imperf. tense:* secgende wæs, 'was saying,' 3028.

wēste, *adj.*, WASTE; *acc. sg. m.* wēstne, 2456.

wēsten, *st. m. and neut.*, WASTE, 1265; *dat.* wēstenne, 2298 (see note).

wīc, *st. neut.*, [WICK] dwelling, 821, etc.; *often in pl.*, 125, etc.; *dat. pl.* wīcun, 1304. [*Lat.* vīcus.]

wīcan, *st. v.*
  ge-wīcan, *st. v., intrans.*, WEAKen, give way, 2577, 2629.

wicg, *st. neut.*, horse, steed, 234, 286, 1400, etc.; *pl.* wicg, 2174. [*Cf. O.E.* wegan, 'carry.']

wīc-stede, *st. m.*, [WICK-STEAD] dwelling-place, 2462, 2607.

wīd, *adj.*, WIDE, extended, long, *of space and time*, 877, 933, 1859, etc.

wīd-cūð, *adj.*, [WIDE-COUTH] widely known, 1256, etc.; *gen. absolutely*, wīd-cūðes (i.e. Hrothgar), 1042.

wīde, *adv.*, WIDELY, 18, etc.; *qualifying a superlative*, wīde mǣrost, 'the most famous far and wide,' 898.
  wīdre, *compar.;* wīdre gewindan, 'to flee away more widely, escape further,' 763.

wīde-ferhð, *st. m.*, [WIDE-life], *only used as acc. of time*, for a long time, from generation to generation, 702*, 937, 1222.

wīd-floga, *w. m.*, WIDE-*FLI*er (the dragon), 2346, 2830.

wīdre, see **wīde**.

wīd-scofen, see under **scūfan**.

wīd-weg, *st. m.*, WIDE-WAY, way leading afar, highway; *acc. pl.* geond wīd-wegas, 'along distant ways,' 'far and wide,' 840, 1704.

wīf, *st. neut.*, WIFE, woman, 615, etc.

wīf-lufu, wīf-lufe, *w. f.*, WIFE-LOVE, love for one's wife, 2065. [See Sievers[3] § 218, N. 1.]

wīg, *st. m. or neut.*
(1) war, battle, 23, 65, etc.; *dat.* and *instr.* wigge, 1656, 1770 (see note), 1783.
(2) war-prowess, valour, might, 350, 1042, 2323, 2348.

wiga, *w. m.*, warrior, 629, etc. [*P.B.B.* x. 511.]

wīgan, *st. v.*, war, fight, 2509.

wīg-bealu, *st. neut.*, war-BALE, the evils of war, 2046.

wīg-bil, *st. neut.*, war-BILL, war-sword, 1607.

wīg-bord, *st. neut.*, [war-BOARD] war-shield, 2339.

wīg-cræft, *st. m.*, war-CRAFT, war-might, 2953.

wīg-cræftig, *adj.*, war-CRAFTY, mighty in battle, 1811.

wīgend, *st. m.* (*pres. part.*), warrior, 3099; *acc. sing. or pl.* wīgend, 3024, *nom. pl.* wīgend, 1125, 1814, 3144, *gen. pl.* wīgendra, 429, etc.

wīg-freca, *w. m.*, war-wolf, warrior, 1212, 2496.

wīg-fruma, *w.m.*, war-chief, 664, 2261.

wigge, see **wīg**.

wīg-getāwa, *st. f. pl.*, war-equipments, 368. [*See* **gūð**-geatwa.]

wīg-gryre, *st. m.*, war-terror, 1284.

wīg-heafola, *w. m.*, [war-head] war-helmet, 2661.

wīg-hēap, *st. m.*, war-HEAP, band of warriors, 477.

wīg-hete, *st. m.*, war-HATE, 2120.

wīg-hryre, *st. m.*, [war-falling] slaughter, 1619.

wīg-sigor, *st. m. or neut.*, war-victory, 1554.

wīg-spēd, *st. f.*, war-SPEED, success in war, 697.

wigtig, see **witig**.

wīg-weorðung, *st. f.*, idol-WORSHIP, sacrifice, 176. [*P.B.B.* x. 511. *Cf. Goth.* weihs, 'holy.']

wiht,
  I. *st. f.*, WIGHT, being, creature, 120 (see note), 3038.
  II. *st. f. neut.*, WHIT, AUGHT, 2601 (*see* onwendan), 1660, 2857 (see note); *acc.* for wiht, 'for aught,' 2348; *with gen.*, 581.

III. *Adverbial use*, AUGHT, at all; *almost always negative* (*with* ne), naught, NOT **at** all, no WHIT. (1) *Acc.*, *with* ne *or* nō: 541, 862, etc.; nō hine wiht dweleð ādl ne yldo, 'sickness or age hinders him not a whit,' 1735.
(2) *Dat.*; *with* ne, 186, 1514, etc.; *affirmatively*, 1991.

wil-cuma, *w. m.*, [WILL-COMER] welcome guest, 388, 394, 1894.

wil-dēor (= wild dēor), *st. neut.*, [WILD DEER] wild beast, 1430.

wile, see **willan**.

wil-geofa, *w. m.*, WILL-*GIV*er, joy-giver, 2900.

wil-gesīð, *st. m.*, [WILL-companion] willing *or* loved companion, 23.

willa, *w. m.*, WILL, wish, desire, desirable thing; joy, pleasure; sake: 626, etc.; *dat. sg.* tō willan, 'for his pleasure,' 1186; ānes willan, 'for the sake of one,' 3077; *gen. pl.* wilna, 660, 950, 1344; *dat. pl.* willum, 'according to our wishes,' 1821; *so* sylfes willum, 2222, 2639. [*Cf. Goth.* wilja.]

willan, *irreg. v.*, WILL: *pres. sg. 1st* wille, 318, 344, etc.; wylle, 947, etc.; *2nd* wylt, 1852; *3rd* wile, 346; wyle, 2864; wille, 442, 1371, etc.; wylle, 2766; *pl.* wyllað, 1818. *Negative forms:* nelle = ne + wille, 679, 2524; nolde = ne + wolde, 706, 791, 2518, etc. *With omission of inf.* nō ic fram him wolde, 543.

wilnian, *w. v.*, desire, 188.

wil-sīð, *st. m.*, [WILL-journey] willing journey, 216.

wīn, *st. neut.*, WINE, 1162, 1233, 1467. [*From Lat.* vīnum.]

wīn-ærn, *st. neut.*, WINE-hall, 654.

wind, *st. m.*, WIND, 217, etc.

win-dæg, *st. m.*, strife-DAY, day of strife, 1062.

windan, *st. v.*, *intrans.*, WIND, twist, 212, 1119, 1193, etc.; *pp. dat. sg.* wundini golde, 'with twisted gold,' 1382 (see note).

æt-windan, *st. v.*, *with dat. pers.*, WIND away, escape, 143.

be-windan, *st. v.*, WIND about, brandish, enclose, grasp, mingle, 1031, 1461, etc.; *pp.* galdre bewunden, 'WOUND about with incantation, encompassed with a spell,' 3052.

ge-windan, *st. v.*, *intrans.*, WIND, turn, flee away, 763, 1001.

on-windan, *st. v.*, *UN*WIND, 1610.

wind-blond, *st. neut.*, [WIND-*BLEND*] tumult of winds, 3146.

wind-geard, *st. m.*, dwelling of the winds, 1224.

wind-gerest, *st. f.*, [WIND-REST] wind-swept resting-place, 2456 (see note).

windig, *adj.*, WINDY; *pl.* windige, 572, 1358.

wine, *st. m.*, friend, *esp.* friend and lord, friendly ruler, 30, 148, 170; *gen. pl.* winigea, 1664; winia, 2567.

wine-dryhten, **wine-drihten**, *st. m.*, friend-lord, friend and lord, friendly ruler, 360, 862, 1604, etc.

wine-gēomor, *adj.*, friend-sad, mourning for the loss of friends, 2239.

wine-lēas, *adj.*, friendLESS, 2613.

wine-mǣg, *st. m.*, friend-kinsman, relative and friend, loyal subject; *pl.* wine-māgas, 65.

winia, **winigea**, see **wine**.

winnan, *st. v.*, [WIN] strive, fight, 113, 506; *pret. sg. 3rd* wan, 144, 151, won, 1132; *pl.* wunnon, 777.

wīn-reced, *st. neut.*, WINE-house, wine-hall, 714, 993.

wīn-sele, *st. m.*, WINE-hall, 695, 771, 2456.

winter, *st. m.*, WINTER, year, 1128, etc.; *gen. sg.* wintrys, 516; *pl.* wintra, 147, etc.

wīr, *st. m.*, WIRE, wire-work, filagree, 1031, 2413.

wīs, *adj.*, WISE, 1413, 1845, 3094 (see note), etc. *Weak forms: nom. m.* wīsa, 1400, 1698, 2329; *acc. sg.* wīsan, 1318.

wīsa, *w. m.*, WISE one, guide, 259.

wīs-dōm, *st. m.*, WISDOM, 350, 1959.

wīse, *w. f.*, WISE, fashion; *instrumental acc.* (Grein), ealde wīsan, 'in the old fashion,' 1865.

wīs-fæst, *adj.*, [WISE-FAST] wise, 626.

wīs-hycgende, *adj.* (*pres. part.*), WISE-thinking, 2716.

wīsian, *w. v.*, *with acc. rei*, *dat. pers.*, *or absolutely*, [make WISE] point out, show; direct, guide, lead; 2409, etc.; *pres. sg. 1st* wīsige, 292, etc.; *pret. sg.* wīsode, 320, 402, etc.; wīsade, 208 (see note to l. 209), etc.

wisse, see **witan**.

wist, *st. f.* (*from* wesan):
(1) weal, 128, 1735.
(2) meal; possibly 128, but see note.

wiste, WIST, see **witan**.

wist-fyllo, *st. f.*, food-FILL, abundant meal; *gen. sg.* wist-fylle, 734.

wit, *st. neut.*, WIT, 589.

wit, *pers. pron.* (*dual of* ic), we two, 535, etc.

wita, *w. m.*, wise man, councillor, *pl.* the WITAN, 778; *gen. pl.* witena, 157, etc., weotena, 1098.

witan, *pret. pres. v.*, [WIT] know, 764, 1863, 2519, etc.; *pres. sg.* 1*st and* 3*rd* wāt, 1331, etc.; *negative*, nāt, 681, etc.; 2*nd* wāst, 272; *pret. sg.* 1*st and* 3*rd* wiste, 646, etc.; wisse, 169, etc.; *pret. pl.*, wiston, 181, etc.; wisson, 246: tō ðæs ðe hē eorð-sele ānne wisse, 'to where he knew that earth-hall to be, knew of that earth-hall,' 2410; *so*, 715; *pres. sg.* 1*st*, ic on Higelāce wāt...þæt hē, 'I know concerning Hygelac, that he,' 1830*; *negative*, sceaðona ic nāt hwilc, 'I know not which of scathers, some foe,' 274; 3*rd*, God wāt on mec (*acc.*), þæt mē is micle lēofre, 'God knows concerning me that I would much rather,' 2650.

  ge-witan, *pret.-pres. v.*, know, 1350.

wītan, *st. v., with acc. rei and dat. pers.*, [WITE] reproach, blame, 2741.

  æt-wītan, *st. v., with acc. rei*, TWIT, blame, charge; *pret. pl.* ætwiton wēana dǣl, 'charged [him] with their many woes,' 1150.

  oð-wītan, *st. v., with acc. rei and dat. pers.*, reproach; *inf.* ne ðorfte him ðā lēan oðwītan mon on middan-gearde, 'no man on earth needed to reproach him (or them: see note) with those rewards,' 2995.

gewītan, *st. v.*, depart, go, 42, 115, 123, 210 (see note), etc.; *often with reflex dat.* 26, 662, 1125, etc.; *often followed by inf.* (*in many cases best rendered by a pres. part.*) 234, 291, 853, 2387, etc.; *pp.*, *dat. sg. m.*, þæt ðū mē ā wǣre forð gewitenum on fæder stǣle, 'that thou wouldst aye be to me when dead in a father's place,' 1479.

witian, see **weotian**.

witig, *adj.*, WITTY, wise (applied to the Deity), 685, etc.; wigtig, 1841. [*P.B.B.* x. 511.]

witnian, *w. v.*, punish, torment; *pp.* wommum gewītnad, 'tormented with plagues,' 3073.

wið, *prep. with dat. and acc.*, WITH (*with acc.* 152, etc., *with dat.* 113, etc.), *can often be rendered by Mod. Eng.* '*with*,' *especially with verbs denoting strife, such as* winnan, 152; *but* '*against*' *is a rendering more generally satisfactory*, 326, etc.; *sometimes* towards (*acc.*) 155, 1864; by (*acc.*), 2013, 2566; from (*dat.*), 827, 2423. *With acc. and dat. in the same sentence:* 424–6; gesæt þā wið sylfne...mǣg wið mǣge, 'he sat then by [the king] himself, kinsman with kinsman,' 1977–8: wið duru healle, 'to the door of the hall,' 389*; wið earm gesæt (*see* note to l. 749); forborn bord wið rond[e], 'the shield was burnt up to the boss,' 2673; wið Hrefnawudu, 'by (over against) Ravenswood,' 2925.

wiðer-ræhtes, *adv.*, opposite, 3039.

wiðre, *st. neut.*, resistance, 2953.

wlanc, see **wlonc**.

wlātian, *w. v.*, look, look for, 1916. [*Cf. Goth.* wláiton, 'to look round'].

  in-wlātian, *w. v.*, to gaze in, 2226*.

wlenco, *st. f.*, pride, bravado, daring; *dat.* wlenco, 338, 1206, wlence, 508.

wlītan, *st. v.*, gaze, look, 1572, 1592; *pret. pl.* wlitan, 2852.

  giond-wlītan, *st. v.*, look through, view thoroughly, 2771.

wlite, *st. m.*, countenance, 250. [*Cf. Goth.* wlits.]

wlite-beorht, *adj.*, of BRIGHT aspect, 93.

wlite-sēon, *st. f.*, sight, 1650.

wlitig, *adj.*, beautiful, 1662.

wlonc, **wlanc**, *adj.*, proud, 331, 341, 2833, 2953; *with dat.* ǣse wlanc, 'carrion-proud,' 1332.

wōc, see **wæcnan**.

wōh, *adj.*, crooked, wrong; *dat. pl.* him bebeorgan ne con wōm wundor-bebodum wergan gāstes, 'he knows not how to protect himself against the crooked wondrous commands of the cursed spirit,' 1747 (if so punctuated, but see note).

wōh-bogen, *adj.* (*pp.*), crooked-BOWED, coiled, 2827.

wolcen, *st. neut.*, WELKIN, cloud; *dat. pl.* wolcnum, 8, etc.

wolde, *pret.* of **willan**.

wollen-tēare, *adj.*, with WELLing TEARS, 3032.

wōm, see **wōh**.

womm, *st. m.*, spot, plague, 3073.

won, *v.*, see **winnan.**

won, wan, *adj.*, [WAN] dark, 702, 1374; *nom. pl. neut.*, wan, 651; *weak form* wonna, 3024, 3115.

wong, wang, *st. m.*, plain, meadow, 93, etc.

wong-stede, *st. m.*, [plain-STEAD] champaign spot, 2786.

won-hȳd, *st. f.*, [WAN-, i.e. un-thought] carelessness, rashness, 434.

wonn, 3154 (see note to ll. 3150, etc.).

won-sǣlig, *adj.*, unhappy; won-sǣli, 105.

won-sceaft, *st. f.*, [WAN-*SHAP*ing] misery, 120.

wōp, *st. m.*, *WEEP*ing, 128, 785, 3146. [*Cf. O.E.* wēpan.]

worc, see **weorc.**

word, *st. neut.*, WORD, 30, etc. *The dat. pl. is common with verbs of saying:* 176, 388, 1193, 2795, 3175.

word-cwide, -cwyde, *st. m.*, WORD-saying, speech, 1841, 1845, 2753.

word-gyd, *st. neut.*, WORD-lay, dirge, 3172.

word-hord, *st. neut.*, WORD-HOARD, 259.

word-riht, *st. neut.*, [WORD-RIGHT] right *or* befitting word, 2631.

worhte, see **wyrcan.**

worn, *st. m.*, multitude, number, 264; *acc. sg.* þonne hē wintrum frōd worn gemunde, 'when he, old in years, remembered the number [of them],' *or* 'remembered many a thing,' 2114. *Qualified by* fela *or* eall: *nom. sg.* worn fela, 'a great number,' 1783; *acc. sg.* þū worn fela...ymb Brecan sprǣce, 'thou hast said a great deal about Breca,' 530; eal-fela eald-gesegena worn, 'a very great number of old tales,' 870; worn eall gespræc gomol, 'the aged one spake very many things,' 3094. *Similarly in gen. pl. governed by* fela: *with gen. sg.* worna fela...sorge, 'very much sorrow,' 2003; *with gen. pl.* worna fela...gūða, 'very many wars,' 2542.

worold, *st. f.*, WORLD, 60, etc.; *gen. sg.* worulde, 2343, worlde, 2711; his worulde gedāl, 'his severance from the world,' 3068.

worold-ār, *st. f.*, WORLD-honour, 17.

worold-cyning, wyruld-cyning, *st. m.*, WORLD-KING, mighty king, 1684, 3180.

worold-rǣden, *st. f.*, the way of the WORLD (rǣden, 'condition,' used to make abstract nouns); *acc. sg.*, 1142 (see note).

worðig, *st. m.*, homestead, court, precincts, street, 1972.

worð-mynd, see **weorð-mynd.**

woruld-candel, *st. f.*, WORLD-CANDLE, the sun, 1965.

woruld-ende, *st. m.*, WORLD-END, the end of the world, 3083.

wracu, *st. f.*, revenge; *acc. sg.* wræce, 2336. [*Cf. Goth.* wraka.]

wrǣc, *st. neut.*, *WRACK*, misery, exile, 170, 3078.

wræcca, see **wrecca.**

wræce, see **wracu.**

wrǣc-lāst, *st. m.*, exile-track, path of exiles, 1352.

wrǣc-mæcg, *st. m.*, banished man, exile, 2379.

wrǣc-sīð, *st. m.*, *WRACK*-journey, exile, 2292; *dat. pl.* nalles for wræc-sīðum ac for hige-þrymmum, 'by no means because of banishment, but out of magnanimity,' 338.

wrǣt, *st. f.*, ornament, jewel; *acc. pl.* wrǣte, 2771*, 3060*; *gen. pl.* wrǣtta, 2413; *dat. pl.* wrǣttum, 1531.

wrǣt-līc, *adj.*, ornamental, curiously wrought, splendid, wondrous, 891, 1489, etc.

wrāð, *adj.*, WROTH, hostile, *absolutely*, foe; 319, 660, etc.

wrāðe, *adv.*, amiss, 2872.

wrāð-līce, *adv.*, WROTHLY, wrathfully, 3062.

wrecan, *st. v.*, *with acc.*, WREAK, drive, drive out, utter, avenge, 423, 1278, etc.; *often* wrecan gid, spel, etc., 'utter, rehearse a lay, legend, or tale,' 873, etc.: *subj. pres.* þonne hē gyd wrece, '[that] then he should utter a dirge,' 2446; *pret. sg.* ferh ellen wræc, 'strength drove out life,' 2706 (see note); *pp.* wearð...on bid wrecen, 'was driven to bay,' 2962.

ā-wrecan, *st. v.*, tell; *with acc.*, gid, 1724, 2108.

for-wrecan, *st. v.*, *with acc.*, drive away, banish, 109, 1919.

ge-wrecan, *st. v.*, *usu. with acc.*, WREAK, avenge, 107, 3062, etc.; *pret. pl.* gewrǣcan, 2479; *with reflex. acc.* 2875; *absolutely*, hē gewræc syððan, 'he took vengeance afterwards,' 2395.

wrecca, *w. m.*, WRETCH, exile, wanderer, adventurer, 898, 1137, F. 27*; *dat.* wræccan, 2613*.

wrecend, *st. m.* (*pres. part.*), WREAKer, avenger, 1256.

wreoðen-hilt, *adj.*, with WREATHed *or* twisted HILT, 1698.

wrīdian, *w. v.*, grow, 1741. [*P.B.B.* x. 511.]

wrītan, *st. v.*, WRITE, engrave, 1688.
  for-wrītan, *st. v.*, cut asunder, 2705.

wrīðan, *st. v.*, *with acc.*, [WRITHE] bind, 964; bind up, 2982.

wrixl, *st. f. or neut.*, exchange, 2969.

wrixlan, *w. v.*, *with dat.* wordum, 'exchange, interchange, words,' 366, 874.

wrōht, *st. m. and f.*, strife, contest, 2287, 2473, 2913. [*Cf. Goth.* wrōhs, 'accusation.']

wudu, *st. m.*, WOOD:
  (1) a wood, 1364, 1416.
  (2) a spear; *acc. pl.* wudu, 398.
  (3) a ship, 216, 298, 1919; *nom. sg.* wudu wunden-hals.

wudu-rēc, *st. m.*, WOOD-REEK, smoke, 3144*.

wuldor, *st. neut.*, glory; *gen. sg.* wuldres, 17, etc. [*Cf. Goth.* wulþrs.]

wuldor-torht, *adj.*, glory-bright; *pl.* 1136.

Wuldur-cyning, *st. m.*, Glory-KING, the King of glory, 2795.

wulf, *st. m.*, WOLF, 3027.

wulf-hlið, *st. neut.*, WOLF-slope; *acc. pl.* wulf-hleoðu, 1358.

wund, *st. f.*, WOUND, 2711, etc.; *acc. sg.* wunde, 2725, etc.

wund, *adj.*, WOUNDed, 565, etc.

wunden-feax, *adj.*, with WOUND, i.e. twisted, hair, 1400.

wunden-hals, *adj.*, [WOUND-neck] with twisted *or* curved prow, 298.

wunden-mǣl, *st. neut.*, [WOUND-sword] sword with winding, curving, ornaments, 1531*.

wunden-stefna, *w. m.*, [WOUND-STEM] ship with twisted *or* curved stem, 220.

wunder-fæt, *st. neut.*, WONDER-VAT, wondrous vessel; *dat. pl.* 1162.

wundini, see **windan**.

wundor, *st. neut.*, WONDER, 771, etc.; monster, 1509: *nom. acc.* wundur, 3032, 3062, etc.; *acc.* wunder, 931; *dat.* wundre, 931; *gen. pl.* wundra, 1607; *dat. pl. adverbially*, wundrum, 'wondrous(ly),' 1452, 2687*.

wundor-bebod, *st. neut.*, WONDER-command, wondrous command, 1747.

wundor-dēað, *st. m.*, WONDER-DEATH, wondrous death, 3037.

wundor-līc, *adj.*, [WONDERLIKE] wondrous, 1440.

wondor-sīon, *st. f.*, WONDER-sight, wondrous sight, 995.

wundor-smið, *st. m.*, WONDER-SMITH, mystic-smith, 1681.

wundur-māððum, *st. m.*, WONDER-jewel, wondrous jewel, 2173.

wunian, *w. v.*, [WON]:
  (1) *intrans.* dwell, remain, 284, 1128, etc.; *with dat.* wīcum wunian, 3083.
  (2) *trans.* indwell, inhabit, 1260, 2902.
  ge-wunian, *w. v.*, *with acc.*, dwell with, remain with; *subj. pres. pl.* gewunigen, 22.

-wurðad, see **weorðian**.

wurðan, see **weorðan**.

wurðlic, see **weorðlic**.

wutun, **uton**, = let us, *with foll. inf.*, 1390, 2648, 3101. [*Cf. O.E.* gewītan.]

wyle, **wyllað**, **wylle**, **wylt**, see **willan**.

wylm, **wælm**, *st. m.*, surge, flood, 516, etc. [See Sievers$_3$, § 159, 1 and 2.]

wyn-lēas, *adj.*, JOYLESS, 821, 1416.

wynn, *st. f.*, joy, 1080, etc.

wyn-sum, *adj.*, WINSOME, joyous, 1919; *neut. pl.* wynsume, 612.

wyrcan, *w. v.*, WORK; *pret.* worhte, WROUGHT [*Cf. Goth.* waúrkjan]:
  (1) *with acc.* work, make, 92, 930, 1452; *pret. part. pl.* (*as adj.*) 'disposed,' fæste geworhte, 'steadfast,' 1864.
  (2) *with gen.* achieve; *subj. pres.* wyrce sē þe mōte dōmes, 'achieve glory he who may,' 1387.
  be-wyrcan, *w. v.*, surround, 3161.
  ge-wyrc(e)an, *w. v.*, *trans.*, WORK, accomplish, achieve, 635, 1491, 1660; *subj. pret. pl.* geworhton, 3096; gewyrcean þæt, 'bring it about that,' 20.

wyrd, *st. f.*, WEIRD, fate, 455, 477, etc.

wyrdan, *w. v.*, destroy; *pret. sg.* wyrde, 1337.
  ā-wyrdan, *w. v.* destroy, 1113.

wyrm, *st. m.*, WORM, dragon, 886, etc.

wyrm-cynn, *st. neut.*, WORM-KIN, serpent kind, 1425.

wyrm-fāh, *adj.*, WORM-adorned, snake-adorned, 1698.

wyrm-hord, *st. neut.*, WORM-HOARD, dragon's hoard, 2221.
wyrnan, *w. v.* [*from* wearn].
  for-wyrnan, *w. v.*, refuse, 429, 1142.
wyrp, *st. f.*, change, 1315.
wyrpan, *w. v.* [*from* weorpan].
  ge-wyrpan, *w. v.*, recover; *with refl. acc.* 2976.
wyrsa, *adj. compar.* (*of* yfel), WORSE, 1212, etc.; *gen. pl.* wyrsan, 525; *neut. acc. sg. absolutely*, þæt wyrse, 1739. [*Cf. Goth.* waírsiza.]
wyrt, *st. f.*, [WORT] root, 1364.
wyrðe, *adj.*, WORTHY, 368, 2185.
  wyrðra, *compar.*, worthier, 861. See also **weorð**.
wyruld-, see **worold-**.
wyscan, *w. v.*, wish; *pret. pl.* wīston, 1604 (see note).

Y

yfel, *st. neut.*, EVIL; *gen. pl.* yfla, 2094. [*Cf. Goth.* ubils.]
ylca, *pron.*, the same, ILK, 2239.
yldan, *w. v.*, delay, put off, tarry; *inf.* 739 [*from* eald].
ylde, **elde**, *st. m. pl.*, men, 70, 77, 150, etc.; *dat.* eldum, 2214, 2314, 2611, 3168.
yldesta, see **eald**.
yldo, *st. f.*, [ELD] age, old age, 1736, etc.; *dat.* ylde, 22, eldo, 2111.
yldra, see **eald**.
ylfe, *st. m. pl.*, ELVES, 112.
ymb, **ymbe**, *prep.*, *with acc.*, about, around, concerning, *local, temporal, denoting object, etc.*, 399, etc.; *following its case*, 689; ymb āne niht, 'after one night,' 135, and *cf.* note to l. 219.
ymbe, *adv.*, about, around, 2597.
ymbe-sittend, **ymb-sittend**, *st. m.* (*pres. part.*), [about-SITTING] neighbour; *nom. pl.* ymbe-sittend, 1827; *gen. pl.* ymb-sittendra, 9; ymbe-sittendra, 2734.
yppe, *w. f.*, high seat, throne, 1815. [*From* ūp.]
yrfe, *st. neut.*, heritage, 3051. [*Cf. Goth.* arbi.]
yrfe-lāf, *st. f.*, heirloom, 1053, 1903.
yrfe-weard, *st. m.*, heir, 2731; *gen. sg.* yrfe-weardas, 2453 (see note).
yrmðo, *st. f.*, misery; *acc.* yrmðe, 1259, 2005. [*From* earm.]
yrre, *st. neut.*, anger, 711, 2092.
yrre, **eorre**, *adj.*, angry, 769, 1532, etc.; *gen. sg. used substantively*, eorres, 'of the angry one,' 1447. [*Cf. Goth.* aírzeis.]
yrre-mōd, *adj.*, angry in MOOD, angry-minded, 726.
yrringa, *adv.*, angrily, 1565, 2964.
ys, see **wesan**.
ȳð, *st. f.*, wave, 548, etc.; *acc. sg. or pl.* ȳðe, 46, 1132, 1909.
ȳðan, *w. v.*, destroy, 421. [*Cf. Goth.* áuþs, 'desert.']
ȳðe, 1002, 2415, see **ēaðe**.
ȳðe-līce, *adv.*, easily, 1556 (see note).
ȳð-geblond, **-gebland**, *st. neut.*, BLENDing of waves, surge, 1373, 1593; *pl.* 1620.
ȳð-gesēne, see **ēð-gesȳne**.
ȳð-gewinn, *st. neut.*, wave-strife, 1434, 2412.
ȳð-lād, *st. f.*, [wave-LODE] wave-path, way over the sea; *pl.* 228.
ȳð-lāf, *st. f.*, [wave-LEAVing] what is left *or* thrown up by the waves, the foreshore, 566.
ȳð-lida, *w. m.*, wave-sailer, ship, 198. [*Cf.* līðan, 'to go.']
ȳwan, **ēawan**, **ēowan**, *w. v.*:
  (1) *trans.* show; *pres. sg.* ēaweð, 276; *pret.* ȳwde, 2834.
  (2) *intrans.* appear; *pres. sg.* ēoweð, 1738.
  ge-ȳwan, ge-ēawan, *w. v.*, present, proffer, 2149; *pp.* ge-ēawed, 1194.

ADDITIONAL NOTES

I have to thank many friends and correspondents for drawing my attention to misprints, or for generous help as to difficult passages in *Beowulf*: Mr J. H. G. Grattan, Mr Cyril Brett, Prof. O. F. Emerson and especially Mr Ritchie Girvan.

During the past five years there has been comparatively little discussion of the grammatical problems of *Beowulf*: but special mention must be made of the *Interpretations and Emendations of Early English Texts* by Prof. Ernst Kock, in *Anglia*, xlii. 99 etc. (1918).

l. 24. *lēode gelǣsten.* In support of the interpretation 'may help their lord,' Kock quotes: *gelǣstan hlāforde æt hilde, An.* 411, *gelǣstan frēan tō gefeohte, Maldon*, 11.

33. *hringed-stefna, isig ond ūt-fūs.* Hollander [*M.L.N.* xxxii. 246] suggests **itig*, 'splendid,' O.N. *itr*.

86. Kock takes *earfoðlīce* as an adj.: 'endured an irksome time'; *earfoðlīce þrāge = earfoð-þrāge* (l. 283).

133. Sievers shows that *werig*, applied to the evil spirit, is simply *wērig*, 'weary.' If it were, as Hart thinks, a distinct word, akin to *āwyrged*, 'accursed,' we should expect to find it more often in Late West Saxon in the form *wyrig*. [See *Anglia*, i. 577; *I.F.* xxvi. 225–35.]

249. Bright suggests *is* for *nis*, and would interpret *seld-guma* as 'a rare man,' comparing *seld-cūð*, 'seldom known'; *seld-cyme*, 'a rare visit'; *seld-siene*, 'seldom seen' [*M.L.N.* xxxi. 84].

489. *onsǣl meoto.* When finite verb and noun occur in one half-line, the verb is, in *Beowulf*, normally less stressed than the noun; and hence, in the second half-line, it is the noun which comes first and takes the alliteration, except in cases where the verb, bringing some vivid picture before our eyes, is emphatic [Sievers, *Altgerm. Metrik*, 1893, § 24].

Bright [*M.L.N.* xxxi. 217–23] has a full and interesting discussion of the metrical stress of the imperative: he would read here *onsǣl mētto*, translating 'disclose what thou hast in mind.' But the verb in such a position must, in *Beowulf*, be emphatic; and Hrothgar cannot be adjuring Beowulf to break his stubborn silence, for taciturnity is not Beowulf's weakness.

The examples given by Bright himself show how alien to the technique of *Beowulf* (though not of some other O.E. poems) would be the subordination of the noun to the verb here. Bright quotes 37 half-lines, containing imperative + noun, in *Beowulf*, and *in every instance* the noun takes the alliteration: in the first half-line the verb may, or may not, also have alliteration, but in the second half-line it cannot. The overwhelming probability is therefore that not *onsæl* (which takes the alliteration) but *meoto*, represents the verb, as Holthausen, Klaeber and Sedgefield have held. Kock [*Anglia*, xlii. 105] reads *on sǣl meota* 'think on joy,' comparing *ic on lagu þence, Hy.* 4, 95, *hicgeað on ellen, Finn.* 12; and he takes [*on*] *sigehrēð* as parallel to *on sǣl*, 'think on joy, on conquest's glory for the men.'

765–6. But Kock quotes satisfactory parallels for *þæt* as a relative, in similar circumstances: *swē hwylc mon swā ðęt sīo, þęt ðes londes brūce, Oldest Eng. Texts*, 451; *that war Krist, that thar stuod, Heliand*, 5433.

1008. Schücking interprets both *æfter* and *symle* as adverbs, 'ever after,' comparing *ā symle, Hy.* 4, 114 [*Archiv*, cxv. 421].

1068. *Finnes eaferum.* The question is whether the 'dative of personal agency,' or 'instrumental,' without a preposition, is possible. Klaeber and Lawrence doubt [see *J.E.G.Ph.* xiv. 548; *Proc. Mod. Lang. Assoc. Amer.* xxx. 398]. Green defends it at length, but the parallels he quotes are hardly conclusive [see *Pub. Mod. Lang. Assoc. Amer.* xxxi. 759–97]; Kock quotes a good parallel from Otfrid: *sunton, then wir fallen,* 'sins by which we fall' (iii. 21. 12).

1083. Klaeber [*J.E.G.Ph.* xiv. 548] would now retain *gefeohtan.* For the redundancy *wīg gefeohtan* he compares the *Chronicle,* anno 871, *rāde onridon.*

1106. *syððan.* Kock suggests that this means 'atone,' and is connected with *sēoðan*: "logically, the ideas 'seethe,' 'sacrifice' and 'atone' go together."

1107. *icge.* Brett (*M.L.R.* xiv. 2) compares *incge* (l. 2577) and *inge* (*Exod.* 190) "In all three passages the root meaning 'mighty' would do very well."

1440. *wǣg-bora.* Sedgefield$_2$ renders 'wave raiser,' 'wave causer,' and compares *rǣd-bora* (l. 1325).

1543. For *oferwearp,* 'stumbled,' Brett compares Mid. Eng. intransitive 'overthrow': 'gerte him in the nekke that he overthrew' [see *M.L.R.* xiv. 7]. But *strengest* can perhaps be defended as uninflected accusative: cf. *Rood,* 6, *þæt ic gesāwe...bēama beorhtost.*

1598. For *geweorðan* 'agree' cf. *þæs þe hīe þæs geworden hæfde, Chronicle,* anno 918: *gewearþ þā senatos* (Orosius): *þā gewearð ūsic* (*Satan,* 256) [Hubbard in *J.E.G.Ph.* xvii. 120].

1757. Kock construes *egesan* as dat.-instrumental, and *ne gȳmeð* as parallel with *dǣleþ*: 'spends the treasures, not keeping anxiously the ancient hoard.'

1770. *wigge.* Against Klaeber, Kock argues strongly for the interpretation 'by fighting,' quoting *Ps.* 34, 3, *me...wīge belūc wrāðum fēondum,* where the Vulgate context certainly favours the interpretation of *wīge* as 'by fighting.' Kock further instances *Met.* 1, 22, *Beow.* 1084 and *Widsith,* 120, etc. And Hrothgar had not kept his people out of war: he had often been *on ōre ðonne walu fēollon* (1041–2).

1861. I take the *tt* of *gegrēttan* as merely a scribe's double writing, like *æþellingum* (l. 906) or *gebǣrann* (*Finn.* 40).

1925. Kock reads *bregorōf*: "words meaning 'king,' 'lord' are used as intensives, as we amuse ourselves 'royally.'"

1926. Kock reads *hēa[h on] healle,* comparing *brūn on bāne,* 2578; *giong on galgan,* 2446; *ēadig on eorðan, Gen.* 2147.

1934. *sinfrē[g]a* can mean simply 'husband.'

2051. That Withergyld is the name of the father of the young Heathobard warrior who is stirred to revenge has been suggested with probability by Meed [*M.L.N.* xxxii. 435].

2164. Kock takes both words, *lungre* and *gelīce,* as adjectives: 'swift and all alike'; comparing *frome, fyrd-hwate,* 2476; *hearde, heaðo-scearde,* 2829; *ōmige, þurhetone,* 3049; *ealdum, infrōdum,* 1874. Mr Grattan suggests that *lungre* should be interpreted in its usual sense of 'straightway': 'straightway four horses all alike followed the other gifts.'

2212. My former statement, '*hǣþ* is feminine,' was an error, the ultimate origin of which is probably to be traced to the misreading *hēaure hǣþe* in this passage (e.g. in Holder's edition). *Hǣþ* however is masc. or neut. [see Platt in *Anglia,* vi. 173; Sievers, *P.B.B.* ix. 239; xx. 553].

2223. *þeow.* Lawrence argues powerfully in favour of *þegn* [*Pub. Mod. Lang. Assoc. Amer.* xxxiii. 554–7].

2252. *gesāwon sele-drēam.* Kock, translating 'had seen [the last of] the joy in Hall,' compares ll. 2725–7, and Vergil's *fuimus Troes, fuit Ilium,* 'done are we Trojans, done is Ilion.'

2338. Kock suggests *eall-īren ne[r],* 'a protection all of iron.'

2385. Brett defends *orfeorme,* 'without support,' i.e. 'in the absence of Beowulf.' But the *f*-alliteration of the second half-line is surely against this.

2852. The punctuation in the text is probably correct, for, if *wlītan* were inf., it would depend upon *læg,* which is impossible, as Beowulf is dead.

3005. Brett urges that Thorpe's interpretation gives a meaning to the otherwise meaningless *furður gēn,* 'did deeds of valour beyond the Scyldings' realm' [*M.L.R.* xiv. 1]. We may also note that Beowulf had been adopted by Hrothgar as his son (ll. 947, 1176), and is even called *freca Scyldinga* (l. 1563).

3072. Brett interprets *geheaðerod* as 'fenced out *from*' [*M.L.R.* xiv. 5].
3146. *gelæg*. Pluperfect in sense, like *hwearf* (l. 55), *crungon* (l. 1113) [Kock].

Finnsburg.

Two good editions of the *Finnsburg Fragment* have recently appeared: one by Mr Bruce Dickins in his *Runic and Heroic Poems* (1915), and one by Mr W. L. Mackie, with an excellent discussion of the text, in the *J.E.G.Ph.* xvi. 250–73. But we must not forget that the text of the *Fragment* has come down to us in a very corrupt form. Mr Mackie protests against my description of Hickes' transcript as 'inaccurate': since the original is no longer extant, Mr Mackie urges that we cannot tell how far any errors are due to Hickes.

But there are other transcripts by Hickes, of MSS. which *are* still extant, and from these we can estimate his accuracy. It is no disrespect to the memory of Hickes, a scholar to whom we are all indebted, to recognize frankly that his transcripts are not such as to render them at all a satisfactory substitute for the original MS. Hickes' transcript of the *Cottonian Gnomic Verses* (*Thesaurus* I. 203) shows an average of one error in every four lines, about half being mere matters of spelling, whilst the others are serious. Hickes' transcript of the *Calendar* (*Thesaurus* I. 207) shows an average of one error in every six lines.

And we find in the *Finnsburg Fragment* inaccuracies of exactly the type which Hickes so often commits. For example, Mr Mackie doubts the legitimacy of emending *Garulf* to *Garulf*[*e*]: but Hickes (or his printer) was very careless as to the final *e*; compare *Cal.* 15, 23, 41, 141, 144, 171, 210; *Gn. Verses*, 45.

l. 9. Mackie, following Bosworth-Toller, would make the *a* of *wāðol* long, and connect with *wāþ*, 'wandering.'

30. Mackie retains *healle*, thus making the alliteration fall upon *gehlyn*, the second accented syllable of the second half-line. He appositely cites l. 43 in justification.

36. The emendation *hwearflīcra hrǣw* was made by Grundtvig (1820), but his interpretation (1861) 'piled up corpses' is hardly satisfactory; nor is that of Grein$_2$ 'corpses of the swift.' Mackie points out that *hwerflīc* occurs in Alfred's *Boethius*, xi. 1, *hū hwerflīce ðās woruldsǣlþa sint*, 'how fleeting are these earthly blessings.' The meaning here should then be 'corpses of the mortal,' 'of the dead.'

41. *swānas*. "In Old English *swān* (Modern Eng. *swain*) elsewhere always means 'swineherd,' 'herd.' There is no other example of its use in the general sense of 'men' or even of 'servants.' This first appears in Middle English. If *swānas*, 'men,' is accepted here, one is almost bound to regard it as late Old English, the meaning influenced by Scandinavian *sveinn*, which had already widened its significance"—Mackie. Mackie also defends *hwitne medo*, instancing an eighteenth century recipe 'for making white mead.'

Persons and Places.

For the etymology of Grendel see E. G. T. Rooth in *Anglia*, *Beiblatt*, xxviii. 335. Rooth connects with *grand*, 'sand,' and interprets 'creature of the sand, or of the deep,' comparing *grund-wyrgenne* (l. 1518). Björkman's discussion of Breca, the Brondings and Wealhtheow in *Beiblatt*, xxx. 177 etc., and of Beow and Beowulf in *Engl. Stud.* lii. 145 etc., should also be consulted.